S0-CBH-185

Aid and Ebb Tide

A History of CIDA and Canadian Development Assistance

David R. Morrison

Wilfrid Laurier University Press

In association with

The North-South Institute / L'Institut Nord-Sud

This book has been published with the help of a grant from the Humanities and Social Sciences Federation of Canada, using funds provided by the Social Sciences and Humanities Research Council of Canada.

We acknowledge the financial support of the Government of Canada through the Book Publishing Industry Development Program for our publishing activities.

Canadian Cataloguing in Publication Data

Morrison, David R. (David Robert), 1941-
Aid and ebb tide : a history of CIDA and Canadian Development Assistance

Co-published by the North-South Institute/L'Institut Nord-Sud.
Includes bibliographical references and index.
ISBN 0-88920-304-0

1. Economic assistance, Canadian – Developing countries – History.
2. Canadian International Development Agency – History.
I. North-South Institute (Ottawa, Ont.). II. Title.

HC60.M667 1998 338.91'7101724 C97-932446-7

Published in association with The North-South Institute/L'Institut Nord-Sud

Cover design by Leslie Macredie. CIDA photographs on front and back covers by Roger Lemoyne (copyright © Her Majesty in Right of Canada).

Printed in Canada

for

Alena

Contents

List of Tables and Figures vii
List of Acronyms ix
Chronology of Key Events xiii
List of Ministers and Senior Officials xvii
Preface xix

1. Defining Canadian Development Assistance 1
2. The Early Years, 1950-66 27
3. Maurice Strong and the Creation of CIDA, 1966-70 57
4. Global Expansion and Growing Pains, 1970-77 99
5. Retrenchment and Reorientation, 1977-80 143
6. Rethinking the Mission, 1980-83 177
7. Multiple Mandates and Partners, 1983-89 221
8. A Jolt of Fresh Energy? ODA Policy Reviewed, 1984-89 271
9. Shifting Gears, 1989-93 313
10. Ebb Tide, 1993-98 369
11. Explaining Canadian ODA 425

Appendices

A. Canadian Official Development Assistance: Selected Components, Total, and ODA/GNP Ratio, 1949-50 to 1996-97 453

B. Percentage Distribution of Canadian Government-to-Government ODA by Region, Ten-Year Cumulative Totals, 1950-60, and Five-Year Cumulative Totals, 1960-95 455

C. Top Twenty Recipients of Canadian Government-to-Government ODA at Five-Year Intervals, 1960-61 to 1995-96 456

D. Core/Category I and Non-Core/Category II Countries, 1978, 1981, 1986 461

E. Publicly Financed Technical Assistance Personnel and Students and Trainees Supported by Canadian ODA, Five-Year Intervals, 1965-95 ... 464

F. Canadian ODA: Proportion of DAC Effort and Comparative Standing, Five-Year Intervals, 1960-95 ... 465

G. Percentage Distribution of All Attributable Country-to-Country Aid by Region, Canada and DAC Donors, 1970-71, 1980-81, and 1995-96 ... 466

H. Percentage Distribution of Attributable Country-to-Country Aid by Country Income Level, Canada and All DAC Donors, 1970-71, 1980-81, and 1995-96 ... 467

I. Canadian Multilateral ODA: Proportion of DAC Effort and Comparative Standing, Selected Years ... 468

Notes ... 469

Index ... 587

List of Tables and Figures

Tables

1.1. Canadian ODA by Program Channel and Expenditure Category, 1955-56, 1965-66, 1975-76, 1985-86, 1995-96 8

4.1. Percentage Distribution of Bilateral Aid Attributable by Sector, Canada, 1973-76, and All DAC Donors, 1975-76 125

5.1. Percentage Distribution of Canadian Bilateral Aid Commitments Attributable by Sector, 1976-79 167

6.1. Percentage Distribution of Attributable Canadian Country-to-Country Aid by Income Level of Recipient Countries, 1980-83 200

6.2. Percentage Distribution of Canadian Country-to-Country ODA Commitments Attributable by Sector, 1980-83 207

7.1. Canada's ODA/GNP Ratio, 1983-89 256

7.2. Percentage Distribution of Attributable Canadian Bilateral Aid by Income Level of Recipient Countries, 1979-80, 1984-85, 1989-90, and Percentage Increases, 1979-80 to 1989-90 258

7.3. Percentage Distribution of Polled Opinions about Level of Canadian Aid, 1985-88 269

7.4. Percentage Distribution of Polled Opinions about the Effectiveness of Canadian Aid, 1985-88 269

8.1. Decentralized Posts 306

8.2. Statistical Overview of Decentralized Posts, 1989-90 308

9.1. Percentage Distribution of Allocable Bilateral (Geographic Programs) and Country-to-Country ODA by Sector, 1988-89, 1990-91, and 1992-93 354

9.2. Percentage Distribution of Polled Opinions About Level of Canadian Aid, 1989-93 367

Figures

9.1. CIDA and Sustainable Development 320

10.1. Index of Real Government Program Spending since 1988 414

List of Acronyms

APF	Agency Programming Framework
ASEAN	Association of Southeast Asian Nations
AUCC	Association of Universities and Colleges of Canada
BHN	Basic human needs
CALA	Canadian Association for Latin America and the Caribbean
CCIC	Canadian Council for International Cooperation
CEA	Canadian Export (Exporters') Association
CESO	Canadian Executive Service Overseas
C-FAR	Citizens for Foreign Aid Reform
CGIAR	Consultative Group on International Agricultural Research
CIDA	Canadian International Development Agency
CIDB	Canadian International Development Board
CIEC	Conference on International Economic Cooperation
COCOA	Conference on Canadian Overseas Aid
CPPF	Canadian Project Preparation Facility
CPR	Country Program Review
CUSO	Canadian University Service Overseas (now simply CUSO)
DAC	Development Assistance Committee of OECD
DEAP	Development Education Animateur Program
DFAIT	Department of Foreign Affairs and International Trade
DIP	Development Information Program
DRIPP	Développement Régional Intégré de Petit-Goâve à Petit-Trou-de-Nippes
EAB	External Aid Board
EAITC	External Affairs and International Trade Canada
EAO	External Aid Office
EDC	Export Development Corporation
EIP	Educational Institutions Program
ENGO	Environmental non-governmental organization
ETAB	Economic and Technical Assistance Branch
FACE	Food Aid Coordination and Evaluation Centre
FAO	Food and Agriculture Organization
FEARO	Federal Environmental Assessment Review Office
FSUs	Field Support Units
G7	Group of 7 Industrial Countries

GEF	Global Environment Facility
GNP	Gross National Product
HRD	Human resource development
IAE	International Assistance Envelope
ICFID	Interchurch Fund for International Development
ICHRDD	International Centre for Human Rights and Democratic Development
ICDS	Institutional Cooperation and Development Services Division
ICERDC	Interdepartmental Committee on Economic Relations with Developing Countries
ICOD	International Centre for Ocean Development
IDA	International Development Association of the World Bank
IDB	Inter-American Development Bank
IDEA	International Development Executives Association
IDO	International Development Office of AUCC
IDRC	International Development Research Centre
IETCD	Interdepartmental Economic and Technical Cooperation Division
IFAD	International Fund for Agricultural Development
IFIs	International Financial Institutions
IGCA	Interdepartmental Group on Capital Assistance
IGTA	Interdepartmental Group on Technical Assistance
IMF	International Monetary Fund
INC	Industrial Cooperation Program
INGO	International non-governmental organization
IPFs	Indicative planning figures
IT&C	Department of Industry, Trade and Commerce
LDC	Less-developed country
LLDC	Least-developed country
MAF	Mission Administered Funds
MEPAD	(Report on) More Efficient Project Aid Delivery
MPs	Members of Parliament
NAFTA	North American Free Trade Agreement
NGI	Non-governmental institution
NGO	Non-governmental organization
NICs	Newly industrializing countries
NIEO	New International Economic Order
ODA	Official Development Assistance
OECD	Organisation for Economic Co-operation and Development
OIC	Overseas Institute of Canada
OPEC	Organization of Petroleum Exporting Countries
PAC	Partnership Africa-Canada
PAM	Project Approval Memorandum

PCO	Privy Council Office
PIM	Project Identification Memorandum
PPP	Public Participation Program
RBM	Results-Based Management
RDBs	Regional Development Banks
SADC	Southern African Development Community
SADCC	Southern African Development Coordination Conference
SALs	Structural adjustment loans
SAP	South Asia Partnership
SAPs	Structural adjustment programs
SCAAP	Special Commonwealth Africa Aid Programme
SCEAIT	Standing Committee on External Affairs and International Trade
SCFAIT	Standing Committee on Foreign Affairs and International Trade
SECALs	Sector adjustment loans
SIDA	Swedish International Development Agency
SJC-CFP	Special Joint Committee of the Senate and of the House of Commons Reviewing Canadian Foreign Policy
SMR	(CIDA's) Strategic Management Review
SUCO	Service Universitaire Canadien Outre-mer
SUNFED	Special United Nations Fund for Economic Development
SWC	Status of Women Canada
TCS	Technical Cooperation Service
TFO	Trade Facilitation Office
UK ODA	United Kingdom Overseas Development Administration
UN	United Nations
UNCTAD	United Nations Conference on Trade and Development
UNDP	United Nations Development Program
UNEPTA	United Nations Expanded Program of Technical Assistance
UNESCO	United Nations Educational, Scientific and Cultural Organization
UNFPA	United Nations Fund for Population Activities
UNHCR	United Nations High Commission for Refugees
UNICEF	United Nations Children's Fund (formerly International Children's Emergency Fund)
UNIDO	United Nations Industrial Development Program
UNRWA	United Nations Relief and Works Agency for Palestinian Refugees
US AID	United States Agency for International Development
WFP	World Food Program
WHO	World Health Organization
WID	Women in Development
WUSC	World University Service of Canada

Chronology of Key Events

1949 • First Canadian contribution to UN Expanded Program of Technical Assistance.

1950 • Canada joins Colombo Plan for Co-operative Economic Development in South and Southeast Asia; India, Pakistan, and Ceylon become main recipients of bilateral aid under the Colombo Plan.

• Technical Cooperation Service (TCS) set up in Department of Trade and Commerce.

1951 • International Economic and Technical Cooperation Division (IETCD) established in Department of Trade and Commerce, absorbing TCS; Nik Cavell appointed administrator of IETCD.

1958 • IETCD upgraded as Economic and Technical Assistance Branch (ETAB) within Department of Trade and Commerce, with Orville Ault as director.

• West Indies Aid Program and Commonwealth Technical Assistance Program (for Commonwealth African countries) initiated.

1960 • Start of first UN Development Decade; industrial countries urged to transfer 1 per cent of their combined national incomes to developing countries.

• Canada joins Development Assistance Group of the Organisation for European Economic Co-operation, reconstituted as the Development Assistance Committee (DAC) of the Organisation for Economic Co-operation and Development (OECD) in 1961.

• ETAB replaced by External Aid Office (EAO), under a director general with the rank of deputy minister reporting to secretary of state for External Affairs.

• Full bilateral aid programming extended to Commonwealth African countries under the Special Commonwealth Africa Aid Programme (SCAAP)

• Canada subscribes to International Development Association (IDA), set up as a soft loan arm of the World Bank.

1961 • Modest technical assistance program started in francophone Africa; capital assistance extended in 1964.

1962 • Canada supports establishment of World Food Program.

1963 • Newly elected Liberal government under Lester Pearson announces major increase in Canada's aid effort, involving new soft loan program.

- First Canadian aid to Latin America through loan program administered by the Inter-American Development Bank (IDB).

1964
- Canadian government transport authorized for Canadian University Service Overseas (CUSO).
- Canada supports founding of African Development Bank.

1965
- CUSO becomes first development NGO to receive financial support from government of Canada.
- Canada becomes charter member of Asian Development Bank.

1967
- Pearson government pledges to meet international aid targets "within a short period of time."
- EAO establishes Non-Governmental Organizations (NGO) Program.
- Canada supports establishment of Commonwealth Technical Assistance Program, forerunner of Commonwealth Technical Cooperation Program (founded in 1971).

1968
- Government of new Liberal Prime Minister Pierre Trudeau upgrades EAO to Canadian International Development Agency (CIDA), with Maurice Strong as first president, reporting to secretary of state for External Affairs.
- Canadian government aid mission to francophone Africa, led by Lionel Chevrier, part of a major effort to use aid to support Ottawa's position regarding Quebec's ambitions for international recognition.
- Canadian Council for International Cooperation (CCIC) set up as umbrella organization representing NGOs.

1969
- Report of the Commission on International Development, chaired by former Prime Minister Pearson, urges DAC donors to contribute 0.7 per cent of GNP to ODA by 1980 at the latest.
- CIDA sets up Business and Industry Program.

1970
- First Canadian government aid policy statement, *International Development*, based on review led by CIDA and published as one of six booklets emerging from the Trudeau government's foreign policy review.
- Legislation founds International Development Research Centre (IDRC).
- CIDA launches bilateral programming in Latin America.

1971
- Report of the House of Commons Subcommittee on International Development Assistance, chaired by Georges Lachance.
- CIDA founds Development Education Program, forerunner of the Public Participation Program (PPP).

1974
- CIDA sets up International Non-governmental Organizations (INGO) Program.

1975
- After lengthy interdepartmental process, cabinet approves *Strategy for International Development Cooperation 1975-1980*.

- Canada's ODA/GNP ratio reaches 0.53 per cent in 1975-76 (0.55 in the 1975 calendar year), the highest level ever.

1976 • Report of the House of Commons Subcommittee on International Development, chaired by Maurice Dupras.

1978 • CIDA sets up Educational Institutions Program in NGO Division.

1979 • Business and Industry Program replaced by Industrial Cooperation Program (INC).

1980 • Report of the Parliamentary Task Force on North-South Relations, chaired by Herb Breau.

- Report of the Independent Commission on International Development, chaired by Willy Brandt, former chancellor of the Federal Republic of Germany.
- CIDA creates Institutional Cooperation and Development Services (ICDS) Division.

1982 • Report of the House of Commons Subcommittee on Canada's Relations with Latin America and the Caribbean, chaired by Maurice Dupras.

- Founding of Petro-Canada International Assistance Corporation (PCIAC).

1983 • Trudeau government promises to achieve ODA/GNP ratio of 0.7 per cent by 1990.

- Creation of International Centre for Ocean Development (ICOD).

1984 • CIDA sets up Business Cooperation Branch.

- Appointment of Canadian Emergency Coordinator/African Famine to oversee Canadian response to severe famine in Ethiopia and other parts of sub-Saharan Africa.
- Approval of WID (Women in Development) Policy Framework.

1985 • Progressive Conservative government of Brian Mulroney, after first honouring the pledge to reach ODA/GNP ratio of 0.7 per cent in 1990, sets back target date to 1995.

1986 • Report of the Special Joint Committee of the Senate and of the House of Commons on Canada's International Relations, chaired by Tom Hockin and Jean-Maurice Simard.

- ODA/GNP target of 0.7 per cent deferred to the year 2000.
- CIDA establishes Africa 2000 Program.

1987 • Publication of *For Whose Benefit?*, report of the House of Commons Standing Committee on External Affairs and International Trade, chaired by William Winegard.

- Report of World Commission on Environment and Development, chaired by Gro Harlem Brundtland, prime minister of Norway.

1988 • Cabinet approval of *Sharing Our Future*, Canada's new aid strategy.
• Legislation sets up International Centre for Human Rights and Democratic Development (ICHRDD).

1989 • First of several cutbacks in the ODA budget; effective abandonment of 0.7 per cent target.

1991 • CIDA adopts sustainable development framework.
• Creation of International Assistance Envelope (IAE) with a non-ODA reserve for assistance to Eastern and Central Europe and the former Soviet Union.
• Report of Groupe Secor on Strategic Management Review of CIDA.
• Abolition of Petro-Canada International Assistance Corporation (PCIAC).

1992 • Abolition of International Centre for Ocean Development (ICOD).

1993 • Leak of draft International Assistance Policy Update.

1994 • Report of the Special Joint Committee of the Senate and of the House of Commons Reviewing Canadian Foreign Policy, chaired by Allan MacEachen and Jean-Robert Gauthier.

1995 • Publication of *Canada in the World*, the foreign policy of the Liberal government of Jean Chrétien, including new statement of aid policy.
• Transfer of programming responsibility for non-ODA support to Eastern and Central Europe and the former Soviet Union to CIDA from the Department of Foreign Affairs and International Trade.
• Deep cuts in the aid budget and a projection of a decline in the ODA/GNP ratio to the lowest level since the 1960s; elimination of several programs, including CIDA's Public Participation Program.
• Release of CIDA's new policy on poverty reduction and other policy papers.

1996 • Introduction of Results-Based Management (RBM) Policy.

List of Ministers and Senior Officials

Ministers Responsible for Canada's Development Assistance

Lester Pearson, Secretary of State for External Affairs, 1948-57
  Clarence Decatur Howe, Minister of Trade and Commerce, 1948-57
Sidney Smith, Secretary of State for External Affairs, 1957-59
  Gordon Churchill, Minister of Trade and Commerce, 1957-60
Howard Green, Secretary of State for External Affairs, 1959-63
Paul Martin, Secretary of State for External Affairs, 1963-68
Mitchell Sharp, Secretary of State for External Affairs, 1968-74
Allan MacEachen, Secretary of State for External Affairs, 1974-76
Donald Jamieson, Secretary of State for External Affairs, 1976-79
Flora MacDonald, Secretary of State for External Affairs, 1979-80
  Martial Asselin, Minister of State for CIDA, 1979-80
Mark MacGuigan, Secretary of State for External Affairs, 1980-82
Allan MacEachen, Secretary of State for External Affairs, 1982-84
Jean Chrétien, Secretary of State for External Affairs, 1984
Joe Clark, Secretary of State for External Affairs, 1984-91
  Monique Vézina, Minister of External Relations, 1984-86
  Monique Landry, Minister of External Relations, 1986-93
Barbara McDougall, Secretary of State for External Affairs, 1991-93
  Monique Vézina, Minister of External Relations, 1993
Perrin Beatty, Secretary of State for External Affairs, 1993
André Ouellet, Minister of Foreign Affairs, 1993-96
Lloyd Axworthy, Minister of Foreign Affairs, 1996-
  Pierre Pettigrew, Minister for International Cooperation, 1996
  Don Boudria, Minister for International Cooperation, 1996-97
  Diane Marleau, Minister for International Cooperation, 1997-

Directors General of the External Aid Office

Herbert Moran, 1960-66
Maurice Strong, 1966-68

Presidents of the Canadian International Development Agency

Maurice Strong, 1968-70
Paul Gérin-Lajoie, 1970-77
Michel Dupuy, 1977-80
Marcel Massé, 1980-82
Margaret Catley-Carlson, 1983-89
Marcel Massé, 1989-93
Jocelyne Bourgon, 1993
Huguette Labelle, 1993-

Preface

The transfer of capital and expertise from industrial country donors to developing country recipients through Official Development Assistance (ODA) has been a noble but flawed means of promoting economic and social development and overcoming global poverty. The enterprise has had to contend with colossal human and biophysical challenges and vastly unequal relations of wealth and power. In addition, donor governments have undermined the effectiveness of their foreign aid by pursuing multiple and often conflicting objectives—political and commercial as well as humanitarian. Aid agencies have also been buffeted by internal conflicts and organizational constraints, as well as by pressures from elsewhere in government, from domestic business and other non-governmental interests, and from a shifting transnational discourse on development. Nonetheless, there have been successes as well as failures, and there are still manifest needs for non-market resource transfers to support the development efforts of the world's poorest peoples and countries.

Aid and Ebb Tide examines Canada's mixed record in meeting those needs by reviewing the history of its development assistance program—from modest beginnings after the launch of the Colombo Plan in 1950, through provision of significant and comparatively generous resources to developing countries in the 1970s and 1980s, to a decline in the face of neo-liberalism and cutbacks in the 1990s. In particular, the book explores the politics, major policies, and organizational dynamics of the aid program. Publication coincides with the thirtieth anniversary of the Canadian International Development Agency (CIDA), the organization chiefly responsible for designing and delivering Canada's ODA.

Several themes recur throughout the study: interdepartmental conflict over aid policy and delivery, organizational and cultural changes within CIDA, motives and objectives of foreign aid, Canada's ODA volume and record in meeting international targets for resource transfers, choice of recipient countries, programming priorities, terms and conditions attached to development assistance, Canadian involvement in multilateral aid, CIDA's relations with its partners in the voluntary and business sectors, and efforts to strengthen public support for initiatives to promote international development.

Focusing on these important themes for understanding and assessing Canada's performance as an aid donor, a comprehensive history of that experience fills an important gap in the already rich literature on Canada's North-

South relations. As it looks primarily at the Canadian side of the equation, however, *Aid and Ebb Tide* can offer only a partial evaluation of Canadian ODA. Much more research needs to be undertaken in recipient countries to examine the human impact and developmental effectiveness of projects and programs on a case-by-case basis.

The book is based mainly on sources available in the public domain—Canadian government, parliamentary, non-governmental, and international documents and reports; press reports (many from CIDA's excellent Paper Clips service, now lamentably suspended); statistical data; and secondary materials, published and unpublished. Although I did not seek formal access to confidential documentation, I was able to draw upon several key official documents that have not been circulated publicly. In addition, I conducted over 120 interviews—a few on-the-record (with CIDA's presidents), and the rest with public servants and others on a not-for-attribution basis. Valuable for "reality-testing," the interviews supplemented documents with personal recollections, interpretations, and judgements.

It is ten years since Roger Young, then senior research officer at the North-South Institute, suggested that I undertake a short history of CIDA to mark the Agency's twentieth anniversary. The project took much longer to complete than either of us anticipated. Once immersed in the material, I decided to expand both the historical sweep and the scope of the investigation. Following a sabbatical leave that proved insufficient to complete the groundwork, I spent several years juggling research and writing with heavy academic administrative responsibilities. In the meantime, development assistance was profoundly affected by global political and ideological changes. About one-quarter of the book deals with the past decade, which has been a difficult time for CIDA and the Canadian aid program.

I want to thank the North-South Institute for sponsoring this study and providing superb logistical and generous financial support. The project has spanned the presidencies of Bernard Wood, Maureen O'Neil, and Roy Culpeper, who all offered beneficial advice and encouragement. I am particularly indebted to Roger Young and Clyde Sanger. Roger's guidance and practical assistance were enormously helpful during the early stages of the research. I then worked closely with Clyde, the Institute's recently retired director of communications. I value greatly his profound knowledge of the subject and sharp editorial eye, and his good humour and patience during what at times seemed like an endless period of gestation. He also prepared the index. Michelle Hibler, Clyde's successor as director of communications, provided much-needed help with organizational matters. During their time at "North-South," Marcia Burdette and Gerald Schmitz supported my research efforts in various ways and offered astute observations on early draft chapters. I also received insightful comments from Alison Van Rooy, a research officer at the Institute, a Rhodes Scholar, and a former student at Trent University. Gail Anglin, the information specialist, deserves recognition for her excellent service in securing needed documentation. These and other staff members made the North-South Institute a warm and welcoming place to work during my visits to Ottawa.

Three particularly well-informed readers made thoughtful criticisms and suggestions after reviewing the complete text: Cranford Pratt, emeritus professor of political science at the University of Toronto and the pre-eminent scholar in the field of Canada's North-South relations; Bill McWhinney, a founder of CUSO and a former senior vice-president of CIDA; and Allan Thornley, who lived much of CIDA's history from his vantage point as a writer of speeches and official documents. Lewis Perinbam, for many years vice-president of CIDA's Special Programs Branch, read some of the historical chapters and was a fount of useful information. Anonymous readers selected by Wilfrid Laurier University Press and the Aid to Scholarly Publications Program provided additional commentary. All of this feedback made for a better book, while I alone am responsible for its deficiencies.

I am pleased that Wilfrid Laurier University Press agreed to publish *Aid and Ebb Tide*, and have enjoyed working with Sandra Woolfrey, the director, Carroll Klein, the managing editor, and Doreen Armbruster, the production coordinator.

Past and present senior executives in CIDA and what is now the Department of Foreign Affairs and International Trade—and many, many other public servants, politicians, NGO representatives, development activists, academics, and consultants—were enormously helpful and cooperative in facilitating my research. I cannot thank individually the many people who provided materials and granted me time for interviews, but their contributions to this study cannot be overemphasized.

A vote of thanks goes to Gwynne Roseborough of Peterborough for her cheerful and expert help in formatting tables and text. Many others at Trent University provided assistance of various sorts, which I gratefully acknowledge. This book has been published with the help of a grant from the Humanities and Social Sciences Federation of Canada, using funds provided by the Social Sciences and Humanities Research Council.

I appreciate the encouragement, patience, and forbearance of Alena, Dan, Mike, and (on her frequent visits) my mother, Frances, during the long hours I spent writing in the attic. Alena Heitlinger has provided tremendous support, including scholarly and stylistic advice. This book is dedicated to her with a very special thank you.

Trent University
Peterborough, Ontario, Canada
May 1998

David R. Morrison

Chapter 1

Defining Canadian Development Assistance

The Cold War and decolonization in Asia framed Canada's decision in 1950 to offer capital and technical assistance through the Colombo Plan for Co-operative Economic Development in South and Southeast Asia. Since then, Canada has disbursed over $50 billion in official development assistance (ODA) to countries in Africa, Asia, the Caribbean, and Latin America.[1] A reticent player in Western aid efforts in the 1950s, the Canadian government became more enthusiastic in the 1960s, a time of optimism, idealism, and prosperity when support for international development captured the imagination of growing numbers of Canadians.

Creation of the Canadian International Development Agency (CIDA) in 1968 symbolized a commitment that led to expansion of the aid program to most parts of the developing world, making Canada one of the more generous donors among industrialized countries. As a percentage of gross national product (GNP), ODA allocations reached a crest in 1975, fell, then rose again in the 1980s amid changing ideas about development and periodic bouts of aid fatigue. There has been a drastic ebbing since 1989, driven by immediate pressure to reduce the federal deficit, and by dramatic changes in a world order transformed by the fall of communism, the rise of global markets and ethnic conflict, and the ascendancy of neo-liberal ideology.

This book examines the shifting contours of Canada's aid efforts, focusing in particular on the political, policy, and organizational history of CIDA's first thirty years.

Canada and International Development

Canada's response to the enormous economic and human challenges confronting the developing countries of the South has its roots in a history unburdened by involvement as a colonial power or major actor in the developing world. As a smallish middle power, Canada has been firmly committed to the

---

Notes to Chapter 1 are on pp. 469-73.

United Nations and other international organizations, and well disposed to multilateral peace-keeping and problem-solving. A bilingual and bicultural heritage provided membership in the Commonwealth, as well as an incentive to create in la Francophonie yet another association of states cutting across the North-South divide.

Before 1950, few Canadians had worked or travelled in what became known as the Third World—missionaries and their families, and still smaller numbers of government, business, and military people. Not many more had even indirect connections with what were seen as distant and exotic lands. Contacts increased in the 1950s and 1960s, with growing numbers of international students coming to Canada and more Canadians—many of them young volunteers—travelling and working abroad. Since the mid-1970s, personal ties to the Caribbean, Latin America, Asia, and Africa have been augmented by growing numbers of immigrants and refugees from those regions.

Wealthy and blessed with an abundance of resources, Canada has developed as an industrial capitalist country with a political culture based on the values of economic and political liberalism. Nonetheless, it has shared with developing countries problems arising from extensive foreign economic control and a trade profile oriented towards the export of primary products and the import of manufactured commodities. Moreover, as a late industrializer with a small population thinly stretched across a continent, Canada has had a strong (though seemingly weakening) tradition of state intervention in the marketplace, in the provision of communications and transportation infrastructure, and in the creation of welfare measures to moderate regional, class, and ethnic disparities.

At least until recently, this attachment to positive liberalism domestically found expression in what Cranford Pratt called "humane internationalism"—"an acceptance that the citizens and governments of the industrialized world have ethical responsibilities towards those beyond their borders who are suffering severely and who live in abject poverty."[2]

With few exceptions, non-aid economic relations with developing countries have been of little consequence for those countries or for Canada. Apart from the activities of a handful of Canadian-based resource and manufacturing firms, and the substantial presence of Canadian banks and financial institutions in the Commonwealth Caribbean, private investment in the developing world has been slight. So too has Canada's trade with developing countries—among the lowest of the industrial nations, in part because of the enormity of commercial links with the United States and the absence of colonial ties, but also because of Canada's own rich resource base. Moreover, Canadian firms have had limited success in capturing markets in the South, and domestic political forces have shaped trade policies that have been among the most protectionist and restrictive in the North.

All of these factors have influenced Canada's relations with the developing world, as have the dominant preoccupations of Ottawa's postwar foreign policy—East-West security concerns, commercial interests, a desire to maintain credibility among the major Western powers (especially after Canada's admission to the G7 in 1976) and, above all, economic and political relations with the US. Also important have been efforts to court the image of a sympathetic, caring, and progressive Northern power, and to respond to humanitarian impulses among the Canadian public. Although there are now serious questions about its future, foreign aid has been the dominant expression of Canada's North-South relations since the 1960s.

The Nature of ODA

What became known as official development assistance resembled colonial development and welfare programs initiated by some European imperial powers in their overseas territories before, during, and after World War II. While both involved concessional resource transfers (that is, grants and subsidized loans) for infrastructural projects, and various forms of budgetary support, ODA is distinguished by the modifier in the more generic term "foreign aid." The transfers occur between sovereign states, in some cases mediated by international agencies that are creatures of sovereign states.

The notion that states have some responsibility for human well-being beyond their own boundaries was embedded in the 1945 founding charter of the United Nations, which called upon members to "employ international machinery for the promotion of the economic and social advancement of all peoples."[3] Over the next few years, members funded several new UN agencies to take on humanitarian and developmental mandates. Meanwhile, planning for a postwar economic order at the Bretton Woods Conference in 1944 led to creation of the International Monetary Fund (IMF) and the International Bank for Reconstruction and Development (the World Bank). Though not envisioned at the time, these two international financial institutions (IFIs) came to play key roles in shaping the destiny of developing countries. The UN agencies and the World Bank were later joined by regional development banks (RBDs) as the main conduits for multilateral aid.

Bilateral or government-to-government assistance to developing countries began with Point Four of President Harry Truman's inaugural address in January 1949. It proposed that the US commit itself to "a bold new program for making the benefits of our scientific advances and industrial progress available for the improvement and growth of underdeveloped areas."[4]

Congress passed the *Act for International Development* in 1950—the same year that Canada, Australia, and New Zealand joined Britain in bilateral aid efforts through the Colombo Plan in the newly independent Commonwealth states of the Indian sub-continent.

Foreign aid came to mean a number of things in the years that followed. As Ivan Head, former president of the International Development Research Centre, commented, it

> projects a false sense of philanthropic generosity to governments endeavouring to find a noble description for such activities as the overseas disposal of surplus agricultural products. Indeed, "foreign aid" is such an all-embracing term that it can contain without apparent embarrassment military weapons, massive public works projects, humanitarian relief, and university scholarships. Not all of them, obviously, are developmental.[5]

ODA, the narrower technical concept, does at least exclude military aid, as well as export credits extended to developing countries at market rates of interest.

Western donors agreed in 1969 to define Official Development Assistance as: "those flows to developing countries and multilateral institutions *provided by official agencies*, including state and local governments, or by their executive agencies, each transaction of which meets the following tests:

> a) it is administered with the *promotion of the economic development and welfare of developing countries as its main objective*, and,
> b) it is concessional in character and contains a *grant element of at least 25 per cent*.[6]

ODA resource transfers may be in the form of cash, kind, or expertise. Non-repayable grants qualify, as do loans if they are made on concessional or "soft" terms. Economic support for both current and investment expenditures count, along with humanitarian assistance and emergency relief. The expenses of administering aid programs, initially excluded, have been counted since the early 1980s. So too have various imputed costs, including, most recently, those for the first year of resettling refugees.[7]

Although ODA must satisfy both conditions a) and b) above, the key condition operationally is concessionality of transfers for non-military purposes. These are then assumed to promote "development and welfare." Whether an ODA grant or loan is developmental is a question that is both value-laden and, within a particular conception of development, empirical. There have been many different, often competing ideas about what constitutes good development: roads, bridges, electricity, and other components of physical infrastructure; high-level education and training for institution-building and capacity-strengthening; support for filling "gaps" in local savings and foreign exchange; reform of agricultural practices and technologies; primary education and health care, clean water, and other basic human needs; empowerment of poor rural and/or urban communities; and on and on—transforming the role of women, cleaning up the environment, promoting human rights and civil society, transforming state-market relations, etc.

The picture is even more complex since the so-called main objective of promoting economic and social development has to compete with myriad others. Bilateral aid in particular is rooted in a mix of strategic, political, commercial, and non-developmental humanitarian concerns that may coincide or conflict with, or may simply be irrelevant to, developmental ones.

After the collapse of communism in the Soviet Union and Central and Eastern Europe, donors debated whether assistance for "countries in transition" should be counted as ODA. The outcome was a decision to extend eligibility to the ex-Soviet Asian republics, but to exclude the more advanced European economies.[8]

Forms of ODA

Unlike multilateral non-food aid, which provides cash to international organizations, most bilateral or government-to-government assistance involves transfers in kind of goods and services. These have been offered in the form of development projects, commodities (or lines of credit for commodities), and technical assistance.

Projects have been the most important component of Canadian bilateral aid over the years. In keeping with different conceptions of development, they have been enormously varied, ranging from major capital works (dams, railways, etc.) to cattle-breeding and crop storage, to efforts aimed at improving community-based water supplies and productive opportunities for women.

Commodity aid entails donations of commodities or lines of credit that enable recipients to obtain goods up to a specified value. Food has been a mainstay of Canadian aid, along with potash, metals, forest products, steel rails, railway locomotives and rolling stock, and communications equipment. Commodities, if they are needed, save scarce foreign exchange. Sometimes made available for free distribution in emergencies, they have most often been given to recipient governments to sell on local markets. Actual practices have been inconsistent, but the preference has been to have the local currency proceeds from such sales placed in counterpart funds to help finance ongoing or new development projects. Program aid (commodities, lines of credit, and balance of payments support) is quick-disbursing compared with project aid and much less burdensome administratively.

Technical assistance involves the provision of donor country expertise abroad, and the education and training of recipient country nationals in the donor country, their home countries, and/or third countries. (Appendix E summarizes data on technical advisers, students, and trainees supported by Canadian ODA over the years.)

Five Decades of Canadian Development Assistance

A variety of transitory arrangements were made for administering Canadian aid in the 1950s, when it was assumed that the activity would be temporary like the Marshall Plan in postwar Europe. In 1960, under pressure from the US and the old colonial powers to shoulder a greater share of development assistance efforts, Canada became a founding member of the Development Assistance Committee (DAC) of the Organisation for Economic Co-operation and Development (OECD). That same year, the Canadian government set up a small External Aid Office (EAO) attached to the Department of External Affairs. Then, in 1968, EAO was turned into the Canadian International Development Agency, which still reported to the Secretary of State for External Affairs, but now through a president with the rank of deputy minister.

The Bureaucratic Nexus

CIDA has operating responsibility for bilateral, voluntary, business, food, and international humanitarian aid channels. In 1995, it also assumed responsibility for delivering non-ODA aid to Central and Eastern Europe and the former Soviet Union.[9] The Agency shares jurisdiction over multilateral aid, chiefly with the Department of Finance, which represents Canada at the World Bank and the International Monetary Fund. CIDA oversees relations with UN development agencies, regional development banks, and most multilateral technical assistance programs (including those run by the Commonwealth and la Francophonie). The Department of Foreign Affairs and International Trade (External Affairs, among earlier incarnations) has controlled some smaller budgets for scholarships and international organizations.

CIDA's budget represents about three-quarters of the total ODA effort. In addition to the departments of Finance and External/Foreign Affairs, several small development-oriented crown corporations have been involved in aid delivery: the International Development Research Centre (IDRC) since 1970, Petro-Canada International Assistance Corporation (PCIAC) from 1982 to 1993, the International Centre for Ocean Development (ICOD) from 1983 to 1994, and the International Centre for Human Rights and Democratic Development (ICHRDD) since 1990. (Only passing reference is made to these organizations in the pages that follow, though each merits its own history.)

CIDA has always had to work closely with External/Foreign Affairs, the senior partner in foreign policy-making, and the organization in charge of the diplomatic missions that deal directly with governments of aid-receiving countries. Trade officials (in Industry, Trade and Commerce, which was subsequently merged into External Affairs) have consistently pushed to have the aid program serve commercial ends. Finance, always heavily involved on the multilateral side and in determining aid volume, developed a strong interest in bilateral programming when debt and structural adjustment became significant issues on the aid agenda in the 1980s.

The departments of Agriculture and Fisheries and Oceans have been major players in food aid, often as champions of the domestic interests they represent. Other departments—for example National Health and Welfare, Transport, and Environment—have at various times tried to persuade CIDA to finance some of their initiatives. Meanwhile, Treasury Board has been the gatekeeper on the size of the Agency's establishment and its programming authorities.

CIDA has sometimes been characterized as a "policy-taker" rather than "policy-maker." That was certainly the case with EAO and other forerunners, which operated under the watchful eyes of senior departments. With the formation of CIDA as a distinct entity in 1968 came the desire to play a lead role in shaping not only aid policy, but also other aspects of Canada's relations with developing countries. As we shall see, while the Agency lost repeated skirmishes to extend its influence beyond the realm of ODA, and has always had to accommodate pressures from elsewhere in government, it did achieve considerable relative autonomy over programs within its own operating sphere.

Aid channels and organizations. By providing snapshots at ten-year intervals, Table 1.1 illustrates the growing complexity of the Canadian aid program. It also reflects the greater latitude allowed in recent years to count administrative expenditures and imputed costs as ODA.

Most of Canada's official development assistance has been bilateral or multilateral (though the bilateral share declined steeply in the 1990s). Food aid, delivered both bilaterally and multilaterally, has always been a significant component of Canada's development assistance. (It is subsumed in the other totals in Table 1.1 and then broken out separately.)

Other channels have become increasingly significant. Since the late 1960s, public funds have been made available to support, on a responsive basis, the development and humanitarian relief efforts of non-governmental organizations (NGOs) and institutions (NGIs) in the voluntary sector. The Industrial Cooperation Program (INC) is a business-oriented program aimed at encouraging joint ventures, technology transfer, and other private-sector linkages with developing countries. Responsive programming for both voluntary sector and for-profit sectors grew rapidly after 1980. International

Table 1.1
Canadian ODA by Program Channel and Expenditure Category, 1955-56, 1965-66, 1975-76, 1985-86, 1995-96 ($ million)

	1955-56		1965-66		1975-76		1985-86		1995-96	
Channel/Category	Amount	%	Amount	%	Amount	%	Amount	%	Amount	%
Bilateral[a]	25.32	86.2	85.78	70.1	507.73	56.2	816.22	36.3	898.57	33.5
Multilateral	2.44	8.3	34.04	27.8	331.65	36.7	864.62	38.5	904.92	33.7
Voluntary sector[b]	0.02	0.1	0.49	0.4	35.29	3.9	22.33	9.8	257.38	9.6
Industrial Cooperation	—	—	—	—	0.11	—	27.83	1.2	63.66	2.4
Humanitarian assistance	1.60	5.5	1.05	0.9	2.00	0.2	25.85	1.2	59.02	2.2
Crown corporations[c]	—	—	—	—	24.46	2.7	114.00	5.1	93.07	3.5
Administrative costs[d]	—	—	—	—	—	—	172.30	7.7	157.68	5.8
Other[e]	—	—	1.00	0.8	2.27	0.3	6.46	0.3	250.01	9.3
Total	29.37	100.0	122.35	100.0	903.51	100.0	2,247.61	100.0	2,684.31	100.0
Food aid total[f]	0.49	1.7	34.62	28.3	221.04	24.5	347.80	15.5	260.39	9.7
Bilateral	0.49	1.7	31.47	25.7	116.57	12.9	163.13	7.3	114.97	4.3
Multilateral	—	—	3.15	2.6	104.47	11.6	150.30	6.7	126.34	4.7
NGOs/INGOs	—	—	—	—	—	—	34.37	1.5	19.08	0.7

a In 1995-96, includes $9.04 million in official debt relief of loans made by the Export Development Corporation, the Canadian Wheat Board, etc. Also includes $7.64 million in CIDA scholarships.

b Includes provincial government contributions to NGOs as well as CIDA's International NGO Program. The disbursements shown in 1955-56 and 1965-66 (before the formation of the NGO Program) included a $15,000 grant to the Red Cross (in both years) and the first year of support for CUSO in 1965-66.

c International Development Research Centre (IDRC), Petro-Canada International Assistance Corporation (PCIAC), International Centre for Ocean Development (ICOD), and International Centre for Human Rights and Democratic Development (ICHRDD).

d Following a decision by the Development Assistance Committee of OECD to allow inclusion of administrative costs in ODA, Canada began to include them in 1982.

e Until the late 1980s, "other" included only scholarship programs. Beginning in 1987-88, CIDA began to count the "imputed costs" of ODA-sponsored foreign students (waiver of differential fees, etc.). The Development Information Program set up after *Sharing Our Future* was included in the "other category" beginning in 1990-91. An imputed cost for services rendered by other federal departments was added in 1991-92 and fees levied by the Public Works Department in 1992-93. Then, in 1993-94, Canada began to count as ODA the costs of settling refugees from ODA-eligible countries during their first year in Canada. This last change resulted in an enormous jump for "other." The total of $250.1 million included: refugee costs, $153.02 million; imputed student costs, $68.66 million; Commonwealth Scholarships, $8.9 million; Development Information Program, $2.31 million; and miscellaneous (including government fees, imputed costs of service, interest, etc.), $17.12 million.

f Food, aid, included above in bilateral, multilateral, and voluntary sector totals, is broken out separately here.

Source: Calculated from CIDA, Historical ODA System, and CIDA, *Statistical Report on Official Development Assistance, Fiscal Year 1995-96* (Hull: Canadian International Development Agency, 1997), pp. 8, 45-47, 61, 72. Columns may not add precisely to totals because of rounding.

humanitarian assistance for emergency relief in the wake of natural and, increasingly, human-made disasters expanded dramatically in the early 1990s.

CIDA's mission and culture. Despite all the cross-pressures on Canada's aid program and its organizational vicissitudes, CIDA—especially in the minds of many long-serving employees and retirees—has exemplified (to quote one of them) "a whole new idea in government." Paul Gérin-Lajoie, the Agency's second president, observed: "Unlike any other department, [CIDA] does not start from the springboard of representing Canadian interests abroad, so much as from the other end of representing certain interests abroad—that is, the interests of the world's poorest people—back to Canada."[10] While conflicts with External Affairs and other departments have differed little from other bureaucratic turf wars, this vision has been a powerful motivation to act independently and, often in the face of intense pressures, to push for developmental integrity. The persistence of this vision also helps to explain the description of CIDA's culture as "idealistic" by a team of management consultants who studied the Agency in 1991:

> The high sense of mission found in most employees and managers reflects the strong belief that strictly developmental criteria and absolute respect for the culture and orientation of recipient countries must prevail over any other considerations. Historically, consideration for Canadian economic interests abroad, and the use of profits or benefits to motivate firms or individuals, are looked at with suspicion, if not contempt. This . . . is supported by the "welfare state mentality" still prevalent in the Canadian public service.[11]

Although the consultants also identified a "group think syndrome," resulting in part from "periodic assaults and challenges on CIDA's management practices" from inside and outside of government, the institutional culture has in fact been strongly individualistic as well. Enthusiasm for CIDA's developmental mission, together with lack of agreement on what constitutes good development, produced within the Agency what one senior official characterized as "1000 points of policy."

CIDA in comparative perspective.[12] Most OECD countries were already part of a nascent international aid regime when they organized or reorganized themselves for ODA policy-making and delivery in the 1960s. Arrangements differed markedly. Unlike the Nordic countries and Switzerland, but like most other industrial country donors, Canada has never had a legislated basis for its development assistance. While parliamentary committees have carried out several aid policy reviews, most of them thoughtful and non-partisan, neither the House of Commons nor the Senate has exercised the oversight of their counterparts in the Nordic countries, the Netherlands, and Germany—let alone the extreme interventionism of the American Congress.

Some larger donors—such as France, Germany, and Japan—devised complicated bureaucratic arrangements that fragmented responsibilities for policy-making, separating policy from delivery. In this respect, CIDA's relationship to Foreign/External Affairs has been more typical: an aid agency or department exercising a fair degree of autonomy over developmental content and program implementation, working as part of, or in close association with, a foreign ministry that sets the overall parameters of foreign policy.

Unlike US AID, which has its own network of field offices, CIDA has again been more typical in managing its overseas operations through foreign ministry posts. For most of the Agency's history, a tenth or less of its complement has been stationed in embassies and high commissions abroad in small aid sections that have had limited administrative, monitoring, and liaison responsibilities. Beginning in the 1980s, increasing use was made of field support units, staffed by Canadian and locally engaged contract personnel. In the meantime, the Agency was not alone in making more use of private-sector firms and non-governmental organizations and institutions for project implementation as ODA resources grew more rapidly than personnel.

The complexity of the developmental challenge, rapid swings in wisdom about how best to meet it, and criticisms of aid effectiveness have confronted all aid agencies, but CIDA stands out as having had a peculiarly endemic penchant for continual reorganization. One potentially far-reaching initiative in the late 1980s saw the Agency briefly join a donor trend towards greater decentralization of decision-making authority to the field. High start-up costs, budget cuts, and political obstacles soon curtailed the process: decentralization was first scaled back, then reversed altogether in 1992.

Playing a major role in the field of multilateral assistance, CIDA has differed from some aid agencies (such as US AID and Swedish SIDA) that are responsible only for bilateral assistance. It is like Britain's Overseas Development Administration (UK ODA) in this, but not other ways. For example, UK ODA has been able to rely heavily on the overseas network of the British Council to support technical cooperation, and has thus had less need for devolution to the private and voluntary sectors. Early on, UK ODA developed considerable expertise in macro-economic analysis. In contrast, while CIDA built up in-house sectoral expertise (since diminished), it has had more of a generalist tradition associated with operational details of project implementation and, more recently, with management of contracts for executing agencies.

Like their American counterpart, UK ODA and CIDA (which in 1977 lost its authority to carry over unspent funds) have had to wrestle with the contradiction between planning for long-term development and spending annually lapsing funds. Many continental European donors have enjoyed more flexible arrangements.

The Europeans and the Americans have been more forthcoming about sharing evaluation results than either the British or the Canadians, who share a tradition of administrative secrecy,[13] though recent emphasis on accountability and transparency has led to greater openness in CIDA.

Official Justifications for the Canadian Aid Program: A "Trinity of Mixed Motives"

The Canadian government's initial justification for joining the Colombo Plan was couched unequivocally in the rhetoric of Cold War security and support for the American-led Western alliance. Fears of communist expansion in Asia—similar to those prompting the Marshall Plan for the reconstruction of war-torn Europe—motivated Truman's Point Four. Lester Pearson, Canada's secretary of state for External Affairs, told the House of Commons in February 1950: "If South-East Asia and South Asia are not to be conquered by communism, we of the free democratic world . . . must demonstrate that it is we and not the Russians who stand for national liberation and economic and social progress." His stirring words were matched by John Diefenbaker, then speaking on behalf of the opposition: "50 million dollars a year . . . would be cheap insurance for Canada, for the opinion of Asiatic representatives [at Colombo] was that this plan, if launched in time, would do much to halt communism in Asia."[14]

Official discourse gradually changed. Pearson's "Methodist-inspired humanism"[15] came to the fore in a 1955 speech:

> [The] genuine desire of Canadians to help others who are less fortunate, the recognition that the more quickly other people's standards of living rise the better off we shall all be, the conviction that economic and social progress are essential to a durable peace . . . all of these seem to be more solid and more fundamentally significant reasons for providing assistance. . . . It is a sorry commentary . . . that without [the communists] and the threat which they represent we might not so readily have done what we should have been doing anyway.[16]

Pierre Trudeau made several rousing appeals for an enlightened response to the plight of the world's disadvantaged after he became prime minister in 1968. In a convocation address at the University of Alberta in May of that year, he declared:

> Never before in history has the disparity between the rich and the poor, the comfortable and the starving, been so extreme; never before have mass communications so vividly informed the sufferers of the extent of their misery. . . . We are faced with an overwhelming challenge. In meeting it, the world must be our constituency.[17]

Speaking to the Canadian Jewish Congress in 1974, Trudeau asserted: "If Canada's presence in the world were to be judged by a single criterion, [it should be] Canada's humanism, its pursuit of social justice. . . . Canada's foreign policy would be nothing if it were not caring."[18]

Successive governments have proclaimed the importance of humanitarianism as *a* foundation for Canadian aid. Most recently, *Canada in the World*, the 1995 policy statement of Jean Chrétien's Liberal administration, called international assistance "one of the clearest international expressions of *Canadian values and culture*—of Canadians' desire to help the less fortunate and of their strong sense of social justice—and an effective means of sharing these values with the rest of the world."[19]

In common with most official efforts to justify Canada's involvement in international development, however, the 1995 statement was put in the context of mixed humanitarian, political, and commercial rationales—a "trinity" of motives, as Keith Spicer called it in *A Samaritan State?*, his lucid and often acerbic study of the early years of Canadian aid. Among early versions of this "familiar and cherished litany" was a "homespun plea" from J.M. Macdonnell, MP, to the House of Commons in 1961:

> There are . . . three obvious arguments. . . . First of all, there is the humanitarian argument. If these people were going to bed hungry just across the road from us we would not go to bed until we had done something about it. Second, there is the political argument which is that it is tremendously in our interests . . . that these underdeveloped countries shall develop economically under free institutions and not under communist institutions. . . . Then there is the third argument, which some people rather deprecate because it sounds as if we were doing for our own interests. I have no objection to doing something in our own interests as long as it is in the interests of other people too.[20]

Typically the trinity of motives has been translated into objectives: Canada could assist with development efforts and provide disaster relief—thereby responding practically to humanitarian impulses—and simultaneously pursue foreign policy and commercial goals.

International Development, the white paper published in 1970 as a volume of the Trudeau government's *Foreign Policy for Canadians*, asserted that "the economic and social development of developing countries" was the "primary objective" of Canadian development assistance," but that aid programming had to be "sensitive" and "relevant" to "other Canadian objectives" such as strengthening multilateral institutions, fostering national unity, and "supporting the expansion of Canadian commercial interest overseas."[21] Endorsing the notion of development as primary, a 1971 House of Commons committee urged that these other objectives not "distract Canadian attention from the central task at hand."[22] As we shall see, this plea set the stage for twenty-five years of sparring between parliamentarians and government representatives, with MPs taking the high road in arguing for developmental supremacy and poverty alleviation in the event of conflicting objectives, and ministers and bureaucrats generally opting for "flexibility" and "balance."[23]

For several years, CIDA's official objectives were defined in the following open-ended fashion:

> To facilitate the efforts of the peoples of developing countries to achieve self-sustainable economic and social development in accordance with their needs and environment by cooperating with them in development activities, and to provide humanitarian assistance, thereby contributing to Canada's political and economic interest abroad in promoting social justice, international stability and long-term economic relationships for the benefit of the global community.[24]

Political and foreign policy objectives. Definitions of Canada's "political interest abroad," still firmly embedded in anti-communism, were gradually broadened. In the 1950s, the Commonwealth link—though forged by little more than quite disparate experiences of British colonialism—provided English-Canadian politicians with an emotionally convincing rationale for an aid program that expanded from Britain's former colonial territories on the Indian sub-continent to emerging Commonwealth countries in Africa and the Caribbean.

During the late 1960s and 1970s, the federal government used foreign aid to court support from France's former African colonies in order to combat efforts by the government of Quebec to obtain international recognition. More generally, ODA has been employed as part of a larger effort to promote national unity by projecting Canada's linguistic duality on the world stage.

Although the francophone African case stands out as an exceptional use of development assistance for specific international leverage, Ottawa has pursued other, more general objectives such as: enhancing Canada's prestige and goodwill in both industrial and developing countries, augmenting its capacity and influence as an "honest broker," and promoting multilateralism. At various times as well, the aid program has been a vehicle for conveying a sense of difference from US foreign policy. In recent years, Canada has joined other donors in making ODA conditional on recipient country performance in such spheres as human rights, governance, and economic policy reform. Gender equity and environmental sustainability have been actively promoted as well.

Meanwhile, the justification of aid as a means of promoting international security, which had mainly Cold War overtones until the collapse of communism, was sometimes couched in North-South terms. Trudeau buttressed his calls for social justice with a warning about the consequences of not acting:

> We must recognize that, in the long run, the overwhelming threat to Canada will not come from foreign investments, or foreign ideologies, or even—with good fortune—foreign nuclear weapons. It will come instead from the two thirds of the people of the world who are steadily falling farther and farther behind in their search for a decent standard of living.[25]

The argument for aid on security grounds other than the East-West conflict invited scepticism before the 1990s.[26] More recently, the notion of "common security" has gained currency in the context of post-Cold War globalization. In *Canada in the World*, the Chrétien government asserted that international assistance "contributes to *global security* by tackling many key threats to human security, such as the abuse of human rights, disease, environmental degradation, population growth and the widening gap between rich and poor."[27]

Commercial advantage. Seldom advanced as a primary rationale, the benefits of aid for the Canadian economy have been strongly promoted by business and from within government, especially by trade ministers and officials. A 1959 cabinet memorandum on aid allocations argued the advantages of selecting capital projects on the basis of their contributions to the Canadian economy: "They not only provide employment for Canadians, . . . but also tend to have an appreciable impact on the operations of Canadian manufacturers of capital goods. . . . Moreover, a completed project . . . stands as an enduring monument of Canadian friendship and goodwill."[28] Food aid was quite explicitly seen and defended as a mechanism for stimulating an ailing agricultural economy and disposing of mounting domestic surpluses, especially in the 1950s and 1960s.[29]

A paper prepared by the Department of Trade and Commerce in 1968 summarized what by then had become conventional wisdom. If aid succeeded, there would be long-term benefits for the Canadian economy: "the Third World will be wealthier, will purchase more, and will offer a larger commercial market for Canadian exports." Moreover, beyond short-term benefits for individual firms and sectors supplying goods and services for overseas projects, foreign assistance had the potential to stimulate the development of new products and skills, give Canadian enterprise international experience, smooth out "the peaks and troughs in demand at home and abroad for particular goods and services," and relieve depressed industries and regions.[30]

During the "stagflation" of the late 1970s, the government, with business support, increased pressure on the ODA program to deliver commercial returns, emphasizing stronger long-term "mutually beneficial bilateral relationships between our developing partners and Canada."[31] A persistent theme thereafter, it was pushed vigorously in recessionary periods, especially in the early 1990s during Brian Mulroney's second Conservative administration.

In 1995, *Canada in the World* called development assistance:

> an investment in *prosperity and employment*. It connects the Canadian economy to some of the world's fastest growing markets. . . . And, in the long-run, development cooperation can help lift the developing countries out of poverty. This means that it contributes to a stronger global economy in which Canadians, and other peoples, can grow and prosper.[32]

Leading Characteristics of Canada's Aid Program

Although there is no necessary relationship between the quantity and the quality of development assistance, the share of a donor country's national income devoted to aid has been a significant indicator of its commitment to international development. After a slow start, Canadian aid began to grow rapidly in the mid-1960s. Over the next decade, the External Aid Office and CIDA oversaw a dramatic increase in disbursements, spurred on by Canada's promise to make steady progress towards the ODA target for donor countries endorsed the UN General Assembly in 1970—0.7 per cent of GNP. Canadian aid grew by 67.5 per cent in real terms in the 1970-75 period, almost four times average DAC growth, and third only to Sweden and Norway (which started at lower levels).[33] DAC's annual report for 1975 confidently predicted that Canada would be among donors reaching 0.7 per cent by 1980.[34]

Jean-Philippe Thérien characterized Canada's "singularity" among Western donors as arising "from its lying between the G7 and the like-minded nations in its commitment to development cooperation."[35] After 1975, however, its proportional effort became more aligned to the G7, which Canada joined on American prompting in 1976, than to "like-minded" Denmark, Norway, Sweden, and the Netherlands. All of these went on to achieve well above 0.8 per cent, sometimes reaching 1.0 per cent. Canada's ODA/GNP ratio of 0.53 per cent in 1975-76 was the highest ever attained.[36]

From 1975 to 1980, Canadian aid (as measured in 1981 $US) fell by 8 per cent,[37] and the ratio dropped to 0.43 per cent. During the 1980s, it fluctuated in a range of 0.43 to 0.50 per cent, second to France among the G7, though still well above the DAC average.

Beginning in 1989, when the deficit-cutting agenda took hold, development assistance was slashed more heavily than other federal program spending. Most industrial donors also cut back their aid, but Canada's free fall was staggering by comparison. From a respectable fifth within the OECD in ODA volume in the mid-1980s, Canada dropped to ninth in 1996, well behind much smaller Netherlands and Sweden and barely ahead of Denmark. The collapse in proportional effort was even more dramatic—from sixth among the twenty-one DAC members in ODA/GNP ratio as late as 1994 to eleventh just two years later![38] Canada's per capita ODA contribution of US$64 in 1995-96 was less than one-quarter that of the average of the Nordics, and a mere thirteenth among DAC donors.[39] A slight reprieve in planned cuts for 1998-99 will likely yield a ratio in 1999-2000 of 0.27 per cent rather than the 0.25 per cent that had earlier been feared. Just over half of the proportionate effort a decade earlier, 0.27 per cent will be the lowest level since 1965-66 and well below the average of DAC donors excluding the US, whose abysmal performance—0.12 per cent in 1996—drags down the overall average.[40] Unless this trajectory is reversed, Canada's reputation as a generous aid-giver will be in tatters.

Recipient countries: A global reach.[41] The choice of recipient countries is a crucial determinant of ODA effectiveness. Two issues are particularly important: first, though with no guarantee of success, potential impact is greater if resources are concentrated in selected countries rather than widely dispersed; and, secondly, the poorest countries with the weakest capacity to mobilize resources from internal and international markets are in greatest need of concessional transfers. In comparative terms, Canada has a weak record on concentration, and a better-than-average one on assisting the poorest countries.

The geographical spread of Canada's bilateral aid has been unusual among DAC donors. Britain, France, Belgium, the Netherlands, and other ex-colonial powers concentrated efforts largely within their former colonial empires and spheres of influence. Japan, the Nordic countries, Australia, and other large and small donors tended to specialize along regional or ideological lines. In contrast, Canada's global reach across Asia, Africa, and the Americas has resembled that of a superpower and a major power—the United States and Germany—but without approaching either's economic clout or international political interests.

Rapid proliferation of assisted countries in the 1960s and early 1970s occurred through a combination of accident and design, the joint product of a growing aid budget and an underlying political calculus—the Commonwealth-plus in Asia, a balance between Commonwealth and francophone states in Africa, and Commonwealth and broader responsibilities within the Western Hemisphere. The use of ODA as a "diplomatic calling-card"[42]— in small amounts for a large number of countries—was common enough among most donors. For Canada, however, this wide dispersal also meant a low degree of concentration on a designated group of priority recipients.[43]

"We envy the Swedes and the Danes" was the comment of a long-serving CIDA officer when reviewing Canada's extraordinary range of recipients, its lack of regional concentration, and its relatively marginal aid presence even in core countries. From the mid-1970s onwards, repeated attempts to achieve greater concentration met resistance from politicians and diplomats who were worried about damaging existing relations and keen to take on new challenges. As Martin Rudner noted, there were as well new pressures from "influential domestic constituencies, ranging from export interests to immigrant communities and internationally-oriented associations and institutions, who tend to demand aid for countries of interest to themselves."[44]

Even though the choice of recipients had little to do with levels of development, large initial allocations to the Indian sub-continent, and subsequent expansion to former British and French colonies in sub-Saharan Africa, tilted bilateral allocations towards low-income countries. When donors became increasingly accountable on these matters—because of the plight of the least-developed and those most affected by the energy and food crises of the early 1970s—Canada was able to show that the bulk of its ODA went to the poorest countries.[45]

As we shall see, efforts by CIDA planners to entrench this as policy, and secure a more development-oriented eligibility framework, were challenged by other bureaucrats who wanted aid programming to respond more fully to commercial and diplomatic priorities. The conflict yielded a compromise in the late 1970s—a two-track approach, which maintained the commitment to the poorest countries but focused more energy on strengthening Canada's long-term economic relations with middle-income countries and other high-growth economies, especially in East and Southeast Asia. Bilateral allocations to some of the poorest recipients were hit hard by cutbacks in the 1990s: total Canadian aid to the least developed countries fell from 0.15 per cent of GNP in the mid-1980s to a mere 0.06 per cent in 1996.[46]

Programming priorities: Chasing fashions. All public policy domains exhibit fads, fashions, and pendulum swings, and foreign aid, far from being an exception, has been especially prone to frequent twists and turns. To some extent, the changes have been driven by a well-meaning desire to find workable and relatively simple solutions for complex human, social, and material problems, and to do so in a hurry. As Roger Riddell observed, "In their eagerness to achieve quick and tangible results from their interventions, donors have projected an image suggesting that they know the answers and that these answers lie comfortably and consistently within the context of the assistance they have to offer." At the same time as insisting that effective development requires patience and a long-term perspective, "donors have constantly changed the details of their programme approaches (. . . frequently proclaiming that single and specific constraints provide the fundamental barrier to development), while also failing to learn from past experience."[47]

Continually changing priorities have also reflected sweeping global changes, altered ideological assumptions, shifts in political and commercial objectives, and efforts to make development assistance more saleable to sceptical taxpayers. Often failing to stay the course as they have flitted about from one priority to another and taken on more and more responsibilities, aid agencies have undermined their own credibility and, more importantly, their professed efforts to achieve sustainable development.

Like other donors, but with more alacrity than most,[48] CIDA has associated itself with new fashions and policy thrusts: physical infrastructure, food and commodity aid, and technical assistance in the early years; agriculture and social development in the late 1960s; the poorest countries and basic human needs in the 1970s; human resource development, poverty alleviation, structural adjustment, women and development, and the environment in the 1980s; and sustainability, private-sector development, human rights/democracy/good governance, and peace-building in the 1990s.

Although Canada has frequently experienced both time lags and marked discrepancies between policy declarations and the reality of project implementation, there have been exceptions: in both rhetoric and practice, CIDA has been a leader internationally in women in development and gender analysis; in time, a similar claim may be made in the sphere of environmental sustainability. As one of two major food donors (along with the US), Canada has also been at the forefront of efforts to develop, with variable success, an approach to food aid that contributes positively to development and food security rather than encouraging dependency. In addition, though many new priorities in the 1980s and 1990s led to a less focused effort overall, programming in the field was substantially reoriented from conventional infrastructure projects to an emphasis on human resource development and capacity-building.

Terms and conditions: Divergent impulses. Two important indicators of aid quality are its impact on long-term indebtedness and the extent to which ODA is tied to procurement of goods and services in the donor country. In Canada's case, generous, concessional terms of aid have been accompanied by stringency on procurement tying.

Prescient about the dangers of debt in the early years, Canadian policymakers extended most assistance in the form of grants. A loan program was added in the mid-1960s, but with very soft terms—no interest, and repayment over fifty years with a ten-year grace period. Accounting for half of the bilateral program in 1969-70, lending gradually declined to under 10 per cent by the mid-1980s; even in 1970, the grant element of total Canadian aid was 94 per cent,[49] a level equalled or exceeded thereafter. ODA was put on an all-grants basis for least-developed countries in 1977 and all others in 1986. As debt strangulation deepened in the 1980s, the government took steps to forgive the aid-related debts of most African, Caribbean, and Latin American recipients. Unlike some other donors, Canada has consistently been in compliance with DAC-approved norms for concessionality.[50]

In response to criticisms that tied aid inflates costs for uncompetitive goods and services, and skews development priorities by restricting projects to what donors are prepared to supply, successive governments have defended the practice as a means of securing domestic business support for ODA and demonstrating to the public that aid dollars create jobs in Canada. Although DAC data for the 1970s and early 1980s were disputed by CIDA, these suggest that Canadian development assistance was always tied at levels substantially above the donor average.[51] Following an easing of restrictions in 1988, recent comparative figures have pegged Canada somewhat closer to, though still well short of the DAC average.[52] Meanwhile, a generally poor record for supplying competitive inputs improved, especially after a dwindling of efforts to use ODA for dumping surplus steel rails and railway equipment.

CIDA avoided other forms of conditionality until the late 1980s, when it joined the donor community in supporting economic policy reforms advocated by the World Bank and the International Monetary Fund. Increasing proportions of bilateral support for seriously indebted countries, especially in Africa, were made conditional on acceptance of Structural Adjustment Programs that pushed for open markets, less government, and "getting the prices right." This conversion to neo-liberal orthodoxy provoked intense criticism from the non-governmental development community on both economic and social grounds—especially for the negative impact of adjustment on the poorest and most vulnerable.

The human rights performance of recipient governments became a concern among development activists in the 1970s. Three parliamentary committees between 1982 and 1987 challenged Canadian authorities to withdraw or curtail ODA allocations in cases of serious abuse, and to use aid as a tool for human rights development. While human rights, democracy, and good governance have been programming priorities since the early 1990s, Canada's record on aid/human rights conditionality has been uneven and controversial.

Multilateral assistance: Middle-power enthusiasm. Multilateral assistance (except food aid) is free of procurement restrictions and less prone to manipulation for non-developmental purposes. As a result, despite strong criticisms over the years, multilateral agencies have been championed as vehicles for delivering "purer" development assistance and strengthening international solidarity.

From a cautious and tight-fisted participant in the 1950s, Canada became an active supporter of multilateral assistance in the 1960s, when Ottawa realized that multilateralism could be pursued in the sphere of aid as well as security. Canada went on to rank highly within DAC in the breadth of its institutional commitment and in the share of its ODA channelled multilaterally (typically between 30 and 40 per cent).[53] Though with less enthusiasm, it continued as an active player in the 1980s, a time when the Reagan administration in the US was openly hostile to multilateral agencies and there was much closer donor scrutiny of their performance. With a sharp scaling back of commitments in the 1990s, Canada's future role has come increasingly into question. Multilateral aid as a percentage of total ODA has dropped below the DAC average and Canada's share of donor country contributions has plummeted.[54]

Non-governmental programming: Professionalizing altruism. Canada's leadership in supporting the development efforts of NGOs and NGIs has been highly acclaimed, and its programming initiatives in this field have been widely copied. Appointed as Director General of the External Aid Office in 1966, Maurice Strong (later CIDA's first president) was determined to tap the energy and experience of citizens by expanding voluntary work for international development. He persuaded his superiors to approve two innovative forms of financial support: first, core funding for Canadian University Service Overseas (the forerunner of CUSO) and other volunteer-sending NGOs, even though they had considerable latitude in determining their own priorities, and, second, grants of public funds to match, on a project-by-project basis, donations raised by NGOs for activities they wanted to pursue.

In the early 1970s, CIDA began funding community-based development education through what became the Public Participation Program (PPP). Support was extended as well to international NGOs (INGOs) such as the International Planned Parenthood Federation. Later in the decade, universities and colleges (long used as executing agencies in bilateral projects) became eligible for responsive funding matched to in-kind contributions. Similar arrangements were extended to cooperatives, trade unions, professional associations, and municipal organizations.

Heightened emphasis on programming for basic needs and human resource development opened new opportunities for NGOs and NGIs to provide services for bilateral projects in the 1980s. Then, with cutbacks in the 1990s, officials began to question the number and complexity of NGO funding arrangements, as well as the impact of extensive responsive programming on the overall coherence of Canadian aid. As CIDA became more intrusive in its demands for managerial accountability, difficult choices were made about long-standing commitments.

Bonded by mutual dependence and a shared commitment to development assistance, CIDA and the non-governmental community have frequently been at odds over finance, organizational autonomy, and programming priorities. NGOs have been among the Agency's most persistent critics on procurement tying, food aid, human rights, structural adjustment, poverty reduction, and many other issues.

Business cooperation: Seeking distant profits. CIDA-INC, the Industrial Cooperation Program, has been defended as an effective means for stimulating entrepreneurial initiatives in Canada and abroad, and condemned as a thinly disguised vehicle for promoting Canadian commercial advantage that has little to do with development in recipient countries.

Maurice Strong believed that good development could be promoted abroad, along with enhanced support for development assistance in Canada, by persuading businesses to seek out profitable opportunities in the Third World. He was especially keen about joint ventures involving small and medium-sized enterprises that had never operated outside of North America. The Business and Industry Program, established in 1969, offered grants for starter and feasibility studies to explore such opportunities. Canadian businesses, which had always been the main suppliers of goods and services for the bilateral program, showed little interest at first in this sort of responsive programming.

Intermittent efforts to attract more attention culminated in creation of the Industrial Cooperation Program in 1978. Facilities for pre-investment starter and feasibility studies were transferred to the new program, and given much higher funding ceilings. As part of the thrust in the late 1970s to bring greater commercial returns from Canadian aid, INC set up a facility to provide financial and logistical support for firms seeking contracts from the World Bank and other multilateral agencies. It also funded training and management consultancy work undertaken by firms and business associations, as well as promotional materials, travel, and networking in support of international private-sector linkages. It grew rapidly in the 1980s and has been hit less by cutbacks than other programs in recent years.

Public outreach and support: A bumpy road. By allowing spending on public outreach to count as ODA, DAC has encouraged efforts to stimulate support for aid and international development. CIDA's special programs for NGOs and business have sought, among other goals, to foster greater public awareness and encourage growth of a helpful political constituency. These objectives also led to support for NGO development education programs and the Agency's own involvement in promoting publications and audio-visual materials.

Meanwhile, from the mid-1970s to the early 1980s, CIDA's public affairs personnel became more reactive as they had to deal with horror stories about Canadian aid circulated by journalists and opposition parliamentarians.

Although some were unsubstantiated, others were given credibility by the Auditor General's criticisms of administrative shortcomings. Public support for aid, as measured in opinion polls, showed signs of weakening. CIDA then devoted considerable, perhaps excessive, energy to improving financial and managerial systems and reducing the risks of bad press about embarrassing errors in the field.

A parliamentary committee urged in 1980 that "the awareness and involvement of Canadians in North-South concerns" be encouraged by raising expenditures for such purposes to 1 per cent of ODA, more than double the budgetary allocation at that time.[55] Though the Trudeau government did not agree to the proposed target, activity increased. In appointing a new president of CIDA in 1983, the prime minister chose in Margaret Catley-Carlson someone especially gifted at reaching out and rekindling support for the aid program. Her efforts coincided with a generous response from Canadians to the plight of Ethiopians afflicted by drought and civil war in 1984-85. Polls showed public approval for aid on the upswing to an all-time high.

After another parliamentary committee highlighted outreach as a priority in 1987, the Mulroney government promised to achieve the 1 per cent threshold in what was then a growing ODA budget. There were several new initiatives—but the commitment was short-lived, and public support for aid fell off sharply with the 1990-92 recession and the preoccupation with deficit reduction. Both the Tory administration and its Liberal successor began to question the use of public funds to promote support for an aid budget they were curtailing. Canadian-based development education activities were among the hardest hit by budget cuts.

The Organization of the Book

Besides recounting the history of CIDA and aid policy-making, the chapters that follow deal with several recurring themes that have been summarized in this introduction. These include: interdepartmental struggles over aid programming, organizational and cultural changes within CIDA, debates about the objectives and developmental impact of Canadian aid, ODA volume and comparisons with other Western donors, choice of recipient countries, programming priorities, terms and conditions of Canadian aid, Canada's contributions in the sphere of multilateral aid, CIDA's relations with its domestic partners in the voluntary and business sectors, and the Agency's efforts to strengthen public support for international development.

Chapter 2 provides an overview of the early years of Canadian aid from 1950 to 1966. Chapters 3 to 10, organized around the terms of CIDA's seven presidents, carry the story forward to 1997. While the choice of presidencies as time periods is arbitrary, it does have a logic beyond simple convenience. The president of CIDA has not only enjoyed the power and prestige of a deputy minister, but has often played a more public and visible role than the conventional Ottawa mandarin. This remained true even when the Agency was shifted from the general oversight of the secretary of state for External Affairs, the norm in the Trudeau and early Chrétien years, to the specific responsibility of a junior minister during the Progressive Conservative administrations of 1979-80 and 1984-93 and again under the Liberals after 1996.

As Phillip Rawkins observed:

> The role of the president is to mediate between CIDA and the government of Canada and, on a day-to-day basis, to represent the agency in its dealings with developing countries and other donor agencies. Most critical is the capacity of the agency's chief executive officer to secure the resources and space for manoeuvre in government essential to the fortunes of CIDA and its work-force. The president must also play the central role in determining broad directions, while demonstrating to the staff empathy with the central values of the agency.[56]

Nevertheless, though CIDA has often been identified with the person of the president by development activists, parliamentarians, academics, and the media, it must be emphasized that the Agency's history represents the talents, labours, and frustrations of hundreds of dedicated Canadians. Some of them are named in the pages that follow, and many more deserve to be.

On Explaining Canadian ODA

The book concludes in Chapter 11 by returning to the question "Why Canadian aid?" After an examination of contrasting images of motives and objectives, it reviews and assesses efforts in the policy-oriented and scholarly literature to explain Canada's aid performance.

Developmentalist critiques written from a policy-oriented perspective have tried to understand the uneven impact of Canadian ODA on the promotion of economic and social development in recipient countries. Much of the answer lies, of course, in unequal global relations of wealth and power, and all of the complex economic, political, social, and biophysical challenges in the developing countries themselves. Developmentalists claim, however, that the risks of development assistance—not least its inherent cultural arrogance—have been compounded by the many and often conflicting ambitions that Canada and other aid donors have sought to realize through their aid programs.

The question of what drives multiple expectations and other aspects of ODA policy-making in Canada has been the subject of considerable scholarly debate, chiefly between proponents of two schools of thought—statist and dominant class. The statist perspective argues that development policy reflects mainly the preferences of political leaders and senior bureaucrats, rather than those of recipient countries or non-state domestic actors such as business and NGOs. A leading proponent of this view, Kim Richard Nossal, has contended that the aid program is shaped not by the conventional trinity of humanitarian, political, and commercial motives, but rather by the pursuit of prestige, organizational maintenance, and the limitation of public expenditures.[57]

The dominant-class approach, rooted in Marxist and neo-Marxist analysis, agrees that foreign aid has served many purposes and that state actors have dominated decision-making. However, its advocates assert that ODA has been primarily an instrument for supporting the globalization of capitalist relations of production and entrenching the wealth, power, and privilege of dominant classes in both North and South. Cranford Pratt has been the most prolific analyst of Canadian ODA policy-making over the past thirty years. Now professor emeritus of political science at the University of Toronto, he has been a persistent critic of the "reluctance of the government of Canada, a comparatively liberal and humane country, to respond to ethical concerns as fully as public opinion would permit in its development assistance and other policies relating to global poverty."[58] Though not a Marxist and receptive to some statist assumptions, Pratt has argued that the dominant-class thesis is the most convincing one for understanding Canada's relations with developing countries.[59]

This author agrees that statist and dominant-class perspectives have provided valuable insights, not least in their convincing rejection of a pluralist model that views state officials as mere mediators among contending societal interests. Neither explanatory framework, however, is able to account for the complex history of Canadian foreign aid. Indeed, both fail to direct sufficient attention to the actual processes of political brokerage and interest mediation that have shaped multiple, often-conflicting objectives and policies, and undermined the coherence of Canadian aid.

These processes—state-societal, state-centred, and transnational—have in turn been mediated by organizational and managerial factors. Accordingly, Chapter 11 revisits the historical evidence about the impact on aid policy of domestic interest groups, intra-governmental politics, the international aid regime, and organizational behaviour. Some significant conclusions emerge: that non-state domestic actors have had a greater impact on policy-making than statists would have us believe; that, despite manifest sensitivity to the needs of capital and specific business lobbies, CIDA has been more responsive to the interests and demands of NGOs and NGIs than dominant-class theorists have suggested; that developmental impulses within the Agency have been muted as it has tried to accommodate itself to the political and commercial objectives pursued by more powerful interests elsewhere in government; that an increasingly influential transnational discourse among multilateral and bilateral donor agencies has had a profound effect on CIDA's programming priorities and its relations with domestic interests, other bureaucratic players, and recipient countries; and that the translation of policy into operational reality has been frustrated by bureaucratic impediments, disbursement pressures, regulatory controls, and inadequate evaluation. All of these factors, together with severe budget cuts in recent years, help to explain why Canadian ODA, amid undoubted successes, has fallen short in helping the world's poorest people and countries.

Chapter 2

The Early Years, 1950-66

Development assistance to the emerging Third World at first took a back seat to diplomacy and security in Canada's postwar international relations. The Cold War, fear of Soviet expansion, American leadership of the Western alliance, the decline of Britain, European reconstruction, NATO, the UN, and the Commonwealth defined the main preoccupations of Canadian foreign policy during what is often portrayed as a golden age of liberal internationalism. As we have seen, it was the link between security and the Commonwealth that put foreign aid on Canada's public policy agenda. In his *A Samaritan State?* Keith Spicer observed: "The colossal shadow of new-born People's China cast . . . the appalling prospect that Mao Tse-tung's guerilla triumphs might be retold against impoverished, inexperienced and dislocated administrations throughout Asia." Set against that threat was an "exhilarating vision of a free, multi-racial Commonwealth" as representatives of the UK and the old white dominions sat down in 1950 with their counterparts from India, Pakistan, and Ceylon in the Ceylonese capital of Colombo.[1] Canada's decision to join the Colombo Plan was tempered, however, less by enthusiasm and more by caution and fiscal parsimony.

From 1950 to 1960, the uncertain commitment to foreign aid was mirrored in organizational confusion that drained the energy of many dedicated participants. Still, while the activity was marginal in terms of overall government operations, parliamentary appropriations grew, and the geographical scope of bilateral assistance spread from former British colonies in the Indian sub-continent to other regions of Asia, and to newly independent members of the Commonwealth in Africa and the Caribbean. A few ambitious capital projects were undertaken, a modest technical assistance program was launched, and arrangements were made for delivering food, commodity, and emergency aid. The terms of country-to-country aid—a high degree of concessionality, but supply tied heavily to the procurement of Canadian goods and services—established what would become lasting norms. The stage was also set for extensive involvement in multilateral aid programs, not so much by contribu-

---

Notes to Chapter 2 are on pp. 473-79.

tion levels, which were small, as by active participation in a growing number of organizations.

Creation of the External Aid Office in 1960 coincided with the first United Nations Development Decade and a realization among Western donors that development assistance would involve longer-term efforts than originally foreseen. However, it was not until the mid-1960s that the Canadian government, prodded by the United States and the former colonial powers, made a commitment to contribute at least a "fair share" to the overall aid effort.

A sizeable new loan scheme with soft repayment obligations was added to what had been essentially an all-grants program, and by 1966 Canada was becoming a significant donor in terms of funding levels. With domestic political and cultural concerns prompting expansion into francophone Africa and Latin America, the program became more widely dispersed throughout most of the developing world. The earlier tight-fisted attitude to multilateral institutions gave way to more generous levels of support. Meanwhile, Canadian University Service Overseas (CUSO) was the first voluntary development agency to receive public funding.

Under the watchful eye of senior departments, the External Aid Office, led by its first director general, Herbert Moran, overcame much of the administrative chaos that plagued its predecessors in the 1950s. It remained a rudimentary operation, however, with limited capacities for planning, supervising field operations, and reaching out to explain foreign aid to the Canadian public.

Part I: Tentative Beginnings, 1950-60

Australia and Ceylon made a joint proposal for transfers of capital and technical assistance from the United Kingdom and the white dominions to the newly independent and soon-to-be-independent Asian territories of the old British Empire.[2] Canada had donated more than two billion dollars to European reconstruction as a logical extension of its wartime commitments and a contribution to Western efforts to contain communism. The prospect of financial transfers to geographically and culturally remote and distant lands was another matter—the recent communist revolution in China notwithstanding.

Lester Pearson, Canada's secretary of state for External Affairs, had already helped transform the British Empire into a new Commonwealth of Nations by playing a key role in enabling India to remain a member on becoming a republic. Though doubtful about the aid scheme, he agreed to participate in the January 1950 meeting of Commonwealth foreign ministers that gave birth to the Colombo Plan. As John Holmes reported, the decision to attend was made "on the grounds that it would be unwise to let the Asian members think Canada was uninterested in their problems and that it would be all to the good to have a 'North American' view heard, especially on economic matters."[3] The US was also keen to see the Commonwealth involved in efforts to thwart communism and maintain access to Asia's raw materials and potential markets.

Convinced of the scheme's desirability while in Colombo, Pearson returned to Ottawa hoping to persuade his colleagues to take part.[4] Holmes recalled that the cabinet was sharply divided: "Prominent among the old guard was the minister of agriculture, Jimmy Gardiner, who never hesitated to make known his view that the problems of Indian poverty could be solved by a sale of the pooled jewellery of the Maharajahs."[5] Prime Minister Louis St. Laurent was sceptical as well. So too were the Department of Finance and the Bank of Canada, which worried about the balance of payments and budgetary implications of rearming for the Cold War.[6]

Cabinet agreed only to Canadian attendance at a follow-up meeting in Sydney, Australia. In May 1950, Robert Mayhew, the minister of Fisheries, headed a delegation that was told to

> resist any attempts that might be made to oversimplify the problem of raising the standard of living in these countries by expressing it in exclusively financial terms without regard to the social conditions which stand in the way of increasing agricultural and other production. They should also look with suspicion at overly grandiose schemes of development. Ordinary handpumps may be more suited to some regions than vast irrigation works; and ploughs may be more needed than tractors.[7]

In retrospect, such advice seems inspired, but the Canadian government's chief concern was to avoid becoming fiscally overextended.

Years later, Douglas LePan, Mayhew's principal adviser, remembered that Canadian participants had been warned against making any financial commitment

> until the needs of the area had been carefully assessed, . . . until the possibilities of self-help and mutual aid among the underdeveloped countries themselves had been thoroughly explored, and until procedures had been suggested to ensure that whatever external financial aid might be available would be put to effective use. Only in the field of technical assistance were we given any leeway.[8]

The government announced a month later, in June 1950, that $400,000 would be made available in 1950-51 for the technical assistance program of the Colombo Plan. It was not until February 1951, however, following further consultations in London and "no fewer than six meetings of Cabinet"[9] that

Pearson asked Parliament to approve a Canadian contribution of $25 million for capital assistance in 1951-52, "a previously unheard-of sum of money for such a purpose."[10]

The Colombo Plan was in fact not a plan but a consultative group of donor and recipient countries engaged in government-to-government rather than multilateral relations with one another. Canadian participation thus marked the beginning of bilateral aid.

Meanwhile, Canada's active support for the UN and its agencies had, even before 1950, led to some official involvement in multilateral aid activities—funding for UNICEF, emergency relief for refugees in the Middle East, and small grants for the administration of training programs and the recruitment of Canadian experts. Responsibility was divided across several departments and agencies: Finance, External Affairs, and the Bank of Canada for financial contributions to such agencies as UNRWA and UNHCR, and—to cite further examples—Agriculture (FAO), External Affairs (UNESCO), and National Health and Welfare (WHO) for training programs and the provision of Canadian technical expertise. The establishment in 1949 of the UN Expanded Program of Technical Assistance (UNEPTA) prompted interdepartmental discussions on coordination of such activities. Hugh Keenleyside, director of UNEPTA and a former federal deputy minister, pressed for active Canadian participation—though, as with the Colombo Plan, agreement to take part had to overcome stiff resistance in cabinet and the Department of Finance.[11] The initial contribution was $850,000 rather than the $1 million sought by External Affairs.[12]

Institutional Experimentation and Inadequacy[13]

Although the Colombo Plan and foreign aid were seen as short-run and transitory, institutional mechanisms were needed to coordinate training, recruitment of experts, and other aspects of technical aid, as well as for administering prospectively much larger sums of money for capital projects. A kaleidoscope of acronyms ensued. In September 1950, a five-person Technical Cooperation Service (TCS) was set up within the Department of Trade and Commerce, with responsibility for technical assistance under the Colombo Plan and UNEPTA. (Jurisdiction for other UN programs remained elsewhere.) Two months later, a permanent Interdepartmental Group on Technical Assistance (IGTA) was formed to consider future policies and procedures in the light of Canadian resources, and to supervise the work of TCS. A rather unwieldy twenty-five members were drawn from nine departments and agencies under the chair of External Affairs.

In September 1951, the Technical Cooperation Service was absorbed within a new International Economic and Technical Cooperation Division

(IETCD) of Trade and Commerce. With the Interdepartmental Group on Technical Assistance retaining oversight of technical assistance, responsibility for capital allocations and projects was shifted to a smaller Interdepartmental Group on Capital Assistance (IGCA), commonly known as the Colombo Plan Group. External Affairs chaired IGCA, which represented as well the interests of Trade and Commerce, Finance, and the Bank of Canada. Funding decisions for multilateral aid remained with individual departments and were not considered within this framework.

The person hired as administrator of IETCD was one of only two employees in the early years who had any Third World experience. Nik Cavell had spent many years in Asia in the Indian Army and in business. A flamboyant extrovert, whose forte was promotion rather than management, he was more effective in securing projects than in developing a solid bureaucracy. He was on the road for three or four months a year, the only one in the division to travel outside Canada.

Although Cavell took charge of capital assistance, the Technical Cooperation Service was left to operate as a separate solitude under its own director, John Macdonald, an able administrator seconded from National Health and Welfare. Making TCS a bright spot amid considerable turmoil for a brief period in 1952-53, he brought all technical aid activities into the unit, set up advisory panels to obtain expert advice from other departments and organizations, commissioned informational brochures for recipient countries, and prepared operating manuals for internal use.

IETCD is remembered less for its substantive accomplishments than for its marginality in the hierarchy of foreign policy. It was plagued by organizational confusion, continual staff turnover, and low morale. An institutional history, written by a long-time CIDA insider, portrayed the period in rather dismal terms:

> The program proceeded in an unstructured manner, improvisation was common, ad-hoc solutions abounded, record-keeping was minimal, selecting and briefing of experts and trainees remained inadequate or worse, long-term planning was unknown, and reports from the field were spotty to non-existent. The atmosphere in many of our Missions abroad was that political analysis was the true art of the diplomat, that career advancement lay therein, and that aid administration was drudgery. . . . [The] popular view of the transient nature of aid . . . led to the conviction held by career civil servants that the aid field was a career backwater. This, in turn, led to difficulty in attracting first-class men and women in the numbers required.[14]

These problems were worsened by fragmentation of responsibilities for the implementation of capital projects among various agencies outside IETCD, including the Defence Construction Ltd., the Canadian Commercial Corporation, and the Office of International Programmes and Contributions in the Department of Finance.

Continual reorganization (seemingly coded into the DNA of Canadian aid administration) further bedeviled the work of IECTD, as did the peculiar policy-making and reporting arrangements under which it worked.

> Doubtless, the personnel and administrative policies, as indeed the professional talents, of chief officials, were not always best suited to aid administration. But the underlying causes of the general malaise could be imputed only to the complexity of foreign aid itself, and to cabinet policies fixing the scope and framework of administration. These major defects in cabinet direction were, on the one hand, a deliberate short-term view of aid and, on the other, a divided political responsibility for its administration.[15]

As Spicer explained, the decision to place administration of the external aid vote within the Department of Trade and Commerce "theoretically split responsibility for policy and administration between two ministers, each exclusively accountable to Parliament for a distinct aspect of aid." However, within the interdepartmental groups, the Department of Finance exercised tight budgetary control, while External Affairs, which chaired the committees, also "kept a quasi-administrative planning and negotiating role through its Economic Division. . . . Doubtless, close personal relationships of committee members . . . made harmonization of the three departments' interests easier," but "intrinsic differences in outlook and aspirations" created continual conflict.[16]

Though determined to keep aid firmly subordinated to foreign policy, External Affairs was apparently content to see much of the administrative burden shouldered in Trade and Commerce. One official recalled to Spicer: "we were well aware that [External Affairs] was not equipped to deal with recruiting engineers and such creatures. We had qualms about the implications of having this under T. & C. . . . but the practical advantage of a proper office, and most of all, the patronage of C.D. Howe in the Cabinet, seemed more important." Another said that External Affairs had no desire in 1950 to endanger security in its own quarters by having "a lot of foreign trainees milling about there."[17] Yet another retired civil servant told this author that the lessons of potential commercial advantage for Canada had been well learned during the wartime experience under the Mutual Aid scheme with Britain. "Trade and Commerce wanted it bad. Aid was trade and trade was aid. The two were seen as inextricably tied together."

This basic state of disarray prevailed until 1960. Among myriad organizational changes, two stand out as being particularly noteworthy. First, the Technical Cooperation Service and its successors gradually took over policy-making as well as administration in the sphere of technical assistance, which was obviously of less interest than capital aid to the senior bureaucrats. The Interdepartmental Group on Technical Assistance gradually ceased to function. Secondly, after Nik Cavell left to become high commissioner in Ceylon in 1958, IETCD was upgraded within Trade and Commerce as the Economic and Technical Assistance Branch (ETAB). Dr. Orville Ault, a former teacher and a less colourful figure than Cavell, moved from the Civil Service Commission to become director. He set up a Program Planning Division (alongside divisions dealing with capital assistance, technical assistance, and finance and administration) to bring greater coherence to planning and project appraisal. However, little was accomplished; within months, the chief of program planning (brought in from the Ontario government), the assistant director, and a new special adviser on education had all resigned. Ault asked for an information officer, but was turned down on grounds that the aid program was supposed to be responsive, not promotional.[18] The fundamental malaise remained.

Program Growth and Diversification in the 1950s[19]

Canada's bilateral aid grew from $25.3 million in 1951-52 to $61.2 million in 1959-60, by which time the Economic and Technical Assistance Branch had an establishment of twenty-one administrative officers. Allocations for multilateral programs, outside ETAB's domain, were $5.8 million. Canada was still a comparatively small donor, standing eighth among Western countries in total volume of what was later defined as ODA,[20] and was under strong pressure to contribute more.

Geographical distribution defined by the Commonwealth. As founders of the Colombo Plan hoped, the United States and American dollars were soon brought into the scheme, which was expanded to several non-Commonwealth countries in Asia. Canadian participation in the early years, however, remained largely defined by the Commonwealth connection. From 1950 to 1960, India received $148.4 million (53.8 per cent) and Pakistan $100.6 million (36.5 per cent) of Canada's $275.8 million contribution to Colombo Plan countries. Ceylon and Malaysia received 6.5 and 1.1 per cent respectively (and Singapore much less), leaving just 2 per cent for non-Commonwealth countries.[21]

That India and Pakistan, the most populous of the Asian Commonwealth countries, received the largest shares is hardly surprising. The presence of diplomatic missions in those countries, the absence of direct representation in most others, and momentum once programs were established ensured that they would continue as major recipients. Their governments' ability to persuade Canadian officials of superior absorptive capacity was important as well. Cavell told the House of Commons Standing Committee on External

Affairs in 1955 that "India, Pakistan and Ceylon have planning boards and five-year plans. . . . Still more backward countries . . . have not as yet been able to evolve realistic plans. . . . We shall not give them any capital assistance until they have plans into which we can fit that assistance."[22]

Although allocations remained highly concentrated in the 1950s, the seeds of a widely dispersed program were being planted. With the Commonwealth connection continuing to define eligibility, many new candidates for Canadian aid emerged as decolonization raced through Africa and the Caribbean.

Enthusiasm for the Commonwealth reached its apogee when John Diefenbaker served as prime minister from 1958 to 1963. He had seen his hopes for a major Commonwealth trading initiative dashed by the time his government hosted a Commonwealth Trade and Economic Conference in Montreal in September 1958. As Wynne Plumptre observed, "other important matters had to be found to take pride of place on the agenda."[23] Diefenbaker used the Montreal conference to announce a major expansion of the Canadian aid program. First, the annual commitment to the Colombo Plan itself was increased from $35 million to $50 million for each of the next three years. Secondly, a new West Indies Aid Program was launched to provide $10 million over five years in capital and technical assistance to the Commonwealth Caribbean. Thirdly, Ghana's independence and the anticipated emergence from colonial rule of Nigeria and other British African territories prompted a new Commonwealth Technical Assistance Program[24] to provide funds to Commonwealth countries outside the Colombo Plan area; an initial $500,000 was committed for 1959-60. Finally, the Montreal Conference gave birth to the Commonwealth Scholarship and Fellowship Plan, which involved exchanges among the industrialized countries of the Commonwealth, but was conceived mainly as a technical assistance program for Third World members.

"I believe," Diefenbaker declared, "our first consideration in external aid programs should be to raise the living standards within the Commonwealth, for I consider the Commonwealth the greatest instrument for freedom that the world has ever seen."[25] Speaking to the UN General Assembly two years later, the Tory prime minister talked about Canada's "family concern for those countries achieving independence within the Commonwealth."[26] As Spicer commented: "This emotional, quasi-mystical feeling of Commonwealth kinship, while rarely shared (though often exploited) by member nations of non-British stock, brings many English Canadians . . . to feel that Commonwealth aid is a unique fraternal obligation."[27]

Generous terms and stringent procurement tying. Two features that defined the quality of Canadian bilateral aid were put firmly in place during the program's first decade. The first was a high level of concessionality. While other donors typically made much of their ODA available in the form of loans, Canadian decision-makers strongly favoured providing aid on an all-grants basis in order to avoid adding to the debt load of recipient countries.[28] The second was a dogged determination to keep the program firmly tied to the purchase of Canadian goods and services. Politicians, trade officials, and businesses had witnessed the commercial benefits of the wartime and postwar Mutual Aid program with Britain, and expected as a matter of course that foreign aid to developing countries would generate similar returns, along with political goodwill.

Aid for modernization. To the extent that the ad hocery of the 1950s was based on any coherent sense of what the enterprise was about, it was a rather uncritical acceptance of dominant conventions among larger aid donors, especially the US. Little cultural or political sensitivity characterized "big push," "growth with trickle down," and "modernization as westernization" perspectives.

The notion of development as an investment-driven process leading to a "take-off to self-sustaining growth" became closely identified with Walt Rostow, who popularized the work of other economists and sailed with the prevailing ideological winds in *The Process of Economic Growth*[29] and *The Stages of Economic Growth: A Non-Communist Manifesto*.[30] There were major debates about how to achieve take-off, but for aid planners it lay in support for industrial growth through roads, railways, power and irrigation dams, and other major infrastructural projects. Rostow's stage theory of economic growth was, as one long-serving aid official put it, "all the rage" among his colleagues until the late 1960s. He told the author: "None of us at all knew anything about aid. Sort of on the outskirts were old China hands and children of missionaries who had grown up abroad and knew something about the problems of development. Nobody listened to them. They were yesterday. We were going to install the industrial revolution." He went on to talk about a project for fishery mechanization and refrigeration in Ceylon that ended up as a complete failure because it had been seen as a purely technical matter.

Canada's bilateral aid was at first dominated by major capital projects. In fact, almost one-third of all Canadian Colombo Plan aid during the 1950s, and close to two-thirds of capital assistance, was absorbed by just three massive undertakings—the Warsak hydro and irrigation scheme in Pakistan and, in India, the Kundah hydro development and steam locomotives.[31] Although the first major project approved in Pakistan was a cement factory, physical infrastructural projects in power generation, transportation, and telecommunications made up most of the rest of the capital assistance.

The coincidence of Asian drought and an American grains surplus led to the initiation of food aid after Congress passed Public Law 480 in 1954. Aid programs also began to supply industrial commodities. In due course, the theory of foreign aid came to recognize ODA as filling, at various times and in differing combinations, two gaps in developing economies—investment-related shortages in local savings and trade-related shortages in foreign exchange. Food and commodity aid helped fill both of them.[32]

Food and commodities accounted for almost as much of Canada's bilateral program as capital projects during the 1950s. Wheat aid was included in the first bilateral allocation to India in 1951-52, though the Indian government was reluctant to see the shipment count towards Colombo Plan commitments. Canadian authorities, who also found it difficult at first to rationalize food aid as developmental, accepted an approach devised by the US: donated wheat would be sold in ration shops in India and Pakistan to generate "counterpart funds," which would then be used to finance local costs of capital projects.[33] (That was the principle; the actual practice has remained chaotic over the years.)

Food aid was provided sparingly until Diefenbaker came to power on a wave of prairie populist support in 1957. "In view of the fact that we have in Canada a tremendous surplus of wheat," the new prime minister said, also taking note of the ever-present food shortages in the Asian Commonwealth, "we would naturally hope, if not expect, that these countries would take a large share of wheat and flour under the Colombo Plan."[34] Food aid allocations soared from 3.0 per cent of total Canadian ODA in 1956-57 to 27.7 per cent in 1957-58 and 46.6 per cent just a year later.[35]

Non-food commodity aid was introduced in 1954 after the government of Pakistan requested industrial raw materials and consumer goods. As with other matters, the response in Ottawa was cautious, but procedures were worked out so that commodities donated for current or later consumption would qualify as assistance for long-term development by saving foreign exchange and generating, as with food aid, counterpart funds.[36] Metals (especially aluminum, copper, nickel, and steel) accounted for the lion's share of this support, which also included fertilizers and pesticides, asbestos, railway ties, wood pulp, and newsprint.

Technical assistance—education and training and the provision of Western expertise—was seen as a minor priority in the development canon of the early 1950s. It soon became apparent, however, that capital assistance to Asia was not achieving the wonders wrought by the Marshall Plan in postwar Europe. One reason, of course, was that aid flows were very small by comparison (except those for South Korea, Taiwan, and other areas of strategic interest to the US). In addition, growing numbers of practitioners and academic observers argued that economic development required investments in technology and human resources as well as transfers of physical capital.[37]

In Canada's case, technical assistance lagged far behind capital and commodity aid, accounting for less than 4 per cent of total bilateral ODA during the 1950s. At any given time, there were approximately thirty Canadian experts abroad, and some three hundred students and trainees in Canada. Towards the end of the decade, technical assistance became a higher priority with the change in development wisdom and the drive to political independence in the Caribbean and Africa, where levels of education were much lower than in Asia. In contrast to Cavell, Ault was especially enthusiastic about education and training.

Bilateral emergency relief, not restricted to developing countries, was channelled through IETCD and ETAB, and largely administered by the Red Cross.[38] While relief of suffering from floods, droughts, and earthquakes was the most common sort of activity, the biggest project involved resettlement of Hungarian refugees who came to Canada in the wake of the 1956 uprising.

Modest support for multilateral assistance. In 1952, the Department of External Affairs had expressed a hope that Canada's Colombo Plan contributions for technical assistance would in due course be absorbed within UNEPTA to avoid duplication. Nothing further was heard in this vein. After four years of effort, developing countries secured General Assembly approval in 1957 for a Special United Nations Fund for Economic Development (SUNFED) that was to provide substantial low-interest capital for developmental purposes. The victory was hollow, however, as Western donors were not prepared to fund a multilateral development bank they could not be sure of dominating. Canada joined the United States and the United Kingdom as the only members of the General Assembly to vote against SUNFED, which subsequently "died on the vine for lack of donors."[39]

Canadian authorities were similarly chary about other multilateral initiatives, but did support the Americans in establishing alternatives to SUNFED that were more amenable to Western control and broadened the base of burden-sharing: first the UN Special Fund in 1958, and then the International Development Association (IDA) as a soft loan window within the World Bank.[40]

As David Protheroe commented, Canada in the 1950s, "in stark contrast to the security field," did not "look much like a sympathetic, initiative-taking and accommodation-seeking middle power with a professed vital stake in the multilateral aid system." Still, the 9.2 per cent of Canadian aid channelled to multilateral organizations in 1959-60 was almost twice the 4.9 per cent average of all Western donors in 1960.[41]

Assessing the Experience in the 1950s

There were successes and failures in the first decade of Canadian aid, just as in later periods. However, while the fledgling aid bureaucracy was dedicated and hard-working (if somewhat naive), the successes owed little to considered policy or effective organization. An administrative officer sent on a tour of Colombo Plan countries early in 1960 wrote a report that simultaneously captured the poignancy of an initial Third World experience and the need for a more serious Canadian approach to aid:

> [One] begins to grasp what no amount of conversation or informed reading can ever adequately convey, that is the incredible and degrading poverty in which the vast majority of Asians are condemned to live and die. . . . The area is a wilderness of famished bodies, decrepit buildings, rags, filth and the stench of decay—in short an assault upon the senses made more intense by contrast with the opulent scenery of countries like Ceylon and Indonesia and the wealth of Westerners and occasional native magnates in large cities everywhere. Without labouring the point, it is clear that the prevalence of these conditions points an all-too-obvious moral for the planners and financiers of economic development in the region, namely that not a penny nor a minute can be spared for any purpose that does not lead directly to a permanent and measurable diminution of poverty. In this elemental penury, money spent on "frills" is not just misappropriated in the broad sense of the word; it is literally embezzled from the prostrate populations and hence better not spent at all.

He complained about the absence of a Canadian frame of reference for the Colombo Plan. "The result is time-wasting confusion and disagreement among officials in Ottawa and complete disarray in several Missions abroad."[42]

Part II—The External Aid Office, 1960-66

At the end of the 1950s, the American government launched a campaign to increase both the number and contributions of other Western donors. The US was then providing approximately three-fifths of ODA; with pressure building on the national balance of payments, "US Congressmen were growing tired of shouldering the world aid burden so largely by themselves."[43] Other important catalysts were the increasing tempo of decolonization in Africa and elsewhere and deepening concern about competition from the small but growing aid programs of the Soviet Union and Eastern Europe.

American efforts to extend burden-sharing led to the creation of the Development Assistance Group within the Organisation for European Economic Co-operation in 1960 and its institutionalization as the Development Assistance Committee (DAC) of the reconstituted Organisation for Economic and Co-operation and Development the following year. Prompted by the new Kennedy administration, member countries adopted a "Resolution on the Common Aid Effort" in March 1961 urging "an expansion of the aggregate volume of resources made available to the less-developed countries and to improve their effectiveness." The resolution stressed the importance of putting development assistance on "an assured and continuing basis," and called for a study of the "principles on which Governments might most equitably determine their respective contributions to the common aid effort."[44]

Although DAC lacked formal authority, yearly meetings and periodic working groups became important focal points for exchanging perspectives and experiences among aid donors. Annual reports of the DAC chairman published by the secretariat in Paris became the leading source of statistical data on development assistance and other North-South flows, and a barometer of current thinking within the international aid establishment. Member countries agreed at the outset to submit themselves to regular reviews by representatives of other donors.

The agenda for these reviews was already apparent in Chairman James C. Riddleberger's 1961 report: he called for increased aid, criticized hard financial terms on loans to low-income countries, appealed for "joint efforts to reverse the trend towards more tying of aid" to donor procurement, urged more effective coordination among DAC members, and advocated strong support for multilateral agencies (recommendations not unlike those repeated annually for the next thirty-five years).[45] The World Bank, new regional development banks, and a growing network of UN agencies provided further points of contact for bilateral donors, as did various aid consortia and international conferences.

The idea of a quantitative target for resource transfers from rich to poor countries gained currency during this period. The World Council of Churches called in 1958 for a commitment of 1 per cent of national income. In proclaiming the 1960s the United Nations Development Decade, the General Assembly set two specific objectives: achieving a 5 per cent annual growth rate in the developing countries by 1970, and increasing resource transfers as soon as possible to 1 per cent of the combined national incomes of industrial countries.

A New Organizational Approach to Canadian Aid

Another outcome of American pressure for greater burden-sharing and the realization that foreign aid would be a long-term phenomenon was the reorganization or establishment of aid ministries and agencies in several Western countries. The growth of Canadian ODA and unsatisfactory institutional arrangements for aid policy and delivery also prompted efforts in Ottawa to develop a stronger, more coherent organizational framework for the aid program.

Ault's Economic and Technical Assistance Branch proposed in February 1959 that it assume the major role in policy formation.[46] The Colombo Plan Group came to a different conclusion, however, and Ault was transferred. Wynne Plumptre, assistant deputy minister of Finance for Economic and International Affairs,[47] drafted a proposal that was ultimately presented jointly to the cabinet by the secretary of state for External Affairs, the minister of Trade and Commerce, and the minister of Finance. Noting that "the administrative arrangements in Ottawa no longer are entirely adequate to the need," the cabinet memorandum stated:

> Canada's aid programmes have grown substantially in terms of total money expended, in terms of geographic area covered and in terms of their importance as a manifestation of this country's foreign policy. In view of their growth, these Canadian programmes seem bound to come more and more under public surveillance not only at home but also in foreign countries where they are likely to be subject to comparison with similar efforts by other donors, old and new, friendly and unfriendly. . . . In the present three-way sharing of responsibility powers are not clearly defined. Consequently there have been delays in reaching inter-departmental agreement and this, in turn, has impeded the eventual policy decisions on issues both large and small. There is, therefore, an urgent need for improved administrative arrangements if Canada's aid programmes are to achieve their maximum effect.

On August 24, 1960, the cabinet approved a recommendation to "bring the administration of aid programmes under the supervision and control of . . . the Minister responsible for economic aid votes in Parliament and for Canadian external relations." An External Aid Office (EAO) was to be established, headed by a director general reporting to the secretary of state for External Affairs and acting in consultation with an External Aid Board. The new arrangements took effect on November 1, 1960.[48]

Policy-making and Administration

The director general, given the rank of deputy minister, and EAO were charged with responsibilities that went well beyond the uncertain mandates of IETCD and ETAB:

> (a) [to administer] Canada's assistance programmes covered by the general aid votes of the Department of External Affairs;
>
> (b) to keep these programmes under constant review and, as appropriate, to prepare recommendations on them and related matters to Cabinet; to prepare submissions to Treasury Board on financial questions relating to economic assistance;

(c) to ensure co-ordination in the operations of other departments and agencies of government concerned with various aspects of economic assistance programmes;
(d) to consult and cooperate as appropriate with international organizations and agencies;
(e) to consult and cooperate as appropriate with Canadian voluntary agencies active in under-developed countries;
(f) to co-ordinate Canadian efforts to provide emergency assistance in the case of disasters abroad; for this purpose to achieve the necessary liaison with the Canadian Red Cross Society and other appropriate Canadian organizations.

The director general was named as chair of the External Aid Board (which replaced the Colombo Plan Group); other members were the deputy ministers (or their alternates) of Finance, Trade and Commerce, and External Affairs, and the Canadian executive director of the World Bank.[49]

The first director general was Herbert O. Moran. After an early career in corporate law, he had joined the armed services during the Second World War and had gone on to demonstrate considerable organizational ability as General Burns' staff officer in charge of repatriating Canadian troops. He then entered the Department of External Affairs, where he rose to the position of assistant undersecretary of state before serving eight years abroad as ambassador to Turkey and high commissioner to Pakistan. Hoping to receive a European posting on his return from Rawalpindi, and well aware of the intensity of political debate about foreign aid in the United States, he at first resisted the invitation to assume the External Aid post. In August 1960, after lengthy discussions, he agreed reluctantly on three conditions: that the term be limited to two years, that the starting date be deferred to January 1961 to allow sufficient time to put an organization into place, and that three senior officers be seconded to work with him from each of the three senior departments.[50]

As things turned out, EAO began functioning—without office accommodation—well before the end of 1960, and staffing support from the other departments, though welcome, was less extensive than anticipated. The new director general first had to find somewhere to house the operation, and then to deal with difficult organizational problems. Not impressed with many of the personnel inherited from the ETAB, he was disturbed to learn that little had been done to honour the 1958 commitments to expanded programming in the African and Caribbean Commonwealth and to the Commonwealth Scholarship Plan.

Despite his difficult start, Moran remained as director general until 1966. Long-time employees recalled that he ran EAO like an embassy. Stern in manner and demanding with subordinates, he promoted a more professional orientation than had existed in EAO's predecessors, and was able to use an upgraded and more permanent organization to recruit able personnel. He understood official Ottawa, and was able to work effectively in interdepartmental fora as a junior partner to External Affairs.

Although he introduced many operational improvements, Moran was more a doer than a thinker and did not bring a dynamic policy vision to the job. Broad matters of policy were left to External Affairs, with Trade and Commerce and Finance continuing to play active roles as well. As a result, like IETCD and ETAB, EAO was run essentially as an implementing agency. It also remained largely a bilateral operation, with even the multilateral aid responsibilities of External Affairs remaining firmly under the wing of the senior department. A veteran of EAO observed:

> The External Aid Office was completely out of that. Not only was it out of it, Moran and the others weren't particularly anxious to do it. In terms of intelligence about what was going on in the developing world and at the UN, [involvement in multilateral aid] was absolutely essential. That was one of the real weaknesses of EAO.

A creative policy role for EAO was hindered as well by rapid program growth, especially in Moran's last three years. Someone who joined the staff in the early 1960s recalled: "We were so busy trying to stay alive [under mounting pressures] that we had no time to think about policy and where we were going." The overall approach to delivery changed much less than the level of activity. Formal policy remained one of responding to recipient country requests. Laudable in principle, this approach was often lamentable in practice because decisions were taken without any systematic study of conditions in developing countries or of Canadian capabilities. Capital and technical assistance activities remained functionally separate, and even the linkages among programs for education, training, and recruitment of experts (now called advisers) were weak, creating conflict and wasteful duplication of effort.

For most of the period, operations personnel had only indirect contacts with the field: written communications with missions abroad and debriefings of returned advisers and contractors. Long-distance phone calls were frowned upon—even in Canada! Procedural changes, though many, were hit and miss. The less-than-adequate filing system brought over from Trade and Commerce remained in place throughout the Moran period. As workload expanded, the program became notorious for delay. And, as ever since, the external regulatory environment slowed the approval process even further. In the early 1960s, for instance, Treasury Board rules decreed that all technical assistance projects of over $1000 had to have the minister's approval.[51]

While policy and planning capacities were limited, Moran and his associates did get cabinet's authorization for two important tools that began to clear the way for a more coherent approach: the right to keep all funds appropriated by Parliament on a non-lapsing basis,[52] and the authority to engage in five-year forward planning. Together, these two provisions created the possibility of shifting from short-term and ad hoc responses to developing country requests, toward longer-term commitments made after systematic analysis of how Canadian assistance could be effective in meeting recipients' plans and needs.

Pleas for development expertise and a field presence. Meanwhile, in the spring of 1962, the newly founded Overseas Institute of Canada, a citizens' umbrella group and forerunner of the Canadian Council for International Cooperation, and the University of Western Ontario co-sponsored a Conference on Canadian Overseas Aid (the COCOA Conference). It brought together representatives from the UN, the World Bank, business, universities, Canadian voluntary organizations, and aid programs.

Several concerns were raised about the administration of the Canadian aid program. The authors of the conference report noted that the "basic principle of Canadian administration of foreign aid is to manage the program with a small administrative staff, which arranges for the use of whatever outside experts are needed whenever the need arises." They expressed regret that "current recruitment efforts [for EAO staff] are directed towards obtaining experts in administration rather than in external aid, economics, or knowledge of recipient countries," and advocated establishing a career service that would recruit people with these various forms of expertise from both outside and within government.[53]

> Establishment of a career service might help to eliminate a criticism of another type—the lack of expertise in external aid as such on the part of those administering the program in the field. The complete reliance on regular diplomatic personnel for field administration and evaluation has raised considerable objections. For the present, such reliance has the advantage of ensuring maximum coordination between aid policy and foreign policy. . . . [Some] engineers have been attached to diplomatic missions, under ambassadorial control, to provide technical advice to the diplomatic staff. As long as the present system continues, however, it would seem desirable to make external aid specialists out of some Foreign Service Officers, achieving such an aim through both recruiting and training methods.[54]

The report also suggested that EAO set up a small permanent staff of technical experts, who would develop systematic inventories of external expertise, help with recruitment of consultants, and offer specialized advice on projects. They "could also be used in the field to provide much needed coordination in technical assistance activities."[55]

The advice did not strike a responsive chord in EAO, and—though the establishment grew from 60 in 1960 to 350 in 1966—there was not even a single professional economist working as such at the end of Moran's tenure.[56] To the extent that a coterie of professional staff was developed, it was in engineering and related to the design and implementation of capital projects. Many of the people recruited during this period, engineers and generalists alike, had military backgrounds.

Just at the end of the Moran era, Keith Spicer also made a strong pitch in *A Samaritan State?* for a career service, aid specialists, and decentralization to the field. He argued strenuously against "unreal" objections that officials had cited to him—that there would not be enough openings for "young men of ambition or to justify creation of new civil service classifications"; that there would be too few applicants for a career aid service; and, specifically about postings abroad, that the current level of Canadian assistance did not warrant them. Spicer concluded:

> The career service is . . . an urgent and logical imperative of an expanding Canadian aid programme. Long ago this wise investment in human resources was understood by the United States and other large donors, even though excessive professionalism and bureaucratic sclerosis have marred some of their efforts. . . . [Until] this reform is achieved, aid policy itself will be shackled—not by the public's refusal of increases in aid, but by the administration's growing impotence to exploit them.[57]

Actually, by the time Spicer's book was published in 1966, EAO had taken a modest step towards establishing a direct presence in developing countries. The first of three field liaison officers was in New Delhi and two more were about to be posted to Africa. However, the decision to train and second these people was a pragmatic response to a complaint from External Affairs about the growth in aid-related work in Third World posts, rather than an affirmation of the case for a field presence.

Programming in the Moran Era

The increase in Colombo Plan support and new Commonwealth African and Caribbean initiatives in 1958, along with creation of the External Aid Office in 1960, suggested that the Canadian aid program was poised for a period of rapid growth. However, while the broader international context also favoured such an outcome, it was delayed until the Liberals returned to power under Lester Pearson in 1963.

When Howard Green, Diefenbaker's secretary of state for External Affairs, was asked in March 1960 in the Standing Committee of the House of Commons on External Affairs whether Canada would respond to the UN target with substantial increases, he replied in defiance of the facts that "Canada's participation in these programmes is very good. In our opinion it is better than any other nation."[58] A year later, he defended the record again, but added: "Mind you, in some ways we are an underdeveloped country. There is quite a difference between the capacity of Canada and that of some of the older countries, such as the United States, West Germany, and the United Kingdom, to provide aid of this kind."[59]

Not long afterwards, the Conservative government, mired in economic and other domestic doldrums, reduced contributions to the Colombo Plan from $50 million to $41.5 million in each of 1962-63 and 1963-64. Support for Commonwealth Africa and the Caribbean was increased by about $3 million over earlier annual levels, but the overall reduction was substantial.[60] ODA/GNP ratios calculated subsequently revealed a drop from 0.20 per cent in 1960-61 to 0.13 per cent in 1962-63.[61] Paul Martin, external affairs critic for the Liberals, condemned the cutback for confusing "desirable retrenchments in Canada with the glaring need that faces underdeveloped countries."[62] David Lewis of the New Democratic Party called it "an act of meanness in a world which cries out for generosity."[63]

Officials were embarrassed by 1962 DAC figures that showed Canadian aid as a percentage of GNP falling well below that of other members. Canada's DAC delegate reacted defensively, arguing that the data made Canadian performance look weaker than it actually was. It was his veto of a recommendation to publish these data that delayed for a few years their inclusion as a standard feature of DAC's annual reports.[64]

At this stage, American pressure on Ottawa to increase aid and assume broader responsibilities in the Western Hemisphere outside the Commonwealth was probably counterproductive. It certainly did not help that John Diefenbaker's growing conflict with President John F. Kennedy over defence policy extended to external aid. With sharp recession and growing unemployment in Canada, the prime minister became ever more determined to resist Kennedy's admonitions to increase defence and aid spending.[65] Canadian-American relations featured prominently in the 1963 general election, and, although a minor issue, both Diefenbaker and Green reacted angrily to an official report on the American aid program that made comments about other donors, including the desirability of a larger Canadian program. Green saw it as "another case of Americans trying to tell Canada what to do."[66]

Press commentary generally agreed that Canadian aid efforts had been insufficient. This reproach haunted Diefenbaker so much that he later produced in his autobiography a proud catalogue of what he saw as his government's aid achievements, expressing incredulity about "domestic and international criticism that Canada was not doing enough!"[67] Some of the critical commentary came from articulate supporters of the aid program who attended the COCOA Conference in 1962. Voicing concern about the government's cutbacks, they were not sanguine about a positive response:

> Despite the apparent general support of the external aid program by "informed" public opinion, it is doubtful whether Canadian taxpayers (and, of course, their representatives in Parliament) are willing to absorb an important increase in aid expenditures. Most of the public is not very well informed about the existing program, and they know less about its objectives. Even informed circles, aware as they are of competing demands for the expenditure of the tax dollar, are reluctant to see other programs sacrificed for the sake of external aid. It is precisely at Cabinet level, where crucial aid decisions are taken, that the pressure of other demands is most strongly felt.

Noting that "aid has no vociferous and well-organized 'constituency,' " the conference report concluded that any considerable increase was unlikely "as long as the public remains uninformed and unconvinced."[68] A public opinion poll conducted by the Canadian Peace Research Institute late in 1962 found that 51 per cent of respondents considered the Canadian aid program "about right," 23 per cent thought it was "too much," and 3 per cent were opposed to any aid.[69]

Despite the low public profile of the ODA program, official demeanour changed after the Liberal election victory in 1963. While the skirmish over aid volume had been only an isolated incident in the election campaign, Pearson pledged to restore the austerity cuts, and Peyton Lyon speculated that the accompanying press support for increases in Canadian aid may have contributed to the new government's subsequent decision to enlarge the program.[70] Wynne Plumptre, who represented Finance on the External Aid Board for several years, gave due credit to Paul Martin, the new secretary of state for External Affairs, though "I rather wish that . . . he had not been so apparently obsessed by the comparative statistics. There are much better reasons for expanding our aid."[71] Prime Minister Pearson also supported greater commitment, though without the depth of passion about international development, or the time to devote to it, that characterized his post-political career.

Announcing a substantial increase in aid allocations in November 1963, Martin said:

> our Canadian effort cannot be viewed in isolation but rather as part of a broad collective effort. We would be failing in our responsibilities both to the developing countries and to other advanced countries with which we are associated, if we did not ensure that Canada played its proper role in this common aid effort.

The major innovation was a loan scheme with an initial ceiling of $50 million per annum that would undertake development lending on very soft terms—no interest, fifty years repayment, and a ten-year grace period.[72] Grants were to be increased as well. All opposition parties welcomed the announcement, although Diefenbaker, now leader of the opposition, reserved judgement on the loan program until he had a chance to study it. Tommy Douglas, leader of the NDP, urged even more rapid expansion, aimed at reaching 2 per cent of Gross National Product.[73]

In 1965, DAC endorsed the UN target of 1 per cent of donor country GNP for transfers of private and official sources of finance to developing countries.[74] Pearson accepted it for Canada in 1966, though without specifying a date for achievement. A year later, he assured the House of Commons that "we aim" to reach it "within a short period of time."[75] At that stage, even after three years of aid budget growth, Canada stood third among (by now) fifteen DAC donor countries in per capita income, yet only thirteenth in the net flow of private and official resources to developing countries expressed as a percentage of national income.[76] However, when DAC later did retrospective calculations on ODA as distinct from other transfers, Canada in 1966 ranked sixth (out of seventeen DAC members) in dollar volume, accounting for 3.12 per cent of DAC ODA, up from 1.39 per cent in 1960. In relative terms, at 0.33 per cent of GNP, the ranking was ninth, below the DAC average of 0.41 per cent. Still, the Canadian percentage represented a jump from 0.16 per cent and last place (out of nine) in 1960.[77]

By 1965-66, the last full year of Moran's stewardship, bilateral allocations had more than doubled to $85.8 million from a low point of $33.1 million in 1962-63. Multilateral grants and advances from other federal departments and agencies had expanded more than fivefold since 1959-60, to $34.0 million.[78] (Real growth was substantial as these were years of low inflation.) Given government commitments, Canadian aid was poised to achieve much higher levels of growth, although—with the facility to carry over unspent funds—the bilateral program was beginning to experience difficulty in disbursing as rapidly as monies were appropriated by Parliament.[79]

Geographical Distribution: Towards a Global Reach[80]

New programs in yet more parts of the developing world were launched in the early 1960s, ensuring that the Canadian aid program, however large or small, would be global and widely dispersed rather than concentrated. Although the basis for further diversification was well established by 1960, only seven Asian countries had by then received more than $1 million in Canadian bilateral aid since 1950. Ten other Colombo Plan recipients had received token amounts, and programs had been started in Ghana, Nigeria, and the (then) West Indies Federation. By the end of the 1962-63 fiscal year,

97 per cent of all bilateral assistance had gone to just four countries: India, Pakistan, Ceylon, and Malaysia.

Just four years later, there were fifty-nine active bilateral recipients (not including regional programs): eleven under the Colombo Plan, five in the Commonwealth Caribbean, thirty-four in Africa, and nine in Latin America. Presence was only token in many of these countries, but programming had nonetheless begun. Despite this proliferation, allocations remained heavily concentrated in the Colombo Plan area, especially India and Pakistan. In 1965-66, India received $39.9 million and Pakistan $19.4 million, compared to less than $20 million for all of Africa; within that continent, only Nigeria ($3.8 million), Ghana ($2.0 million), and Tanzania ($1.1 million) received more than $1 million.[81]

The Commonwealth Caribbean. The first focus of the Caribbean program, the nascent West Indies Federation, was seen as a project that Canada, with its own federal institutions, was especially well placed to foster. When the Federation broke up on the eve of independence in 1962, separate programs were established for Jamaica and Trinidad and Tobago, as well as for several of the smaller islands that remained (and, in some cases, still are) British dependencies. In 1963, three years before independence, an aid program was initiated in Guyana, at least partly in response to British and American concerns about the political agenda of the Jagan regime and Alcan's fears about the safety of its investments.[82]

Commonwealth Africa. Late in 1960, the earlier African initiative was expanded by the creation of a new umbrella for aid relations, the Special Commonwealth Africa Aid Programme (SCAAP). Ghana and Nigeria were the focal points for SCAAP. Canada's aid presence in Ghana, destined to be substantial and relatively stable considering that country's political vicissitudes, was for a time upstaged by support for Nigeria, with which, as John Schlegel observed, there was a "mutual concern for bilingualism, multicultural societies and a common federal structure."[83]

Although less overt than at the birth of the Colombo Plan, Cold War rivalries played a role in the expansion of Canadian aid in Commonwealth Africa. Nowhere was this more apparent than in Tanzania, where foreign policy disputes with Britain, the US, and West Germany led the governments of those countries to urge greater Canadian involvement as a counterweight to growing Chinese aid. As earlier in Ghana and Nigeria, development assistance was supplemented by military support.[84] Tanzania's membership in the East African Community gave yet further impetus to Canadian aid, which was extended directly to Community institutions and in increasing quantities to Kenya and Uganda, the other member states. (Like the West Indies Federation, the East African Community was short-lived.)

By the mid-1960s, bilateral programming was also beginning in Zambia, Malawi, Botswana, Lesotho, and Swaziland.

Francophone Africa. In a curious way, John Diefenbaker's passion for the Commonwealth served as a catalyst for an extension of Canadian aid to francophone Africa. The coincident timing of the Canadian government's new Commonwealth initiatives, Quebec's Quiet Revolution, and decolonization within the African empires of France and Belgium led to critical commentary from French-speaking journalists and intellectuals. In 1960, André Laurendeau complained, "Le Commonwealth n'est pas l'humanité," and Jean-Marc Leger wrote:

> Pourquoi serait-il impossible que le gouvernement central décide une fois pour toutes de tenir compte de la situation particulière résultant pour le Canada de sa bi-ethnicité? Et, chaque fois où dans le cadre du Commonwealth un programme quelconque d'assistance est institué, d'y joindre un programme analogue en faveur des nombreux Etats de langue française?[85]

Their pleas struck a responsive chord in External Affairs where Marcel Cadieux, then a deputy under-secretary, pushed strongly for a program in French-speaking Africa.[86]

Towards the end of 1960, Ottawa dispatched Pierre Dupuy, ambassador to France,[87] on a fact-finding mission to several newly independent French-speaking countries of Africa. He recommended establishment of a distinct regional aid program for francophone Africa, identified possible projects in Tunisia and Senegal, reported some interest in Canadian capital goods, and suggested opening an embassy in Dakar, Senegal with multiple accreditation to other states in the region.[88] There was little enthusiasm for a new venture in the External Aid Board, but Cadieux persuaded Howard Green, secretary of state for External Affairs, that it would be "in the national interest." The outcome, announced in April 1961, was a positive, if hardly dramatic decision to commit $300,000 a year in educational assistance.[89] EAO was responsible for administering the program, but Cadieux chaired a committee set up with representation from the federal and Quebec governments and various educational interests to advise on allocations. Dakar and Tunis, both considered as sites for a diplomatic mission, were bypassed in favour of Green's choice, which was Yaoundé, apparently because he had recently learned with pleasure that Cameroon "was a bilingual country just like Canada."[90]

Canada's willingness to extend aid at first drew little response in the former French colonies, either among African officials, the products of what they regarded as a superior educational system in metropolitan France, or among the French themselves, who were hostile to this perceived intrusion on their territorial prerogatives. Although the presence of missionary priests from Quebec provided an entrée for the program, lack of Canadian experience and slowness in establishing official representation resulted in inability to spend even the small amount of money allocated. Further complexity stemmed from the desire of the strongly nationalist Lesage government in Quebec to gain its own international presence and to exclude the federal government from any activity that encroached upon provincial jurisdiction over education.

The COCOA Conference of 1962 drew attention to these difficulties, and advised the government to concentrate aid in the Commonwealth, where political ties and common administrative structures would ensure that "Canadian aid can be more effectively utilized."[91] Shortly thereafter, however, Cadieux and other senior officials in External Affairs who were worried about Quebec's growing assertiveness in international matters, persuaded Paul Martin and the new Liberal government to reject this sort of anglo logic, which also reflected the disposition of senior people in EAO.[92] The annual allocation for French-speaking Africa was increased to $4 million in 1964-65, capital projects became eligible for support, and efforts to penetrate the francophone countries were intensified. Moreover, "the capacity to deliver programs was improved . . . by the decision to open posts in Senegal and Tunisia in 1966."[93] A close witness of these events told the author:

> Paul Martin saw more clearly [than Howard Green] the domestic political benefits as well as the international political benefits of an aid program, and was interested in involving the province of Quebec, which we did mainly through Father Lévesque and the clergy generally. I think we had half of the Roman Catholic Church under contract at one point!

The new commitment still failed to generate much interest in the former French colonial empire, but a substantial project was approved in French-speaking Rwanda, a former Belgian UN trusteeship territory. The Right Reverend Father Georges-Henri Lévesque was given the mandate of guiding a new national university through its formative years as its first rector. According to a well-placed observer, this initiative was strongly opposed by EAO and senior officials in External Affairs, who saw no demonstrable Canadian interest in Rwanda. However, as the founder of the Faculty of Social Sciences at Laval University, a former vice-chairman of the Canada Council, and an intellectual force in the Quiet Revolution, Father Lévesque had strong political support among francophones in the federal cabinet.

Despite the higher priority on francophone Africa, Spicer wrote in 1966 that "Even a thirteen-fold increase to four million dollars in 1964-65 left Canada's yearly allocation to the eighty million people of these twenty-one French-speaking African states less than double the Canadian aid given that year to the four million people of the Commonwealth Caribbean."[94] He advocated a more ambitious program, but one small in scale compared with the actual growth that occurred in the late 1960s when, as we shall see in Chapter 3, development assistance to francophone Africa was used aggressively as a tool for foreign and domestic policy purposes.

Latin America. The final geographic initiative during the Moran years was in Latin America. While Diefenbaker resisted American pressure to extend Canadian ODA to the Americas beyond the Commonwealth Caribbean, the Pearson government took steps that eventually culminated in creation of a full regional program in Latin America. Following the 1963 decision to increase Canada's aid effort, an interdepartmental working group broached the idea of channelling assistance to individual Latin American countries through World Bank consultative groups. The External Aid Board subsequently rejected direct bilateral assistance on grounds of "manpower shortages, language difficulties, dispersion of our aid effort and administrative problems."[95] The Board did endorse, however, a proposal for a Canadian loan program in the area under the auspices of the Inter-American Development Bank (IDB) as part of the new $50 million soft-loan scheme.

Although this approach was adopted partly to avoid a new administrative burden, the chief rationale was to escape making political choices among countries of the region. Nonetheless, it was not long before the Department of Trade and Commerce and Canadian engineering firms began lobbying for specific projects,[96] and church groups active in the region began to push for a technical assistance program. EAO officials expressed reluctance about becoming more involved while also admitting "the lack of logic in the choice of the present recipients."[97]

A Continuing Tough Line on Tied Aid

Although the terms of Canadian bilateral aid became marginally harder with introduction of the loan program, DAC lauded Canada for its commitment to substantial concessionality, highlighting the conscious policy of ensuring that Canadian aid did not add to mounting debt in developing countries.[98] However, Canada was unyielding to DAC pressure on the issue of procurement tying. The program remained completely tied to the purchase and use of Canadian goods and services, and, in the absence of a Canadian merchant marine, recipient countries were expected to cover all shipping costs themselves.[99] The minimum domestic content of goods was pegged at 80 per cent.[100]

An internal EAO document argued that untied aid offered advantages to less-developed countries and was in principle desirable, but that volume and concessionality "are probably more important." Conceding that DAC had a legitimate concern with tying and minimizing "any impairment that may result" through the provision of uncompetitive goods, the paper suggested that there were explicit trade-offs for donors:

> [We] must take account of the possibility that an improvement in quality by a reduction in tied aid might entail a reduction in total aid, and that undue emphasis on untied aid could be a deterrent to augmenting aid efforts generally. . . . It may be that we should accept the continuance of a certain proportion of tying in bilateral aid programmes as inevitable and perhaps even necessary in the interests of maximizing the total aid effort.[101]

Preventing a drain on the balance of payments was frequently cited as the main justification for tying, and, as Moran told a Commons committee in 1961, tied bilateral aid "makes possible the expenditure of public funds in Canada. Under a multilateral program you have no control over your funds."[102]

Aid administrators also saw the presumed domestic political advantages as important as well. A leading figure in the External Aid Office put it this way:

> We were reaching out wherever we could to try and satisfy the public that development assistance carried benefits for Canada. One instrument we had was tied aid—the money spent in Canada with its benefits to Canadian companies. . . . Aid was a new concept in those days and people said, "What the hell is this? You're just taking some of our taxpayers' money and giving it to foreigners." So we were looking for ways to say to the people, "That's not quite the way development assistance works."

On the basis of his long experience in the Department of Finance, Plumptre argued: "Better a million dollars' worth of aid on which you can depend for continuing year-to-year support, even though the prices involved are (say) 20 per cent above competitive world prices, than half or a quarter that sum which lacks continuing support but can be used to shop for the best bargains in the world."[103]

The rigidity of tying created particular difficulties in the Commonwealth Caribbean where, in the absence of food or commodity aid, there were no counterpart funds available to cover local costs. Under pressure from British and West Indian governments, the External Aid Board asked cabinet for authority to spend in special circumstances up to 25 per cent of a project allocation on local costs, including shipping. The government announced its agreement to this limited degree of flexibility at a Commonwealth Caribbean-Canada Conference held in Ottawa in July 1966.[104]

Programming: Shifting Contours in the 1960s

Within the Colombo Plan area, food and commodity assistance continued to match capital projects in importance, except during years of cutbacks, which were managed largely by decreases in food aid. Food as a percentage of Canadian ODA declined from over 20 per cent in 1961-62 to under 4 per cent the next two years. Not coincidentally, the reductions occurred during years of diminished wheat stocks and above-average commercial exports. The Canadian Wheat Board and farm interests pushed for an increase after a bumper crop in 1962. With establishment of a separate food aid program in 1964-65 (announced by Martin in the November 1963 package), allocations returned to levels above 20 per cent a year, and, with huge shipments to India in 1966-67, reached the highest level ever of 57 per cent in that year.[105]

Capital projects. While food and commodity support were restricted to the Colombo Plan region, capital projects in all geographic areas continued to be predominantly in transportation, especially locomotives and steel rails, and power generation and transmission.[106] As former officials admitted to the author, locomotives and steel rails were among the least competitive of goods provided under the aid program, but they came from depressed Canadian industries and regions and had strong political backing.

Higher priority on technical assistance. With expansion into Africa and changing aid discourse, technical assistance, which had accounted for only 3 to 4 per cent of expenditures in the 1950s, reached 12 per cent of the grants program in 1965-66. The number of students and trainees in Canada under EAO auspices grew from 709 in 1960 to 2,964 in 1966; Canadian advisers and teachers abroad rose from 21 to 824.[107] Much of the increased administrative establishment was involved in the placing and supporting trainees and advisers. Given their jurisdiction over education, the provinces became actively involved in providing organizational support for Canadian aid.

The pool of qualified Canadians available to offer specialized training programs in Canada and undertake aid postings overseas, though growing, remained severely constrained until the late 1960s. Universities played a key role in the expansion that did take place, offering more places in regular undergraduate and graduate programs as well as special courses under contract with EAO.[108] What later became a substantial program of official support for linkages between Canadian and developing country universities also had its beginnings during Moran's tenure. The director general told DAC during the 1965 review of Canadian aid:

> We have found that one of the most effective forms of assistance to institutions of higher education is through the contractual arrangements we make with individual Canadian universities. In this way, a particular Canadian university accepts the responsibility for the provision of a minimum number of professors over a period of years as well as the training in Canada of counterparts with all costs, including any required equipment, being met from government aid funds. Under such an arrangement, the overseas university receives the direct support

and has available the full resources of a Canadian university and also the opportunity for the establishment of valuable continuing links between the two institutions.[109]

While universities were able to provide some of the expertise that was in short supply, they also generated recruits for less specialized work abroad. There was no shortage of energy and enthusiasm among recent graduates who accepted teaching and other posts under the auspices of the fledgling Canadian University Service Overseas (CUSO).

Challenges to conventional programming. The guiding philosophy of Canadian aid—growth through capital and technical transfers—remained unchanged during the Moran era. However, debates in academic, voluntary agency, and policy-making circles outside of Canada about whether aid was tackling unequal income distribution, unemployment, agricultural underdevelopment, and poverty began to penetrate informed discussion within the country. At the COCOA Conference in 1962, Dr. G.C. Monture, a distinguished Canadian of Mohawk descent who had considerable international experience, criticized "Canada's almost total preoccupation" with providing hydro generating facilities to India. As Franc Joubin recalled, "His vigorous criticism surprised, and appeared to confuse, some of the senior bureaucrats present who regarded Canada's external aid program as being nearly ideal."[110] The Overseas Institute of Canada followed the COCOA Conference with a Workshop on Canadian Participation in Social Development in 1963;[111] another OIC conference in 1965 called for "balanced" Canadian effort incorporating "both *social* and *economic* factors in the approach to developing countries."[112]

Multilateral Activism[113]

From a reluctant participant in the growing multilateral aid system through most of the 1950s, Canada became an active supporter in the 1960s. The change reflected acceptance of the norm of burden-sharing among Western donors and also the extension of middle-power multilateralism from the sphere of security into that of aid. After the decision to expand development assistance in 1963, the multilateral system held the additional attraction of a resource outlet with minimal administrative workload. Canadian contributions to multilateral aid agencies reached a level of 27.8 per cent of ODA in 1965-66, far higher than the DAC average of 5.6 per cent.[114]

Support was increased for existing UN agencies (Canada for a time became the second largest donor to UNRWA and UNHCR), and energy was channelled into creation of the United Nations Development Program (UNDP) through a 1965 merger of UNEPTA and the UN Special Fund. As we have seen, Canada's food aid policy in the early years was driven by the simple assumption that there was a happy coincidence of interest between humanitarian need abroad and disposal of the surplus production of Canadian farmers. Nonetheless, the founding of the World Food Program in 1962 owed much to Canadian initiatives, however self-interested the motives, dating back to Diefenbaker's earlier proposal for a world food bank.

Little more than a passive supporter when the International Development Association was founded under the auspices of the World Bank, Canada became active in the work of the new agency. Canadian representatives were among those who failed to persuade the United States that IDA should have authority to make grants as well as concessional loans. Relations with regional development banks were initially cautious. As noted above, Parliament approved late in 1963 a five-year scheme that provided loans for Canadian procurement of up to $10 million annually through the Inter-American Development Bank. In keeping with long-standing policy to remain aloof from inter-American organizations, actual membership in the IDB was declined at this time. Canada supported establishment of the African Development Bank in 1964, and became a charter member of the Asian Development Bank in 1965.[115]

Connecting with the Voluntary Sector and the Public

The director general and his associates were reluctant to offer more than moral support to voluntary agencies involved in international development. However, as high commissioner to Pakistan, Moran had encouraged formation of a CUSO forerunner, Canadian Overseas Volunteers (organized by Keith Spicer). Although it took a lot of persuasion, he eventually recognized as worthy of consideration CUSO's requests for direct government assistance for its volunteer placement program. Paul Hellyer, the minister of National Defence, agreed in 1964 to use Royal Canadian Air Force transport training missions to take CUSO volunteers to central locations overseas. Despite Paul Martin's reservations, a further breakthrough came in 1965 when $500,000 in federal funds were committed to the organization for the next fiscal year.[116]

Apart from Overseas Institute of Canada conferences, which brought the official and voluntary interests in aid together, and occasional speeches by the director general to service clubs and the like, EAO kept a low public profile. It did receive hundreds of letters from Canadians with ideological concerns about aid (positive and negative), complaints about the program and/or specific projects, and ample advice on how to run it more effectively. These were duly answered. Unlike Ault, Moran was permitted to hire an information officer, but public relations remained essentially responsive rather than proactive.

Moran Moves On

Herb Moran's intended two years had stretched almost to six when he accepted an appointment as ambassador to Japan in 1966. During his tenure, Canada's official development assistance had grown from less than $70 million annually to $122 million, and a program involving a few capital projects and food aid in four Asian countries had expanded to almost sixty countries in all areas of the developing world. However, organizational arrangements, though much improved when contrasted with the 1950s, were still far from adequate. Policy and analytical capacities within EAO were underdeveloped and technical expertise was limited. Delivery in the field continued to depend upon Canadian diplomats, for whom developmental issues were often secondary, and consultants, who were supervised from Ottawa by bureaucrats with no direct involvement or experience in developing countries.

Although Moran lacked an ambitious policy agenda, it is arguable that no Ottawa insider could have achieved much more during the early 1960s. Foreign aid was still a novel, relatively marginal government activity, and the three senior departments dominating the program—External Affairs, Finance, and Industry, Trade and Commerce—had ingrained traditions and objectives. They were about to be challenged by a dynamic and ambitious outsider.

Chapter 3

Maurice Strong and the Creation of CIDA, 1966-70

The rapid growth in parliamentary appropriations for development assistance after 1963 and the strong, if qualified, commitment of Prime Minister Pearson (and later of Prime Minister Trudeau) to meet international aid targets opened the door in the late 1960s to unprecedented dynamism in both organizational and programming terms. The period and its legacies are inextricably connected with the leadership of Maurice Strong, who succeeded Herb Moran as director general of the External Aid Office in September 1966. Strong, a self-made millionaire with no prior experience in government, spearheaded efforts to transform EAO into an agency that would take responsibility for multilateral as well as bilateral aid, and help shape Canada's trade and other policies towards developing countries. The creation of the Canadian International Development Agency in 1968 symbolized these ambitions, which, though far from fully realized, established CIDA as a significant player on the Ottawa scene.

At a practical level, the presence of an energetic entrepreneur at the helm made life difficult for many bureaucrats, but ensured that the whole operation was subjected to fundamental rethinking. Strong recruited some remarkably able people from the private and public sectors to take on senior responsibilities—and, as the establishment virtually doubled, returned CUSO volunteers and others injected youth, commitment, and enthusiasm into the organization. Although EAO/CIDA remained highly centralized in Ottawa, officers now travelled abroad and more of them were posted to Canadian embassies and high commissions. Amid considerable organizational change and turmoil, the project and the recipient country emerged as fundamental units of operation.

Parliamentary allocations for external aid increased substantially, faster in fact than the capacity of EAO/CIDA to disburse. As a result, the volume of unexpended appropriations mounted steadily. A global bilateral program, already in the making when Strong took over, moved closer to its final shape

---

Notes to Chapter 3 are on pp. 480-87.

as the program in francophone Africa was expanded aggressively and another was launched in Latin America. Although large projects for economic infrastructure, along with food and commodity aid, continued to dominate government-to-government transfers, technical assistance expanded and aid planners became more conscious of the social dimension of development.

Meanwhile, what proved to be long-lasting policies on terms of aid were fashioned, and multilateral assistance came of age. Strong also stimulated significant innovations in responsive programming and public outreach with the establishment of the NGO and business programs, and in development research with the creation of the International Development Research Centre. Spurred on by some fundamental challenges to orthodox thinking about the place of aid in international development, he hoped to accomplish more through an ambitious policy review during his last year in office, but it fell short of his expectations.

To a large extent, the Strong era has to be understood as a special historical opportunity shaped by the novelty of the activity and its prominence in Canada during a period of cultural and economic upheaval. It was an opportunity that Strong and his close associates exploited with vigour.

From External Aid to International Development

Strong was appointed just as "trade not aid" became the clarion call for many developing countries and for liberal critics in the North. It was a direct challenge to the protectionist practices of industrial country governments, which had chosen the soft option of development assistance in preference to adjusting their own economies.[1] Meanwhile, within radical academic circles and some southern countries, the international trade option was being challenged by a vision of self-reliant development and relative disengagement from transnational capitalism. Though divergent, liberal and radical critiques contributed to efforts aimed at devising common developing country policies on opening access to Northern markets and regulating the activities of multinational corporations. The UN Conference on Trade and Development (UNCTAD)—which met every four years beginning in 1964—became the main forum for discussion of proposals advanced by the "Group of 77," named after the "Joint Declaration of the 77 Developing Countries" presented to the UN General Assembly in 1963.[2]

Amid growing debate about non-aid dimensions of international development, development assistance came under increasingly sharp attack in the latter half of the 1960s. American contributions started declining after 1964 in the wake of bitter controversy in Congress and as the US Administration was becoming more deeply mired in Vietnam. Academic and popular commentaries were questioning the value of ODA—from the right as an unwarranted and wasteful intervention in the marketplace that undermined capitalism, and from the left as a tool for strengthening the capacity of capitalism to exploit and underdevelop the Third World.[3] As Göran Ohlin observed, "Already in the 60s there was talk of 'aid fatigue' and also criticism of the profligate life style of elites in the countries receiving aid. . . . A German newspaper coined the phrase that 'the poor in rich countries were helping the rich in poor countries.' "[4]

Within multilateral and bilateral agencies themselves, doubts were increasing about the efficacy of pursuing economic growth as *the* pathway to development, if development implied such goals as a more equitable distribution of incomes and the reduction of poverty. In aggregate terms, developing countries slightly exceeded the growth target set for the 1960s by the UN in 1961. Much of the gain was negated, however, by rapid population increases. There was little evidence of "trickle down": while wealthy elites had become richer, many more people were living in absolute poverty. Widespread improvements in life expectancy and literacy were accompanied by unemployment and underemployment that were reaching critical proportions. Green revolution technology was increasing crop yields, especially in parts of Asia, but per capita agricultural production elsewhere was stagnating or, in sub-Saharan Africa, declining.

The Appointment of Maurice Strong

Strong, who left school at the age of sixteen, was only thirty-three in 1962 when he capped a meteoric rise in business by becoming president of Power Corporation. He was active in community and voluntary organizations, among them the Overseas Institute of Canada, CARE, and the Red Cross; as international president of the YMCA, he promoted its world service program in developing countries. He had also spoken out about Canada's international role, suggesting that a greater contribution could be made in global development than in defence.

Strong's name was suggested to Prime Minister Pearson by J. Roby Kidd of the Overseas Institute of Canada. In correspondence with Kidd, Pearson agreed that Strong was "an exceptionally good man to take the job."[5] Strong himself recalled that he had conversations about an expanded and broadened Canadian role in international development with Ed Ritchie, then assistant under-secretary of state for External Affairs. These led to discussions with Paul Martin and ultimately the prime minister, before the announcement of what for Ottawa was an unorthodox but inspired appointment. One of Strong's colleagues in the EAO commented:

> At the symbolic level, the choice of person by the government to head the new drive, a businessman, a man who was extremely well connected in a lot of fields, put an accent on the direction this was to take. It was already perceived that the level of involvement was going to be quite high. It was going to be sustained over a long period of time, and it was going to be ultimately at its core a business relationship.

Strong's Agenda[6]

Reflecting on the context of his appointment, Strong recalled: "There was an awareness in the government and elsewhere that aid was not just a short-term phenomenon—that it would have to be integrated more into our own governmental apparatus, on a more permanent basis, and that multilateral, trade, and other issues would have to be more closely attuned to our foreign aid efforts."[7] He was concerned about the fragmentation of Canada's approach to developing countries when he met Pearson to discuss his possible selection. He indicated that he would be interested, "provided that the External Aid Office became the focal point for the coordination of both multilateral and bilateral assistance with a commitment to the concept of international development; and that we would have input in the policy side in respect of a whole series of measures, only one of which was direct assistance."

The prime minister readily agreed, and Strong took office confident that he had a mandate from the top to reshape the role of EAO. However, "when I got to Ottawa I was shocked to realize that an agreement with the prime minister doesn't mean a damn thing unless it is translated into something to which the bureaucracy can react." It was one of several lessons for the new director general about the workings of government as he set about "to remake the whole thing" through a much longer and more arduous process than he had imagined.

Strong gradually learned by trial and error how to work through and around the established processes, ruffling feathers along the way but also earning respect. Some colleagues perceived him as mistrustful of bureaucracy, uncomfortable with established procedures, and impatient when things moved slowly; as one noted, "we always seemed to be telling him that his ideas wouldn't work." Often this advice was correct, but another associate recalled his surprise about the degree of independence and flexibility Strong achieved.

Some of Strong's colleagues thought that he went too far in introducing practices derived from business, and several commented on his managerial weaknesses as well as his strengths. Most agreed, however, that he had a great ability to recognize talent and a profound respect for competence. He consulted widely, listened, and learned. Peter Towe, Moran's deputy director, stayed on to provide continuity during the first year, and was one of a number of key people Strong credited for helping him survive the transition to the public service milieu. Another was Denis Hudon, recruited by Strong and Towe from the Department of Finance.[8]

The task of upgrading the role of EAO required support from the senior departments that had dominated policy-making. Strong was the newcomer and the junior player—but, as chairman of the External Aid Board, he could convene meetings of a committee that contained the most powerful mandarins in Ottawa, among them R.B. Bryce and Louis Rasminsky, then deputy minister of Finance and governor of the Bank of Canada respectively. Strong found both the vagueness of the Board's terms of reference and the deep commitment of many of its members helpful in dealing effectively, from his standpoint, with interdepartmental skirmishes over jurisdiction and status.

By virtue of his deputy ministerial status, the new director general was also an *ex-officio* member of other committees of deputies where he could contribute his perspectives on a range of foreign and domestic policy issues. On occasion, when the going got tough, he would take a more political route and use his direct access to Paul Martin or Lester Pearson (and later to Mitchell Sharp or Pierre Trudeau)—but he became well aware that nothing infuriated senior mandarins more than an end run.

Strong diagnosed lack of analytical capacity as a fundamental weakness of EAO, in terms both of its developmental mission and his own organizational ambitions.

> It was amazing. We had some very bright people in External Aid. . . . Certain individuals had policy ideas but there was no organized policy capability at all. I realized that to win our policy role we had to develop policy capability. Of course, the World Bank was the major element—as it still is—in the policy field.

Recruitment of Denis Hudon was one measure taken to develop an independent capacity in the policy domain and to forge links between the bilateral and multilateral programs. Hudon had long been involved in official Canadian liaison with the international financial institutions and the technical assistance programs of the UN, and was Canada's executive director of the World Bank when he joined EAO in 1967. He brought knowledge of the international scene and his executive directorship with him, thus giving EAO a direct link with the Bank. He was later given overall responsibility for integrating the various bits and pieces of bilateral aid, developing a systematic approach to project and program appraisal, and creating a capacity to relate aid to other aspects of Canadian policy towards the Third World.

The External Aid Office Becomes CIDA[9]

By 1968, with several of these initiatives well under way, EAO could no longer be seen simply as a weak adjunct of External Affairs. Despite scepticism of senior officials about Strong's ability to secure approval for renaming the operation the "Canadian International Development Agency," he was able to win support in the External Aid Board and overcome the initial reservations of Secretary of State for External Affairs Sharp.[10] Prime Minister Trudeau announced on May 29, 1968: "In order to stress the true objectives of our aid programme, we shall change the name of the External Aid Office to the Canadian International Development Agency."

At one level the change merely brought Canada into line with the United States, the United Kingdom, Sweden, and other donors who had recently adopted similar nomenclature to symbolize, at least rhetorically, a shift from aid as charity to international development as partnership. At another, however, the new name captured Strong's organizational and policy ambitions. It also coincided with the philosophical position held by Ivan Head, the new prime minister's foreign policy adviser, and with the position Trudeau advanced in one of his first public speeches after assuming office:

> As Canadians we must realize that international co-operation, particularly in the field of economic assistance, in order to remain effective, must take on a new form. From the present pattern of commodity and food assistance, of gifts of manufactured goods and loans of money, we must, in response to the economic needs of the developing countries, turn more and more to preferential trade agreements.[11]

In discussing the creation of CIDA, Mitchell Sharp also emphasized the government's commitment to a broader conception of international development:

> "Give away" programmes of aid must increasingly be supplemented by a much more complex and sophisticated set of arrangements in the fields of trade, investment, education, science and technology, designed to support and strengthen the self-help efforts and initiatives of the less-developed nations. In short, the activities in which we are involved in the name of civilization are no longer aid, with its connotations of "handout" and "hand-up," but international development in the truest sense of partnership.[12]

It was a flight of fancy somewhat loftier than the reality of Canadian endeavour, present or future, but doubtless well intentioned.

Strong recalled that he had originally favoured converting EAO into "something like a crown corporation" with a legislative mandate to give it more autonomy and greater operational flexibility than a normal government department. However, he became convinced after several months in office that a crown corporation would not

> square with my central concerns . . . to have our aid program become development-oriented and to have the Agency become one that was not only a giver of funds but a policy centre within the Canadian government on all things affecting international development. . . . It became clear after I became more familiar [with government] that the price that operating independence brings is you don't have a policy role. You may have occasional lobbying capacity in your special area, but you are not part of the normal processes of policy development and interdepartmental consultation.[13]

As for clarifying the status of the operation and giving it a legislative basis,

> Again I learned—I was very naive in those days about government—that we were still a weak instrument compared to the strong departments. As soon as we started to crystallize legislation, I sensed that this was going to draw an awful lot of fire. Immediately we started to make our mandate explicit, the other departments were going to be operating to whittle it down. . . . I finally realized that the vague status we had was perhaps the best we could hope for at that time. . . . Although it's true that we couldn't state absolutely that our mandate gave us the right to do x or y, nor could anyone else say that our mandate did not give us that right.

The actual legal basis for CIDA could hardly have been vaguer. A cabinet memorandum of August 29, 1968 referred to the 1960 and 1962 orders-in-council setting up the External Aid Office and to the prime minister's May statement. The memorandum stated simply: "That it is now considered that the name 'External Aid Office' implies Canada is primarily concerned with aid as such rather than with all aspects of co-operative international development." The subsequent order-in-council (1968-1760) of September 9, 1968 merely substituted new titles for old ones and specified no functions or responsibilities. Although the label "agency" perhaps suggested some difference from "department," nothing was spelled out. Despite periodic discussions since then, no further action has ever been taken to modify CIDA's official status.

The only other matter covered in the memorandum and the order-in-council was somewhat more controversial than the change from EAO to CIDA and the associated renaming of the External Aid Board as the Canadian International Development Board:

> That, in the light of the increasing usage of the term "Director General" to designate positions within the Public Service at levels well below that of Deputy Minister, it is further considered that this title has lost some of its original meaning and fails to reflect appropriately the rank and importance of the position of *chief executive officer* of an organization responsible for administering Canada's programmes of international development; that it is considered that a

> more appropriate title for the position would be "*President, Canadian International Development Agency*."[14]

Thus it was that Maurice Strong succeeded in having a deputy ministerial position dignified with the corporate title of president—in effect, president of a department of government, a curious anomaly that has survived seven changes since that time. Again, just as "agency" evokes the image of something distinct from a department, so does "president" suggest a symbolically different position from that of deputy minister. This symbolic difference was also substantive in two significant legacies enjoyed by Strong's successors until the mid-1980s: a public profile for the president of CIDA as an advocate of the international development program and a considerable independence from day-to-day ministerial involvement.

For people working in EAO, the change had no immediate practical effect. Two comments typify recollections of the event as, more than anything else, signifying greater organizational autonomy:

> On the ground it was not evident that there was a major transformation. Institutionally and in terms of funding, these were not dramatic jerks. . . . It was quite substantive, though, in terms of corporate role, scope, and power.

> In terms of continuing with our policies, continuing with our same problems, there was no change at all. . . . The change of name was psychologically important. . . . It was a transition in affirming the independence of the aid program from any one department.

Other Institutional Initiatives

The late 1960s was a period of unparalleled opportunity to recruit excellent people to EAO/CIDA: the budget was growing fast, Treasury Board permitted rapid expansion in the establishment (from 350 to almost 600), the challenge of international development was fresh in the Canadian context, and it appealed not only to idealism but also to a sense of adventure and/or the exotic. A pool of young people with Third World experience and enthusiasm for the cause of international development was available in the first generation of returned CUSO volunteers. Many joined EAO/CIDA. Ex-priests and others with missionary experience continued to come into the service. The military remained an important recruitment pool, especially for people with engineering qualifications. It was sometimes an uneasy mix of value orientations and administrative styles, but career prospects in the field were such that the Agency was able to recruit ten of the top fifteen graduates accepted into the federal government's administrative trainee program in 1969.

Strong was also able to reach out to some quite senior people in government and the private sector and persuade them to join the operation, at least in its formative period. They in turn drew in others. Mention has already been made of Denis Hudon, who became deputy director general and later vice-president of Planning and Economics. Hudon looked to the Export Credits Insurance Corporation and recruited Fergus Chambers as director of an Economics Division to develop further the policy capability that Strong sought. Donald Tansley, deputy minister of Health in Saskatchewan during the medicare crisis, was deputy minister of Finance in New Brunswick when he received a call from Strong inviting him to consider a CIDA vice-presidency.

Others were brought in as special advisers. One of the most distinguished was John Bene, president of Weldwood of Canada, a substantial forest products firm. Although he agreed to join CIDA for a year or two, he ended up staying on for several more both as a resource person on agro-forestry and as a key recruiter of people with sectoral competence in other fields. Another was Joseph Hulse, a food scientist, who went on to become executive vice-president of the International Development Research Centre (IDRC) and the author of many distinguished scientific publications. Yet another was Clyde Sanger, who joined CIDA as special adviser on communications. Formerly the *Guardian*'s correspondent in East Africa before joining the *Globe and Mail*, he had just published *Half a Loaf*, a critical study of Canadian aid based on extensive travels in the field. He too moved on to IDRC and eventually the North-South Institute, while remaining active as a respected journalist.

Organizational experimentation. Before the change of name, Strong had already presided over what *Canadian Business* called a "quiet revolution" that "has shaken the office to its roots."[15] In fact, disbursements slowed down while the whole operation was subjected to a thorough review.[16] The Bureau of Management Consulting Services of the Public Service Commission was commissioned in January 1967 to undertake "a study of the External Aid office to delineate its functions and objectives, and to make appropriate recommendations for its organization . . . and relationships."[17] Meanwhile, one of Strong's special advisers began a review of methods and procedures for assessing, processing, and implementing aid projects. Task forces, in some cases involving outside consultants, examined past activities and prospects in a number of regions and sectors.

A senior management seminar discussed interim reports in July 1967, a final organizational report was issued in September, and a new organization was put in place on October 1 of that year. Three branches were created, ostensibly to pull together various components of the existing program and to take account of the enlarged role being sought for EAO: (1) Planning and Economics, with responsibilities for long-range program planning, economic analysis, multilateral aid, technical liaison, program evaluation, and relations with voluntary agencies, business, and the provinces; (2) Operations, with responsibilities for project development and implementation in both the technical and capital spheres (though, with shifting permutations and combinations, separate divisions were maintained for various aspects of technical and capital assistance); and (3) Finance and Administration, with overall responsibilities for support services, including greater emphasis on the personnel function and career development.[18]

Within this framework and equipped with the five-year forward planning authority recently secured by Moran, first rudimentary steps were taken towards developing criteria for country eligibility, economic analyses of major recipient countries, longer-term programs for these countries, and cost-benefit approaches to project assessment. All these measures signified an intention to move beyond the responsive ad hocery of the early years to an era of somewhat more coherent planning. A more professional approach to preparing Canadians for placements abroad was reflected in creation of the CIDA Briefing Centre in 1969.

Efforts were also made to improve analytical capacities for matching sectoral emphases with available Canadian human and material resources. One of the people involved in these efforts to strengthen planning had, before the process began, "been horrified by the blind offers that were being made" to recipient countries.[19] The task forces concluded that EAO staff and desk officers should travel abroad. One report stated:

> Immediate contact with developing countries and their representatives in situ would greatly improve their knowledge of local conditions and requirements and would help in formulating assistance plans on a more sound and firm basis. Work in the office on their return could be handled with [fewer] delays and a more thorough appreciation of all aspects involved.[20]

What seems obvious and commonplace in retrospect represented a dramatic break from the practice of the pre-Strong years.

Of equal importance, the management study recommended "that positions for field officers be established in centres of Canadian aid activity abroad, and that they form part of the staff of the High Commission [or embassy] to which they would be attached."[21] There was an existing protocol between EAO and External Affairs governing communications and reporting arrangements for three liaison positions established during the Moran era. What was now being proposed, however, involved major jurisdictional and practical problems for External Affairs.

Relations between EAO and External were difficult and strained during months of negotiations that eventually culminated in agreements on several issues. Among these was a statement setting out responsibilities for field officers, who were responsible through the chain of command to the head of mission, who in turn was responsible for aid matters to EAO. Although no delegated decision-making authority was contemplated at this stage, field officers were expected to undertake extensive liaison with recipient governments and Canadian projects and personnel, to initiate proposals, and to play a key role in monitoring project implementation.[22] By 1969, there were twenty-one of them.[23]

In addition, Strong hired SNC, the Quebec consulting firm, to manage offices on behalf of CIDA in francophone African countries where there was no Canadian diplomatic representation. This end run angered officials at External Affairs, but, as Elaine Dewar commented, it was this sort of "mingling of public and private in the cause of public policy that was Maurice Strong's signature on events."[24]

Constant restructuring, by now a tradition, continued. Among several additional organizational alterations, one major shift stands out. Implemented in 1970 by Donald Tansley, it moved CIDA's bilateral program towards a focus on the project as the basic unit of administration, and the recipient country as the main focus of planning and operations. The changes were introduced because incorporation of the various aspects of technical and capital aid into an Operations Branch had not led to the effective coordination and integration that had been sought. Operations Branch had been organized along functional lines in five divisions: advisers, capital assistance, education, engineering, and training. Within each, desk officers were unrealistically expected to understand the needs of 70-odd recipient countries across three continents, while simultaneously maintaining specialized sectoral knowledge and expertise in Canadian procurement. Moreover,

> The structure made no adequate provision for systematic monitoring of ongoing projects, the prognosis of possible difficulties and initiation of remedial actions, and the evaluation of completed projects. . . . [It] was also necessary for Canadian Posts to correspond with several officers in order to deal with the various projects with which the Post was concerned.[25]

Shortly after joining CIDA in 1968, Tansley concluded that what was needed was a reorganization along geographical lines, with overall responsibility for any one project assigned to one person, no matter how many components and other people were involved.[26] He sustained this conviction during a year of travel in Africa and Asia to review the performance of the Agency's technical assistance programs. Upon his return as vice-president Operations in the spring of 1969, Tansley initiated a process that culminated in the reorganization of Operations Branch into four geographic divisions (Colombo Plan, Commonwealth Africa, Francophone Africa, and the Caribbean and Latin America), and four sectoral and technical ones (engineering, manpower, training resources, and contract administration).

Although Planning Branch remained paramount in matters of country program planning and project approval, each project, once approved, was assigned to a project officer in Operations who assumed managerial responsibility, working in consultation with officers from the relevant geographic or sectoral divisions. The plan called for the project officer to carry ten to twenty projects, all in the same region and, if possible, all in the same country. Meanwhile, officers in resource divisions assumed more specialized responsibilities focused on sectoral expertise and Canadian procurement. But the reorientation was gradual: it would be another four years before technical assistance divisions ceased to have implementation responsibilities.[27]

All this restructuring failed to resolve some fundamental management problems. George Cunningham, in his comparative study of aid agency management, observed: "Co-ordination between the two branches (Planning and Operations) was bad and there was little interchange of personnel. The result was that those who planned aid activities were denied the experience gained by implementation and those who implemented had imperfect opportunity to feed back their ideas to the planners."[28] And, despite Strong's professed concern for effectiveness, an associate noted: "one of the big gaps was evaluation. I mean it was a dirty word in CIDA at that stage. Everybody was so busy getting onto the next thing. . . . There was no corporate memory."

New Programs

While organizational experimentation was implanting some lasting approaches and discarding others—amid a fair degree of chaos and confusion—three new programs contributed to the excitement and enthusiasm of the time. All bore the mark of Maurice Strong's entrepreneurial leadership, two became permanently incorporated within CIDA, and the third sparked a new organization.

The Non-Governmental Organizations (NGO) Program

Strong's active participation in community and voluntary work convinced him of the desirability of reaching out "to harness the substantial resources which exist in the private sector." In one of his first public speeches as director general on January 26, 1967, he told the Empire Club of Toronto:

> The concept of individual responsibility and private initiative is basic to the Canadian way of life. We would like to see our government aid programs complemented and supplemented by an increasing amount of private initiative on the part of voluntary service organizations, church groups, cooperatives and business and industry. Private agencies can do so much to create . . . direct per-

> sonal channels . . . between Canadian citizens and the peoples of the developing world.

The timing for an ambitious public outreach program was right: public interest in fund-raising for international development was obvious in the massive success across Canada of "Miles for Millions" walkathons in 1967. The Centennial Commission, set up to orchestrate celebrations for the 100th anniversary of Canadian Confederation, and EAO provided logistical and financial support for these efforts and for associated speaking tours and community gatherings.[29]

After establishing a small liaison unit for voluntary agencies in 1966, Strong commissioned Lewis Perinbam, a Malaysian-born Canadian, to study how their relationship with the official aid program could be strengthened. Perinbam was then at the World Bank, having previously served as secretary-general of the Canadian National Commission for UNESCO and, in 1961-62, as CUSO's founding executive secretary. His report provided the basis for a Non-Governmental Organizations Program, unveiled in November 1967, and he himself was persuaded to join CIDA as director of the Special Programs Division a year later. He became vice-president for Special Programs in 1974, and remained in this post until his retirement from the Agency in 1991.[30] Although management was not his forte, Perinbam was a persistent gadfly in the executive group and a constant source of new ideas.

The NGO program provided core funding for CUSO (and potentially for other agencies whose activities served key CIDA priorities) and, on a project-by-project basis, grants to other NGOs to match funds they themselves raised for their own work in developing countries. Perinbam summarized the objectives as follows:

> First of all was the desire to go beyond the confines of government-to-government relationships and to tap the enormous resources, experience, expertise and knowledge that resided outside of government. . . . I think the overriding consideration here was not the business of giving money to NGOs but to enable government to tap and gain access to the resources that resided in the non-governmental sector. The second consideration was to make it possible for a large number of voluntary organizations who possessed a wealth of experience and capacities to collaborate with the government in the whole international development field. . . . The third was to find ways to enable Canadians to participate in international development. Unless Canadians could have a sense of participation, this whole thing would seem very remote from them. Participation was also a means of building enlightenment and informed support for the whole international development endeavour.

He also emphasized a fourth concern related to the development process itself:

> The NGO sector was a way of stimulating, supporting and strengthening the voluntary sector in developing countries. . . . In a way, many of these activities were a means of creating a world that would be more hospitable to the democratic idea, to the idea of the open society. And this was a non-doctrinaire, a non-political approach by simply sharing with the developing world something of the benefits that accrued to us.[31]

The Treasury Board had serious qualms about the unorthodoxy of transferring public monies to private agencies, but the NGO program was launched with an initial budget of $5 million in 1968-69. Over $3 million was allocated—$2.3 million to CUSO and the rest to more than fifty other agencies. Among activities supported were educational radio programming in Tanzania, community development in Jamaica and India, and a clean water project in Peru. Spending increased to $8.6 million in 1969-70 as the number of agencies and institutions wishing to take advantage of the program mushroomed.[32] CIDA also provided funding to help found the Canadian Council for International Cooperation (CCIC). It replaced the underfunded and understaffed Overseas Institute of Canada as a non-profit umbrella organization to coordinate and support the work of NGOs, to promote greater public participation in development assistance, and—not least—to enlarge the political constituency seeking an enhanced Canadian role in international development.

The Business and Industry Program

Among NGOs receiving CIDA funds was the Canadian Executive Service Overseas (CESO). It was established on Strong's initiative to tap the skills of people from Canadian business and industry (often after retirement) for short-term assignments in developing countries. CESO became one of the most successful ventures of its sort and continues to provide a creative developmental outlet for Canadian business expertise.[33] Less successful initially was the Business and Industry Program, begun in 1969 as the second leg of the non-governmental initiative. Strong explained his rationale for setting it up:

> Well, business and industry are the prime conveyors of economic development—the prime instruments. And Canada did not have the same relationship that many big countries had with the developing world . . . the United States, for example. Many developing country people were familiar with big U.S. corporations or had gone to major U.S. universities and colleges. . . . Of course, the former colonial powers, like France and the Netherlands, had cadres of people who had been actively, on their side, involved in the developing world. . . . So there were natural linkages between the developing countries and the other major countries offering development assistance. Canada had far fewer of those kinds of relationships. So, we felt we needed to take special measures to introduce industry into the development process.[34]

As originally conceived, the program was designed to assist "Canadian business and industrial firms in the establishment of enterprises which could make an important contribution to the development of the countries concerned."[35] Informational materials on investment opportunities were prepared, and funds were made available for starter and feasibility studies of such opportunities.

It would be several years, however, before an expanded and revamped program attracted much notice. The few non-branch-plant Canadian firms with international horizons did not need such a program, while the vast majority of small- and medium-size businesses looked to the United States if they had any long-term interests beyond the domestic economy. There was growing business interest in development assistance, to be sure, but it was overwhelmingly confined to sales opportunities arising from bilateral aid tied to procurement of Canadian goods and services. Still, though the ground was infertile in the late 1960s, the seed that was planted eventually took root as the Industrial Cooperation Program, which expanded rapidly in the 1980s.

The International Development Research Centre (IDRC)[36]

Yet another legacy of the period partly attributable to Maurice Strong was the creation of the International Development Research Centre. IDRC's distinctive approach to fostering indigenous research capabilities within developing countries emerged from a lengthy planning process, but it was Strong's impetus that generated that process.

> [We] recognized that we needed to look at fundamentals, not just transferring assistance to developing countries. We needed to look at science and technology as the principal source of economic development in our era, and the need of developing countries not just to have the hardware, but to have very special and sensitive assistance in developing their own science and technology capabilities.[37]

Strong had been toying with the idea of establishing a research program within EAO. Then, in informal discussions about what to do with the Montreal site of "Man and His World" once Expo 67 was over, he floated the idea of locating there a major centre for international development research, which might have a focus on domestic public policy analysis as well. As originally conceived, it was to be a think-tank concerned with "improved methods for extending the benefits of modern industrial and technical progress to the whole community of man."[38]

Strong raised the idea with several people, including Pearson. Without informing senior officials that he intended to do so, the prime minister used the opportunity of an after-dinner speech to the Canadian Political Science Association at Carleton University in June 1967

> to raise the challenge of finding new instruments for concentrating more interest and more resources on the application on a global basis of the latest technology to the solution of man's economic and social problems. One idea for a new Canadian initiative to meet this challenge which is being considered by the government is the establishment of a research centre for international development. It might even be on the site of Expo 67. . . . We cannot, even if we wished, become a great power in a political or military sense. But we have already proven in our peace-keeping efforts that we can make a good contribution to world order. Perhaps it will now prove possible for us to add a new dimension to our modest role in the world community by providing for this centre for research.[39]

"Apoplectic" and "livid" were adjectives used in two different interviews with leading participants to describe the response of certain mandarins to the prime minister's speech. Strong was condemned for having made an end run directly to the top without first securing interdepartmental support. Marcel Cadieux, under-secretary of state for External Affairs, was particularly upset, precisely at a time when delicate negotiations were under way on the issue of posting EAO field officers to missions abroad. However, Pearson, himself a veteran of bureaucratic wars, knew what he was doing. Strong weathered the storm and assembled "a galaxy of senior officials" on a steering committee to consider the proposal. Reservations and concerns abounded, but they were overcome, not least because of the inspired choice of a consultant, Wynne Plumptre, principal of Scarborough College and, as noted earlier, a former senior official in the Department of Finance.

The bureaucratic hurdle was cleared, the first Throne Speech of the new Trudeau government contained a commitment to the proposal, and Strong participated in drafting legislation. David Hopper, first president of IDRC, and Geoffrey Oldham, brought to Ottawa from the University of Sussex as an adviser, were crucial in "breaking new ground" when IDRC "established, as its primary objective, the support of research that was not only located in developing countries and designed for their benefit, but was actually to be carried out, as far as practicable, by the scientists of the developing countries themselves."[40]

The Bill provided a legislative mandate, an international board, free use of funds untied to Canadian procurement, and operating independence—all attributes that were inappropriate for CIDA, but which, as Clyde Sanger observed, were "born out of the frustrations . . . Maurice Strong encountered as CIDA president."[41] Well received in the House of Commons Standing Committee on External Affairs and National Defence, the legislation was symbolically strengthened by deleting "of Canada" from the proposed title.[42] It was finally given royal assent in May 1970,[43] long after Strong's original idea for the Expo 67 site had been dropped in realization that the politics of location would have subverted the substance of the proposal.

Ongoing Programs: Continuity and Change

Parliamentary appropriations for development assistance continued to rise rapidly during the Strong era, growing from $247.9 million in 1966-67 to $383.7 million in 1970-71.[44] During the fiscal retrenchment early in Trudeau's first term, the development assistance budget was one of the few not frozen;[45] in fact, it was increased by 17 and 13 per cent in 1969-70 and 1970-71, respectively ($50 million and $45 million). Reported ODA lagged behind appropriations, but increased from $210.7 million in 1968-69 to $345.4 million in 1970-71. Canada remained the sixth-largest DAC donor through this period, accounting for 4.85 per cent of total flows in 1970, up from 3.12 per cent 1966. As a percentage of GNP, Canadian ODA fell from 0.34 in 1966-67 to 0.28 in 1968-69, and then rose to 0.40 in 1970-71. Whereas Canada's relative standing in 1966 was ninth and below the DAC average, in 1970 it was sixth and above the average of 0.34 per cent (which had been declining, along with the relative performance of the United States and Britain).[46]

Canada's volume performance would have been more impressive if the bilateral program had been able to spend more of a cumulative undisbursed cash balance, which reached $417 million in 1970-71.[47] Appearing before the Commons Standing Committee on External Affairs and National Defence in 1969, Strong attributed the magnitude of undisbursed funds to the normal time lag between allocations and actual spending, and to the reviews he had commissioned to improve CIDA's effectiveness in the field.[48] In *Half a Loaf*, Sanger concluded that slow-moving bureaucracies in recipient countries bore some of the responsibility, but that much of the fault lay in centralization of decision-making in Ottawa.[49] Cunningham suggested that the disbursement problem was exacerbated "by the fact that recipients, knowing Canadian aid is non-lapsing, tend first to use aid from other countries which might otherwise be lost."[50] A major factor was CIDA's slow and cumbersome project approval and contracting procedures, a problem that has bedeviled the Agency ever since.

Geographical Distribution

A small bilateral program concentrated in a handful of Asian countries in the 1950s had already expanded to almost sixty recipients by the time Strong became director general of EAO in 1966. By 1970-71 (the last year planned during his presidency), government-to-government aid was being channelled to seventy-two countries—seventeen in Asia, fifteen in anglophone Africa, twenty-one in francophone Africa, twelve in the Caribbean Commonwealth, and seven in Latin America. There were also regional programs for the University of the West Indies and the East African Community. Disbursements of $1 million or more went to thirty-five of these recipients that year.[51]

Despite this proliferation, allocations remained highly concentrated in the Colombo Plan area, especially India and Pakistan. India received $103.1 million and Pakistan $47.5 million in 1970-71, compared to $54.4 million for all of Africa; within the latter, the largest country totals were Ghana ($7.0 million), Nigeria ($6.6 million), and Tunisia ($5.5 million). Four other countries received over $4 million: Sri Lanka, Guyana, Algeria, and Colombia.[52]

The Colombo Plan and the Commonwealth. While most Canadian ODA in the Colombo Plan area continued to go to Commonwealth countries, the one Asian country explicitly selected for an enlarged presence during the Strong era was Indonesia after the fall of the Sukarno regime. Bureaucrats in External Affairs and CIDA, who often differed on such matters, agreed on this choice, which the 1970 Foreign Policy Review said was made because of Indonesia's "extensive natural resources" and "strategic location."[53] Recent discovery of oil and Vietnam-era concern about communist expansion in South-East Asia and the Pacific were significant geopolitical factors for External Affairs. However, an aid planner recalled that the Agency also pushed hard to have Indonesia recognized as a country of concentration because that nation of farflung islands had developmental needs that matched Canada's commercial and technical capabilities.

A Canadian mandate extending across the Commonwealth Caribbean was solidified in 1966 following agreement with the British and Americans on a division of labour that assigned Canada particular responsibilities for water resources, air transport, education, and agriculture.[54] It was government policy after 1966 to expand aid rapidly in the Commonwealth Caribbean. For several years thereafter, pressure to disburse in the area exceeded ability to commit, and was thus yet another factor encouraging proliferation of recipients.

Within Commonwealth Africa, the Canadian presence in Ghana, Nigeria, and East Africa was extended southward to small bilateral programs in Zambia, Malawi, Botswana, Lesotho, and Swaziland. Gambia and Sierra Leone were the only Commonwealth African countries that were by and large excluded.

Although the most dramatic use of external aid in pursuit of Canadian foreign and domestic policy goals occurred in francophone Africa, the ODA-related issue that prompted the most political controversy within Canada was the Nigerian civil war. Little public or media attention was paid to the conflict for almost a year after it erupted in mid-1967. Then, suddenly, during the summer of 1968 and only weeks after Trudeau's landslide electoral victory, the plight of secessionist Biafra became a *cause celèbre*. As John Schlegel summarized it, the Liberal government's policy was "dependence on international law and non-intervention, participation in a neutral observer team, respect for Nigeria's territorial integrity, support for the UN's initiatives and the initiatives of the OAU [Organization of African Unity]."[55]

Trudeau was preoccupied with his own quite different secessionist threat, but as Granatstein and Bothwell argued:

> Had the prime minister stuck to official formulas while striking the requisite attitude of responsible concern, he would not have heard much about Biafra.... But one day in August 1968 when Trudeau was interrogated by reporters on Parliament Hill about Biafra, he merely replied 'Where's Biafra?' The answer was juridically correct, but politically horrendous, since it implied arrogance, indifference, and ignorance to the television audience. Trudeau managed to offend precisely those liberal and humanitarian segments of opinion whose views he had previously been thought to share.[56]

Fanned by sympathetic church and non-governmental groups, the story was kept alive by the media until December. The Commons Standing Committee on External Affairs devoted several sessions to the situation and Canada's policy, and the House itself spent more time discussing Nigeria/Biafra in the fall of 1968 than either the Soviet invasion of Czechoslovakia or the Vietnam War.

The most hotly debated issue was whether the Canadian government should support direct relief efforts in the secessionist state above and beyond aid channelled through the International Committee of the Red Cross, whose presence was accepted by the Nigerian federal authorities. Trudeau and his colleagues resisted pressure for such action on grounds that it would violate the principle of non-interference in Nigeria's internal affairs. A grant for Canairelief, a coalition supporting direct relief and seen as sympathetic to the Biafran cause, was finally announced, but never delivered, just before the civil war ended with reunification in January 1970. Although this decision upset the Nigerian government, the postwar relationship was cordial and the level of Canadian assistance for relief, reconstruction, and development was stepped up.

Aid to francophone Africa: A major foreign and domestic policy initiative.[57] Standing out among the mix of foreign policy, domestic, commercial, and developmental factors contributing to geographical expansion was an intensification of the drive to enhance Canadian aid presence in francophone Africa. David Dewitt and John Kirton, in presenting their thesis that the late 1960s marked a shift in the thrust of Canadian foreign policy from "liberal internationalism" to "complex neo-realism," argued that "this transition was initiated in the 1960s when significant Canadian aid began to be deployed in specific francophone countries for the domestic political purpose of meeting the challenges to Canadian foreign policy from Quebec and France."[58] Douglas Anglin suggested that Ottawa, in setting out "to buy francophone African goodwill with aid offers," chose "perhaps the most dramatic new direction in foreign policy ever undertaken by a Canadian government."[59]

The small francophone Africa program, expanded after the Liberals returned to power in 1963, was part of a larger bilingual, bicultural strategy to counter the alternative nationalist strategy of Quebec leaders for enhancing provincial autonomy. As we saw in Chapter 2, there was little interest among France's former African colonies. Nor was there within EAO. As one old hand put it, "Nobody was anxious to push [the program]. French was non-existent . . . It didn't take off until Quebec's involvement in international affairs."

That involvement had been increasing through the 1960s, and a brief summary is in order to place the expansion of aid to French-speaking Africa in context. The new provincial government of Jean Lesage opened a "Délégation générale du Québec" in Paris in 1961. Shortly thereafter,

> Paul Gérin-Lajoie, then a member of the Quebec cabinet, echoed the calls of President Bourguiba of Tunisia and President Senghor of Senegal for the establishment of an association of "la Francophonie" in which Quebec would become a member. He pursued his ideas in a series of speeches in Quebec where he stressed Quebec's right to undertake international activities within the fields under her jurisdiction.[60]

Both as minister of Youth and later as minister of Education in charge of Quebec's newly secularized system, Gérin-Lajoie challenged any aspects of Ottawa's technical assistance activities that encroached upon provincial jurisdiction over education. The future president of CIDA was seen by a senior EAO officer during the Moran period as "the biggest burr in our saddle."[61]

Gérin-Lajoie and his colleagues also continued to promote Quebec's international recognition, and secured a cultural entente with France in 1965. Daniel Johnson's Union Nationale government, elected in 1966, accelerated the pace of international initiatives by opening direct relations with francophone African countries in 1967. As Louis Sabourin noted, "in other circumstances, such exchanges might not have created any problems, but the whole political climate in the evolution of Quebec-Ottawa relations had already begun to deteriorate."[62] General de Gaulle made his famous "Vive le Québec libre" speech in Montreal in July 1967, Johnson was calling for "égalité ou indépendance," and René Lévesque issued his manifesto calling for a sovereign Quebec.

Among field studies of Canadian aid commissioned by Strong was one by Henri Gaudefroy, whose report in January 1967 on his tour of francophone African countries provided the basis for a memorandum to cabinet later that year.[63] Serious difficulties had been "encountered in identifying . . . sound projects for Canadian aid financing under existing policies and procedures," and $13.5 million of the $34.5 allocated to the region remained uncommitted. Gaudefroy cited as obstacles: the ready availability of aid from France and elsewhere, Canada's limited diplomatic presence and experience in the region, and the perception of African governments that Canada was a minor source of assistance with restricted capabilities. "These obstacles were compounded of course by the fact that administrative customs and practices, among others the use of the metric system of measurement, are very different from those to which Canada is accustomed."

Despite the problems Gaudefroy identified, the cabinet memorandum asserted that "it is essential to obtain agreement as soon as possible with the governments of the independent French-speaking African states, concerning the initiation of additional worthwhile projects and thus reduce significantly the backlog of uncommitted funds." After noting the humanitarian case for more assistance to an area where needs were great, and the "significant political influence in Africa" Canada stood to gain through a positive response to these needs, the document continued:

> Finally, and this strictly domestic consideration is undoubtedly the most urgent and compelling one, it is essential, in the present context of federal-provincial relations, that Canada should reflect in its External Aid programme the bicultural character of the country. Such a policy is a necessary demonstration of the Government's conviction that it has both the capability and the will to provide for the full and effective expression in Canadian activities abroad of both of the two main cultural groups of this country.

Several proposals were suggested to facilitate a policy that would as well "circumscribe any possible attempts by provincial governments to undertake independent programmes in the field of foreign aid."

Later in 1967, Trudeau, then minister of Justice, attended a law conference in Togo and, at Strong's urging, visited a number of other francophone countries. On his return, he reported to Pearson that Quebec's aid projects were as yet small and insignificant, but stressed the urgency of expanding Canada's diplomatic presence in the region and of expanding federal government aid; "to do our job we must spend more time and money at it," Trudeau wrote.[64]

The conflict with Quebec reached crisis proportions for the federal government soon afterwards when the government of Gabon invited Quebec but not Ottawa to a conference of francophone education ministers in February

1968. Canada suspended diplomatic relations with Gabon. Amid intense international and domestic political negotiations over the next two years, the development assistance program in former French colonies was the primary vehicle for expanding official Canadian presence in the region. It proved to be an effective way of ensuring that francophone African governments understood Ottawa's position on external relations.

Recommending the dispatch of a high-level mission to francophone Africa, the 1967 cabinet memorandum had reluctantly conceded that "it would be difficult in the circumstances not to invite [provincial authorities in Quebec] to participate." In the context of the Gabon crisis, however, Quebec was not invited to join the team that toured the region in February and March of 1968. It was led by Lionel Chevrier, a long-time Franco-Ontarian member of the federal Liberal cabinet.

> Chevrier was told by Martin to offer assistance to the francophone states for a specific political reason: to illustrate that Ottawa was the source of greater aid than Quebec could ever aspire to. However, there was to be no assistance to those African states who were following a course of action inimical to Canada's federal structure or sympathetic to Quebec's aspirations.[65]

The mission was given authority to make immediate commitments of funds, and developmental considerations were secondary. As Granatstein and Bothwell observed, the "connection between aid and attitude was almost shamelessly explicit in the Canadian expedition."[66] A CIDA officer recalled: "Foreign policy dominated the program for three or four years. You were under a strong obligation to get something off the ground—even if the projects were not so hot. A lot were not very good." Chevrier, however, did ease CIDA's disbursement problem: forty-nine projects were approved in Morocco, Algeria, Tunisia, Niger, Senegal, the Ivory Coast, and Cameroon.[67] Annual allocations to francophone Africa rose from $12 million in 1967-68 to $32 million in 1969-70 and doubled to $64 million in 1970-71.[68]

Politically, the drive into francophone Africa brought more French Canadians into CIDA and active involvement in aid work abroad. More immediately, French African states became more helpful to Ottawa. Government leaders in Cameroon, the Ivory Coast, Niger, Senegal, and Tunisia stated publicly that they would support the federal position and not negotiate with the provinces. As Sanger explained, a good relationship with Niger blossomed:

> In return for some timely, if modest, help in 1970 in getting Canada accepted as a full member of the Francophone states' Agence de Coopération Culturelle et Technique (while Quebec, despite French manoeuvres, was given lower status as "a participating government"), Canada became deeply involved in a large development assistance program in Niger. This includes some $31 million to

> help build the Route de l'Unité et l'Amitié, a 265-mile road. . . . Whether this road will prove to be an expensive bit of nonsense, leaving herdsmen and others to continue their trek southwards into Nigeria along more natural routes, will be interesting to watch.[69]

Latin America. In due course, the logic of hemispheric politics undoubtedly would have drawn Canada into an extensive aid relationship with Central and South America. Of all the regional bilateral programs, however, the one that evolved in Latin America was the only one that stemmed to any significant extent from non-governmental initiatives. Business interest in winning capital projects under the Inter-American Development Bank scheme was soon matched by growing pressure from religious groups for a Canadian technical assistance program. Protestant missions urged action, but the strongest calls came from Roman Catholic orders in Quebec, with their long history of missionary work in Latin America.[70] Also a factor was a special emotional attachment towards the region felt by many French-speaking intellectuals, both within and outside the Catholic Church. J.C.M. Ogelsby observed:

> There has been much written and stated about a certain supposed affinity between French Canadians and Latin America. This is the *Latinité* concept that holds that peoples of Latin origin have some common heritage that differentiates them from others. This idea is not widely held in French Canada, but over the years it has had enough support among intellectuals to make it part of their view of the world. And as editor of . . . *Cité libre*, Trudeau included occasional editorials and articles on Latin America. They tended to reflect a sympathy for social and economic changes.[71]

Although there was little enthusiasm in External Affairs or EAO for greater involvement in Latin America, the balance of forces within the federal government shifted when Trudeau became prime minister in 1968. Announcing in May of that year his decision to conduct a major foreign policy review, he said:

> We have to take greater account of the ties which bind us to other nations in this hemisphere—in the Caribbean, Latin America—and of their economic needs. We have to explore new avenues of increasing our political and economic relations with Latin America where more than four hundred million people will live by the turn of this century and where we have substantial interests.[72]

Five cabinet ministers and some thirty officials toured nine Latin American countries later that year. Other than a call for intensification of existing relations, the formal policy towards Latin America did not change much in the subsequent foreign policy review, not least because of bureaucratic inertia. CIDA, however, responded to the prime minister's challenge and began planning a new program. Launched in 1970, it was oriented mainly to technical assistance in agriculture, forestry, fisheries, and community development.[73]

Although francophone Africa was more important geopolitically as a battleground for the Canada-Quebec conflict, the decision to embark on bilateral programming in Latin America also reflected a desire to project a stronger bilingual and bicultural image externally. The region further balanced the anglo tilt towards the Commonwealth, and opened up additional culturally challenging opportunities for French Canadians to participate in international development. Strong's successor, Paul Gérin-Lajoie, also used the Latin American program as a way to enhance the francophone presence within CIDA.

The issue of concentration. By the mid-1960s, Herb Moran was becoming increasingly concerned about the growing administrative burden on the aid program, as well as the doubtful rationality of simply allowing the pressures at work to continue driving proliferation. He and his senior colleagues also questioned the absence of any explicit criteria for country selection that consciously weighed developmental, political, and economic considerations. In April 1966, shortly before he left office, Moran secured cabinet support for a formal policy endorsing concentration:

> The requirements of these [developing] countries far exceed availabilities. Canadian aid should therefore be directed and largely limited to those less developed countries where Canada has important interests, which are mobilizing and making effective use of the resources available to them and where Canadian assistance will clearly contribute to increasing the effectiveness of the development effort.[74]

No indication was given, however, about how "important interests" or "the effectiveness of the development effort" were to be defined or measured.

Maurice Strong was temperamentally suited to build, not contain—but CIDA's annual review for 1968-69 emphasized the government's policy of achieving greater effectiveness through concentration.[75] Ten countries or regions were designated as areas of concentration: India, Pakistan, Ceylon, and Malaysia (in the Colombo Plan region), Nigeria and Ghana (in anglophone Africa), Tunisia, Cameroon, and Senegal (in francophone Africa) and the Commonwealth Caribbean as a whole. DAC's annual report for 1969 took the policy of concentration at face value and listed Canada along with Japan and the Scandinavian countries as donors that "have decided to concentrate their aid on a few selected countries of 'first choice.' "[76]

The allocations memorandum to the cabinet for 1968-69 actually announced phasing out programs "of marginal interest." The 1969-70 memorandum noted, however, that discussions about curtailing or reducing programs had encountered strong opposition from Canadian posts abroad.

"Furthermore, it was not advisable to phase out any of the countries of Francophone Africa."[77] As a result, the issue was deferred pending reconsideration during an overall review of aid policy that commenced early in 1969.

Changes in Terms and Conditions

The terms of the Canadian aid program remained highly concessional during Strong's tenure, although the proportion of the bilateral program allocated to loans rose from 38.5 per cent in 1965-66 to 50.8 per cent in 1969-70 and 49.6 per cent in 1970-71.[78] Also, while sparingly used, a new category of harder development loans was introduced with terms of 3 per cent interest, thirty years maturity, and a seven-year grace period.[79]

As for procurement tying, it will be recalled that some loosening of restrictions was announced in 1966 so that, in special circumstances, up to 25 per cent of a project allocation could be spent on local costs and shipping. CIDA gained some additional flexibility in November 1968 when Treasury Board agreed to reduce the required Canadian content of each project from 80 per cent to two-thirds of total Canadian costs. It was agreed as well that a lower content could be approved by cabinet or Treasury Board. This change enlarged the scope of what Canadian suppliers could provide to the aid program, a boon to CIDA planners and several firms. Approved local costs were exempted from the content regulations, as were small projects under $50,000 and miscellaneous equipment purchases under that level.[80] Canadian policy continued to reject quite firmly, however, DAC enjoinders to move towards greater general untying or, failing that, towards allowing purchases from developing country suppliers.

Progressive Challenges and Traditional Programming

The emergence of a more forceful developing country presence on the world scene, and changing sensitivities in donor-recipient relations, gave rise in the late 1960s to symbolic changes in diplomatic language used to describe these relations: "aid" had become "development assistance" and was becoming "development cooperation" among "partners." The economic growth and modernization models that shaped ODA efforts were being criticized in academic circles and aid practitioners were doing a lot of rethinking. Earlier preoccupation with capital and technical support for industrial development was giving ground to concerns about the agricultural sector, population, and social issues, as well as the need to expand opportunities for developing country exports. The organizational reforms within EAO/CIDA encouraged reappraisal of what Canada was doing, and new people in policy analysis and planning were challenging conventional approaches.

Addressing a teach-in on international development at the University of Toronto in 1970, Strong said:

> Speaking personally, I have a lot of respect for some of the views of those who think aid can do (and has on occasions done) harm in encouraging people of the developing countries in the wrong kinds of activity, and in loading them with economic and social costs quite out of line with what they ultimately see as their best long-term interests, and in supporting existing power structures and institutional arrangements which are admittedly inadequate.

After rejecting the argument that aid should be abandoned—"It could all too easily provide an excuse for us to fall back to the laissez-faire days of unconcern and irresponsibility"—he recognized that

> Even at their best, present foreign aid programs represent just a first primitive step toward the evolution of an international system which will have built into it more continuing and impersonal mechanisms for the transference of resources in order to remove poverty and equalize opportunity on a global basis. . . . Growth by itself is clearly not enough. Alongside it must go a restructuring of institutions, and a reordering of value systems.[81]

Change was more rapid at the rhetorical level, however, than in the actual content of Canadian bilateral operations and the mindset determining it.

Technical assistance. Technical cooperation (as it was now called) remained a high priority, but—unlike the case earlier in the 1960s—it did not increase as rapidly as capital projects and commodity aid. The number of students and trainees studying in Canada declined from 2,964 in 1966 to 2,608 in 1970, although third-country training had been started and increasing numbers of CIDA-supported students were enrolled elsewhere.[82] The overall decline reflected a lessened need in Colombo Plan countries that was not yet offset by growing numbers from Africa. Another factor already at work was mounting pressure to disburse, much easier to do through large capital projects than through highly labour-intensive training programs. It was also the end of an era of high demand for primary and secondary school teachers. The number of technical and professional advisers did increase over the second half of the 1960s, and the deployment of university-based personnel remained relatively stable.

Food aid and agriculture. The simple notion that food aid was an unmixed blessing, both for prairie farmers and the malnourished in the Third World, was subjected to increasing criticism in the 1960s. While it was recognized that judicious use of the food channel could help developing countries build buffer stocks and conserve scarce foreign exchange, there were serious potential pitfalls as well. Not only did the cycle of surplus production in the North not always coincide with need in the South but, within recipient countries, food aid (other than for emergency relief) often depressed agricultural prices, thereby reducing incentives to invest in agrarian reform and domestic food production. Food shipments also had the potential of interfering with local dietary and consumption patterns in ways that worsened the urban bias of development strategies and long-term dependency upon imports.

Food aid fell from over 50 per cent to just under 30 per cent of Canadian ODA during the Strong era. Most was in the form of wheat and flour, although the dairy lobby successfully pushed for greater use of skim milk.[83] CIDA tried to portray food aid in a positive light,[84] and made a conscious effort to look more closely at the developmental implications of the program.

Although Canada had little expertise in tropical agriculture, the question of how best to contribute in this sphere was central in the field studies Strong commissioned. Dean Fred Bentley of the University of Alberta led a 1967 task force to India, which encountered considerable scepticism but defined a potential Canadian role in dryland farming and water surveys.[85] While the effort to adapt was genuine, EAO/CIDA repackaged existing projects to make it look as though Canadian aid was more in the vanguard of change than it actually was.[86] That phenomenon was to recur often in response to shifts in developmental fashions.

Infrastructural and commodity aid. The bulk of bilateral allocations in all regions continued to go into large-scale infrastructural projects in the spheres of transportation, communications, power generation, and irrigation. Commodity aid remained an important form of Canadian assistance in India, Pakistan, and other Colombo Plan recipients. The pressure to disburse arising from the rapid increase in parliamentary appropriations, reinforced by the highly visible growth of unexpended balances, made infrastructural projects and lines of credit for commodity aid natural temptations for aid administrators because, as Appavoo observed, "they allowed for the expenditure of large sums of money with the same or even less administrative effort than several smaller projects."[87] This factor coincided with traditional thinking about development and worked against innovation.

More Multilateral Activism

Multilateral aid flows grew quickly during the Strong era as EAO assumed more managerial responsibility and it became public policy to enhance the level of Canadian contributions. ODA channelled multilaterally rose from $34.0 million in 1965-66 to $47.3 million in 1966-67, and reached $67.5 million by 1970-71.[88] Canada continued to play an active role in UN agencies, including discussions on reforming UNDP after Sir Robert Jackson's study in 1969. Support was given as well to the establishment in 1967 of a Commonwealth Technical Assistance Program, forerunner of the Commonwealth Technical Cooperation Program (founded at the Commonwealth Heads of Government Meeting in Singapore in January 1971).[89] In the meantime, Strong used the External Aid/Canadian International Development Board as a vehicle for discussing multilateral aid.

Strong became alternate Canadian governor of the World Bank—a position since maintained by successive CIDA presidents in support of the governor, who is the finance minister. Sharp, then minister of Finance, advocated quadrupling donor contributions during the second IDA replenishment in 1967, and thereby had a positive impact upon the eventual decision to increase available funds by 60 per cent.[90] Increasingly, Canada played a significant role in regional development banks. It became one of two non-regional members of the new Caribbean Development Bank in 1969 (the other was Britain).

CIDA's president and other senior officials became active and visible in a number of other international development fora as well. The annual Tidewater meetings bringing together the DAC chairman, the president of the World Bank, heads of major bilateral donor agencies, and developing country leaders started when Strong suggested that such people needed to get away from the formality and posturing of DAC meetings to a setting where they could converse more openly and freely. He also offered vigorous support for tropical agricultural research institutions and was a prime initiator of the Consultative Group on International Agricultural Research (CGIAR) shortly after he moved from CIDA to head the UN Commission on the Environment.

CIDA's new emphasis on multilateralism was symbolically represented in the content and format of annual reviews issued under Strong. They began with a discussion of global issues and Canada's contributions to multilateral agencies and institutions before reporting on the bilateral program.

Rethinking the Mission

Toward the end of his tenure, Strong launched an ambitious re-examination of Canada's international development policies and the place of aid within them. It took place at the same time as a major international review, in which Lester Pearson played a prominent role.

The Pearson Commission

Growing concern about the future of aid and conflict about the nature of development prompted George Woods, president of the World Bank, to suggest in 1967 that a "grand assize" of distinguished persons be appointed to assess the experience to date, "clarify the errors and propose the policies which will work better in the future."[91] His successor, Robert McNamara, invited Pearson, who had just stepped down as prime minister, to chair the Commission on International Development.

Pearson's report, submitted in September 1969, supported many trade reforms that industrial countries had been resisting—such as a non-reciprocal preference scheme for developing country exports, supplementary financing for temporary loss of export earnings, and buffer stocks to stabilize commodity prices. It urged developing countries to be more open to private investment, and developed countries to offer better incentives to encourage such investment. On the aid front, the commission called for softer loans, recognition of debt relief as a legitimate form of aid, greater untying of bilateral ODA to cover local costs and procurement in developing countries, and an increase in the proportion of aid flowing to multilateral institutions to at least 20 per cent by 1975. Above all, developed countries were asked to increase total resource transfers to developing countries to a minimum of 1 per cent of GNP by 1975. (UNCTAD II In New Delhi in 1968 replaced national income with GNP as the denominator for the 1 per cent target, thereby setting a higher threshold.)

Pearson also added a new target to the lexicon: each donor's net disbursements of ODA (as defined that year by DAC) "should . . . reach 0.7 per cent of its GNP by 1975 or shortly thereafter, but in no case later than 1980."[92] This objective was endorsed by the UN General Assembly when it proclaimed the Second Development Decade in 1970. As the DAC average at the time was 0.34 per cent,[93] and the target was tied to growing donor economies, its achievement required considerably more than a doubling of the existing level of support.

The Pearson commission defined the goal of international development as putting "the less developed countries as soon as possible in a position where they can realize their aspirations with regard to economic progress without relying on foreign aid." The goal would take time to achieve.

> But can the majority of developing countries achieve self-sustaining growth by the end of the century? For us the answer is clearly yes. In our view, the record of the past twenty years justifies that answer. We live at a time when the ability to transform the world is only limited by faintness of heart or narrowness of vision. We can now set ourselves goals that would have seemed chimerical a few decades ago and, working together, we can reach them.[94]

All that was needed was an act of political will. As Patricia Marchak commented, the report, "though compassionate and well-intentioned," lacked sophistication "in its structural analysis of poverty. . . . [The] expectation that matters would change if only everyone was informed about the existence of poverty was at best rather innocent."[95] The politics, the problems, and the obstacles were a good deal more intractable—as Strong's parallel review would also show.

Maurice Strong's Review

Prime Minister Trudeau came to office committed to an overall review of Canadian foreign policy. Late in 1968, he agreed to Strong's request to incorporate within it an international development component that CIDA would lead in preparing. Strong hoped to produce a document that would articulate "some of the new streams of thinking and action" already under way, that would be exciting, and that would "stake out territory far in advance, giving us a sense of direction and some targets to achieve."[96]

Planning Division was assigned detailed responsibility, but much of the impetus for critical appraisal of existing policies and new ideas was expected to come from a group of consultants, mostly academics. They were asked to prepare papers on key themes and participate in seminars chaired by Strong and attended by members of the Canadian International Development Board and senior CIDA officials. The main issues defined at the outset were: purposes of development assistance, level, terms, multilateral aid and donor coordination, geographical allocation, sectoral concentration, the role of the private sector, and trade and other alternatives to direct aid.[97]

Purposes of Canadian aid. Considerable attention was devoted to the motives and objectives of Canadian aid, in part to achieve a clearer sense of direction for Canadian efforts, and in part to develop a convincing public rationale for an expanding program at a time when "aid fatigue" was growing, especially in the US.

A day-long seminar was devoted to discussion of a paper on "Canada's Purpose in Extending Foreign Assistance," written by Professor Stephen Triantis of the University of Toronto very much in the tradition of Machiavelli giving advice to the Prince. Triantis began by drawing a distinction between the objectives of development abroad—among them economic development, famine relief, and population control—and Canada's motives for giving aid—the familiar humanitarian, economic, and political trinity. He expressed doubt about the depth of the public's humanitarian concern, except in response to disasters, and suggested that "the philanthropic motive might at best account for governmental foreign aid of modest proportions."[98] As for economic motives, if one took "only the economic costs and benefits into consideration, our aid entails a loss for Canada. Generally, it would seem that, having decided on and practised foreign aid, we have tended to develop some economic arguments *ex post facto* in order to justify it."[99]

Political motives were much more important in Triantis' view. While sceptical about broad claims regarding peace and security, he suggested that foreign aid "may be used to induce the underdeveloped countries to accept the international *status quo* or change it in our favour." In this respect, it provided the opportunity "to lead them to rational political and economic developments and a better understanding of our interests and problems of mutual concern."[100] Relations with other donors were important as well.

On how to promote foreign aid among the electorate, Triantis discussed the appeal of a "Sunday School mentality":

> First, it appears noble and unselfish and can serve in pushing into the background other motives . . . [that] might be difficult to discuss publicly. Second, it is vague and, hence, it serves well our system of government in which it is not considered always necessary or desirable . . . fully to advise the public about the true costs of, and benefits from, various public policies.[101]

Nevertheless, Triantis cautioned against an "all-out" humanitarian campaign that might lead to backlash if the public "became conscious of the costs involved and compared foreign aid to other welfare expenditures."[102] Instead, despite the tenuous validity of peace and security argument, "partly because it is vague, it is easy to 'sell.' . . . It would seem foolish to drop a questionable argument if it is serving us well." Observing that "our real motives may not be very helpful in an effort to sell to the Canadian public a given aid package," he also advocated pushing the "advancing our exports" argument to court business support.[103]

Discussion of Triantis' paper in the Development Assistance Review Committee was wide-ranging and inconclusive. Among unattributed comments summarized in a subsequent aide-mémoire were the following:

- Our aid program until now has not been intellectually coherent.
- All governments state the wrong motives for their international aid.
- We should give underdeveloped nations enough aid to keep them quiet.
- A principal foreign policy objective is to find a policy which will help the best possible relationship with the United States.[104]

Only passing reference was made to the concern with national unity that had in fact been a major political preoccupation within the aid program over the previous two years.

About one-quarter of a subsequent background paper prepared for a three-day conference in May 1969 by CIDA's Planning Division dealt with motives and objectives. The document summarized the three broad motives, noting the imprecision of the philanthropic and the weakness of the case for the economic. The political motive was presented in terms of security (noting the lack of evidence), desirability of an enlarged Canadian "role in the international community of nations," and promotion of national unity and identity within Canada.[105] In reverse order, it was suggested that each could be matched with an objective:

- [The] first would be the political objective to establish within the recipient countries those political attitudes or commitments, military alliances or military bases that would assist Canada or Canada's western allies to maintain a reasonably stable and secure international political system.
- A second objective might be the establishment of markets for Canadian products and services.
- A third objective might be the relief of famine and personal misery.[106]

The paper proceeded to argue that "the basic problem which concerns Canada about the developing countries is their poverty and all the problems that it can lead to; thus the increase of their wealth and their ability to use and distribute it becomes the major and central objective." This fourth objective

> is not an alternative to those above. . . . [There] is *nothing inconsistent* between economic development and the previous objectives. But the main difference is that Canada's development assistance efforts would be directed to improving the general welfare, strength and viability of the recipient country and the first objectives would become *secondary and incidental* to this general process.[107]

Within this hierarchy of objectives, there was at least the implicit presumption that developmental objectives ought to prevail in the event of a conflict. However, this was not spelled out as clearly as it would be later in a thoughtful article by Grant Reuber of the University of Western Ontario, one of the participants in the review. Reuber (a future Ottawa mandarin) urged that "CIDA's task, which inevitably will be very difficult, be not made any more difficult by asking the agency to compromise its primary responsibility of aiding development in the LDCs in the most effective way possible in order to advance a series of objectives that conflict with this major responsibility."[108]

A call for a "quality program." Reuber's own discussion paper, on how to promote economic development through aid, lamented the ad hocery and passivity of Canadian decision-making. He suggested that "the generally low quality of the projects put up to Canada may simply reflect the fact that in the past Canada has been prepared to support low quality projects."[109] He called for an activist approach, involving:

- Membership in a "Good Guys Club" of small donors with "no particular axe to grind." . . . [It] could offer developing countries policy advice that might "be viewed with much less suspicion than views and advice emanating from major donors."

- Concentration of bilateral project aid emphasizing "development criteria" and "a hard-headed approach" within a limited number of recipients and in designated sectors of Canadian expertise.
- Active participation in multilateral agencies.

Reuber argued that pursuit of a quality program would require creation within CIDA of a top-flight capacity for economic analysis. Further strengthening of analytical capability would come from annual policy reviews that would draw upon the expertise of "distinguished international scholars. . . . What is being proposed is that we abandon our amateur status and join the big-time professional league in discussions of general development policies."[110] Looking back at the review experience, one of the CIDA personnel not surprisingly quipped, "The academics made us a little nervous."

Volume. The consultative phase of the review took place just before the Pearson commission recommended a donor ODA target of 0.7 per cent of GNP. However, both Agency personnel and consultants pushed to secure official commitment to UNCTAD's call for transfers of 1.0 per cent (including official export credits). They also sought a firm timetable for reaching this level by 1975.

The summary discussion paper subsequently prepared by CIDA noted a consensus among participants "that the developing countries can use as much aid as donor countries can make available," and "that the Canadian economy has the ability to make the resources available for any level of programme within the range of current public discussion." The constraint was budgetary: "Aid expenditures must . . . compete directly for priority with other growth expenditures such as health, education, welfare, and regional development."[111] Senior representatives on the International Development Board from other departments were reportedly in sympathy with continued movement towards international targets, but agreed with Finance that it would be unwise to make any firm commitment to a timetable or a date for achievement.[112]

Eligibility and concentration. Participants in the review were convinced of the need for greater concentration in fewer countries (in contrast to what we have seen was actually happening). They agreed as well that criteria were needed. Reuber suggested six: (1) political importance Canada attaches to development in particular countries; (2) economic needs of countries; (3) Canada's ability to meet those needs; (4) past performance and likely prospects for using foreign and domestic resources effectively for development; (5) level and types of aid available from other donors; and (6) "the extent to which, directly or indirectly, Canada can expect to influence countries for the purpose of improving their economic performance—i.e., the opportunity open to Canada to exert beneficial leverage effects through its aid." With respect to this last argument in particular, he suggested concentrating bilateral aid in smaller countries rather than large ones "where our efforts are likely to disappear into a yawning chasm."[113]

The summary discussion paper reproduced these criteria for further deliberation. As for sectoral specialization, however, it made only a general pitch[114] in place of Reuber's recommendations that Canada specialize in education at all three levels, agriculture, fishing and fish processing, minerals surveying and mining, electric power, and communications.[115]

Terms and conditions. There was general agreement that the existing high level of concessionality should be maintained in a bilateral program divided roughly equally between grants and loans with soft terms to minimize the debt burden of recipients. In contrast, the issue of procurement tying provoked lengthy debate, both in seminars with consultants and during informal interdepartmental discussions. Benjamin Higgins of McGill University reviewed the literature on tying, citing evidence about broad developmental and direct costs (estimated at between 12.5 and 40 per cent) imposed upon recipients. He concluded: "[The] gains in terms of projecting the Canadian image and in terms of national security (that is, accelerating the development of LDCs) would exceed the losses in terms of promoting Canadian exports, if Canada took the lead in unilateral untying, at least for countries in the 'quality' programme." In turn, any losses for Canada's exports or balance of payments could be minimized by carefully working out projects "designed to fit Canadian human and natural resource patterns."[116]

Officials in Planning Division accepted the evidence about the harmful effects of tying, but believed that these could be minimized by careful planning that avoided all but the most competitive Canadian inputs. The summary discussion paper noted the recent easing in tying restrictions, and set out the advantages of further action—greater project flexibility and closer observance of DAC norms—as well as the disadvantage of a weakened Canadian identification with the program and increased budgetary vulnerability in the event of a worsening balance of payments situation.[117]

Multilateral aid. The issue of Canadian identity in the aid program, the allied question of securing continued public and especially business support for it, and balance of payments considerations featured prominently in debate on what overall share should go, untied, to multilateral agencies.[118] A background paper by Louis Sabourin of the University of Ottawa recognized that certain objectives were better met by bilateral aid, but argued for a dramatic increase in multilateral contributions, perhaps to as much as 50 per cent of the overall ODA budget (compared to the recent level of 15 to 20 per cent, somewhat above the DAC average of 11 per cent). The strength of multilateral agencies (especially the World Bank) in policy analysis, and Canada's interest in international institutions, were generally seen as solid arguments for going beyond levels determined by international agreements on burden-sharing.[119]

NGOs and business. Although Strong himself was enthusiastic about an expanded role for non-governmental interests, and had already launched the NGO and Business and Industry programs, the review did not devote much time to the matter. Given the economistic bias of participants, there was scant appreciation of more than the political advantage of channelling public monies to NGOs. There was little discussion of a lengthy paper produced by the Private Planning Association on ways of encouraging more active Canadian business involvement in Third World countries.[120]

Trade and other non-aid issues. Also given short shrift was the broader issue of non-aid approaches to international development. It was agreed that immigration did not offer a viable alternative to development assistance, and could harm developmental prospects by accelerating the brain-drain.[121] Participants discussed preferential market access for developing country exports and measures to stabilize the prices of primary commodities, both major demands by Third World representatives in UNCTAD and other fora. They were divided both on the merits of then-current proposals and on the potential effectiveness of Canadian action.

As none of the consultants pushed hard to make non-aid matters central, and various departmental representatives expressed jurisdictional qualms, the summary discussion paper offered little more than a call for further analysis and discussion.[122] Despite Strong's own desire to make CIDA the centre of all Canadian international development efforts, it was clear that the Agency's actual role was still restricted to planning and delivering the aid program.

The White Paper: *International Development*

The consultative process concluded with a three-day conference of participants, chaired by Mitchell Sharp, in May 1969. The government's white paper, *International Development*, was subsequently drafted within CIDA and a cabinet-approved version was published in 1970 as one of six booklets comprising *Foreign Policy for Canadians*.

Why Canadian aid? On motives and objectives, the white paper followed the structure of the earlier summary discussion paper by setting forth motives that were then largely repeated as objectives. Despite Triantis' advice to play down humanitarian sentiment, the section on motives was grounded in an extension of positive liberalism to the international sphere:

> [All] individuals in a society have both rights and obligations toward other citizens in that society, because the potential of that society cannot be realized unless the potential of each of its members is also realized. . . . It is a sense of

> obligation to the less-affluent that underlies a progressive tax system, a system of free general public education, widespread pension plans, regional development plans, and general health-care programmes; all of these programmes are designed to provide a distribution of opportunities and rewards . . . that is consistent with the sense of justice and obligation of Canadians. It was in large measure an extension of this sense of social obligation and justice to the people in the less-fortunate countries that helped provide public support for the transfer of large amounts of Canadian resources to those countries in the post-war period.

This argument prefaced perhaps the only memorable passage amid the dry prose of the document: "A society able to ignore poverty abroad will find it much easier to ignore it at home; a society concerned about poverty and development abroad will be concerned about poverty and development at home."[123] A strong statement in itself, it was also crafted to confront head-on any objection to foreign aid on grounds that "charity begins at home."

The white paper contended that the morally correct course of action also reflected Canadian interests. Without accepting a "fair share of the responsibilities of membership in the world community, . . . we could not expect to find . . . support for Canadian policies amongst other nations." Development assistance could also strengthen international institutions in confronting common global challenges such as population growth, environmental problems, and technological change. More immediately, it "provides an initial source of financing for export of Canadian goods and services . . . and provides Canadians with the kind of knowledge and experience which help support the expansion of Canadian commercial interest overseas." Finally, by "providing an outward-looking expression of the bilingual character of Canada, our development assistance role also helps contribute to our sense of internal unity and purpose."[124]

Turning from motives to objectives, *International Development* stated:

> The Government regards the economic and social development of developing countries as the *primary* objective of the Canadian development assistance programme. . . . Toward this objective, all allocations and commitments of development assistance funds should be measured *chiefly* against criteria relating to the improvement of economic and social conditions in the recipient countries.[125]

If developmental goals were primary, others were presumably secondary, but the document did not say so explicitly; nor did it raise the possibility of conflicts among them. Rather, it emphasized that the development assistance program must be "sensitive" and "relevant" to "other Canadian objectives," such as: supporting the conduct of external relations, linking Canada's efforts to the common ends of developed countries, giving greater opportunities for expression of Canadian know-how and experience, and making Canadian goods and services more widely known and used. "Broadly speaking, the opportunity for gaining international understanding of Canada's national interests and objectives will be enhanced by an increasing development aid programme."[126]

Although perhaps subsumed under "common ends of developed countries," the use of aid to promote global peace and security received only a fleeting reference in the white paper. Political sensibilities may account for the absence of any mention of the Cold War, though it was still prominent in the earlier summary discussion paper, which had talked of a desire to "thwart the expansion of unwanted political ideologies and systems." Also, while that paper had recognized the tenuous relationship between development and political stability in the short run, it asserted that "foreign aid and economic development in the less-developed countries will help to reduce poverty, forestall political disorder . . . and maintain international stability."[127]

Perhaps Sharp was responsible for toning down the security argument in favour of a stronger moral one. He certainly did so in a speech to the Canadian Manufacturers' Association a month later:

> The assumption that the developed nations' interests are served best by maintaining the status quo through the judicious supply of aid is both arrogant and unfounded. . . . There are countries where one can only hope that in due time the development assistance they receive from us and from others will give to the people the sinews they need to rise and cast aside the cruel weight of unjust and unprincipled government.[128]

Given the timing, his comments were clearly a rejoinder to discussion in the Review committee, especially the views advanced by Triantis.

A few new policy directions. The document reaffirmed some existing policies: generous loan terms, increased support for NGO and business involvement, and creation of IDRC. Little was said about programming priorities, although the commitment to continuing food aid acknowledged criticisms and said that it had to be provided "with discretion."[129] Sectoral concentration based on Canada's "special competence" was foreseen in the white paper, but no examples were offered.[130] On non-aid matters, the white paper noted that "these subjects touch upon issues whose primary considerations lie outside the Canadian development assistance programme." As they related directly to the progress of developing countries, however, the "Government . . . is concerned to ensure that its policies in these matters take into account its development assistance objectives."[131]

The most significant policy innovations actually announced in *International Development* reflected compromises on the intertwined issues that generated the most controversy during the consultative phase—procurement tying in the bilateral program and the overall share of multilateral aid. On the former, in order "to improve the flexibility of the Canadian programme to meet specific requirements of high development priority," procurement conditions would be liberalized to cover shipping costs on all goods made available through ODA, and "to make available up to 20 per cent of total bilateral allocations on a completely untied basis for projects and programmes of particularly high development priority." As the previous policy had restricted every individual project to an untied maximum of 25 per cent, including shipping costs, and little use had as yet been made of that authority, the potential change from previous practice was substantial. A further commitment was made to work with other donors towards a more general agreement on untying.[132]

Further untying was foreseen, and a strong commitment to multilateral institutions was expressed, in a pledge to increase "within the next five years" the proportion of multilateral assistance to 25 per cent of the overall program.[133] Falling short of of a dramatic increase, this target still represented a commitment to go beyond the minimum burden expected of Canada internationally and the Pearson commission's recommendation of 20 per cent.

The policy on volume was more cautious. While mentioning neither a specific target nor a timetable, the document did promise that ODA funds would be increased over the coming years "to move towards the internationally-accepted targets." More specifically, "the Government will endeavour to increase each year the percentage of national income allocated to official development assistance"; this commitment "will enable" the aid budget "to grow on a regular and dependable basis that will provide a substantial increase in the proportion of Canadian resources allocated to development assistance by the middle of the decade."[134]

The white paper addressed, in general and open-ended terms, how to choose aid recipients and how to achieve a reasonable degree of concentration within them. On country eligibility, Reuber's list of criteria was presented in a modified form as "a number of principles" by which bilateral aid "can" be allocated. "Historical factors which support a special sense of concern" replaced political importance for Canada, and any direct reference to the potential for exercising developmental leverage was deleted. Degree of poverty, proximity to self-sustaining growth, developmental performance, availability of good projects and programs to match Canadian expertise, and concentration in the interests of improving effectiveness and impact were cited as principles to inform allocation decisions. No guidance on how to attach relative weights was offered, apart from the comment that "each leads to difficult anomalies if used as a sole criterion."

A commitment was made to allocate approximately 80 per cent of bilateral funds over the next three to five years to an unspecified number of "countries of concentration." The remainder would go to other countries, mostly for education and technical assistance, and also "for occasional capital projects of high development priority."[135] Not mentioned was the introduction in 1970 of Mission Administered Funds (MAF), small allocations for local projects disbursed directly by Canadian diplomatic posts, that relieved some of the pressures for full-scale bilateral programming. Though sometimes little more ambassadorial slush funds, MAF (subsequently renamed Canada Funds) have also supported some excellent and cost-effective grassroots projects.

The new policies on procurement tying and multilateral aid, along with signals about increased funding and a more activist approach to country and sector specialization, were important as they carried cabinet backing. However, *International Development* fell far short of the exciting, forward-looking document that Strong had wanted, or even a less ambitious codification of policy to provide guidance for delivering the aid program. George Cunningham suggested that the review process was "probably a good deal more ambitious than that of the Pearson commission which was taking place at the same time." Yet the end product of the Canadian review was a slight pamphlet, "half of which is devoted to arguing a case for aid like a simple propaganda appeal to doubtful members of the public, and half to policy intentions often expressed in vague terms."[136]

Strong agreed in retrospect that the white paper was disappointing:

> I remember being quite sad about the policy review. . . . I had hoped this would be an exciting new thing, that it would catch fire politically among Canadians, that it would give us a major new framework. But I was wrong on that. . . . It couldn't be made as exciting as I had hoped when I first started it because I could see during the process of consultation that some of the things we were already doing, when we put them in a policy document, people would start to react against them. And I became very concerned [as with the earlier process of considering legislation for CIDA] that the end result . . . might end up with more fetters on us. . . . I became very concerned about the document itself producing resistance to things we were already doing simply because we were articulating them as policies.

As a result, "we reduced the document to a non-threatening level" and made it "relatively unexciting. . . . I became very cautious about it and was never proud of the [final] document because I felt that it not only didn't go much beyond what we were doing—in fact, to some degree, it even downplayed some of the exciting things we were already doing."[137] Cunningham reported that some of the participating academics saw the white paper as an indication that the review had little impact on the aid program, though "the operation was useful in confronting officials with the ideas of those outside."[138]

A Parliamentary Critique

Cunningham went on to suggest that the outcome might have been different if there had been direct parliamentary involvement in the review process.

> Experience seems to suggest that fundamental re-examinations of development policy are more likely to have an effect if they are directed at government by or through committees of the legislature. Groups of consultants are disbanded when they have finished their work but Members of Parliament, once indoctrinated by the radical ideas of academics and lobbyists, can keep up a continuing pressure on governments for changes of policy.[139]

Developments in the 1980s would partially validate this hypothesis. However, *International Development* was in fact reviewed by a parliamentary committee, which invited testimony from academics, NGOs, multilateral agencies, and CIDA. It produced a document more radical than the white paper,[140] which then vanished with no discernible impact on the policy process.

Georges Lachance chaired a Subcommittee on International Development Assistance, which drew from the membership of the House of Commons Standing Committee on External Affairs and National Defence. The subcommittee agreed with the moral case for aid advanced by the government, and—while "acutely conscious of the gravity of . . . needs at home"—it saw "no conflict between . . . meeting these domestic needs and . . . international development abroad." It also echoed Trudeau in claiming that "there can be no durable peace or stability on the planet as long as the gulf between rich and poor is allowed to persist or widen."

The subcommittee endorsed the government's commitment to economic and social development as the primary objective of the aid program, asserting that none of the other "real and legitimate" interests set out in *International Development* "should distract Canadian attention from the central task at hand."[141] As we shall see, Lachance's entreaty would be echoed again and again by parliamentarians.

Although much has changed internationally and in developing countries since 1970, the overall impression garnered from reading the Lachance report is *plus ça change*. It endorsed policy initiatives in *International Development*, but went much further, expressing concerns that have either remained on the agenda for reform, or have been brought back from time to time by members of the Canadian development community and subsequent parliamentary committees.

The subcommittee called for a definite timetable for achieving the Pearson Commission's target of 0.7 per cent of GNP by 1975-76. Canada was urged to take an active role in international negotiations aimed at replacing tied aid with international competitive bidding, and, failing an agreement, to proceed without delay to untying Canadian funds for procurement in developing countries. Further decentralization of CIDA to the field, including limited project-approval authority, was recommended to speed up decision-making and improve responsiveness to recipient country needs.

The subcommittee report also emphasized the human dimension of development assistance, stressing the need for a better balance between capital projects and social and equity concerns. Environmental questions were seen as requiring more attention. NGOs were viewed as particularly effective instruments for social development, and the subcommittee recommended greater and more flexible funding arrangements for them. It also advocated more strenuous efforts (including investigation of an equity facility) for assisting Canadian firms to make meaningful long-term contributions to strengthening Third World economies. Concerned that much of the public support for the aid program was "somewhat passive and acquiescent," and that Canadians "may not be immune much longer to the 'weakening of will' " apparent in some donor countries, Lachance called for "vigorous new efforts at public education and involvement."[142]

Above all, the Lachance report declared, "a firm political will at the highest level" was needed to ensure that development assistance was effectively integrated and coordinated with policies on access for developing country exports, commodity price stabilization arrangements, and immigration.[143] CIDA's policy review had pulled punches. Strong did not when, after stepping down from the presidency, he appeared before the subcommittee. Referring to testimony from Professor Gerald Helleiner and other witnesses who "were extremely critical" of the white paper's failure to address non-aid issues, he said:

> I think many of these comments are very well taken. There has been a movement within government for some time to give CIDA a much greater voice in these affairs and I can say with the all the strength I can command that this is something which simply must be done. It does not make sense at all to operate a development assistance programme in isolation from other important policy areas by which Canadians affect the development of a developing world.[144]

Strong Departs

During the almost five years that Maurice Strong served as director general and president, the Canadian development assistance program was transformed from a marginal operation into a central facet of Canada's external relations. It was a time of considerable creativity in terms of process and substance, and a period that—despite the disappointment of the policy review and ongoing organizational uncertainty—left a number of permanent imprints on programs, policies, and operations. The need for coherent planning was also recognized, and solid steps were taken to make it happen. However, the day-to-day reality was closer to a comment from one of Strong's colleagues: "A little chaotic always. Lots of mistakes. Everything slow as hell because, I suspect this is still the case, the central agency procedures designed for domestic matters were pretty cumbersome in an operation like CIDA's."

Still, this last respondent typified other comments about the Strong era by adding: "It was a fun organization to work for. . . . Foreign aid was drawing some of the brightest people around—brightest and most idealistic." Another observed: "Strong was the first one to put the real interests of the aid program on top." As Strong left to assume his new responsibilities with the UN Commission on the Environment late in 1970, the Agency's resident artist circulated a cartoon. It showed the former president running at full tilt, tossing pieces of paper over his shoulder. CIDA employees trailed behind, trying to catch them. Each one was labelled "idea."

Chapter 4

Global Expansion and Growing Pains, 1970-77

Like his predecessor, Prime Minister Trudeau appointed a well-known public figure from outside the Ottawa establishment to head the aid program—Paul Gérin-Lajoie, one of the architects of Quebec's Quiet Revolution. The appointment simultaneously removed a strong nationalist from provincial politics, ensured vigorous expansion of Canadian aid to francophone Africa and Latin America, and injected enthusiasm into a project to have CIDA and the ODA program reflect Canada's cultural and linguistic duality. Gérin-Lajoie occupied the position for just over six years, until February 1977. After the heady days of Strong, it proved to be an exciting but increasingly difficult period for CIDA.

Spurred on by Canada's promise to make steady progress towards the 0.7 per cent ODA/GNP target, total Canadian ODA exceeded $900 million in 1975-76 and reached 0.53 per cent. CIDA had problems managing a rapidly growing budget, however, and the Agency became a target for increasing public scrutiny and criticism, as well as for the ambitions of other departments. Internationally, industrial and developing countries alike experienced painful adjustments, and conflict between them intensified as the North resisted demands for a New International Economic Order (NIEO). Meanwhile, doubts were growing about the appropriateness of Western aid efforts, especially—in a time of severe food shortages—their apparent urban and industrial biases.

These factors stimulated imaginative rethinking about Canada's role in international development. Gérin-Lajoie was highly sensitive to shifting currents in international and Third World discourse, and strongly supported creativity and experimentation. He also continued Strong's efforts to secure a central role for CIDA in influencing Canada's non-aid relations with developing countries. These concerns converged in a protracted process leading to publication of the Agency's *Strategy for International Development Coopera-*

Notes to Chapter 4 are on pp. 487-98.

tion 1975-1980. Although it enshrined progressive rhetoric on assisting the poorest countries, meeting basic human needs, and untying to permit procurement in developing countries, the obstacles confronting a grand policy framework were even greater than in 1969-70, not least because of CIDA's rapid growth and visibility on the Ottawa scene.

The new president's approach within CIDA, like Strong's, encouraged free-wheeling behaviour somewhat disdainful of bureaucratic conventions, but Gérin-Lajoie put more effort than his predecessor into representing Canada abroad and less into developing close links with leading Ottawa mandarins. He also failed to maintain managerial control over the Agency. Amid major administrative restructuring and considerable organizational infighting, serious weaknesses in operational effectiveness and financial accountability gradually became apparent. Problems of morale and high staff turnover fed hostile questioning from opposition members of Parliament and press accounts of "horror stories" in the field. From mid-1974 until Gérin-Lajoie's resignation in 1977, considerable time and energy went into "fire-fighting" media and parliamentary criticisms.

The Global Context: The NIEO and Basic Needs

While the gap between rich and most poor countries continued to grow in the 1970s, differentiation increased within the developing world. East Asia's "four little tigers" (South Korea, Taiwan, Hong Kong, and Singapore) earned the acronym NICs (newly industrializing countries), oil-exporting countries secured enormous hard currency surpluses after the Organization of Petroleum Exporting Countries (OPEC) raised oil prices dramatically in 1973 and 1974, and some non-oil, but resource-rich developing countries were able to adjust to the oil shock. Others suffered a severe imbalance in their international payments that was magnified by a sharp downturn in commodity prices after 1974. The worsening plight of very poor nations was reflected in their designation by the UN as least-developed countries (LLDCs). Most of these were in sub-Saharan Africa and South Asia, areas also hit hard by food shortages early in the decade.

Another catalyst for differentiation was a burgeoning Eurodollar surplus that was created by the Nixon administration's decision to withdraw from the Bretton Woods system of fixed exchange rates in 1972 and later magnified by the infusion of recyclable petrodollars. Many upper and middle-income countries secured access to this surplus through commercial bank loans at low and seemingly manageable rates of interest, supplementing support from official aid sources of aid. Meanwhile, low-income countries remained almost solely dependent on ODA as a source of external financing.

The flow of DAC aid in the 1970s failed to keep pace with economic growth in the donor countries. Although Norway, Sweden, and the Netherlands surpassed the 0.7 per cent target, the average in 1977 was 0.31 per cent, down from 0.34 in 1970. Still the largest donor, the US reduced its proportionate effort from 0.31 to 0.22 per cent.[1] Meanwhile, Arab OPEC countries became major contributors of multilateral and bilateral aid, largely earmarked for other countries in the Middle East and the Islamic world.

Despite diverging economic interests and ideological and regional conflicts, governments of developing countries continued efforts within the Group of 77 (now expanded) to develop a common agenda for international structural reform. The Conference of Non-Aligned Nations meeting in Algiers in 1973 called for a New International Economic Order (NIEO). A year later, the Sixth Special Session of the UN General Assembly adopted a program of action designed to level the playing field between North and South; among other objectives, the NIEO called for preferential access to markets in industrial countries for developing country exports.[2]

The so-called North-South Dialogue, which focused on NIEO proposals, dragged on over the course of the decade, driven by hope that industrial countries would make concessions in exchange for energy security. The developing countries discovered, however, that their bargaining clout was limited in the face of determined efforts by the US and most OECD members to resist what were characterized as unwarranted interventions in the marketplace. Moreover, the capitalist countries of the North, confronted by monetary instability and the OPEC and NIC challenges, had their own problems of rising unemployment and inflation. Positions hardened on both sides.

Discourse on development assistance shifted considerably, though the impact was more conceptual than practical. The failure of "trickle down" was apparent everywhere, most poignantly for the Americans in South Vietnam, which had been touted as a major aid success story before the war.[3] Increasing attention was devoted in the late 1960s and early 1970s to devising employment-generating and rural development schemes. Then, a big push for change came from Robert McNamara, president of the World Bank, in a speech to the Bank's governors at Nairobi in September 1973:

> The basic problem of poverty and growth in the developing world can be stated very simply. The growth is not equitably reaching the poor. . . . The data suggest that the decade of rapid growth has been accompanied by greater maldistribution of income in many developing countries and that the problem is most severe in the countryside. . . . One can conclude that policies aimed primarily at accelerating economic growth . . . have benefitted mainly the upper 40 per cent of the population and the allocation of public services and investment funds has tended to strengthen rather than offset this trend.[4]

The Bank sponsored a major study, *Redistribution with Growth*,[5] which, though largely skirting the issue of redistributing income and assets, emphasized the desirability of tapping new growth to raise the productivity of the poor. This orientation represented a significant departure from the earlier "growth equals development" perspective. Led by the World Bank, the international donor establishment embraced a commitment to meet the basic human needs (BHN) of those living in absolute poverty, especially in the poorest countries. These needs were defined as productive employment, adequate nutrition, clean drinking water, shelter, primary health care, and basic education.[6]

The concept of BHN remained somewhat fuzzy. Often, it was simply appropriated to relabel continuing activities; it also tended to promote narrowly technocratic programming that viewed the poor as target groups rather than participants in development. However, it legitimated poverty reduction as a fundamental goal of development assistance. Moreover, aid donors came to respect as developmental, rather than dismiss as mere welfare, small-scale community-based projects. Organizationally, this resulted in a larger share of ODA for NGOs.

Portrayed by Western development agencies as complementary to the developing world's NIEO aspirations, the emphasis on BHN was greeted with suspicion by many governments in the South. Efforts to make ODA conditional on meeting them were resented,[7] while the new orientation

> threatened to distract attention from the problems connected with underdevelopment and from the industrialised countries' joint responsibility for them. Consequently, the basic-needs approach was frequently dismissed for placing emphasis on income distribution within developing countries rather than on income inequalities between countries as the NIEO did. As a result of these disparate views, the multilateral discussions between North and South became a dialogue of the deaf.[8]

Monsieur le président

Back in Ottawa, Paul Gérin-Lajoie was an intriguing choice for the presidency of CIDA. He had served in Jean Lesage's Quebec cabinet from 1960 to 1966 spearheading the organization of a secular school system in the province and becoming its first-ever education minister. As vice-premier, he also played a key role in efforts to achieve special status for Quebec through constitutional reform and the development of separate international relations with France and (as we saw earlier) francophone Africa. After the Union Nationale election victory in 1966, he remained in opposition but eventually "got tired of waiting around for Lesage to retire" as Liberal leader.[9] Although at odds with Trudeau over the issue of special status for Quebec, Gérin-Lajoie secured a federal appointment in 1969 as vice-chairman of the Prices and Incomes Commission. He was appointed president of CIDA in November 1970. Moran's bête-noire was now CEO.

A former official lamented that "the meaning of the Gérin-Lajoie appointment was that the aid program was being subordinated to the interests of internal Canadian unity." Despite that controversial judgement, however, there was a strong case for appointing someone with a high profile, and a proven record of mobilizing public opinion, to promote an activity for which there was uncertain political support. Discussing his expectations with Gérin-Lajoie, Trudeau commended the ex-minister's work as an educator and communicator, and urged him to devote energy to creating greater public awareness of the challenges of international development.[10]

Gérin-Lajoie worked tirelessly to raise the profile of Canada's aid program at home and abroad. Within CIDA, his managerial weaknesses were generally acknowledged—but, while he made enemies, he commanded fierce loyalty from supporters who saw "PGL" (as they fondly called him) as committed and inspirational. One long-serving officer said, "Maurice Strong gave us structure and geography, but PGL gave CIDA its soul."[11] As external pressures mounted, many employees developed a fortress CIDA mentality, believing that, whatever their failings, the organization and the president were striving against adversity to fulfil a developmental mission.

When Gérin-Lajoie came under heavy press and parliamentary attack, many of his staunch defenders were correct in seeing an anglo backlash against a high-profile francophone.[12] At the same time, however, his style did invite criticism. One particularly cynical former colleague commented:

> The difference between Strong and Gérin-Lajoie was quite simple. Both of them were political animals—intensely political and ambitious. But Maurice Strong saw his political ambitions and his political future tied to doing a good aid job, having a legitimate program. . . . Gérin-Lajoie saw the aid program as a pork barrel to sort of buy his way around the international system. Whether you did a good technical or respectable development . . . was of a second priority, though I won't say he wasn't concerned.

Gérin-Lajoie continued to act as a minister, styling his executive group the "President's Committee." His personal staff of six might seem commonplace today, but it was larger than what other deputies, and even most federal ministers, enjoyed in the early 1970s. He had twelve of his major speeches, themselves largely ghost-written, edited and typeset in a series of booklets entitled *Thoughts on International Development*.[13] He spent several thousand dollars redecorating his office twice during his first few months—one of his senior officials warned that he "would get hammered" for this. Travelling abroad with a large entourage, Gérin-Lajoie was treated as "le président." While such flamboyance and imperial grandeur were frowned upon in Ottawa, he impressed host governments in developing countries, communicating eloquently and forcefully a profound sympathy for their problems and aspirations.

Policy Development

Just ten days after assuming office, the new president announced that he would emphasize the social objectives of aid. Speaking to the Lachance Subcommittee on International Development Assistance in February 1971, he elaborated:

> It is by now widely acknowledged that the Sixties witnessed a concentration on economic development and on growth rates measured in terms of Gross National Product, with too little account taken of the social development of the people affected. . . . [a] complete preoccupation with economic growth and a neglect of the social effects—the opening up of wide gaps in living standards within a country's population, for example—can bring great dangers to that country. . . . Our assistance program has already begun to emphasize . . . how best to help the least privileged in any country with which we work.[14]

Soon after a November 1971 meeting of the Group of 77 developing countries, which approved an early formulation of the NIEO, Gérin-Lajoie endorsed many of its demands.[15] He expressed readiness to respond to the plight of least-developed countries after UNCTAD III in 1972—and, when OPEC raised oil prices in 1973, a willingness to redesign policies to assist those developing countries hardest hit. With signs of deepening famine in parts of Africa and Asia, PGL announced that CIDA would put more emphasis on agriculture and basic human needs. He readily endorsed McNamara's challenge to donors and recipients to come to grips with absolute poverty. In short, as each new problem or theme emerged internationally, Gérin-Lajoie and CIDA—at least the talented advisers and speech-writers in his office—were quick to embrace it, earning for Canada during this period a reputation for being in the avant-garde of the donor establishment (except on the issue of procurement tying.)

This rapid response at the rhetorical level to shifting concerns can be characterized as profound idealism and commitment, as a desire to win respect internationally as a progressive donor, or as simple faddishness. However, Gérin-Lajoie, the politician, did view the developing world as his constituency. In a 1971 speech, he claimed that "CIDA is different from all other government departments in one outstanding respect. It is the single representative which the less favoured countries have in Canadian Government councils, the single voice of clear support on which they should be able to count from the outset."[16] PGL characterized his approach as "listening to the world."[17]

Towards a Strategy for International Development Cooperation, 1975-80

Changes in thinking about international development and the role of foreign aid influenced a lengthy and difficult process leading to publication in September 1975 of CIDA's *Strategy for International Development Cooperation 1975-1980*.

In the fall of 1972, barely two years after the release of *International Development*, the President's Committee decided that CIDA needed a new policy framework for the second half of the decade. When Gérin-Lajoie told Agency personnel of the project early in January 1973, he requested a completed draft for presentation to the minister within two months. By the end of January, the target had been set back to September 1973.[18] It was July 1975, however, already well into the first year of the strategy, when Cabinet approved the final version. It reflected more than a score of revisions that emerged from intense debates, both internal and interdepartmental.

The impetus for a new strategy.[19] Several factors contributed to the strategy initiative. Although CIDA planners were afraid that rapid increases in aid volume would overstretch the Agency's human resources, Gérin-Lajoie wanted to achieve a goal that eluded Strong: a definite timetable for reaching the international ODA target of 0.7 per cent of GNP. Like his predecessor, PGL was keen to see the Agency play a larger policy role in non-aid matters, especially enhancing market access for developing country exports. There was also the challenge of keeping development assistance on the political agenda during the period of minority government from 1972 to 1974.

At the same time, the late Harry Hodder, vice-president of Policy Branch, was eager to develop a clear role for his new branch. Long a creative force within EAO and CIDA, he is remembered for once quipping "CIDA is a very large animal with a very small brain." Hodder was particularly troubled about how to manage a program that was growing much faster than personnel resources. If, as Gérin-Lajoie hoped, the 0.7 threshold could be achieved by 1980, sweeping administrative efficiencies and less labour-intensive mechanisms for resource transfers would be needed.

Hodder also worried about how to meet a cabinet directive to reduce the number of countries eligible for Canadian aid when political and bureaucratic pressures kept encouraging proliferation. Within the Agency, he and PGL were under pressure from junior officers who wanted a stronger Canadian commitment to NIEO reforms and help for the poorest people in recipient countries. A study was launched on how Canada could better support LLDCs.[20]

A challenge from Industry, Trade and Commerce. The need for a new aid policy review seemed even more urgent when CIDA was confronted by a major initiative from the Department of Industry, Trade and Commerce (IT&C). Back in 1968, IT&C had produced a lengthy position paper defining its "basic role" in the aid program as ensuring "that Canadian bilateral aid allocations make the maximum possible contribution to Canadian economic development, without compromising the contribution of these allocations to Third World development."[21] This document had identified several priorities: increasing aid to rapidly growing developing countries where markets for Canadian products "will materialize in the near rather than the distant future," encouraging capital assistance projects, especially those with a high engineering content, and involving Canadian business in project selection. IT&C also cautioned against further procurement untying.

Members of the Aid Operations Division of the International Financing Branch of IT&C were among the most assiduous 'CIDA-watchers' in the Ottawa bureaucracy. They increased their pressure on the Agency in January 1973 by circulating a draft proposal calling for a more active IT&C role in ODA decision-making. "Because countries, sectors and projects for Canadian aid . . . were almost invariably selected on other than commercial grounds," the authors[22] contended, "the Department of Industry, Trade and Commerce has had to attempt to maintain an ongoing commercial input on a more or less ad hoc basis."[23] CIDA's recent focus on LLDCs was attacked as one more initiative giving primacy to countries of little commercial or political interest to Canada.

IT&C argued that the aid program could support a broader strategy for creating new developing country markets for Canadian goods and services, especially those high in value added and technological sophistication, and, at the same time pursue CIDA's developmental objective because the more advanced recipient countries had the best potential for rapid growth. The authors called specifically for a new "commercial aid program" that would "consciously and explicitly" direct seed money to countries of higher market priority for Canada.[24] This program would be administered by CIDA in close consultation with IT&C and business. Meanwhile, CIDA would retain a "pure aid program," concentrated in a small number of poorer countries, increasingly focused within sectors of internationally competitive Canadian capability but largely freed from formal procurement tying.

A year of false starts. Hodder wanted a tight time-frame for the strategy exercise, partly to thwart IT&C designs and recapture the initiative for CIDA. He retained his vice-presidential status, but was redesignated special adviser to the president on the strategy; a Strategy Unit was set up and attached to the president's office rather than Policy Branch.[25] In an Agency-wide memo, Gérin-Lajoie gave the project "highest priority," and encouraged all CIDA officers to "submit their own views to Hodder without clearance through the normal channels."[26] Open sessions organized for staff input enhanced a feeling that their participation was valued.

Meanwhile, Hodder decided to keep the process largely within the bureaucracy. He told the President's Committee: "Academics had a major involvement in the previous examination of our programs in 1969 but many contributions were tangential, attributable in part to a lack of familiarity with the operations of our programs and the policy and other constraints to be faced."[27]

In response to IT&C's challenge, the Strategy Unit proposed an alternative: sectoral studies undertaken

> in full cooperation with the business community and IT&C, to identify where Canada now has and will have in future capabilities relevant to the needs of our clients. The direct involvement of the business community will be one of the most important aspects of this exercise both to solicit business support and understanding as well as to formulate on a continuing basis a strategic approach to Canada's commercial penetration of the markets of the Third World.[28]

In addition, throughout early 1973, Gérin-Lajoie stepped up efforts to court business support for Canadian aid.[29] These attempts to forestall further pressure from IT&C encountered intense opposition within the Agency, especially from younger, more radical officers who categorically rejected any concessions pointing towards a more commercially oriented program. Successive drafts of the strategy tried to steer a middle course, but internal conflict continued to simmer. As Glyn Berry put it in his exhaustive case study of the process, Hodder was engaging in "anticipatory accommodation" so that a document could proceed relatively unscathed through the "interdepartmental gauntlet," while his in-house critics focused on "purely developmental criteria."[30]

Meanwhile, weeks stretched into months as the Strategy Unit took on an ever-growing list of concerns, many of which required lengthy study. Unable to secure agreement on an agenda in the President's Committee or elsewhere, and tiring of the uncertainties of working with PGL, Hodder left the Agency at the end of 1973.

A strategy takes shape. After Hodder's departure, the Strategy Unit moved to Policy Branch. Distanced from politics at the presidential/vice-presidential level, his erstwhile junior colleagues sought to achieve consensus within CIDA by shifting away from concerns about organizational efficiency and commercial responsiveness, to an analysis of global change and how Canada should respond to the plight of LLDCs and other countries hit hard by energy and food crises. They also pushed for a priority on meeting the basic needs of the poorest. As Berry observed, however, the objective was less to seek sweeping changes in Canadian policies towards developing countries than—in the words of a key player—"to shift those policies two notches if possible, but certainly one notch towards the progressive."[31]

Early in 1974, the Strategy Unit fashioned what would be the organizational framework of the final document—a general analysis of global trends and Canada's role in North-South matters, followed by a section outlining specific objectives and commitments. Several in-house task forces were set up to develop positions on country eligibility and concentration, terms, bilateral resource transfer instruments, cooperation with the Export Development Corporation, and multidimensional approaches to international development. As those now in charge of the project accommodated much of the developmental critique that had been directed at Hodder's efforts, the process moved ahead more smoothly within CIDA. Once drafts began to circulate outside the Agency, however, many of the modestly progressive edges were soon blunted.

The New Strategy: Issues and Outcomes

The strategy reasserted the primacy of development objectives,[32] promising to concentrate assistance "in those countries which are at the lower end of the development scale . . . and which are most severely affected by current world economic conditions." In turn, the reorientation of the World Bank from growth with trickle-down to growth with equity was reflected in a priority on "meeting the basic needs of their populations. Canada will give the highest priority to development projects aimed at improving the living and working conditions of the least privileged sections of the population in recipient countries."[33]

Although non-developmental goals were not catalogued explicitly, the strategy quoted the phrase in the 1970 white paper about being sensitive to other national objectives, and stated that the program would be compatible with the government's foreign policy.[34] The text referred to mutual benefits that might flow from new forms of cooperation with developing countries enjoying significantly increased export earnings, and argued that the benefits of tying a substantial portion of bilateral aid to domestic procurement "indicate that the cost of the aid program to Canadian society is less than volume alone would suggest, be it in times of world prosperity or hardship."[35]

The contextual analysis. CIDA's perspectives survived the interdepartmental editing process to a greater degree in the analytical section of the final document (Part I) than in policy statements (Part II). Part I suggested that global economic dislocations in the early 1970s had raised "the possibility that resources necessary for economic growth may . . . cease to be in adequate supply to meet the needs of all countries, and that the environment may not support . . . growth at a rate sufficient to provide a decent standard of living for the entire world population." The intolerable prospect of a widening gap between rich and poor meant that "redistribution of economic activity and consumption from rich to poor is then seen by the developing world to be the only route for the improvement of their situation."[36]

The OPEC oil shock had brought home the vulnerability of all countries to external instability.

> [The] industrialized countries will increasingly find their future prospects linked to the viability of a new relationship between themselves and the Third World, which, in turn, will require unprecedented commitments by the international community. In view of the disastrous consequences of allowing the present structural imbalances in the world to persist, there is no satisfactory alternative [to] . . . the creation of an international economic system which will provide a more equitable distribution of resources and opportunities to all people.[37]

There was a need for increased aid that would challenge "the mistaken belief that maximizing economic growth rates can alleviate poverty through the 'trickling down' of benefits to the poor."[38] However, from the vantage point of developing countries, aid was only a small part of the much larger requirement for trade, monetary, and other reforms such as those advocated by the Group of 77.

Part I went on to argue that Canada was favourably placed to support the evolution of a new relationship between industrialized and developing countries:

> Its past development assistance performance, as well as its lack of imperial or colonial ambitions, has gained Canada a favourable reputation as a relatively progressive and unbiased participant in Third World affairs. For historical and cultural reasons, Canada also enjoys special links with Commonwealth members and Francophone countries out of proportion to its economic power.[39]

Although "approaches may differ," Canada shared interests with developing countries in such matters as orderly marketing arrangements and stable prices for primary export commodities, a non-discriminatory multilateral trading system, sovereignty over natural resources, and reforms of international shipping and the Law of the Sea. Canadians as consumers had a stake in securing easier access to "some competitive products" made in developing countries.

Textual additions such as "approaches may differ" and "some competitive products" reflected a weakening of assertions about the complementarity of Canadian and developing country interests. These revisions appeared in the interdepartmental editing process, which also ensured that no precise commitments were made to any of the reforms sought by the Group of 77, and that statements about Canada's capacity included domestic concerns about recession, inflation, and a deterioration in the balance of payments.

A multidimensional Canadian approach to international development. Part II, the policy section, was organized into twenty-one points. Point 1 proclaimed:

> In renewing its firm commitment to international development cooperation, the Government undertakes to harmonize various external and domestic policies which have an impact on the developing countries, and to use a variety of policy instruments in the trade, international monetary, and other fields in order to achieve its international development objectives.[40]

The Lachance committee had earlier concluded: "until there is more general acceptance of the broader conception of development cooperation and of the legitimacy of a broader CIDA role, the viewpoints of aid officials are unlikely to prevail over those of other agencies with differing perspectives." It advocated an integrated strategy for international development that would give CIDA an enlarged policy role in sensitizing other government departments to developmental implications of policies, and in coordinating interdepartmental communications and consultation.[41]

Neither Lachance nor Strong's best efforts had made much headway with a multidimensional approach, but the Strategy Unit took up the challenge with vigour in 1974-75. By that time, there was at least greater interest elsewhere in the bureaucracy in some of the broader issues. Apart from the francophone Africa initiative, Third World concerns had remained marginal in External Affairs until 1972 when Paul Martin, Sr., now a senator, represented Canada at UNCTAD III in Santiago, Chile. Martin was furious about the inadequacy of official preparations,[42] an experience that led to regular interdepartmental discussions on North-South matters. Ivan Head, the prime minister's adviser on foreign affairs, was a key player among those—a minority—who argued that it was in Canada's interest to pay more attention to the Third World, and to adjust trade and other policies creatively. The need to take such questions seriously became even more urgent after the 1973 OPEC oil price shock. In 1974, the specialized Interdepartmental Committee on Economic Relations with Developing Countries (ICERDC) was struck with External Affairs in the chair.[43]

After a CIDA task force on multidimensional development attempted to crystallize positions on non-aid matters in 1974,[44] the Strategy Unit proposed that the Privy Council Office undertake a review of all aspects of international development policy. Other departments immediately opposed what they saw as an attempt to force policy decisions prematurely and encroach on their territory.[45] As a result, CIDA had to be content in the strategy with announcing ICERDC's creation and its mandate: "to review policies that affect Canada's economic and other relations with developing countries, to examine their consistency, to propose policies consistent with a broad approach to our relations with developing countries, and to prepare coordinated policy positions for international meetings affecting Canada's relations with developing countries."[46]

In fact, the actual work of ICERDC, largely limited to preparation for international conferences, fell well short of a thoroughly multidimensional approach. And it remained true that "while CIDA is accorded an important role in 'aid,' her involvement in trade, tariffs, monetary matters and so on is merely tolerated."[47] Once more, CIDA had failed to move beyond its role as an aid agency.

To digress briefly, one outcome of concern about the broader context of aid was the founding of the North-South Institute as an independent, non-governmental agency dedicated to providing professional, policy-relevant research on North-South issues. CIDA sponsored a consultation on the Multidimensional Approach to Development in March 1975, which brought Agency people together with Irving Brecher from McGill University, Gerald Helleiner from the University of Toronto, Glen Milne from the Privy Council Office, and Bernard Wood from the Parliamentary Centre. On the issue of how to foster a support base outside of government, they concluded:

> Private sector resources were judged to be surprisingly slender. The number of experts in the universities is small, and the obvious institutions such as IDRC and the Institute for Research in Public Policy have carved out different areas of specialisation. While there has been much discussion about the need in Canada for an institution similar to the Overseas Development Council (USA) or the Overseas Development Institute (UK), proposals for a "Canadian Development Institute" have not come to fruition. Such an agency, with a capacity to research, to lobby, and to educate, would serve interests wider than the multi-dimensional alone, but would be invaluable to the latter.[48]

The idea was supported enthusiastically, and the North-South Institute was set up in 1976 with initial funding from the Donner Canadian Foundation, IDRC, and CIDA. Bernard Wood left the Parliamentary Centre to become executive director. The multidimensional issue was a central preoccupation for the Institute's founders. So too was concern that criticism of CIDA and the Canadian aid program, growing since 1974, was superficial and undermining public support for international development. Informed criticism was needed, but from a vantage point of strategic support for a more enlightened Canadian approach to North-South relations.

The international ODA target. Point 6 of the strategy reaffirmed the government's "determination to achieve the official United Nations target of 0.7 per cent of GNP and to move towards this target by annual increases in the proportion of Official Development Assistance to GNP."[49] Although it is arguable that "determination" is stronger than "will endeavour," the position in the strategy was little different from that in the 1970 white paper. During the bargaining process, CIDA had to abandon Gérin-Lajoie's goal of reaching the target by 1979-80. Moreover, in response to Treasury Board efforts to expunge all references to 0.7 per cent, the Agency even had to delete a statement pointing out that the current growth rate, if sustained, would achieve that level by the end of the decade.[50]

Priorities for country eligibility and concentration.[51] Of all the issues in the strategy exercise, geographical distribution consumed the most time and energy within CIDA, and generated the greatest interdepartmental conflict. By 1972, the list of countries that had at some stage been recipients of Canadian aid stretched to more than ninety entries. In March of that year, cabinet called for reductions in total recipients and countries of concentration. CIDA's allocations memorandum for 1972-73 suggested three criteria for declaring recipients ineligible: high GNP per capita, large revenues from oil sales, and persistent slowness in planning and implementing projects. These factors were at best marginal, however, when the 1973-74 eligibility list deleted eighteen occasional recipients who had "no permanent place in the scheme of Canadian assistance."[52] George Cunningham observed in 1974: "CIDA officials acknowledge . . . that the idea of countries of concentration, which was new to Canada until a few years ago, is manifested more in intention than in fact."[53]

IT&C's pressure to divide the aid program into commercial and pure components had a catalytic effect on making eligibility and concentration major preoccupations within the Strategy Unit. A task force was set up to examine past experience and develop proposals that would reclaim the initiative for CIDA.[54] Its report found that "some countries have been declared eligible on the basis of low per capita GNP and evidence of firm commitment to development; others were declared eligible in spite of the fact they clearly did not qualify for assistance according to the same criteria." Several decisions had clearly contradicted "general statements concerning the primacy of development." The task force summarized its conclusions about the past as follows:

- The decision-making process has been informed by various developmental, political and commercial considerations introduced from time to time on an ad hoc, case-by-case basis.
- No standard weightings have been applied to the argumentation of various departments for the inclusion/exclusion of countries; the result has been inconsistency and sometimes outright contradiction in discussions on eligibility.

- It has been relatively easier to add a country to the eligibility list than to remove the same country or another.
- A variety of development "criteria" appear and re-appear in such discussions but they have never been applied on an across-the-board, systematic, and consistent basis. They do however provide a guide to the criteria which the Canadian Government has considered relevant to the problem of eligibility.[55]

The task force set out "to render more explicit and systematic the assumptions and logical processes underlying decisions on eligibility and allocations, to disentangle and examine their development, political and commercial elements, and, finally, to illuminate and systematize future decisions."[56] It based its analysis on two premises: "that the differing impact of the energy crisis has highlighted *the need for the community of donors to channel both emergency and longer term aid to those countries which need it most*," and that, while other objectives were not always mutually consistent with the paramount purpose of ODA to foster development, CIDA's mission could be more effectively pursued during the process of "blending" objectives if development criteria were clearly formulated.[57]

While conceding that External Affairs and IT&C would continue to push non-developmental concerns, the task force argued that eligibility and allocation decisions should be shaped primarily by developmental need, as defined by level of per capita income, social indicators, an assessment of development effort and commitment, and, to the extent possible, a forecast of future prospects and foreign exchange availability. Matching recipient needs with Canadian capacities, and appraising a country's ability to plan and implement effective development programs, while both germane, were best left to annual country programming exercises rather than to decisions on eligibility (i.e., to CIDA rather than interdepartmental negotiations).

Using classification schema based on levels of development and GNP per capita, the authors noted that a large part of Canada's bilateral ODA had gone to the poorest countries. "*The assumption of the Task Force has been that a substantial drift 'upward' from CIDA's historical category shares (i.e., in favour of the relatively well-off nations) would be a regressive step*, tantamount to a transfer of resources from the Maritimes to Alberta."[58] They recommended, therefore, that the bulk of bilateral funds be directed to developing countries under $200 per capita (in 1971 $US), that 20 per cent of the program be devoted to LLDCs by 1980, and that the portion of CIDA disbursements going to upper-income developing countries (those with per capita incomes in excess of $375) not exceed 8 per cent. The task force also suggested ranges of 40-45 per cent for Asia, 37-43 per cent for Africa, and 9-12 per cent for the Americas (close to recent experience, but slightly skewed towards Africa as a lower-income region).

The report made a strong case for greater concentration among fewer recipients, suggesting that the number of countries receiving significant amounts of government-to-government assistance be reduced to fifty by 1980. It recommended dropping recipients from the upper-income category, especially those with below-average developmental performance and/or those with good foreign exchange prospects. Jamaica, which had been an especially high priority (and remained so), was cited for possible deletion along with Trinidad and Tobago, Chile, Costa Rica, and Gabon. To ease the transition—and maintain the "diplomatic calling card" aspect of aid—the task force recommended that up to $200,000 a year be made available to non-program countries, including those not currently receiving Canadian grants or loans.

Shortly thereafter, Allan MacEachen, Mitchell Sharp's successor as secretary of state for External Affairs, asked CIDA to examine the implications of reducing the number of recipient countries to thirty. In response, the Agency defended fifty as achievable without unduly antagonizing existing recipients, and realistic in accommodating developmental and non-developmental goals without sacrificing one to the other. Once the issue was opened to interdepartmental consultation, IT&C continued to argue for a two-tiered system—core programming in a few countries, with the balance going to a new Global Fund to advance Canadian commercial interests. External Affairs advocated channelling at least 75 per cent of bilateral ODA to twenty or thirty countries, reserving the rest for a more broadly defined global fund.[59]

The interdepartmental debate yielded a strategy text that essentially maintained the status quo. Point 8 declared that the ODA program "will direct the bulk of its resources and expertise to the poorest countries of the world. . . . Particular attention will be given to the hardcore least developed countries identified by the United Nations." Up to 10 per cent (rather than the recommended limit of 8 per cent) "will be allocated to upper income developing countries."[60] (External Affairs had objected to the lower ceiling, fearing that it threatened the Caribbean program.[61]) In addition, Point 2 discussed new relationships with oil-exporting and upper-income countries that "will emphasize reciprocal interests and mutually beneficial exchanges rather than development assistance."[62] No reference was made to any ranges for the major geographical areas.

Point 9 promised to concentrate bilateral ODA "on a limited number of countries selected on the basis of need, commitment to development, general Canadian interests, and the geographic distribution of other donors' bilateral assistance." Although the criteria were focused more clearly on development than those in the 1970 policy, the temporizing reference to "general Canadian interests" left a question mark about operational significance. In a further concession to trade promotion, another statement indicated that the government would occasionally provide "a positive response to development projects that are submitted for Canadian consideration and are outside the ambit of regular programs." The document did not set a number for program countries, but included the proposal to make available up to $200,000 a year to non-program countries.[63]

The strategy might well have reflected a greater commercial tilt had there not been intervention from the political level. Early in 1975, MacEachen made it known that he opposed a large commercial element in the aid program.[64] Trudeau made two more of his powerful appeals for greater attention to North-South issues at Duke University in 1974 and at the Mansion House in London in 1975.[65] These were frequently quoted in defence of CIDA's position. Moreover, the prime minister himself argued against a stronger commercial orientation when the completed strategy came before the Priorities and Planning Committee of cabinet in July 1975.[66]

Terms and conditions. The concessionality of Canadian development loans, ODA debt relief, and procurement tying became major issues during the strategy process. The Department of Finance attempted to open up the terms of development lending, suggesting that a matrix of varying interest rates and repayment requirements be established for recipients at different levels of development. External Affairs argued for a "third window" offering loans to upper-income countries on terms of 4 per cent interest, twenty-five years repayment, and a seven-year grace period. Hodder was initially receptive, but junior officers objected, arguing that the original 0-50-10 formula be retained as the norm, and that harder loans on the 3-30-7 formula be offered (as they had been) only sparingly to higher-income recipients.[67]

Neither the matrix approach nor the third window was incorporated in the strategy, but CIDA conceded in Point 12 that the "terms of assistance will be flexible and will be adapted to the economic conditions of each partner country." The possibility of parallel financing in concert with the Export Development Corporation was also raised in Point 16. As a trade-off, CIDA won statements committing Canada to maintenance of at least a 90 per cent grant element in the bilateral program and support for efforts to improve the terms of overall ODA flows internationally.[68]

On the related issue of debt relief, the Strategy Unit failed to secure either of its objectives—a formal policy on debt rescheduling, or a joint CIDA-Export Development Corporation study of implications of official debt forgiveness for countries experiencing serious repayment problems. Finance was adamantly opposed to a general policy on debt relief and was joined by Treasury Board in rejecting the proposed study. Instead, officials in Finance managed to get their own wording for Point 15,[69] which said: "The Government recognizes the serious problem of indebtedness for developing countries and will continue to take a forthcoming attitude towards the provision of debt relief on a case-by-case basis and when exceptional circumstances warrant it."[70]

CIDA made more headway on the issue of procurement untying, although it did not seek a general change in the 1970 policy. In fact, Gérin-Lajoie supported a largely tied program, and the group pushing for a more developmental orientation in aid policy recognized that they lacked a convincing case as only about one-half of the existing untying authority was being used. In other words, it was certainly possible to untie more of the existing program to meet local costs; the constraint was practice within CIDA rather than policy.[71]

What PGL, sensitive to international and domestic criticisms of tying, did seek late in the process was a specific breakthrough on the issue of untying development loans for competitive bidding by developing country suppliers.[72] A commitment to take such action would put Canada among the majority of DAC members abiding by a 1974 memorandum.[73]

Early drafts of the strategy circulated outside CIDA omitted any reference to untying. According to Berry, when a recommendation to allow developing country procurement appeared in a later draft, it was viewed as violating an interdepartmental entente that untying would not be raised.[74] Finance opposed the move and IT&C, especially upset, insisted on consulting business. CIDA officials met twice with the Canadian Export Association, which not surprisingly registered strong opposition.[75] Gérin-Lajoie appealed to MacEachen for support, noting that there would be strong criticism from NGOs if the strategy evaded the issue, especially since other donors had moved further than Canada. Complete untying was out of the question, the president said, but a modest opening to developing countries would help strengthen their industrial capacities.[76]

CIDA subsequently managed to secure as Point 14: "The government will liberalize the CIDA procurement regulations by *immediately* untying its bilateral development loans so that developing countries would be eligible to compete for contracts."[77] The issue was debated in the Priorities and Planning Committee of Cabinet where the text was approved on an informal understanding that no more than 10 per cent of the bilateral program would be untied in this way without further cabinet-level approval.[78] Point 14 also promised that the government would study the implications of untying allocations to other donors, in situations where immediate assistance was needed but could not readily be met by Canadian capabilities. What appeared to be a dramatic concession turned out to be a pyrrhic victory, however, as we shall see in Chapter 5.

Programming priorities. Many compromises in the strategy reflected real or anticipated interdepartmental conflict. Provisions relating to the content of the bilateral program were also shaped by contradictory forces, though largely within CIDA itself. On the one hand, there was a desire to associate closely with the World Bank's emphasis on rural development and basic human needs; such a reorientation called for smaller-scale and more labour-intensive projects with larger local-cost components. On the other hand, rapid growth in aid volume was still outstripping CIDA's administrative resources, and the bilateral program remained highly tied to Canadian procurement. These factors reinforced a preference for large capital-intensive projects and a search for more liquid transfer instruments.

The contradiction was reproduced in the strategy. Point 5 made a commitment to meeting the basic needs of people in the poorest countries. As well, "Canada will give the highest priority to development projects and programs aimed at improving the living and working conditions of the least privileged sections of the populations in recipient countries and at enabling these people to achieve a reasonable degree of self-reliance."[79] Point 13 gave several reasons for increasing the liquidity of the bilateral program through "selective but more widespread use of general program assistance to key sectors of the economy, lines of credit, tied and untied food and commodity assistance, and general support to indigenous institutions (such as development banks)."[80]

Point 7 conveyed a determination to focus aid more sharply on sectoral priorities that would address basic needs—food production and distribution, rural development, education and training, public health and demography, and shelter and energy. "Greater specialization in fewer sectors will improve the quality of Canadian development expertise and allow for a more rational and efficient use of Canadian resources." What was actually proposed, however, involved a broadening of sectoral emphases to new priorities on rural development, health, population, and housing—without dropping any of the existing ones. Another clause stated that "Canada will continue to offer its assistance in sectors such as transport and communications where Canadian expertise and technology are appropriate and competitive."[81] It was inserted on the insistence of External Affairs and supported by IT&C.[82]

Critical arguments about the potentially harmful impact of food aid preceded the statement that

> Canada, like other donors, must continually weigh the choices between the provision of assistance for investment in productive sectors, including agricultural production, as against the immediate consumption demands of food-deficient countries. But until 1980, the precarious level of food stocks stands out above other factors and the prospect that these can be rebuilt in the developing countries is remote.[83]

Point 18 reiterated a commitment made by MacEachen at the World Food Conference in Rome in 1974 to supply one million tons of grain in food aid in each of the following three years. It also raised the possibility of untying up to 20 per cent of food aid for procurement in third countries, mainly in the developing world.

Other channels. While the bilateral program was its chief focus, the strategy dealt as well with shares for other channels. Point 4 pledged that "Canada will continue to support actively and participate in international institutions as important forums for building cooperative relationships and for mobilizing and channelling resources for development." Particular references were made to the World Bank, IDA, and Commonwealth and francophone institutions. Canadian contributions would continue to rise, up to a maximum of "about 35 per cent" of ODA disbursements apart from food aid.[84] Since food aid had been averaging 20 to 25 per cent of ODA, and about one-fifth of it was channelled multilaterally, the new target for multilateral aid was about 30 per cent of total disbursements, 5 per cent above the commitment in the 1970 white paper. As we shall see, the new guideline was soon exceeded.

Point 11 pledged continuing support for research organizations that promoted innovations and strengthened indigenous research capability. The international agricultural research institutes and IDRC were cited, and a commitment was made to strengthen IDRC-CIDA cooperation. Point 17 on "diversity of channels" recognized NGOs, otherwise ignored in the review; they were praised for their growing capacity to mount substantial programs and were promised 6 to 10 per cent of non-food ODA. Point 19 on emergency relief flagged the need to ensure that it did not distort longer-term development efforts.[85]

Public participation. Point 21 was highlighted in a separate section of the strategy:

> Though the official program of development cooperation may be financed and administered by the Government, it will be organized in such a way as to support, strengthen, and intensify the widest possible participation of all sectors of the Canadian community: individuals and voluntary non-profit organizations, the governments of the provinces, the several departments of the federal and provincial governments, universities, and the business sector. To support such efforts, the Government will implement an improved and expanded program to ensure that relevant information on all dimensions of international development is made available to the public.[86]

This point did little more than restate Strong's philosophy, but, as we shall see, CIDA was by 1975 facing a rather more difficult challenge in its relations with politicians, the media, and the public.

Launching the Strategy

The strategy document was finally unveiled by Allan MacEachen at a meeting of the Ottawa diplomatic corps on September 2, 1975. The next day, the minister summarized the contents in a speech to the UN General Assembly.[87] In his preface to the document, he suggested that the strategy provided basic principles and approaches to shape policies, bench-marks from which to assess Canadian performance in the coming years, and a moving framework that encouraged adaptation to rapidly evolving and unforeseen circumstances. Press coverage was minimal but generally favourable, with most attention devoted to what were seen as moves towards greater country concentration, sectoral specialization, support for the poorest, and untying.[88]

As Berry commented, however, the document was not a strategic action plan, but rather a collection of existing positions and principles with little operational meaning. Several of the generalities were such that "bureaucratic bargaining in the future would be constrained to no greater degree than in the past."[89] By and large, the outcome demonstrated, as had Strong's review, CIDA's limitations in negotiating policy with its more senior governmental partners. Looking back in an interview with the author, Gérin-Lajoie contended that the strategy exercise was less important for the final product, which was an anti-climax, than for its value as an educational process within the Agency and other departments.[90]

A Parliamentary Review

There was no parliamentary involvement in the policy review, a curious anomaly in view of Gérin-Lajoie's political career and the progressive policy positions so recently advanced by the Lachance subcommittee. Some opposition parliamentarians were paying attention to CIDA, however, and the president was often distracted during 1974-75 by partisan attacks on aspects of the aid program and his management of the Agency. One result of this stormy period was the appointment of another subcommittee on international development under the aegis of the House of Commons Standing Committee on External Affairs and National Defence. Chaired by Liberal Maurice Dupras, the subcommittee really owed its existence to the persevering efforts of a Conservative, Douglas Roche, a strong internationalist somewhat detached from most of his caucus colleagues.

With an open mandate to deal with any matters regarding international development, the subcommittee held thirty meetings from July 1975 to April 1976, heard testimony from twenty-three witnesses, and reviewed forty-eight written submissions. On the eve of UNCTAD IV in Nairobi, it issued a report, which—like Lachance—was more radical than the official document that preceded it. The Dupras report took up the challenge of developing an integrated, multidimensional Canadian policy on all aspects of North-South negotiations. Sensitive to domestic cross-currents on several issues, it put forward thoughtful proposals on commodities, trade, technology transfer, and Canada's potential for leadership. It called for a more systematic approach to the growing debt burden, and urged Canada to press for international procedures for converting ODA debts to grants where appropriate for the poorest countries.[91] On development assistance, it argued that

> It is important to stress the continuing role of aid since the debate on the "new international economic order" has often focused primarily on "non-aid" aspects of cooperation. . . . The structural changes now sought in international economic relations aim at expanding the possibilities for self-help by the developing countries. However, . . . many countries, especially the poorest, have little prospect of benefitting from these opportunities for a long time to come.[92]

Moreover, the current account deficits of non-oil developing countries now were vastly greater than ODA flows.

The Dupras report expressed concern that available aid was falling far short of needs, yet most industrial countries were contributing much less than internationally agreed targets, and there was a danger of efforts lagging even further. Recognizing pressures of fiscal restraint and competing demands, the subcommittee was nonetheless "convinced of the extraordinary and superseding importance of the needs of the developing world, and strongly urges against any loss of momentum in the Canadian movement toward the international aid targets."[93] It sought a firm commitment to 0.7 per cent of GNP by 1980 and an endorsement of 1.0 per cent as a longer-term goal. It also supported making aid flows more predictable and automatic through various forms of international taxation.

The subcommittee stressed the complementarity of increasing aid volume and simultaneously improving quality. Contrasting the good Canadian record on concessionality with the weaker one on tying, it urged that the commitment to allow developing country procurement be fulfilled quickly. The priorities of the strategy on the poorest countries—basic needs, rural development, and food self-sufficiency—were endorsed, along with CIDA's intention, as brought forward in testimony, of concentrating on smaller projects and programs with a direct impact at the local level.

On eligibility, "a very high priority must be placed on concentrating Canadian development cooperation in countries where there is a demonstrated commitment by their governments to development and to the efficient and equitable distribution of the benefits of development among their people."[94] In this respect, the report suggested that the relationship of aid to human rights violations be studied further by the parent committee. This matter was new to the aid policy debate in Canada, having only just recently been given prominence by US President Jimmy Carter. New as well was a call for comprehensive evaluation of project and program effectiveness and management; this too reflected international debates, as well as doubts spawned by growing media allegations about Canada's aid failures in the field.

The Dupras report, like Lachance before it, was put on a shelf to collect dust.

Program Evolution

As the policy process unfolded within the Strategy Unit and senior levels of CIDA, the fundamental reality for the Agency was phenomenal growth and extraordinary pressure to disburse.[95] Though there were $50 million and $30 million cuts from planned levels in 1973-74 and 1975-76 respectively, annual appropriations increased on average by 15 per cent during Gérin-Lajoie's first five years: from $383.4 million in 1970-71 to $783.7 million in 1975-76. But that was only one factor feeding the pressure. Shortly after he assumed office, PGL made a commitment to speed up the allocation and disbursement process so as to clear the $400 million backlog in approved but undisbursed funds.[96] Beginning in 1973-74, disbursements began to draw significantly upon the accumulated pipeline. As a result, total ODA rose even more rapidly, from $345.4 million in 1970-71 to $903.5 million in 1975-76.

During 1975-76, ODA as a percentage of GNP reached 0.53 (0.55 in the 1975 calendar year), the highest level up to that time or since. Canada's performance among DAC donors actually dropped in relative (GNP) terms from fifth in 1970 to eighth in 1975, but remained the sixth-largest in volume terms, almost overtaking the British program and accounting for 6.36 per cent of DAC flows (up from 4.85 per cent in 1970). The ODA/GNP ratio declined to 0.49 in 1976-77, Gérin-Lajoie's last full year. Total disbursements in the fiscal year 1976-77 were $963.3 million, a current dollar increase over the previous year but negated in real terms by rapid inflation.

Geographical Distribution[97]

The bilateral program grew less rapidly than overall ODA, but doubled in size to more than $500 million during the Gérin-Lajoie presidency. In accord with evolving policy and sensitivity about differentiation within the developing world, allocations to LLDCs rose from 12 per cent of bilateral aid in 1972 to 18.9 per cent in 1975—and, with the classification of Bangladesh as an LLDC, to 28.1 per cent in 1976.[98] CIDA informed DAC in 1976 that five-year indicative planning figures for 1977-82 called for a distribution of 79.3 per cent to countries with a GNP per capita of less than $200 US in 1973, 11.0 per cent to countries in the $200-$375 range, and 9.7 per cent to those above

$375. This last group was actually allocated 10.6 per cent in 1975—down, CIDA reported, from 17 per cent in 1971.[99] Meanwhile, the prospective debt burden of recipients decreased as loans fell from 49.6 per cent to 19.3 per cent of total government-to-government assistance during Gérin-Lajoie's tenure.

If one steps back from aggregate numbers to look at distributional shifts among recipients, it is harder to detect coherent patterns during the 1970s in terms of levels of development. Most oil and gas producers—Nigeria, Algeria, Trinidad and Tobago, and Ecuador—experienced a noticeable decline, but Indonesia emerged as a major recipient. Some least-developed countries—Malawi, Tanzania, and the Sahelian countries—were allocated more than previously, while programming began in Haiti[100] and Nepal. However, major flows to middle-income countries continued in such cases as Tunisia and Jamaica (the latter being in straitened financial circumstances) or increased substantially in others such as Colombia.

On concentration, the compromise in the wake of the strategy debate was to divide the list of sixty-odd principal recipients into program countries, for which there was to be sustained planning, and project countries, for which disbursements would be made on a case-by-case basis. In 1975-76 there were thirty-four programs and thirty-one project countries.[101] A year later, the number of program countries was pared to twenty-six, but largely by treating groups of recipients in some regions as programming units (the Sahel, the Leeward and Windward Islands, and Botswana-Lesotho-Swaziland).[102] The list of programs stabilized around thirty at the end of the Gérin-Lajoie period. It is set out in Appendix D.

The new classification promoted a sharper distinction between program and project countries; in due course, approximately 80 per cent of bilateral ODA went to the former, 15 per cent to the latter, and 5 per cent to others. For the top ten recipients, however, the bilateral program became *less* intensive during the 1970s. This group received 70.9 per cent in 1970-71 compared to 66 per cent in 1975-76. By 1980-81—still within a five-year planning cycle begun while Gérin-Lajoie was president—the figure was down to 52.9 per cent. The share of the top twenty fell as well, though not as much.[103]

Regional and country changes. Although practice did not live up to rhetoric, there was a further, specific reason for diminishing concentration—a dramatic drop in Canadian ODA to India. Probably, India's pre-eminence within the bilateral program would have continued in gradual decline, especially since a 1973 External Affairs review of Canadian policy towards the sub-continent had questioned whether aid was helping Indian development.[104] Moreover, India itself had been reducing its dependence on external assistance.

The crucial factor that accelerated the decline, however, was New Delhi's announcement in May 1974 that it had successfully tested a nuclear device in the Thar desert. Indian authorities had given a commitment that only peaceful purposes were contemplated when they accepted CANDU technology from the Atomic Energy Co. of Canada (AECL). Prime Minister Trudeau, in the midst of an election campaign, deplored the action and announced immediate suspension of nuclear aid. The experience of imposing conditions on aid was new and traumatic for Canadian aid officials. Ongoing non-nuclear projects were allowed to continue, but severe constraints were placed on new initiatives. There was a sharp retreat from infrastructural projects and lines of credit (because they were fungible), and a much smaller allocation was channelled into agricultural and people-oriented activities. The effect on regional shares, especially a shift from an Asian domination to rough parity between Africa and Asia, is clear in Appendix B.

Conflict within the Indian sub-continent had already altered the configuration of the bilateral program earlier in the Gérin-Lajoie era. The civil war in Pakistan raised for Canada the dilemma (as Biafran crisis had earlier) of whether to give humanitarian relief to a secessionist state. While Ottawa was careful not to violate the code of non-intervention, it provided considerable support to the East Pakistan area through the Red Cross and the World Food Program, as well as to refugees who fled to India.[105] Once India's invasion ensured independence for Bangladesh, Gérin-Lajoie was quick to make a site visit, aid workers returned to projects, and new forms of assistance were provided. Bangladesh became the largest recipient of Canadian ODA by 1977-78. Normal relations were restored with Pakistan, which continued to receive substantial Canadian support.

Considerable expansion occurred in francophone Africa and Latin America. PGL took a strong personal interest in each, and early in his tenure pledged to build them up alongside the "mature and well-rounded" programs in Asia, Commonwealth Africa, and the Commonwealth Caribbean.[106] As a result of the Chevrier mission, disbursement levels in francophone Africa now matched those in anglophone Africa, and, in accordance with policy, they were kept in tandem as expenditures quadrupled to over $100 million in each between 1970-71 and 1975-76.[107] Approximately half of CIDA's core programs were in Africa by 1977.

Latin America did not match the foreign policy saliency of francophone Africa, but, as mentioned in Chapter 3, both regions were seen as opportunities for enhancing French Canadian involvement in development assistance efforts. Gérin-Lajoie devoted considerable time and energy to travel and diplomacy in the region, and drew upon a network of ex-missionaries and others with Catholic Church experience in the Americas to spearhead programming. Important as well were commercial objectives and direct pressure from the Department of Industry, Trade and Commerce. In 1976-77, disbursements reached $26.5 million, slightly more than in the Caribbean.

Other political factors also shaped the bilateral program during the early to mid-1970s. Canadian advisers were withdrawn from Idi Amin's Uganda in 1972 on grounds that their security was threatened.[108] Pressure from NGOs and support groups for non-military assistance to southern African liberation movements, while strongly opposed by some Conservative MPs, eventually culminated in a decision to provide funding through the NGO program.[109] In addition, aid to African "front-line" states was stepped up—one of the reasons why Tanzania emerged as Canada's largest aid program in anglophone Africa in the late 1970s and early 1980s. (Other factors were its status as an LLDC, Trudeau's friendship with President Julius Nyerere, the international aid establishment's embrace for a time of Tanzania's experiment in socialism and self-reliance, and the prominence within CIDA of Karl Johansen, an emigrant from Tanzania to Canada.[110])

A technical assistance program was started in Cuba in 1973, expanded the following year to provide capital support, and then cancelled in 1978 after parliamentary and media criticism of Fidel Castro's decision to send Cuban troops to support regimes in Angola and Ethiopia.[111]

Progressive Talk, Traditional Programming

There was a wide gap between progressive declaratory statements and what was happening in the field during the Gérin-Lajoie era. The president placed great emphasis on social development, yet the Agency's 1974 DAC Aid Memorandum was revealing:

> Because CIDA planning and programming is done along institutional (multilateral) or country lines, the social aspects of development frequently do not receive direct consideration. At the present time, there is no explicit requirement that project analysis take into consideration questions of income distribution, employment, the role of women, etc. However, there is increased awareness of these issues.[112]

Several factors worked against labour-intensive, basic needs-oriented programming: bureaucratic inertia, a long lead-time between conception and implementation of projects, CIDA's administrative capacities, Canadian resource limitations, and, not least, pressure to disburse.

Although CIDA's data on sectoral distribution have been notoriously unreliable, Table 4.1 suggests the extent to which bilateral aid remained skewed towards large capital projects in power generation, transport, and communications. It also shows that Canada devoted higher shares to these spheres than the DAC donor community as a whole, and lagged well behind average DAC performance in all social spheres, especially health and population.

Technical assistance. Pressure to disburse worked against not only social development, but also ongoing programming in technical assistance. This was especially true after 1972, when staff increases in CIDA were small in comparison with a rising budget, and specific bureaucratic mechanisms for administering technical assistance were disbanded. As Phillip Rawkins explained: "The aid bureaucracy preferred to move away from this 'messy' area to concentrate its efforts on the quicker-disbursing, high-dollar infrastructure and technology transfer projects."[113]

Table 4.1
Percentage Distribution of Bilateral Aid Attributable by Sector, Canada, 1973-76, and All DAC Donors, 1975-76

Year	Planning[a]	Public utilities	Agri-culture	Industry and trade	Educa-tion	Health	Social infra-structure
Canada							
1973	0.7	66.5	6.8	4.6	19.4	2.3	0.6
	(2.4)	(223.0)	(23.1)	(15.4)	(66.2)	(7.9)	(2.2)
1974	—	52.8	7.8	6.5	26.0	2.6	4.3
	—	(164.8)	(24.5)	(20.4)	(81.1)	(8.1)	(13.5)
1975	2.6	61.9	6.0	11.4	10.9	4.1	3.0
	(7.3)	(174.3)	(17.0)	(32.2)	(30.8)	(11.5)	(8.5)
1976	9.3	41.3	29.1	8.3	6.5	2.5	3.0
	(32.0)	(142.3)	(100.5)	(28.6)	(22.4)	(8.6)	(10.4)
All DAC							
1975	2.0	25.1	17.4	15.8	22.5	9.3	7.9
1976	1.8	28.1	17.6	15.7	20.6	10.3	4.8

a And public administration.

Source: Adapted from OECD-DAC, *Development Co-operation: Efforts and Policies of the Members of the Development Assistance Committee 1974*, pp. 250-51; ibid., *1975*, pp. 224-25; ibid., *1976*, pp. 236-37; and ibid., *1977*, pp. 192-93. The figures in parentheses are in $US million. Data for all DAC donors are not available for 1974 and 1975. No data were produced for years before 1973. DAC defines bilateral aid as everything that is not multilateral, i.e., what CIDA now calls country-to-country aid.

Although more technical assistance was being channelled through integrated projects, the number of Canadian educators and advisers serving abroad (including volunteers posted by CUSO and its francophone equivalent, SUCO) declined from 3,080 in 1970 to 2,289 in 1976. The number of students and trainees funded by Canadian ODA (in Canada and third countries) went down from 2,757 to 1,686.[114] Overall, the share of technical assistance in bilateral expenditures fell from 13.4 per cent in 1970-71 to 10.3 per cent in 1975-76, rising again to 13.2 per cent in 1976-77 (a cutback year).[115] Figures in Table 4.1 show that expenditures on education and training also fell well below DAC norms.

Agriculture and rural development. Another change apparent in Table 4.1 was a huge jump in reported disbursements for agriculture between 1975 and 1976. Much of this was undoubtedly achieved through creative relabelling. After the global food crisis in 1973, however, CIDA did take the challenge of agricultural development more seriously. Some innovative approaches to regional and village-based programming were initiated in the Sahel following a major famine relief effort, and ambitious (and subsequently controversial) experiments in integrated rural development were undertaken in Haiti, Colombia, and Lesotho.

An Agency task force in 1974 recognized that lack of Canadian expertise was a major obstacle to significant refocusing on agriculture, fisheries, forestry, and other renewable resources.[116] It recommended steps to strengthen Canadian capabilities, and CIDA subsequently reported plans to channel 30-33 per cent of bilateral disbursements to renewable resources projects between 1977-78 and 1981-82.[117] Detailed sectoral guidelines were produced in 1976 for rural development and renewable resources, as well as for social development and community services, and infrastructure and environment.[118]

Food aid.[119] For the first time, food aid topped $100 million in 1970-71, with $100.3 million of the $104.2 million total used to provide 1,254,000 metric tons of Canadian wheat and flour through bilateral and multilateral channels—the highest volume ever. That same year, Canada followed the lead of the US and introduced a supply management scheme to limit wheat production. Falling supply, record demand, and rising general inflation contributed to a dramatic increase in world prices, so that a nominal rise in wheat aid to $113.5 million in 1973-74 purchased only 637,000 tons.

After failed harvests in many parts of Asia and Africa in 1972 and 1973, a crisis atmosphere prevailed when a World Food Conference was convened in Rome in November 1974. The conference was preceded by vigorous lobbying efforts by the Canadian Council for International Cooperation (CCIC), Oxfam, and church groups to secure a stronger Canadian commitment to food aid and the broader reforms of the NIEO. To the annoyance of some in Ottawa's official delegation, the NGOs sent representatives to Rome to keep up the pressure and maintain direct communication links with opposition MPs and the media back home.

The results of the conference fell well short of the expectations of the UN organizers and developing country participants, and Canadian NGOs were disappointed with the performance of MacEachen and his delegation. However, Canada was one of the few industrial countries (Australia and Sweden were the others) to make firm commitments: a minimum supply of one million tons of cereal grains for human consumption in each of 1975-76, 1976-77, and 1977-78 (one-tenth of total pledges sought by conference organizers); an increase in non-grain foodstuffs to a value of about $45 million annually in each of the next three years; and an immediate reallocation of $50 million to increase food and fertilizer shipments to countries most in need. Food aid accounted for about 25 per cent of total ODA in 1975-76 and 1976-77, more than double the two previous years.

Although questions about the long-run developmental value of food aid remained, the Canadian program after 1974 was no longer based simply on surplus disposal. It remained a factor, however, especially after an effective lobbying campaign by the Dairy Farmers of Canada led to a quadrupling of skim milk aid.

Multilateral Aid: The Fastest-Growing Component of Canadian ODA

Multilateral aid increased more than sixfold from 1970-71 to 1976-77, from $67.5 million to $422.1 million. The absolute growth was larger than that of the bilateral program, and the multilateral share of Canadian ODA rose from 19.5 per cent in 1970-71 to 36.7 per cent in 1975-76, and a high point of 43.7 per cent in 1976-77.[120] Performance in these last two years was well above the strategy target of approximately 30 per cent, reflecting largely the difficulties of finding bilateral outlets as quickly as appropriations accumulated. As Protheroe commented, "the high multilateral share should not be seen as fully a conscious pro-multilateralism, [but] the rising trend of Canadian multilateral targets in the 1970s did show a sincere and growing commitment to the developmental advantages of multilateral aid."[121]

Noteworthy initiatives in the multilateral sphere during the Gérin-Lajoie period were the assumption of full membership in the Inter-American Development Bank in 1972, as part of Canada's new thrust into Latin America,[122] and a formative role in setting up the African Development Fund, a new soft loan facility in the African Development Bank.[123]

Canada promised at the World Food Conference in Rome to channel at least 20 per cent of food aid multilaterally, largely through the World Food Program (WFP). While this merely confirmed current practice (like so many official commitments), about half of the increase in food aid in 1975 and 1976 was provided through the WFP.

During these two years, Canada was the largest donor to the WFP, surpassing the US. Canadian support at Rome was also important in establishing the International Fund for Agricultural Development (IFAD), a new agency conceived largely as a way of recycling OPEC's financial surpluses into innovative and grass-roots rural development efforts.[124]

New NGO Initiatives

Still marginal in the Agency's overall activity, the NGO program was given steady encouragement by Gérin-Lajoie and continuing vitality and inventiveness by Lewis Perinbam, who became vice-president (Special Programs) in 1974. Despite qualms in Treasury Board about financial control, disbursements rose from $9.1 million in 1970-71 to $42.2 million in 1976-77[125] as the program's incentive structure encouraged creation and growth of new NGOs. CIDA also began to realize the valuable role NGOs could play in community-based programming aimed at meeting basic human needs. With the recruitment of Romeo Maione, an experienced labour activist, to head the NGO Division, the program's links with organized labour, Canadian-based community organizations, and francophone institutions were strengthened.

Two important programming initiatives were taken during this period. One was the International NGO (INGO) Program, founded in 1974 to provide funding for the development work of international voluntary organizations such as the International Planned Parenthood Federation and the International Council for Adult Education. In securing modest assistance for INGOs, Perinbam had to contend with more scepticism from Treasury Board, and with opposition from some domestic NGOs who registered their displeasure about being bypassed in this way.[126]

The other innovation was an experiment in support of NGO development education activities, approved with great reluctance by Treasury Board in July 1971.[127] The Development Education Program provided a matching grant to CCIC for a four-year "Development Education Animateur Program" (DEAP), which placed seven development educators into five regions of the country. DEAP, along with CUSO's Mobile Resources Centre, which was also funded, gave birth to dozens of volunteer-based learner centres across the country. (They were modelled in part on the London Learner Centre, which was set up on a voluntary basis in 1968.) The objective was to spread knowledge about the developing world beyond official circles and the Ottawa-Toronto-Montreal triangle. Soon CIDA was providing grants for learner centres and other community-based development education activities and such national coalitions as the church-sponsored "Ten Days for World Development."

As Jean Christie pointed out in an historical essay on development education in Canada, there were tensions between CIDA and development activists from the outset of their relationship:

> CIDA's conception of the work . . . was that it would give the public an understanding of Canada's aid program internationally, encourage participation in international organizations, and generate support for CIDA's work. This was not exactly what the NGOs had in mind. . . . [Most] were specifically interested in pointing out ways in which the Canadian government and corporations supported the very structures which perpetuate underdevelopment and poverty.[128]

CIDA funds supported groups that voiced strong criticisms of the official aid program, and often even more damning opposition to other government policies (or lack thereof) towards the Third World. As Blair Dimock noted, "CIDA's public education efforts certainly stimulated the much desired awareness and interest they were designed for, but not necessarily the tone or content expected."[129]

Relations with Canadian Council for International Cooperation (CCIC) were particulary tense during and after the World Food Conference in Rome in 1974. Politicians and civil servants in the official delegation were infuriated by NGO activities that were largely financed by CIDA and supported by information leaked by sympathetic Agency personnel. "The experience of having . . . preferred constituents create serious problems" led some officers to conclude that they had "created a monster" that "was threatening to worsen the Agency's own political security within the government."[130] While CIDA cut funding for the CCIC in 1975, it did institutionalize the Development Education Program, which acquired its familiar acronym, PPP, as the Public Participation Program. The Agency also became embroiled in political struggles within the NGO movement, most notably a feud between CUSO and SUCO, its French-speaking equivalent.[131]

Business and Industry

Many within the Agency regarded the Business and Industry Program with suspicion, and there was little business interest in the original pre-investment incentives program. Some CIDA executives, however, shared Strong's vision of more active corporate involvement beyond the traditional spheres of engineering and equipment exports. Gérin-Lajoie himself showed little interest until Canada hosted a meeting of the United Nations Industrial Development Organization (UNIDO) in 1972. Wanting to demonstrate CIDA's commitment, he supported a reorganization of the program that put greater emphasis on publicizing opportunities for Canadian investment in developing countries. The budget for investment feasibility and starter studies was increased.[132]

Following Canada's endorsement of the Declaration on Industrial Development Cooperation issued in 1974 by UNIDO in Lima, CIDA sponsored several initiatives emphasizing "reciprocal interests and mutual benefits rather than purely development assistance." The most significant was an

Experimental Program in Industrial Cooperation (EPIC), launched in 1976; teams were dispatched to nine middle-income countries in search of industrial projects that matched skills, technology, and management capabilities in the Canadian private sector.[133]

Provincial Government Involvement

Cooperation with the provinces was given a more concrete basis with establishment of the Voluntary Food Aid and Agricultural Development Program in 1976.[134] An initiative of Premier Allan Blakeney of Saskatchewan after the Rome conference, it provided federal funding for the costs of transporting to recipient countries foodstuffs, commodities, and services supplied by the provinces. Also during this period, the four western provinces established international development programs similar to one already run by Quebec. These provided modest additional sources of public funding for NGOs, especially for development education.

Organizational Change and Turmoil[135]

CIDA is acknowledged as one of the most successful experiments in bilingualism among federal departments. Achieved amid considerable anxiety and conflict, this ranks as perhaps the most durable legacy of the Gérin-Lajoie years. An English-speaking colleague described his experience in the President's Committee:

> What Gérin-Lajoie did was brand new in the federal government at that time. He was determined that there had to be more use of French, and he used as much French as he did English in the President's Committee. This was very hard on two or three of us. . . . But he had the most sensible way of handling that. He'd speak in French and he'd know . . . that I hadn't gotten most of it. Then in English he'd say: "In other words, maybe we can put it this way," and he'd go through the whole bloody thing again. . . . It was a very sensitive way to handle the issue, but he made his point. There was going to be a French stamp to the Agency. Even at that time, CIDA had the largest proportion of francophone officers of any department in Ottawa. So he had a good base.

Still more French-speaking personnel were recruited, and the new bilateral division for Latin America joined francophone Africa as an administrative unit with French as its chief working language. One long-serving officer recalled that the director of personnel, a strong believer in management by conflict, announced the decision without any prior warning. It created quite a stir among some English-speaking employees, some of whom allegedly retaliated by leaking confidential External Affairs documents written in the aftermath of Pinochet's 1973 coup in Chile.[136] A few anglophone officers complained directly to Mitchell Sharp, but the minister, in supporting Gérin-Lajoie, conveyed a clear signal that French would become a full working language throughout the Agency, not simply in a francophone Africa ghetto.

PGL strengthened CIDA's commercial base in French-speaking Canada through active use of the contract approval process to build up Quebec-based suppliers and engineering and consultancy firms, especially SNC and Lavalin. He also established a business liaison office in Montreal (the only one until much later). During his tenure, Ontario's share of CIDA contracts dropped from 40 per cent in 1971 to 26 per cent in 1976, while Quebec's grew from 38 to 55 per cent.[137]

Personnel Problems[138]

In the short run, Gérin-Lajoie's determination to raise the status of French was a minor factor that contributed to personnel difficulties. More serious was the nature of the work. Many young and idealistic recruits, especially returned volunteers, were disillusioned by the political, commercial, and bureaucratic milieu of the aid program, especially its bilateral core. The president's relative lack of interest in management and a high level of organizational infighting upset others. These problems were in turn deepened by the fluidity and organizational chaos inherent in a context of rapid expansion.

Considerable on-the-job learning was necessary to accommodate a dramatic staff increase in the early seventies. The establishment grew by 40 per cent between 1970-71 and 1972-73, reaching 843 by December 1972.[139] Thereafter, personnel growth levelled off, rising only marginally to a total of 937 in December 1974 and 969 in December 1977.[140] Aid spending continued to rise rapidly, however, and workload pressures increased, even as steps were taken to make disbursements less labour-intensive. Meanwhile, career advancement depended on a job transfer rather than a positive evaluation in an existing position.

As a result of these factors and the public relations problems discussed below, CIDA was still able to attract good people, but it was becoming more difficult to keep them. More complaints were being registered about poor morale. Staff turnover and departures were becoming endemic, especially at the senior level.

Continuing Reorganization[141]

The president's leadership style, interbranch territorial ambitions, and rapid employee and program growth led to further rounds of organizational change. Running through CIDA's almost chronic restructurings was a preoccupation with the issue of how best to harness the skills and energies of people in a number of overlapping categories: planners and operations personnel, generalists and specialists, and geographical and sectoral experts.

Gérin-Lajoie's first reorganization in May 1971 created the position of executive vice-president to take charge of day-to-day management, leaving the president free to concentrate on "broad policy questions, new policy initiatives, and external relations."[142] The division of line responsibilities between two powerful branches, Planning and Operations, ended when the Planning and Multilateral Institutions divisions of the old Planning Branch were placed directly under the executive vice-president. The arrangement was short-lived. Jacques Gérin was appointed vice-president Operations when Donald Tansley assumed the executive vice-presidency. Gérin, who joined CIDA after a distinguished career in professional engineering (and then went on to hold senior positions in several federal departments), secured support for a further reorganization in October 1971. Planning Division was disbanded and its personnel were absorbed within a restructured Bilateral Branch. One of those affected recollected: "Some of us more bitter planners said, 'Well, the Agency has just shot its brains out.' " Whatever the merits of the scheme, it brought planning and implementation under one vice-president, although it still left an awkward division between a geographical approach to some aspects of programming and a sectoral approach to others, notably technical assistance.

Other changes in 1971 included creation of a Policy Branch under a new vice-president (Hodder), elevation of the Information Division to a Communications Branch under a director general, and grouping of NGO and Business and Industry divisions in a Special Programs Branch.

Vice-president Gérin was a key player in yet another reorganization in 1972. Multilateral Programs Division was given branch status with its own vice-president. In Bilateral Branch, the mixture of functional and geographical approaches to administering bilateral aid gave way to a more fully geographical one. However, two more years of further experimentation elapsed before it was finally decided to integrate technical assistance activities within the geographical framework (for those affected, yet another source of personnel anguish and disgruntlement).

By 1974, the reconstituted Bilateral Branch was planning and delivering its programs entirely through five area-based divisions: Asia, Caribbean, Commonwealth Africa, Francophone Africa, and Latin America. Two sectoral divisions, Engineering and Human Resources, provided specialized advice but no longer had direct responsibilities for project administration. However, not all technical resources were placed within Bilateral; special advisers remained outside, and various other aspects of operations support—such as relations with consultants and contract administration—were assigned to an Administration Branch.

Several more changes took place over the next few years—the disappearance and reappearance of the executive vice-presidency, creation of a separate branch for special advisers, and a shuffle through varying combinations of finance, administration, and personnel functions.

Operational Changes

Continual reorganization was accompanied by efforts to strengthen operating procedures. The details need not detain us, but two developments were of lasting importance. One related to country planning and budgeting. Beginning in 1974-75, Treasury Board imposed annual disbursement ceilings on ODA. Based on the level of parliamentary appropriations (set below planned spending levels) and some portion of the accumulated pipeline, the expenditure caps were intended to intensify pressure on CIDA to eliminate the backlog of unspent funds. As a result, the Agency shifted from appropriations to disbursements as the basis of forward budgetary planning, and introduced Indicative Planning Figures (IPFs)—five-year rolling projections of expenditures in major country programs.

The second change involved a more systematic approach to program planning and project management. As CIDA's annual review to DAC in 1974 explained: "The procedure in the past to obtain approval of bilateral projects was to submit a memorandum to the Project Review Committee, composed of CIDA Vice Presidents and senior resource personnel, at a fairly advanced stage in the planning process, at which point it was often difficult to reject or modify the proposals." The new system required prior submission and approval of a Project Identification Memorandum (PIM). Once a project was fully developed, a Project Approval Memorandum (PAM) was submitted to the Project Review Committee for consideration before making a recommendation to the president and/or the minister. Logical framework analysis derived from US AID was introduced to guide the preparation of PAMs.[143]

Interdepartmental Conflict

Conflict over the substance of the aid program was inherent in the differing mandates of CIDA and other departments. An intensification of territorial bickering was probably inevitable as the Agency became more visible in terms of personnel and spending power. In addition, under Trudeau, External Affairs suffered a decline in its earlier preeminence and was among federal departments that experienced budget cuts, while CIDA emerged relatively unscathed.

Leadership was a factor as well. Maurice Strong's aggressive promotion of the Agency generated a network of CIDA-watchers in External Affairs, Finance, the Treasury Board, and Industry, Trade and Commerce. While Strong managed interdepartmental conflict by playing an active role in deputy ministerial fora, with occasional recourse to political end runs, PGL charted his own course, leaving responsibility for interdepartmental relations largely to his subordinates. When he travelled, he frequently made commitments without consulting External Affairs. In addition, as Sanger noted, Gérin-Lajoie

> explored the idea . . . of setting up special aid missions, separate from normal diplomatic embassies and with authority to commit considerable funds. These ideas were thought impertinent by Trade and by External Affairs, and were squashed, although something of a compromise was made in the Eastern Caribbean where the Canadian High Commissioner based in Barbados has always been a CIDA officer on secondment.[144]

Cooperation at the assistant deputy ministerial/vice-presidential level was cordial at first,[145] but the Gérin-Lajoie era was marked by increasingly strained relations between CIDA and other elements of the Ottawa bureaucracy. As we saw in the strategy experience, the Agency was perceived by others as out of tune with Canadian interests—while, within CIDA, other agencies were likewise seen as wrong-headed. Although compromises and trade-offs were reached, the structures and the personalities of the time did not lend themselves to genuine consensus on most issues. As CIDA's view of the global situation and the most appropriate role for Canada within it got more out of step with perspectives elsewhere, and as aid expenditures and staffing levels grew, CIDA-watchers intensified actions to limit the Agency's freedom to manoeuvre.

The Agency's relationship with External Affairs emerged briefly into the public view in the fall of 1976 after a cabinet shuffle that moved Allan MacEachen from External Affairs to Deputy Prime Minister and House Leader, and Donald Jamieson to External Affairs from Industry, Trade and Commerce. MacEachen apparently agreed to the transfer only if CIDA continued to report to him and he remained as co-chair of the Conference on International Economic Cooperation (CIEC), which was then the world's main forum for North-South negotiations. Trudeau was initially receptive, but Basil Robinson, under-secretary of state for External Affairs, and Michael Pitfield, clerk of the Privy Council, strongly opposed splitting CIDA from External. Territorial prerogative was a factor, but so too was concern that the aid program and its sizeable budget would be divorced even further from foreign policy, especially given Gérin-Lajoie's penchant for independence.

The conflict simmered for five months, during which MacEachen kept his CIEC responsibility and CIDA reported through Jamieson. In February

1977, the prime minister resolved the dispute by saying that the Agency would stay in the External Affairs portfolio, although he did not rule out assigning it elsewhere in the future.[146] The issue was not buried. Several other OECD countries had separate ministers for international development, an arrangement earlier sought by the Lachance subcommittee and now supported by Douglas Roche, opposition critic on aid matters.[147] As we shall see in Chapter 5, the Conservatives became wedded to the idea and appointed a minister of state for CIDA after winning the 1979 election.

An Emerging Crisis in Program and Financial Accountability

The introduction of country programming, project cycles, and logical framework analysis indicated a growing professionalization and sophistication in the management of the Canadian aid program—but, as growth accelerated, serious weaknesses appeared. One fundamental inadequacy was the lack of effective evaluation. The Agency admitted to DAC: "While it would be desirable to be able to report that CIDA rigorously assesses the success or failure of its projects according to a primary criterion—whether the project assisted the host country to achieve a greater degree of self-reliance and increased capacity to advance its own human and socio-economic development—this is not always the case."[148] In fact, this was almost never the case. The process of allocating funds for programming was idiosyncratic: one senior manager recalled, perhaps with a touch of hyperbole, that financing for a project depended on the mood of a rather crusty official in Administration Branch who held the purse-strings.

A senior administrator of the time told Phillip Rawkins:

> We had a great deal of money and very little knowledge of where the money went. There was very little formal planning or country programming and we had none of the equipment (i.e., computer based management and information systems) that we have now. . . . In the bilateral [divisions], we didn't know what our commitments were and we didn't have a firm grasp on our financial planning.

As Rawkins observed, the basic concerns of CIDA's centralized desk officers were to maximize disbursement and ensure that tying regulations on Canadian sourcing were met. The Agency "had paid relatively little attention to putting in place quality controls or financial systems, to developing clear guidelines, or to training project officers in program and project management."[149]

The Auditor General began expressing grave concerns about the lack of effective integration between programming and financial planning and controls, and undertook a full special audit in 1975-76. Some of the ensuing criticisms reflected the unfamiliarity of the Auditor General's staff with the risks and uncertainties of development assistance—for example, the failure of students and trainees to return to their home countries, the tendency for project costs to increase because recipient governments did not (or could not) contribute their agreed-upon shares, and, perhaps less excusably, the spoilage of food aid.

Other charges, however, raised serious questions about the Agency's financial controls and accountability: incorrect reporting of "significant disbursements" under the wrong program designations, contributions made under vague memoranda of agreement with recipients, delegation of more than $2 million in sub-contracting authority to architects and engineers working abroad with no effective monitoring by CIDA, "overcommitments of varying magnitude up to 300%" above disbursement ceilings, contracts signed before certification of available funds, retroactive authorization of purchases, etc.

In all, the Auditor General made ninety-two recommendations, eighty-seven of them aimed at tightening up all facets of the Agency's work.[150] Meanwhile, Treasury Board, which had watched developments in CIDA with increasing alarm, was gearing up for an operation to impose fundamental financial and administrative constraints on the Agency during the presidency of Michel Dupuy—who was also to inherit another internal management review begun during Gérin-Lajoie's last few months in office.

CIDA's Troubled Public Image

Because it put public support for foreign aid at risk, harsh criticism of CIDA in the media and Parliament in the mid-1970s was the most damaging of all the growing pains during the Gérin-Lajoie presidency. Until 1973, the press and the three major political parties paid little attention to the aid program, expressing occasional support for the effort in general and CIDA in particular.[151] What criticism there was tended to come from NGOs and academics who wanted a more radical, developmentally oriented aid program, and a coherent Canadian international development strategy linking aid with preferential trade and reforms in the international order.[152]

Before the tide really began to turn, Gordon Pape reported in the *Gazette* (Montreal) on a seven-week tour of CIDA projects in Africa early in 1973. He concluded that Canadian foreign aid "is being usefully and beneficially spent," though some projects "have not been fully thought out." Giving examples, including a semi-automated bakery in Dar es Salaam that would become one of the most notorious CIDA horror stories,[153] he quoted doubts and criticisms voiced by Canadian aid workers, and suggested that pressure to disburse "the embarrassing backlog of unspent aid funds" was a major problem.[154] Gérin-Lajoie replied directly, defending the projects Pape cited on grounds that they had been requested by recipient governments: "developing countries must chart their own course of development." Nevertheless, "mistakes are the inevitable price to be paid when innovation and some risk-taking must be brought to play in a race to prevent malnutrition, poverty and underemployment from creating widespread social and economic chaos."[155]

Late in the summer of 1973, some Conservative members of Parliament began asking specific questions about aid allocations that imputed doubtful wisdom or worse.[156] Shortly thereafter, three MPs who toured North Africa with Gérin-Lajoie expressed concerns about the effectiveness of aid administration. Pierre De Bané, a Liberal parliamentary secretary (who was born in Palestine), was quoted as saying that some Canadians in Tunisia had "admitted to me they were racist. That is, they did not appreciate the Arabs with whom they were working." Denying the allegations, CIDA promised to increase its sensitivity to local conditions through greater decentralization to the field.[157]

Troubles within Latin America Division (relating to the decision to make French its working language) were reported in January 1974.[158] Soon, lines of communication opened up between disgruntled CIDA employees and ex-employees, parliamentarians, and the media. Opposition MPs were told of a study of rapid staff turnover in CIDA undertaken for the Agency by Price Waterhouse. When Gérin-Lajoie declined to make it available to the Standing Committee on External Affairs and National Defence, the committee passed a motion in May 1974 demanding its release. Tensions rose, but the minority government of Pierre Trudeau was defeated in the House of Commons before the committee's powers were put to the test.[159]

The tempo of negative comment accelerated and the tone became more sensational after Trudeau's reelection with a majority. The following is a typical example from the press:

> Ask about the CIDA program and you'll get a story that's full of the "focus on man," "the quest for economic and social justice," "humanitarian support for liberation movements" (which presumably frees local money for guns and ammunition!), and plenty of executive travel to identify problems that are already well documented. Most alarming of all the propaganda is to hear that . . . CIDA's funds . . . [are] dispersed and managed bilaterally in 67 countries all over the world—countries such as Algeria, Sri Lanka, Belize, Burma and Zaire (which incidentally was able to afford a $100,000 diamond as a token of affection for Mrs. Hubert Humphrey back in 1968!)[160]

Innuendos about PGL's style were coupled with stories of mismanagement in Ottawa and abroad. At the instigation of the prime minister himself, the Agency appointed a full-time parliamentary liaison officer in the autumn of 1974.[161]

Although Communications Branch did some creative public outreach during this period,[162] its time and energy became more and more absorbed in "fire-fighting." Coinciding with public relations difficulties arising from CCIC's attack on the government at the World Food Conference, allegations were made in the press that food aid to Bangladesh had been stolen and resold.[163] CIDA was also accused of trying to disguise the size of its controversial Cuban program.[164]

Ottawa's two daily newspapers tried to outdo each other in a lively campaign of CIDA-bashing during the winter of 1974-75. Patrick Best of the *Ottawa Citizen* wrote several articles that attacked Gérin-Lajoie (among other things, for the expense incurred in redecorating his suite of offices), and reported on turnover, morale problems, and MPs' complaints that the Agency's use of external consultants was excessive.[165] Richard Gwyn in the *Ottawa Journal* quoted departing employees' comments about CIDA—"'Banana republic,''scandal,''administrative chaos,''a sick joke'"—and offered a catalogue of more horror stories. "Outside CIDA hardly anyone knows how its vast budget is spent, on what, or why, whether well or badly. CIDA, complained one MP recently—not an opposition critic but a Liberal backbencher—'is a state within a state.'"[166] The *Journal* also published a series of investigative articles by Christopher Cobb and Robert McKeown, which again divided attention between stories about Gérin-Lajoie and allegedly failed projects.[167] Editorials in both papers called for independent investigations by the Standing Committee on External Affairs and National Defence.[168] While general support was voiced for foreign aid, the overall impression conveyed was one of mounting waste and mismanagement. Around this time, Trudeau reportedly described CIDA as "Canada's sleeping conscience" when he showed up at the Agency for a surprise noon-hour visit to deliver a pep talk to beleaguered staff.

Opposition MPs returned to the onslaught in January 1975 using press reports as a basis for demanding a special parliamentary investigation. The prime minister and other government spokespersons replied that ample opportunity to probe CIDA's spending would be afforded during the usual Standing Committee review of estimates.[169] The assault continued during a one-day debate in February, which Robert McKeown called "Pillow warfare!" when "sledge hammers were at hand."[170] Confronted by a determined Conservative campaign to set up a special subcommittee on international development, Allan MacEachen finally agreed not to oppose such an initiative if it came from the Standing Committee on External Affairs and National Defence.[171]

The minister appeared before the Standing Committee on April 10 in conjunction with its annual review of CIDA's estimates. He promised new guidelines to govern the aid program (a reference to the forthcoming strategy), and tabled a document presenting the Agency's perspective on several projects that had been publicly criticized.[172] He also spoke at length about the complexities of development:

> History tells us that development in Canada, as in most other industrialized countries, has been a messy process, riddled with inefficiencies and even waste, marred by abuses and controversies. . . . So we should be prudent when we are tempted to question the usefulness of the Route de l'unité in Niger. The CPR, a century ago, also led nowhere. . . . Development is difficult, even in the best of conditions. And conditions are even more dismal in most developing countries today than they were a century ago in the stony stretches and frozen bogs of northern Ontario.

CIDA had learned much through trial and error, MacEachen said, and the new guidelines would reflect these lessons.[173]

A well-crafted speech, it made little impact on opposition critics who were incensed that neither the remarks nor the accompanying document had been circulated in advance.[174] Over the next few weeks, Gérin-Lajoie and his senior officials appeared several times before the committee. Neither CIDA nor opposition MPs gave ground to one another in a series of acrimonious exchanges. Two motions calling for the establishment of a subcommittee to examine the Agency's financial affairs were defeated on division.[175]

Douglas Roche found the whole experience unsettling. In the forefront of Conservative efforts to get agreement on setting up a subcommittee on international development, and highly critical of Gérin-Lajoie, he lamented in an article in *Saturday Night*:

> The CIDA debate is another example of the shallowness of politics. Whatever the season, Ottawa offers a perpetual climate of gamesmanship and image-making. Charge, counter-charge, and confrontation make the headlines. And politicians live by headlines. CIDA should certainly be examined, but not in a climate of hostility. . . . We worry about a CIDA road that goes nowhere, Gérin-Lajoie's style of living, or local officials blocking food delivery. What we ought to be concerned about is a global crisis characterized by rapidly increasing numbers of people, gross income inequalities, unequal consumption of food and mineral resources, insufficient health, education, housing, and transportation services, increasing unemployment, and environmental deterioration.[176]

Roche's caucus colleagues—notably Claude Wagner and Dan McKenzie, whose primary interest lay in stirring up a CIDA scandal to embarrass the government—failed to force a parliamentary investigation of the Agency. However, Roche and a few like-minded MPs kept pressing for a special committee to review the whole range of Canada's relations with the Third World. They finally succeeded in securing the appointment of the Subcommittee on

International Development whose progressive and non-partisan report in 1976 was discussed earlier in the chapter. In an effort to stimulate greater public awareness and involvement in North-South issues, Roche, Andrew Brewin of the NDP, and Liberal Irénée Pelletier undertook a ten-day, eight-city tour across Canada in January 1976.[177]

Meanwhile, the storm of bad publicity subsided after May 1975. Gérin-Lajoie told the Ottawa chapter of the Society for International Development that CIDA would have to account to the public more fully and more often.[178] He and MacEachen both tried to put a positive face on the experience,[179] as did CIDA's annual aid memorandum to DAC:

> Within the last six months, the media and some Members of Parliament have expressed new interest in the volume, policies and administrative procedures of the official development assistance program. A number of articles appeared in the national press criticising various aspects of aid administration or specific aid projects, leading to questions in Parliament and more intense study of CIDA spending estimates by the House of Commons Standing Committee. With few exceptions, however, critics preface their remarks by stating their support for Canada's aid effort and urging that more, not less be done.[180]

Despite efforts to rationalize the highly public battering of CIDA, both the president and the Agency continued to suffer from a serious credibility problem, as well as a siege mentality heightened by ongoing interdepartmental conflict. Public opinion polls suggested that support for Canadian aid, though declining, was soft.[181]

A Change of Leadership

Gérin-Lajoie remained in office until early 1977. Given his length of service and the difficulty of recovering from a public relations debacle such as CIDA's without a change of leadership, his imminent departure had been anticipated for well over a year. The *Ottawa Citizen* speculated in August 1976 that he would be replaced by Michel Dupuy, a career diplomat who had been heavily involved in the development of Canada's North-South policies.[182] Shortly thereafter, the *Globe and Mail* reported that Dupuy's appointment "has apparently been delayed by a number of developments including the difficulty of finding another job for the incumbent, Paul Gérin-Lajoie."[183]

By the time Dupuy's appointment was made official six months later (to take effect on March 1, 1977), CIDA had gone through two more rounds of adverse publicity. The first followed publication of the Auditor General's special audit in November 1976. Coming when the press appetite for CIDA horror stories had been whetted, the report offered yet two more—an expenditure of $828,000 to refit a fishing vessel for Colombia that subsequently proved unfit for navigation (it came to be known as "the boat that wouldn't float") and a $63,900 consignment of seed potatoes to Haiti that had to be destroyed upon arrival.[184]

The second came when Morton Shulman alleged in the *Toronto Sun* that CIDA officials in Haiti were spending money foolishly for unauthorized purposes.[185] CIDA challenged the accuracy of the story, and even the *Sun* later admitted that the muckraking columnist had been in error both on Haiti and in a subsequent column on Montserrat.[186] However, Shulman was the catalyst for a revival of earlier stories and the launch of new editorial criticisms.[187]

In an emotional farewell at a reception just before his retirement—to private consultancy rather than a government position—PGL praised the spirit and dedication of CIDA employees and criticized those in the media who "had attacked CIDA without checking the facts." He concluded by saying that he believed in justice, not charity, and added that "justice need not exclude charity, either at home or abroad." Fittingly, Gérin-Lajoie announced that Treasury Board approval was being sought for a new program to stimulate broader awareness of the complexities of international development. Among its components would be grants for new courses in international development journalism at Laval University and the University of Western Ontario.[188] His departure also coincided with publication of the last annual report of his presidency. *Canada and Development Cooperation* provided more details about the aid program, and offered a more radical perspective on North-South relations, than any previous or subsequent report.[189]

Gérin-Lajoie left behind a much larger aid program than the one he had inherited. He reached out to developing countries and insisted that their agendas influence CIDA's thought and action. He bequeathed a legacy of progressive policy development that extended the Agency's sights well beyond past practice, and offered a series of guide-posts by which to assess subsequent performance. He strengthened the bilingual character of the Agency and Canada's aid presence abroad.

Other than this last achievement, however, the advances were threatened by developments both within and without. Program growth was outstripping the capacities of the CIDA's human resources and its financial and administrative systems. Increased visibility and obvious growing pains reinforced determination elsewhere in the bureaucracy to rein in an upstart that was seen as too independent and insensitive to domestic and foreign policy goals. Media horror stories and partisan political debate about CIDA's effectiveness heightened the Agency's institutional vulnerability, and threatened to undermine public support for an expanding aid program. As one participant in the strategy process put it, "CIDA got its policy as its world was crumbling."

Chapter 5

Retrenchment and Reorientation, 1977-80

A former CIDA executive summarized his perspective on the organization's institutional history. Under Maurice Strong, it emerged as "a third player" in Canadian foreign policy alongside established interests in External Affairs and Industry, Trade and Commerce. In that formative period, the Agency developed an independent "mandate" and "capability." Thereafter, "the history of the aid program . . . was to see that third capability diminish. It was driven out, subordinated, homogenized in with the other two. That's the history of the aid program in those twenty years. In a nutshell, it was bureaucratized." As he saw it, CIDA's efforts to resist the process during Gérin-Lajoie's presidency merely accelerated the inevitable outcome. An External Affairs document in 1976 suggested that the secretary of state for External Affairs, "to whom both [the Department and CIDA] report, must sometimes feel that he is driving an ill-matched team of horses."[1] This situation was to change under Gérin-Lajoie's successor, Michel Dupuy, who served for three years from March 1977 to March 1980.

When his appointment was announced, Dupuy told the *Ottawa Journal* that "I was born in the game" of international relations, a reference to his late father, Pierre Dupuy, a distinguished Canadian diplomat.[2] The younger Dupuy was a graduate of Oxford, L'institut des études politiques, and the Sorbonne; he was as well author of a published doctoral thesis, *L'Assistance technique et financière aux pays insuffisamment développés*. Aged forty-seven at the time of his CIDA appointment, he had been in the Department of External Affairs since 1955 and had held several portfolios dealing with developing countries. An assistant under-secretary of state since 1971, he was Allan MacEachen's principal adviser on North-South policy, serving as chairman of the Interdepartmental Committee on External Relations with Developing Countries and deputy co-chairman (under MacEachen) of the Paris

Notes to Chapter 5 are on pp. 498-507.

Conference on International Economic Cooperation.[3] The press release announcing Dupuy's appointment spelled out his mandate:

> The prime minister has asked Mr. Dupuy to focus his attention on means to ensure that Canadian aid reaches those who need it most, whilst remaining compatible with the development priorities of recipient governments. He is also being asked to emphasize sound financial management, and close co-operation with the other departments of the Canadian government that have an interest in the development and implementation of Canadian aid policy. Finally, Mr. Dupuy is being urged to respond positively to the well motivated concerns expressed about Canadian development assistance, and to co-operate actively with the parliamentary sub-committee in its on-going review of CIDA policy and programs.[4]

Although phrased in generalities, the announcement contained clear directives about enhancing managerial effectiveness, overcoming interdepartmental conflict, and improving the public image. Dupuy himself was fond of maritime metaphors; he saw his major tasks as "tightening all the bolts" on the ship and moving it closer to the rest of the fleet.[5]

The new president's tenure was unquestionably a difficult one. When Dupuy assumed office, CIDA was in a state of virtual receivership in the wake of the Auditor General's 1976 report. He was an outsider brought in to "clean house," and for his first few weeks the Agency suffered the humiliation of relinquishing all of its spending authorities to the Treasury Board until new procedures were worked out. Dupuy inherited as well a process of internal reorganization that was bogged down in institutional inertia and sharp conflicts over territory and principle. He had marching orders to integrate CIDA within the foreign policy apparatus, a process implying programming as well as organizational changes that were unwelcome to many insiders, and to NGOs and members of the broader development constituency. Shortly after taking office, he also had to superintend the Agency's move from crowded headquarters in downtown Ottawa to the Place du Centre in Hull; many Agency employees were disgruntled about the relocation to this vast, cold, and impersonal complex.

Just as steps were being taken to overcome perennial disbursement difficulties, especially within the bilateral program, ODA budgets were cut back substantially from planned levels over three successive fiscal years. After the difficulties of adjusting to rapid growth earlier in the decade, learning how to retrench became the priority. Then the election in 1979 of a Progressive Conservative government after sixteen years of unbroken Liberal rule added further complexity and uncertainty.

It is a moot point whether anyone could have survived this period of office with a positive image. One officer who had lived through Moran,

Strong, and Gérin-Lajoie said that it was a relief to return to "Ottawa normalcy" with a career civil servant at the helm, and that Dupuy's experience as a foreign service officer and his skills as a diplomat were helpful in overcoming strained relations with External Affairs. Many who worked with Dupuy, however, found him wanting. Two quotations typify such assessments: "He consulted to a fault, so much that he hardly ever made a decision." "Tough times need tough people, not compromising bureaucrats." Another respondent, who agreed that changes were needed, thought that the president was excessively defensive, and appeared to lack confidence in an organization that had much to be proud of. Dupuy recruited some top-flight managers to assist him at the vice-presidential level, but his own administrative leadership was tentative and uninspiring.

While Dupuy did have a clear perspective on broad matters of policy, it was one that many in CIDA saw as narrowly focused on short- and medium-term Canadian interests at the expense of longer-term developmental objectives. Other preoccupations and the change of government forestalled plans to develop a formal policy framework to succeed the strategy for 1975-80. There was, however, a de facto change towards a "two-track" approach to country eligibility: on the one hand, it maintained the commitment to channel the bulk of Canada's ODA to low-income countries including LLDCs; on the other, it increased efforts to use aid as a means of strengthening relations with selected middle-income countries.

As Western countries sought ways of coping with high inflation and unemployment in the late 1970s, Canada was not alone in putting much greater emphasis on securing domestic economic benefits from aid. However, it was one of only five DAC donors to cut back on ODA in real terms; only New Zealand and Australia had weaker records from 1975 to 1980.[6]

Meanwhile, special programs for NGOs and business achieved greater recognition as important channels for Canadian ODA, the former in support of anti-poverty and basic needs thrusts, and the latter in efforts to strengthen commercial and investment links. A new program in institutional cooperation was initiated to encourage the development of longer-term linkages between developing country institutions and Canadian universities and other non-profit institutions. Public outreach activities were expanded and then contracted in the wake of spending reductions.

Restructuring and Retrenchment

Two aspects of organizational reform preoccupied CIDA's senior executives during the Dupuy years. The first was externally imposed and involved creation of extensive procedures for financial planning, accounting, and monitoring, along with closer oversight of Agency activities by Treasury Board and the Comptroller General. The second was internally driven and focused on a "Corporate Review" of management structures—the review that had been initiated shortly before Gérin-Lajoie's departure. The catalysts for both were the Auditor General's 1976 report and the mounting parliamentary and press concerns about waste and mismanagement.

New external controls. An overhaul of financial controls and reporting procedures was essentially dictated to CIDA by the Auditor General, the Comptroller General, and Treasury Board. A colleague recalled accompanying Dupuy to a meeting with a senior official of the Board and being told: "Tell your troops that the goddamn crusade is over."

> We had "policemen" coming out of our ears. . . . We all recognized that it was too much of a shoestring operation before, so we did need some system, but the manner . . . was very much dictated by the outside. The problem was that Michel was not prepared to resist. Mind you, we maybe didn't have much choice.

Dupuy told the author that he had to go outside the Agency because he could not find people within CIDA with the time and experience required for the task. Other respondents agreed, however, that Dupuy's lack of forcefulness was a particular liability in these dealings, which had a devastating impact on morale.

The new president was but a month in office when the Agency's non-lapsing authority was removed: from now on, the only way to avoid loss of any unexpended, year-end surplus was to spend annual appropriations within the twelve-month fiscal year. This change required an entirely new approach to planning disbursements and managing cash flows.[7] Meanwhile, Treasury Board worked systematically through each of CIDA's major programs, designing frameworks for financial management, which set stricter expenditure limits for project approvals by the president, the minister, and the Board itself. A plethora of checks and double-checks in accounting and information systems was introduced as, more and more, concern for financial accountability came to dominate the Agency's activities.[8] As Granatstein and Bothwell observed, "CIDA was almost literally turned around. Instead of facing outwards, it guarded its rear."[9]

The Corporate Review.[10] While the Auditor General's criticisms prompted the decision to undertake a management review and determined much of its agenda, endless infighting and ongoing dissatisfaction with the 1972 organizational structure and subsequent changes also provided considerable grist for the mill. At issue was the still unresolved question of how to fashion project teams with clear lines of responsibility and accountability among country-focused project managers, sectoral specialists, and those involved in procurement of goods and services. Cutting across this issue was conflict between Bilateral Branch and various divisions within other branches that supplied professional expertise and operations support. Within Bilateral, it was felt that project delivery was impeded by the Branch's lack of direct control over ill-coordinated support resources. Elsewhere, including the president's office, some organizational means of counter-balancing a too powerful Bilateral Branch was seen as desirable. The politics of succession to the vice-presidency of Bilateral further complicated the picture.

Gérin-Lajoie appointed Pierre Sicard as vice-president, Corporate Review, on January 1, 1977, beginning an extensive Agency-wide process over the next seven months (which included Dupuy's first five in office). It examined the distribution and coordination of branch responsibilities and the problems identified by the Auditor General, especially the undue length of CIDA's project cycle, expenditure controls, procurement practices, and program evaluation. Several structural changes were agreed upon without great difficulty: assignment to Policy Branch of responsibility for designing Agency-wide evaluation procedures; creation of the Food Aid Coordination and Evaluation Centre in the Multilateral Branch; and division of the Finance and Administration Branch into a Comptroller's Branch, and a Personnel and Administration Branch.[11]

Much more contentious was a recommendation, under review since 1975, to consolidate sectoral and professional expertise currently scattered among the Bilateral, Special Advisers, and Administration branches in a new Resources Branch with major responsibilities for project implementation. In effect, the proposal harkened back to the old split between Planning and Operations, except that now Bilateral would draw up country plans, and Resources would play the lead role in implementation. The scheme aroused strong opposition in Bilateral Branch,[12] which proposed instead that it take over sectoral expertise and support services.

Dupuy found himself in the eye of a storm. After lengthy and acrimonious discussion, the President's Committee finally worked out a compromise. As proposed, a new Resources Branch would draw together the Special Advisers Branch, the Engineering and Human Resources divisions of Bilateral, and the divisions of Finance and Administration dealing with contracts, consultant selection, and procurement. Lead responsibility for project implementation would remain in Bilateral, however, with the possibility foreseen that Resources might manage "certain projects as requested by client branches, under the direction of the client branches."[13] In turn, divisions within Resources would control the selection of cooperants (advisers in the field) and contract negotiations with Canadian consultants and suppliers.

The Corporate Review proposed these arrangements as transitory from January 1978 to October 1980. At that point, following further reorganization within Bilateral Branch (merging the two Africa divisions and the Latin America and Caribbean divisions), both Bilateral and Resources branches would be dissolved and reshaped into three geographic branches. The text of the Corporate Review envisioned the final structure as having the "following features":

- Three Area Vice-Presidents reporting directly to the President, responsible for all bilateral program activities in Africa, Asia and the Americas. It is possible that the Area Branch Vice-Presidents will also be assigned responsibility for the Agency's activities relating to the regional multilateral institutions operating in their respective areas, and the responsibility for providing input in the development of the NGO programs and projects ongoing in their territory.
- Each Area Branch will be equipped with a Resources Division made up from staff transferred from the Resources Branch.
- Each Resources Division will be organized on a sectoral basis, as appropriate to the makeup of the Area Branch program. Projects will be managed using the project team philosophy.

The responsibilities of the executive vice-president would shift to a senior vice-president, who would also coordinate the activities of the new area branches.[14]

Elaborate proposals for implementation were submitted to Treasury Board in November 1977, and approved shortly thereafter.[15] Those that called for immediate action were introduced in 1978, but others did not take place on schedule. The Latin America and Caribbean divisions were integrated in January 1979, but francophone and anglophone Africa retained their separate identities. In June 1979, an internal report revealed that there was "a dwindling impetus to implement" the proposed changes. Internal opposition had effectively thwarted the split of Bilateral into three area branches that would absorb personnel from Resources within them. A Corporate Review Implementation team, appointed in July 1979, found that twenty-five of the original fifty-six recommendations had not been acted upon.

At the end of March 1980, shortly after Marcel Massé replaced Dupuy, the two presidents issued a joint memorandum announcing: "Decisions have now been taken *to bring the Corporate Review Implementation to a close* in order to stabilize the Agency's structures, so that we may get on with other important tasks that we face." Citing financial restraint, unforeseen in 1977, as a principal reason "why our world did not unfold quite as we expected," the memorandum stated:

> We confirm the underlying rationale of the geographic structure for Bilateral Programs. . . . We are, however, of the view that the proposal to adopt a "3As" [Africa, Americas, and Asia branches] is not the most appropriate. We will retain the present arrangement. . . . Within . . . Bilateral . . . there will be four area divisions: Asia, Americas, and the two Africas, as at present. We have also decided that Resources Branch should remain intact as an organizational entity. . . . The present size of our program and the very severe constraint that we have on technical and specialist resources further support the view that keeping this critical mass of talent in a single organizational unit is warranted and necessary.[16]

A stronger emphasis on evaluation. The question of how to evaluate the efficiency and effectiveness of public policies received growing attention within Western governments and international institutions in the 1970s. Within aid agencies threatened with budget cuts, more energy was devoted to strengthening project and program evaluation—both to improve effectiveness and to demonstrate positive results to sceptical politicians and publics.

The establishment of an Evaluation Division in CIDA's Policy Branch in 1973 reflected this general movement, but its initial activity was limited to a few ad hoc reviews of projects and programs without any consistent methodology. As soon as new procedures for financial and operational audits were in place, Dupuy and the President's Committee—spurred on by the Auditor General's criticisms and pressure from Treasury Board—gave high priority to the development of a systematic, Agency-wide approach to evaluation. In 1978, Policy Branch created a standardized approach for evaluating short and medium-term outcomes of projects, and project officers began to apply it on a routine basis the following year. Work continued on making programming more responsive to feedback from project evaluations, and on developing procedures for broader program and corporate evaluations.[17]

Interdepartmental and Ministerial Relations[18]

Whatever his deficiencies as an administrator, Michel Dupuy was well suited to fashion a new interdepartmental relationship in which CIDA would be recognized as a source of expertise on many aspects of Canada's North-South relations, on the one hand, but would assert less independence from External Affairs as the lead foreign policy agency, on the other. That was the relationship envisaged by Michael Pitfield, clerk of Privy Council, and by Allan Gotlieb, whose appointment as under-secretary of state for External Affairs coincided with Dupuy's to CIDA. This new approach emerged as part of a broader scheme to refashion the foreign policy apparatus. Its impetus stemmed from earlier interdepartmental conflict, confusion over who was to speak for the government on North-South issues, and continuing failure to develop an integrated Canadian policy on the New International Economic Order.

Pitfield became a member of both the Interdepartmental Committee on Economic Relations with Developing Countries and the Canadian International Development Board in 1977. From then until the defeat of the Trudeau government in 1979, he used these and other means to work towards a more integrated interdepartmental consensus on foreign policy led by External Affairs, but attuned to the concerns of the prime minister and the Privy Council Office.

ICERDC, chaired by Dupuy on behalf of the under-secretary before 1977, had done little more than develop positions for international conferences. Nevertheless, it had already eclipsed in importance both the CIDB (which Gérin-Lajoie seldom convened) and the Interdepartmental Committee on Development Assistance (which brought together interdepartmental representatives at the assistant deputy level). Gotlieb assumed the chair of ICERDC in 1977. In a speech two years later, he spelled out his conception of the committee's role:

> The Under-Secretary chairs the Interdepartmental Committee on Economic Relations with Developing Countries which has a broadening mandate to preside over Canada's economic relations with the Third World. It shapes instruments of policy such as our programme of development assistance. It also deals with a broad range of Canadian trade and financial issues as they affect our relations with developing countries.[19]

While the statement gave an overblown conception of the actual degree to which an integrated approach to North-South issues had been achieved, ICERDC became heavily involved in a number of aid policy issues, especially a reassessment of the strategy and attempts to define a new approach to country eligibility. Moreover, the proposition that "development assistance would be tied into and made responsive to overall governmental and foreign policy objectives" was acknowledged in an agreement that all aid policy papers emerging from CIDA's Policy Branch would require the co-signature of the president and the under-secretary. CIDA during the Dupuy years became much more a purely implementing agency.

The Conservatives acted on their long-standing pledge to make the Agency more politically accountable by appointing a separate minister of state for CIDA after they won the 1979 federal election. Senator Martial Asselin was assigned the task in a reporting relationship to Flora MacDonald, the new secretary of state for External Affairs. The Senator was given responsibility for the Agency's day-to-day operations, but MacDonald made it clear that she was responsible for policy.[20] Asselin made a few controversial statements about the need for changes in management systems but, in press statements and an appearance before the Commons Committee on External Affairs and National Defence, it was clear that he had much to learn.[21] As the government was defeated after just nine months in office, the arrangement ended before it was really tested.

Aid Volume: Flagging Commitment and Retrenchment

Budgetary stringency became a fact of life during the Dupuy presidency, and the official commitment to 0.7 per cent of GNP, though not formally abandoned, was increasingly meaningless. As we saw in Chapter 4, Canada's performance slipped from 0.53 in 1975-76 to 0.49 in 1976-77. This was partly the result of a spending cap that limited the increase in total disbursements in 1976-77 (from the accumulated pipeline and new appropriations) to an 8 per cent increase from $903 to $975 million. However, disbursements were almost $12 million below the allowable limit, a shortfall that would have been much higher without last minute increases in advances to multilateral institutions;[22] these raised multilateral aid to 43 per cent of ODA, substantially above the strategy guideline. With the ending of non-lapsing funds, the 1976-77 shortfall was lost. In total, an accumulated pipeline of $148.4 million approved by Parliament for Canadian development assistance disappeared.[23]

The inability to disburse all resources available for bilateral programming continued to plague CIDA in 1977-78.[24] Once more, the Agency had to resort to the multilateral channel (41 per cent) to ensure that it spent close to its approved funding ceiling. The ODA/GNP ratio remained at 0.49 per cent. Thereafter, the constraint on growth was less CIDA's capacity to disburse, which was improving, and much more fiscal austerity.

Even before severe restraint began in 1978, the Trudeau government had backed away from the pledge in the strategy to achieve annual increases in the proportion of ODA to GNP. A report prepared by the Commons Subcommittee on International Development in May 1977 called for an immediate, real increase in ODA and a return to the course set out in the Strategy.[25] At CIEC and OECD ministerial meetings in June, Canadian representatives indicated, in light of slippage the previous year, that there would be a substantial improvement in the aid effort.[26] An internal CIDA document in July, however, defined the position as "setting aside of the 0.7% target in favour of a regularly growing 'Floor Commitment,' in other words stabilization around 0.5% to 0.52% of GNP."[27]

The floor looked more like a ceiling a year later. In June 1978, Parliament approved a 14.6 per cent increase for 1979-80, which would have put the ratio above 0.5 per cent.[28] Just two months later, however, Trudeau returned from the Bonn G7 summit determined to cut a mounting federal deficit. CIDA was required to take a share of a planned lapse in 1978-79, which amounted to $85 million. In 1979-80, the budget was frozen at the original appropriation level of the previous year, resulting in a further cut of $133 million.[29] As a result, the GNP ratio dropped from 0.49 per cent in 1978-79 to 0.47 per cent in 1979-80.[30]

Later in 1978, Policy Branch prepared a speculative essay on whether to redefine or rescind the 0.7 commitment. The authors suggested that contributions other than ODA could be counted, for example, any structural adjustment expenditures and unemployment benefits in Canada that assisted Third World exports, some Export Development Corporation loans, and joint ventures in fields like renewable energy. "The alternative would be to state that the 0.7% objective is no longer valid in itself, since it has become obsolete and since it is not very clear why the situation would be better at 0.7% than at 0.5%." If this course of action were chosen, compensatory options might include stronger positions in support of other Third World demands, greater procurement untying, and more support for joint ventures. "It is possible to question the 0.7% objective without necessarily losing face. Indeed, innovation will become all the more essential . . . since . . . pursuit of the 0.7% objective is illusory in view of current constraints."[31]

The UN target became even more illusory after Joe Clark and the Progressive Conservatives came to power in the spring of 1979. Flora MacDonald was viewed as a friend of the aid program, but she warned early in her ministerial tenure that little growth could be anticipated.[32] Finance Minister John Crosbie spoke bluntly to the IMF meeting in Belgrade in October 1979, acknowledging

> that Canada's economic woes such as inflation, unemployment, and severe budgetary and current account deficits might seem to be insignificant in relation to the problems facing most developing countries. [But he added:] "Nevertheless they are serious indeed in any economic context. They are viewed seriously by the average Canadian. Further increases in the transfer of resources are difficult to justify until our own economic position improves."[33]

Sinclair Stevens, who gained a reputation as "the slasher" as Treasury Board president under Clark, had said of CIDA while in opposition: "I am convinced we could be spending half as much and getting twice the benefits."[34]

Aid was a prime target in spending cuts announced in the Estimates for 1980-81. The inflation rate was running at 9.6 per cent, and overall government expenditures went up by 11.3 per cent, but the aid budget was increased less than 2 per cent from $1.21 billion to $1.23 billion. As a result, ODA, which had been running at 2.3 per cent of federal spending, dropped to 2.0 per cent in 1980-81.[35] The North-South Institute exclaimed: "The most recent projections of Canadian aid levels, falling to 0.37 per cent of GNP in 1981, will shock the international community."[36] In fact, the Department of

Finance recommended in 1979 that 0.35 per cent become the norm.[37] Although the trend line was moving rapidly down to that threshold, MacDonald claimed nonetheless that Canada was still committed to achieving 0.7 per cent. She added: "I do not expect to see that figure reached this year and I do not want to raise any false expectation."[38]

The budgetary reductions before the Tories took office resulted in a decline in Canada's ODA/GNP ratio to 0.43 per cent in 1980-81, below the level in 1972-73.[39] Despite claims of growing "aid fatigue" in the donor community, the overall DAC average actually improved from 0.35 per cent in 1975 to 0.37 in 1980. Canada remained above the donor average, but fell to seventh place in total contributions in 1980, behind the Netherlands, and to ninth out of the seventeen members in ODA/GNP ratios. Canadian ODA accounted for just 3.95 per cent of all DAC flows in 1980, down from 6.36 per cent in 1975 and 4.85 per cent in 1970.[40]

After accommodating the 1978-79 cuts fairly easily, CIDA had to make painful choices when planning for 1979-80 and 1980-81. Some projects were stretched out and, where there were as yet no legal obligations, others were cancelled. Although all channels suffered decreases, bilateral aid absorbed a disproportionate share because multilateral commitments were longer-term and more difficult to break; in addition, the Department of Finance was able to protect contributions to the international financial institutions.[41] It was a lesson heeded by CIDA management, which, as we shall see in subsequent chapters, tried to find ways of protecting the bilateral core of the program.

Policy Development

Even though Dupuy's mandate was primarily managerial and the Agency during his presidency was preoccupied with administrative and financial difficulties, the president's personal impact was greatest in the policy sphere. Shortly after his arrival, he assembled senior and middle managers at a forum in Arnprior. One of the officers in attendance recalled how he and other colleagues were taken aback by Dupuy's forthright message: that external aid should serve Canada's foreign policy objectives, and that a principal concern was economic survival in the face of tough global competition from newly industrializing countries and established industrial powers.

> It was a clear and coherent vision. . . . If you accepted the assumptions, it was right. A lot of people didn't accept the assumptions, including myself. Certainly we should be competitive and push our trade interests, but development assistance is not an appropriate vehicle to do that. It doesn't help competitive Canadian interests. In fact it undermines our competitiveness and the use of development assistance for patently commercial and political objectives doesn't

> reinforce our strength and our status in developing countries. It undermines it. But that was certainly not the way Michel saw things, and it was certainly not the way the powers in External Affairs, Finance, and IT&C saw it.

Although Dupuy's political style was not as assertive as his analysis, a preoccupation with Canadian concerns was increasingly a factor in the interpretation of existing policy and in planning for a new strategy for the 1980s.[42]

In July 1977, Policy Branch undertook a mid-term review of the strategy for 1975-80 for the President's Committee. The strategy's analytical section was characterized in retrospect as weak because of the interdepartmental compromises it embodied. These in turn "have meant that the recommendations of the second part (the twenty-one points), although well-intended and denoting a remarkable surge of innovation, remain of a general nature and invoke at times contradictory interpretations."[43] The basic themes of the document had lost nothing of their pertinence, but circumstances in the developing world were changing; moreover, there was growing uncertainty about how to apply "a somewhat inoperational strategy," and about the degree of commitment to it by senior management. After rejecting outright abandonment, Policy Branch identified three options: A, marginal change to make twenty-one points more operational; B, major revision to select clearer objectives "and an accelerated operationalization of points responding closely to the new perception of the demands of international cooperation"; or C, formulation of a new strategy for the 1980s.

The authors recommended Option B for 1978-79 and 1979-80, and a start on active planning for Option C. Five themes were suggested: (1) a focus on internal disparities within developing countries, leading to a massive attack on poverty and malnutrition through efforts to satisfy *basic human needs*; (2) support for global structural changes and resource transfers to foster *self-reliant development*; (3) enhanced sensitivity to the relationship between *environment and development*; (4) active promotion of *social justice and respect for human rights*; and (5) acceptance of interdependence—imbued with solidarity—and the possibility of pursuing *mutual interests* in international cooperation.[44] The themes mirrored accurately then-current discourse within the international donor community.

In December 1977, Dupuy issued "Directions for the Agency: From Now Until the 1980s." Affirming that the strategy for 1975-80 still governed the ODA program, he indicated that "far from being cast in stone, the strategy contains a flexibility which becomes even more important as we must constantly adapt our cooperation program to reflect the evolution of Canada and the world at large." He announced that the President's Committee had adopted an "option called B" that reflected two components. First, "the recent evolution of the Canadian economy as well as its short and medium-term prospects require that CIDA strive to ensure that its activities maintain or generate employment and economic benefits in our own country. We must also aim at strengthening mutually beneficial bilateral relationships between our developing partners and Canada." Secondly, there would be heightened emphasis on two objectives "already defined in the Strategy"—the support of self-reliance and the satisfaction of basic human needs.[45] Environmental and human rights concerns were not included in the official version of Option B.

Dupuy's definition of mutual interests was more short-term and more Canadian-centred than the one advanced by Policy Branch. It was also set out as the first priority, though it should be pursued "while not neglecting our essential mandate which is international development." Apart from recognizing the particular capabilities of NGOs in grass-roots projects, the document was not forthcoming about how to reconcile the goals of self-reliance and basic needs satisfaction with recommendations to maximize the use of Canadian goods and services, especially components with high value-added content.

In addition, Bilateral Branch was asked to develop appropriate transfer mechanisms for promoting commercially oriented and mutually beneficial relations with selected countries "where some of the basic needs are already satisfied" and there were "viable self-sustaining commercial prospects."[46] Both "Directions for the Agency" and Dupuy's speeches[47] revealed an apparently untroubled advocate of the proposition that there was no inherent conflict between Canada's economic interests and developmental priorities in the Third World.

Policy Branch began developing proposals for a new strategy for the 1980s and suggested that its inauguration coincide with an important international occasion, perhaps the launch of the Third Development Decade at the UN General Assembly in 1980. "Such an impact is indispensable, internationally, to strengthen Canada's image in the field of co-operation, and, nationally, to elicit a better response from federal departments, Parliament and the public."[48]

By 1978, however, much of the active work on reviewing existing policy and charting new directions had been appropriated by the Interdepartmental Committee on Economic Relations with Developing Countries, where External Affairs played the lead role. An ICERDC task force drawn from IT&C, Finance, the Treasury Board, and the Privy Council Office as well as CIDA undertook a reassessment of eligibility criteria. It concluded that too much emphasis had previously been given to LLDCs and too little to foreign policy objectives. A suggested formula would weight factors according to a ratio of 40:25:20:15 for need, political relations with Canada, economic performance, and commercial relations respectively. In approving the proposal, ICERDC urged that more aid be focused on promoting bilateral relations with rapid-growth developing countries, especially those in the middle-income range.[49]

While a desire to have foreign aid serve domestic economic interests was long-standing, this new, hard-nosed approach was supported by Donald Jamieson, secretary of state for External Affairs from 1976 to 1979, who was much less interested in CIDA's developmental mission than MacEachen had been. It was also legitimated by similar trends elsewhere. Aid fatigue in donor countries was accompanied by growing irritation over the stalemate in North-South negotiations and mounting concern over domestic stagflation and public-sector deficits. Efforts to secure commercial benefits from ODA were reflected in the introduction of an aid-trade fund in Britain, and in the aggressive use of ODA monies in parallel with export promotion credits, especially by France and Japan.

Canadian business pressure to harness the aid program more directly to commercial interests also intensified. This was a major issue for the Export Promotion Review Committee, chaired by Roger Hatch, president of CANPOTEX, and made up of leading business executives. It was appointed by the minister of Industry, Trade and Commerce at the end of 1978 to examine ways of improving government export promotion and support services. A few months later, the Liberal government was defeated at the polls, and the committee did much of its work under the Conservatives (1979-80), reporting just before the Clark government fell. *Strengthening Canada Abroad*, the committee's report, accused CIDA of taking "an overly philanthropic giveaway approach to aid." Arguing that Canada could do more for development by integrating aid and trade strategies, Hatch called for a larger bilateral program that would come from reduced contributions to multilateral institutions. Existing bilateral ODA was too widely dispersed and too oriented to nations that "are too underdeveloped for much meaningful trade to result." Hatch recommended that part of an enlarged bilateral budget be reserved for parallel financing with the Export Development Corporation, and that the rest be concentrated in "fewer countries to whom Canada's technical capabilities are most useful, and with whom there is trade potential." Criticizing CIDA for failing to maximize Canadian content through tied aid, the committee urged that sourcing of goods and services be shifted to a separate office that would serve CIDA, IT&C, and the Export Development Corporation.[50]

Alternative Policy Perspectives

The Hatch report made a case for converting the aid program largely into an instrument for trade promotion. While there was no possibility of such an extreme position finding favour within government, articulate expressions of dissent helped counteract a movement in that direction. Stout resistance came from within CIDA itself, and the NGO community was strongly opposed. Shortly after Dupuy spoke to the Empire Club in Toronto in December 1977 about benefits that aid generated for Canadian business, Douglas Roche complained in the House of Commons:

> If any final proof is needed about the confusion of purpose in Canada's foreign policy, Mr. Speaker, let us consider the sorry spectacle of CIDA officials now justifying Canada's aid budget on grounds that it is good for the Canadian economy. Is the Department of Industry, Trade and Commerce so bereft of ideas to promote the sale of Canadian goods abroad that the government must insist that CIDA become a sales agency? The management of the economy must be even worse than we imagined if CIDA, an agency that was started to express the humanitarian concern of Canadians for the poor of the world, is now to be used to prop up industry, trade and commerce.

Roche said that there was nothing inherently wrong with tying aid to Canadian procurement, provided that it promoted development. However, he attacked the "myth" that, at 0.23 per cent of GNP (roughly half of total ODA), tied aid was important for the Canadian economy. There were benefits for Canada from international development, "and we should not hesitate to point them out." But

> True aid is an investment in the long-range development of people. If CIDA persists in explaining itself on grounds of immediate commercial returns to Canada—when that return is insignificant anyway—it will seriously jeopardize that substantial body of public opinion that supports CIDA on the grounds that it is actually helping the poorest people.[51]

To buttress his case, Roche cited the first major critique of Canada's performance in the sphere of international development published by the North-South Institute. In *North-South Encounter*, the Institute expressed disappointment about lack of Canadian leadership on most major issues reviewed by the CIEC in 1975-77. It also published an "interim report card" on the strategy for 1975-80, which assigned poor marks for inaction or contradictory performance on most of the twenty-one points. The Institute regretted CIDA's failure to move as yet on the commitment to allow developing country procurement, and advocated greater untying to meet local costs for projects aimed at meeting basic human needs.[52]

The Economic Council of Canada, which sponsored several studies on Canada's relations with developing countries, published an overview entitled *For a Common Future* in 1978.[53] It argued that Canada should respond positively to the challenge of international development by adjusting rather than protecting. On ODA, the Economic Council rejected arguments for short-run commercial advantage and measures involving inefficient subsidization of Canadian industries.[54] It endorsed the general thrusts of the strategy for

1975-80, especially emphasis on the poorest countries, and offered several recommendations for making the aid program more effective and efficient: rigorous evaluation, concentration on fewer countries, and untying for procurement both in developing countries and—on the basis of reciprocal agreements—in other donor countries (though only after domestic adjustment measures reached a threshold point).[55]

For a Common Future also urged integration of all aspects of North-South policy,[56] but maintained that there ought to be a clear demarcation between the promotion of Third World development and Canadian commercial interests. Asserting that CIDA's business and industry programs for pre-investment starter and feasibility studies fell into the latter category, the report urged shifting them to the Export Development Corporation or Industry, Trade and Commerce.[57] The authors departed from the conventional consensus on multilateral aid, querying whether it was necessarily more effective than a reformed bilateral program would be. However, this stance was related to the loss of Canadian control over resources—rather than of commercial advantage—and to concern that multilateral disbursements had risen well above the strategy guideline to cope with CIDA's bilateral disbursement problem.[58]

Meanwhile, throughout the period from 1977 to 1979, Roche and a handful of opposition MPs continued to push for a major parliamentary review of CIDA and all aspects of Canadian aid policy. Besides aid management and the orientation of Canadian assistance, procurement tying, volume slippage, and ODA sensitivity to human rights[59] were among issues members wanted to examine in greater detail. The Subcommittee on International Development was reconstituted in 1977 with terms of reference to study both Canada's role in the North-South dialogue and the effectiveness of Canada's aid programs from the perspective of the strategy for 1975-80.[60] Given the timing of CIEC meetings, the subcommittee decided that global negotiations were more urgent, and undertook a review of Third World debt problems. The aid study was deferred. Despite opposition requests, the government did not renew the subcommittee's mandate in subsequent sessions.

The Conservative election victory in the spring of 1979 at last seemed to create the opportunity for a parliamentary review. Douglas Roche was named parliamentary secretary to Flora MacDonald. Many observers thought that Roche deserved the new CIDA portfolio in Cabinet, but he was bypassed in favour of Senator Asselin, a francophone.

The Tory Interregnum

In August 1979, Prime Minister Clark confirmed en route to the Commonwealth heads of government meeting in Zambia that exhaustive reviews of foreign policy and aid would soon be undertaken.[61] Shortly thereafter, civil servants in External Affairs and CIDA began drafting discussion papers for referral to the Standing Committee on External Affairs and National Defence, or possibly a joint committee of the House and the Senate. Both Clark and MacDonald favoured a populist process with extensive public hearings.[62]

As part of the exercise, Roche secured Tory caucus support for a thorough, independent, and "tough-minded" management review of CIDA—by a broad-based team of business people, NGO representatives, and politicians—that would then be submitted to the parliamentary committee.[63] He also urged that a Canadian advisory council on international development be set up as an ongoing "watchdog" with a similarly representative membership.[64]

Interested groups began developing submissions for the parliamentary hearings. CCIC produced a comprehensive "Framework for Canada's Development Assistance" in November 1979. It called for reaffirmation of the 0.7 per cent target, a fundamental commitment to meeting the basic human needs of the poorest groups in the poorest countries, elimination of tying provisions by 1985, more funding for NGOs, and greater sensitivity to human rights performance.[65]

MacDonald gave some indication of her own thinking during the fall of 1979, and generated not a little controversy. She pledged that Canada's external relations and foreign aid would take human rights into account, a stance that won support from the NGO community. However, her tendency to engage in tub-thumping moralism evoked doubts about the effectiveness of her approach;[66] at the same time, she raised the hackles of the Canadian Export Association, which feared a loss of trade opportunities.[67]

On more than one occasion, the minister suggested that the government's own aid efforts should concentrate on economic infrastructure, leaving greater responsibility for social development to NGOs and the private sector.[68] She said that any increases in aid during the period of austerity would likely be in "soft" areas like technical cooperation and the provision of Canadian advisers.[69] She also voiced strong support for the work of NGOs and a desire to increase their funding.[70]

For those who saw her as a progressive Red Tory, MacDonald caused consternation by asking whether greater effort ought to go into securing economic benefits from Canadian ODA. Dwelling on that theme in a speech to the Empire Club, she mused:

> I look at the distribution of effort that our Department of External Affairs and our aid programmes have, and I wonder why we are so deeply committed in certain parts of the world. What are Canada's real interests in this involvement? It certainly doesn't have to do with trade; our commerce with most of those countries is minimal. . . . Even more generally, I wonder on what basis we have

> chosen to participate in individual aid programmes. Have we taken into account the economic returns Canada may expect in both the short and long term? How good are we at assessing projects from the point of view of actually helping real development, and of doing ourselves some good at the same time?

She opened herself to subsequent ridicule with the following statement:

> Ever since the Second World War Canada has been cultivating the image of an international nice-guy. We're friends to everyone, the honest brokers. We've spent billions on aid and untold man-hours of effort in being as upright and noble to the third world as we can be. And yet last month in Havana the non-aligned countries cheerfully branded us as imperialists. Pakistan is one of the very largest recipients of our aid programmes, but it led the attack.[71]

Writing in the *Gazette* (Montreal), André McNicoll noted that confusion and uncertainty over foreign aid policy since the election turned to bewilderment with the Empire Club speech, which "sent shock-waves through the multitude of aid organizations."[72] Peyton Lyon, a former diplomat and distinguished commentator on Canadian foreign policy, praised the minister for her generous response earlier in the year to the plight of Vietnamese "boat people," but her remarks on aid policy prompted him to write: "In opposition, Flora MacDonald earned, and seemed to welcome, the 'Red Tory' label. In office, she seems determined to convert the label to 'Redneck Tory.' "[73]

The minister herself responded to mounting criticism by claiming that she was raising questions "in order to provoke a discussion of foreign policy. . . . [If] I can pose provocative suggestions or questions, it will get people thinking about it."[74] In retrospect, David Cox suggested that MacDonald "was well aware of the vulnerability of the aid budget and the consequent need to increase public awareness of the merits of the aid programme. This purpose tended to be obscured by her statements which, lacking clear direction, perhaps even strengthened the hand of those in the government who were not strong supporters of aid."[75]

"Canadian Aid Policy": CIDA's 1979 discussion paper. The long-sought review did not occur, of course, as the Clark government was voted down in the House of Commons in December 1979 and lost the February 1980 election to Pierre Trudeau's Liberals. Discussion papers prepared by the bureaucracy were being printed the very day the government fell. Although they were not distributed, the new Liberal government later agreed to place them in the public domain.[76]

Discursive and open-ended, the discussion papers were as bland and bureaucratic as Flora MacDonald's statements were colourful. Although the one on "Canadian Aid Policy" did not survive as government policy, it provides a revealing snapshot of official thinking at the end of the Dupuy presidency. It marked yet another shift in the declarative language of official thinking away from the primacy of development to an External Affairs perspective emphasizing ODA as an instrument of foreign and domestic policy.

Development assistance was to be subsumed within the totality of Canada's relations with the Third World, in a coherent set of policies reflecting national interests, "which can be classified as economic, political, social and security." All were discussed in terms of their benefits for Canadians, sometimes particular groups. The political category (curiously separated from security) included Canadian "interests such as those of the [Canadian] business community in the wealthier developing countries and the humanitarian groups in the poorer developing countries." The economic interest was defined entirely in the light of potential gains for Canada. In contrast, the social interest dealt with developing countries:

> Many Canadians believe that the principles of social justice which have been applied in Canada should be reflected in Canadian objectives in the developing countries. Concerns about basic human needs and human rights underlie much of the public's thinking about the Third World. Part of the Canadian interest may therefore be defined as the development of programs and policies designed to help the disadvantaged countries and peoples of the world.[77]

In this characterization of ethical concern as a mere political issue, we see for the first time in a major government document on Canadian aid policy a determinedly "realist" position with little concession to the idea that the government ought to act internationally on the basis of collective moral responsibility.[78]

The discussion paper argued as well that popular perceptions needed updating:

> Many Canadian attitudes date back to the early post-war period. . . . We saw the Third World as an area of poverty which stirred our national humanitarian conscience. . . . What many Canadians have not fully appreciated today is just how much the Third World has changed in the past twenty-five years. . . . Its economic evolution has been uneven and vast poverty remains. . . . This tends to conceal . . . the progress it has achieved, particularly in the middle-income countries, as well as the opportunities offered to Canada for economic partnership.[79]

In turn, among

> the most important decisions to be taken on the future of aid policy is the overall orientation of that policy. . . . In other words, what should be the balance between the various motivations which may be summarized as lying between pure altruism at one end of the spectrum and narrow self-interest at the other end?[80]

Conveying little sense of challenge or excitement, or of then-current international debates, the document suggested that trade-offs were required among developmental, political, economic, and humanitarian interests. Limited budgetary growth meant that tough decisions would be needed about the shares of various aid channels: "expansion of one will be at the expense of another."[81]

"Canadian Aid Policy" lauded the effectiveness of NGOs in assisting small, basic human needs projects and in encouraging support for Canada's aid effort among the Canadian public.[82] Recently reorganized business and industry programs were portrayed as valuable in increasing business support for international development. "The program attempts to give priority to the poorer developing countries but, by virtue of its nature and its more comprehensive eligibility list, it also complements the bilateral program activities by providing a means of cooperating with rapidly industrializing developing countries as the more traditional aid mechanisms are phased out."[83]

The document made the usual case for geographical concentration and suggested need, developmental effort, and Canadian interests as criteria that could be taken into account for determining eligibility.[84] It took no position on regional distribution (merely observing that there was now rough parity between Africa and Asia),[85] but flagged the issue of what balance Canada should achieve between poor and middle-income countries. The text observed that aid had a lesser impact in LLDCs, though their need was great. In contrast, the "needs of middle-income countries are more in line with Canadian commercial capabilities, and a reasonable amount of aid from Canada can be useful to reinforce the maturing economic and political relationships we wish to develop with them."[86]

In clear deference to MacDonald's views, the policy paper recognized human rights performance as a relevant criterion for eligibility decisions. It also claimed—another exercise in relabelling—that past decisions to suspend aid to Uganda, Kampuchea, and Equatorial Guinea had taken human rights into consideration.[87] While the Clark government's recent decision to declare Vietnam ineligible was similarly characterized, no suggestions were offered for addressing human rights concerns systematically or consistently.[88]

Discussion of procurement tying observed that the practice "remains a matter of conflicting views and wide debate about its merits, impact and rationale." On terms, the possibility of more lending on intermediate terms was broached, especially "if programs are expanded in the middle-income countries." The role of ODA in debt relief was also mentioned.[89] A review of sectoral priorities reported that increasing emphasis was being given to sectors "which are important from the point of view of Canadian technological capability—e.g., energy, transportation and communications."[90] The policy paper also urged taking better account of the role of women in development, admitted CIDA had fallen short in the sphere of technical cooperation, and recognized the need for stronger monitoring and evaluation of programs.[91]

Volume and the international aid target were left for the last section. The fall in the ODA/GNP ratio was noted in tandem with an assertion that "Canadian performance compares reasonably well with the largest DAC donors and consequently with the DAC average." Understating what had been painfully obvious since 1978, the authors observed that the 0.7 per cent target "does not in itself provide stability for the planning of Canadian aid at the program and project level where a three to four-year planning horizon is required for greater effectiveness."[92]

Programming Highlights during the Dupuy Era

For all its ambiguities, the strategy was supposed to guide the aid program at least until 1980. It was not ignored, but restructuring and retrenchment limited possibilities for innovation. Moreover, the heavier emphasis on Canadian interests undercut efforts to extend programming in the interests of the poorest of the poor, while the plethora of external controls and fear of horror stories bred caution and a preference for the status quo.

Geographical Distribution

As we saw, eligibility was the prime issue in policy discussions between 1977 and 1980 that resulted in an undeclared two-track policy of channelling the bulk of bilateral aid to LLDCs and other low-income countries, while giving higher priority to Canada's economic interests in aid relations with selected middle-income and rapid-growth economies. Allocations to the least developed actually rose from 28.1 per cent of bilateral aid in 1976 to 38.8 per cent in 1979, before slipping back to 34.5 per cent in 1980.[93] The share of government-to-government aid channelled to Africa (where most LLDCs are located) continued to rise, reaching 48.7 per cent in 1979-80 (up by more than 10 per cent from two years earlier); this compared to 40 per cent to Asia and 11.2 per cent to the Americas.[94]

The strengthening of political and commercial links to more prosperous developing countries meant that they too received increased bilateral aid, leaving less for the low-income group in between. Reneging on the strategy commitment not to exceed an allocation of 10 per cent to countries with annual per capita incomes of $375 or more (in 1973 $US), CIDA began to experiment with different data bases in its annual DAC memoranda. Using 1976 $US as the standard, the Agency reported that recipients with per capita incomes greater than $400 received 25.7 per cent of bilateral allocations in

1978. Countries with per capita incomes of more than $450 (US 1978) received 23.0 per cent and 19.9 per cent in 1979 and 1980, respectively.[95] In a "smoke and mirrors" exercise the following year, $US 625 was picked as a norm; this fudging of figures dropped allocations to middle-income countries—as now redefined—to 10.3 per cent.[96]

While there were no changes in the list of program countries in place at the end of the Gérin-Lajoie presidency,[97] a large loan program was begun in Egypt, which, CIDA observed, "is of special interest in that the relatively high level of that country's economy can cause significant commercial benefits to accrue to Canada."[98] It was later designated as a core recipient. The Caribbean was flagged as a priority by MacDonald, leading to a decision to maintain bilateral commitments there as cuts were being made elsewhere.

Terms and Conditions

Despite talk about lending on harder terms, most loans were still offered on a fully concessional basis and the overall program became more heavily grants-based. Canada announced at the CIEC meeting in 1977 that outstanding ODA loans to the LLDCs would be converted to grants, and that all new bilateral aid to these countries would be offered as outright grants.[99] Parliamentary approval for cancellation of loans with a book value of $231.8 million was obtained early in 1978.[100] By 1980, grants constituted 86.5 per cent of government-to-government transfers, up from 80.7 per cent in 1976.[101]

Procurement tying: Backtracking on commitments.[102] The bifurcation between a generous policy on concessionality and a stringent one on untying continued, as lobbying by the Canadian corporate sector succeeded in scuttling the 1975 commitment to permit developing country suppliers to bid on ODA loan contracts. CIDA officials had hoped to implement the measure by the end of 1976 following consultations with the Canadian Export Association. Not satisfied that proposed guidelines provided sufficient protection for Canadian interests (even though CIDA agreed to exclude participation by most newly industrializing countries), the CEA early in 1977 urged Jamieson and Dupuy to back down altogether. Draft regulations were first amended to exclude potash, railway equipment, and consulting engineering services, and then quietly buried. The 1979 "Canadian Aid Policy" paper acknowledged that "Because of domestic political pressures, the partial untying measures of the 1975-80 strategy have not been fully [*sic*] implemented."[103]

The North-South Institute deplored the "gap between Canada's proposed determination on the one hand to help developing countries develop their capacities to export goods and services, and Canada's extreme reluctance on the other hand to allow them to compete for the opportunity to supply under Canadian aid programmes."[104] It also pointed out that movement to a stronger basic needs orientation required further relaxation in the untying authority to meet increasing local costs. In declaring the time ripe for "informed decisions," the Institute noted that it had requested and seen recent studies by Treasury Board on the potential impact of untying on the Canadian economy, "but pending declassification of these studies, cannot make specific reference to them without clearance." The government, CEA, and other business organizations were urged to bring "all of their analysis into the public domain."[105] In its 1977 review of Canada, DAC criticized inaction on the untying commitment.[106]

Given the intensity of business opposition to the modest step recommended in the strategy, it is not surprising that the government was unwilling to make Treasury Board's findings available at that time. Eventually declassified in 1984, an analysis undertaken in 1976 found that recipients had borne excess costs of 14 per cent on bilateral disbursements in 1974-75. These were estimated to be 25 per cent for capital equipment and services, 11.7 per cent for primary commodities, and 2.5 per cent for food aid. The report suggested that several factors were responsible: the "weak position of certain Canadian producers, the exercise of monopolistic power by some Canadian firms and the fact that Canada is in an unfavourable geographic situation from some points of view." It also mentioned the indirect costs of accepting aid that might not be in accord with development priorities.[107]

In assessing the impact on the Canadian economy, the Treasury Board study suggested that *full* untying of grants and loans would have yielded:

- a maximum loss of $37.6 million in Canadian production, less than eight per cent of bilateral disbursements, plus some further losses in the service sector;
- little impact on market penetration for new products; and
- an additional balance of payments deficit of at most $100 million, representing one-quarter of 1 per cent of Canada's current account payments in 1974.

While the impact of full untying was thus estimated as relatively minor, the study did show that particular sectors would be affected more seriously than others—producers of railway and telecommunications equipment, the general construction sector, and some agricultural goods (flour, rapeseed oil, and skim milk powder). Selected consulting firms stood to lose up to 25 to 30 per cent of their business. Nonetheless, the report concluded, "in the event of full-scale untying of the bilateral aid program, *the added sacrifice Canadians and, in particular, fixed capital holders would have to make would not be considerable and would not exceed the benefits for developing countries, especially when the relative circumstances of Canada and the nations being compared with it are considered*."[108]

The study also examined the more limited implications of implementing Point 14 of the strategy on untying for procurement in developing countries.

If this step were restricted to the purchase of goods and limited to loans, "it was estimated that 5 per cent of the contracts, at the most, would have been awarded to developing countries." Basing their estimate on Dutch and American experiences with this sort of untying, the authors noted that the effect would probably be even less if (as would have been the case) CIDA excluded Singapore, Hong Kong, and South Korea from participation. Analysis of 1974-75 data revealed that less than 3 per cent of what were identified as "total excess costs" would have been eliminated by developing country procurement. "*It may therefore be concluded that the real advantages of untying of aid at source for countries receiving aid can only be gained by extending it to other industrialized countries.*"[109]

Programming Priorities

With a caveat once more about the unreliability of CIDA's data on sectoral distribution, Table 5.1 sets out CIDA's bilateral commitments for the years 1976 to 1979, highlighting sectors defined as priorities in the strategy. A declining proportion was devoted to agriculture and rural development and to the conventional emphases on power generation and transportation. The share of education and training continued to drop and that of other basic needs remained low, though with a greater emphasis on potable water projects (reflected in the totals for "Health, Welfare, Housing and Water Supply"). Although precise data were not made available, more bilateral aid was offered in the form of liquid transfers, especially commodity lines of credit and parallel financing with the Export Development Corporation.

We examined several factors during the Gérin-Lajoie era that impeded movement towards more labour-intensive, basic needs-oriented programming of the sort that declaratory statements supported. These factors included inertia among operations personnel, a slow and cumbersome planning process, limitations in CIDA's capacities and Canadian resources, and pressure to disburse. Inflexibility owing to budget cutbacks replaced the last of these in the late 1970s, but the others remained. These factors contributed as much as explicit policy considerations—the greater tilt towards commercially oriented programming—to the failure to reorient the bilateral program more heavily towards basic needs.

New financial controls and closer regulation by Treasury Board made project planning even more cumbersome and, given human resource constraints, reversed the gradual process of devolving more responsibility to officers in the field. Roger Ehrhardt observed that tighter control became the "reflex reaction" to criticism after the Auditor General's 1976 report. "Now, like other government departments, CIDA must function within a web of regulations imposed on it by outside departments. Many of these regulations are

Table 5.1
Percentage Distribution of Canadian Bilateral Aid Commitments Attributable by Sector, 1976-79

	1976		1977		1978		1979	
	$M	%	$M	%	$M	%	$M	%
Agriculture and rural development[a]	130.9	29.5	121.9	20.5	180.3	23.6	110.4	17.9
Education and training	22.1	5.0	50.7	8.5	24.9	3.3	20.7	3.3
Health, welfare, housing, and water supply	53.6	12.1	37.5	6.5	47.2	6.2	67.1	10.9
Power production and distribution	33.2	7.5	69.2	11.7	134.6	17.6	185.2	30.0
Transport	69.4	15.6	180.2	30.4	241.1	31.6	84.7	13.7
Communications	0.7	0.2	1.9	0.3	—	—	37.2	6.0
Subtotal	309.8	69.8	461.4	77.8	628.0	82.3	505.3	81.8
Other funds allocable by sector	133.8	30.2	132.1	22.2	134.9	17.7	112.1	18.2
Total funds allocable by sector	433.6	100.0	593.5	100.0	762.9	100.0	617.4	100.0
Not allocable by sector[b]	234.8	—	354.8	—	534.1	—	174.0	—
Total commitments	678.5	—	949.0	—	1,297.0	—	791.4	—

a Includes fertilizers and multisector commitments.
b Includes debt relief (1977, 1978).

Source: CIDA, *Memorandum to DAC 1978*, p. 27, and ibid., *1979*, p. 24. DAC defines bilateral aid as everything that is not multilateral—i.e., what CIDA now calls country-to-country aid.

inconsistent with the Agency's developmental mandate." A willingness to engage in risk-taking and a capacity for first-hand monitoring, both highly desirable for basic needs programming, were set back by organizational changes that themselves diverted time and energy from innovative programming.[110] Judith Tendler found in her study of the American aid program that "Aid institutionalized its toleration of criticism by coming to identify with the very interests of the bureaucratic entities which it was trying to fend off."[111] A similar process was occurring in CIDA.

Efforts to strengthen food aid. According to the Auditor General in 1976, the food aid program suffered from a lack of operational coordination among several responsibility centres.[112] Before his criticisms were made public, Treasury Board initiated a joint CIDA/Board study of food aid. Criticizing the ad hocery and inadequacy of past efforts, it recommended creation of a single unit in CIDA that would oversee a more coherent approach to planning, allocating, and evaluating disbursements.[113] An interdepartmental working group was set up to develop proposals for ICERDC, which approved a new Food Aid Policy in June 1978. CIDA then established a Food Aid Coordination and Evaluation Centre (FACE) in Multilateral Branch to play an integrating role among the various operating branches that disbursed foodstuffs.[114]

The interdepartmental process had provoked strong debate about the role of food aid, with CIDA advancing a number of proposals on developmental grounds that failed to secure approval.[115] In keeping with the evolving ethos of the Dupuy era, the new policy made explicit concessions to national interests. Nonetheless, it established guiding principles that strengthened the developmental parameters for food aid allocations:

- that food aid is humanitarian, and is given to address the nutritional needs of the poorer segments of recipient country populations;
- that food aid is considered primarily as complementary to the recipient's agricultural strategy;
- that food aid should take account of Canada's economic interest, through surplus disposal and increased value added to agricultural commodities;
- that food aid should be consistent with the general goals and specific objectives of Canada's foreign policy and overall development assistance efforts.[116]

The review occurred during years when Canada fulfilled the tonnage commitment for grains made at the Rome conference in 1974. Food aid accounted for almost a quarter of ODA from 1975-76 through 1977-78, before dropping back to less than 20 per cent thereafter as a result of successive rounds of budgetary cutbacks. This flexibility reflected the government's unwillingness to commit food aid expenditures for more than a year in advance. Williams and Young commented: "It is difficult to imagine food aid reaching its potential contribution to short-term food security when political considerations may dictate reductions just at a time when need is increasing."[117]

Reductions satisfied many in the NGO community, however, where support for food aid at the time of the 1974 World Food Conference had given way to mounting scepticism about its potentially harmful impact on local production and consumption patterns. CCIC's 1979 policy paper called for a complete phasing out of food aid, except for emergencies.[118]

Other Channels

Increasingly anxious to generate greater domestic commercial returns from tied bilateral aid, Liberal and Conservative trade ministers alike urged a reduction in multilateral contributions down at least to the level of 30 per cent or so specified in the strategy for 1975-80.[119] The Hatch report was especially dismissive of multilateral aid, complaining of inadequate returns to Canadian firms and recommending drastic cuts both in support levels and the number of assisted agencies.[120] Determination at the political level to scale down future multilateral commitments was apparent in negotiations during 1979 to replenish the soft loan funds of the International Development Association of the World Bank in the early 1980s. For the first time, Canada opted for a lower share, pledging a contribution level of 4.30 per cent to the sixth replenishment of IDA, down from the 5.83 per cent provided for the fifth.[121]

While the share of multilateral ODA was thus projected to decline in the 1980s, it actually fell only marginally. With high inflation, the real value of multilateral contributions dropped as current dollar levels rose from $422.1 million in 1976-77 to $493.4 million in 1979-80, but the overall share went down only from 43.2 per cent to 40.3 per cent.[122] As mentioned earlier, prior commitments to UN agencies and the international development banks ensured that much of the budget-cutting in the late 1970s came at the expense of bilateral programming.

After a period when the multilateral channel was viewed in CIDA as little more than a safety valve for instant disbursement, the policy and programming capabilities of Multilateral Branch were strengthened under a new vice-president appointed in 1978—Margaret Catley-Carlson, a future CIDA president.[123]

Rapid growth in the NGO Program. CIDA doubled current dollar funding for NGOs from $42.2 million in 1976-77 to $77.5 million in 1979-80.[124] Although the rate of increase was moderated during the cutback years, both Dupuy and MacDonald supported continued growth even as total ODA stagnated. An appreciation of the particular effectiveness of NGOs in mounting grass-roots, basic needs-oriented projects was an important factor, especially in the context of sluggish movement in that direction within the bilateral program. Another was the desire to strengthen the domestic development constituency at a time when aid was slipping in the government's priorities and in public support. As funding grew for the Public Participation Program, the voluntary sector continued to voice strong criticism of CIDA in a "love-hate" relationship founded on a mutual concern to promote an expanding aid program.[125]

The universities and a new program in institutional cooperation.[126] Canadian universities had participated in bilateral projects since the 1950s and had occasionally obtained funding from NGO Division to support their international activities. However, the matching grant approach to NGO funding did not suit their situation. Nor were there satisfactory mechanisms for consultation with CIDA. A new program in "institutional cooperation" represented the culmination of a lengthy and often frustrating process to find both an appropriate responsive mechanism for funding initiatives from the universities and a means of strengthening the Agency's liaison with them.

Attempts to develop more effective cooperation went back several years. In 1968, the Association of Universities and Colleges of Canada (AUCC), under contract with CIDA, commissioned Professor Norma Walmsley, a political scientist (and later the founder of Match International), to survey the international activities of Canadian universities. Her report, published in 1970, recommended establishment of an interuniversity council that would coordinate the involvement of the universities in international development and encourage them to establish linkages with Third World institutions. The proposal secured support neither from AUCC, which saw it as too ambitious, nor from CIDA, which feared a loss of control.

Professors Gerald Helleiner and Cranford Pratt did a subsequent report for CIDA and a number of consultations and workshops were held over the next few years. These efforts yielded a Higher Education Cooperation Plan in September 1974 that foresaw collaboration among CIDA, IDRC, the universities, and other higher education institutions to strengthen research capabilities, institutions, and facilities in developing countries. A provisional advisory council was set up to advise CIDA on proposals for university participation in projects within existing program channels. The process soon foundered, however, because it was difficult to reconcile the criteria with norms prevailing in Bilateral and Special Programs branches.

In 1977, Michael Oliver, president of Carleton University, chaired a committee that drew up a proposal based closely on Walmsley's. Oliver's group recommended that the provisional body be reconstituted as a Council for Cooperation in Higher Education with a full-time secretariat. Advisory to

CIDA on university involvement in bilateral projects, the council would have its own funds to allocate in response to proposals from Canada or abroad for Canadian-developing country university linkages.

While CIDA and IDRC balked at the notion of setting up what would have been a new ODA institution operating at arm's length, both liked the idea of a small secretariat within AUCC that would play a coordinating and information disseminating role. Oliver became the first director of AUCC's International Development Office (IDO) when it was established with funding from CIDA and IDRC in 1978. That same year, a new Educational Institutions Program (EIP) to promote university linkages was set up in NGO Division.

The creation of IDO stimulated fresh thinking in the Special Programs Branch of CIDA about how to foster and fund longer-term linkages involving not just the universities, but also community colleges, the cooperative movement, trade unions, and professional associations. Responsibility for all of these, supported by new eligibility criteria approved by Treasury Board, was transferred to a new Institutional Cooperation and Development Services (ICDS) Division in April 1980. CUSO, WUSC, and volunteer-sending programs were also put under the development services wing of the new division, leaving a reconstituted NGO Division with responsibility for project-oriented NGOs that operated on a matching-funds basis.[127] The move was initially greeted with suspicion by many in the NGO community, who feared a loss of resources and diminished access to CIDA; however, as we shall see, there would soon be rapidly expanding opportunities for NGO programming, both conventional and new, as well as for institutional cooperation.

Business and industry: An ambitious new program in industrial cooperation. The goals of broadening business support for the aid program and expanding the involvement of the Canadian private sector in developing countries underpinned the other major initiative in Special Programs—the creation in September 1978 of a program in Industrial Cooperation (INC) to replace the old Business and Industry Program.

Based on the experience of the Experimental Program in Industrial Cooperation in 1976, INC accorded well with Dupuy's conception of where the aid program should be moving. It was "designed not only to respond to innovative requests for assistance from developing countries and Canada, but can also initiate activities to promote mutually beneficial linkages." It was targeted more at small and medium-sized businesses than at CIDA's traditional suppliers, thus tapping an enlarged constituency. It was also oriented towards developing longer-term relationships, encouraging "Canadian firms to establish or expand operations in developing countries either through joint ventures or other forms of business cooperation, and to assist developing countries themselves to create an environment conducive to this activity."[128]

The pre-investment starter and feasibility study facilities were transferred to INC, and given higher funding ceilings ($10,000 and $100,000 respectively). The new program was also encouraged to fund travel and other activities that would disseminate information to the Canadian private sector about Third World opportunities and to recipient countries about potential Canadian interests. Equally broad was the authority to provide assistance—unrelated to specific investment projects—for such matters as management training for developing country nationals, language and specialized preparation for Canadians going abroad on business, and institutional linkages for business and industry associations. In addition, provision was made for industrial credits to enable selected developing countries to use Canadian expertise to help strengthen capacities in industrial planning, export marketing, and private-sector development.[129]

Two more programs were added to INC's responsibilities in 1979. First, business resentment about the relatively poor success rate of Canadian firms bidding for multilateral aid contracts—an issue highlighted by the Hatch committee—prompted creation of a Canadian Project Preparation Facility (CPPF) within INC to assist Canadian companies "in obtaining a fairer share of multilaterally funded business."[130] Second, and less Canadian-centred, was a venture begun in 1979 to promote exports to Canada from developing countries. Operated on behalf of CIDA by Canadian Executive Service Overseas (CESO), the Trade Facilitation Office (TFO) had a mandate to work with Canadian importers on behalf of all developing countries, especially "the poorest countries without adequate trade representation in Canada."[131] Potentially of greater developmental value than many INC facilities, TFO remained low-key and insignificant.

Personnel with trade commissioner and private-sector experience were hired to oversee INC, and the program was launched with considerable fanfare and media exposure, especially in the business press. Spending rose rapidly, from $250,000 in the last year of the old program, to $460,000 in 1978-79, $3.95 million in 1979-80 and $7.21 million in 1980-81.[132]

Mixed Results in Improving the Public Image

The initial press reports about Dupuy conveyed, as he wished, the image of a "no-nonsense" bureaucrat determined to overcome CIDA's managerial weaknesses.[133] However, hopes that a change in the presidency would overcome negative perceptions of the aid program were only partially realized. During Dupuy's first few weeks in office, the media continued to look to CIDA for sensational copy. The *Toronto Sun* carried a "CIDA dossier" of horror stories shortly after Dupuy's appointment.[134] A few months later, following CIDA's rebuttal of an article in the *New York Times Magazine*, the *Ottawa Citizen* gave an account of the exchange under the headline "CIDA denies giving 500 cattle for barbecue to Amin."[135]

Gradually, the frequency of this sort of publicity diminished, and CIDA ceased to be the hot issue that it was during the last half of Gérin-Lajoie's presidency. However, allegations of waste and ineptitude still dogged the Agency from time to time. Some came from recycled versions of the old horror stories,[136] which lived on for years, but some were new. A CTV *W5* documentary in October 1979 showed broken-down Canadian forklift trucks rusting away at the harbour in Dar es Salaam, Tanzania. The "boat that wouldn't float" came back to haunt the Agency after the Auditor General undertook a comprehensive audit of CIDA during the 1978-79 fiscal year. He reported that an additional $745,000 had been spent from March 1976 to June 1979 "for repairs, modification, equipment, stability tests and hiring of crew, bringing the Agency's total cost for the vessel to $1.4 million." After the Colombian government still refused to accept the boat for use in a CIDA fisheries project, the Crown Assets Disposal Corporation eventually sold the vessel for $133,000.[137]

After all the effort that had gone into overcoming the weaknesses criticized earlier, the Auditor General's comments were discouraging, damning the Agency with faint praise:

> CIDA has recently taken a number of positive steps towards improving its overall management processes, such as establishing the Resources and Comptroller's Branches. However, there still appears to be insufficient recognition or understanding of the importance of financial management and control as a fundamental responsibility of line management. . . . The development of effective financial management and control systems needs to be given *greater priority*.[138]

The report also identified major deficiencies in the management of bilateral projects, expressed concern about lax control over funds entrusted to NGOs, and recommended extensive improvements in food aid delivery, procurement practices, and consultant contract procedures. Recognizing recent improvements, the Auditor General said that more had to be done to strengthen internal systems for evaluation and information feedback. In his formal reply, Dupuy expressed broad agreement with the criticisms and recommendations, gave assurance that remedial measures were under way, but regretted that "I am still not satisfied that the current rate of progress will permit us to introduce all of the improvements we have planned within our set time frame of completion in 1980."[139]

A few critics—notably the *Toronto Sun* and a small right-wing lobby, Citizens for Foreign Aid Reform (C-FAR)—seized on any evidence of waste or mismanagement to undermine the legitimacy of the aid program.[140] Some of the critical media coverage went beyond these issues, however, to raise broader questions about developmental effectiveness. A documentary on CBC's *fifth estate* in April 1978 focused on the implications of procurement tying, the technological bias of bilateral ODA, and the trend towards greater commercialization.[141]

CIDA continued to increase resources for publications, audio-visual aids, and educational materials, although these efforts were subsequently affected by budget cuts.[142] As we have seen, Dupuy took the task of outreach seriously. He worked especially hard to strengthen CIDA's links with the voluntary sector, the universities, and business. However, while his emphasis on how the aid program benefited domestic economic interests undoubtedly reassured CIDA-watchers in the bureaucracy, it provoked strong concern from NGOs, academics, and the small group of internationally minded MPs led by Douglas Roche. In seeking closer relations with CIDA's constituencies, Flora MacDonald upset some of them with her mixed messages.

Meanwhile, the Hatch committee's disdainful dismissal of CIDA demonstrated that Dupuy's courtship of business and the creation of INC had not appreciably increased support in the corporate sector.[143] A *Financial Post* poll of top corporate executives during the 1979-80 election campaign found that 78 per cent of respondents opposed any further increase in the foreign aid budget.[144]

A Gallup poll in June 1978 revealed less support from the public at large for expanding the aid program than in December 1974. On each occasion the following question was put: "Do you think that Canada should or should not increase aid to underdeveloped countries to assist them to become more self-sufficient in the future?" There were more positive than negative responses in both polls, but the spread of 53.3 per cent to 35.0 per cent in 1974 dropped to 44.3 per cent to 42.1 per cent in 1978.[145] While diminished support reflected the tougher times of high inflation and low growth in the late 1970s, CIDA's image problems over this period undoubtedly contributed as well. The 1978 poll was published just before the August budget cuts.

When the Tories came to power a few months later, a *Weekend Magazine* survey revealed that 33 per cent of respondents thought aid expenditures were "too high," compared with 41 per cent "about right" and only 18 per cent "too low." Asked whether they thought Canadian aid was effective, 44 per cent said yes and 31 per cent said no. On procurement tying, the poll found that 61 per cent "think that countries receiving Canadian money should be required to purchase Canadian goods even if they can get a better deal elsewhere."[146]

Assessing the Dupuy Years

Soon after Pierre Trudeau and the Liberals regained power in the February 1980 election, Michel Dupuy was appointed as Canada's ambassador to the United Nations and replaced at CIDA by Marcel Massé. Dupuy's three years had been difficult for the Agency and the aid program. From a developmental standpoint, they were unquestionably a time of retreat. Liberal and Conservative governments both reneged on the commitment to move steadily towards the ODA/GNP ratio of 0.7 per cent. The balance of mixed objectives informing policy and programming tilted more heavily towards the pursuit of commercial and political interests. A greater preoccupation with financial and managerial accountability was unavoidable, but it left less scope for creativity and risk-taking. One long-serving officer commented: "CIDA was like a college in the early '70s with noon-hour seminars, cultural growth, and a lot of intellectual ferment. Then the internal atmosphere changed. It became more like working for the headquarters of a bank—dull and deadly."

The strategy for 1975-80 was a product of that earlier ferment, though tempered by interdepartmental compromises. It remained the official policy framework through the Dupuy years—but, while not ignored, its ethos was out of harmony with the harder national interest perspectives that dominated official thinking about the aid program in the late 1970s. It came more and more to represent an obstacle to get around, rather than a set of guide-posts for action.

The North-South Institute did a "final report card" on the strategy shortly after Dupuy stepped down, judging the government's performance as unsatisfactory ("D") or a failure ("F") on thirteen of the twenty-one points. Among the thirteen were the commitments to comprehensive and organic planning for development cooperation, continued support for international institutions, more focused sectoral priorities, steadily rising volume, heightened geographic concentration, untying for developing country procurement, and (perhaps with less justification) greater involvement of the Canadian community. The only "A" was assigned for ongoing support to IDRC and international research institutes. The priority assigned to the poorest countries and the commitments on food aid were each given a "C."[147]

In contrast, from their vantage point, CIDA's old mentors—External Affairs and IT&C—had reason to be pleased with Dupuy's success in integrating CIDA within the foreign policy apparatus. He did less well, however, in achieving the other imperatives of the Ottawa mandarinate—establishing effective managerial and financial control over the aid program and creating a solidly positive public image for it. In the press, the parting judgements were mixed. John Best of the *Ottawa Journal*, a long-time sceptic, wrote that "Dupuy's major accomplishment was to give CIDA the efficient system of financial management which it had sorely lacked."[148] A few days later, after the Auditor General's Report for 1978-79 was released, an editorial in the same paper pronounced:

> CIDA is in a managerial mess. There are far too many overlapping responsibilities and, in consequence, no clear lines of accountability. The agency spends vastly unjustifiable amounts of money and man-hours on poor accounting practices, on grossly over-staffed public relations programs and ambitiously expensive schemes to complicate simple management functions through computerization.

In the newly appointed Marcel Massé, the editorial concluded, CIDA "possesses its first good administrator in many a year. . . . The agency's top leadership did not take the necessary hard decisions. Mr. Massé, one hopes, will do better."[149]

Chapter 6

Rethinking the Mission, 1980-83

When Marcel Massé became CIDA's fourth president in 1980, he inherited an Agency that was dispirited by retrenchment and mired in organizational infighting. Morale had been sapped as well by CIDA's declining relative autonomy within the bureaucracy and growing displacement of its developmentalist ethos by immediate preoccupations with financial accountability and commercial and foreign policy goals. Parliamentary and media criticisms still frequently projected negative images of Canadian aid. During his brief tenure, Massé sought to confront these problems by challenging the Agency to rethink its mission and many of its policies and practices. In so doing, he attempted to put development back at centre stage in CIDA, though in ways that were pragmatically attuned to political and organizational constraints.

Massé also enjoyed the prospect of substantially increased resources following a decision to reverse the downward slide of Canada's ODA/GNP ratio. The key factor was Pierre Trudeau's return to power in the federal election of February 1980. Heeding a plea to support recommendations of the Brandt Commission on International Development Issues, Trudeau was determined to free some time from constitutional and other domestic concerns to play a leadership role in revitalizing global negotiations between North and South. After a Parliamentary Task Force on North-South Relations, chaired by Herb Breau, argued that an increased ODA budget was essential for a credible prime ministerial initiative, the cabinet agreed to restore progress towards the 0.7 per cent target.

In its final report, the task force called for a constructive response to the aspirations of the South, including a more developmentally oriented aid program. The aftermath was less positive: the government's actions fell well short of Breau's recommendations, and Canada's ODA growth was curtailed during the recession of 1982-83. Trudeau's own North-South initiative faltered in the face of intransigent opposition from the US and Britain. Meanwhile, the parliamentary non-partisanship that characterized the work of the

---

Notes to Chapter 6 are on pp. 507-17.

task force gave way to bitter divisions over human rights and Canadian policy in the Americas when a Commons committee undertook a review of Canada's relations with Latin America and the Caribbean.

Within CIDA, there was a renaissance of sorts. Massé exposed senior and middle managers to trends and debates within development discourse. He himself expressed a strong preference for reorienting ODA away from mega-projects towards the human dimension of change, and pushed CIDA to develop more sharply focused sectoral emphases and country eligibility criteria. Government decisions added more core countries, offering opportunities for new forms of aid relations. The higher priority on rapid-growth economies continued, but more emphasis was put on fostering longer-term relationships rather than immediate export promotion.

Tackling persistent organizational problems, the new president tried to develop more coherent programming for major recipients through an approach aimed at achieving an Agency-wide country focus. Efforts begun under Dupuy to improve management systems made progress with the assistance of two able senior vice-presidents, first Margaret Catley-Carlson and then Bill McWhinney. Externally, Massé worked to strengthen CIDA within the Ottawa bureaucracy and to increase its control over the ODA budget. Two new small agencies received shares of that budget—Petro-Canada International Assistance Corporation (PCIAC) and the International Centre for Ocean Development (ICOD).

CIDA was still dogged under Massé by bad press about failed projects abroad and at home. Some NGOs and academics remained critical of tendencies for commercial and foreign policy objectives to override developmental imperatives, and several commentators lamented the absence of a new strategy to replace Gérin-Lajoie's 1975 document.

Efforts to Revive North-South Dialogue

Before examining CIDA during the Massé presidency, it is useful to look at broader efforts, both international and Canadian, to break the impasse in North-South talks and push international development higher up the public policy agenda in the industrial world.

At the Global Level: The Brandt Commission

Nearing the end of his time as president of the World Bank, Robert McNamara looked to a panel of distinguished world citizens once more, this time hoping to counter aid fatigue and get global negotiations back on the rails. Willy Brandt, the former West German chancellor, agreed to chair an Independent Commission on International Development Issues with carefully balanced representation from the North and the South. (Joe Morris, president-emeritus of the Canadian Labour Congress, was the one member from Canada.)

The Commission's report, *North-South: A Programme for Survival*, was published in 1980. Like Pearson a decade earlier, Brandt appealed to international morality as a source of strengthened political will, but based the case as well on claims of mutual interests:[1]

> The North-South debate is often described as if the rich were being asked to make sacrifices in response to the demands of the poor. We reject this view. The world is now a fragile and interlocking system, whether for its people, its ecology or its resources. Many individual societies have settled their inner conflicts by accommodation, to protect the weak and to promote principles of justice, becoming strong as a result. The World too can become stronger by becoming a just and humane society. If it fails in this, it will move towards its own destruction.[2]

Reflecting the upheavals of the 1970s, Brandt was more pessimistic than Pearson. The call for action, though, was more sweeping, seeking common ground on much of the NIEO agenda and urging "massive" new resource transfers to reduce international income equalities. Industrialized countries were urged once more to achieve the ODA/GNP target of 0.7 per cent, now by 1985, and 1 per cent by 2000. A plea was made to place development finance on a more predictable and long-term basis, preferably through some form of universal progressive taxation, along with levies on international trade, arms production or export, and the global commons, especially seabed minerals.

The Brandt report also called for increased lending by multilateral development banks, and consideration of a world development fund, with decision-making more evenly shared between developed and developing countries than in existing institutions. It also proposed a summit of world leaders to break the North-South deadlock and launch an emergency program for 1980-85.[3]

The Parliamentary Task Force on North-South Relations

One of several policy-oriented House of Commons task forces set up by the new Liberal government in 1980, the Parliamentary Task Force on North-South Relations was part of Trudeau's campaign to persuade other Western governments to take the North-South dialogue and Brandt seriously. The task force was asked to examine relationships between developed and developing countries in the areas of food, energy, trade, balance of payments, "development issues, including official development assistance and assistance to the most poor," and other matters under negotiation in international fora.[4] There were clear expectations that it would raise the public profile of North-South issues in Canada, and court domestic political support for Trudeau's initiative.

Though broadly focused on all aspects of Canada's relations with developing countries, the task force provided the first opportunity for a major parliamentary review of Canadian ODA since the Lachance subcommittee in 1970-71.[5] Herb Breau, Liberal MP for the New Brunswick riding of Gloucester, accepted an invitation from the Prime Minister's Office to chair the task force of seven. The Conservatives named Douglas Roche as vice-chairman; another key member was Father Bob Ogle of the NDP, who, after years of service in Brazil, was a strong exponent of liberation theology. They took on their work with great energy and determination.

An interim report and aid volume. Established in May 1980, the task force held public hearings almost immediately with witnesses from government, the NGO community, and business. Mindful of the upcoming special session of the United Nations on global negotiations in August, Breau and his colleagues prepared an interim report at the end of July. It supported action along the lines advocated by Brandt, and offered two conclusions about public outreach in Canada: first, that "public understanding and support is both lacking in this country and essential to any real progress" and, secondly, that the required educational effort should emphasize positive accomplishments and advantages of development cooperation rather than "fears and threats."

The main focus of the interim report was on slippage in Canada's ODA/GNP ratio since the mid-1970s. "This has occurred despite declared Government policy to achieve the official United Nations target of 0.7 per cent of GNP and to move towards this target by annual increases in the proportion of Official Development Assistance to GNP."[6] The text recognized the "tight fiscal position of the federal government" and "the difficult task of reconciling the many competing demands of Canadians on resources," but asserted that

> there are compelling arguments for keeping our commitments. Canada has a long tradition of dedication to development cooperation and we have built up a good reputation in developing countries. If we do not live up to our many pledges to move towards the 0.7 per cent target, we will seriously weaken our dedication and damage our reputation.

With strong support from Mark MacGuigan, the new secretary of state for External Affairs, and knowing that the prime minister and Allan MacEachen (now finance minister) were sympathetic, the interim report recommended "immediate steps to prevent any further decline in the share of our GNP which goes to ODA and begin once more to move towards the 0.7 per cent target."

MacGuigan, scheduled to address the UN General Assembly on August 26, hoped to use the occasion to renew Canada's pledge to 0.7. There was still no agreement in cabinet, however, and he ended up saying merely that the Canadian government would "make every effort to ensure that important North-South problems are given greater attention and urgent consideration internationally."[7] The *Ottawa Citizen* accused the minister of empty rhetoric.[8] Shortly thereafter, despite reservations on fiscal grounds, the Cabinet Committee on Planning and Priorities agreed to renew the pledge to the UN target.[9] MacGuigan returned to the General Assembly on September 15, 1980 to make a brief statement: "We shall now move upwards once again and our ODA will reach a level of 0.5 per cent of GNP by the middle of the decade. Our intention thereafter is to accept the need to reach an ODA level of 0.7 per cent of GNP by the end of the decade and we shall employ all our best efforts to reach this objective."[10]

Media reaction was generally positive, though critical that progress towards the target would be so slow. Columnist John Best sounded a note of caution:

> At a time of high unemployment, minor or only very sluggish economic growth and surging inflation at home, increasing numbers of Canadians may feel that this country should solve its own problems before worrying about solving others. Already you can hear such refrains. And cabinet ministers, politicians all, will be tempted to heed them. External affairs ministers have fought such battles before, and lost.[11]

The final report. The desire to broaden public support for increased aid and other policy initiatives remained a major preoccupation of the task force. At Roche's urging, the first recommendation of its December 1980 final report called on the government to allocate 1 per cent of the ODA budget "to encourage the awareness and involvement of Canadians in North-South concerns" by channelling resources through existing private organizations and fostering creation of new ones. The government was urged as well to exercise more candour and openness about the successes and failures of development.[12]

Greater popular support was cited as one of three requirements for a more prominent Canadian role as a bridge-builder between North and South. The others were an integrated and comprehensive public policy for international cooperation (something the North-South Institute urged be in place by the spring of 1981 at the latest),[13] and a mandate for Parliament to oversee North-South issues on a continuing basis. To accomplish the latter, the task force recommended setting up a permanent standing committee on North-South relations.[14]

Generally speaking, the task force responded sympathetically to developing country concerns about trade and other matters, and to positions advocated by NGOs and others in the Canadian development community. It devoted particular attention to the mixed objectives of development assistance. During testimony, CIDA's then acting president, Margaret Catley-Carlson, had highlighted the issue in responding to a question about the effectiveness of Canadian aid:

> Effective as what? As a foreign policy tool? As a tool to transform an economy? As a tool to promote markets for Canadian commodities? As a transfer mechanism to the poorest countries or as a transfer mechanism to the poorest people?—not the same thing. As a means to increase food production? As a tool to put their productive sector in touch with ours? As a means of transforming regimes and social structures in developing countries?[15]

The task force expressed unhappiness about the multiplicity of often contradictory expectations imposed on ODA:

> The concept of development assistance is hardly thirty years old. The reasons given for it have been many and varied. Some have argued that it is a way to promote trade. Others have seen it as a means to win friends and frustrate adversaries. Still others want aid to promote their particular concerns or values in developing countries. We think it is time to say simply that *aid is to aid*. Its purpose is to promote human and economic development and to alleviate suffering.

A homely analogy to barn-raising developed the position further:

> Lacking some of the skills, tools and materials to build a barn, a farmer calls on his friends to assist him. . . . Each neighbour helps, is personally involved in the project and contributes what he or she has to give. This help is an act of solidarity. No doubt it may in the future allow the neighbours to ask for help in return. Their involvement in the project gives them some influence on the way it is carried out. . . . But their *reason* for helping is not principally self-interest, nor a desire to wield influence, nor the opportunity to unload their own possessions. It is the simple desire to help.

Similarly, "Canada should give [ODA] because it is needed, because it is right to help and because it has, despite all the problems during the last three decades, produced positive economic and social change in developing countries."[16]

Breau urged government to "reaffirm and strengthen" the basic human needs of the poorest people in developing countries as *the* central objective of Canadian ODA, and to uphold the priority on assisting the poorest countries. "We reject suggestions that an increased share of aid should go to other countries because they offer more promising markets for Canadian goods and services."[17]

While a majority on the task force rejected the fully blown critique of tied aid advanced by CCIC and others, the report did argue that "decisions concerning procurement of goods and services required for aid projects should be made . . . consistent with development assistance objectives." It regretted that CIDA had not made full use of its current untying authority, especially in view of the requirement of basic needs programming for more funds to meet local costs. The government was urged to free the Agency from the 80 per cent tying rule.[18]

Witnesses from Industry, Trade and Commerce and the private sector urged greater use of aid funds for export promotion, especially for mixed credit and parallel financing with the Export Development Corporation.[19] In response, the Breau report expressed unequivocal opposition: "The use of Official Development Assistance as part of export promotion is not acceptable."[20]

On other aid-related issues, the task force welcomed the decision to increase the ODA/GNP ratio and emphasized the importance of linking volume to national income as a means of discouraging future slippage.[21] It called on the government to achieve 0.57 per cent—above the previous high point in 1975—rather than just 0.5 per cent by 1985.[22] The report favoured greater concentration in fewer countries as one means of making aid more effective, a strengthened field administration as another, and a return to the practice of carrying funds forward as yet another. Higher levels of support for IDRC and emergency humanitarian assistance were proposed as well.[23]

A detailed chapter on food aid argued a thoughtful case for using non-emergency assistance as a temporary expedient in support of measures to promote food self-sufficiency.[24] The report also called on industrialized countries to achieve energy conservation themselves, as they promoted energy self-sufficiency in developing countries, and to assist those most seriously affected by the oil shocks of the previous decade.[25]

Familiar claims were recited about the respective advantages and disadvantages of bilateral and multilateral channels; rather than recommending a fixed ratio between them, the task force suggested that both share in the real growth of ODA, with proportions determined by how best to meet basic human needs of the poorest. Praising the work of NGOs in this respect, the report recommended increasing their share of the aid budget and directing their way bilateral funding for small projects in agriculture, health, and rural development. The support for NGOs and a plea to strengthen women's basic education and development skills[26] were the two major shifts in policy discourse not anticipated in the strategy for 1975-80.

The official response. The Breau report was well timed to support the prime minister's initiative to increase the attention paid internationally to North-South issues. Trudeau held talks in Middle Eastern, African, and Latin American capitals late in 1980 and early in 1981 in preparation for a number of key conferences: the G7 summit in Canada in July 1981, the Commonwealth Conference in Melbourne in October, and then—in response to the Brandt report—a meeting of heads or state and government from North and South in Cancún, Mexico, also in October. Amid this flurry of activity, Roche complained about the lack of an official response to the recommendations of the task force and an opportunity to discuss them in the House of Commons.[27] His own Tory party, however, turned down an arrangement whereby each of the Liberals, Conservatives, and NDP would give time to permit a three-day debate on the North-South dialogue and foreign policy.[28] In the event, there was only a one-day debate—on June 15—when the government also tabled its reply to the task force.

The response lauded the task force for increasing public awareness, generating all-party support for a distinctive Canadian role in the North-South dialogue, and producing constructive policy proposals. It voiced general approval for most of the recommendations—but in flat, bureaucratic prose with much hedging and caution on specifics. The recommendation to spend 1 per cent of ODA on development awareness in Canada yielded only a promise to make outreach a higher priority. The government agreed that greater country concentration would be desirable, as would expanded participation of NGOs in bilateral programming. It promised as well to increase resources for NGOs, IDRC, and emergency assistance. With some reservations, it also endorsed the task force's approach to food and energy.

The response did not address the proposition that "aid is to aid," and the satisfaction of basic human needs became "one of the central thrusts" rather than "the central objective" of the aid program. The question of accelerating movement towards the UN volume target merited only a study. The government denied that existing procurement regulations had been a major developmental constraint. It promised to review the question of non-lapsing funds. It also hinted that multilateral aid might not grow as rapidly as bilateral.[29]

The ensuing parliamentary debate focused more on issues of security and arms control than on international development, although the prime minister reiterated his government's commitment to North-South reform.[30] The task force report, when mentioned, was cast in a positive light, but only Roche devoted detailed attention to it. He criticized the weak responses to many recommendations, especially the failure to pledge 1 per cent of ODA for public outreach. He also regretted that the response neither outlined a new international development strategy, nor made a commitment to develop one.[31]

The Subcommittee on Canada's Relations with Latin America and the Caribbean

While no action was taken to create a standing committee of the House on North-South relations, another parliamentary study was launched in March 1981 when a subcommittee of the Standing Committee on External Affairs and Defence was established to examine Canada's relations with Latin America and the Caribbean. The chairman was Maurice Dupras, who had previously chaired the Subcommittee on International Development in the mid-1970s.

Within church and NGO circles, attention was increasingly focused on human rights abuses and refugees fleeing civil strife in the countries of the southern cone and Central America. Meanwhile, trade officials and some business firms saw new opportunities for Canadian exports and investment, especially in high-growth economies such as Brazil, Venezuela, and Mexico. Concerns about regional security were growing as well, especially after Ronald Reagan escalated Cold War confrontation in Central America and the Caribbean.

The government hoped that the subcommittee would focus on trade,[32] but Roche, Ogle, and some other members (including Flora MacDonald) were more interested in human rights and the politics of development. The subcommittee commissioned two academic studies that reflected these concerns,[33] and an interim report issued in December 1981, while not directly critical of American policy, put forward a perspective on regional conflict at variance with the Reaganite view:

> The evolution of political, economic and social structures in these regions arises from the legitimate human desire to improve living conditions and to achieve justice. Any attempt, therefore, to characterize the process as derived essentially from an alien ideology should be resisted. Moreover, social change in these countries will evolve from a wide range of development models. . . . Canada should recognize and support such pluralism in Latin America and the Caribbean.[34]

The interim report also stressed that internal reforms "must be complemented by changes in the international system where too often economic forces cripple the development process."[35] On ODA, the subcommittee agreed with the task force that the central objective of the aid program "should be to improve the lives of the poorest people and the prospects of the poorest countries. . . . [Other] important Canadian interests, such as trade, should not be allowed to dilute or interfere with this basic commitment." Support was voiced for concentrating ODA in the lower-income countries in the Caribbean and Central America, and for building a special development relationship with the Commonwealth Caribbean.[36]

Though approved unanimously by the parent standing committee, the interim report provoked strong negative reaction among right-wingers in the Tory caucus who disliked the emphasis on human rights and development rather than trade, the implicit critique of American policy, and a call for increased aid for Nicaragua's Sandinista regime. After four members of the subcommittee (including MacDonald) returned from a brief visit to El Salvador early in 1982, and supported the Liberal government's decision not to provide observers for that country's somewhat suspect elections, Conservative MPs Sinclair Stevens and Robert Wenman themselves travelled there as unofficial observers. Conveying positive impressions upon their return, they shouted down a request in the House for an extension of the subcommittee's mandate. The extension was granted, however, after Roche agreed to give up his membership to Stevens.[37]

The subcommittee produced three more reports: one on Central America and the Caribbean in July 1982, another on South America in November 1982, and a final submission also in November. The proceedings, both open and closed, were marked by acrimony, and the language of the reports was hotly contested. Stevens and five other Tory MPs insisted on a formal dissenting opinion in the July report, and no less than five minority opinions were appended to the final report.[38] Debates swirled around the issues mentioned above, with positions based largely on whether members accepted the majority view that regional problems were mainly rooted in poverty and underdevelopment, or a minority perspective that saw them chiefly as a reflection of struggle between the free world and communist totalitarianism.

As far as the aid program was concerned, contending positions were staked out on human rights and country eligibility, with the majority endorsing the anti-poverty, basic human needs orientation of the interim report. Strong support was voiced for Canadian and international NGOs that provided direct help to the poorest.[39] The July report also urged the government to increase the share of aid funds administered by field staff, and to make greater use of local personnel and products in recipient countries.[40]

The government's response to the final report was tardy and uninspiring; it contained little of significance for ODA policy apart from discussion of human rights conditionality and the place of the Americas in the aid program (matters to which we shall return).[41]

Trudeau's Initiative Ends with the Collapse of North-South Negotiations

Brandt had launched his appeal for a global Keynesian approach to international development just as Margaret Thatcher and Ronald Reagan came to power in their respective countries determined to bury the legacy of Keynes in their domestic economies. Both leaders agreed reluctantly to attend the twenty-two-nation summit on Cooperation and Development in Cancún in October 1981. Co-chaired by Trudeau and Mexican President Lopez-Portillo, the meeting quickly degenerated into a futile exchange of positions. The North-South dialogue then faded into scarcely audible whispers after Mexico announced in August of the following year that it could not meet payments on its foreign debt. While the developing countries had up to that point overestimated their bargaining strength, any hope for a New International Economic Order evaporated "in the wake of the worst global recession in fifty years, the collapse of oil and other commodity prices, an enormous debt overhang in Africa and Latin America, growing trade protectionism among governments in the North, and, within many of the latter, a neo-conservatism interested in international development only if state interventionism yields to the 'magic of the marketplace.' "[42]

Canadian politicians were now preoccupied with recession at home. The Brandt Commission visited Ottawa in December 1982 prior to releasing a follow-up report, *The Common Crisis*. It received a "cool reception" from the prime minister, who was quoted as saying he was not prepared to give "Mr. Brandt or any other organization a blank cheque on the future."[43]

Marcel Massé as CIDA President

Meanwhile, back in March 1980, Marcel Massé came to CIDA with an impressive track record. A Rhodes scholar with arts and law degrees from McGill and Montreal, a diploma in international law from the University of Warsaw, and an Oxford B.Phil., he had had a formative Third World experience as a Crossroads Canada volunteer in Senegal. It was there he met Josée M'Baye, who became his wife. After briefly practising law, he spent almost four years in the Administration and Economics Division of the World Bank (from 1967 to 1971). He continued his public service career in Ottawa as an economic adviser in the Privy Council Office (PCO), and in New Brunswick, where he rose to the position of chairman of the Cabinet Secretariat under Premier Richard Hatfield.

Returning to the PCO in 1977, he was chosen two years later by Joe Clark to replace Michael Pitfield as secretary to cabinet and clerk of the Privy Council. Massé was just thirty-eight when he became Canada's top public servant. The opportunity was short-lived, however, as Pitfield was brought back following Pierre Trudeau's reelection. Massé accepted the prime minister's offer of the CIDA presidency, happy to resume his involvement in international development. Michel Dupuy was shifted to New York as Canada's ambassador to the United Nations.[44]

A former senior colleague observed: "For the first time in the history of CIDA, we had a president who by virtue of his background and own life was singularly equipped to be head of a development agency." Within the Agency, Massé's presidency was seen in retrospect as a second "golden age," a period when morale soared, programming and organizational capacities grew stronger, and much of the enthusiasm of earlier times was rekindled. One respondent commented: Massé "broke the image of management as bean-counting by getting us to think in broader and more imaginative ways." He was especially admired for his intellectual curiosity and analytical prowess. Another colleague recalled:

> Marcel introduced a much "colder" analysis of development, not discarding humanitarianism but bringing in the approach of a surgeon vis-à-vis cancer. He was more systematic about development issues, and a lot more strategic in looking at what was feasible rather than believing in our dreams. . . . I would say that Marcel brought us renewed belief in what we were doing. . . . [He] certainly improved our image in town and across Canada.

Assessments outside the bureaucracy were not invariably positive. One external critic appreciated Massé's efforts to create an overarching intellectual framework for aid policy, but thought that the outcome was too diffuse and open-ended to be of much practical use. Within the NGO community, Massé was seen as too pro-business and some of his initiatives were viewed with suspicion.

A common source of regret in CIDA was that Massé's term as president was so short. He served only thirty-one months (five fewer than Dupuy) before being transferred to External Affairs in October 1982. Effectively, his tenure was even shorter because he took sick leave for several months in 1980 while recovering from a complicated appendectomy. (Though absent from his duties during this time, he spent his convalescence updating his knowledge of development literature.)

Massé's Vision

Massé returned to full-time development work in 1980 more uncertain about the task than during his World Bank days. Then, the way ahead appeared to be through capital investment and straightforward technology transfer.[45] However, he said, "too much emphasis was put on capital and physical resources and too little priority given to the human element."[46] Speaking early in 1981, Massé affirmed his support for the reorientation—in both the Bank and CIDA—towards basic human needs:

> [We] have come to understand development not only as building an economic infrastructure, but as being part of, and influencing, the social evolution of a whole people. Understood in this way, development involves the organization of the society, its human relations, its beliefs, attitudes, standards, division of responsibilities, awarding of privileges, its social values and the means by which the society protects and perpetuates these.[47]

The change in understanding, he continued, "is now leading us to what I will call for lack of better words 'the cultural model' . . . [Within] this model, in order to foster proper development, we must first start by understanding people." Economic growth must now "be judged in terms of its contribution to the adaptation of a group of people to their total environment, rather than as a value in itself."[48] On another occasion, Massé suggested that "We are slowly moving from the era of the economist to the era of the sociologist, the person who asks the deeper question—what do these people in the developing world really want, and what do their cultures need?"[49]

Massé promoted the cultural model in part because, as he said, he had an operational objective:

> My "model of development" was still vague and uncertain because it was a way of looking at development rather than a definition of development. What I was trying to inculcate in terms of motivating our project and development people was that they first had to make the effort to understand who they were trying to serve and what these people wanted.[50]

Getting people to ask fundamental questions about the nature of their work was the basic goal during three-week "search conferences" held at Mont Ste-Marie, first for senior managers and later for country program directors. Participants were exposed to management training techniques and to dynamic and controversial speakers who addressed development issues from across the ideological spectrum. Brainstorming about the future and scenario-building were used to highlight changing patterns in North-South relations, shifts in international production and trade, growing differentiation among developing countries, and the significance of non-economic factors in development. According to Massé, the sessions were designed to "blow up people's minds, not to teach them the truth," and to give them "a way in which they see their day-to-day actions relating to goals they believe in."[51]

A close observer characterized these seminars sceptically as "pleasant sabbaticals." People who shared the experiences, however, saw them as formative for themselves and the organization. Whether or not the search conferences had a substantive impact upon the CIDA's approach to development, they were effective in building morale, organizational self-confidence, and a renewed sense of mission.

Policy Development within CIDA

The search conferences were one means of tackling what Massé perceived as a policy vacuum within the Agency. The period covered by the strategy for 1975-80 was coming to an end, and, as we have seen, that document had not served as an effective guide to action. Its broad goals co-existed uneasily with the government's heightened emphasis on Canadian interests and there was growing uncertainty about priorities in terms of sectors, country eligibility, and delivery channels. CIDA's own efforts to craft a new approach for the 1980s had been superseded first by more active involvement in policy issues by External Affairs and other departments, then by preparations for the Clark/MacDonald foreign policy review. The notion that a revised aid strategy might emerge from that review died with the change of government.

Initiating an internal review of all aspects of policy, Massé wanted to reconcile the concerns of the parliamentary task force with the government's foreign policy and commercial priorities, and to establish clearer operational guidelines he could defend as developmental. The exercise culminated in a policy paper for cabinet, which, once approved, became the basis for the "Agency Programming Framework (APF)." It was distributed within CIDA in December 1981. The document set out "the following general principles . . . to guide ODA programming in the 1980's":[52]

a) real growth in funding for country-to-country programming;
b) concentration of bilateral assistance on a smaller number of countries;
c) concentration of *up to* 80 per cent of country-to-country assistance on lower income countries with 1978 annual per capita incomes below $625;
d) allocation of *at least* 20 per cent of country-to-country assistance to middle-income countries with which Canada wishes to strengthen long-term political and economic ties;
e) greater integration of all aid channels in pursuit of defined country objectives, in order to improve the effectiveness of development assistance;
f) concentration of country-to-country programming in three broadly defined priority areas of agriculture and food production, energy, and human resource development;
g) establishment of a higher priority upon non-governmental participation in development cooperation;
h) maintenance of a level of participation in multilateral organizations that "is commensurate with our international responsibilities and with their effectiveness as development instruments" and that is sufficient to permit an active presence in key institutions;
i) increased support for International Humanitarian Assistance, aimed at making recipients more self-reliant in coping with natural and "man-made" disasters;
j) continuation as an active food aid donor; and

k) increased funding for improving research capabilities in developing countries.

The APF also included a new "Aid Eligibility Framework," an elaboration of how country focus programming was intended to work, five-year indicative planning figures for major recipients, and a detailed discussion of the three sectoral priorities (all discussed below).

While phrased in general terms, the document pulled together operating principles and signalled a sharper focus on key questions. There was to be more clarity about the status of recipient countries and an attempt to achieve greater concentration in fewer of them. Low-income countries would continue to receive the bulk of Canadian ODA, but a higher share would be available for building long-term relationships with selected middle-income countries. An emphasis on government-to-government aid would give way to a more integrated country-to-country approach, with the Canadian non-governmental sector playing a greater role. Human resource development would be emphasized and designated—along with agriculture and food production, and energy as sectoral priorities—replacing the longer and less-focused list in the strategy for 1975-80. The message was that systematic planning should replace ad hocery in country programming. Nuanced in the document (and subsequently confirmed) was a decision to reduce multilateral aid as a proportion of total ODA.

Clearer integrated guidelines within the Agency were not accompanied by such clarity in the government's communications with the public. Though the APF was leaked and given limited circulation by CCIC, it did not become a public document; nor was a new official strategy forthcoming by the end of Massé's tenure. John Tackaberry suggested that repeated postponements stemmed from a concern within CIDA that a new policy paper might become a target for later criticism of the sort that the North-South Institute and others levelled when assessing outcomes of the strategy for 1975-80.[53]

Massé admitted as much in a subsequent interview with the author, but in the form of a critique. Such a formal policy statement, he argued, would give an impression of simplicity not inherent in the business of development, would emphasize unimportant quantitative targets at the expense of important qualitative goals, and would impose limits upon action in the context of rapidly changing circumstances. Far preferable to a formal strategy, in his opinion, was a dynamic process linking policy guidelines and operations through the annual preparation of Indicative Planning Figures (IPFs) for delivery channels and recipient countries, and the development of integrated Country Program Reviews (CPRs).[54]

Organizational Changes under Massé

For Massé, an organizational structure "must be subservient to the long-term objectives you are trying to realize." CIDA in his view needed reorganization to facilitate smaller scale, people-to-people projects and, more broadly, to impose a stronger developmental logic on allocation decisions rather than leaving them to the vagaries of the intra-agency competitive struggle for funds. Speaking to a CIDA-NGO consultation early in 1982, he explained:

> We've got a multilateral vote and a multilateral branch, a bilateral branch and a special programmes branch. Why? Because that's the way they have grown. Now you all know when you organize by function, whoever is in charge is of course convinced that his function and his programmes are the most important ones, and then the fight takes place as to who should get the most money. That is how empires are built.[55]

He now intended to introduce a country focus approach that would start with a specification of program objectives, based on the needs of a particular country, and only then determine the most appropriate channels of intervention. "*In sum*, what 'country focus' entails is a fundamental change in the manner by which the planning process deals with the programs to be adopted. . . . The main focus thus shifts from the concerns of CIDA's various programs to the full scope of needs in each of the developing countries assisted by Canada."[56]

Universities, colleges, other institutions, and occasionally NGOs had been used as executing agencies by Bilateral Branch in the past. As we have seen, the parliamentary task force urged more reliance upon NGOs in particular, a direction that Massé supported because "the NGO projects that have been executed in the last few years—and those that I've seen that are presently being planned—are better instruments to realize . . . development as we now understand it, than almost any other channel of delivery in the agency."[57] Indeed, a significant impetus for country focus was to find a way of channelling more resources to the non-profit sector without, as one participant in the experience put it, "a lot of blood-letting." After the upheavals and cutbacks of the Dupuy era, the bilateral "pipeline" was relatively empty, and NGOs were seen as a crucial means of filling it.

The new organizational approach was to apply to all core countries (and regions in the case of non-core recipients). The key player was the country program director, who worked with a country programming team (including officers familiar with each delivery channel) to prepare a three-year country program review for consideration, amendment, and ultimate approval by the President's Committee.[58] For Massé, the process involved

> some of the best days of my week because these discussions made you discover all kinds of new things. The country program directors would come with plans on which they would have spent tens and tens of hours, on which they would have put together all the knowledge that they could get either personally or through consultants. They'd have to come and check their goals for the country with the goals of the organization. And we'd spend three, four, five hours on a country. By doing it, we refined the goals of the organization and the goals we were seeking in the country.[59]

A pilot experiment with country focus was undertaken in Jamaica and gradually extended to a few other country desks before full implementation in September 1982.

Although the change was more conceptual than structural, it was accompanied by a major reorganization that had its genesis in the Corporate Review of 1977. Bilateral Branch was at last broken down into smaller branches corresponding with the "4As"—Anglophone Africa, Francophone Africa, Asia, and the Americas. Two reporting levels between the president and the project manager were eliminated, and the matrix approach to achieving interaction between the Resource Branch, Comptroller's Branch, and the old bilateral divisions was now extended to interaction with other programming centres in the Agency, especially Special Programs.[60] An area coordination group was set up in Resources Branch to maintain liaison between the 4As.

Country focus subsequently had an impact on the way CIDA operates, especially in terms of projecting country expenditures and encouraging active interbranch consultation. However, the actual experience fell well short of the level of rationality and flexibility sought by Massé. Before long, country focus as a label lost the conceptual content given to it by Massé and was used simply as an adjective to describe projects for which geographic branches employed NGOs, universities, and other institutions as executing agencies. These projects often became a source of intense jurisdictional disputes between Special Programs and the 4As. Such difficulties were in turn compounded by worries about whether NGOs and NGIs could be held as accountable for their performance as private-sector firms, and by complaints of unfair competition from consultants and businesses. As we shall see, country focus also became a bone of contention within much of the voluntary sector.

Managerial reform. Massé's efforts to reorient CIDA programming depended on having reliable management systems in place. The Auditor General's 1979 criticisms led to an exercise initiated by Dupuy "to coordinate the various management initiatives undertaken by the Agency in recent years." Work culminated at the end of 1980 in a plan approved by the Comptroller General for implementation over a four-year period.[61] CIDA confidently reported to DAC that, "When fully in place, the Plan will constitute a coherent and comprehensive mechanism to meet CIDA's needs and priorities with respect to financial management and control systems for the 1980s."[62]

The process of managerial reform up to this point had been focused on financial control and accountability, rather than rapid and effective delivery of aid projects in the field. Indeed, the demands of financial control systems with all of their checks and double-checks were slowing the whole process down. While the simplified reporting structure in the new 4As organization promised to improve the situation, Massé and McWhinney commissioned a major internal review of project approval and implementation processes in 1982. It produced the "Report on More Efficient Project Aid Delivery," or MEPAD report for short. It was sharply critical of the Agency's performance:

> CIDA's ability to respond in a timely fashion to aid requests has become a problem of crisis proportions. The complexities and difficulties associated with project approval are adversely affecting the morale of CIDA officers, . . . productivity . . . and the ability of the agency as a whole to respond effectively. Ultimately, the reputation of the agency both nationally and internationally is affected by this serious problem.[63]

The two to three years taken from the time of project identification to the commencement of work in the field was slower than other donors and "out of keeping with the mandate of CIDA." "[A] number of Posts have pointed out that CIDA is considered by recipient countries as the source of last resort. . . . Canada is often left with the projects which are difficult to undertake, or marginal in effect."[64]

Assuming a substantial increase in the ODA budget through the 1980s but little growth in staff, the report made forty-eight proposals for improving aid delivery. These included greater use of less labour-intensive transfer instruments such as lines of credit, rearrangement of the project cycle so that activities could take place simultaneously rather than sequentially, improved personnel and training practices to reduce staff turnover, use of more consultants in the field to provide monitoring and logistical services, and measures to speed up processes for contracting, consultant selection, and procurement.

MEPAD led to many concrete measures. Perhaps the most significant came in response to a recommendation that each project should be implemented by a single outside executing agency. "Thus CIDA Officers will manage managers rather than the details of a project, although they will still monitor all projects at an appropriate level of detail."[65] There had already been considerable movement in this direction, but from now on the practice of contracting out project management was to become the norm. The report side-stepped the question of whether aid effectiveness would be improved by decentralizing to the field greater responsibility for project decision-making.

Such a move had been strongly urged by Suteera Thomson in a much-publicized study for the Science Council of Canada on CIDA's role in agricultural and rural development.[66]

In addition, both the Breau task force and the Subcommittee on Latin America and the Caribbean had pushed for more decentralization. MEPAD did call, however, for improved supervision and evaluation of projects by setting up experimental project-monitoring and evaluation groups in recipient countries. Seen as desirable as a way of easing the workloads of Canadians in diplomatic posts, this measure would also encourage greater use of local personnel and NGOs as executing agencies.[67]

Interdepartmental relations Though playing within the post-Gérin-Lajoie rules of the interdepartmental game, Massé used his skills in bureaucratic politics and his knowledge of the Ottawa scene to restore to CIDA elements of the policy-making authority lost under Dupuy. Questions such as country eligibility remained issues for interdepartmental negotiation, but Massé's forcefulness, his preoccupations with efficiency and transparency, and the reactivation of policy dynamism internally all helped to give CIDA a more central role in shaping policy. ICERDC (the Interdepartmental Committee on Economic Relations with Developing Countries), disbanded during the Tory interregnum, was not reconstituted. Massé sat on the more broadly focused Committee of Deputy Ministers on Foreign and Defence Policy, and CIDA was represented on a number of committees at the assistant deputy level, including one on economic development. Informal processes of interdepartmental consultation also became more common and routine.

CIDA under Massé also gained more effective influence over the entirety of the ODA budget. As clerk of the Privy Council under Prime Minister Clark, Massé had been involved in developing an "envelope" approach to budgetary control, which became the basis of a refined Policy and Expenditure Management System introduced by the Liberal government in 1980. Within this framework, CIDA was designated to play a lead role in preparing annually a five-year strategic overview of ODA.[68] CIDA's previous allocations memoranda had dealt only with the Agency's own budget, while the Department of Finance had independently sought funds for the World Bank. It was the feeling in CIDA that Finance had considerably more clout during the years of cutbacks, and that the Agency's budget had become a residual within the reduced ODA allocation. Now, under the new system, the overall shares for CIDA, the IFIs, IDRC, and other ODA agencies were reconciled within a single plan prepared by CIDA after extensive consultation.

The pendulum swung towards greater control by CIDA of the ODA agenda despite a succession of measures aimed at further integrating various services operating abroad under the authority of the Department of External

Affairs.[69] With Michael Pitfield back at the helm in the Privy Council Office, the Trudeau government endorsed in 1980 a proposal for a consolidated foreign service of senior officers from External Affairs, Industry, Trade and Commerce, Manpower and Immigration, the Canadian Government Office of Tourism, and CIDA. Four career streams were subsequently created: political and economic affairs, development assistance, social affairs, and commercial and economic affairs. Heads of post, drawn from any of these streams, were given authority over all staff, regardless of function, but reported to the respective departments, which initially retained separate operational identities.

In January 1982, the process was taken a step further when the prime minister announced that External Affairs would assume responsibility for trade promotion as well as foreign policy and immigration. The Trade Commissioner Service, along with the trade policy and trade promotion sections of Industry, Trade and Commerce, were incorporated within a revamped Department of External Affairs. As Kim Nossal reported, "Only CIDA was left unscathed by reorganization, although officials hinted that its turn would come."[70]

The Agency was nonetheless affected profoundly. Marcel Massé, whose agenda for reorienting CIDA was just hitting full stride, was named undersecretary of state for External Affairs in October 1982. Expected to overcome the organizational and interpersonal chaos that accompanied the clash of diplomatic and commercial cultures, Massé orchestrated yet another reorganization in External Affairs aimed at making the "shotgun marriage" work. His efforts met with scant appreciation. Leaving External Affairs in 1985 with his reputation for managerial genius tarnished, he was posted to Washington as Canadian executive director at the International Monetary Fund.

Massé left the Agency in the good hands of Bill McWhinney, who served as acting president in 1982-83. A volunteer in Ceylon in the early 1960s, McWhinney served as executive secretary of CUSO from 1962 to 1966,[71] when he became interim executive director of the Company of Young Canadians. After working as a consultant in the External Aid Office, he joined the federal public service, eventually moving to CIDA from Treasury Board. While an excellent manager, his task as an interim appointee was to maintain a holding operation. The Agency waited ten long months for a permanent successor to be named.

New institutions. The Massé era witnessed establishment of two new ODA institutions, the first since IDRC in 1970. Petro-Canada International Assistance Corporation (PCIAC) was conceived by the Liberal government as a component of its National Energy Program in November 1980, after the failure of a Canadian-supported initiative to create an energy affiliate within the

World Bank group. Oil prices were then climbing after the second OPEC oil shock (to what would be record levels, before collapsing) and energy problems within the Third World were once again acute. PCIAC was set up to "act as a direct delivery mechanism for Canadian ODA to assist oil-importing countries to reduce or eliminate their dependence on imported supplies."[72] It was authorized to participate in oil and gas exploration and to provide technical assistance in petroleum exploration, development, and production. The new agency became operational in 1982 as an independently managed subsidiary of Petro-Canada, reporting through the minister of Energy but dependent for funding on the ODA vote.

The International Centre for Ocean Development (ICOD), announced at the Commonwealth Heads of Government Meeting in Melbourne in 1981,[73] was set up following the signature by 119 countries of the UN Convention on the Law of the Sea in December 1982. Based in Halifax with funding from the ODA budget (but reporting through the minister of Fisheries), ICOD was constituted as an independent crown corporation with a mandate to help developing countries build up their indigenous capacities in ocean resource management and utilization, especially for food production. The Centre specialized in research, training, and the exchange of information and expertise.[74]

Program Profile in the Early 1980s

Canada's ODA rose by half a billion dollars from $1,308.1 million[75] in 1980-81 to $1,797.1 million in 1983-84 (the year after Massé's departure as president).[76] But this was a time of high inflation. In constant 1988 $US, the increase was substantially less—from $1,554 million in 1980 to $1,697 million in 1983.[77] Also, even though Canada's GNP fell during the 1982-83 recession (thus suppressing the GNP denominator), the ODA/GNP ratio rose only slightly. Following a DAC decision to allow administrative expenses to count in ODA totals, the ratio for the 1983 calendar year was 0.45 per cent, compared to a recalculation of 0.43 per cent for 1980. (It should be noted that this decision had the effect of inflating ratios by at least .01 per cent).[78] The upward trend reflected the commitment to achieve 0.5 per cent by 1985, but actual growth was modest because CIDA needed time to adjust from retrenchment to renewed expansion. Moreover, planned disbursements were cut by $75 million in 1982-83 and $155 million in 1983-84.[79]

At a ratio of 0.45 per cent in 1983, Canadian ODA contributions remained well above the DAC average, which at 0.36 was slightly below the 1980 level. These shifts were reflected in an increase in Canada's percentage of overall DAC donor flows from 3.94 in 1980 to 5.18 in 1983 (the level of the early 1970s but still below the peak years of 1975 and 1976). In comparative terms, Canada passed the Netherlands in total contributions in 1983, regaining sixth place among DAC donors, but remained in ninth place in GNP ratio (except in 1981 when the standing was eighth). The Netherlands, Norway, and Sweden all exceeded 1.0 per cent of GNP during some of these years, becoming the first DAC members to do so.[80]

Eligibility and Geographical Distribution[81]

Massé's concern to develop coherent principles for Canadian aid was reflected in a new eligibility framework approved by the cabinet in 1981. It was built on old distinctions between program, project, and other recipients but within the broader country focus perspective. Countries were classified as I (Core), II-A (Middle Income Non-Core), II-B (Transitional) and III (Other Eligible):[82]

- Category I: Major recipients of Canadian ODA. Multi-year programming. All aid instruments and delivery channels used.
- Category II-A: Development assistance to middle income countries to strengthen long-term political and commercial links. Selected instruments. Flexible response to opportunities with minimal administrative burden. Broadly defined strategy worked out for each geographic area without multi-year program planning.
- Category II-B: Recipients moving up to core or down to III. Selective instruments; only exceptional use of traditional bilateral approaches.
- Category III: Minimal presence through strictly responsive programming—Mission Administered Funds, Special Program channels, and food aid where appropriate.

The planned shares for the three categories were 75, 20, and 5 per cent respectively. Since program countries as a group had typically received 80 per cent, this guideline foresaw less concentration, presumably to create more space for initiatives in middle-income countries. The list of recipients by category and geographic area is reproduced in Appendix D. The framework also included Categories IV and V for developing countries explicitly excluded by cabinet directive,[83] and for states and territories that qualified for ODA under DAC rules but did not receive Canadian aid.[84]

New core countries. The prospect of more resources encouraged addition of four new core countries/regions during the early 1980s: Zimbabwe, SADCC (the Southern African Development Coordination Conference), China, and Thailand. In addition, Rwanda, where programming was long-standing, was upgraded from non-core to core status. Bolivia and Belize, relatively small recipients, were dropped as core countries as was El Salvador.[85]

Three factors—Canada's commitment to the front-line states facing South Africa's apartheid regime, the Commonwealth link, and the prospect of expanded relations with one of the more developed countries in sub-Saharan Africa—all contributed to an immediate decision to establish a sizeable program in Zimbabwe as soon as Robert Mugabe achieved political power in 1980.

The launching in 1983 of a major program within the SADCC framework was riskier and less predictable. SADCC was established in 1980 as a partnership among front-line states eager to reduce their dependency on South Africa by accelerating their economic development through coordinated regional efforts. Angola, Botswana, Lesotho, Malawi, Mozambique, Swaziland, Tanzania, Zambia, and Zimbabwe were charter members. CIDA subsequently became the largest bilateral contributor to regional projects aimed at reconstructing and developing transportation, communications, and energy infrastructures, and at strengthening human resources and institutions. Major core programs were retained in Tanzania, Zambia, and Zimbabwe, but Botswana, Lesotho, and Swaziland were shifted to non-core except for their participation in SADCC projects.

China and Thailand were both designated as core countries in 1981. In China's case, the decision was made soon after its 1980 admission to the World Bank opened the door to ODA eligibility under DAC rules. As a low-income country, it could be justified by Canada's commitment to channel the bulk of bilateral assistance to the poorest. However, mutual interests and the extension of the government's policy of "concentrated bilateralism" to newly industrializing countries provided the major motivation for targeting both China and Thailand, a middle-income country.

While commercial objectives were important in China and Thailand, Massé was determined to develop new programming within a longer time horizon than earlier trade-inspired initiatives. For him, the key to successful bilateral aid was the development of long-term relationships. As he said in an interview with a business magazine:

> Our function is not just to provide aid to a number of countries, as many people think. Our main interest is in establishing a real collaboration with African, Asian and Latin American countries. In order to make them equal partners in international trade we must first help them build a developed infrastructure to assist in raising their living standards. In the future these efforts will provide us with broad markets for our industrial production and will guarantee our supply of raw materials.[86]

The international aid establishment was by then questioning the value of mega-projects, and Massé believed that Canadian interests would be better served by concentrating less on immediate export opportunities, which in any case were few, and more on effective human resource development and strategic networking with local government, business, and educational elites. The change reflected as well a new, self-confident attitude on the part of Asian leaders. As an officer in Asia Branch put it, "They didn't want junk just because a grant was available. They said, 'You provide what we want, not just what you want to give us.' "

The Chinese themselves were most interested in expanding opportunities for education and training in the West, and the president took a strong personal interest in shaping a program that emphasized links with Canadian institutions of higher education. These were important features in the Thai program too, and in a revamped one in Indonesia. Massé described the approach as "the multiplication of contacts at the thinking level."[87]

Shares by income level and region. The two-track policy adopted during the Dupuy years was made more explicit under Massé, both by pursuing longer-term relationships with selected middle-income and high-growth countries and by reducing the targeted share of low-income recipients from 90 per cent (under the 1975-80 strategy) to 80 per cent. Canada's commitment to the poorest countries was, however, still substantial. At the UN Conference on LLDCs in Paris in 1981, the government promised to increase the ODA share of the least developed from all channels to 0.15 per cent of GNP, up from the then-current level of 0.11 per cent.[88] As Table 6.1 indicates, the proportions of country-to-country aid allocated to LLDCs and middle-income recipients both rose at the expense of "other low-income" from 1980 to 1983.

Table 6.1
Percentage Distribution of Attributable Canadian Country-to-Country Aid by Income Level of Recipient Countries, 1980-83

Income level	1980	1981	1982	1983
Least developed	32.8 (178.8)	30.4 (191.5)	34.3 (237.9)	36.6 (227.7)
Other low income	49.7 (270.7)	47.1 (296.8)	47.2 (327.2)	39.4 (245.5)
Middle income	17.4 (94.8)	22.5 (141.9)	18.5 (128.5)	24.0 (149.5)

Source: Calculated from OECD-DAC, "Aid Review 1984/85: Report by the Secretariat and Questions on the Development Assistance Efforts and Policies of Canada" (Paris, 1984), Table 4, p. 15. The figures in parentheses are $ million. The data are for what DAC calls bilateral aid, i.e., everything that is not multilateral, hence the broader label "country-to-country," which subsumes NGO, business, and humanitarian relief channels, as well as contributions from the development crown corporations.

As we saw in Chapter 5, bilateral disbursements to Africa began to exceed those of Asia for the first time in the late 1970s. That pattern continued in the 1980-83 period, with shares for Africa and Asia of 48 and 42 per cent respectively. Contributions to Latin America and the Caribbean fell below 10 per cent. These patterns reflected earlier commitments: new planning figures for Asia and the Americas called for Africa and Asia each to receive 42 per cent and the Americas 16 per cent.[89] The pursuit of mutual interests and longer-term relationships with rapidly growing middle- and low-income countries figured prominently in the establishment of the Asian target, as did normalization of relations with India.

Trade prospects in the Americas were seen as excellent until the severity of the debt crisis became apparent in mid-1982, but decisions to increase the shares of Latin America and the Caribbean were related more to a growing foreign policy focus on hemispheric security and a heightened public interest in issues of political conflict, development, and human rights.

Official concerns about political turmoil in Jamaica, the presence of a radical leftist regime in Grenada, and instability elsewhere in the region were important in prompting the Department of External Affairs to undertake a comprehensive review of Canada's relations with the Commonwealth Caribbean in 1980. The review highlighted the link between politics and development, and urged an increase in Canadian aid.[90] In January 1981, the government designated the Commonwealth Caribbean as a priority area in its external relations. Then, while resisting pressure to become formally associated with President Reagan's Caribbean Basin Initiative, the Canadian government announced in June of that year that aid to the region would be doubled between 1982 and 1987.[91] Jamaica was a principal beneficiary, becoming by far the largest recipient in the Americas during the 1980s.[92]

Cancellation of core country designation for El Salvador came after a suspension of bilateral aid to both that country and Guatemala in March 1981 on grounds that escalating violence under military regimes made aid work impossible.[93] Meanwhile, modest bilateral programming was undertaken in Nicaragua amid strong support for the Sandinista regime from Canadian church groups and NGOs. The government was more prepared to expand support to Honduras (already a core country) and Costa Rica; Mark MacGuigan announced in February 1982 that Canada would increase ODA contributions to Central America to $106 million over the next five years, more than double the level of the previous five.[94]

By then, the Subcommittee on Canada's Relations with Latin America and the Caribbean was enmeshed in polarized conflict over Canadian foreign policy in the region. Though divided, it subsequently recommended that bilateral assistance to El Salvador and Guatemala not be resumed until their governments made substantial progress in reducing human rights violations. It also suggested that further aid to Nicaragua be conditional upon its maintaining armed forces solely for purposes of self-defence.[95] More generally, the subcommittee recommended that Central America and the Commonwealth Caribbean both be made regions of concentration in Canadian foreign policy.[96]

The government's response testily pointed out that the Commonwealth Caribbean had already been so designated in 1981 and that decisions to increase ODA substantially in both regions had been announced.[97] Meanwhile, though Haiti remained a core country, aid to the Duvalier regime was cut back sharply when CIDA, as we shall see below, cancelled a massive integrated rural development scheme.

Human rights conditionality. NGOs, church and solidarity groups, and the media exhibited a lively concern about the linkage between foreign aid and human rights during the early 1980s. The issue emerged as a major and contentious matter for the parliamentary subcommittee. The majority's final report recommended that "Canadian development assistance should be substantially reduced, terminated or not commenced . . . where gross and systematic violations of human rights make it impossible to promote the central objective of helping the poor." In less extreme situations, the subcommittee urged that the non-governmental sector be the main delivery channel—especially NGOs working directly with the poor—and that assistance be given to "organizations which are struggling to maintain and protect civil and political rights." It also suggested increasing aid as a positive encouragement to regimes that demonstrated an improved record.[98]

Appearing before the Standing Committee on External Affairs and National Defence in March 1983, Allan MacEachen (who had recently returned to his old External Affairs portfolio) expressed agreement about terminating or cutting aid in cases of serious human rights abuses. He also endorsed a subcommittee statement urging caution in tying assistance directly to human rights performance.[99] At a conference on human rights and foreign policy a few weeks later, he voiced scepticism about suspending aid in other than extreme situations; without international support, Canadian action would be ineffective and would only harm the poor.[100] The government's formal response to the subcommittee was supportive in principle, but worded carefully so as to maintain operational flexibility.[101]

Action on human rights during the period under review was limited. The most clear-cut was a decision in 1980 to remove newsprint from the list of commodities that Guyana was eligible to purchase under a line of credit "when it became clear that newsprint was not reaching the opposition press and Canada was thus indirectly contributing to a climate in Guyana of denial of political and civil rights."[102] T.A. Keenleyside argued that the government employed a human rights rationale for the 1981 suspension of bilateral aid to

El Salvador and Guatemala "only ex post-facto in the face of growing interest in aid-rights linkage." More significant in reality, he contended, were "the administrative impossibility of carrying out the program and the risks to Canadian field personnel under prevailing circumstances."[103] The government did terminate assistance to Surinam in 1983, citing human rights violations as the rationale, but there was as yet no test of the government's resolve in situations where there was significant Canadian presence.

Terms: Aid and Trade Promotion

Canadian ODA remained highly concessional and closely tied to Canadian procurement during the early 1980s. While the North-South Institute and academic critics continued to press for greater untying, the major issue on terms for the bureaucracy was the use of ODA for trade promotion. It was now common practice for many OECD governments to offer aid funds in parallel with promotional export financing to help their firms win major contracts in richer developing countries. The French had gone one step further and pioneered the use of *crédit mixte*, which involved blending ODA funds with official export credits to subsidize concessional financing packages.

Despite pressure to seek commercial advantage from the aid program, especially after 1977, the Canadian government did not follow these trends immediately. CIDA had long been involved in parallel financing with the World Bank and the regional development banks (funding contracts for Canadian suppliers), and the strategy for 1975-80 had called for greater cooperation between the Agency and the Export Development Corporation (EDC) in activities "that meet the operating criteria of both institutions."[104] In 1975 and 1976, CIDA provided modest support for infrastructure and training for a sugar complex in the Ivory Coast and a cement plant in Indonesia, both of which primarily involved EDC and commercial bank financing.[105] No further arrangements of this sort were made in 1977, and only four more projects were approved by the end of 1979.[106] CIDA was quite insistent on applying developmental criteria before agreeing to participation. As for mixed credit, Canadian officials took the same line as their American counterparts—that it was an undesirable form of market interference.

Growing demands from business for action on both fronts—parallel financing and mixed credit—were put forcefully in the 1979 Hatch report. It urged meeting *crédit mixte* competition by setting aside bilateral funds "so that parallel financing arrangements can be entered into systematically, as a matter of course, when they are needed to win an important contract." Hatch also recommended that EDC be responsible for assembling financing packages and negotiating all terms with host governments.[107] In effect, it was a call for a mixed credit facility rather than parallel financing; CIDA would have no role apart from providing funds and sitting on a proposed Export Trade Development Board.

Confronted by this territorial incursion (and, at the time, possible further budget cuts), the Agency reacted swiftly. An overview of the Bilateral Program, prepared during the 1980 federal election when Dupuy was still in office, recommended establishment of an "export financing facility" or "third window" targeted at middle-income countries that would: (1) finance commercially oriented projects with significant potential for export promotion; (2) provide flexibility to respond quickly to commercial ventures requiring guaranteed funding; and (3) undertake parallel and co-financing with partners in the private and public sectors.[108]

Meanwhile, Industry, Trade and Commerce circulated a paper reiterating arguments about the desirability of increasing aid to middle-income countries, establishing a commercially oriented global fund, and involving IT&C directly in project selection. The authors also urged creation of a mechanism allowing trade officials to play a central role in seeking out CIDA/EDC parallel financing opportunities. They expressed regret about the trade-distorting effects of *crédit mixte*, but left no doubt about their strong support for meeting competition head-on.[109]

As we shall see in Chapter 7, the concept of an export financing facility or aid-trade fund, in which CIDA would play the lead role, remained on the policy agenda. In the short run, however, the government decided to establish a *crédit mixte* facility within EDC. Operational in January 1981, it was empowered to use "Section 31" funds (from the government's discretionary account) to offer competitive financing terms when there was evidence that foreign competitors were offering subsidized credit. Concessional or grant elements in any resulting loan package were not counted as ODA.

At the same time, CIDA stepped up its programming in middle-income countries, and increased substantially its participation in parallel financing projects and lines of credit with the EDC.[110] Some of these joint ventures with EDC used aid (or the threat of its withholding) as a lever for obtaining contracts. Linda Freeman documented a particularly blatant case involving the sale of locomotives to Tunisia in 1982.[111] At least one financing package—the Bukit Asam project in Indonesia—remained unused because Canadian suppliers were uncompetitive.[112] Nevertheless, in the view of business, the mechanisms for meeting credit competition were still inadequate—parallel financing because of the need to meet development criteria, and the mixed credit facility because it could be accessed only in defensive circumstances in non-core CIDA countries (a restriction relaxed in 1983).[113]

Potential returns for Canadian firms also motivated the search for co-financing opportunities with OPEC donors. By 1982, there were forty-five such projects approved or under consideration.[114] As Martin Rudner observed, these arrangements exposed Canada to the propensity of Arab donors "to wield development assistance as a weapon of foreign policy in international disputes, in inter-Arab rivalries, and in particular in their economic campaign against Israel."[115] He documented a case in Sri Lanka where work on a jointly financed irrigation project was suspended after that country's government renewed diplomatic relations with Israel.[116]

The New Programming Priorities[117]

Though pressure from political and business leaders to increase commercial returns from Canadian ODA was intense, Massé did exhibit a determination to achieve programming coherence in the field. This concern was reflected in the discussion of sectoral priorities set forth in the Agency Programming Framework, which stipulated that 80 per cent of country-to-country funds would be directed towards the three areas of agriculture and food production, energy, and human resource development. The mix could vary from recipient to recipient, with every country program review presenting a detailed analysis of needs in each sphere and how best CIDA could respond to them.

The APF section on agriculture and food production emphasized food self-sufficiency as well as transportation, storage, and marketing. Programmers were urged to support projects benefiting small farmers, women and, more generally, the poorest rural populations. The long-standing commitment to agricultural research was endorsed, along with the importance of "strengthening national planning in central agencies to ensure the development of appropriate agro-food systems and national policies."

In the field of energy, self-sufficiency ("not necessarily independence") was also cited as the objective. A mix of activities was foreseen, involving both "traditional support" for power generation and transmission, and "innovative activities to assist recipients to identify, develop and utilize other sources of energy," especially from renewable and locally available sources. The APF suggested that Canadian expertise could be helpful in energy planning, conservation, "proper resources management," and forest management.

Promoting human resource development. Identification of "human resource development" (HRD) as the third major sectoral priority marked the most significant departure from recent practice. As noted above, Massé was strongly influenced by emerging scepticism about mega-projects in international development circles. Subscribing to the World Bank's recent analysis of poverty and human development,[118] he was also convinced of the desirability of investing in people to achieve both economic growth and redistributive social goals. The APF cited reasons for making HRD a high priority:

> In the shorter term, human resource development means education and training to meet the immediate need for skilled technical, managerial, and administrative personnel, and measures directed towards specific target groups to facilitate their participation in the main economic system of the country. These target groups can include women, landless, rural/urban poor, young people in isolated communities, etc. In the longer term, human resource development means the eradication of poverty through education and training, health, nutrition, population control, sanitation and water programmes.[119]

Arguing that "capital formation and technological change can be fully effective only if they are firmly rooted in the social and cultural environment of each country," the policy urged careful analysis of human resource needs in each country program review. With respect to the need for skilled personnel, the APF called for more technical assistance to strengthen the capacity of crucial central agencies of recipient governments, and for more scholarships, training programs, and institutional linkages. It made several suggestions for meeting basic needs of the poor and the dislocated, including compensatory training and relocation for those adversely affected by development projects, provision of skills and credit to rural populations, and new initiatives in basic education related to nutrition, food production, primary health care, literacy, and sanitation and water management. A separate section called for programming to ensure that women "participate in and share fully the benefits of development."

CIDA's recent track record in what was now called the HRD sector had been unimpressive. Confronted by restrictions on staffing, and complex bureaucratic and financial controls, Massé and Senior Vice-President McWhinney floated the idea of setting up a Third World Foundation to take over primary responsibility for education, training, and other types of HRD programming. Modelled loosely on technical cooperation agencies in Germany and other donor countries, it was conceived as a privately incorporated but publicly funded body that would help with coordination of the international development work of universities, colleges, the cooperative and labour movements, volunteer-sending organizations, and some other NGOs. The private sector would also participate in the training activities of the Foundation, which would as well take over CIDA's Briefing Centre.

Massé and McWhinney believed that such a body could operate more flexibly and creatively than CIDA, and give Canada's efforts in HRD greater visibility. Some NGOs reacted to the proposal with suspicion, however, and several senior managers within CIDA opposed further devolution of the aid program. The idea was dropped in 1983. By that time, Massé had left, spending growth had slowed, and MacEachen argued that the time was not ripe for yet another new institution.[120]

Within the Agency, a new HRD-oriented program called Management for Change was launched in September 1981. During his time as clerk of the Privy Council, Massé had suggested a Canadian initiative to strengthen public administration in developing countries. Announced by Joe Clark at the 1979 Commonwealth Heads of Government Meeting in Lusaka, the commitment remained little more than a concept until Lewis Perinbam gave it some substance in Special Programs Branch. Designed for senior-level executives in the public and private sectors, the Management for Change Program was given an open-ended mandate "to develop innovative ways of strengthening the management capabilities of developing countries."[121] International networking was central to activities that included conferences, seminars, and short-term work assignments.

Sectoral distribution. As noted above, the new Thai and Chinese programs, and the revamped one in Indonesia, emphasized education, training, and other forms of HRD. These activities and the general renewal of technical cooperation are reflected in Table 6.2, which shows an increased share for education in the sectoral distribution of country-to-country spending from 1980 to 1983. Otherwise, the data suggest that new sectoral priorities had not yet had an appreciable impact on programming. Food aid accounted for between 15 and 20 per cent of overall ODA in the early 1980s (18.4 per cent in 1983-84 when allocations were $332.5 million); a balance tipped towards multilateral disbursements swung back to rough parity with the bilateral channel during the Massé years.[122]

Table 6.2
Percentage Distribution of Canadian Country-to-Country ODA Commitments Attributable by Sector, 1980-83

	1980	1981	1982	1983
Agriculture	21	37	13	23
Public utilities	16	35	26	19
of which: energy	(8)	(1)	(10)	(5)
Industry	5	5	11	12
Education	1	7	10	9
Health and social infrastructure	6	1	6	5
Other, multisector, and unspecified	51	15	34	31
Total	100	100	100	100

Source: OECD-DAC, "Aid Review 1984/85: Report by the Secretariat and Questions on the Development Assistance Efforts and Policies of Canada," Table 8, p. 21.

Other Channels

While the Trudeau government resisted some of Hatch's recommendations for tying the aid program more strongly to domestic commercial goals, it did agree to increase the share of bilateral aid at the expense of multilateral commitments for the period from 1981 to 1986 "as a means of improving the commercial benefits derived from aid."[123] The policy was supported by Massé and his senior managers, who thought that bilateral programming had borne too much of the budget-cutting burden in the 1970s. CIDA also had an interest in constraining the power of Finance to set contributions levels for the international financial institutions, which meant that other channels had to take what was left over in the aid envelope. The cabinet accepted a specific recommendation to hold the IFI share within a range of 18 to 22 per cent of total ODA. (The actual share between 1977-78 and 1980-81 had fallen between 22 and 23 per cent.)

As Protheroe observed, the late 1970s and early 1980s were generally a period of "disquiet within the multilateral aid system."[124] Canada was not as begrudging as many other donors, but it was no longer the champion of the system it had been in the late 1960s and early 1970s. As noted in Chapter 5, Ottawa bargained for a reduced share of the sixth replenishment of IDA in 1979. When the new Reagan administration balked at meeting the American commitment two years later, Canada,

> like most donors (but not the UK, Austria, Belgium, Denmark, Italy and some small Third World donors), took a tough line and invoked the pro-rata trigger clause reducing its own contributions to IDA-6 in retaliation against the American cuts for 1982. Moreover Canada did not participate in the $500 million rescue plan for 1982.[125]

Canadian negotiators later helped forge a compromise that extended the life of IDA-6 by maintaining established commitments for an extra year. The result made possible a further reduction in the target range for IFIs, down to 18 to 20 per cent of ODA in 1983; actual disbursements declined to 19.5 and 18.9 per cent in 1982-83 and 1983-84 respectively. Overall, the share of multilateral shrank from 40.2 per cent in 1979-80 to 35.6 per cent in 1982-83, but grew again to 37.2 per cent in 1983-84—well above the DAC average and the 30 per cent level sought by politicians.[126]

Other noteworthy developments in the multilateral sphere included adoption by CIDA of guiding principles for funding UN and other international development institutions; and, when full membership in the African Development Bank was opened to non-African states, the assumption by Canada of a seat on the board of directors.[127]

New guidelines for humanitarian assistance. CIDA had long been involved in humanitarian assistance through core funding of such organizations as the International Committee of the Red Cross, UNHCR, UNRWA, and UNICEF. These agencies were also used as direct conduits for emergency relief, as were various Canadian and international NGOs. There was, however, little systematic policy governing this aspect of the ODA program until the approval in 1983 of a set of guiding principles for action in cases of natural and human disasters.[128] Up to 1980, annual humanitarian relief expenditures typically fell within the range of $10 to $30 million (including core funding grants), a tiny fraction of the ODA budget.[129] With a devastating drought gripping the Horn of Africa, however, the humanitarian channel was about to assume much greater significance.

Non-governmental organizations: Rapid growth and turbulent change. Recorded ODA channelled through the voluntary sector rose 119 per cent from $89.7 million in 1980-81 to $197.3 million in 1983-84. The latter sum represented 10.8 per cent of Canadian aid, up from 6.9 per cent only three years earlier.[130] The increase was not all for responsive programming, as it included some $30 million in bilateral country focus activity.[131] The revamped NGO Division and the new Institutional Cooperation and Development Services Division shared roughly equally in the growth. The universities played a prominent role in country focus programming, especially in the new programs for China and Thailand with their heavy emphasis on human resource development and Canadian partnerships.

Increasingly, CIDA looked to the voluntary sector not only for political support and effective grass-roots programming, but also for program management capabilities. The Agency intensified efforts to devolve labour-intensive responsibilities to external executing agencies. Country focus was part of this thrust, as was the introduction of block funding for some larger NGOs. So too were financial transfers to CIDA-sponsored NGO coalitions, which were given the authority to distribute funds under watchful Agency eyes. The first of these was the Reconstruction and Rehabilitation Fund, set up in 1980, to enable NGOs to respond quickly to humanitarian emergencies. Then, in 1981, the South Asia Partnership (SAP) was established to bring together previously unlinked indigenous NGOs in the Indian sub-continent and Canadian counterparts, especially for small-scale self-help projects in the rural sector.[132]

Within the NGO community, CIDA's initiatives met mixed reactions. Funding growth was welcomed, but there were concerns that country focus might lead to greater CIDA domination and a reduction in responsive funding for projects conceived by NGOs themselves or in concert with their overseas partners. These fears were at first heightened when CCIC obtained a leaked copy of briefing notes used by Massé to explain country focus to CIDA officers at a November 1981 meeting. NGOs were deeply upset about not being consulted on a proposal that had far-reaching implications for their relationship with the Agency and that could be interpreted as an alternative rather than an addition to the existing NGO programming. Reportedly furious about the leak, Massé later attempted to assuage NGO concerns at a consultation in February 1982.[133]

A few larger agencies, such as WUSC and CARE, embraced the opportunity to work as bilateral executing agencies, but others remained doubtful. CCIC was especially sceptical about country focus. The organization's leadership was angry for other reasons as well. First, CIDA had begun separate consultations with the International Development Executives Association (IDEA), which involved chief executives of large NGOs—some who were members of CCIC and some who had withdrawn because they regarded the Council as too radical. Secondly, the Agency played a lead role in setting up a new development education organization, the Futures Secretariat, which CCIC and many NGOs saw as an effort to undercut their own "dev-ed" work. As we shall see below, the Futures Secretariat was short-lived.

While relations between CIDA and individual NGOs had their ups and downs, the Agency announced in 1983 that funding for SUCO, the Quebec counterpart of CUSO, would be terminated in April of the following year. It was an unprecedented step. Three years after finally severing by-then tenuous links with CUSO, SUCO had become hopelessly mired in ideological and organizational turmoil. It had also fallen short of targets for placements of volunteers and was deeply in debt. The organization mounted a campaign on nationalist grounds aimed at reversing the decision, but secured little support. CIDA promised only to assist those currently serving overseas with the completion of their contracts and their passages home.[134]

Industrial Cooperation Program: A hit with business. The business constituency was a major beneficiary of the increased tilt towards middle-income countries, the growth of parallel financing, and the decision to expand the share of bilateral aid. In addition, unlike the old Business and Industry Program, the Industrial Cooperation Program generated such a positive response that CIDA had difficulty fulfilling requests, especially for access to the Canadian Project Preparation Facility. In October 1980, Mark MacGuigan announced a doubling of annual funding for INC from $9 million to $18 million.[135] Marcel Massé was also enthusiastic about the program, not least because it gave a stake in Canadian ODA to "a large number of small winners."[136] In 1983-84, the allocation grew to $28.7 million, 1.5 per cent of aid spending.[137]

INC sponsored trade missions and exhibitions to promote Canadian products and services. It added more new programming dimensions, among them (in 1980) the Canadian Technology Transfer Facility for testing and adapting in developing countries proven technology already in use in Canada, and (in 1981) the Canadian Renewable Energy Facility for supporting experimental research and development by potential Canadian suppliers.[138] INC also funded a pilot project to investigate joint ventures with Canadian investors in Cameroon; an office was set up in Yaoundé by the Canadian Export Association.

The Subcommittee on Canada's Relations with Latin America and the Caribbean gave serious consideration to yet another proposal for expanding Canadian investment in developing countries—a facility to provide equity capital from public and private sources to promote joint ventures in developing countries in partnership with Canadian firms. There had been intermittent discussion about the possibility of setting up something like the Commonwealth Development Corporation in Britain or the Swedfund in Sweden. Most recently, the Hatch report had recommended an equity participation fund "to reduce the overall risk to Canadian firms."[139] The idea was then pursued energetically by the Canadian Association for Latin America and the Caribbean (CALA), a lobby group supporting expanded Canadian business links within the hemisphere.

CALA presented a detailed proposal to the subcommittee for a Canadian overseas investment agency that would receive some public funding but be run as a private-sector institution by business people. With a focus on small and medium-sized Canadian firms, it would assume the functions of INC, and—though conceived as "primarily an entrepreneur and not a financier"—it would as well take modest equity participation in joint ventures. CIDA would be represented on an executive council and have "an ultimate veto" over country selection and development criteria ("which one hopes would seldom have to be exercised").[140]

The subcommittee endorsed the concept as a means of establishing "Canadian beachheads" in Latin American and Caribbean markets, suggesting as well that ODA goals would be advanced by the potential stimulus to economic growth.[141] The government's official response was silent, reflecting CIDA's resistance to the idea of losing a popular private-sector program, and scepticism from the Finance and Treasury Board about using aid funds for risky equity ventures.

A Still-Troubled Public Image

Massé's success in revitalizing CIDA from within was not matched in the Agency's public relations. He certainly took outreach seriously, actively seeking opportunities to promote Canada's aid program. Though he evoked some suspicion within the NGO community, he impressed many business people, intellectuals, and development activists with the depth of his knowledge and his analytical prowess. His personal warmth and charm were also readily apparent in face-to-face encounters. In larger gatherings and on television, however, he appeared remote and somewhat too cerebral to connect with a popular audience. Neither he nor his public affairs staff made much headway in countering the scepticism and the negative images that continued in much of the media coverage of CIDA and its work in the field.

C-FAR (Citizens for Foreign Aid Reform), the virulent right-wing lobby formed in 1976 to campaign against CIDA and Canadian ODA, was especially busy in the early 1980s. Paul Fromm and his associates wrote letters to the press, circulated a newsletter to MPs and other opinion leaders, and scrambled after media interviews. They recycled old horror stories to illustrate "CIDA's dark history of financial sloth, faulty accounting procedures, and inadequate stewardship of public funds."[142] Fromm and James P. Hull also published a book-length diatribe in 1981 entitled *Down the Drain? A Critical Re-examination of Canadian Foreign Aid*.[143]

Several papers ran stories about C-FAR's campaign,[144] and some columnists continued CIDA-bashing from a similar perspective.[145] The Agency tried to counter the campaign, and Douglas Roche circulated an extensive point-by-point rebuttal to MPs and the media.[146] C-FAR's views were embraced, however, by some of his fellow Tories, notably Ron Stewart[147] and John Gamble. In announcing his campaign for the Conservative leadership in 1983, Gamble said it was "lunacy" for the government to go into debt so that it could give money to "socialist dictatorships." He had earlier gone on record as favouring an 80 per cent cut in the aid budget.[148] Both C-FAR and Gamble were generally seen as representing an extreme fringe, but their views received wide circulation.

So too did those of Robert Carty and Virginia Smith, whose 1981 *Perpetuating Poverty: The Political Economy of Canadian Foreign Aid*[149] was a popularly written critique of aid from a left-wing perspective. Carty and Smith cited several CIDA projects as evidence for their contention that aid was part of the problem of poverty and underdevelopment, not a solution. CBC TV aired a documentary called "Up the Down Escalator" in September 1982 that added more grist for the mill by criticizing CIDA's performance in Tanzania in terms of the Agency's stated objective of helping the poorest people in the poorest countries. It suggested that there was a structural defect in an aid organization that employed one thousand people in Ottawa and only fifty-four in the field, an observation echoed by several journalists.

Polls indicated that support for Canada's aid program was positive but weak.[150] A programming fiasco in Haiti did not help, although Massé did his best to counter adverse publicity. Meanwhile, concerned about aid fatigue and the horror story syndrome, the North-South Institute undertook a series of well-publicized evaluations of CIDA's bilateral programs aimed at focusing attention on the developmental implications of the Agency's work. A ministerial initiative to set up a "Futures Secretariat" was a similarly motivated but ill-conceived venture that ended in embarrassment. So too did an effort within CIDA's Public Affairs Division to develop a new communications strategy.

Cancelling the DRIPP Project in Haiti[151]

Massé was drawn into one of CIDA's biggest-ever public relations challenges about a decision to cancel a major integrated rural development project in Haiti known by the acronym DRIPP (Développement Régional Intégré de Petit-Goâve à Petit-Trou-de-Nippes). It had been initiated in 1974 in the wake of Robert McNamara's Nairobi speech and soon after Paul Gérin-Lajoie decided, against the advice of senior planners, to try bilateral programming in Haiti. As Philip English noted in his evaluation of CIDA's Haiti program for the North-South Institute:

> DRIPP was to be a CIDA showpiece. Here was a project which would epitomize the new basic needs approach in one of the neediest countries, proving that CIDA was abreast of the latest development wisdom and able to reach the truly poor. Here the honourable priorities outlined by CIDA in its 1975-80 strategy statement would ring true, with no question of mere Canadian self-interest.[152]

The project was extraordinarily ambitious. It sought to combat rural poverty through simultaneous improvements in education, health, transportation, and agricultural development among 300,000 people in an area of 1,700 km^2. The methodology of integrated rural development was new (and, as experience elsewhere would show, flawed), Canadians had little expertise in the field, and the host Duvalier regime was notorious for its corruption, brutality, and lack of commitment to the rural poor. Altogether, disaster waiting to happen!

Although little was done to raise rural productivity during DRIPP's first five years, there were some positive achievements such as new clinics and improved secondary roads. However, equipment and materials disappeared, costs were overrun, funds were unaccounted for, and relations with the Haitian authorities were bad. According to a former official in the Canadian Embassy, CIDA officials in Hull, though well aware of serious concerns, nonetheless planned for a new five-year phase after receiving a generally positive evaluation in March 1980 (when Massé joined CIDA).[153] When it then proved difficult to work out differences with the Haitians, particularly over management controls and finances, an audit was ordered early in 1981. According to Massé, by now fully involved, the upshot was to negotiate an intermediate phase of only eighteen months "with very strict conditions . . . making the Haitians very clearly aware that if the rules of the game were not enforced . . . we would withdraw."[154] An agreement was signed in July 1981.

After catching wind of a potential story, CTV's *W5* sent a film crew to Haiti a few weeks later. Bill Cunningham, executive producer of *W5*, claimed:

> Until we went to Haiti to investigate this project, the Canadian International Development Agency's failure . . . was carefully hidden for seven years. Our arrival . . . in mid-November caused CIDA officials considerable anguish. After all, they had just finished the $21 million initial phase of the project and, in August, had received approval to spend another $8 million on an intermediate phase to be spent over a period of 18 months.[155]

On November 28, 1981, Mark MacGuigan announced that the project had been cancelled "en raison de l'impossibilité pour les gouvernements haitien and canadien de s'entendre sur des mécanismes de contrôle et de gestion acceptables pour le gouvernement canadien."[156] CIDA telephoned to advise CTV of the decision, under the impression, Cunningham presumed, that "we were to air our Haiti segment the following evening."[157] CTV took credit for the cancellation when the program was eventually screened in January 1982. In an all-time low point for CIDA's public relations, hundreds of thousands of Canadians witnessed the Haitian project manager appearing to pass out on camera in the face of tough questioning by CTV. Meanwhile, the videotape was shown to a group of MPs on the Subcommittee on Latin America and the Caribbean just before their departure on a study trip that included Haiti.

The affair received considerable attention from the subcommittee. Called as a witness, Massé became unusually flustered when complaining about the way his own forty-minute interview with Henry Champ was edited down to two minutes. He denied categorically that the CTV investigation had influenced the cancellation.[158] Philip English's study, however, suggested that at least the timing was influenced by fear of a media scandal.[159]

There was a flurry of negative comment in the press after the documentary was shown, when the MPs visited Haiti, and again after the project was discussed by the subcommittee.[160] The controversy was nonetheless mild compared to what it might have been if the cancellation had not occurred. While CIDA was criticized for undertaking the project and not getting out earlier, Massé took credit for making a tough decision, claiming in CIDA's 1981-82 annual report that "it was the only responsible step to take. Canada's international reputation as an efficient donor was reinforced."[161]

As English observed later, "CIDA managed to deflect some blame to the Haitians and generate benefits for itself." But, he added: "If CIDA's withdrawal was justified, it was for somewhat different reasons. Rather than questions of image and public relations in Canada, it is the nature of the beast which CIDA had created which deserves attention." It was a classic case of negative consequences flowing from the pressure to spend. "While many lessons were drawn from this experience, the main conclusion is that DRIPP was too ambitious and grew too quickly, in terms of CIDA's knowledge and capabilities and Haiti's absorptive capacity at local levels and in government."[162]

The North-South Institute's Bilateral Evaluations

English's study was one of four country-based evaluations of Canadian bilateral aid that emerged from an ambitious research project launched by the North-South Institute in January 1980. Media coverage of Canadian ODA was an important stimulus, as Roger Young, the Institute's senior research officer, later explained:

> [Research] related to Canadian aid . . . remained modest relative to the large and growing expenditure on aid in Canada. Significantly, detailed awareness of the nature of Canadian aid policies and programs seemed almost non-existent in comparison with the less analytical yet highly critical media coverage of aid in Canada. There was a serious danger that public opinion and policy decisions could be badly biased by criticism based on single project "snapshots" that would be generalized to the overall aid program.[163]

Since most of the Institute's funding came from CIDA, it sought and secured non-governmental support for this project. The main source was a $275,000 grant from the Donner Canadian Foundation.

The objective of the research was to assess the developmental effectiveness of Canadian foreign aid in the 1970s in selected countries. The Institute signed an agreement with CIDA for access to documentation on condition that final drafts would be submitted to a liaison committee that "would read and if necessary provide a formal written response to the drafts."[164] The agreement was initially controversial among the researchers, but Young reported afterwards that they had excellent access and no pressure to censor texts. The Institute initially selected eight countries, two from each of CIDA's regional programs. Following a preliminary review of documentary and statistical materials in Ottawa, four were chosen for intensive field research—Bangladesh, Tanzania, Senegal, and Haiti.[165]

The studies of Bangladesh and Tanzania (by Roger Ehrhardt and Roger Young respectively) were published along with a preliminary overview of findings in June 1983.[166] English's evaluation of the Haitian experience was released the following February, and the report on Senegal (by Réal Lavergne with Philip English) in 1987.[167] Each presented an account of successes and failures. The verdict was most negative in Haiti, but even there English commented favourably on projects in the educational sector and on the work of NGOs. Overall, the Institute concluded that the coherence of the aid program was being undermined by a crisis of mixed and changing objectives. Foreign policy, commercial, and short-term humanitarian relief considerations tended to crowd out the objective of long-term development. Not enough Canadian aid was reaching the poor, especially in rural areas; the technological bias of aid tying was a factor, and so too was the tendency to avoid risks. Over-centralization of personnel and decision-making authority in Ottawa, cumbersome and time-consuming procedural regulations, lack of field-based experience, and inadequate capacities to store and retrieve corporate memories were seen as weakening CIDA's effectiveness.

The release of the first two evaluations and the general conclusions was well timed, coinciding with the appointment in June 1983 of Margaret Catley-Carlson as CIDA's new president. The reports also received extensive coverage in the press, which for the most part dwelt not on project failures but on the case for reforming the aid program. The argument for decentralization was embraced especially forcefully.[168] In the House of Commons, Douglas Roche urged the government to act on the reports by producing at last a development strategy for the 1980s focused on reaching those most in need.[169]

The Futures Secretariat[170]

While the North-South Institute's bilateral evaluations contributed to more thoughtful discussions on CIDA in the media, an effort by Mark MacGuigan to broaden support for Canadian aid ended in failure. When the minister agreed to address the UN General Assembly in August 1980, he was eager to announce something tangible as he did not yet have authority to renew Canada's 0.7 per cent commitment. What emerged was a pledge to establish a "Futures Secretariat" in CIDA "to inform and involve our citizens."[171] When interviewed after his speech, MacGuigan said he sensed that increased aid was neither strongly opposed nor solidly supported by Canadian taxpayers. "But," he continued, "what I would like to see is a Canadian public which itself so much wants to help the developing world that they are besieging the government with pressure, with requests, with admonitions to do something of this kind."[172] He wanted public pressure, not just support, and his proposed Futures Secretariat would contribute to that end.

The idea was inspired by Lewis Perinbam, who used "Futures Secretariat" at a conference earlier that summer as a possible name for an international brains trust of distinguished world citizens along lines suggested by the Brandt Commission.[173] Following MacGuigan's surprise announcement, bemused CIDA officials (including Vice-President Perinbam) found themselves responsible for implementing an ill-defined commitment to set up a new Canadian institution housed within CIDA. CCIC immediately condemned the proposal on grounds that it would duplicate the development education work of NGOs and give government an excuse for inaction.[174] NGO representatives and others invited to a CIDA consultation on the Futures Secretariat in October 1980 said they wanted no part of an initiative that might emerge as a propaganda vehicle for CIDA and the government.

A working group, chaired by Perinbam and including CCIC and NGO representatives, recommended shortly thereafter that the Secretariat become a citizens' advisory council on international development, which would meet two or three times a year and be co-chaired by the minister and the external affairs critics of the opposition parties. It would include representatives of the NGO community, and reach out to sectors of the Canadian public not normally exposed to development education work and/or predisposed negatively to the radical message of many development activists. Enthusiastic at first, MacGuigan backed off when he was warned about potential political pitfalls by Under-Secretary Gotlieb and other officials in External Affairs. Then, in January 1981, the minister announced that the Futures Secretariat would be a non-governmental organization. CCIC, which had supported a citizens' council, was aghast at the notion of a government-sponsored NGO and withdrew from the working group.

The Futures Secretariat was launched as a "non-governmental" entity after MacGuigan convened a March 1981 conference of carefully chosen representatives of business, labour, church, educational, and women's groups. Many of these went on to serve on a thirty-person Board chaired by Kurt Swinton, an industrial engineer with considerable experience in voluntary organizations, notably as president of the Couchiching Institute. In June, Swinton announced the appointment as president of David MacDonald—who, before his defeat in the 1980 federal election, had served as a Conservative MP for fifteen years and minister of Communications under Clark; he was also a Red Tory with strong interests in development and human rights. There was talk of an infusion of $500,000 from the government and an ambitious goal to match that amount from private donations. Plans were still vague—indeed, Swinton was quoted as saying that the Board's ideas were numerous and "half-baked."[175]

Supported by grants of $100,000 from CIDA and $50,000 from IDRC, MacDonald assumed office in September 1981. After hiring a staff of ten, he got off to an auspicious start by orchestrating a media briefing prior to the Cancún Conference. Thereafter, difficulties abounded. Although MacDonald had been Swinton's choice to show that the Futures Secretariat was not a Liberal gimmick, the two began quarrelling immediately about the organization's mission. Little headway was made on developing a plan of action, an application for charitable donation status was delayed, and CIDA began to complain about a lack of financial accountability. Some Board members called on MacDonald to resign. Meanwhile, CIDA devoted a full page to the Secretariat in its 1980-81 annual report. Beyond restating the desirability of helping Canadians become more aware of global interdependence, however, the text gave no indication of what the new body was actually doing.[176]

Budgetary proposals finally produced in January 1982 were seen as too grandiose, and CIDA's recommendation to Treasury Board for new funding was cut back from $177,000 to $93,000. Also unimpressed, Treasury Board turned down the request. By April 1982, the Board of the Secretariat was in disarray, there was little to show for several months of work, and the organization was unable to pay its employees or its bills. Staff members were laid off. The cabinet finally approved, in June 1982, a further grant of $50,000 to cover debts and MacDonald's salary to the end of that month.

The formal demise of the Futures Secretariat came that fall. Swinton and other critics blamed MacDonald's leadership and administrative failings, while MacDonald saw himself and the Secretariat as victims of Liberal partisanship. Richard Harmston, then executive director of the CCIC, ascribed the collapse to a failure to resolve the contradictions of being both government-sponsored and supposedly voluntary.[177]

Other Outreach Initiatives

Even as CCIC and CIDA were bickering over the Futures Secretariat, they cooperated on a national survey and review of NGO-based development education activities. A report by the Coopérative d'animation et de consultation of Montreal in May 1982 endorsed the parliamentary task force's recommendation to channel 1 per cent of ODA to development education, and urged that all of these resources be allocated by CIDA's NGO-oriented Public Participation Program. (PPP's annual expenditures had grown from $600,000 in 1971-72 to $5.4 million in 1982-83; 1 per cent of ODA that year would have amounted to a budget of $16.7 million!) The report recommended increased funding, especially for local groups with a solid community base. It also encouraged NGOs to offer more training in educational techniques and media relations, and to reach out more broadly, especially to senior levels of the school system, business, and local and provincial governments. The recommendations informed "An Operational Strategy for Development Education in the 1980s," ratified by CCIC in the fall of 1983.[178]

Within CIDA's Public Affairs Branch, work continued on audio-visual and other educational materials, especially those targeted towards school-age children. Massé's high-level networking was helpful as agreements were sought with provincial departments of education to include international development in formal curricula.

Meanwhile, there was consternation about an Adcom Research poll undertaken for CIDA that confirmed very low public awareness of the Agency's lead role in Canada's international development activities.[179] Ann Jamieson, director general of Public Affairs, proposed a new communications strategy late in 1982. "Our challenge," she argued, "is to show [Canadians] they are in their present [economic] predicament precisely because the world economy is out of sync, that [the economic downturn] cannot be corrected by Canada alone. However, they will have to be told this by sources . . . outside government if it is to be believed."[180] Therefore, active efforts were needed to influence "opinion leaders" to carry the message forward and project a more favourable perception of CIDA and its activities. Jamieson spelled out ways of courting MPs, journalists, and members of the business and development communities to become "doers." She also envisioned a more active public relations role for a new president, once one was appointed. "The agency must convince Canadians that it is an efficient, effective and responsible institution with which to trust Canada's activities in development and a sizeable budget."[181] Jamieson saw the need for additional outside expertise and a five-fold increase in spending on information and publicity—up to $4 million a year. Discussion was only beginning when David Vienneau of the *Toronto Star* obtained a copy of the document and accused CIDA of planning a propaganda campaign. Once more, there was embarrassment.

A Period of Uncertainty

The Jamieson affair occurred during the ten-month hiatus between Massé's sudden departure for External Affairs and the arrival of his successor as president, Margaret Catley-Carlson. Although Bill McWhinney handled day-to-day affairs ably as acting president, uncertainty over the succession threatened to snuff out the fires kindled during Massé's brief tenure. Massé had revitalized the Agency's sense of developmental mission, strengthened its capacity to engage in interdepartmental policy and budget struggles, and—through country focus—challenged its traditional bureaucratic practices and interbranch rivalries. His time was too short to embed these changes firmly in CIDA's culture and operations.

The Agency's sense of loss was compounded by the prospect that the 0.5 per cent target for 1985 would fall victim to a deepening recession. It also looked as though the aid program would experience even tougher times if, as anticipated, the Conservatives won the federal election expected in 1984. It did not help that Massé left behind a legacy of strained relations with the

Canadian development community, and largely unsuccessful efforts to strengthen public outreach.

Rumours abounded about possible candidates for the vacant position—including Michael Pitfield after he announced in October 1982 that he was stepping down as clerk of the Privy Council.[182] But the months dragged on. John Walker, a veteran on the CIDA beat for Southam News, characterized the Agency as drifting leaderless and aimlessly "in a sea of Government indifference."[183] Meanwhile, Douglas Roche continued his lonely quest for an aid strategy for the 1980s, failing to pin down the ever-wily Allan MacEachen when the minister appeared before the Committee on External Affairs and National Defence in March 1983.[184] Catley-Carlson's appointment was finally announced in June, but she was unable to assume the post until September 1983.

Chapter 7

Multiple Mandates and Partners, 1983-89

Margaret Catley-Carlson, CIDA's fifth president, assumed office when Western aid programs were in the doldrums. During her tenure from 1983 to 1989, she devoted enormous time and energy to enhancing support and participation from CIDA's main Canadian constituencies—NGOs, non-governmental institutions, and business—and to getting new groups and interests involved. She also conveyed stronger, more positive images about ODA and Canadian efforts to parliamentarians, the media, and—though harder to reach—the general public. "Partnership," first used to convey a desirable posture towards aid recipients, became the buzzword to describe relationships between CIDA and Canadian interests.

A more populist, Canadian-oriented approach suited well the ministers who assumed responsibility for the aid program after Brian Mulroney's Progressive Conservatives won office in 1984. Wanting to make CIDA and Canadian aid more business-friendly, the Tories put considerable effort into private-sector and trade initiatives. However, initial fears that they would convert the Agency into little more than an export promotion agency proved exaggerated, especially after an extraordinary public outpouring of humanitarian concern about the African drought in 1984-85. As secretary of state for External Affairs, Joe Clark, together with his high-quality staff, exercised a benign influence upon the ODA program. Moreover, the Conservatives' ideological stance accommodated shifting greater responsibility for delivery not only to the for-profit sector, but also to non-profit organizations and institutions.

There were as well growing international and domestic pressures to make ODA more sensitive to environmental sustainability, human rights performance, and the role of women; Catley-Carlson's commitment proved crucial in mobilizing an Agency-wide focus on women in development.

Notes to Chapter 7 are on pp. 517-31.

While deficit reduction was used to justify backtracking on commitments to increase the ODA/GNP ratio, Clark fought hard to preserve the aid budget, which continued to grow until 1989. CIDA's person-years were frozen, however, as the Tories attempted to downsize the civil service and devolve more work to the private sector. This factor—coupled with a higher-volume program, more sectoral commitments, and a further proliferation of recipient countries—accelerated dramatically the process of contracting out. Most of the Agency's line officers became managers of contracts rather than development projects. Reorganization remained a fact of life. Meanwhile, greater politicization of consultant selection and aid programming was apparent after the Conservative government gave a junior minister day-to-day responsibility for the CIDA.

Catley-Carlson's positive leadership helped the Agency steer a course through growing complexity and often contradictory expectations. By emphasizing openness to interdepartmental consultation, she maintained good relations with External Affairs, Finance, Treasury Board, and even the Auditor General. However, the sharper developmental focus that Massé attempted to instill blurred, and morale suffered as professional officers accommodated more demands and lost their hands-on relationship with development projects.

As the Agency wrestled with its multiple mandates and accommodated more partners, the Auditor General and critics in Parliament, the media, and the development community continued to raise questions about the coherence and effectiveness of Canada's aid program. There were ample opportunities to voice such concerns when the Tories finally launched the public review they had been clamouring for since the mid-1970s. The review and its aftermath (including CIDA's 1988 strategy, *Sharing Our Future*) are examined in the next chapter.

A New President, a New Communications Mandate

A career civil servant like her two predecessors, Margaret Catley-Carlson rose quickly through the ranks of External Affairs after graduating in political science and economics from the University of British Columbia and studying at the University of the West Indies. In addition to postings dealing with Europe and trade policy, she held several assignments involving developing countries. These included an early tour of duty in Pakistan, the UNCTAD conference in Chile in 1972, and the Conference on International Economic Cooperation in Paris in 1976-77. After working closely with Michel Dupuy on the CIEC assignment, she was thirty-six when he invited her to join CIDA as vice-president, Multilateral Branch in 1978. She moved up quickly to senior vice-president, and served as acting president for several months in

1980 when Marcel Massé was on sick leave. Soon after a reassignment to External Affairs as an assistant under-secretary in 1981, she returned to development work as deputy executive director of UNICEF in New York.[1]

Tough Challenges for Aid in the Mid-1980s

When Catley-Carlson became president of CIDA in September 1983, Western economies had been going through their deepest recession since the Second World War and the times were not propitious for foreign aid in Canada or the other OECD countries. Economic prospects in Asia were promising and East Asia's "four tigers" were experiencing spectacular growth, but development in Africa and Latin America was imperilled by an enormous debt overhang, the collapse of oil and other commodity prices, and growing trade protectionism among the industrial countries. Aid fatigue was on the rise in the North once more, fuelled by harder times, a sense that much ODA had been futile, and the neo-conservatism of Thatcher and Reagan. The North-South dialogue had collapsed and Pierre Trudeau, just two years after championing its resurrection, was now castigating the Group of 77 for demanding too much.[2]

Although the government was formally committed to raising Canadian aid to 0.5 per cent of GNP by 1985, Canada's average annual *decline* of ODA in real terms for the period 1977-78 to 1982-83 had been 2.0 per cent, the third worst among DAC countries and far below the average *growth* among members of 4.8 per cent.[3] CIDA had been rejuvenated intellectually and strengthened organizationally under Massé and McWhinney; internal morale was higher and a sense of corporate mission was clearer than in the late 1970s. However, while polls continued to demonstrate general support for Canadian aid efforts, media horror stories from Haiti, Tanzania, and elsewhere had reinforced public images of waste and ineptitude. Even sympathetic outsiders saw the absence of an official strategy for the 1980s as evidence of drift, confusion of purpose, and indecision.[4]

Internationally, the donor establishment was worried about dwindling public support and resources. Concerns about "whither aid?" sparked several studies, both official and independent, which, while predisposed to support development assistance, were aimed at assessing the historical record and contributing to reinvigoration. One major study was commissioned by a Task Force on Concessional Flows set up by the World Bank and the IMF. In *Does Aid Work?*, consultants under the direction of Robert Cassen concluded that much of the public discussion of aid had been distorted, and "that the majority of aid is successful in terms of its own objectives."[5] They found, however, that many aid efforts had been unsuccessful, that the record in sub-Saharan Africa was especially disappointing, and that there was much room for strengthening coordination among donors and recipients.

In a meticulous and comprehensive analysis of the ODA experience for the Overseas Development Institute in London, Roger Riddell wrote:

> To the extent that donors attempt, on often flimsy evidence, to maintain that on the whole aid does work reasonably well, then ammunition is provided to the critics who, without too much digging around, are able to counter these positive assertions with the evidence of aid projects and programmes that have gone wrong. . . . Thus donor bias supporting the generalisation that aid works not only inaccurately portrays our present state of knowledge, it also indirectly plays into the hands of those who argue that in general aid does not work and who even more misguidedly use this conclusion to maintain that therefore it *cannot* work. . . . [The] case for aid and the case against the critics can be sustained without aid's mistakes and uncertainties being concealed.[6]

One of those critics was Graham Hancock, whose *Lords of Poverty* (published soon after the Cassen and Riddell studies) called for the demise of a "development business" that seldom helped the poor and that underwrote "the privileged lifestyles of the international civil servants, 'development experts,' consultants and assorted freeloaders who staff the aid agencies themselves."[7]

Maggie the Communicator

When Prime Minister Trudeau asked Catley-Carlson to assume the CIDA presidency early in 1983, he stressed—as he had with her predecessors—the importance of reaching out to Canadians to promote international development and Canadian aid.[8] It was a task she took on with verve and vitality, proving a superb choice for tackling the image problem that had plagued CIDA for the past decade. Her energetic speech-making, often to standing ovations, was important. So too was her personality—affable, unpretentious, approachable, direct. She was comfortable being called Maggie. When visiting developing countries, she liked to go into a village, sit on someone's floor, and talk with women about their lives and needs.

Right at the outset, Catley-Carlson decided that it was the wrong psychology to tell people how dreadful things were and then appeal for their support. Instead, she developed an approach that became a hallmark for the hundreds of speeches she gave during her tenure: keep the message clear and simple, outline areas of demonstrable progress (higher literacy, lower infant mortality, smallpox eradication, etc.), assert that aid works, give one or two concrete success stories, and then go on to the particular theme of the address.[9]

Catley-Carlson was equally effective in strengthening CIDA's ties with its primary constituencies—NGOs and business. Her political superiors, Liberals and Tories alike, were especially anxious to put CIDA's relations with the business community "on a more professional and non-apologetic footing."[10] She was good at stroking: "The NGO program is probably Canada's biggest development success story";[11] "if we are to carry out a bigger, better, more effective program, we need to draw skilfully on the best Canada has to offer to the developing world—and most of that best lies in the huge reservoir of skills and capacities constituted by Canada's private sector."[12]

She claimed credit for CIDA as well, but always gave pride of place to partnership between government and the private and voluntary sectors. As she put it to the Canadian Institute of International Affairs:

> All that CIDA . . . can do is serve as a *facilitator* of development—by receiving and analyzing the proposals put forward by developing countries, by matching some of them against Canadian capabilities, and then by recruiting the best resources Canada can offer—companies, institutions, individuals—and financing their work.

Catley-Carlson also made a plea (echoed in other talks) for help in putting the message across:

> I am only one voice, and a public servant, so there are limits. I think, however, it is high time for those who believe in human development and international cooperation to charge into the marketplace of ideas, and to put our case with renewed energy and conviction. For too long, the cynics and skeptics have held the floor and the public has begun to believe their dismal message that the world is getting worse and there is nothing we can do. . . . I am not asking you to become flacks for CIDA, but . . . I am asking you to do what you can to see that international cooperation, the Third World, and even poor old, much-abused CIDA get a fair shake in the essential debate on this great world problem.[13]

Quickly developing excellent relations with the media and parliamentarians, she tackled the horror story problem head-on:

> I don't regard it as odd that we've had our own Edsels. . . . [These] are spread with great amounts of panache by the Canadian press, so that the impression is often left that we do nothing other than get into disastrous projects in Haiti and leave forklift trucks rotting on the dock in Tanzania. We do that. We get our own dry holes. We also have a lot of success stories.[14]

When Catley-Carlson said things people did not want to hear, she usually managed to avoid giving offence. To those pushing for a sharper developmental focus in the aid program, one more oriented to poverty reduction and less motivated by commercial objectives, she defended long-established policy compromises:

> I think that, in Canada, opposing tied aid is a little bit of the Canadian inferiority complex manifesting itself. In other words, it's suggesting that anything that is made in Canada and exported under the aid program must almost by definition be uncompetitive or unsuitable from an international standpoint. Well, 30 cents of each dollar in each of our pockets comes from Canada's ability to export. If we were uncompetitive and if we could only supply unsuitable goods and products, this would simply not be the case. So I don't have any problem with the morality of tied aid.

But, she added, "that's not to say that a lot of other people don't."[15] She supported strongly the emerging orthodoxy about the private sector as *the* engine of economic growth,[16] another unpopular viewpoint within the NGO/humanitarian constituency. However, she also advised business that CIDA was not a commercial development agency, and defended multilateral aid when private-sector pressure sought a reduction in favour of more bilateral programming.[17]

Catley-Carlson wanted as well to persuade Canadian constituencies that they were part of a larger collective effort. Allan MacEachen, Liberal secretary of state for External Affairs, agreed to convene a two-day national colloquium on "Partners in Development" in March 1984. Representatives of business, NGOs, universities, labour and cooperative movements and others, including members of Parliament, were convened for a freewheeling discussion of aid policy. Not surprisingly, sharp differences of opinion were voiced on tied aid, the "relationship between 'pure' development goals and trade objectives," and human rights.[18] This town-meeting format was not tried again, but, throughout Catley-Carlson's presidency, consultations between CIDA and a multitude of Canadian interests were more extensive than ever before.

Though positive about Catley-Carlson's communications skills and successes, some observers were critical of the well-patented approach she employed to put across her message. It was not that she shied away from the seriousness of a crisis, such as the African drought, or the magnitude of developmental challenges, or that she actually asserted that there were easy answers. Rather, her style seemed to convey the *impression* that there were simple and workable solutions. Moreover, she talked a lot about development "out there," yet her message came across as Canadian-centred.

Probably most frustrating was her effectiveness in accommodating a multiplicity of perspectives on aid policy. The North-South Institute, among others, saw this as reflecting a "disarray of objectives" in which the promotion of long-term development was "often the first to be crowded out."[19] As Phillip Rawkins put it, "her conviction that CIDA was 'not a policy maker, but a policy taker' seemed to many to sum up the lack of focused effort to deal with development goals."[20]

After the Conservative victory and the appointment of junior ministers with responsibility for the aid program, Catley-Carlson assumed a lower profile and no longer received as much media coverage as in her first year. She continued an active round of speaking engagements, however, dwelling more on international issues and less on Canadian policy. She always evoked upbeat enthusiasm and encouraged partnerships among CIDA, Canadians, and the developing world. Her immediate political superiors, Monique Vézina to 1986 and Monique Landry thereafter, appropriated much of the Catley-Carlson approach, though neither was a gifted public speaker in French or English.

Catley-Carlson encouraged growth in the Agency's public outreach programs as well. The Public Participation Program became a separate division within the Special Programs Branch, and expanded its support for community-based development education efforts. Several initiatives emphasized young people. Following discussions with provincial ministries of education, PPP in 1987 funded teachers' associations to bring global issues into Canadian classrooms—arguably CIDA's most enlightened and forward-looking move in this field.[21]

In 1988, a Youth Initiatives Program was launched in Special Programs to foster links between young Canadians and their counterparts in developing countries; the program funded overseas exchanges and assignments as well as development education projects in Canada.[22] Meanwhile, the Public Outreach Unit within Public Affairs Branch launched two bilingual magazines, targeting the eight-to-eleven and twelve-to-fifteen age groups, and produced several other educational materials (including the popular "World in Development" maps).

The Policy Agenda under Catley-Carlson

Soon after her appointment, the new president suggested that the essentials of Canadian aid were sound and would be retained: the emphasis on the poorest countries and people, sectoral specialization in agriculture, energy, and human resources, a stable share of the aid budget for multilateral organizations, and growing resources for NGOs and business as long as the promised level of ODA growth materialized. Besides building public awareness, her new priorities were: enhanced private-sector cooperation in Canada and abroad, more effective integration of women in development, and a stronger emphasis on environmental issues.[23] Catley-Carlson was also keen to expand CIDA-funded opportunities for education and training.

Each of these issues became a focus of policy development. The Liberals proposed an Aid-Trade Fund after the 1982-83 recession accelerated the drive for commercialization of Canadian aid. The Tories were even more eager to use aid for commercial advantage when they assumed office. However, the severe drought and famine that intensified in Ethiopia, Sudan, and other areas of sub-Saharan Africa exerted a different pull. So too did Catley-Carlson's determined effort to move beyond token advocacy to a comprehensive approach to the role of women in development. Policy work on environment and development was more tentative, with rhetoric outpacing action.

Aid, Trade, and a Change of Government

Trade expansion and international competitiveness were watchwords for Canadian foreign policy throughout the 1980s. As we have seen, the Trudeau government decided to increase bilateral aid at the expense of multilateral, explicitly to increase domestic commercial benefits.

A 1983 External Affairs trade policy paper noted that CIDA had stepped up its consultations with business, had regularly sought the views of other departments on eligibility and allocations, and had become further exposed to trade priorities through representation on the board of the Export Development Corporation and the Export Trade Development Board (set up in response to the Hatch report). Meanwhile, Canadian business was pushing for further integration of aid and trade policies, especially more concessional financing. The trade policy paper concluded: "Although all of the business community's expectations cannot be met without running the risk of negating real developmental considerations which form the primary objective for Canadian official development assistance, there is nevertheless considerable scope for Canada to pursue commercial objectives in its aid program."[24] Especially good opportunities were seen for agricultural and fisheries products, capital equipment, and high technology.[25]

Trade promotion officials and Ed Lumley, minister of state for Trade, wanted a proactive and firm-driven *crédit mixte* fund with resources well beyond those then available through EDC. The Department of Finance was afraid that such a fund would soon exhaust discretionary resources and create yet another pressure on the escalating federal deficit. Since the government was committed to "best efforts" to achieve the ODA/GNP target of 0.7 per cent by 1990, Finance proposed tucking any increase in concessional financing into the expanding aid budget.[26]

For CIDA, which wanted to protect ODA in the event of a Conservative election victory, the prospect of a new business-oriented facility was attractive, though not at the expense of the existing program. A compromise was fashioned that satisfied bureaucratic contenders—except EDC, which wanted to house an expanded facility. First, in the Speech from the Throne in December 1983, the Trudeau government pledged unequivocally to reach 0.7 per cent by the 1990-91 fiscal year. It also promised to channel more resources through NGOs, cooperatives, and other non-profit bodies.[27] Then, Finance Minister Marc Lalonde announced in his February 1984 budget that up to one-half of the increase over 0.5 would be made available for a new Aid-Trade Fund within CIDA.[28]

Planned ODA growth was such that up to $1.3 billion was foreseen for the new fund by 1990-91. While details had not yet been worked out, officials indicated that CIDA would actively encourage Canadian firms to seek out export opportunities. Depending on circumstances, financial packages would combine varying proportions of EDC loans on hard terms with interest-free CIDA loans. Although subject to appraisal for developmental content, these would be quick-disbursing and available in any CIDA-eligible country without regard to country planning or eligibility status. The fund would be aimed at near-NICs such as Algeria, Mexico, Malaysia, and the Philippines, and at increasing Canadian sales in China and India. Extensive consultations with business were promised.[29]

The Aid-Trade proposal worried many critics, who saw in it not only more subsidies for uncompetitive exports, and yet another forlorn effort to convert aid-financed sales into longer-term commercial relationships, but also—in developmental terms—a Canadian aid program even more heavily skewed towards mega-projects and middle-income countries.[30] The DAC secretariat also expressed reservations, querying whether the Aid-Trade Fund would violate recently negotiated principles for the use of aid in association with export credits.[31]

Catley-Carlson conceded that the facility would be of primary interest to more-developed countries, but, presumably because it would be financed from additional resources, she denied that "this will affect the past Canadian strategy of trying to help the poorest countries."[32] Frank Petrie, a former trade official who had just taken over as president of the Canadian Export Association, applauded the government's announcement:

> There's certainly no sin in ensuring that there's going to be good fallout from the Canadian aid program for the Canadian economy. I don't think the government's proposed Aid-Trade Fund will deflect from the developmental priority. . . . All the exporters I've talked to have realized that the aid program has to be used for developmental purposes primarily, although I think that a lot of people aren't quite clear about the aims of the aid program.[33]

An internal review. Within CIDA, the Liberal government's decisions to increase ODA to 0.7 per cent and launch the Aid-Trade Fund prompted a review of policies and procedures to follow up the earlier MEPAD exercise. Douglas Lindores, vice-president, Multilateral Branch (and later senior vice-president), was asked to examine ways of delivering "a substantially increased volume while maintaining and indeed improving aid effectiveness." In "Options for the Future," he concluded that "the current policy framework for Canadian ODA does not form a consistent whole." Policies reflected "the compromises and balances that the government felt the aid programme had to strike among various and (sometimes) competing objectives and constituencies." Balancing contradictory objectives was especially difficult in agriculture and human resource development because many needs in these spheres could not be met through Canadian goods and services.[34]

Lindores was not as sanguine as the president (in her public remarks) about grafting yet another priority onto the existing program. The Aid-Trade Fund and "a general government desire to make the programme more responsive to Canadian business interests" appeared to require reconsideration of sectoral emphases (perhaps even to be replaced by a theme-oriented approach), and reexamination of the policy of channelling 80 per cent of bilateral resources to the poorest countries. To the extent that internal trade-offs could be achieved, however, it might be possible "to continue to work towards respecting Canada's international undertaking to channel 0.15% of GNP to the least developed."[35]

While observing that business would object to untying procurement to allow international competition, Lindores advocated more flexibility to meet local costs in low-income countries, at least LLDCs, and for projects related to basic human needs. Business opposition might be offset "by the emphasis being placed on our commercial interests through the Aid-Trade Fund and the expansion of responsive activities such as the Industrial Cooperation Programme and Lines of Credit."[36]

The aid-trade initiative also offered the prospect of a quick-disbursing mechanism to help the Agency spend a rising budget with relatively fixed human resources. Lindores suggested that, if the new facility grew as anticipated, marginal increases in the NGO program, food aid, humanitarian assistance, multilateral technical cooperation programs, and bilateral liquid transfers "should permit the target to be met without major administrative resource implications for the Agency." Both the Aid-Trade Fund and an expansion of lines of credit assumed, however,

> that the limiting factor on the export of Canadian goods and services under concessional financing terms is the lack of such financing. This fact is far from proven and there is evidence from the operations of our existing lines of credit that the availability of concessional financing may not be able to overcome the essential lack of competitiveness of Canadian goods and services in many areas. If this should prove to be the case, then it cannot automatically be assumed that the Aid-Trade Fund will actually disburse the level of resources made available to it.[37]

Large projects were now less in demand because of debt and high maintenance costs, and many governments had become more sophisticated in dealing with aid donors.

These reservations notwithstanding, Lindores claimed that "the basic utility of such a mechanism is consistent with a large body of opinion within CIDA itself." While EDC was making a bid for the facility, he argued the importance of keeping it in CIDA to safeguard its developmental integrity, to help the Agency build a more constructive relationship with the private sector, and to minimize the risk that business would accept ODA money from EDC and then return to CIDA "for what wasn't [available]—the rest of the bilateral programme."

A new branch was suggested as an umbrella for the fund, the Industrial Cooperation Program, and other business-oriented activities.[38] Sensing that such a step would sit well in the event of a Conservative electoral victory, the President's Committee secured Treasury Board approval to establish a Business Cooperation Branch. It began operations in July 1984.

A new government. Lindores' review and preliminary planning for the Aid-Trade Fund occurred on the eve of the summer 1984 federal election. The short-lived Liberal administration of John Turner (when Jean Chrétien served as secretary of state for External Affairs) announced no changes in the aid program (apart from a budget cut), and the election campaign was devoid of discussion of foreign policy issues—with one exception, a speech to business people by Sinclair Stevens, who had been opposition critic for external affairs since Brian Mulroney defeated Joe Clark for the Tory leadership in 1983.

There was nervousness in foreign policy and international development circles about the prospect that Stevens might keep the portfolio in a Conservative cabinet and pursue a right-wing agenda. However, belying his reputation as the "slasher" (as president of the Treasury Board under Clark in 1979-80), and the image he conveyed in his minority report on Latin America and the Caribbean in 1982, Stevens did not signal any dramatic departures from established policy in his remarks to the Canadian Association for Latin America. On development assistance, he promised that a Conservative government would honour the pledge to achieve 0.7 per cent by 1990, develop a closer relationship between trade and aid, and make more use of NGOs, all echoes of existing Liberal policies. If Stevens departed from the status quo, it was to emphasize long-standing concerns about the proliferation of recipients and the desirability of reviewing allocations to countries that were systematically violating human rights. According to a press report, he drew chuckles when he announced: "We will review the mandate, objectives, resources and effectiveness of the Canadian International Development Agency."[39]

Those who dreaded Stevens were relieved when Joe Clark was chosen as secretary of state for External Affairs. One of several newcomers to Ottawa, Monique Vézina, was named minister of state for External Relations with specific responsibilities for CIDA and French-speaking developing countries. In his first ministerial press briefing, Clark said that the new government's foreign policy would place a "very high emphasis" on international trade. However, pending a review of foreign policy and ODA, he indicated that the essentials of the aid program would stay in place, including Canada's 0.7 per cent commitment.[40] Work on the Aid-Trade Fund was suspended while an interdepartmental committee undertook a study of export financing.

From Aid-Trade to Trade and Development.[41] A consultation paper on export financing was published early in 1985. Some cautionary notes were sounded about using aid for trade promotion: a larger allocation of ODA resources to support concessional financing "would likely involve a departure from CIDA's current mandate"; it was not in Canada's long-term commercial interests to become associated with projects that might ultimately be of limited value to recipient countries; and it was essential not to damage Canada's reputation by subsidizing the sale of uncompetitive goods and services.

Nonetheless, the report recommended consideration of three options—more flexible parallel financing, an aid-trade mechanism, and/or greater use of EDC's *crédit mixte* program, with concessional funds counted as ODA.[42] Following consultations with business,[43] the Aid-Trade Fund was reborn in May 1985 as the Trade and Development Facility. It was still to be located in CIDA and funded out of half of ODA increases in excess of 0.5 per cent of GNP. Now, however, since Finance Minister Michael Wilson had twice cut planned aid spending (and set back the target for 0.7 per cent from 1990 to 1995), projected funding for the Facility up to 1990-91 would drop to $550 million from $1.3 billion.[44]

Work commenced on the revised proposal early in 1985. Once more, there were debates within the bureaucracy about how to reconcile developmental appraisal with commercial opportunity. CIDA officials were especially worried that companies would pre-empt the Agency by making firm commitments that, if pulled back, would create embarrassment and that, if not, would force cuts in other programs. Meanwhile, business spokespersons declared a preference for "one-stop shopping" at the Export Development Corporation without the hassle of proving developmental worth. Although details were still unresolved, Geoffrey Bruce, CIDA's vice-president for Business Cooperation, informed the *Financial Post* in August that, as with the previous proposal, the Facility would be exporter-driven and quick-disbursing. It would be open to all CIDA-eligible countries, probably without geographical quotas, but restricted to "priority" projects; sales of defence and luxury items and "the building of monuments" would be expressly precluded.[45]

The high visibility of the Facility continued to attract criticism from NGOs and the media. Nigel Martin, executive director of CCIC, complained: "We're commercializing aid and doing nothing more than trying to encourage Canadian exports to the Third World instead of giving aid to those who need it most—the poor."[46] The *Globe and Mail* strongly opposed the scheme: "Canada has a duty to trade and to aid; but to do both in combination is to do neither well."[47] Madame Vézina claimed, however, that the Facility would create "thousands of jobs. . . . I do not understand those who are saddened by this prospect."[48]

In view of the dismal historical record of the Canadian private sector in penetrating Third World markets, visions of commercial success were dubious. They were soon dashed in any case when the Tory government's concern about the federal deficit proved more compelling than accelerated trade promotion through aid. In February 1986, just weeks before the program was to begin, Wilson's budget cut the level of planned ODA growth yet again, deferring 0.7 per cent to the year 2000 and maintaining the 0.5 per cent level until 1990. Although aid was now projected to increase at the growth rate of the Canadian economy, bringing the Trade and Development Facility on stream would have offered little scope for expanding other programs and meant cuts for some. The absence of a growth trajectory, the uncertainty and "lumpiness" of exporter-driven requests for aid-trade funds, and the negative political fallout of persisting in these circumstances all contributed to the Facility's demise.

Instead, the government announced that concessional funding from the Export Development Corporation under Section 31 for aid-eligible countries would be reported as ODA, over and above what was planned on a formula basis. CIDA would be consulted about "developmental soundness" of projects, but would not undertake formal appraisals. Again, the DAC secretariat was critical: "This implies that there is a fundamental difference between the rigorous appraisal procedures applied to traditional ODA projects and those to be used in assessing ODA eligibility in the case of Treasury-financed mixed credits." It also rebuked Canada for not consulting other DAC members about the change.[49]

It was clear, though, that a reversion to *crédit mixte* under Section 31 would involve modest funding when compared to the proposed Trade and Development Facility. A lot of energy had gone into an effort that, as Martin Rudner noted, had come after "international trade subsidization through associated financing had already passed its historic peak and had begun to ebb."[50] While cancellation of the Trade and Development Facility did not signal a diminution of CIDA's interest in courting business, the scale of such activity no longer threatened to overwhelm the aid program. Meanwhile, the African famine had been tilting the Agency's policy agenda in a very different direction.

The African Crisis

In the early 1980s, there was serious economic and social decay almost everywhere in sub-Saharan Africa. Debt was rising, export revenues were falling, population growth was outstripping food production, and environmental degradation was worsening. Institutions were crumbling and many countries were afflicted by civil strife. In addition, a wide swath across the north of the region—reaching from Ethiopia in the east to Senegal and Mauritania in the west—was devastated by the worst drought of the century. So too were many parts of southern Africa, especially Mozambique and Angola. Famine conditions were already intense by 1984 when a remarkable number of Canadians and citizens of other industrial countries were galvanized to take action or donate money by horrible images of human suffering that reached electronically into their homes.

The worst situation was in Ethiopia, where drought was aggravating a catastrophe wrought by human cruelty and neglect. Following the overthrow of the old imperial order of Haile Selassie, the country was convulsed by civil war and ideological turmoil resulting from centuries of exploitation and despotism. The Food and Agriculture Organization of the UN had been appealing to the world for help since 1982. Canada, through CIDA and some NGOs, provided food aid in amounts greater than any other Western donor, but the response everywhere was woefully inadequate until the autumn of 1984. More than a year earlier, Eugene Whelan, then minister of Agriculture, had proposed a $20 million emergency scheme to take food to millions of starving "unreachables" in isolated areas of the country. "But, say sources close to the former Liberal government, a document detailing the scheme was blocked in cabinet committee when such key players as Allan MacEachen, then external affairs minister, and Jean-Jacques Blais, then defence minister, could not be convinced of the gravity of the situation."[51]

A serious response from Northern aid donors came only after desperate relief workers persuaded television crews from Europe and North America to come to Ethiopia and do some filming. The effect was astounding. As Joe Clark commented, "People in High River don't read FAO reports. They do watch television." Two minutes and eleven seconds of airtime on the CBC National News in October 1984 prompted "a sudden outpouring of emotion and money."[52]

On November 1, Clark named David MacDonald, the ex-minister and former head of the Futures Secretariat, as Canadian Emergency Coordinator/

African Famine. Reporting directly to Clark, and working out of CIDA in liaison with Vézina and Catley-Carlson, MacDonald was asked to assess the gravity of the crisis, propose concrete steps for government assistance, work with NGOs in mobilizing Canadian support, seek help from the provinces, and cooperate with other donors and international agencies. Two weeks later, a government that had just reduced planned aid expenditures for 1985-86 by $180 million created a $50 million Special Fund for Africa. It included up to $15 million to match private donations dollar-for-dollar.[53]

The breadth and depth of public response remained remarkably high through the winter and spring of 1984-85. The flow of private donations was such that Clark had to return twice to cabinet to secure matching funds of almost $36 million, two-and-a-half times the level originally approved.[54] Church groups, schoolchildren, voluntary organizations, and—taking a lead from Bob Geldof in the UK—musicians and entertainers got involved. Municipal and provincial governments were also active. Moreover, Mulroney's earlier surprise appointment of former Ontario NDP leader Stephen Lewis as ambassador to the United Nations gave Canada an eloquent and passionate voice in international fora; a volunteer teacher in Nigeria in the 1960s, Lewis emerged as a champion for the African cause. Maurice Strong also played a prominent role as executive coordinator of the United Nations Office of Emergency Operations in Africa.

The actual emergency operation was bedeviled by all the chaos inherent in a disaster—spoilage and inappropriate diversion of food and relief supplies, and also in the Ethiopian case warring sides in a civil conflict trying to gain political and military advantage from aid. Nevertheless, considering the difficulties, international efforts were creditable and many lives were saved. The Canadian contribution was especially well orchestrated by the joint efforts of MacDonald's office and a coalition of NGOs, Africa Emergency Aid, which also broke new ground: it was "the first time NGOs had played such an active part in making program decisions on the use of CIDA funding"[55] (as opposed simply to allocating funds).

Reporting on his first four months, MacDonald made several recommendations to the Standing Committee of the House of Commons on External Affairs and National Defence (SCEAND).[56] At its hearings in April 1985, the committee supported extending MacDonald's mandate for a further year, strengthening the government-NGO partnership, increasing public education and outreach, and making available another public fund to match private donations. Above all, it highlighted the need to move beyond relief to development by tackling the underlying causes of the crisis:

> [Development] assistance to Africa is a long-term problem to which Canada should make a long term commitment. . . . We should see to it that our aid dollars are used to best advantage. At present a clear strategy is lacking. Canada cannot simply react to the plans of others. . . . In particular, Canada's aid program should be designed to maximize benefits for the poorest people. We need to clarify our own goals.

The committee's chairman, William Winegard, was determined to move from rhetoric to action, serving notice that SCEAND would undertake an in-depth review of all aspects of Canada's development assistance programs and policies.[57]

Working with a clear mandate (unlike his experience with the Futures Secretariat), MacDonald had delivered, and his term was extended to March 31, 1986. This time, he was authorized to move beyond relief coordination to longer term studies and a program of outreach within Canada. The government's fiscal agenda stood in the way of commitment to more matching funds, but an $18 million African Recovery Fund was made available, to be allocated largely through Africa Emergency Aid.

During his extended term, MacDonald led evaluation missions to eleven African countries, remained heavily involved in monitoring and international networking, and undertook a busy round of activities aimed at maintaining Canadian commitment.[58] However, the immediacy of the crisis had passed, donations were falling off, and much of the outreach involved the "converted preaching to the converted."[59] The most ambitious aspect of this activity was "Forum Africa," a series of community meetings across the country, which culminated in a three-day National Forum Africa in Ottawa in February 1986. Catley-Carlson assessed CIDA's lessons from the crisis for those in attendance:

> A trauma such as the African famine shakes a development agency to its core. What has been the most profound change in CIDA's thinking, post-1984? It is a realization that the single-project approach to development, which works well in North America and often in Asia, just won't work in Africa because the leap is too great. . . . The second lesson is, in a nutshell, "fix—don't build." The available dollars can do more good, faster, if we use them not to create costly projects from scratch, but to get what already exists back into good running condition.[60]

Toward a longer-term Canadian initiative. In his final report, MacDonald made several recommendations for what he called a "Decade for Africa." He called on the government to give Africa a special place in the ODA program, with steadily increasing levels of support progressively freed from procurement tying. Self-sufficiency in food production, trade liberalization, and debt relief were suggested as high priorities. He urged further strengthening of "partnership," both between Canadians and Africans and among Canadian

NGOs and institutions. In addition, more African students "should be assured fair access to Canadian colleges and universities," and Canadian partners should establish a "Canada-Africa Centre" to administer and distribute a matching fund of $50-60 million annually.

MacDonald also suggested giving responsibility for the initiative to the minister for External Relations, "assisted by a senior-level order-in-council appointment, bringing together the responsibilities for Africa in the Department of External Affairs and CIDA." This new arrangement would involve creation of an early warning and emergency preparedness unit; the full integration of all aid programs in Africa, both anglophone and francophone; the coordination of interdepartmental policies on aid, trade and finance; and the creation of a consultative committee on Africa with advisory and outreach responsibilities.[61]

By this time, Monique Vézina had become caught up in the African crisis, and wanted to leave her ministerial mark by launching a special program. As Hugh Winsor commented, "She seems to have come some distance from the first impression that seeped out—that she was more concerned about who in Canada got CIDA contracts than what those contracts were for."[62] MacDonald's "Decade for Africa" was viewed as too far-reaching and costly to be considered in its entirety. Moreover, the administrative recommendations had no support within the bureaucracy, where they were seen as a thinly veiled effort by MacDonald to carry on with increased jurisdiction over vast parts of CIDA and External Affairs.

Despite testy moments between Vézina and MacDonald, especially during his extended term, his proposals for strengthening longer-term partnerships formed the kernel of Africa 2000, launched by Vézina in May 1986. With $150 million in funding for the first five years, Africa 2000 made a fifteen-year commitment to small-scale projects in agriculture, reforestation, food security, and women's participation.

A total of $75 million was to be disbursed by a successor body to Africa Emergency Aid, whose members had indicated their wish to continue collaborating. Partnership Africa-Canada was organized shortly thereafter. As Madame Vézina told the House of Commons, "I am counting on the NGOs to be our very first partners in *Africa 2000*." Canadian companies would be invited to join as "our second partners," and would be encouraged to foster small-scale enterprises. A new administrative unit in Special Programs Branch would oversee the program, aiming to put in place "more than 2000 small projects . . . helping to meet the essential needs of the African people" by the end of 1987.[63]

Supporting the program as a step in the right direction, MacDonald voiced disappointment that nothing was announced on aid untying, debt, trade, or his notion of an integrated approach to African programming.[64] (He himself, however, was given a continuing role in Africa shortly thereafter as Canadian ambassador to Ethiopia.)[65] The *Ottawa Citizen* thought that Africa 2000 was "rich with good ideas—but shamefully short on funds," involving as it did a diversion from existing resources.[66]

Vézina proposed another initiative soon afterwards to the UN General Assembly—a multilateral mechanism modelled on Africa 2000.[67] "Its role would be to make available to local communities, village councils and volunteer organizations in Africa, funds and technical expertise to help them to carry out projects of their own choosing to meet their needs in the fields of desertification, conservation of ground cover, and food production." Canada was prepared to contribute $20 million over five years. When UNDP later set up the Africa 2000 Network in 1989, Canadian support was confirmed by Monique Landry, Vézina's successor.[68]

Women in Development

While aid-trade and the African crisis required policy responses from CIDA, the major initiative within the Agency was a remarkably successful effort to move the issue of women in development (WID) from the margins to the centre of programming. In an interview marking CIDA's twentieth anniversary in 1988, Catley-Carlson looked back on the major accomplishments of her presidency as *Sharing Our Future* (the 1988 strategy examined in Chapter 8), the transition between governments of two different parties, and the expansion of partnerships with Canadian voluntary organizations and businesses. "And if I were to add one, I would say the whole 'Women in Development' initiative, because I think Canada has become a world leader in the area of women in development, and I am very proud of that."[69]

Dating back to the appointment of the Royal Commission on the Status of Women in 1967, feminists in key positions in the federal cabinet and bureaucracy had succeeded step-by-step in making women's issues matters of serious public policy. Some worked actively in the UN and other international fora with like-minded women from other countries on proposals that, once adopted, were used to legitimate domestic Canadian objectives. The nerve centre of these activities—initially a coordinator in the Privy Council Office—was upgraded to an agency in 1976, as Status of Women Canada (SWC). SWC and the minister responsible were mandated to ensure that women's concerns were integrated into overall governmental planning and decision-making. Under a policy adopted that year, all departments were directed to examine the impact on women of their proposals, include an analysis of implications for women in cabinet documents, and designate a person or unit to oversee these activities.[70]

The 1976 policy emerged from a review of the government's record in advancing women's equality undertaken the previous year in preparation for the World Conference of the International Women's Year in Mexico City. In her opening statement as head of Canada's delegation in Mexico City, Coline Campbell, MP, reported that CIDA endorsed the principles of full integration and equality of women in development programs; she pledged high priority to special programs designed to improve the condition of women in developing countries.

CIDA's representative on the delegation, Hylda Bateman, recommended formation of "an action-oriented Steering Committee within the Agency to devise strategies for sensitizing all personnel concerned with policy, program planning and operations on the concerns of women in the development process."[71] In line with SWC policy, a one-person "responsibility centre" for integrating women into Canadian development projects was created within Policy Branch in 1976.[72] Michel Dupuy reiterated the Agency's commitment in 1977 when hosting a colloquium attended by thirteen DAC donors who agreed to step up efforts to make recipient countries aware of women's basic needs.[73]

Some small-scale projects targeted at women accompanied these early efforts to put WID on CIDA's policy map. The Agency also supported in 1976 the creation of MATCH, the first developmental NGO in the world run exclusively by and for women.[74] Despite active advocacy by the WID coordinator, however, overall programming did not reflect much awareness of gender issues. Suteera Thomson interviewed several planning and project officers during 1978 and 1979 for a study of CIDA's role in promoting food security. Of fifty respondents, forty-one found it difficult to answer her questions about women's involvement in projects.[75] It was time, she concluded, to move beyond rhetoric to action.[76] The policy-performance gap was apparent in other donor agencies as well—including US AID, even though it was assigned a legislated mandate in 1973 to promote women's integration.[77]

Following the 1980 Copenhagen Conference to mark the mid-point in the UN Decade for Women, pressure from Canadian and Nordic representatives was crucial in securing DAC's agreement to give WID more emphasis in statistical reporting and in annual reviews of members' performance.[78] In 1981, CIDA was a charter member of DAC's WID correspondents group and helped prepare "Guiding Principles to Aid Agencies for Supporting the Role of Women in Development." Approved by DAC members at their High-Level Meeting in November 1983, the Guiding Principles asserted:

> DAC Members recognize that development is a total process. It must involve both men and women in order to be effective. Substantial gains will only be achieved with the contribution of both sexes, for women play a vital role in

> contributing to the development of their countries. . . . However, development activities have too often been designed in a way which takes insufficient account of the role of women as decision-makers, as producers and as beneficiaries, and of the fact that the income of women is crucial to the raising of the standard of living of the family.

DAC members were urged: to make their policies explicit in the form of legislation or ministerial directives; to ensure that WID directives were integrated in all aspects of policy and project planning, implementation, and evaluation; and to develop comprehensive approaches to gender analysis, data collection, and accountability. Particular emphasis was put on giving women access to productive resources and opportunities for education and training.[79]

That High-Level Meeting was Catley-Carlson's first as president, and she promised to promote WID within CIDA. The Agency reported later that the Guiding Principles were a major source of inspiration for the development of a new Agency-wide strategy that would move away "from the traditional advocacy approach to WID towards a more professional approach based on accountability."[80] However, finding a practical and effective means of doing so was proving difficult.[81] The first draft of a strategy prepared by an enlarged WID Unit in Policy Branch was turned back by the President's Committee on grounds that it staked too much on claims of equity and social justice, and not enough on women's economic impact. It also risked giving the undesirable impression that CIDA knew what was in the best interests of Third World women. What was wanted, the WID Unit was told, was a solid approach that could not be dismissed in Canada or abroad as feminist propaganda or cultural imperialism.

A way out of the impasse came from what Catley-Carlson described as a "chance conversation" with Peter MacPherson, then director of US AID, about the WID training course offered by the Harvard Institute for International Development. Two CIDA people were sent on the course, which offered what had been missing in the earlier draft strategy—a careful analysis of women's work and experience based on research on gender roles and, even more importantly, on case studies of actual development projects and situations. The developmental importance, and not just the moral imperative of WID, could be demonstrated convincingly from data that went beyond well-known UN statistics—women perform two-thirds of all the world's work and produce half the world's food, yet receive 10 per cent of the world's income, and own 1 per cent of the world's property[82]— to examine concrete experiences such as the following from Bolivia:

> World Bank people were anxious to help the mountain herders increase the production of wool, gathered from llamas. They instructed the men in a de-licing procedure involving dipping the llamas in a chemical solution. Bolivian men,

> however, do not look after llamas. They listened to the lessons with polite indifference and didn't ask, or didn't hear, if it mattered what time of day the animals were dipped. Women, picking up what information they could from the men, wearily dipped the llamas one evening when the regular chores were done. That night the wet llamas died of exposure.[83]

Harvard personnel were contracted to provide three-day seminars for CIDA officers (the President's Committee took the second course), and to prepare in-house Agency trainers. Meanwhile, the WID Unit, under the able leadership of Elizabeth McAllister, produced a second draft of the policy paper that became the "WID Policy Framework." Approved by the President's Committee in November 1984, the policy emphasized the necessity of involving both women and men to make development effective, and of ensuring "that development intervention impacts on women as positively as possible and that women are enabled to have a positive impact on development." The goal of realizing "the full potential of women as agents and beneficiaries of the development process" required the integration of WID in all aspects of the Agency's work, as well as women-specific programming.

The Framework set out operational objectives:

- To develop mechanisms to integrate WID into corporate planning and management systems, and to operationalize WID policy in a manner that is measurable and reviewable.
- To develop explicit plans to include and to benefit LDC women and girls in . . . Country Program Reviews, program and project design, and in sectoral policies and guidelines.
- To develop specific strategies for increasing the representation of women in training and scholarship programs.
- To develop methods to collect sex-disaggregated data in order to identify and to eliminate unintentional discrimination in development programs and projects, and to develop a data base to plan country programs and projects.

Other objectives dealt with training CIDA personnel, extending the Framework to consultants, promoting WID multilaterally, and developing communications strategies directed towards the Canadian public and potential beneficiaries in developing countries.[84]

Although work proceeded on many fronts, energies during 1984-85 were concentrated on expanding the Framework into a corporate action plan. The key to overcoming obstacles previously experienced in CIDA and other donor agencies lay in diffusing responsibility for detailed planning and implementation from the WID Unit to all parts of the Agency. With strong support from Vézina, Catley-Carlson, and the President's Committee, an Agency-wide WID Steering Committee was constituted under the vice-president for Policy. While there was strong top-down support, the success of the organizational strategy rested on a bottom-up development of plans based on widespread consultation by branch task forces.

The goal of getting all professional employees to acquire ownership of WID was further strengthened by training sessions using the Harvard methodology; 75 per cent participated by 1986[85] and all by 1988, when the training program was offered to many executing agencies as well.[86] A signal that performance on WID objectives would be included in employee job appraisals provided another strong incentive. Although the "big push" met resistance from some, and sceptical resignation from others who saw WID as another flash-in-the pan fad, even some of the most tough-minded engineers were won over by the training course.

By the end of 1985, a comprehensive Action Plan for 1985-86/1990-91 was in place. Unveiled publicly by Vézina in June 1986, it spelled out continuing and planned activities.[87] The minister also announced that $25 million of the $150 million earmarked for Africa 2000 would be channelled to special programs and multilateral efforts to enhance women's access to education, technology, and credit. In addition, a $10 million fund was announced for projects integrating health into development activities.[88] Stevie Cameron commented in the *Ottawa Citizen*:

> Put in the context of CIDA's statistics, you wonder why it wasn't a larger share. . . . Still, the $25 million is a good start, and as one cynical observer pointed out at the splendid lunch Vézina threw . . . when she made the announcement, it's a lot more than the government has ever given Canadian women's programs in order to achieve change. All they do here about day care, for instance, is study it—expensively and endlessly.[89]

Cross-agency groups went to work on several fronts: reshaping procedures to incorporate WID guidelines in all programs and projects, developing gender-differentiated data bases and ways of measuring performance on WID goals, devising means to make Agency staff accountable for WID, securing access to WID expertise in Canada and recipient countries, and increasing women's participation in education and training programs. The WID Unit itself participated in this work, and continued to develop a comprehensive workbook for programming and project personnel.

Piece by piece, the Action Plan became operational. WID issues now had to be addressed in each project identification memorandum, in all management plans, and in terms of reference for executing agencies. A WID Annex was added to the standard project approval memorandum, and approaches to evaluating WID performance were put in place. A target of 50 per cent women was set for scholarships and training places. A gender-based data bank was developed. WID training was extended to businesses and NGOs, and special outreach programs were established. Dialogue with recipients was increased, reportedly with generally positive results. A full-time WID expert was hired, and the WID Unit was transferred from Policy Branch to Professional Services (formerly part of the Resources Branch), symbolizing a transition from policy formulation to ongoing implementation.[90]

Meanwhile, CIDA became even more active in promoting WID in international fora. An Expert Group on Women in Development was officially established within DAC in 1984,[91] and Canada held the chair during 1984-85. The Nairobi conference marking the end of the UN Decade for Women in 1985 provided a strong incentive to get the Framework in place and move forward with the Action Plan. Canadian delegates played a key role both in ensuring that the deliberations did not get bogged down in the acrimony that had often characterized North-South gatherings, and in drafting "Forward-Looking Strategies to the Year 2000," the main document that emerged from the conference.[92] CIDA itself provided funding for several Third World delegates, and participated actively in discussions on WID. (Monique Landry was a member of the Canadian team in Nairobi and, on becoming minister of External Relations in 1986, continued to offer strong ministerial support.)

CIDA has been a follower of international trends on most policy issues, but it has been a leader on WID. After Nairobi, the Agency was in the forefront of efforts to encourage multilateral institutions to adopt WID programming criteria and claimed credit for several positive outcomes.[93] CIDA also became a major supporter of the UN Development Fund for Women, which funds innovative pilot projects for Third World women, and Women's World Banking, an international NGO established to advance women's entrepreneurial activities. When asked by the author to name any activities in which CIDA had provided leadership, senior DAC officials in Paris consistently mentioned Women in Development. One less-than-sympathetic official described WID as a "Canadian fixation."

As she approached the end of her tenure, Margaret Catley-Carlson was justifiably pleased with WID as a success story in corporate management.

> I don't know if after five years we can say we've changed the lives of some women. Yes, I think we can. If you look at the number of women who now have access to credit because of an organization like Women's World Banking, that have access to health care because of the push we've put on things, the number of women scholars that—if we hadn't set quotas, that nasty word—we've put into scholarship programs. . . . I think we can say that we're actually making a dent in how the women of the world have access to the benefits of development. I feel very good about that.[94]

Environment and Development

The relationship between environment and development, though first highlighted at the Stockholm conference in 1972, became a major issue for aid donors (other than US AID) only in the mid-1980s. The Canadian government, under both Liberals and Conservatives, wanted to be seen in the vanguard of progressive thought and action on global environmental matters, not least because of the dispute with the Reagan adminstration over acid rain.

Geoffrey Bruce, later to become CIDA's vice-president for Business Cooperation, was Canada's delegate to the UN Environmental Program early in the decade. He played a key role in campaigning for the General Assembly's endorsement of the World Commission on Environment and Development, which began work in 1984 under the chair of Gro Harlem Brundtland, Norway's prime minister. Maurice Strong was one of the commission's twenty-two members, drawn from North and South, and Canadian Jim MacNeill, former OECD environment director, served as secretary general. CIDA provided $800,000 in funding for the commission,[95] the only bilateral aid agency to offer financial support.

While CIDA tried to look like a leader on the environment, the Agency's track record had been much weaker than its words. Shortly after Stockholm, Clyde Sanger (then with IDRC) analyzed changes required in Canada's aid program if commitments made at the conference were to be taken seriously. Greater expertise was needed in land management, fisheries resources, and hygiene; and more untying was essential for projects that would entail high local costs.[96]

There was, however, little follow-up until 1975, when the Agency entered into a cooperative agreement with the Department of the Environment to organize joint workshops on environment, basic needs, and self-reliance under the rubric "eco-development." The Sectoral Guidelines produced by Policy Branch in 1976 focused heavily on environmental concerns, especially the volume on "Infrastructures and Environment." It drew upon procedures in the 1973 order-in-council setting up the Federal Environmental Assessment Review Office (FEARO) to administer environmental assessment for all projects involving federal monies, properties, or lands.[97] No steps were taken, however, to make the guidelines or recommendations of the joint workshops operational. Nor did CIDA consider itself bound by the FEARO process for projects undertaken abroad.[98]

Finding a mix of adequate and inadequate programming, an external evaluation of CIDA's environmental performance in 1979-80 by an interdisciplinary team of researchers concluded that the best projects owed more to the initiative of individual officers and consultants than to coherent policies and procedures. On balance, the study's authors judged performance as falling far short of the Agency's claims for itself. They urged senior management to make a strong commitment to environmentally sound development, and to integrate effective operational guidelines into all phases of the project cycle. They also called for systematic training of Agency personnel and consultants, a reliable corporate memory to improve learning from past lessons, greater decentralization to the field, and a relaxation of tying requirements. They suggested consideration of a special responsibility centre in the Agency, though with some wariness in view of the ineffectiveness of the WID office at that time.[99]

An environmental specialist hired by Policy Branch in 1983 produced an information paper that catalogued projects deemed to be environmental or to contain environmental components. Using a rather generous definition of "environmental" and "natural resources" (and the established practice of relabelling activities), he concluded that about 12 per cent of CIDA's commitments in 1981-83 were for such projects.[100] Shortly thereafter, Canadian officials took part in the development of DAC guidelines on the environment and development assistance, and on environmental assessment, which were subsequently approved by the OECD Council.[101]

The order-in-council on the Environmental Assessment Review Process was amended in 1984 to include CIDA projects.[102] Senior Vice-President McWhinney argued that a new policy, with environmental impact assessment as its centrepiece, ought to be a high priority. Catley-Carlson was less convinced of the need for urgency until well into 1985, when CIDA agreed to make a presentation to the Brundtland commission on the environmental experience of bilateral aid agencies. A consultant was hired to develop a statement, and the tempo of work on a new corporate policy picked up.

An early draft of the discussion paper for Brundtland proposed a conceptual approach for linking environment and development; reviewed lessons from experience, positive and negative (including the human and biophysical costs of dams and other mega-projects); and recommended a policy based on the complete integration of mandatory environmental impact assessment in all stages of the project cycle. It indicated as well that CIDA's new policy would soon be announced.

Catley-Carlson, however, did not want a document that presented a "quasi-repentant" thesis, that was less than laudatory about the Agency's past performance and current capabilities, that referred to failures in general terms, and that alluded to a policy still in formation. A new submission was quickly prepared by the Public Affairs Branch. Filled with pretty pictures, it alternated between descriptive material on the environmental problems of developing countries and all the good things that CIDA was doing. There was a passing reference to some projects that "failed because they were not environmentally sound, and therefore not sustainable," but the blame was assigned mostly to recipient governments rather than development agencies. The words sounded progressive, but there was little substance to interest the commission.[103]

In June 1986, a month after the Brundtland hearing, the President's Committee approved a new, more proactive policy on environment and development with three main components.[104] First, beginning July 1, all bilateral projects and programs would be screened for environmental implications—which, if significant, would trigger a full environmental impact assessment. Similar procedures would be developed for Special Program and Business Cooperation initiatives, and monitoring would be undertaken of multilateral bodies receiving Canadian ODA. Secondly, "environment enhancing projects" would be encouraged in the spheres of "Natural Resources Environment" (agriculture, forestry, and fisheries) and "Human Resources Environment" (population, health, and human habitat).[105] Thirdly, CIDA would promote "a greater degree of environmental awareness" in Canada, recipient countries, and multilateral organizations. Especially important would be education, training, and institution-building with an environmental emphasis. Implementation would require the designation of one person in each branch to act as environmental coordinator.

In addition, Treasury Board would be asked to add personnel to the environmental advisory unit in order to develop information systems for screening and assessment procedures, to prepare manuals and training programs, to supervise consultants, to gather baseline data, and to establish a resource centre. Finally, the minister would be asked to designate "environment" as a priority programming emphasis like WID.

The advisory unit was expanded to six shortly thereafter. Environmental assessment procedures became operational within bilateral branches in November 1986, but not in Business Cooperation or Special Programs until April 1988.[106] In fact, implementation moved slowly. With senior management preoccupied during this time by the parliamentary review and the preparation of a new strategy, commitment at that level was not as strong or determined as it had been with women in development.

Landry did designate environment as a major cross-sectoral priority, timing the announcement to coincide with the April 1987 publication of *Our Common Future* (the report of Brundtland's World Commission on Environment and Development).[107] Somewhat disingenuously, she claimed two months later, when releasing a published version of the "new" environmental strategy, that CIDA was the first government agency to adopt policies reflecting the Brundtland report.[108] The document was in fact a repackaging of CIDA's June 1986 policy paper, with material from the May 1986 submission to Brundtland, and pictures.

Meanwhile, although the Brundtland commission itself said little that was new to students of environment and development, it did reflect considerable educational and political work since 1972 to forge a consensus on the proposition that international development and the preservation of the environment, far from being contradictory, are inextricably linked. This change of consciousness was accelerated by industrial disasters such as Bhopal and Chernobyl, and by growing knowledge about how the link between poverty and the environment had degraded land and depleted resources, making forests shrink and deserts spread. What was needed to tackle these problems was a global commitment to "sustainable development," defined in *Our Common Future* as "development that meets the needs of the present without compromising the ability of future generations to meet their own needs."[109] The concept was not original, but Brundtland's popularization dramatically increased its circulation—and debasement—in development discourse.

As for CIDA's environmental strategy, Patricia Adams of Probe International—a virulent critic of aid agencies and mega-projects—claimed that "in reality, all CIDA has done is adopt . . . rules that other federal departments adopted long ago." She specifically condemned the lack of openness of the Agency's procedures as contrary to Brundtland's call for public scrutiny and approval.[110] Many environmentalists also queried the depth of the new commitment when the Agency financed in 1988 a feasibility study of the massive Three Gorges dam that China wanted to build on the Yangtze River. CIDA later tried to defuse controversy by releasing the consultants' appraisal, which was positive on both technical and environmental grounds, together with detailed replies to criticisms advanced by Probe International and others.[111] However, the issue of Canadian involvement, past and prospective, remained the subject of intense debate.

While introduction of mandatory environmental screening in project identification and approval procedures was a major step for CIDA, implementation of the proactive elements of the policy moved more slowly. Policy-making capacity was strengthened by the appointment of a special adviser on environment (at the rank of director general) late in 1988 and a director for sustainable development early in 1989.[112] The Agency also hired a group of consultants to propose ways of pursuing sustainable development more effectively. In their report, Jim MacNeill and his associates urged CIDA to adopt sustainable development as an overriding goal infusing all aspects of the Agency's work. They cautioned, however, that such a commitment "will require much more than a change of rhetoric in the Agency's speeches and documents. It will require major changes in CIDA's policies and in the way in which CIDA designs, negotiates and delivers Canada's ODA programs and projects."[113] The authors advocated a thorough merger of economic, social, and ecological dimensions of analysis in order to move beyond narrow environmental policies concerned solely with ameliorating the effects of economic development "through after-the-fact repair of damage already done."[114] They made seventy-odd hard-hitting recommendations, including a call for more rigorous environmental assessments that incorporated recipient country involvement. They argued as well that public release of an assessment ought to be "a condition for providing support to a project."[115]

The President's Committee had trouble digesting MacNeill's radical language, but decided to proceed with work on an overarching policy on sustainable development. In a speech just before she was transferred in 1989, Catley-Carlson called "sustainable development . . . the most important concept . . . to emerge during the 1980s." It meant rethinking everything in new ways and required "a new kind of economic growth . . . that is qualitative as well as quantitative."[116] Whether and how it would be applied to the work of CIDA were questions left for her successor. Meanwhile, Prime Minister Mulroney announced to the UN General Assembly in September 1988 that the federal government would establish in Winnipeg an International Institute for Sustainable Development (IISD), "which will promote internationally the concept of environmentally sustainable development." He also voiced support for a proposed global conference on sustainable development in 1992, twenty years after Stockholm.[117]

Organizational Change

Conservative ministers of state for External Relations, Monique Vézina from 1984 to 1986 and Monique Landry thereafter, had responsibilities for francophone relations and Africa (apart from the explosive south), but they were essentially ministers for CIDA. They moved with their support staffs into executive offices at CIDA's headquarters in Hull and became heavily involved in the day-to-day affairs of the Agency. Both were neophytes in Parliament. Madame Vézina, a long-time activist in the *caisses populaires* movement in the Gaspé Peninsula, had no prior experience in foreign affairs. Madame Landry, a physiotherapist from Ste. Thérèse, had been active in the Mulroney faction of the Conservative Party and had served on the board of the Quebec Association of Liquor and Wine Stores; between 1984 and 1986, she was parliamentary secretary first to the secretary of state and then to the minister of International Trade.[118]

The minister was now public spokesperson for Canada's aid program. Catley-Carlson's role became more like that of a conventional deputy minister, devoting considerable time and energy to the service of the minister and her office and (as noted earlier) less to public outreach. The president developed an effective working relationship with both ministers, but mutual mistrust and tension often characterized interaction between CIDA personnel and ministerial aides. Some of these difficulties stemmed from closer political scrutiny of the management and delivery of aid programming than under Liberal secretaries of state for External Affairs. While the latter had been concerned about major policy initiatives and big contracts for goods and services, Vézina and Landry became more fully involved as well in decisions about consultant selection, NGO funding, and contracts for universities and other institutions.

Both ministers were especially interested in Quebec suppliers,[119] in the regional distribution of contracts, and in spreading the benefits of work for CIDA as widely as possible.[120] They and Tory MPs made frequent public announcements about the Agency's largesse; Landry in particular enjoyed the limelight of press conferences and media releases bearing her name.

Creating visibility for the aid program, the ministerial publicity also gave it a previously absent partisan political cast. Early in 1987, Roger Young of the North-South Institute complained that CIDA was becoming a "smorgasbord" for hungry Canadian domestic interests rather than a legitimate development agency. The effectiveness of Canadian ODA was endangered because Vézina and Landry, in search of new partners, were inviting unqualified firms and organizations to bid for contracts. The problem was exacerbated, Young claimed, by ministerial intervention in selection processes that traditionally had been left mainly in the hands of public servants.[121] Vézina, wrote Martin Rudner, "made no secret of her role in channelling procurement contracts to Conservative party 'friends.' This politicization of procurements has created vested interests in tied aid that overshadow, and even dominate, mere aid/trade concerns."[122]

Douglas Roche (who did not stand for reelection in 1984) and other Conservative MPs had long argued that putting a junior minister in charge of CIDA would ensure a strong voice for the aid program in cabinet. Concretely, though, neither Vézina nor Landry had much clout. That ODA survived budget-cutting as well as it did during the first Mulroney administration was much more the result of Joe Clark's seniority and tenacity.

Aid Delivery

Clark, Vézina, and Landry were committed ideologically to delivering more of Canada's ODA through the private sector. With her long experience in the credit union movement, Vézina was supportive of NGOs and not-for-profit organizations as well as small business. Landry, less sympathetic to the voluntary sector, was especially enthusiastic about expanding business involvement. The broader Tory agenda to squeeze the civil service and contract out aspects of government work accelerated dramatically a process in CIDA that was under way before the election of a Conservative government.

As we saw in Chapter 6, anticipation of substantial ODA growth, coinciding with a near freeze on the Agency's personnel, led to a decision in 1982 that officers would manage executing agencies rather than projects. Early in 1984, Douglas Lindores' "Options for the Future" devoted considerable attention to the implications of "hands-off" management—how to ensure effective delivery "in the face of the often questionable capability, motivation, and trustworthiness of parts of the Canadian supply base"; how to achieve accountability; and how to confront the contradiction that many officers had joined CIDA to do development, not to be contract managers.[123] With respect to this last issue, Rawkins observed:

> Handling disbursements and achieving cash targets were difficult but manageable and clearly defined objectives. "Hands-off"—managing the overall process while leaving "micro-management" to contractors—was a different matter. In the curious intimacy of CIDA, probably strengthened by the leadership style of the mid-1980s, there was a strong sense of personal accountability for projects. Officers felt uneasy about leaving everything to the executing agency.[124]

More and more, that is what happened as the work of consultants expanded from project implementation to planning, and then to monitoring and evaluation. Between 1983-84 and 1988-89, authorized person years in CIDA (i.e., full-time-equivalent public servants) rose by 6 per cent from 1,082 to 1,146, while consultants registered with the Agency grew from 2,500 to almost 5,500, and the number of contracts executed skyrocketed by more than 350 per cent—about three times the rate of increase in projects funded.[125] Costs went up appreciably as well.[126] The move to hands-off management and the burden and complexity of contract management took a toll on morale. As one respondent put it, working for CIDA was now "a lot less fun."

There were other implications as well. Lindores reported in 1984 that professional personnel were worried "that the Agency had devoted so much time to its processes in recent years that it had fallen far behind other bilateral and multilateral agencies in the assessment of world development problems and trends."[127] Among several officers who voiced similar concerns when interviewed by the author towards the end of the decade, one reckoned that CIDA was less able to do in-house development policy work than in the 1960s and 1970s. Looking back on Canada's performance in the 1980s, the DAC secretariat was blunt about the lack of developmental coherence in CIDA's supposedly country-focused bilateral programs in the 1980s—they tended to be largely a collection of "enclave projects" with "many Canadian experts hired on a contract basis with a horizon rather limited to the particular project"; there was "little attempt to address economic and development problems on a wider basis."[128]

The Auditor General on bilateral programming. The "enclave project" syndrome was also an outcome of the regulatory environment developed after the Gérin-Lajoie era. As Rawkins observed: "CIDA Officers were encouraged to devote their attention to contracting, monitoring, and evaluation, at the expense of the 'front end' of the cycle—planning and building strategic, developmental relationships (and hence country-based knowledge)."[129] Lindores recognized that the "controls were so successful . . . that is possible that we now manage more to the needs of our regulatory environment than to the needs of our clients."[130]

The Auditor General continued to press for tightening up financial and managerial controls. His office undertook a further detailed audit of CIDA during the 1983-84 fiscal year, focusing on bilateral program management. While still urging strict compliance to the regime of existing controls (which he found greatly improved), the Auditor General commented at length on the Agency's performance in the field. Based on site visits to thirty-one bilateral projects in ten core countries and a cursory review of thirty others, his report identified several key deficiencies: a management structure that was essentially invariable without regard to size or complexity of projects, insufficient technical support for project team leaders in Hull and those responsible for implementation in the field, inadequate on-site monitoring by field officers, and "information used to make project decisions [that] was not always accurate, complete or timely."[131] The report complained as well of inadequate learning from past experience and mistakes.

The Auditor General lambasted CIDA for moving so slowly from project identification to mobilization; a study of eight projects in Indonesia revealed that the average elapsed time from project requests to the placement of consultants for implementation was 5.4 years. Procurement inadequacies were also identified.[132] While these criticisms probably reinforced the enclave project mentality, the report stressed as well that country program reviews, though not used much, focused more on the past than on forward planning.[133]

Reorganizing support functions. The Auditor General's report was a catalyst for Lindores' study and a subsequent review of Resources Branch undertaken by an internal task force. The latter concluded that the Branch—some two hundred employees—was too large and had too many disparate functions to be managed effectively by a single vice-president. The upshot was its dissolution and the creation of two new branches (in addition to Business Cooperation) in July 1984. Housing sectoral experts and professionals (now clearly performing support rather than line functions), the Professional Services Branch was responsible for recruitment and selection of consultants for project work. Operations Services contained the Area Coordination Group (which was responsible for developing operational policies and procedures for the four geographic branches) and took charge of procurement, the technical and legal aspects of contracts, and the recruitment, training, and briefing of cooperants. The Consultant and Industrial Relations Group was relocated from the old Resources Branch to Business Cooperation, which assumed primary responsibility for liaison with business.[134]

CIDA also tried to strengthen its technical expertise and field capacities. The project monitoring and evaluation groups set up on an experimental basis in the early 1980s became the model for field support units. Consisting of Canadian and locally engaged contract personnel, these were organized and staffed by executing agencies, and assigned responsibilities for planning, monitoring, expert advice, administration, logistics, and evaluation under the supervision of Canadian posts. They grew from four at the end of 1984 to thirty-one in 1988.[135]

Appearing before the Commons Standing Committee on Public Accounts in the spring of 1985, Catley-Carlson expressed confidence that speedier and more effective project delivery would result from the single executing agency approach, reorganization of professional and operating services, establishment of field support units, the improvement in corporate memory and evaluation systems, and other changes emanating from the 1982 MEPAD Report.

She reminded members, however, that "the origin of the problem . . . was that over the previous five years, CIDA's attention was directed to the establishment of increasingly complex and numerous control systems designed to minimize the risk of failure or of financial or other embarrassment to Canada." Inevitably, there was a trade-off between accountability and developmental efficiency and timeliness. The most recent recommendations of the Auditor General "have their financial merits," but every time new procedures or training requirements were added "in a situation of fixed administrative resources," there was a challenge "to determine the true administrative and financial cost . . . and to achieve a balance between that cost and the need for timely delivery of bilateral programs."[136]

Pressure for greater decentralization. Within CIDA, Douglas Lindores discovered that "There is no subject on which the Agency appears to be more unanimous than on the need for more decentralization. The opinion was widely expressed that a significant transfer of planning and programming functions to the field would lead to much more relevant assistance." In "Options for the Future," however, he concluded that expansion of field support units was probably the limit of what CIDA could achieve. A transfer of Agency personnel and decision-making authority abroad confronted seemingly insurmountable obstacles—high costs of maintaining public servants overseas as foreign service officers, confusion about lines of responsibility in an integrated foreign service, potential difficulty in negotiating support and auxiliary services with External Affairs, and demands of the regulatory and accountability environment.[137]

That might have ended the matter, but it became an issue for the Public Accounts Committee after the North-South Institute's bilateral evaluations in 1983 had criticized CIDA for overcentralization and insufficient experience in the field. The Auditor General's 1984 report echoed these conclusions. Catley-Carlson broached the issue when she appeared before the committee: "Nowhere is the impact of the Canadian regulatory environment on the form and functioning of the aid program more clear than in the allocation of human resources to the delivery and monitoring of programs. A very conscious policy has been pursued to allow maximum amounts of assistance to be delivered with minimum field staff." She defended this approach, reviewed the reasons for it, and cited two countries where Canada was delivering an aid volume roughly comparable to that of the US with a fraction of US AID's field staff. Cautiously, the president then appeared to invite further discussion: "It is possible to regard the current Canadian system as an extremely cost-effective, high-productivity approach to high levels of program delivery with minimal human resources. It is also possible to regard the program as under-administered, overcentralized, slow and risk-avoiding. Much depends on the angle of vision."[138]

The issue was prominent during the committee's three public hearings on CIDA and in deliberations on the African crisis by the Standing Committee on External Affairs and National Defence.[139] As discussion ensued, Catley-Carlson conceded the hypothetical desirability of greater field presence, but was resolute in arguing that full-blown decentralization was utterly inconceivable in the Canadian context. She listed the obstacles Lindores had summarized in his paper and added another: "a centralized form goes well with a highly tied aid program, which we have, if you do not have in the field, the kind of commercial representation of Canadian firms which would allow you to take some of the same sourcing decisions from the field."[140]

In its October 1985 report, the Public Accounts Committee urged the government to "allow greater decentralized decision-making and allocate additional expert staff to the field."[141] The government's response in May 1986 claimed that decentralization was in fact occurring in the context of the single executing authority approach, the growth of field support units, and recent decisions to give diplomatic missions responsibilities for managing cooperant contracts and engaging local consultants. "In summary, within current constraints, shifts in decision-making from headquarters to the field can be made through the use of private-sector resources to assist embassy personnel." Those constraints were under review, however, and "further decentralization options will be considered" in the light of recommendations coming from the current parliamentary review of ODA policies and programs.[142]

As we shall see in Chapter 8, parliamentarians became convinced that full-scale decentralization was imperative.

Program Profile during the Catley-Carlson Era

Pierre Trudeau made the commitment to achieve 0.7 per cent of GNP by 1990-91 shortly before he announced his retirement. Columnist John Best quipped that the outgoing prime minister was a "generous fellow" for agreeing to spend $5 billion or so a year, but "there is only one small rub: . . . it will be left to his successor or successors as prime minister to find ways of redeeming the pledge. It will hardly be an easy task."[143] Interim spending projections called for an increase from $1.8 billion in 1983-84 to $2.9 billion in 1987-88. The actual amount that would have been required in 1990-91 was $4.7 billion,[144] a further increase of $1.9 billion or 65 per cent over the final three years. In fact, Canada's ODA expenditures in 1990-91 were $3.02 billion, 0.45 per cent of GNP.

Backtracking on ODA Targets

Backtracking on growth, though not formally on the commitment, began even before the Conservative election victory in September 1984. John Turner's government, scrambling to demonstrate fiscal responsibility in support of electoral promises, announced in August 1994 that $56 million of identified "savings" of $300 million could be achieved from ODA "which will not need to be spent this year."[145] It was not a one-time cut, but a reduction in the base for further spending projections.

Meanwhile, during the election campaign, Mulroney endorsed the goal of 0.7 per cent by the end of the decade. Clark confirmed the pledge in the UN General Assembly on September 24, 1984. "Despite serious economic problems at home," he said, "we shall not turn our backs on the world's disadvantaged peoples."[146] Looking for ways of bringing down the federal budget, Finance Minister Wilson was not as sanguine. The C.D. Howe Institute put foreign aid on its agenda for spending cuts, and the Business Council on National Issues claimed that pegging the ratio at 0.42 per cent would result in annual savings of $500 million by 1988.[147] In his November 8 economic statement, Wilson set back the date for 0.7 to 1995 and announced an interim target of 0.6 by 1990. Though the commitment to 0.5 in 1985-86 remained, $180 million would be saved in that fiscal year by moving to a slower growth path.[148] Officials in Finance wanted a steeper slowdown, but Clark and the public response to the Ethiopian crisis blocked the way.

Wilson's May 1985 budget cut an additional $50 million from the 1985-86 spending base,[149] bringing total reductions (including the Liberal one) to $286 million. The North-South Institute estimated that Canadian aid over the five-year period to 1990-91 would be reduced by $1.6 billion as a result. Although the Finance Minister claimed the additional cut would not compromise the commitment to 0.6 per cent by 1990, the aid budget would have had to increase by 17 per cent in 1986-87 and 11 per cent a year thereafter for that target to be achieved.[150] This, the Institute predicted, would be a "severe test" in the context of continuing budgetary austerity.[151] Indeed, it was more severe than Wilson was prepared to consider. In introducing his February 1986 budget, he rejected the planned growth path as unsustainable. Projected spending would be reduced by $83 million in 1986-87 and $205 million in 1987-88, and held at the 0.5 per cent ratio until the end of the decade (still requiring an average increase of 8.7 per cent a year). Only in 1991 would the ratio begin to rise towards 0.6 per cent in 1995.[152]

Shortly thereafter, Clark defended this second retraction in a speech to the diplomatic corps. Arguing that all sectors had to contribute to deficit reduction, he tried to put a positive face on the decision by pointing out that ODA spending over the next five years would be $13.6 billion, compared to $8.7 billion over the previous five. (These of course were current dollars, not adjusted for inflation.) Moreover, the minister promised, not only would ODA remain formula-funded, with 0.5 as the base in each of the next five fiscal years, but it would be as well the fastest growing component of Ottawa's discretionary spending. He also confirmed a commitment to the elusive 0.7 per cent, now in the year 2000.[153] There were cries of "broken promises" and "betrayal" from editorial writers and development interests.[154]

As we shall see in the next three chapters, however, these curbs on ODA growth during the first Mulroney administration were mild when compared to real spending cuts and an effective abandonment of 0.7 during the government's second term, and to even steeper reductions after the Liberals returned to power in 1993.

Missing the revised target.[155] Between 1983-84 and 1988-89 (the year before the fiscal axe fell), Canadian ODA grew from $1,812.0 million to $2,930.7 million, an average increase of 8.9 per cent a year.[156] Passing $2 billion in 1986-87, CIDA's own expenditures stood at $2.3 billion in 1988-89. Although the expenditure path was geared to 0.5 per cent, economic growth was rapid during this period and the target was barely achieved in only one fiscal year, 1986-87, though twice in the calendar year used by DAC (see Table 7.1). Meanwhile, the ratio for all DAC members remained in the 0.35-0.36 per cent range. Canada's share of total OECD flows was highest in 1984—5.66 per cent—and stood at 4.99 per cent in 1988, in both cases below peak years in the mid-1970s. In 1984 and 1985, Canada was the fifth largest DAC donor, ahead of the United Kingdom, but then fell to seventh behind both Britain and Italy. Using the ODA/GNP ratio as a measure of effort, Canada passed Australia and Germany to move from ninth to seventh place in 1984. That ranking was maintained until 1989 in all but one year.

Table 7.1
Canada's ODA/GNP Ratio, 1983-89

Fiscal year		Calendar year	
1983-84	.45	1983	.45
1984-85	.49	1984	.50
1985-86	.46	1985	.49
1986-87	.50	1986	.48
1987-88	.48	1987	.47
1988-89	.49	1988	.50

Source: See Appendix A and CIDA, *Memorandum to DAC*, for the relevant years.

Eligibility and Geographical Distribution[157]

In looking for ways of streamlining CIDA's operations, the Lindores report was pessimistic about achieving greater country concentration: "Despite Cabinet approval of a policy to concentrate bilateral programming on a more limited number of eligible recipients, it has not proven possible to implement the decision in the face of special case pleading by Ministers, other government departments, and on occasion, CIDA itself."[158] The pattern continued under the Tories, especially during Clark's tenure as secretary of state for External Affairs. He wanted Canada to be sympathetic and involved each time there was a new disaster or global challenge.

The defeat of the Marcos regime in 1986 prompted a quick decision to indicate Canada's support for democracy in the Philippines and earmark yet another Asian nation for a longer-term relationship. External Affairs and CIDA had earlier decided to channel increased aid through a coalition of Canadian and Filipino NGOs rather than through a corrupt and discredited government. Thus, only weeks after the change in regime, Vézina was able to announce a new $5 million, NGO-based program aimed at improving living standards and employment opportunities for the poor and landless.[159] In July 1986, Clark visited President Aquino in Manila and promised that CIDA would upgrade the Philippines to core country status and undertake substantial programming.[160] A five-year $100 million commitment was made in October, emphasizing private-sector development and institution-building as well as poverty alleviation.[161] The jump in bilateral aid to the Philippines was the most dramatic in CIDA's history—from less than $500,000 in 1985-86 to $22 million in 1986-87.

While no other countries attained core status during the late 1980s, Mozambique, Ethiopia, and the Sudan—all racked by civil strife, drought and famine, and desperate poverty—received major increases in bilateral ODA. Walter McLean, a Conservative MP with strong links to Africa dating from his missionary days in the 1960s, successfully supported NGO efforts to upgrade Mozambique. Though not designated as "core," it was made a "country of concentration" eligible for bilateral aid under the umbrella of the Southern African Development Coordination Conference.[162] Following Brian Mulroney's commitment at the 1987 Commonwealth summit in Vancouver, a new Canadian Education Program for South Africa was set up "to assist the disfranchised majority in order to prepare them for full participation in a post-apartheid society."[163] Modest programming was started in Uganda, after a fourteen-year hiatus, when Yoweri Museveni restored relative stability in 1986. That same year, following Joe Clark's mission in search of trade opportunities and a Canadian role in the Middle East peace process, Jordan was shifted from Category III to II and began getting Canadian aid for the first time ever.

Data on the percentage of bilateral aid channelled to CIDA's leading recipients reveal the extent of diminishing concentration during the last half of the 1980s. In 1985-86, 53.4 per cent went to the top ten and 72.7 per cent to the top twenty; by 1990-91, those proportions had gone down to 43.2 per cent and 61.6 per cent respectively.[164]

Shares by income level and region. Table 7.2 shows that bilateral flows to LLDCs kept pace with increases to other low-income and middle-income countries between 1984-85 and 1989-90, altering the trend of the previous half decade. Given the Tories' emphasis on trade promotion, this might seem surprising. What the shift reflected in part was the enormous increase in food and other aid to Africa and to Bangladesh. Also, some of the increase in funding for middle-income countries came in the Industrial Cooperation Program, outside of the bilateral budget. Nonetheless, of the top ten bilateral recipients in 1989-90, three were in the middle-income group (Jamaica, Cameroon, and Morocco), and a fourth (Indonesia) was at the top of the low-income category—as was Egypt, which stood eleventh.[165]

Table 7.2
Percentage Distribution of Attributable Canadian Bilateral Aid by Income Level of Recipient Countries, 1979-80, 1984-85, 1989-90, and Percentage Increases, 1979-80 to 1989-90

	Distribution (percentage)			Increase (percentage)	
	1979-80	1984-85	1989-90	1979-80 to 1984-85	1984-85 to 1989-80
Least developed	39.5 (227.5)	35.6 (296.5)	35.7 (329.6)	30.3	11.2
Other low income	42.4 (244.8)	42.5 (354.2)	42.6 (393.2)	44.6	11.0
Middle income	18.1 (104.5)	21.9 (182.2)	21.7 (200.4)	77.8	10.0

Source: Adapted from CIDA, *Annual Report 1981-82*; ibid., *1981-82*; ibid., *1985-86*; and ibid. *1989-90*, using the UN classification of LLDCs and the World Bank classification of countries by income level. (Excludes regional programs except Sahel, which is counted as LLDC.) The figures in parentheses are in $ million. These data are for bilateral (government-to-government) flows; those in Table 6.1 are country-to-country data prepared for the DAC.

The 1981 policy to equalize the bilateral shares of Africa and Asia at 42 per cent (then at 48 and 42 respectively) and to increase the Americas to 16 per cent (from 10) achieved close to the desired outcome by 1983-84 when the shares were 43, 42, and 15. Despite the African crisis, disbursements actually fell below those to Asia in 1985-86 (42 and 44 per cent respectively), but were substantially greater once more by 1987-88 (45 and 38 per cent respectively). As we shall see in Chapter 8, a new policy then called for stabilization at roughly these levels. In the meantime, the relative share of the Americas rose to 16 per cent.[166] A House of Commons Committee on the Peace Process in Central America asked in 1988 for an additional allocation to the Americas of $100 million over five years for a Special Fund for Central America;[167] the government agreed, though the fund was carved out of the existing regional allocation after a steep budget cut in 1989.[168]

Human rights concerns. NGOs and church groups continued to push for making aid conditional on human rights performance. The issue was highlighted in concrete terms when the Mulroney government restored modest programming in El Salvador in 1984 and Guatemala in 1987 after controversial elections brought civilian governments to power in those countries. Both actions led to sharp criticism, as did Canada's larger presence in Honduras at a time when that country was being turned into an armed camp by American support for the Nicaraguan contras.[169] Human rights abuses and civil strife prompted questioning at various times of Canadian aid to Guyana, Ethiopia, Sudan, Zaïre, Sri Lanka, and Indonesia.

Programming in Haiti, cut back after cancellation of DRIPP, was increased substantially after the Duvalier dynasty was deposed in February 1986. Canadian aid then came under strong criticism when General Namphy disrupted and cancelled elections in November 1987, and stage-managed a presidential contest the following January. After twice reviewing the status of the program, the minister suspended government-to-government aid, while agreeing to maintain a sizeable poverty-oriented program channelled through NGOs.[170] By then, two parliamentary committees had made a major issue of human rights conditionality, and the government was wrestling with how to develop a more proactive policy. As we shall see, a major test of resolve would come in June 1989 when Chinese authorities brutally suppressed the pro-democracy movement in Tiananmen Square. Only three years earlier, Prime Minister Mulroney had announced a doubling of Canadian aid to China.[171]

Terms: Debt Relief and Structural Adjustment

Although Canada shied away from leadership on international debt issues in the 1980s, the government did take some exemplary actions on aid-related debt, past and present. Clark attempted to ease the pain of the 1986 budget cut by announcing that the bilateral loan program would be discontinued on April 1, 1986, and that the Canadian aid program would be placed on an all-grants basis.[172] Two months later, Vézina informed the UN that Canada would extend a moratorium to sub-Saharan African countries on repayments of ODA loans for an initial period of five years, with reconsideration for extensions.[173] The amounts involved—$250 million over fifteen years on a total debt of $700 million—were insignificant in the light of some $150 billion (US) owed to Africa's creditors. However, as the *Gazette* (Montreal) commented, that "drop in the bucket . . . is causing ripples":

> [By] delaying the repayment, Canada is giving the countries a much-needed breather and is lessening the real value of the amount owed. It is setting an example for other creditors to emulate. Already the Netherlands and the Nordic countries have announced similar plans. And it is showing solidarity with the wishes of Africans, who increasingly are showing they want to do what they can to solve their own problems instead of simply blaming them (not without reason) on colonialism.[174]

Further measures followed in 1987 when outright forgiveness of ODA debt was extended to sub-Saharan African countries at conferences of heads of government of la Francophonie in Quebec and the Commonwealth in Vancouver.[175] (These steps got generally favourable responses in the press, except for a questioning of the human rights record of some beneficiaries, especially Zaïre.) Also during 1987, the Standing Senate Committee on Foreign Affairs reviewed the debt crisis in Africa and the Americas, and made several recommendations for further Canadian action.[176]

The debt crisis opened wide the door for the IMF and the World Bank to make adjustment loans to indebted countries conditional upon policy reform. Fuelled by a zealous conversion to the new neo-conservative orthodoxy, the Bretton Woods institutions pushed for open markets, "getting the prices right," reducing external and fiscal imbalances, privatizing public enterprises, downsizing the state, and promoting the private sector as *the* engine of development. SAPs (structural adjustment programs), SALs (structural adjustment loans), and SECALS (sector adjustment loans) exacted tough measures and, at least in the short run, hit hardest at the disadvantaged: "the people who have lost jobs, seen their limited purchasing power decline, experienced a deterioration in their already inadequate access to health care and unpolluted water, and so on."[177] Bilateral aid agencies were encouraged to join in "policy dialogue" and make their liquid program aid conditional on the reforms sought by SAPs and SECALs.

With its close ties to the Fund and the Bank, the Department of Finance was especially keen to see Canada play an active role in support of structural adjustment. CIDA under Catley-Carlson participated but with some scepticism and reluctance.[178] Program assistance was already increasing, driven by disbursement pressures and a recognition that some of the most indebted recipients in Africa were in dire need of help to maintain infrastructure, basic services, and international payments. Gradually from 1987 onwards, program aid was tied formally into the adjustment framework, though with little clarity and even less fanfare; it was the focus of discussion in the President's Committee only once before 1989.[179]

What did get publicity was the Agency's concern about the social costs of adjustment. Speaking to the Ottawa chapter of the Society for International Development in 1988, Catley-Carlson said:

> Our key problem, I think, is to find optimum ways to make vital adjustments—to enable the developing countries to live up to that name, strengthen their economies, and generate more jobs and income—while at the same time not putting the burden on the poor, who already bear far more than their share . . . in a single phrase, adjustment with a human face.[180]

This was one of several references during this period associating CIDA with UNICEF's campaign to temper adjustment programs with a "human face," that is, measures to soften the worst effects on the poor and most severely affected; in Ghana, CIDA was a key player in setting up PAMSCAD (Plan of Action to Mitigate the Social Costs of Adjustment) in 1987.[181]

CIDA's Changing Program Priorities

While women in development and the environment were major preoccupations, Catley-Carlson also pushed hard to increase support for education and training, which she strongly believed promoted sound development and made good long-term friends for Canada. Human resource development was now supposedly a major sectoral priority, yet the proportion of Canadian aid devoted to the educational sector at the beginning of her presidency was small by comparison with other bilateral donors that had Canada's linguistic advantages. Indeed, DAC even chided CIDA in 1984 for its weak performance in the area.[182]

With the decision to contract out more of the aid program, the labour-intensity of technical cooperation was no longer as pressing an issue. The Canadian Commonwealth Scholarship and Fellowship Plan was increased from 500 to 700 awards in 1984, and a new program was started in 1985 to provide 350 scholarships annually to university students from francophone countries.[183] Universities, colleges, research-granting agencies, and private firms and institutions responded enthusiastically to increased CIDA funding. Provincial governments were keen as well to seek new markets for "competitive Canadian knowledge services."[184] By 1989, there were 12,052 CIDA-sponsored students and trainees, up from only 1,705 in 1983.[185] Meanwhile, broader questions about human resource development were a major focus in the parliamentary policy review.

Data on sectoral distribution, always suspect, became even more unreliable as CIDA multiplied its mandates and took on new themes and issues. Also, DAC changed its reporting categories during the 1980s. What data there are suggest that sectoral distribution, defined conventionally, was relatively stable with three exceptions: the relative shares of education and program aid increased, while the share of agriculture went down. The health sector remained a low priority in the bilateral program, though higher on the multilateral side where CIDA made substantial contributions to AIDS-related work and to international campaigns for child immunization. Canada's response to the African famine led to high levels of emergency food and non-food assistance.[186]

As a proportion of total ODA, food aid rose from an average of 15 per cent in the early 1980s to just over 18 per cent in 1983-85. That level was still well below the average of 25 per cent in the mid-1970s.[187] The humanitarian crisis in Africa prompting the increase also reinforced the case for longer-term developmental approaches linking food aid to eventual agricultural and food self-sufficiency. The Breau task force on North-South relations had already made that argument forcefully, but there was considerable disagreement in Canada and internationally about how to do so. CIDA's corporate review of food policy in 1983 pushed the emerging consensus within the donor community that non-emergency food aid should be made conditional upon macro-economic policy reform. A new statement of the Agency's objectives for food assistance was somewhat lower key on this issue, emphasizing the potential of "accelerating the pace of development by freeing foreign exchange and generating domestic resources for investment."[188]

Other Channels

The World Bank, regional development banks, and UN agencies experienced bleak times in the 1980s—an often-hostile administration in the US, a lower priority among donor countries seeking more domestic benefits from aid dollars, and, in part as a result, growing scepticism about roles, managerial competence, and developmental effectiveness. As David Protheroe observed, Canada's posture "reflected a less automatic supportiveness of organizations, a firmer attitude towards reciprocity and burden-sharing, and an augmented concern with managerial efficiency relative to innovation." Nonetheless, he judged Canada's "new tough-mindedness" as "constructive": "continuing funding while working from within, diligently, for reform."[189]

American opposition to increased funding for the World Bank dominated negotiations for IDA replenishments covering the 1985-87 and 1988-90 periods. Ottawa was among those voicing support for greater generosity, and, while still tough on burden-sharing, was more willing than in 1979-81 to countenance slightly higher proportionate contributions. Canada's share was 4.5 per cent in the seventh replenishment (up from 4.3 in the previous one), and 5.0 per cent in the eighth—4.75 per cent was seen as the normal share of the burden and 0.25 per cent as a one-time contribution to help compensate for lower American contributions.[190] (That quarter per cent was fought over by Finance and CIDA; the Agency resented shifting more resources to the multilateral account of the very Department of Finance that had just imposed the 1986 ODA cut.)[191] In Protheroe's view, Canada's policy preferences during these negotiations "were among the most enlightened—for instance, its strong support for a geographical shift in favour of Africa on the grounds of need, its opposition to American proposals to attach interest rates to IDA loans and shorten maturities, and its advocacy of a relatively moderate proportion of policy-based lending in IDA."[192]

In the regional development banks (under CIDA's direct jurisdiction), Canadian representatives until the late 1980s also counselled moderation in policy-based lending, a position at variance with the US. As well, they pushed the Asian Development Bank to fund more projects with an anti-poverty focus. In response to concern about governance in the RDBs, especially the African, CIDA initiated systematic monitoring and evaluation of all of them.[193]

The Agency also placed UN development agencies under close scrutiny, asking tough questions about Canadian funding and participation. At the same time, Canada remained a strong supporter and helped with the shortfall created by declining American contributions. Especially important was the rescue in 1986 by Canada and other donors of the UN Fund for Population Activities. Had they not provided full compensation, the UNFPA would have collapsed after the US withdrew all funding, accusing the organization of encouraging abortion and involuntary sterilization in China. Meanwhile, often in the face of intense lobbying from other government departments and domestic interests, CIDA enforced relatively successfully a policy of providing core funding of UNDP and other key agencies, in preference to specialized funds and activities.[194]

Multilateral aid grew from $674.5 million in 1983-84 to $912.5 million in 1989-90. Although the Conservative government maintained the Liberal policy of lowering the proportion of multilateral aid to 30 per cent or less of total ODA, the share reached 39.8 per cent in 1985-86, a year of heavy food aid shipments through the World Food Program. It did not drop below 31.5 per cent during the Catley-Carlson presidency, and stood at just over 32 per cent in 1989-90.[195]

As Protheroe noted, working to counter the general predisposition to cut, "there always seemed to be some element of the multilateral program that the government wished to expand—emergency programming through the WFP, balancing Commonwealth commitments in la Francophonie, upholding values of multilateralism, strengthening Canadian influence in this or that agency, etc."[196] Consequently, Canada remained well above the DAC average (of 25 per cent or so) in the share of ODA devoted to multilateral aid. It slipped, however, from being the third largest DAC contributor to multilateral agencies in 1985-86 (tied with Germany) to seventh from 1987 to 1989. Nonetheless, in the UN system, only the US and Japan made higher ODA contributions in 1988; Sweden moved past Canada into third place in 1989.[197]

Voluntary sector: Good relations, uncertain future. ODA channelled through the voluntary sector grew from $196.2 million in 1983-84 to $304.6 million in 1988-89.[198] An increase of 56 per cent, this was less than the 62 per cent growth in total Canadian aid in that period. Accordingly, the channel's share dropped slightly from 10.8 per cent to 10.3 per cent. However, these data are misleading as indicators of the participation of non-profit organizations in the aid program. Beginning in 1984, CIDA officials decided to record bilateral country focus projects undertaken by NGOs and NGIs in bilateral totals, rather than transferring the amounts to Special Programs as had been the practice during the previous two years.[199] By the mid-1980s, NGOs and NGIs were conduits for bilateral projects worth more than $100 million a year; in

1989-90, country focus disbursements of $126.8 million accounted for approximately 20 per cent of bilateral expenditures.[200]

Within the voluntary sector, continued growth in funding for responsive programming relieved a fear that the traditional NGO program would be displaced by country focus. Moreover, many country focus projects approved for bilateral funding were initiated by non-governmental agencies and/or their partners overseas.[201] What did occur, though, was a sharper differentiation between, on the one hand, non-profit development agencies that depended largely (and in some cases almost entirely) on funding from CIDA and multilateral organizations and, on the other, development and humanitarian fund-raising agencies that also relied on public fund-raising and a volunteer base in churches and communities. Most of the country focus projects were undertaken by a few large organizations in the first category—such as WUSC, CUSO, UNICEF, CARE Canada, and CECI (the Centre canadien d'études et de coopération internationale)—and by the Association of Universities and Colleges of Canada, individual universities, and other institutions.[202] As Rawkins reported,

> Country focus was a boon to harassed desk officers. By proposing to "sole-source" a project to a non-profit organization, a desk officer would avoid the lengthy contracting and consultant selection process. More positively . . . the early Country Focus projects were more likely than other bilateral programs to deal with issues around poverty alleviation and the targeting of aid initiatives on specific populations.[203]

Relations between CIDA and Canadian NGOs were warmer during the Catley-Carlson era than at any time since the late 1960s. Soon after she assumed office, Catley-Carlson invited CCIC's executive to meet for the first time ever with the President's Committee. Formal and informal consultations were frequent thereafter, and both she and Vézina praised the work of NGOs at every opportunity. Moreover, with the relative shift away from mega-projects to human resource development, bilateral and multilateral agencies everywhere were looking to NGOs to deliver people-oriented programming. Although only a few Canadian agencies became major public service contractors under country focus, many more experienced a dramatic change in the scale and scope of their activities. Program funding, first introduced in 1983-84, was gradually extended to organizations with records of satisfactory projects and sound administration. Twenty-two NGOs enjoyed such an arrangement by 1989. Moreover, there was a trend throughout the sector towards more financial dependence on CIDA. Private donations rose steadily during the 1980s, though not as quickly as government support, which during 1987-89 was estimated to provide 40 per cent of NGO revenues.[204]

Many NGOs were troubled about the impact of the changing relationship with government on their mission and autonomy. In an excellent study of Canadian voluntary agencies, Brodhead and Herbert-Copley noted in 1988 that, despite traditional philosophical differences, the increased flow of funding and a higher level of interaction were narrowing the differences between governmental and non-governmental approaches to international development.

> As a result, on the one hand, governmental and multilateral agencies are being influenced by NGOs to meet people's basic human needs, to recognize the key role of women, to give higher priority to human resource development and to overlooked groups such as small farmers, minorities or entrepreneurs. On the other hand, NGOs have subjected themselves to the discipline of the project format . . . [and] have become more institutionalized.[205]

On CIDA's side, Lindores had recognized that building up the capacity of NGOs to deliver more aid might undermine the very characteristics that made them attractive and force them "to institute the types of service and control functions which are characteristic of large bureaucracies."[206] Brodhead and Herbert-Copley expressed unease about these trends, but concluded that the greatest risk to the autonomy of NGOs came "from a loss of internal vitality and self-questioning that can only come from agencies' direct work in the field."[207]

Relationships in the field were also changing in ways that some NGOs found threatening and others worrisome. While CIDA's links to NGOs in developing countries had traditionally been developed through Canadian counterparts, bilateral and multilateral aid agencies were now looking for ways to fund Southern organizations directly. In CIDA's case, Treasury Board allowed diplomatic posts to allocate modest levels of resources to local NGOs through mission administered funds.

By the early 1980s, other approaches were being explored. One involved establishment of government-to-government *microréalisation* funds for small projects undertaken by grass-roots organizations, largely in francophone Africa and Haiti; executed by recipient governments, they were closely monitored by Canadian posts and field support units. Another program, launched in Thailand in 1983, assisted local non-governmental organizations and institutions in implementing small social development projects; the Canadian embassy had administrative responsibility in this case, working with a committee of Thai government and NGO representatives. Another approach, in Bangladesh and Sri Lanka, involved direct funding of large local NGOs. In yet other cases, CIDA negotiated memoranda of understanding with recipient governments that earmarked for local organizations the proceeds from local-currency counterpart funds generated by the sale of Canadian food and/or commodities.[208]

A task force set up by CCIC in 1987 to examine the implications of direct funding included a case study of the Negros Rehabilitation and Development Fund, an $11 million facility based on the Thai model. It was created to assist recovery efforts on the island of Negros in the Philippines where the sugar-based economy had collapsed. The Canadian embassy approved projects recommended by a committee consisting of local people and representatives of the Philippines and Canadian governments. The study alleged that the local members selected by CIDA were identified with landowner interests, and that projects supported landowner-sponsored relief efforts. As a result, the Sugar Workers Union decided not to participate and "controversy surrounding the program . . . has increased significantly with the escalation of violence in Negros. One of the lessons . . . is that the creation of such a fund is unwise when socio-political conditions are so polarized that important representative groups have no other choice but to exclude themselves."[209] CCIC warned as well that direct funding raised the risk that recipient governments would act repressively towards community-based organizations or favour "para-governmental NGOs." It concluded, though, that "there is nothing wrong" with the principle of direct funding. "It is in fact up to the local NGOs to decide whether to accept or refuse contributions from the Canadian government in whatever form." A plea was made that mechanisms not disrupt the "solidarity which should exist between the Canadian and local NGOs." CIDA was also put on notice that Canadian NGOs would inform their Southern counterparts "what they are getting themselves involved in by accepting Canadian public funds."[210]

With some reservations, the CCIC report expressed a preference for cooperative funding arrangements that, like the South Asia Partnership, involved a coalition of Canadian and developing country organizations. A number of other cooperative funding arrangements were in fact established (in some cases with management solely in Canadian hands)—Partnership Africa Canada (the successor to Africa Emergency Aid), Solidarité Canada-Sahel, and Cooperation Canada-Mozambique, among others. Although this approach was not used in Negros, the Philippines Development Assistance Program announced earlier in 1986 did involve a North-South NGO coalition. CIDA used a ratio of 9:1 for matching funds, rather than the usual 3:1, to attract participation from Canadian organizations. As Brodhead and Pratt observed, however,

> The whole process in effect turned on its head the traditional rationale for CIDA's support to Canadian NGOs. The Canadian NGOs were not providing local knowledge and grass-roots contacts that CIDA lacked but, rather, CIDA had identified the "need," which had a significant diplomatic and political purpose, and then induced Canadian NGOs which often had little knowledge of the country, to become involved.[211]

While the Philippines program undertook several worthy projects, its work suffered because neither CIDA nor the Canadian participants understood local political cross-currents.[212]

Industrial Cooperation: Continued growth and promotion. Although the tilt to business was lessened by cancellation of the Trade and Development Facility, Conservative ministers, especially Monique Landry, put high priority on expanding traditional forms of private-sector involvement and opening new doors to CIDA-funded opportunities. Business Cooperation Branch stepped up informal contacts and institutionalized consultations with the Canadian Export (later Exporters') Association and the Association of Consulting Engineers in Canada. In addition, CIDA actively courted the Canadian Manufacturers Association and the Canadian Chamber of Commerce.[213] The Agency commissioned the Conference Board of Canada to study ways of strengthening business participation in the aid program.[214] A new series of information booklets, *The Business of Development*, was launched in 1987 by Landry, who said she wanted to take the "mystery" out of doing business with CIDA.[215] Business Cooperation Branch also increased its visibility through expanded outreach both from head office and, by the end of 1988, from a regional office in Vancouver, as well as the one set up during the Gérin-Lajoie era in Montreal.[216]

The Industrial Cooperation Program moved in 1984 from Special Programs, where it was viewed with some suspicion, to a more congenial setting in Business Cooperation. From 1983-84 to 1988-89, funding for INC increased 111 per cent—far more rapidly than any other program—from $28.7 million to $60.6 million. As a result, INC's share of overall Canadian ODA went up from 1.6 per cent to 2.1 per cent.[217] Growth was especially rapid in China and the second wave of newly industrializing countries of Southeast Asia.[218]

The main draws on INC funding continued to be subsidies for bids on multilateral contracts and grants to explore opportunities for joint ventures, licensing, and technology transfer. The larger budget provided greater scope as well for various forms of international business networking—including missions and exhibitions to market Canadian technology and councils that linked developing country and Canadian business interests. The Lindores report in 1984 queried the "questionable developmental character" of INC's "more promotion oriented activities,"[219] but Tory ministers were happy to equate a high level of Canadian business activity with development in recipient countries.

While bilateral growth increased conventional private-sector participation through the provision of Canadian goods and services, contracting out and the single executing agency approach multiplied many times over the opportunities for private consulting firms, large and small. When the Trade and Development Facility did not materialize, firms were encouraged to be proactive in seeking out export opportunities through an expanded range of lines of credit for Canadian commodities. Though fewer than envisioned, there were still opportunities to tap concessional financing: CIDA disbursed $US 38.5 million and $US 49.4 million in 1987 and 1988 respectively, in association with export credits from the Export Development Corporation. An additional $23.4 million in *crédit mixte* financing from EDC Section 31 funds was reported as ODA during those two years.[220]

An Improved Public Image

During Margaret Catley-Carlson's six years as president, media coverage of CIDA and Canadian aid was much more positive than over the previous decade. The Auditor General provided grist for the horror story mill in 1988 as well as 1984,[221] and investigative journalists highlighted some serious problems in the field.[222] But criticisms were more often focused on policy issues and developmental effectiveness than on allegations of mismanagement or incompetence. The North-South Institute's bilateral evaluations may have helped to change the tone of discourse and many journalists were now better versed about conditions in developing countries. Within CIDA, more careful appraisal, monitoring, and evaluation (and perhaps excessive caution) contributed, and so certainly did Catley-Carlson's skill in public relations.

Opinion polls showed a reversal of the earlier trend towards softening of public support for development assistance. Without doubt, the most significant factor was consciousness of the African crisis. When asked about the one issue or problem facing the world that most concerned them, a fairly consistent fifth answered hunger and poverty. Overwhelmingly, Africa was identified as the continent most in need. As can be seen in Tables 7.3 and 7.4, data from five polls conducted between July 1985 and December 1988 indicated a consistently high level of support for maintaining or increasing Canadian ODA and a remarkably positive evaluation of its effectiveness. A substantial majority wanted Canada to be a world leader in providing aid or at least among the more generous nations.[223] Like earlier surveys, however, the findings also demonstrated a lack of concrete knowledge and major misconceptions about the nature and size of the aid effort (usually underestimated). Disconcertingly for CIDA, few respondents could name the federal agency responsible for Canada's aid program—10 and 15 per cent in 1987 and 1988 respectively; in both years, churches and charitable organizations were identified as making a larger contribution to the program than the federal government.[224]

Table 7.3
Percentage Distribution of Polled Opinions About Level of Canadian Aid, 1985-88

	1985 July (Decima)	1986 February (Decima)	1987 October (NSI)	1987 December (Decima)	1988 December (Angus Reid)
Not enough	24	30	20	34	31
Right amount	59	48	52	45	45
Too much	17	20	17	18	16
No opinion	—	2	11	2	9

Sources: Decima Research, *The Canadian Public and Foreign Policy Issues* (Toronto: Decima Research, 1985), pp. 59, 108; Canadian Emergency Coordinator/African Famine, *Canadians and Africa: What Was Said* (Hull: CIDA, 1986), p. 14; North-South Institute, *Review '87/Outlook '88* (1988), p. 8; Decima Research, *Report to CIDA: Public Attitudes Toward International Development Assistance* (Hull: CIDA, 1988), p. 10; and Angus Reid Associates, *Report to CIDA: Public Attitudes Towards International Development Assistance* (Hull: CIDA, 1989), p. 9.

Table 7.4
Percentage Distribution of Polled Opinions About the Effectiveness of Canadian Aid, 1985-88

	1985 July (Decima)	1986 February (Decima)	1987 October (NSI)	1987 December (Decima)	1988 December (Angus Reid)
Very effective	9	9	14	11	16
Somewhat effective	61	57	52	61	64
Not too effective	24	28	24	21	13
Not at all effective	4	5	5	5	3
No opinion	—	1	5	1	4

Sources: Decima Research, *The Canadian Public and Foreign Policy Issues*, pp. 59, 108; Canadian Emergency Coordinator/African Famine, *Canadians and Africa: What Was Said*, pp. 15, 36; North-South Institute, *Review '87/Outlook '88*, p. 9; Decima Research, *Report to CIDA: Public Attitudes Toward International Development Assistance*, pp. 12-13; and Angus Reid Associates, *Report to CIDA: Public Attitudes Towards International Development Assistance*, pp. 9-10.

A Mid-Life Crisis?

The last of these polls was conducted after an extensive review of aid policies and practices had provided a context for a new strategy that supposedly would guide CIDA into the 1990s. The most significant component of the review was *For Whose Benefit?*—the report of the House of Commons Standing Committee on External Affairs and International Trade. It found in CIDA an organization that had "built up tremendous professional capacities and evolved into an efficient, well-managed bureaucracy." However, the Agency appeared unsure of its role, and had entered "something akin to a mid-life crisis."

> Within the aid program as a whole, there is a continuing tension between the desire to maintain developmental integrity and the pressures to subsume ODA within other foreign policy goals and to make it more responsive to domestic interests. We believe it is both possible and highly desirable to resolve this tension in a way that makes for a stronger, more coherent program and better serves Canada's long-term foreign policy interests.

What was needed was "a fresh jolt of political energy."[225]

Chapter 8

A Fresh Jolt of Political Energy? ODA Policy Reviewed, 1984-89

After Brian Mulroney's triumph in the federal election of 1984, the Tories were at last able to undertake the examination of Canada's aid program they had sought in opposition and been unable to complete during the short-lived Clark administration. The process began with a general review of foreign policy within the bureaucracy in 1984, and ended with publication in 1988 of the first official strategy for the Canadian development assistance program since Gérin-Lajoie's thirteen years earlier.

Unlike the strategy for 1975-1980, which was initiated in CIDA and modified in interdepartmental bargaining, *Sharing Our Future* was substantially shaped by parliamentary committees that conducted extensive soundings outside of government. A Special Joint Committee of the Senate and the House of Commons on Canada's International Relations, which reported in June 1986, devoted more attention to development and Third World issues than anyone had anticipated, but left detailed review of aid policies to the Commons Standing Committee on External Affairs and International Trade (SCEAIT).[1] Beginning hearings in the fall of 1986, SCEAIT published its findings and recommendations in *For Whose Benefit?* in May 1987. Yet another study by a special task force set up by Monique Vézina had virtually no impact on the final outcome even though it was seen as potentially crucial when it was appointed.

Chaired decisively by William Winegard, SCEAIT responded to the views of various Canadian aid constituencies and was most sensitive to developmental and solidarity concerns. The committee sought to instill in the Canadian aid program a more coherent mission based on helping the poorest countries and peoples, and ensuring that development priorities would always prevail in setting objectives. Urging stronger commitments to alleviating poverty and strengthening the human and institutional capacities of developing countries, it recommended relaxing procurement tying to meet local

---

Notes to Chapter 8 are on pp. 531-42.

costs, linking aid to human rights performance, and rethinking criteria for country eligibility. It called as well for improved aid organization and delivery through decentralization to the field, more effective partnership between government and the private and voluntary sectors, and new measures for broadening public awareness and support.

Sharing Our Future, the new official policy, was more attuned than the parliamentary report to commercial and foreign policy objectives, and was more unreservedly populist in catering to domestic Canadian interests. While two of the Winegard committee's key recommendations—a legislated ODA charter and an international development advisory council—were not accepted, the strategy did adopt with modifications several policy and organizational reforms advocated by the parliamentarians, including decentralization. It also affirmed the government's commitments to maintain an ODA/GNP ratio of 0.5 per cent until 1990-91, and then move towards 0.6 and 0.7 per cent in 1995 and 2000 respectively. CIDA and other players in the Canadian aid program planned their activities accordingly, indeed jolted by fresh energy injected by Winegard and his parliamentary associates.

Then came a splash of cold water. In Michael Wilson's first budget after the Conservatives' return to power in the fall of 1988, ODA was cut by almost 6 per cent year over year, and the government's cash allocation by even more. *Sharing Our Future*, touted by Monique Landry as an action plan for the rest of the century, remained a formal commitment, but important components were no longer viable. An ambitious program to decentralize components of CIDA's decision-making started to unravel, beset as well by interdepartmental conflict and managerial resistance within the Agency. Catley-Carlson's departure as president in June 1989 was yet another factor in the strategy's loss of momentum.

The Foreign Policy Review

The review began with a Green Paper prepared in External Affairs. Dubbed the "grey report" by journalists unimpressed with its lack of imagination,[2] *Competitiveness and Security* was revised several times before publication in May 1985, four months after Joe Clark had originally intended. Defining Canada's place in the world largely in terms of bilateral relations with the US, it gave short shrift to North-South issues. A brief section on international development, to which CIDA contributed, was similar in tone and content to the "Aid Policy Paper" prepared for Clark's government in 1979:

> We need . . . to be sure we are clear on where ODA fits into our conception of our own economic and political well-being, our sense of moral responsibility and our overall foreign policy. . . . In seeking the *right balance* in our programs

> abroad, we will have to decide the priorities we wish to attach to humanitarian objectives, to attaining commercial benefits, to sharing in the management and support of the global economy and the global environment and to achieving political stability and progress. Decisions will not be easy. Canadian funds for use abroad are limited.[3]

At least two commentators interpreted this text as a signal that the aid budget would be cut.[4]

The Green Paper also asked whether bilateral aid ought to be made more conditional on the performance of recipient governments in economic management, human rights, and "political like-mindedness." Another set of questions concerned priorities—sectoral, geographic, country income levels, the role of women, the weight assigned to eco-system management, and the balance between bilateral and multilateral channels. The document also observed that "churches, provincial and municipal governments, private organizations, small businessmen and concerned Canadians from all walks of life have demonstrated both a desire and a capacity to help." How, the text asked, could the government best assist Canadians to help others, and how much ODA should be directed through non-governmental channels?[5]

The Special Joint Committee: Constructive Internationalism

As they had in the past, parliamentarians adopted a different tone and emphasis. The Special Joint Committee on Canada's International Relations was set up to carry through the government's commitment to engage MPs and the public in the foreign policy review. Co-chaired by Tom Hockin, MP, and Senator Jean-Maurice Simard, the committee met in the wake of the African crisis and was deluged with oral and written testimony on Third World issues—development, the debt crisis, famine relief, human rights, Central America, and South Africa. Its report, *Independence and Internationalism*, gave much more prominence to these concerns than the Green Paper, and projected a stronger multilateralist orientation symbolized by the phrase "constructive internationalism."

In view of the impending SCEAIT study, the joint committee did not delve deeply into aid issues. Nevertheless, it offered recommendations and observations that dispelled fears about a dramatic change in parliamentary attitudes under the Conservatives. Describing development assistance as "a Canadian vocation," the committee cited testimony from witnesses that CIDA "lacks a clear sense of direction because it is pushed and pulled by political and commercial pressures." It also noted the frequently expressed fear "that the Canadian aid program is being converted into a trade promotion vehicle." In words reminiscent of the Breau task force in 1980, the report then asserted:

> By and large trade and finance operate in ways that are blind to international economic inequalities and mass poverty. . . . Development assistance is one of the few international instruments for counteracting the tendency towards haves and have-nots and for promoting the development of the poorest regions and countries of the world. . . . [It] is vital that development assistance be rededicated to its primary purpose. Accordingly *the committee affirms that meeting the needs of the poorest countries and peoples should remain the primary and overriding objective of the Canadian aid program.*[6]

There was unanimous agreement on making developmental effectiveness a priority. Concerns were voiced about excessive bureaucratization, lack of personnel and decision-making authority in the field, and insufficient public access to evaluation reports. In addition, the committee noted: "Development experts argue that tied aid is a major constraint in meeting the dual goals of aiding the poorest people and integrating women into the development process. . . . We think it is important to maintain Canadian content but essential that procurement not be allowed to distort or detract from development." Lamenting the hobbling effects of "the sometimes parochial and self-seeking nature of national aid programs," the report recommended that Canada "press for closer cooperation among aid donors and remain a strong supporter of multilateral approaches and institutions that encourage such cooperation."[7]

Asserting that there "should be far more to partnership than financial support," Hockin-Simard endorsed the notion that "Canadian development assistance is a partnership between government, volunteers, and private sector." NGOs, seen as "the heart of expanded and revitalized technical assistance programs," should be involved "to the maximum extent possible" in planning and executing capacities. A more active role was envisaged for the private profit sector, especially small and medium-sized Canadian firms. "Many of the poorest developing countries want and need practical, hands-on business experience, particularly as they turn increasingly towards market-oriented economies."[8]

The most far-reaching contributions of the Special Joint Committee, certainly for the aid program, concerned human rights. The committee endorsed the principles for linking ODA and human rights performance recommended by the Subcommittee on Canada's Relations with Latin America and the Caribbean in 1982, and called on Canada to use "its voice and vote" in international financial institutions "to protest systematic, gross and continuous violations of human rights."[9]

Where new ground was broken was in moving from "human rights protection" to "human rights development," a concept championed effectively by Robert Miller, a senior research adviser to the committee.[10] "Canada is not—and should not be—in the business of exporting its own institutions. It can and should be equipped to share its experience and to cooperate with others as they develop their own institutions." Several suggestions were offered: technical assistance for developing electoral institutions and procedures; support for strengthening workers' organizations; encouragement of partnership between human rights research and advisory bodies in Canada and their counterparts abroad; and help in strengthening judicial institutions, the rule of law, local government, and the media. Proposed as the centrepiece of this approach was an International Centre of Human Rights and Democratic Development—a new crown corporation operating at arm's length from government.[11]

Despite acknowledging the fiscal pressures that pushed back the date for achieving an ODA/GNP ratio of 0.7 per cent to 1995 and then to 2000, a majority of members (including many Tories) favoured reinstating 1990 as the target date.[12] On broader issues of international development cooperation, the report urged stronger action on debt and trade. It also devoted considerable attention to foreign students, "an important asset for Canada that has not been sufficiently recognized in terms of improving trade opportunities, increasing cultural contacts and more generally for foreign policy."[13]

The Government's Response

Clark's commitment to enhancing the authority of parliamentary committees was crucial in pushing External Affairs to take the recommendations much more seriously than those of previous committees.[14] The official response acknowledged that "the majority of Canadians wish our aid program to be directed principally at the alleviation of poverty." While reiterating that there were "a number of important objectives," it pledged that "the eradication of poverty will remain foremost."[15] The government was unavailing on the volume target but confirmed women in development as a high priority, promised more support for NGO programming, and pledged increased aid for human resource development (including an expanded CIDA scholarship program).[16]

The reply was cautious about making development assistance more conditional on human rights performance, reiterating an argument that Catley-Carlson had put forth on numerous occasions:

> A balanced approach to human rights issues and development attempts to ensure that repressive regimes will not be rewarded or legitimized through Canadian assistance policies. But it must also ensure that the victims of human rights violations—often the poorest members of society—are not subjected to a double jeopardy by being deprived of needed outside help as well as of their rights.[17]

Uneasy about adopting specific norms, the government agreed "that gross or systematic violations of human rights must be given proper weight in Canadian development assistance policy." It also gave a qualified promise to speak out on human rights abuses.[18]

These commitments on human rights, though limited, went much further than previous official policy. Clark's insistent prodding was even more conclusive in the decision to set up a new institution to promote the development of human rights, a recommendation that bureaucrats in both External Affairs and CIDA wished to sidestep.[19] According to a well-placed respondent, the committee had recommended this initiative in the first place, rather than expanding CIDA's mandate, because the Agency was perceived as "lukewarm" on human rights issues. Following a consultative process undertaken by a non-governmental task force,[20] legislation was passed in September 1988 establishing the International Centre for Human Rights and Democratic Development (ICHRDD) in Montreal. It was the first Canadian ODA agency to emerge from a parliamentary committee initiative.

A Ministerial Task Force

Monique Vézina appointed a Task Force on Canada's Official Development Assistance Program in October 1985 to advise on policy and operational matters and to assist her with the joint committee and Commons committee reviews. It was also asked to identify ways of increasing NGO and business participation in the aid program, and encouraging them "to cooperate more closely with each other for their mutual benefit, that of aid recipients and the national interest."[21] The minister appointed as executive director Jean-Claude Desmarais, Director of the Centre canadien d'études et de coopération international (CECI) in Montreal, an agency active in several countries, especially in francophone Africa.[22]

The task force was beset with organizational difficulties, complicated by suspicion within CIDA that its appointment reflected a Tory minister's mistrust of the bureaucracy after years of Liberal rule. Eventually reporting in August 1986, three months after its original deadline, the group failed to address many issues on which comment had been requested.[23] The recommendations that were made reflected a curious mixture of the bland, the orthodox, and the idiosyncratic.[24]

Desmarais' most radical proposal sought a complete restructuring of how the Canadian aid program was conceived and delivered. The task force suggested a model harkening back to the period before 1970 when planning and operations were organizationally distinct.[25] At the heart of a revamped program would be a planning group to advise ministers on policy, undertake sectoral and macro-level planning, and formulate detailed country programs. "The explicit intent is to remove the day-to-day administrative and monitoring tasks so that time is spent in the areas of respective specialist expertise. As such it would comprise an elitist planning unit for ODA."[26]

The planning group would also determine shares of public funds to be spent in each country by three operational divisions: CANAID, for socio-economic aid channelled through the voluntary sector, CANINVEST, a "commercial-economic counterpart" based on business participation, and an Inter-governmental Assistance Program, for conventional bilateral aid. While the first two of these would depend on the planning group for government financing, they would raise some of their own resources and be semi-autonomous.[27]

Vézina invested considerable political stock in the task force. Whether or not she would have pursued its recommendations is purely a matter for conjecture. By missing its original deadline, the task force found itself reporting instead to Monique Landry. Viewing the report with barely disguised contempt, CIDA's senior management persuaded the new minister to give it a quiet burial. It was published only because SCEAIT asked that it be made available.[28]

The Winegard Report[29]

For Whose Benefit?, SCEAIT's report, was the most important component of the review—both in taking an informed and critical look at Canadian ODA, and ultimately in shaping the new strategy. That a parliamentary committee could have such an important impact on policy reflected in part Clark's determination, as with Hockin-Simard, to ensure that the bureaucracy responded positively. Much of the credit for the content, however, must go to William Winegard, the committee's chairman.

Winegard had many years' experience as a professional engineer, an academic, a university administrator, and a public servant. He had been president of the University of Guelph, an institution especially active in international development work, and Chairman of the Ontario Council on University Affairs, an important provincial government advisory body. He had served on the board of governors of IDRC from 1974 to 1980, and had considerable overseas experience. Deeply committed to international development, he was solidly in the mainstream of the Conservative Party and could not be dismissed as a member of the Red Tory fringe. Approaching age sixty in 1984, he ran successfully for the Conservatives in Guelph, and shortly thereafter was given the committee chairmanship.

As we saw in Chapter 7, one of Winegard's first tasks was to examine Canada's response to the African famine in 1984-85. It was then that he and his fellow committee members decided to tackle a comprehensive evaluation of CIDA and the aid program. Winegard went into the review with an impressive grasp of the issues and a conviction that fundamental reform was needed.

A commanding presence in the committee, he justifiably expected that his views would carry weight. At the same time, he was committed to an extensive and open process.

Ten MPs from SCEAIT were "core participants"—seven Conservatives, two Liberals, and one member of the NDP. Robert Miller and Gerald Schmitz were among the able and committed support staff facilitating the process. Soon after the Special Joint Committee reported, SCEAIT issued a discussion paper inviting individuals and organizations to respond to a number of searching questions in writing and/or at public hearings across the country.[30] The committee then embarked on an ambitious consultation exercise, holding hearings in eight Canadian cities, travelling to Africa (Tanzania, Ethiopia, and Senegal), and spending long hours with officials from CIDA and other departments. Altogether, 107 witnesses gave oral testimony and 280 submitted written briefs. Winegard reported that he and other members also received "thousands of letters, leaving no doubt in our minds that Canadians care and think deeply about the aid program."[31]

Most witnesses came from the international development community—NGOs, concerned citizens, and academics—and several issues kept recurring: CIDA was too centralized in Ottawa-Hull; its programs did not put enough emphasis on alleviating poverty or working with people; developmental opportunities were missed because of excessive procurement tying; there was too much food aid and it was not well integrated into rural development work; and more attention was needed to relieve the human suffering wrought by structural adjustment programs. Greater sensitivity to human rights abuses in making aid allocations, more attention to environmental concerns, an even stronger commitment to WID, and a reversal of funding cuts were other prominent themes.[32]

As the process unfolded, Winegard became convinced that the problems of the aid program stemmed less from what he had suspected at the outset—managerial and organizational weaknesses—and more from a lack of coherence in policy and programming. "After almost a year of studying Canadian official development assistance," the committee's report began, "we concluded that it is beset with confusion of purpose." The text related an incident that participants in the review said was a seminal moment for Winegard:

> The confusion was brought home to us forcefully during a recent meeting with senior Canadian officials. When asked how they would rank the national interest in ODA, one of them replied with great assurance: first political, second commercial and third development. That is one version of development assistance. It is not our version. It is not the version of the Canadian people.[33]

As one insider told the author:

> The analogy that we used several times when discussing the aid program in the committee was that it had become like a grand bazaar where everything was possible. You could sell any kind of good or service under the rubric "development," and it was simply a matter of getting the right idea before the right official and making sure that the bucks were there. . . . If somebody asked "what's development?" the answer would be "it's the sum total of all that stuff."

Prodded by Winegard, the committee began to focus on fundamental questions such as "what is aid for?" and "for whom?" and to examine each issue in the light of basic principles.

When it was published in May 1987, the Winegard report (as it justly became known) asserted that the answer to the question "for whose benefit?" is quite simple: to help the poorest people and countries to help themselves. Only by discharging that mandate does assistance serve Canada's long-term interests, be they defined in humanitarian, political or commercial terms."[34] As David Morrison commented:

> This is a refreshing approach in that it rejects the glib assumption often enunciated by governments that there is a necessary complementarity of interest in ODA between developmental and other concerns such as the support of Canadian industries and exports. As far as the committee was concerned, this is an empirical question that must be answered on a case-by-case basis, with basic developmental objectives taking precedence in the event of a conflict.[35]

A Statutory Mandate for ODA

The committee proposed a legislated mandate for the ODA program that would enshrine a Development Assistance Charter. It suggested the following as a text that would contain "a clear and binding declaration of the fundamental purposes of aid, to guide its managers and to inform Canadians and the people of the Third World":

- The primary purpose of Canadian official development assistance is to help the poorest countries and people of the world.
- Canadian development assistance should work always to strengthen the human and institutional capacity of developing countries to solve their own problems in harmony with the natural environment.
- Development priorities should always prevail in setting objectives for the ODA program. Where development objectives would not be compromised, complementarity should be sought between the objectives of the aid program and other important foreign policy objectives.[36]

The report also urged that CIDA be given the statutory foundation that Maurice Strong once sought and later rejected.[37] While reaffirming that the Agency should remain under the overall responsibility of the secretary of state for External Affairs, SCEAIT thought it was time "to regularize and define the responsibilities of a Minister of International Development in place of the Minister for External Relations." The minister would bring "a strong political commitment and understanding of the Agency's mandate to its operations," and play a key role in the development of policy.

> Twenty years ago CIDA was conceived as an operational agency, delivering goods and services in a supposedly self-evident development process. . . . [Development] now raises a host of policy issues. . . . While the government's position on these issues will not be determined by CIDA, it is essential that the Agency's perspective be expressed forcefully and effectively. In discussions of the debt issue, for example, CIDA should press the case for protecting the interests of the poorest people and countries. Where Canadian trade policies fly in the face of CIDA's attempts to encourage development, that too should be pointed out.[38]

Ironically, that *was* precisely the role that Strong and Paul Gérin-Lajoie had sought for CIDA twenty and more years earlier.

An Overarching Emphasis on Human Resource Development

Despite the Agency's formal commitment to human resource development as one of three sectoral priorities along with agriculture and energy, the report criticized "a strong tendency to treat expenditures on capital equipment and infrastructure as productive investments, while expenditures on people, especially the poorest people, are regarded as unproductive social costs."[39] The case for human development "goes far beyond training in modern management and technology, although that is one of its important facets. More fundamental is the struggle to liberate human potential, which is blocked and often destroyed by poverty and deprivation."[40] Because it was so central in the development process, human resource development ought to be "a kind of prism through which the entire aid program should be viewed" and "a criterion of all bilateral aid rather than only a single sectoral concentration."[41] The committee identified as priorities: strengthening the role of women in development, improving primary health care delivery systems, and supporting educational development, especially at the primary level. At the post-secondary level, SCEAIT sought more emphasis on occupational and technical training, one thousand new open scholarships for core countries, and federal initiatives to remove impediments for ODA-sponsored students to study and gain work experience in Canada.[42]

More generally, the committee recommended "a substantial shift in expenditures from large-scale capital projects to human resource development programs" and urged that capital and infrastructural assistance be provided "only when there are built-in training and technical assistance programs designed to ensure the long-term maintenance and good management of the facilities."[43] A long-standing concern of Winegard was embodied in a call for closer cooperation between IDRC and CIDA and greater use of IDRC research in bilateral and NGO projects. The report commented: "Too much research produces an impressive list of publications and little else. Too much development rests on poorly researched foundations."[44]

Food Aid and Agriculture

Although it had been CIDA policy since the late 1970s to incorporate food aid into efforts for achieving eventual food self-sufficiency in recipient countries, the Winegard committee found Canadian performance still wanting. "Despite the . . . risks associated with food aid—namely, that it can create import dependency, depress the prices paid to small producers and delay needed agricultural reforms—Canada's use of this channel continues to be well above the DAC average." With more than 15 per cent of Canadian ODA going into food aid, and only a fraction of that to emergency famine relief, it was being used primarily as a "quick disbursing program transfer that also satisfies high Canadian tying requirements." SCEAIT recommended that non-emergency food aid not exceed 10 per cent of the ODA budget and that more resources be devoted to agricultural development, especially incentives for small farmers.[45]

Other Sectoral and Programming Emphases

Apart from fundamental concerns with poverty alleviation and human resource development, and a continuing priority on agriculture and food production, the committee recommended a flexible approach to sectoral specialization reflecting the needs of different countries and regions. It also identified issues that warranted new programming efforts. One was rapid urbanization, especially the problem of meeting "the basic human needs of the swelling ranks of urban poor."[46] Another was the environment. The report observed that the 1986 policy still fell short of providing an adequate framework for environmental impact assessment, especially in the energy and forestry sectors.[47]

Structural adjustment. Reviewing recent debates on policy reform, especially in Africa, SCEAIT supported "frank dialogue" with recipients. However, "it should always be borne in mind that the point of such dialogue is not to impose our views, but to strengthen the basic purposes of our ODA in alleviating poverty and supporting self-reliance." Reforms "should be designed to bring real benefits to the poor or, at the very least, to mitigate the effects of adjustment on the poor." The report urged Canadian representatives on governing boards of the international financial institutions to promote approaches to structural adjustment that addressed the impact of conditionality on the poorest. In turn, it called on CIDA to "support investments in social and human development as a concomitant to macro-economic adjustment, so that the burden of policy reform falls least heavily on the poor."[48]

Multilateral aid. While the committee concentrated on bilateral aid and the voluntary and business sectors, it endorsed Canada's long-standing commitment to multilateral aid. It recommended targeting of about one-third of the ODA budget for multilateral programming, above the existing guideline but below the actual level in 1985. The Consultative Group on International Agricultural Research and the International Fund for Agricultural Development were singled out as deserving more Canadian funding.[49]

Some witnesses and committee members advocated shifting responsibility for the World Bank from the Department of Finance to CIDA, in part because of the growing importance of policy-based lending. The report endorsed the existing division of labour, however, citing arguments from officials—first, that ODA was strengthened by having the central financial agency involved in international development and, secondly, that it did not make sense to separate responsibility for the IMF and the World Bank in view of the desirability of harmonizing their policies on adjustment lending.[50]

Humanitarian relief. The committee observed that the existing guideline of allocating 2 per cent of ODA to relief had been exceeded in recent years, and that in 1984-85 the total spent by CIDA's International Humanitarian Relief program and Africa Emergency Aid had risen to 4.2 per cent. It recommended maintaining a base budget of 2 per cent, and allowing an additional 1 per cent to match voluntary relief donations—but from general revenues, not from a reallocation of programmed development assistance.[51]

A New Approach to Eligibility[52]

SCEAIT also tackled the thorny question of country eligibility. The existing three-tier system, established in 1981 ostensibly to achieve greater programming coherence, was subjected to harsh criticism: "It almost invites being held hostage to foreign policy considerations that may have little to do with the basic purposes of the aid program in reaching the poor and promoting self-reliant human development."[53] The report urged abolition of the scheme and designation of no more than thirty core program countries (exclusive of regional groupings) based on criteria such as absolute need, Canada's experience with the country as an aid partner, compatibility of the country's development priorities with those of Canada, demonstrated capacity to use aid effectively (especially for the poor), and respect shown for human rights. The committee called for fully four-fifths of bilateral ODA to go to these core programs.[54]

The report also supported channelling 80 per cent of bilateral aid to low-income countries (stronger than the existing guideline of "up to 80 per cent") and endorsed the commitment of 0.15 per cent of GNP to the least developed. It recognized that a tilt towards Africa was appropriate for a strong anti-poverty orientation, but "we would not want the regional distribution of funds to become unbalanced in ways that might neglect areas less in the public spotlight. Our aid to Asia, the continent that is home to most of the world's poorest people, is already very low on a per capita basis."[55]

Human Rights

SCEAIT joined Hockin-Simard in urging more explicit linkage between ODA and human rights performance. While mindful of political and ideological controversies swirling about the issue, Winegard recommended:

- that there be no preconditions for emergency humanitarian aid on compassionate grounds, but that it be monitored closely to prevent abuses;
- that victims of human rights violations not be forgotten when decisions are taken to reduce or deny aid to governments;
- that human rights criteria developed as part of overall foreign policy "be applied in a universal, consistent and transparent manner";
- that "such criteria, embracing both individual, civil and political rights and socio-economic and cultural rights, be derived from established standards of international human rights law and convention";
- that "verifiable reports of violations, not ideology or strategic interest, be the basis for unfavourable assessments of human rights observance"; and
- that progress on human rights be assessed as part of the overall record of development, "particularly from the vantage point of the poorest people."[56]

To make the guidelines operational, "the Committee sees merit in developing a classification grid for recipient countries that would provide incentives for good behaviour as well as penalties for poor human rights performance." It suggested as well that CIDA and External Affairs prepare an annual ODA-human rights review to be tabled in Parliament and referred both to SCEAIT and the Standing Committee on Human Rights. CIDA was also urged to conduct training courses for development officers, to include human rights evaluations in all country program reviews, and to consult Canadian NGOs in the field when making human rights evaluations. The report echoed the Special Joint Committee with a plea for Canada to "work for changes to allow human rights concerns to be put openly on the agendas of international financial institutions."[57]

Aid Untying

Though careful in examining competing claims, the report challenged existing government policy on procurement tying. On this issue more than any other, the determination to examine fundamentals of the aid program led to a shift in opinion, especially among Tory members who would previously have accepted a defence of tying uncritically.[58] The committee was exposed to considerable debate (including strong support for the status quo from business groups),[59] and was made aware that DAC viewed Canada as one of the worst offenders among OECD donors.[60] The field trip to Africa was also a formative experience.

SCEAIT asserted that procurement tying should act

> as an incentive, not an alternative, to achieving the goal of Canadian international competitiveness. . . . From a development point of view, even more crucial than competitiveness is appropriateness. . . . In affirming the general principle that, where appropriate and competitive, Canadian goods and services should be purchased in preference to those of any other industrial country supplier, the Committee also affirms that the Canadian content of ODA should be driven less by political considerations and fixed percentage rules than by development objectives.[61]

The committee proposed that, as long as Canadian goods and services were competitive and appropriate, they should be purchased in preference to those of any other *industrial country* supplier. However, having made that important concession to domestic business, it went on to propose: that the long-standing 80 per cent rule be relaxed for *local cost and developing country procurement*; that the untying authority be gradually raised to 50 per cent of the bilateral budget; that tying requirements be waived altogether for some LLDCS in sub-Saharan Africa; and that greater untying of food aid be permitted when exportable food surpluses were available in neighbouring countries.[62]

Aid and trade. The report recognized that expanding trade was essential for developing countries. Supporting more vigorous use of CIDA's Trade Facilitation Office, it urged making import promotion a declared objective of ODA policy.[63] The emphasis on import promotion and a reduction in Canada's protectionist barriers was part of a plea to put both sides of the trade ledger into a longer-term perspective. Trade was seen in this light as a way of promoting development for poor majorities in the poorest countries, with the expectation nonetheless "that a strategic increase in aid and trade involvement in some countries can and should repay long-term dividends to Canada."

SCEAIT was critical of efforts to use aid to secure immediate returns for Canadian business, opposing an aid-trade policy that risked "becoming a subsidy for mainly commercial transactions that really ought to pay for themselves."[64] It also urged government support for efforts within the OECD to restrict mixed credits competition, and asked for assurance that concessional export financing offered through the Export Development Corporation not count as ODA unless it met criteria in the proposed Development Assistance Charter.[65]

Decentralizing CIDA

Anticipating that aid budgets were likely to grow less than in the past, the report emphasized the need for more effective delivery. Of all the suggestions for improvement, "none is so compelling or commands such widespread support as decentralization to the field."[66] As we have seen, greater decentralization had been endorsed by the North-South Institute, the Auditor General, and the Public Accounts Committee; it received support as well from NGOs and academics who testified before Hockin-Simard and Winegard.

The committee commended CIDA's recent expansion of field support units (FSUs), as well as growing use of mission administered funds and microréalisation programs for grass-roots projects. In a study made available to SCEAIT, the Agency agreed that more decentralization was desirable, outlined several possible approaches, and urged gradual development of CIDA field offices. Based on the FSU concept, each would employ mostly contract personnel, under a public servant with diplomatic status reporting to the head of post. Rejected largely on grounds of cost was the "person-year transfer approach," involving the transfer of people and functions from headquarters to the field.[67]

Winegard accepted CIDA's arguments that field offices would be cheaper and more flexible, but insisted that full-scale decentralization was an idea whose time had come. "For that to occur, some of the people *and authority* located at CIDA headquarters must be transferred to the field."[68] The committee believed that field-based decision-making was the key to streamlining a cumbersome, rigid, and delay-prone organization that required a loop through Hull for almost every decision. It would improve the quality of project selection and monitoring, involve recipients in all stages of the process, foster reorientation towards human resource development, and secure more effective coordination of aid efforts with other donor countries. SCEAIT also hoped that decentralization would strengthen the field presence of Canadian NGOs, NGIs, and firms, who would work with CIDA "to build long-term, cooperative relations with the people of the Third World. . . . The motto for Canadian ODA should be 'Join Us for Development *in* the Third World.' "[69]

The committee—concerned about cost, and doubtful that a dispersal of staff and authorities to thirty-odd core countries "would permit the development of sufficiently large centres of expertise and planning"—recommended creating five or six regional offices in Africa, Asia, and the Americas, each headed by a deputy vice-president who would have authority to approve projects up to $5 million (the level currently delegated to vice-presidents). Each office or "Canada Partnership Centre" would house twenty to twenty-five professional officers (including program directors for core countries in the region, senior planners, and resource people) and support staff, for a total thirty to forty-five person years.

Although the Agency had estimated that placing forty-five person years in the field might yield a net reduction of only twenty at headquarters, the report urged as close to one-to-one replacement as possible. It did recognize, however, that additional costs for maintaining civil servants in the field would be in the range of $20 to $40 million a year. Decentralization, the committee concluded,

> is not a cost-free process—financially, administratively or politically. Financially, it entails spending a larger portion of the aid budget on administration; administratively, it means losing some control at the centre; and politically, it means accepting the risks of an aid program truly responsive to the needs of our developing country partners. We strongly support substantial decentralization only because we are convinced that its costs are far outweighed by its likely benefits in contributing to a more effective aid program.[70]

As one participant in the review put it: "The developmentalists will never win in Ottawa, but they can in Dar es Salaam."

Improving Evaluation

The committee applauded recent efforts to strengthen accountability, corporate memory systems, and project and program evaluations, "but we note that management and information services are only a supporting aspect of quality control. The front line of development is not at corporate headquarters; it is in the field. This is where the aid relationship succeeds or fails."[71] Noting that a "bottom-up rather than a top-down approach to evaluation" was more likely "to achieve effectiveness in reaching the poorest people," the report recommended that CIDA undertake cooperative evaluations with locally based partners, and make stronger efforts to keep headquarters staff in touch with what was learned in the field. It also urged that longer-range targets be incorporated in planning and project approval documents, and that all evaluations and country program reviews refer back to these targets by attempting "to assess the effect of the aid activity on the poor, women, the environment, human resource development and local self-reliance."

SCEAIT also argued that aid would be improved by exposing evaluations, country program reviews, and other ODA studies to more independent public review.

> We can understand why sensitive information might be withheld, but we believe that a general policy of insularity would not serve the purpose of making ODA more effective, much less build public confidence in the program. The excellent cooperation the Committee received from CIDA at every stage of this study should stand as a model for the future.

The Agency was urged to cooperate closely with other donor agencies, research institutions, and the non-governmental sector to strengthen evaluation, and to work with others to open up evaluation processes in multilateral development agencies.[72]

Strengthening Partnerships

Praising CIDA's domestic partners, the report voiced satisfaction about Canada's leadership in encouraging citizen participation in the aid program. It recognized, however, that "partnerships are not without their complications and limitations." There were irritants as well as positive elements in relations between CIDA and non-governmental sectors, and "very different" perspectives on development and ODA.

> NGOs generally conceive of development as a broad social and economic process requiring strong public sector involvement and small community-based projects, while the business community, quite naturally, places a much greater emphasis upon private sector initiatives and the need to harness the entrepreneurial and commercial capabilities of developing countries. Universities, for their part, emphasize human resource development through advanced education and training.

However, "a pluralistic society must have a pluralistic aid program. The Canadian model of development is one that finds a place for all of these very different, at times competing, partners."[73]

NGOs. The committee applauded NGOs for responding effectively to basic needs of the poorest. Supporting the wish of voluntary organizations to maintain operational independence, it emphasized that country focus projects, while desirable, should not be undertaken at the expense of responsive funding. While SCEAIT was not prepared, as some witnesses urged, to scale down bilateral aid in order to permit a massive redirection of resources to NGOs, it did propose increasing the share of the ODA budget for responsive NGO programming from 5.2 to between 6 and 7 per cent. That would yield more than a twofold real increase by 1995-96 if by then Canadian aid reached the official target of 0.6 per cent of GNP.[74]

Universities and NGIs. The report also endorsed the development work of non-governmental institutions, especially the role of universities and colleges in providing the "thoughtware of development."

> We recognize that in many cases these initiatives may not have an immediate and tangible impact on the poorest people, but we are convinced nevertheless that if the poorest nations of the world are ever to move beyond acute poverty and foreign aid dependency, they will require educated leaders and administrators, as well as a secure institutional base on which to build.

SCEAIT proposed that the combined share of the two responsive programs to which institutions of higher education had access—Institutional Cooperation and Development Services and Management for Change—grow from 2.9 per cent to a range of 4 to 5 per cent, a possible threefold increase by 1995-96.[75]

Business. The committee consistently asserted that the focus of ODA ought to be primarily on development, and only secondarily on Canadian commercial and other objectives. However, it viewed the business community as

> the most underutilized resource in Canadian official development assistance. The Committee . . . would especially like to encourage initiatives that involve a more lasting business commitment to developing countries. The Committee is deeply troubled by the apparent tendency on the part of some businesses to look upon CIDA as a convenient source of tied aid contracts where the partnership ends as soon as the money runs out. This is not good enough.

Long-term commitments were needed to support "the spread and growth of successful, profit-oriented enterprises [that] are vital for self-sustaining economic development."

The committee offered no concrete suggestions, but challenged Canadian business to make more imaginative use of the Industrial Cooperation Program. CIDA-INC in turn was enjoined to respond flexibly, though in ways that would "not sacrifice developmental criteria in the bargain." The report recommended that INC grow as a share of ODA from 1.3 per cent to a maximum of 4 per cent.[76]

An International Development Advisory Council. Winegard saw the tendency for CIDA's relationship with ODA partners to be little more than a cheque-writing operation as a significant source of policy incoherence. His strong views shaped a recommendation for an International Development Advisory Council that would include members of important constituencies such as NGOs, universities, and business, but "not become just another channel for lobbying." Consideration should be given to appointing as members "leading Canadians from various walks of life," and distinguished representatives from developing countries. The role of the Council would be threefold: to advise the minister on long-range policy issues, to buttress the proposed ODA charter by examining and commenting on program and policy evaluations, and to open CIDA to outside policy influence. "In turn, it could play a useful role in encouraging debate of ODA issues and in raising the public profile of CIDA across Canada."[77]

Broadening Public Support

The committee called for vigorous efforts to strengthen public support for development assistance. A prime requisite was ensuring the greatest possible aid effectiveness—" 'greatest possible' because aid is an inherently risky business." While candour and a willingness to acknowledge and learn from mistakes were essential, development education had to be more extensive and effective as well.

Existing outreach activities were found wanting. One aspect, CIDA's public affairs programming, involved considerable effort and was done professionally, but "the Committee believes there is an appalling lack of awareness among Canadians of what CIDA is doing around the world." The other, the Public Participation Program, funded NGOs and others that had done some good work but without much effectiveness in connecting with a wider audience. Moreover (and here we see the scepticism of some Tory members), "the message of development education is sometimes far removed from the medium of development and is based more on ideology than practical experience."[78]

The report recommended a new four-part strategy for development education. First, since "television is now central to any endeavour to reach people's heads and hearts," CIDA should form a "media co-op" with ODA partners that would develop "dynamic media information programs" and track Canadian public opinion on development issues. Secondly, PPP should keep its existing funding share, but be governed by appropriate standards that "differentiate clearly between education and legitimate debate on the one hand and propaganda on the other." Thirdly, the Agency should provide medium to long-term support for "centres of excellence" in Canadian universities that would strengthen international development research and teaching at the post-secondary level and the resource base available for community-based development education. Fourthly, "we want to strengthen the tenuous links between the process of development in the Third World and development education in Canada" by encouraging NGO partners to share their "direct, hands-on experience of development with their fellow Canadians." A more active role in development education was also foreseen for international students and trainees.[79]

Level of Support

Although the committee did not ask the government to reverse its deferral of the commitments to achieve aid flows of 0.6 per cent and 0.7 per cent of GNP until 1995 and 2000 respectively, it sought a legislated guarantee for the 0.5 per cent floor and small, regular increases towards the 1995 target starting in 1988-89.[80]

A New Strategy Emerges[81]

The Winegard report, though hardly a media sensation, received good press coverage and favourable editorial comment. The proposals for linking ODA to human rights performance captured headlines and those for decentralizing CIDA, meeting the needs of the poorest, emphasizing human resource development, and reducing procurement tying received attention as well. NGO representatives and academic commentators responded positively, although some expressed disappointment about the committee's virtual acceptance of the government's timetable for achieving the international volume target. The modest heed given to multilateral aid was also a matter of concern.[82] Pollution Probe, among others, regretted the relative inattention given to the environment and sustainable development.[83] (*For Whose Benefit?* was published a month after the Brundtland report.) Some scepticism was voiced about whether the government would respond meaningfully.

Within CIDA, Policy Branch had provided documents and research support to the committee during the review.[84] In addition, thirteen working groups from across the Agency had contributed to "CIDA 2000," an exercise aimed at clarifying future policy and programming options; it was also used as a conduit to feed ideas to the parliamentarians. As a result, the Agency was well prepared to lead an interdepartmental consultative process that developed material for two cabinet papers approved in August 1987. These in turn informed the government's response to SCEAIT, *To Benefit a Better World*, tabled by Clark and Landry in September (within the one hundred days required by House of Commons rules).

The trite title symbolized a blunting of Winegard's sharp edge from the "poorest of the poor" to a "better world." Nonetheless, much of the committee's reform program was incorporated in a general statement on Canada's official development assistance policies and in specific responses to proposals. Of 115 recommendations, 98 were accepted (some with distinct shifts of nuance), 13 were modified, and only 4 were rejected outright. Indicating that *To Benefit a Better World* was essentially a response to "the widely praised SCEAIT report," the minister announced that a new "comprehensive strategy" was forthcoming.[85]

Keen to leave her mark on a major project, Landry had already won authorization to proceed with what eventually emerged in March 1988 as *Sharing our Future*, CIDA's action plan for the 1990s. Unlike the process that supported the parliamentary review and the official response, *Sharing Our Future* was shaped as a highly confidential ministerial project. Catley-Carlson and senior officials in the Policy Branch worked on the text with staffers from Landry's and Clark's offices and writers from Public Affairs Branch. It was to be the minister's document publicly—but, apart from accommodating Landry's wish to do more for business, it was very much "Maggie's game plan" in response to Bill Winegard's vision.

The core of the strategy contained much of what SCEAIT recommended, at least in modified form:

- a claim that Canada's development assistance efforts would be "guided first by humanitarian concerns";
- a Charter of Development declaring the primacy of developmental goals;
- a strong emphasis on poverty alleviation as a central policy objective;
- a commitment to shift the balance of effort away from large infrastructural projects to human resource development, emphasizing especially the role of women, primary health care, and primary education and literacy, as well as existing emphases on higher education and training;
- a new approach to food aid, promising much greater integration with programming for rural and agricultural development;
- abolition of the three-tiered eligibility framework;
- a promise to exhibit greater sensitivity to human rights performance in determining recipient countries and programs within them;
- liberalized Canadian procurement regulations, allowing higher untying for local costs, especially in Africa and the least-developed countries;
- a significant decentralization of personnel and decision-making authority to the field;
- a concern to respond positively to the interests of non-governmental ODA partners; and
- a revamped and expanded program of public outreach.

Sharing Our Future also confirmed "the Government's objective" of reaching ODA/GNP ratios of 0.6 per cent and 0.7 per cent in 1995 and 2000 respectively. (*To Benefit a Better World* had already announced that growth from 0.5 to 0.6 would begin in 1991-92, not in 1988-89 as the committee recommended.) A statutory floor of 0.5 per cent was rejected.[86]

The Report and the Strategy Compared[87]

The most difficult issues to resolve in *Sharing Our Future* were decentralization and human rights, though for different reasons. On decentralization (to which we shall return later in the chapter), a decision to proceed was taken quickly, but contentious interdepartmental negotiations on implementation delayed publication of the strategy for several months.[88]

Human rights conditionality. The dilemma on human rights was how to respond positively to Winegard without conceding the degree of openness and transparency sought by the committee. Both bureaucrats and their political bosses feared diplomatic embarrassment, business backlash, and intense conflict among parliamentarians if countries were publicly scored on a grid according to human rights performance and ODA eligibility. Some indication of potential volatility was apparent when SCEAIT members named countries they would like to see reprimanded. Winegard himself was on reasonably safe ground when he identified Mengistu's Ethiopia and Pinochet's Chile as candidates for exclusion from government-to-government (as opposed to NGO or humanitarian) aid. Liberal member Roland de Corneille, however, picked a favoured core country with commercial significance when he targeted Indonesia for its aggressive actions in East Timor and other human rights violations. He also suggested taking a close look at Bangladesh, Sri Lanka, and the Philippines (which had only just graduated to core status).[89]

In the response to Winegard, the government expressed scepticism about the possibility of establishing operational criteria for human rights assessment, on grounds that international standards are so general, and that there was such a "diversity of legal systems, social values and traditional structures in the countries in which CIDA functions." Similarly, a human rights country classification grid was rejected in favour of diplomatic channels and less formal means of responding to concerns about violations. However, a commitment was given to make respect for human rights a "top priority" in ODA policy, and to place more emphasis on human rights performance in new programming. The government also accepted recommendations to establish a Human Rights Unit within CIDA and to give Agency personnel training on human rights issues.[90]

No legislated mandate. Winegard had hoped not only that a mandate for Canadian ODA would be enacted by Parliament, but also that a two-day debate on proposed legislation would raise public awareness. Bureaucratic concerns about maintaining flexibility and avoiding a time-consuming legislative process prevailed in a decision not to ask for statutory authorization for a mandate—or, more narrowly, for CIDA. However, *Sharing Our Future* proclaimed an ODA Charter of Principles and Priorities that accepted fully the three principles the committee enunciated—putting poverty first (assisting the poorest countries and people), helping people to help themselves, and ensuring that development priorities must prevail. A fourth was added: "Partnership is the key to fostering and strengthening the links between Canada's people and institutions and those of the Third World."[91]

The sharp edge of the charter was blunted by wording in the accompanying text, which indicated that the old trinity of mixed motives—humanitarian, political, and economic—was alive and well. In wording similar to that contained in the *Estimates* since 1984, the strategy confidently asserted that "Canada's development activities can be and often are supportive of other foreign policy objectives," such as "support for social justice, the pursuit of global peace and security, and the building of a strong international trading system."[92] In fact, the *Estimates* retained the 1984 statement as the "program objective," indicating that it would be implemented in accordance with the ODA Charter, which was appended.[93]

Programming priorities. The charter recognized the "supremacy" of six development priorities: poverty alleviation, structural adjustment, increased participation of women, environmentally sound development, food security, and energy availability.[94] The list, developed during the CIDA 2000 process, omitted human resource development, which was characterized elsewhere in the strategy as the "first priority" and as the " 'lens' through which all of Canada's development efforts are focused."[95] However, whereas Winegard used human resource development in a generic sense to denote a shift in emphasis from infrastructure to people, especially the poorest, *Sharing Our Future*, without defining the concept, tended to equate it with high-level education and training, and new opportunities for Canadian universities, colleges, and private-sector firms. The only operational target mentioned was a doubling of CIDA scholarships over the next five years to a total of 12,000, with about half "likely to be trained in Canada."[96] The document promised action on literacy, basic education, and primary health care, mostly through further education and training of managerial and professional personnel. In this respect, as Martin Rudner argued:

> Despite the emphasis placed on human-resource development and "putting poverty first" in the ODA strategy, in actual practice the educational and training orientations of human-resource development and the strategic targeting of poverty groups do not seem to converge. Most of those offered postgraduate education or technical and occupational training through ODA can be expected to come from better-educated, better-off segments of the developing society.[97]

The committee's concern about the urban poor was incorporated in discussions of poverty alleviation, environment, and women. Although not flagged by Winegard or cited as a priority in the charter, population was also identified as "a major element of . . . programs to meet a number of thematic objectives, including alleviation of poverty, women in development, environment and food security."[98] The strategy included a rather thin section on "initiatives for the Third World private sector"—but, apart from a promise to expand the Trade Facilitation Office, it did not take up Winegard's challenge to make import promotion an ODA objective.[99]

When the list was first unveiled in *To Benefit a Better World*, some observers were surprised to see structural adjustment cited as a priority. Its presence reflected a view within senior management that CIDA ought to have a more focused position on an issue that had emerged as the main preoccupation of the World Bank and the IMF in the 1980s. The strategy defined the goal of structural adjustment as "helping economies cope with debt and reduced export earnings and to improve economic management (while being sensitive to the social and economic effects of this adjustment)." The text, containing a fifteen-point program of concrete action on debt and structural adjustment in the poorest countries, was mostly a rehash of earlier decisions to forgive ODA debt and to contribute to Bank and Fund facilities.[100]

Food aid. The government turned down the committee's recommendation for a cap on non-emergency food assistance. In announcing an intention to increase food aid by 5 per cent a year, however, it simultaneously conveyed a positive message to farm interests and signalled a reduction of the share of food aid in overall ODA—which, to stay at 0.5 per cent of current GNP, would likely rise by 8 per cent or so a year.[101] In *Sharing Our Future*, commitments were made to allocate up to 75 per cent on a multi-year basis to facilitate long-term planning, to provide food aid in ways that would avoid discouraging local production and respect local food preferences, and to help recipient countries reform agricultural policies.[102]

Country eligibility.[103] The strategy abolished eligibility categories, and opened up all forms of Canadian aid to ODA-eligible countries, except those excluded for political, human rights, or economic reasons.[104] Ironically, in view of SCEAIT's desire to make CIDA's policies more transparent, the government was actually able to remove from the public domain information about eligibility priorities (apparent on the old list), leaving as the only source the completely confidential bilateral planning figures approved each year by cabinet. At least *ex post* accountability was promised, however, in a number of overlapping quantitative targets for bilateral assistance over the next five years (based flexibly, it would appear, on a computer analysis of recent experience): 75 per cent on thirty countries or regional groupings; 45 per cent on Africa, 39 per cent for Asia, and 16 per cent for the Americas; 65 per cent to developing countries in the Commonwealth and la Francophonie; and 75 per cent to low-income and small island states.[105]

Not surprisingly, in view of pressure for proliferation, the commitment to the top thirty recipients fell short by 5 per cent of what Winegard recommended. Moreover, in moving from the existing policy of channelling up to 80 per cent of bilateral allocations to low-income countries, towards 75 per cent for these countries and small island states (a designation including a major program in middle-income Jamaica), *Sharing Our Future* immediately raised a question about the depth of the commitment in the ODA Charter to the poorest countries. One further target—50 per cent of total aid to Africa and the least-developed countries of Asia and America—was phrased less categorically than the others ("efforts will be made"). The existing commitment to channel at least 0.15 per cent of GNP to LLDCs was reaffirmed.[106]

The strategy outlined yet another set of criteria for eligibility—a recipient's needs, its willingness and capacity to manage aid effectively, the quality of its economic and social policies, Canada's political and economic relations with the country, the recipient's human rights record, and involvement of its population in the development process.[107] The last reference was new, the link between aid and policy conditionality was stronger than in *For Whose Benefit?*, and there was less explicit focus on poverty alleviation.

Procurement tying. The government had trouble with SCEAIT's recommendations on untying, but gave some ground. Defending the past record and the "current practice of purchasing competitive Canadian goods and services," the strategy conceded:

> Many Third World countries have gained greater capacity to produce skilled people and goods that can be mobilized to contribute to their own development. Furthermore, in the poorest countries, more flexibility is required in Canada's tied aid policy in order to allow local-cost financing of relevant agricultural, grassroots and community projects.[108]

Accordingly, the new policy split the difference between existing guidelines and Winegard's proposals by agreeing to maximum untying levels of 50 per cent in sub-Saharan Africa and LLDCs in other regions, and 33 1/3 per cent elsewhere. In opening up the possibility of significantly higher levels of local purchases, it stopped short of authorizing procurement from developing countries other than the recipient, a practice supported by SCEAIT and indeed first promised in 1975 but never implemented.[109]

Evaluation. The parliamentary committee's concerns about improving and opening up evaluation were largely missing in *Sharing Our Future*. In its initial response, the government promised to develop abstracts of project and program evaluations for parliamentarians, development partners, and others who requested them; it did not, however, acknowledge the value of research or independent, arm's-length evaluations. In turn, the strategy relegated the whole question of evaluation to the issue of information dissemination—welcome to be sure, but a reversion to CIDA's characteristic defensive posture on such matters.[110]

Partnership. When the minister's staff and senior officials developed an approach to the strategy, they looked for an "engine" to tie and pull together the more than one hundred "wagons" in the Winegard report and the government's response. They came up with three themes—improving program delivery (subsuming the issues discussed above), fostering partnerships, and reaching out to Canadians. Considering that the notion of partnership had been given pride of place in CIDA's rhetoric for the previous half-decade, the contention that the "new Partnership Program" was "the biggest innovation of this updated Canadian strategy" smacked of hyperbole.[111] (So too did some of the authors' efforts to lavish praise upon the voluntary sector: "NGOs are as Canadian as hockey."[112])

The concept of partnership was extended, however, and given a new operational twist in a policy to channel 50 per cent of aid dollars each year through:

- domestic and international non-governmental organizations;
- non-governmental institutions;
- development crown corporations (except PCIAC);
- multilateral organizations, including food aid and the IFIs; and
- the business sector.

The other 50 per cent would be allocated through the "National Initiatives Program" of bilateral assistance and other contributions to development decided by the government—multilateral food aid, international humanitarian assistance, scholarships and student fees, and Petro-Canada International Assistance Corporation.

The Winegard report used the epithet "smoke and mirrors" in reference to the ODA estimates tabled annually in Parliament.[113] It was an apt characterization as well for this new policy on funding shares. Since the respective shares of the national initiatives and partnership categories were half/half when the strategy was developed, the immediate practical objective was to protect the bilateral components of the budget from any encroachment that would have resulted from acceptance of SCEAIT's recommendations to increase funding shares for the responsive programs. In fact, the only one of these that was adopted was movement to a 4 per cent allotment for the Industrial Cooperation Program over a five-year period;[114] this increase now had to come at the proportional expense of one or more of the other components of the "partnership program."

Over the longer run, and especially important in the event of funding cuts (which did occur), the new policy attempted to secure the relative share of bilateral aid (which had been especially hard hit when spending was reduced in 1978-81 and 1983-84). It sought, as well, to ensure that decisions about trading off multilateral funding (which was not solely in the hands of CIDA) or responsive funding—in the face of NGO, NGI, and business lobbies—would be considered in relation to one another, rather than bilateral aid.

The government turned down the recommendation to establish an advisory council with representatives of domestic and international partners. Winegard had thought that such a body would harness the "grand bazaar" and strengthen the minister's hand in promoting policy coherence. She thought otherwise and was persuaded that competing claims for membership could provoke unnecessary political conflict. Although *Sharing Our Future* proclaimed that "decision-making authority under the Partnership Program will be decentralized," the statement was hedged with qualifications that seemed to suggest little change from the status quo.[115] Much was made, as well, of policy consultations that were already undertaken on a regular basis.[116]

If the strategy failed to offer much for enhancing participation of non-governmental interests in decision-making, it did deliver something for those interests on several policy fronts. For NGOs, it validated the importance of their work and made several programming changes they had long sought: the emphases on poverty alleviation and human resource development, greater untying, decentralization, and human rights sensitivity. Universities were promised a big increase in scholarships for Third World students, and resources for new centres of excellence in development and area studies.[117] For business, possible losses through greater untying and fewer physical infrastructure projects were offset by promises of better support services in Canada and abroad, a larger role in training programs, a bigger slice of the funding pie for INC, and new general lines of credit in up to twenty countries "of long-term interest to the business community." Landry's preoccupation with broadening for-profit opportunities was reflected in a new requirement that submissions for country focus projects (hitherto the preserve of non-profit development agencies) had to include an analysis of alternative private-sector capacities.[118]

The sensitivity of the Winegard report to domestic interests in the aid program was rooted in a philosophical conception of the nature of development and the mission of ODA. *Sharing Our Future* went well beyond lip service to the developmental goals of the parliamentary committee, but it was more a classic exercise in interest brokerage and populist politics. While it echoed SCEAIT in emphasizing that "Third World peoples and governments must *always* be considered as Canada's first and most important development partners,"[119] the strategy was more preoccupied than Winegard with Canadian partners.

Public outreach. Sharing Our Future reflected SCEAIT's concern about strengthening public support for development assistance and ODA funding. A commitment was made to raise annual spending on development education and information from 0.6 per cent of ODA to the 1 per cent level first sought by the Breau task force in 1980. While there were no allusions to the committee's reservations about the Public Participation Program, and co-funding of traditional "dev-ed" activities was to be continued, it was clear that most new activity would occur elsewhere. Efforts would be stepped up to cooperate with the provinces on increasing global education in the schools. A Media Co-op was endorsed, along with a promise of greater involvement in development education activities by people with developing country experience. New ways would be explored for spreading information about CIDA and international development to all regions of the country, especially to business and the media. An annual "Development Day" would become a focus of special events and programs. Finally, *Sharing Our Future* committed CIDA to carrying out regular public opinion surveys to track public support for ODA and understanding of development issues.[120]

Launching the Strategy

Monique Landry, whose title was now minister of External Relations and International Development, tabled *Sharing Our Future* in the House of Commons on March 3, 1988. Following her press conference later that day, CIDA began distributing thousands of copies of the document across the country. Decorated with colour photos and fancy computer graphics, it began with Landry's "new vision for Canadian Official Development Assistance" and endorsements from Mulroney and Clark. Some journalists poked fun at the visual layout and the fanfare surrounding the launch, but most media commentary was positive, if somewhat restrained since most of the issues had been raised by the Winegard report, and covered again with the publication of *To Benefit a Better World*.

The government was applauded for emphasizing the needs of the poorest of the poor, and for moving on tied aid and decentralization. The compromises on human rights and food aid got mixed reviews. Two issues that drew critical comment were the unbudging position on ODA targets and the promotion of partnership.[121] On partnership, the *Globe and Mail* wrote:

> Development money is scarce, and the risk of such a program is that a number of well-intentioned but ultimately futile projects may be financed. While many non-governmental organizations have proved themselves in the development field, there is less evidence that businesses and other groups have had similar success. If the partnership program is to work, money must be allocated with great care.[122]

The *Winnipeg Free Press* warned that partnership smacked of a "giant boondoggle" that "sounds like a formula for waste on a grand scale that will do little to help the poor but much to help those who claim to be out to help the poor."[123] The North-South Institute later commented:

> [If] Canadian groups of many kinds can use official aid funding (or better still, generate "matching" funding) to bring . . . top quality assistance to the Third World poor . . . Canadians will view these [contributions] as invaluable. . . . If, on the other hand, they should come to suspect that domestic Canadian interest groups are steering the aid program—and that much-needed aid dollars are being used to subsidize the export of second-rate goods or services, or merely to expand the horizons of interested Canadians—taxpayers will rapidly become disillusioned and actively hostile.[124]

The Institute also expressed reservations about some of the outreach proposals, particularly the emphasis on polling and CIDA's preoccupation with raising its own public profile. Promoting awareness undoubtedly merited more resources—but, the Institute asked, "How much should a government agency try to educate the public about the challenges it faces, and the work it is doing, without either engaging, or being seen to engage, in taxpayer-financed propaganda?"[125]

SCEAIT met Landry on March 8, just before she set out on a cross-country tour to promote the strategy. Committee members generally expressed pleasure with the outcome, although the minister was pushed (without much success) to clarify the policy on human rights conditionality. Winegard later went on record as regretting the rejection of an international advisory council. Steven Langdon of the NDP criticized the government's unwillingness to make a stronger commitment on ODA volume, yet "when it comes to dramatically increasing the support for private business in this country through our aid program, you are able to make quite dramatic steps."[126]

The committee held four additional meetings, inviting testimony from CCIC, the Association of Colleges and Universities of Canada, the Canadian Exporters' Association, and Catley-Carlson. Tim Brodhead, CCIC executive director, welcomed much of the substance of *Sharing Our Future* but regretted that the government had fallen short of Winegard on human rights, untying, food aid, and volume. He expressed concern that "stretching 'partnership' to cover such a vast range of possible relationships is going to empty it of meaning."

> It is very hard to see in what sense both the World Bank and a community-based non-government organization in Canada are partners. . . . In effect, the government is saying that anything CIDA is not controlling directly is a partnership relationship. . . . I think there has to be more to it. The notion of some dialogue, some consensus about objectives, and in a sense, even some balance in the power of the partners is more accurately described as a partnership.[127]

Voicing reservations about untying and decentralization, Frank Petrie of CEA complained that "the Charter does not appear to recognize fully the role of the private sector in industrial development." He also said: "We are very nervous about this whole field of human rights, which is not to say we in any way champion what is going on in a lot of countries in the developing world in this regard."[128] When she met the committee, Catley-Carlson quipped characteristically:

> We have been reading with great care and attention the reports of the witnesses you have been calling. . . . I guess my summary observation would be that we have mostly pleased all of them but have not totally pleased any of them, and that perhaps indicates that a reasonable balance among the competing interests has been achieved in the document.[129]

Soon thereafter, Cranford Pratt published a stern critique, depicting *Sharing Our Future* as an exercise in damage limitation and a serious retreat from Winegard's "broad and popular consensus around a humane internationalist aid policy."[130]

Meanwhile, in CIDA, Catley-Carlson pushed for a determined effort to implement *Sharing Our Future*. As we shall see, decentralization was put on the "fast track." Studies were commissioned on how to strengthen programming for poverty alleviation and basic health and education. The broad implications of an emphasis on human resource development were clear, but work was undertaken to define the operational significance of what remained a rather fuzzy, catch-all concept. A training program on human rights was set up. Another exercise focused on determining the practical meaning of making structural adjustment a priority for a bilateral aid agency. Consultations began on implementing commitments to university-based centres of excellence, more scholarships, higher funding levels for INC, and new lines of credit. Manifest Communications were contracted to advise on a new public outreach strategy, and the first Development Day was held on October 3, 1988. Policy Branch started to develop an elaborate, computer-based system to monitor implementation of objectives and benchmarks set out in the strategy; in contrast to 1975, CIDA in 1988 was going to take this one seriously and keep its own report card.

Less to Share

Landry told SCEAIT that *Sharing Our Future* "is intended as a basic guide, in a forward-looking sense, till the turn of the century."[131] The "shelf life" was to be a good deal shorter. Funding cuts were a major factor undermining the strategy. Many of the objectives assumed that resources would rise along with GNP until 1990-91, and then even more rapidly. Planning and consultations proceeded on this basis, and Prime Minister Mulroney solemnly affirmed the volume commitments before the UN General Assembly in September 1988.[132] That was just before the federal election, which returned the Conservatives for a second term. (Clark and Landry both retained their portfolios.[133]) Shortly thereafter, the government indicated a new seriousness about cutting the fiscal deficit.

Rumours circulated that foreign aid would be a major casualty when Michael Wilson, still finance minister, brought down his next budget in April 1989. The amounts predicted fell within the range of $500 to $800 million over three years. NGOs launched a letter-writing campaign to the minister and MPs, and there was some sympathetic press and editorial comment.[134] CCIC and the North-South Institute issued a joint statement two weeks before the budget about how inappropriate cuts would be "when many Third World countries were struggling to cope with crippling debts and sharply reduced living standards, and were taking steps to introduce painful reforms on the understanding that rich countries like Canada would support their initiatives with increased financial resources."[135]

The news on April 27 was worse than anticipated. The cash allocation for ODA in 1989-90 was reduced by $360 million from a base of $2.8 billion (13 per cent) and cumulative cuts over a five-year period amounted to $1.8 billion—more than anyone had predicted. Apart from Defence, which did not suffer an absolute year-over-year cut, expenditure reductions for other departments were paltry. As a result, Official Development Assistance, though only 2.8 per cent of federal spending, sustained over 23 per cent of cutbacks projected for 1989-90 and 17 per cent for 1990-91 (by assuming no more than a carry-forward of the $360 million base reduction).[136] Canada, at the peak of the late-1980s economic boom, removed $360 million from aid spending during a fiscal year in which Canadian GNP grew by $43 billion and a rate of 7 per cent.[137] DAC asked appropriately: "can it be argued that Canada's aid-giving capacity has declined when Canada's economic growth record has been among the strongest in the OECD area in the 1980s?"[138]

Clark exacted from Wilson a compromise that the base cut would be one time only and that formula funding would be maintained. The ODA/GNP ratio would drop to 0.43 per cent in 1989-90, but would then start to grow again—to 0.45 per cent in 1990-91 and then by .005 per cent a year, reaching 0.465 in 1994-95.[139] Somewhat incredibly, a "Backgrounder" on the budget claimed that "the government remains committed to the international target of 0.7 per cent of GNP."[140] Hypothetically, if formula growth were to continue rising .005 per cent annually from the new reduced base, 0.5 per cent would be reattained only in the year 2000, and 0.7 would be achieved in 2040.[141]

The initial impact of the reduced cash level on total ODA was not as severe, because of the timing of deposits of promissory notes to multilateral banks and an increase in the imputed costs of maintaining CIDA-supported students from developing countries.[142] Still, the percentage cut from 1988-89 was 5.6 per cent. CIDA announced the impact on distribution immediately after the budget announcement, maintaining that it wished "to minimize uncertainty for our partners in the private and voluntary sectors and allow them to get on with planning their own affairs." Claiming that the strategy had been used as a blueprint, the Agency announced that all ODA programs would share in the reductions.

Hardest hit were bilateral geographic programming and food aid, cut 12 per cent ($130 million) and 13 per cent ($56 million) respectively. All development crown corporations were affected, especially Petro-Canada International Assistance Corporation which lost 20 per cent of its budget. While the 50:50 split between National Initiatives and Partnership was formally maintained, partners were not cut as heavily in this round.[143] There were major losers in the "partnership envelope"—multilateral food and technical assistance and international NGOs—but funding for domestic NGOs and NGIs was reduced by only 3.2 per cent, from $250 to $242 million. Although the Agency stressed that INC lost much of a planned increase, the business program secured a $10 million increase from $51 to $61 million.[144] When the smoke cleared, Canadian aid had fallen from $2.95 billion in 1988-89 to $2.85 billion in 1989-90, and the ratio from 0.49 to 0.45 per cent.[145]

Although a leak of Wilson's budget speech was the big media story, the harsh ODA cut prompted more than usual coverage of a foreign aid issue. Stephen Lewis, who had stepped down as Canada's ambassador to the UN a year earlier, accused the government of abandoning the Third World in its darkest hour and of taking out its own economic incompetence on those most in need. Editorial comment was almost universally critical of the disproportionate nature of the cuts.[146] Analyzing the politics of the budget, Hugh Winsor remarked: "Reductions in foreign aid, while morally offensive when set against an expanding Canadian economy, affect distant victims who have only a modest domestic constituency. And that part of aid that encourages Canadian companies abroad was maintained or increased."[147] He might have added that most development activists do not vote Conservative.

In the House of Commons, opposition leader John Turner accused the government of turning its back on world poverty and hunger, and the prime minister of lying to the world about Canada's ODA commitment.[148] Landry returned to SCEAIT a week after the budget, this time to receive "the drubbing of her political life."[149] Opposition spokespersons were scathing in their criticisms. André Ouellet (the future Liberal minister of Foreign Affairs who was to oversee a much larger cut in 1995) tried to goad Landry into resigning if the aid budget failed to achieve the promised increase in a year's time. He concluded: "We will be seeing each other again next year, and there will probably be another reduction then. With a minister like you, it is not surprising that your department's funds are being cut."[150] Landry undertook a vigorous round of meetings with business, NGOs, and NGIs. She encountered considerable unhappiness, but faithfully plugged the party line about deficit reduction, always assuring her listeners that the ODA cut was one time only.[151]

The minister and Catley-Carlson used every opportunity to assert that budget reductions would not affect the strategy, other than by delaying some planned expenditures for scholarships, lines of credit, etc. It was now impossible, however, to maintain existing commitments and add major expenses for public outreach, decentralized program delivery, and new forms of programming for poverty alleviation, human resource development, and human rights. Distributional percentages that made sense in the context of expanding resources no longer worked. Even with the increase in funding for INC, there was little scope for achieving the promised 4 per cent share of ODA. Landry made a point of confirming the commitment of 0.15 per cent of GNP to LLDCs, but it just did not add up—both in 1989 and 1990, the level fell to 0.11 per cent.[152]

Even before budgetary pressures began to take their toll, *Sharing Our Future* met a lack of enthusiasm in some quarters of the Agency. The secrecy of the drafting process and the months that elapsed after *To Benefit a Better World* created a sense of detachment among officers that contrasted with the experience of intense involvement during the CIDA 2000 and SCEAIT exercises. There were criticisms of the "smorgasbord" and "keep everybody happy" approach to Canadian interests, and of the tendency (shared with Winegard) to see developmental problems from the vantage point of sub-Saharan Africa. Within Asia Branch, the strategy was viewed as especially irrelevant for the long-term partnerships that Canada was trying to develop in China and Southeast Asia. The scant attention paid to multilateral aid was another source of irritation. Many welcomed the intent of the Charter to put development first, but there was cynicism about whether the commitment was meaningful in operational terms. A mixed review from DAC was upsetting, especially for senior officials who saw the strategy as developmentally progressive.[153] Given the shift to hands-off management and an enormous build-up of demands with scarcely any increase in staff complement, new themes and programming demands did not sit well with many rank-and-file employees. Budgetary reductions intensified the discomfort.

Decentralization: A Short-lived Experiment

Decentralization to the field was, in the end, to become a major casualty of cutbacks and bureaucratic politics. In 1988, however, Clark and Landry decided remarkably quickly to "bite the bullet" and proceed with transfers of personnel and decision-making authority to the field. Major issues of principle were debated and resolved within the government between publication of the Winegard report in May 1987 and approval of cabinet papers that formed the basis of *To Benefit a Better World* in August. Some were relatively uncontentious, though not necessarily in accord with the committee's recommendations. First, at least initially, only bilateral programming would be decentralized; Business Cooperation and Special Programs would remain based at headquarters. Secondly, as bilateral aid involved government-to-government negotiations, decentralized offices would be country-based, not regional (except where there was regional programming). Thirdly, ministerial prerogatives would remain unchanged; no one expected Landry to delegate approval authority for projects over $5 million, but she insisted as well on remaining involved in all consultancy contracts above $100,000.

More controversial, and ultimately the most crucial question, was how to organize decentralized delivery. Senior officials in CIDA still pushed for a field office approach, making heavy use of contracted Canadian and local personnel who would report to a management group of three or four drawn from the Agency. This model was close to existing arrangements in many recipient countries, where a field support unit worked with a small aid section operating out of the embassy. Treasury Board, however, was unwilling to countenance delegation of decision-making authority unless more civil servants were placed in the field. Meanwhile, External Affairs insisted that the head of post had to be responsible for project approval and that any public servants assigned to Canadian missions had to be part of the consolidated foreign service. Clark's agreement with these concerns meant that External Affairs would manage the aid program in the field, with person years either transferred from CIDA headquarters or created anew. Again, this outcome was not one anticipated by Winegard.[154] It ensured that the operation would be very expensive.[155]

Landry and Catley-Carlson had hoped to launch the new strategy within weeks of publishing *To Benefit a Better World*, but decentralization negotiations dragged on for months. Although many in CIDA and External Affairs were enthusiastic about the project, there were sceptics on both sides. Some officers saw the process as an outside imposition, more for reasons of political fashion than aid effectiveness. Discussions about "nuts and bolts" reflected quite different organizational cultures as well as conflicts over jurisdictional turf. Within External Affairs, apprehension about aid decentralization diverting energy from other foreign policy priorities was mixed with a recognition that there were opportunities to offset cutbacks, rebuild, and acquire new resources. On CIDA's side, there were fears of losing control over aid delivery, as well as ODA monies transferred to External Affairs. There was also resentment about the high costs, both capital and recurrent, of following the External Affairs rulebook on diplomatic postings. As one senior official lamented, "interdepartmental discussions sometimes were more of a negotiation between contending interests rather than a joint search for the best way to implement a foreign policy priority."

CIDA and External Affairs signed a memorandum of understanding late in December 1987, which advanced the process to a point where planning could proceed.[156] Treasury Board, however, turned back an initial joint proposal as too costly. It took two months more to secure the Board's agreement on key issues of scope, person years, and budget. The principle of transferring decision-making authority to the field was maintained but the number of posts scheduled for decentralization was cut back. Finally, on March 3, 1988, "after months of suspense," Catley-Carlson was able to announce details to Agency employees.[157] *Sharing Our Future*, released later that day, proclaimed that "almost all of the new initiatives now taking place in Canada's development assistance program can be done well only if there are more aid staff in the field, and if they have more decision-making authority and administrative flexibility."[158]

Identified as Phase 1, the plan involved decentralization to nine diplomatic posts and a number of satellite offices (see Table 8.1). Four of the nine would have responsibilities for ongoing regional programming—Abidjan for the Sahel, Harare for SADCC, Bridgetown for the Leeward and Windward Islands, and Singapore for the Association of Southeast Asian Nations (ASEAN). Aid sections would be headed by Canadian development program directors, supported by senior professional and managerial personnel, and reporting to heads of post. Decentralized offices would assume responsibilities for country program development, sectoral studies, project identification and planning, monitoring, financial management, and evaluation. While procurement and the selection of Canadian consulting firms were to remain centralized, ambassadors and high commissioners would have authority to approve projects up to the $5 million level and contracts for local consultants up to $100,000. In turn, they would be accountable to the president of CIDA for planning and implementing development programs and projects, and would take "functional direction" from Agency vice-presidents.

The approved plan called for an increase in aid-stream person years abroad from the current level of 113 to 230 by 1990, by transferring fifty-seven from CIDA headquarters and adding sixty new positions. Another twenty-two were added to External Affairs in recognition of the Department's increased responsibilities. Most support staff and some professional expertise would be recruited locally. Total start-up and operating costs for the first five years, all to come from the ODA budget, were projected as $260 million, with recurrent expenditures of $50 million a year thereafter. As a result, average annual administrative costs of the aid program would rise by about 25 per cent.

Table 8.1
Decentralized Posts

Place	Date	Satellites
Bridgetown, Barbados	1988	
Dakar, Senegal	1988	Guinea/Conakry
Dar es Salaam, Tanzania	1988	
Manila, Philippines	1988	
Singapore (ASEAN)	1988	
Abidjan, Ivory Coast	1989	Burkina Faso, Mali, Niger
Harare, Zimbabwe	1989	Botswana, Lesotho, Malawi, Mozambique, Swaziland,[a] Zambia
Jakarta, Indonesia	1989	
San José, Costa Rica	1989	Guatemala, Honduras

a The satellite operation planned for Swaziland was delayed and then cancelled.

Source: CIDA, *Annual Report 1989-90*, p. 44, and CIDA, "Administrative Notices: Special Edition on Decentralization," December 21, 1988.

Although no further decentralization was contemplated until Phase 1 had been implemented and evaluated, *Sharing Our Future* promised to expand mission administered funds. As a result, even non-decentralized posts could look forward to a Canadian Fund for Local Initiatives (Canada Fund), "a greatly expanded replacement for MAF with the money and authority to support a larger number of locally managed projects in such vital fields as community development, women in development, basic health care, income-generation, and environmental protection."[159] These allocations did go up, but typically only from $350,000 to $500,000 a year because of budgetary restraint.

The experience of decentralizing.[160] Following seven months of uncertainty since the cabinet decision, there was great pressure in the spring of 1988 to decentralize quickly. Five posts were scheduled in the 1988-89 fiscal year and the other four in 1989-90 (see Table 8.1). One rather harried senior official told the author that he would have preferred a five-year time-frame, but deferred to Catley-Carlson's judgement that the opportunity would be lost if not seized immediately. A handful of people in External Affairs and CIDA were assigned responsibility for a massive project that lacked a coherent game plan because earlier negotiations had focused on structural relationships, not process—let alone developmental implications.

Serious personnel problems were encountered. While several professional officers were eager to accept one posting abroad, there was resistance to ongoing rotational service; fewer women than men came forward; spouses faced difficult career choices and support staff resented that there were fewer opportunities for them than Winegard appeared to have promised. Within decentralized posts, there was little advance orientation on what to expect, and intense logistical pressures to provide office space, houses, and other amenities for a sizeable influx of additional people. New arrivals experienced culture shock, not least within the workplace for those who had no previous experience in diplomatic posts.[161] There were also enormous managerial and communications challenges in putting required systems and equipment in place.

Despite these difficulties, the relocation schedule was achieved (except for one satellite operation). By 1990, the nine decentralized posts and their satellite offices had expanded from 23 to 138 person years (see Table 8.2). Early reports and evaluations were positive. Looking back on the first two years, CIDA was pleased to inform DAC that

> there is improved communication with local representatives and more participation of them in Canadian programming; aid personnel have a far better knowledge of the local milieu; project identification, planning and monitoring is [*sic*] much improved; there is speedier and more timely decision-making; [and] there is increased and more continuous dialogue, mainly at the informal level, and better coordination with other donors.

There was also more untying of funds for procurement of goods and equipment in recipient countries.[162]

While decentralization appeared to be achieving hoped-for developmental objectives, it was a continuing source of managerial and political tensions. From the vantage point of External Affairs, there was concern that operations were having a "tail-wagging-dog" impact on decentralized posts. Moreover, traditional hierarchies were upset when Bridgetown became the second largest post in the Western hemisphere and Harare was bigger than Bonn. At CIDA headquarters, bilateral vice-presidents and other senior officers felt excluded from decentralized operations and had to cope with bifurcated managerial relationships since many country programs remained centralized. In the field, the conflict of cultures and management styles between aid officers and diplomatic/trade officials grew in the decentralized posts because ODA programming bulked so large in local activity and often required separate physical quarters.

Although responsibilities for procurement and consultant selection remained at headquarters, there was business opposition to decentralization. In his testimony to SCEAIT, Frank Petrie of the Canadian Exporters' Associ-

Table 8.2
Statistical Overview of Decentralized Posts, 1989-90

	Estimate of 1989-90 bilateral disbursement ($ million)	Distribution of AID PYS before and after decentralization[a]			Locally engaged staff		
		Before	Additional	After	Staff[b]	Officers	Total
Bridgetown (Barbados)	20.9	2	13	15	8	5	13
Dar es Salaam (Tanzania)	30.8	2	5	7	18	5	23
Manila (Philippines)	26.3	1	6	7	25	0	25
Dakar (Senegal)	33.2	2	13	15	54	2	56
Singapore (Singapore)	3.0	1	4	5	15	3	18
Jakarta (Indonesia)	52.4	2	6	8	17	0	17
San José (Costa Rica)	20.8	1	7	8	16	5	21
Abidjan (Ivory Coast)	63.1	7	35	42	206	7	213
Harare (Zimbabwe)	16.5	5	26	31	50	8	58
	267.0	23	115[c]	138	409	35	444

a Includes satellites for Dakar, San José, Abidjan and Harare.
b Includes chauffeurs and guards.
c Includes fifty-seven transferred from Hull and fifty-eight new. Excludes two PYS in Rwanda.

Source: Groupe Secor, Canadian International Development Agency, "Strategic Management Review: Working Document," October 9, 1991, p. 39/2

ation expressed "strong fear" that small exporters and consultants would be especially disadvantaged. He acknowledged that decentralization

> could improve the quality of aid but we do not think it will speed up the delivery mechanism. Only a few months of the decision process is being moved to the field. The major part of the decision process remains in Canada and should be subject to a major overhaul in order to cut the time to select consultants and the time between project identification and project implementation.[163]

Similar concerns were voiced at CIDA's annual consultation with CEA[164] and persisted in informal contacts—especially with consultants who saw themselves disadvantaged by developing country competitors and with suppliers who complained that decentralized posts were using too much of their new untying authority.

There was also disquiet within the NGO community, notwithstanding earlier rhetorical support for decentralization. Agencies vying for bilateral contracts were affected most directly, but others worried about increased direct funding of southern country NGOs and more CIDA intervention in relations between Canadian and Third World voluntary organizations. There was fear that delivery through External Affairs would weaken the developmental thrust of the aid program. CCIC advised members against rushing to establish separate overseas offices, urging instead stronger links with local NGOs and increased participation in cooperative funding arrangements like the South Asia Partnership.[165]

In an otherwise highly critical 1991 assessment of CIDA post-Winegard, the Interchurch Fund for International Development (ICFID) was cautiously positive about decentralization. It did, however, complain about luxurious and sheltered lifestyles within expatriate diplomatic ghettos—and, from a Zimbabwe case study, about insensitivity to local business in adhering strictly to foreign service regulations requiring all-Canadian content for houses, offices, and equipment. It reported "happily" that CIDA officers had not bypassed locally based Canadian NGOs to relate directly to their indigenous partners, but "there have been several examples of locally hired staff being drawn away from local NGOs by higher salaries. This certainly seems to conflict with CIDA's goal of strengthening local institutions."[166]

A quiet burial. The problems of managing an aid program split between centralized and decentralized modes, and between External Affairs and CIDA, might have been sufficient to end the experiment, especially since there was considerable business opposition as well. The official explanation was cost. Certainly a major catalyst in unravelling the process was the April 1989 budget cut. Landry and Catley-Carlson faced tough questioning from opposition members of SCEAIT when the *Estimates* showed increased administrative expenses in 1989-90 of $86.3 million (including $67.6 million for decentralization). Landry kept reminding the committee that all parties had supported decentralization, but Christine Stewart and Lloyd Axworthy, the Liberal critics for development and external affairs respectively, asserted that their support was contingent on maintaining the commitment to a rising ODA/GNP ratio (now effectively abandoned). Catley-Carlson replied that "the amount of cost sunk in this exercise was such that it was not a good business decision to cut off this expenditure when the exercise is . . . three quarters complete." Besides, she said, decentralization amounted to a mere 2.5 per cent of program costs and was projected to decline to 1.8 per cent. She emphasized how seriously the government had taken Winegard's recommendation and how confident she was of an improvement in the quality of aid.[167]

Soon afterwards, a change anticipated for some months occurred. Catley-Carlson was transferred to Health and Welfare Canada as deputy minister, and Marcel Massé returned to CIDA for a second term as president. By that time, two other key players who helped shape decentralization had also left CIDA—Bill McWhinney, the senior vice-president, and François Pouliot, vice-president of the Policy Branch. When he appeared before SCEAIT in October 1989, Massé was guarded about the experience: it appeared to yield higher quality, but high costs might require trade-offs.[168]

While Massé suggested that two or three years' experience were needed to make a judgement, the clock was ticking much faster. CIDA's decentralization program was the subject of one of several cost-cutting studies commissioned by Treasury Board Chairman Robert de Cotret in December 1989. The review examined three options—recentralizing, streamlining existing decentralized operations, and creating more autonomous aid offices through contracting out. Although the eventual outcome was a combination of the first and the third, at this stage it was decided that streamlining would save costs and preserve the benefits of decentralized program delivery. Phase 2 was cancelled, thirty-eight person years were cut immediately, more were scheduled, and savings of $60.2 million were projected in the period up to 1994-95. It was agreed that CIDA and External Affairs would continue to monitor the experience and make recommendations in 1993 about longer-term directions.[169]

Again, the pace accelerated. In November 1990, DAC—which had commended decentralization—criticized the dramatic increase in administrative expenses to 8 per cent of Canadian ODA, almost double the average for OECD donors.[170] A management study of CIDA by Groupe Secor revealed in 1991 that the expense of bilateral delivery had increased from $85.60 per $1,000 of programming in 1986-87 to $140.60 per $1,000 in 1990-91. However, data from a 1990 evaluation of decentralization revealed that costs had escalated about equally in Dakar and Jakarta, decentralized posts, and in

Bangkok, a centralized operation with a field support unit. Groupe Secor concluded from these "very partial results" that it was not possible "to determine whether the current decentralization model or the FSU-based model is the most cost-effective. In governance terms, however, the Thailand model appears to offer clearer accountability patterns, since the decisions remain in CIDA's HQ."[171]

While further cuts in the ODA budget provided a context for winding down decentralization, Groupe Secor's comment about governance was revealing. Marcel Massé had grown increasingly impatient about sharing field responsibility with External Affairs, and was instrumental in disbanding the foreign service stream for development officers. He also thought that CIDA should become more policy-oriented and less project-driven. Although he believed strongly in the value of field experience, his views became increasingly aligned with the managerial and political pressures already working against decentralization.

"Rationalization" followed "streamlining." The February 1992 budget exacted more cuts from decentralized operations, more person years were withdrawn in 1992-93, and further reductions were planned for 1993-94. By the summer of 1992, although no official announcement had yet been made, journalists learned from disgruntled field employees that decentralization was dead.[172] CIDA's parliamentary *Estimates* confirmed the decision the following spring. As of April 1, 1993, of the 117 person years allocated by Treasury Board in 1988, 66 had been repatriated. Decision-making authorities were shifted back to headquarters, and the last officers completed their tours of duty in September 1994.[173]

From Strategy to Tragedy

Of all the commitments undertaken in *Sharing Our Future*, decentralization probably had the greatest potential for changing CIDA's organizational thinking and behaviour. Although Catley-Carlson fought hard to make it a lasting accomplishment before she left the Agency, its demise was partly a result of dissatisfaction voiced by the very domestic interests she had worked so hard to build up as CIDA's friends in Canada and partners in the field. Unfortunately, through no fault of hers, the energy she devoted to partnership and outreach did not save the aid program from disproportionate cuts when deficit reduction became the order of the day.

The Winegard report still provided a compelling set of benchmarks by which to judge the performance of Canada's aid program and Monique Landry remained a stout defender of "her" strategy as long as she was minister (until January 1993). After Catley-Carlson's departure, however, *Sharing*

Our Future was not taken as seriously within the Agency. While various recommendations had a continuing impact on programming, the total package was not suited to an era of declining resources. Efforts to provide accountability for implementation were abandoned.

To the extent that the strategy had any enduring "strategic" vision, it was in the principles of the Development Charter. While these were values to which the vast majority of CIDA's staff subscribed, they were not translated into operational guidelines to deal with day-to-day bureaucratic and political pressures. When Marcel Massé returned as president, he was quietly yet perceptibly disgruntled about the document. He had a very different vision for CIDA and the future of Canadian aid. In certain quarters within the Agency, it became chic to refer to *Sharing Our Future* as "the tragedy."

Chapter 9

Shifting Gears, 1989-93

Marcel Massé's second term as CIDA president from 1989 to 1993 was a time of turmoil within the Agency and uncertainty for Canadian ODA. Internationally, conventional wisdom about foreign aid was challenged by the fall of the Berlin Wall and the breakup of the Soviet Union, the rise of regional trading blocs and global financial markets, and growing anxiety about the fragility of efforts to achieve sustainable development. Domestically, the Tory government's deficit reduction agenda hit hard at the aid budget and produced considerable dislocation within the federal civil service. Support for aid, as measured in public opinion polls, declined in the context of a deepening recession.

Massé returned to an Agency that he saw as excessively preoccupied with operational minutiae and insufficiently focused on policy reform in developing countries. As he had in his first presidency, he challenged CIDA to rethink its mission and adapt to changing circumstances. This time, however, he encountered resistance to his ideas on development and his organizational vision. Fresh from four years at the IMF in Reagan-era Washington, his contentious views on structural adjustment struck a discordant note for many in CIDA, and provoked disquiet within NGO and academic circles—which further weakened external support for Canadian aid, already eroded by the business community's advocacy of fiscal restraint.

Too late to placate external critics, Massé soon softened his message, accepting more emphasis on the social costs of adjustment and stressing that "economic sustainability" was only one of "five pillars" of sustainable development. A new policy framework proclaimed that the "mission of CIDA is to support sustainable development in developing countries." Pursuing that goal, Massé argued, required "taking a more 'horizontal' approach by working to influence other government policies."[1] Once more, he staked out for CIDA a claim to a larger role than simply aid policy and delivery.

Considerable effort went into strengthening CIDA's environmental policies in advance of the 1992 UN Conference on Environment and Develop-

---

Notes to Chapter 9 are on pp. 542-60.

ment—the Rio Summit. Meanwhile, post-Cold War ideas about the politics of development excited Massé, who actively encouraged policy-making for promotion of human rights, democratic development, and good governance. Disappointed that country program reviews initiated during his first term had become little more than statistical profiles and lists of discrete projects, he pushed again for an integrated approach to country planning, this time through country and regional policy frameworks.

These policy thrusts required stretching fewer dollars over an ever-broadening mandate that still formally included all the commitments of *Sharing Our Future*. Groupe Secor, a consulting firm hired to undertake a strategic management review, concluded that CIDA was overextended, overregulated, underresourced (relative to its responsibilities), and inadequately in control of development content. Although many of Secor's recommendations were rejected when reviewed in-house, its diagnosis informed a cabinet paper that sought approval for greater geographic and sectoral concentration, restructured management systems, strengthened development knowledge, and a de-emphasis on process. Far-reaching changes were envisioned for relations with domestic partners and executing agencies. After protracted delays, the document went before a cabinet committee in December 1992, just after an announcement of the deepest cut in the aid budget since 1989.

Sensing an opportunity to rein in Massé and reassert the primacy of External Affairs, officials in the Department persuaded Barbara McDougall (who replaced Joe Clark in 1991) that it would be unwise to approve organizational reforms before reviewing the fundamentals of aid policy. EAITC (External Affairs and International Trade Canada, as it had become) took charge of developing a draft "International Assistance Policy Update," which endorsed some policy directions being pushed by CIDA but called for more concessional support for former Soviet bloc countries and a diversion of resources away from development in the poorest countries. It also contemplated a shift from long-term commitments to quick-disbursing flexible funds to meet emergencies and changing foreign policy priorities.

Massé and senior officials in CIDA were infuriated, especially by the emphasis on short-term flexibility. Other officials were concerned as well and, in January 1993, leaked copies circulated within the media and the NGO community. Arguing that a full public review of aid and foreign policy should await the outcome of the federal election later that year, CCIC led a successful lobbying effort to halt formal action on the Policy Update. By then, both Monique Landry and Marcel Massé had been transferred, and CIDA was in a state of high anxiety and uncertainty.

Sweeping global changes, budget cuts, Massé's agenda, and foreign policy pressures made *Sharing Our Future* ever less relevant as a set of guidelines for the 1990s—and yet the changing profile of the aid program did reflect some of the strategy's priorities: more bilateral aid was untied, there was a significant shift from infrastructural projects to human resource development, and much higher levels of program aid were earmarked to support structural adjustment in Africa and the Americas. Desk officers took poverty alleviation seriously but the absence of clear operational policies stunted effectiveness. Amid evidence of waning institutional commitment, there was also considerable activity in the sphere of Women and Development and a new policy was developed. As promised, more attention was paid to private-sector development, though mostly in ways that assumed mutual benefits for recipient countries would flow from greater activity by Canadian firms. While bilateral aid was squeezed most heavily in the short run, fiscal pressures and organizational rethinking created uncertainty about the future of multilateral commitments and responsive non-governmental programming. Outreach activities, expanded after *Sharing Our Future*, were cut back just as the polls revealed an ebbing of public support.

Global Winds of Change

The sudden collapse of communism in Eastern Europe and the passing of apartheid in southern Africa marked the end of an era in North-South political relations framed by the Cold War and struggles for decolonization. As a new multipolarity based on regional economic blocs replaced superpower rivalry, the notion of a "Third World" lost its meaning. The disappearance of "the politics of polarized triads" removed from developing countries a security umbrella under which they could profess non-alignment and pursue independent policies and development strategies.[2] In the absence of a credible Soviet model, debt further ensured that the choice now lay between full integration in the global capitalist economy or total isolation and disengagement.

Provided that the dominant rules of the game were accepted—with neoliberal economic reform at the top of the agenda—some nations of the South gained greater opportunities for full incorporation within the global economy. Others, especially the poorest in sub-Saharan Africa with little to offer international capital, faced the prospect of falling further by the wayside even if those in power had no wish to disengage. Moreover, as UNDP data revealed,

> Between 1960 and 1989, the countries with the richest 20% of world population increased their share of global GNP from 70.2% to 82.7%. The countries with the poorest 20% of world population saw their share fall from 2.3% to 1.4%. The consequences for income inequalities have been dramatic. In 1960, the top 20% received thirty times more than the bottom 20%, but by 1989 they were receiving sixty times more.

Extrapolating data on disparities between and within nations, the UNDP dramatized the gulf between the richest and the poorest people world-wide, which had been widening even more rapidly, especially in the 1980s.[3]

For four decades, the potential of ODA to promote human development had been limited in scope, flawed in conception, and weakened by conflicting objectives. The end of the Cold War brought hope for a peace dividend that would free up more funds for aid programming, as well as relieving it of the burden of East-West security concerns. That prospect soon evaporated as Western industrial countries became more tight-fisted in response to both the diminished geopolitical impetus for ODA and a preoccupation with their own fiscal and foreign deficits. Meanwhile, ethnic and regional conflicts diverted potential development assistance into military operations and emergency relief, and Eastern Europe and the former Soviet Union became competitors for declining aid resources. Rather than a peace dividend, the collapse of communism brought politics out of the closet into official aid discourse: "democracy and good governance" joined "sustainability" and "private-sector development" as watchwords for the 1990s.

Massé's Controversial New Vision for CIDA

Massé returned to CIDA in the fall of 1989 after serving as Canada's executive director at the International Monetary Fund. At the time of his reappointment, he was chairing a support group to raise money to help Guyana to clear its debts with the Fund and the World Bank and so become eligible for structural adjustment funding.[4] Appearing before the Standing Committee on External Affairs and International Trade, Massé declared that structural adjustment is "the only way most developing countries can make real headway in their struggle to develop. . . . [Until] you get the basic elements right, so that a country's economic framework makes sense, other investments are often ineffective and may even be utterly wasted."

According to Massé, the "structural adjustment imperative" implied moving CIDA somewhat away from projects to policy-based aid and closer coordination with the IMF and the World Bank (though "I don't mean we should simply follow their lead"). In turn, this required "big strides forward in thinking, in a much more sophisticated way, about what goes into a truly integrated program of development assistance."[5] Moving towards a more knowledge-based organization was also important, he told the committee, in order to strengthen the relationship between process and the substance of development, now that CIDA had evolved "from a system that deals mostly with the nitty-gritty to one where employees spend more of their time on management."[6]

In response to opposition MPs who voiced concerns about the social, environmental, and political implications of adjustment programs, Massé suggested that the Fund and the Bank had demonstrated pragmatism in ensuring "efficient delivery of economic policies."[7] During a subsequent appearance before the SCEAIT in December 1989, he argued that critics were targeting the wrong enemy.

> What we must attack is poverty and impoverishment. . . . But we must not single out . . . structural adjustment. It is quite correct that in a number of countries where structural adjustment programs have been applied . . . incomes per head have decreased, as indeed they should. That is not the proper comparison. . . . [If] you had not applied a program of structural adjustment, incomes per head would have decreased much more than they did with a structural adjustment program.[8]

Parliamentarians were not the only ones taken aback by Massé's espousal of IMF/World Bank prescriptions.[9] As one CIDA official observed:

> A lot of us felt that Marcel's first incarnation had been incomplete. . . . When he came back in, we thought, my God, it's wonderful to have him back. He can finish what he started. . . . He didn't feel that his ideas had changed that much. The rest of us thought that they had changed to a marked degree.

More metaphorically, another commented that it was as if the "messiah" of the first presidency had come back as the "devil's advocate" or, in the eyes of some, the "devil himself." Some policy analysts in the Agency who sought more emphasis on economic reform were pleased to have an advocate at the top. Given conflicting evidence about the economic effectiveness of structural adjustment, however, even they were surprised about the depth of Massé's conviction. His perspective on the social consequences of adjustment—unfortunate but necessary to avoid even worse outcomes—also upset those who saw a special role for Canada in support of UNICEF's "human face" approach.

Most hostile were NGO representatives who for years had seen the IMF and the World Bank as the bêtes noires of international development. Massé and most NGOs simply could not find the same wavelength on this issue and it cast a long shadow on a working relationship that Catley-Carlson had done much to improve.[10] The sharpest attack came from the Interchurch Fund for International Development (ICFID) and the Churches' Committee on International Affairs of the Canadian Council of Churches. They published an assessment of Canadian ODA in October 1991 entitled *Diminishing Our Future/ CIDA: Four Years after Winegard*. Although the paper was critical on several fronts—backtracking on volume targets, aid for trade promotion, and human rights—the main thrust was a condemnation of "the closer and closer integration of CIDA's thinking and policies with those of the IMF." Strongly polemical, the critique nonetheless catalogued impressively evidence of the human devastation wrought by structural adjustment, especially on the poorest. Massé's views on economic reform were quoted and interpreted at length.[11]

The day after *Diminishing Our Future* was released, the *Globe and Mail* summarized the "blistering report,"[12] and a delegation from ICFID met with Massé. He was furious about what he saw as shoddy research and misrepresentation—and a personal attack on him as a development practitioner and a Catholic layman.[13] His bitterness about the experience lingered. In an otherwise conciliatory address to NGO representatives a year later, he said:

> In money terms, the intervention by a group of NGOs in a field where I profoundly think that they are wrong has cost me a billion dollars in my budget over the next five years. That's not a billion dollars to me. It is a billion dollars to starving people who need it. . . . When we have disagreements, we should find ways of solving them that do not affect the people we are working for.[14]

Belying his usual even-handedness, Massé was heard on more than one occasion castigating the ICFID report as "murder by ignorance."

A Framework for Sustainable Development

Long before the conflict with church groups, Massé had become more circumspect in his advocacy of structural adjustment. While still insisting that policy reform, often with painful consequences, was essential for overcoming fiscal and foreign exchange imbalances, he was less assertive in claiming that the IMF and the World Bank had the right answers. He also put more emphasis on understanding the political environment of adjustment and addressing social consequences. (Given mixed evidence of success and "human face" criticisms, Fund and Bank officials themselves became less doctrinaire in the early 1990s.) As a way of avoiding knee-jerk reactions to structural adjustment, Massé started using "economic sustainability," a broader surrogate with fewer emotive connotations, and stressing that economic reform was only one requisite for long-term sustainable development.

Massé supported work already under way on a policy framework using "sustainable development" as an overarching concept for integrating various strands of the Agency's programming. It was a major focus of the President's Committee retreat in March 1991, which adopted the mission statement and schematic presentation set out in Figure 9.1. More than a set of programs, sustainable development was conceived as a process "that needed to be maintained and maintainable."[15] It rested upon "five pillars"[16]— environmental, economic, political, social, and (in an effort to integrate Massé's earlier thoughts) cultural. A discussion paper prepared by Policy Branch stated:

> These five elements (pillars) should not be seen as each standing independently. They are closely linked, and efforts to promote one of the pillars must take explicit account of the implications of the others. Sustainable development can only be achieved . . . when conditions for environmental, economic, cultural, political and social sustainability are met simultaneously.[17]

While no great revelation to students of development who have long stressed the need for an interdisciplinary approach, the framework was refreshing in a policy sphere that had tended to see the economic and the social as separate compartments and to neglect the political.

CIDA's discussion paper recognized that defining sustainable development in precise terms was a "thorny challenge" in view of the great variety of meanings attached to it.[18] Indeed, as Gerald Schmitz observed, since coming into vogue after the Brundtland Commission's report in 1987, the concept had become increasingly elastic and risked "danger of losing whatever critical edge it once had." Moreover, "the suspicion lingers that terms like sustainability have caught on precisely because they are sufficiently ambiguous to allow old orthodoxies to sustain themselves by adopting protective cover."[19]

For Policy Branch, the challenge of operationalizing sustainable development was even more difficult: "it may be easier to . . . [identify] sustainable development by what it is not than by what it is because unsustainable practices are often more evident than sustainable ones." The authors surveyed recent literature to come up with five main requisites: a long-term perspective, respect for diversity and pluralism, emphasis on equity and justice, reliance on participatory approaches, and use of an integrated approach. These in turn were among the themes addressed in a new Agency-wide short course on sustainable development.[20]

Keen to reinvigorate country planning, Massé championed creation of new country and regional policy frameworks, which employed the five pillars as a means of broadening the focus from projects to policy analysis. *Sharing Our Future* remained official policy, and the sustainable development framework was portrayed as a means for making it operational, but the strategy's significance waned in the context of recentralization, budget cuts, Massé's new vision for CIDA, and global changes. Asia Branch, which viewed the document as too Africa-centred, secured approval from the President's Committee for its own mission statement: "To involve Canadians in cooperation for sustainable development in Asia, in a manner that builds relationships and promotes Canada's long-term interests."[21] Although the Branch took poverty alleviation seriously, especially in South Asia, its chief interest lay in intensifying elite-level networking and commercial linkages in East and Southeast Asia. Also, as we shall see, there was growing determination within EAITC to subordinate the aid program more fully to foreign policy priorities.

Figure 9.1
CIDA and Sustainable Development

Mission statement

The mission of CIDA is to support sustainable development in developing countries.

Framework for sustainable development

Sustainable development is an integrating concept. It provides a framework for putting *Sharing Our Future* into effect.

Environmental	*Economic*	*Cultural*	*Political*	*Social*
• Ecosystem integrity • Biological diversity • Population	• Appropriate economic policies • Efficient resource allocation • More equitable access to resources including gender equity • Increasing productive capacity of the poor	• Sensitivity to cultural factors • Recognition of values that are conducive to development	• Human rights • Democratic development • Good governance	• Improved income distribution • Gender equity • Investing in basic health and education • Emphasizing participation of the beneficiaries

These aspects of sustainable development require further review and refinement. This process will involve consultation with CIDA staff and our partners.

Source: Memo to CIDA Staff from Marcel Massé on 1991 President's Committee retreat, March 28, 1991.

Environmental sustainability. Despite designation of environment and development as a major cross-sectoral priority in 1987, the Agency's approach remained ad hoc and compartmentalized until the imminence of the June 1992 Earth Summit in Rio prompted efforts to strengthen policies and integrate them within the broader sustainability framework. CIDA was also actively involved in interdepartmental preparations for the conference.

A new Policy for Environmental Sustainability was published in January 1992. It committed CIDA to three fundamental objectives:

- to help developing countries improve their institutional, human resource and technological capacities to deal with local and global environmental problems;
- to integrate environmental considerations into all aspects of CIDA's decision-making and activities; and
- to work with CIDA's Canadian and international partners to encourage them to integrate environmental concerns into their activities.[22]

The framers of the policy saw environmental NGOs (ENGOs) as crucial players, even though (and perhaps because) they were often among the harshest critics of development assistance. Despite reservations among some senior managers, it was agreed to open up lines of communication and funding opportunities to ENGOs. Annual consultations with the Canadian Environmental Network were initiated in 1992. The Network also assumed management of a new decentralized fund, the Environment and Development Support Program. It was launched to promote environmentally responsible lifestyles through collaborative activities involving Canadian-based ENGOs and development NGOs, their southern counterparts, and aboriginal communities.[23]

CIDA's reticence to become involved in environmental assessment had been a major bone of contention for environmentalists before 1986; thereafter the issue was the secrecy surrounding the process. Anticipating a new *Canadian Environmental Assessment Act*, which would make environmental assessment of all CIDA projects mandatory, the 1992 policy attempted to balance concerns about the sensibilities of non-Canadians with demands for more openness.

> CIDA will respect the sovereignty of partner countries and will adapt approaches for public review of environmental assessments and consultation with affected communities in a manner which respects the foreign nature of projects; it will apply the environmental assessment requirements of partner countries, or international development institutions, when these meet the basic objectives of Canadian law; and it will assist partner countries to develop and apply local environmental planning and assessment capacity. Environmental assessments of CIDA projects will be made available to the Canadian public.[24]

The policy was now stronger, but the burst of energy that brought government departments and NGOs together in constructive dialogue before Rio dissipated after the conference.

Human rights, democratic development, and good governance.[25] Although falling short of Winegard's recommendations, *Sharing Our Future* promised to make human rights a "top priority" in ODA policy. Action to implement that commitment was initially halting. At the political level, Monique Landry admitted in June 1989 that human rights records had not as yet been taken into account in recommendations to cabinet on aid distribution.[26] A one-person human rights unit was set up within CIDA to develop a training program, but at first the preference of officials in both the Agency and EAITC was to leave proactive programming (except in the sphere of women's rights) to the newly established International Centre for Human Rights and Democratic Development (ICHRDD).

Ed Broadbent, former leader of the New Democratic Party, was appointed president of ICHRDD and it commenced operations in 1990. Broadbent used the agency's arm's-length status to good effect, speaking out on international issues and acting as a gadfly to prod stronger Canadian government action. With a modest budget of $15 million over five years, the Centre concentrated, mainly through NGOs, on "front-line activities which prevent or fight human rights violations" and "[which] empower people and benefit in particular the poor, indigenous people, women and children." It provided funds for activities and organizations of various sorts, including human rights institutes and documentation centres, legal aid offices, electoral commissions, and human rights conferences.[27]

The tempo of activity at the political level picked up in the early 1990s. Prime Minister Mulroney used summits of the Commonwealth and la Francophonie in 1991 as platforms to announce a stronger Canadian stance on human rights/ODA conditionality. His action followed a report prepared for the Commonwealth Human Rights Initiative, an independent organization set up to pressure Commonwealth leaders. They were urged, by a committee chaired by former External Affairs minister Flora MacDonald, to adopt a declaration on human rights and set up a standing commission to monitor and report on abuses.[28] Although Mulroney was rebuffed in efforts to advance the committee's agenda at the heads of government meeting in Harare in October 1991, he got considerable publicity back in Canada for his declarations that "the primacy of human rights is a cornerstone of our foreign policy" and "we shall increasingly be channelling our development assistance to those countries which show respect for fundamental rights and freedoms."[29] He was even more assertive in November at the meeting of francophone leaders in Paris.[30]

Media commentary ranged from praise to cynicism (Mulroney was then being touted as a possible secretary general of the United Nations), with concern voiced about whether a coherent policy would be applied consistently.[31] While precise implications of Mulroney's commitment were unclear, a Foreign Policy Framework prepared for Barbara McDougall in 1992 cited as a priority "securing democracy and respect for human values, through promoting human rights, democratic development and good governance."

Meanwhile, Massé was quick to embrace the emerging donor consensus on these themes. While the aid phenomenon and donor-recipient relationship had always been highly political, official policy discussions and prescriptions during the Cold War era were couched in economic and technical terms that ignored the political dimension. The left had long assailed aid agencies for supporting military and other authoritarian regimes that had little regard for human rights or for the needs of the poor. Then, in the 1980s, neo-liberals began to associate autocratic government with a bloated, inefficient state that stood in the way of market-based reform. At the same time, electoral democracy was being rehabilitated in Latin America. But the major catalyst for putting politics on the development agenda was, of course, the end of East-West hostility and the dramatic pace of political change in Central and Eastern Europe.

Like sustainable development, "good governance" has been appropriated to mean many different, often contradictory things. There may be a broad consensus about the desirability of strengthening human security or reducing public expenditures on armaments or curbing corruption, but understandings differ radically on what is needed to make national and local governments more accountable to the people they supposedly serve. Ideologically and practically, there is an enormous gulf between, on the one hand, those who seek economic liberalization, minimal state intervention and low-intensity democracy, and, on the other, those who seek widespread popular participation in public life, empowerment of the poor, and a state capable of counteracting the polarizing effects of market forces.

A variety of contending positions informed calls for new and expanded forms of aid conditionality, raising questions about whether these concerns reflected universal human values or the cultural arrogance of the North. Within CIDA, political sustainability became one of the "five pillars," and the human rights unit was expanded, becoming a four-person Good Governance and Human Rights Policy Division in September 1992. Work started on a comprehensive policy statement. Country and regional desks began to support (though within more constrained political limits) activities similar to those undertaken by ICHRDD. Particular emphasis was put on strengthening institutions of civil society, and providing technical support for conducting and monitoring elections.

Cutbacks, Restructuring, and Downsizing

The dominant preoccupation of CIDA during the second Massé presidency was not with policy but rather with how to cope with declining resources. Although Joe Clark and Monique Landry promised that the $360 million base reduction in 1989 would be one time only, foreign aid remained a favoured target of spending cuts in successive budgets brought down by Michael Wilson and his successor as finance minister, Don Mazankowski. The Tories' reluctance to reduce military spending was in turn legitimated by Iraq's invasion of Kuwait in 1990, Canada's subsequent participation in the Gulf War, and expanded Canadian peace-keeping activities in former Yugoslavia and the Horn of Africa.

The 1989 cutback energized NGOs to lobby actively, and Clark fought visibly to protect the aid program in the 1990 budget. From then on, however, the mood of the development community was more one of anxious resignation as successive budgets kept pruning ODA and putting it into direct competition with assistance to ex-communist states in Eastern Europe and the crumbling Soviet Union.

1990: The NGOs and Joe Clark to the Rescue

During the fall of 1989, Chris Bryant, executive director of CUSO and elected head of the CCIC board, spearheaded a campaign to inform the public about the human costs of aid cuts. NGOs from across the country offered examples from initiatives that had been cancelled or curtailed, including projects for clean water in Nigeria, village pharmacies and sanitation facilities in Burkina Faso, street-market women in Abidjan, cattle inoculation in war-ravaged southern Sudan, and poor rickshaw drivers in Bangladesh. The message—that cuts were hurting the poorest of the poor and undermining Canada's credibility as a donor—received remarkably extensive press coverage, especially during the build-up to Development Day in October.[32] So too did parallel efforts mounted by the Unitarian Service Committee during its annual fund-raising campaign.[33]

Meanwhile, Wilson was rumoured to be targeting another aid cut in 1990. Clark opted to battle more openly this time, emphasizing publicly that the 1989 cut was one time only, and that he was strongly advising his cabinet colleagues against further reductions.[34] In January 1990, he did not deny that he was prepared to put his job on the line to protect the ODA budget. He also told a CCIC delegation that, while he expected the government to honour its commitment, it was important to rally public support. As the Clark-Wilson conflict stirred speculation in the press, several editorials opposed aid cuts and a diversion of ODA to Eastern Europe; some urged Mulroney not to risk a Clark resignation.[35]

In this context, Massé had the latitude to say, when speaking to the Ottawa chapter of the Canadian Institute for International Affairs:

> [It] is my fervent hope, and I pray every night, and probably you should too, that we will be given some increase this year. And, if we were given an increase equal to the rate of inflation which would permit us not to cut programs but even maintain them all in real terms, I think I would feel my prayers had been answered. But I will have to wait until February 20 [budget day] to see if that is true. The government translates the mood of the Canadian population and they are very careful to do just that.[36]

He found it worrisome that 69 per cent of those responding to a recent survey preferred to see development assistance reduced rather than paying higher taxes. Another poll revealed that foreign aid placed third behind subsidies to crown corporations and defence as favoured objects for expenditure reductions.[37] (Although the economy was just starting to slide into recession, Canadians were exhibiting less generosity than earlier, partly because of the Mulroney government's unpopular decision to introduce the Goods and Services Tax.)

When Wilson brought down his 1990 budget, a compromise was evident. Rather than a 9.6 per cent increase that would have resulted from a strict application of the 1989 commitment, growth in ODA spending was capped at 5 per cent in each of the next two years, more or less keeping pace with the Canadian inflation rate at the time. Over a five-year period, cumulative aid expenditures would fall short of projections by $558 million but the government was still able to project an ODA/GNP ratio of 0.47 per cent in 1994-95. Clark saved face, winning plaudits from the NGO community and sympathetic commentators in the press.[38] The most prescient words, however, came from Clyde Sanger of the North-South Institute: "It's a political tradeoff. Joe Clark can say he's done his best under the circumstances, but it's status quo and I don't know if they can go on like this year after year."[39]

1991-92: More Competition for Fewer Resources

Pressure to squeeze aid in the name of deficit reduction did indeed prove unrelenting. At first glance, the February 1991 budget appeared relatively benign as the 5 per cent increase for 1991-92 was preserved. However, announcement of a tighter 3 per cent cap for 1992-93 resulted in a further reduction in planned spending from 1991 to 1996 of $1.6 billion, bringing total cuts since 1988-89 to more than $4.5 billion. Moreover, ODA was rolled into a new "International Assistance Envelope" (IAE), which incorporated assistance for Eastern Europe and the Soviet republics (all subsequently ruled by DAC as "non-ODAable" except for those in Asia). A sum of $47 million for these new recipients was added to the 5 per cent ODA increase for 1990-91, but notice was given that the two components of the IAE would compete directly in future. The government was still committed to an ODA ratio of 0.47 in 1994-95 but relied on "creative accounting" to meet the target: debt relief and EDC concessional credits would become part of "planned" ODA rather than incidental additions, and some environmental initiatives in developing countries funded outside of ODA cash would count as well.[40]

The budget also abolished Petro-Canada International Assistance Corporation. Long reviled by western Tories as an offshoot of the Liberals' National Energy Program in the early 1980s, PCIAC had been starved of resources for several years. Once it was wound up, CIDA took over what little was left of its activities.

The Agency's own estimates were up only 2.2 per cent in 1991-92, in part because it was a year of higher-than-usual note encashments by international financial institutions. This factor—combined with diversion of conventional development assistance into humanitarian relief for victims of the Gulf War, and of conflict and drought in Ethiopia and Somalia—resulted in some cuts in geographic and NGO programming. UNICEF, CUSO, and youth exchange programs were hit especially hard.[41]

The budget and the government's earlier Expenditure Control Program also forced organizational changes within CIDA itself. Anglophone Africa and Francophone Africa were at last merged in a new Africa and Middle East Branch, Business Cooperation and Special Programs were reunited in a Canadian Partnership Branch, and more than forty senior and mid-level officials took early retirement. Among those departing was Lewis Perinbam, who had done so much to shape voluntary programming since his recruitment by Maurice Strong in 1968.[42] As Phillip Rawkins observed: "Others began looking quietly for new jobs. CIDA was no longer a place 'nobody wants to leave.' "[43]

The ODA program lost a strong defender in the fall of 1991 when Joe Clark took over constitutional negotiations with the provinces. Mulroney named Barbara McDougall as his successor at EAITC. By then, with Canada in a deepening recession, attitudes towards aid were hardening. The biennial conference of the Progressive Conservative Party defeated a motion urging a two-thirds reduction in foreign aid, but passed another seeking abolition of the International Centre for Human Rights and Democratic Development.[44] Support for the Reform Party was rising and the aid budget was a prime target in its deficit reduction agenda.[45]

During the build-up to the February 1992 budget, opposition and NGO representatives voiced concerns about McDougall's level of commitment and fears of more cuts.[46] In fact, while the government kept its promise to increase the International Assistance Envelope by 3 per cent in 1992-93, fully one-half of the increment was allocated to Eastern Europe and the (by then) former Soviet Union. The remaining 1.5 per cent for development assistance was insufficient to prevent another round of absolute cuts for geographic, food, and voluntary-sector programming. This was because there were again substantial cash requirements to honour earlier commitments to international financial institutions (reported as ODA when they were pledged). At the same time, a reduction in new commitments to the IFIs (counted as ODA in 1992-93) meant that the 1.5 per cent growth in cash translated into a 3.3 per cent year-over-year decline in projected official development assistance. The government still claimed that 0.47 was attainable in 1994-95 largely because of the recessionary fall in Canadian GNP.[47]

This was also the budget that, while short on real expenditure reductions, took heed of the Reform threat and abolished several advisory bodies and commissions including such valued institutions as the Economic Council of Canada and the Canadian Institute for International Peace and Security. The International Centre for Ocean Development in Halifax was among the victims; as with PCIAC, ICOD's work was scaled back and transferred to CIDA.[48]

More severe cuts yet were to come later in 1992, in the midst of a complex process set in motion in 1990 with the decision to undertake a strategic management review of CIDA.

Towards a Strategic Management Review

The original impetus for a management review came from Monique Landry and her political advisers in response to continuing complaints from executing agents and suppliers about CIDA's slowness, cumbersome regulations, and excessively bureaucratic procedures. Private-sector firms were also chafing about extensive use of sole-sourcing for employing NGOs and NGIs in bilateral (country focus) projects. The 1989 budget cuts, the prospect of more to come, and opposition criticisms of higher operating costs also contributed to a determination to seek outside advice on streamlining aid delivery and making it more cost-effective.

Although the last ministerial initiative of this sort—the 1986 Desmarais Task Force—received a cold shoulder from the Agency, this one was embraced as an opportunity by both Massé and Douglas Lindores, who had replaced Bill McWhinney as senior vice-president in 1988. Massé sought to move CIDA towards his vision of a more cerebral, policy-oriented organization, less preoccupied with process and projects. He also wanted to bring the Agency into line with Public Service 2000 and its proposals for making the federal bureaucracy more entrepreneurial, effective, and client-centred. Lindores, burdened with operational responsibility, wanted to complete the transition to hands-off management in ways that would simplify contracting out, yet not divorce officers from the content of development. Another priority was to find an approach to accountability that would lighten pressures from Treasury Board and the Auditor General to account for all aspects of work done by executing agencies.[49] Landry agreed to a review that would be wide-ranging and strategic in orientation.[50]

Groupe Secor of Montreal secured a $700,000 contract for a year-long study starting in September 1990. Working closely with Massé and Lindores, the consultants agreed to focus on four strategic issues: mandate, relations with stakeholders, accountability, and optimal resource utilization.[51] A research team pored through documents, interviewed some 200 CIDA employees, and held discussions with representatives of non-governmental sectors.

Edginess about the process became public in May 1991, when Dave Todd of Southam News reported fears among "alarmed employees and outside sources" that "Canada's humanitarian reputation as a leading aid donor nation could be badly tarnished if CIDA goes ahead with restructuring next year." According to Todd, planned changes would convert the Agency into a bank rather than "a hands-on agency for delivering foreign aid" with most, perhaps all, work contracted out to the private and voluntary sectors. The number of countries would be reduced substantially and the mix altered to favour those with structural adjustment programs. Finally, he wrote, "several hundred of CIDA's 1,100 staff may be cut."[52]

The story prompted Landry to write a letter to employees, released to the press, which denied that any major workforce reduction was "presently planned." She also claimed that there were no plans to change the number or mix of recipient countries or to remove the Agency's responsibility for implementing aid programs. She stressed that Groupe Secor was doing a management review "to help us improve our delivery mechanisms, not to destroy CIDA," and that *Sharing Our Future* remained CIDA's policy framework. Todd asserted that this latter assurance clashed with Massé's known views.[53] He and Daphne Bramham kept a spotlight on Groupe Secor, observing that Marcel Côté, Brian Mulroney's former director of strategic planning and communications, had resumed a partnership in the organization the day the CIDA study began. Questions of political patronage lingered amid denials of impropriety.[54]

The Secor Report

The consultants reported to the minister in October 1991 and, following translation, their bulky 403-page tome and a summary document were released on November 7.[55] Speaking to private- and voluntary-sector representatives, Landry characterized CIDA as

> a giant in chains, struggling to reconcile its sweeping mandate with constrained resources, cumbersome procedures, [and] rigid controls designed to reassure taxpayers on questions of prudence and probity. . . . To me, it's not good enough to just go on doing things the way they *have* been done, ignoring change.[56]

Secor's text was not as poetic. Cranford Pratt criticized its "pseudo-professional jargon" and quoted a senior CIDA official as quipping that "the report is written in neither official language."[57]

Activities: Scope, cost, and leverage. Linguistic failings aside, the first two sections of the report (on Activities and Organization) were widely acknowledged by CIDA staff and outside observers as a solid analysis of the Agency's managerial weaknesses and dilemmas. It will come as no surprise to readers that the consultants concluded that CIDA was very thinly stretched in terms of geographical spread, sectors, channels, programs, and projects. Renewed attention was drawn to the wide dispersal of recipient countries—158 in all, including 119 in the bilateral channel. Despite the formal commitment to a limited range of programming themes, CIDA's "sectoral contour" was also found to be unfocused across nineteen different areas.[58]

Secor presented disturbing data on the costs of delivering Canadian aid. Overall delivery costs for bilateral aid (fuelled by a dramatic increase in field support unit expenses) rose by 25 per cent in real terms between 1986-87 and 1990-91. As a result, the Agency's cost of delivering $1,000 of aid increased over this four-year period from $52.90 in 1986-87 to $72.60 (37 per cent). Adding in External Affairs field staff supported by ODA funds, the total delivery cost per $1,000 grew even more rapidly—from $85.60 to $140.60 or 64 per cent. Of the $65.00 increase, $31.80 was attributed by Secor to decentralization. In contrast, the cost of delivering $1,000 through the multilateral channel (though for CIDA only) rose from only $6.20 to $8.80. For voluntary programs, the figures were $37 and $44 in 1986-87 and 1990-91 respectively. INC was the second most expensive channel, but, reflecting growing disbursements, the cost per $1,000 declined from $123 to $99.[59]

The report identified six factors as responsible for escalating costs since the mid-1980s: (1) proliferation of countries and sectors, (2) growth in institutions and organizations funded by CIDA, (3) cumbersome, lengthy, and rigid contracting procedures, (4) increased contracting out, (5) decentralization, and (6) costs of ministerial support functions. (The consultants claimed that it was impossible to estimate the last of these with precision.)[60]

Secor attempted to compare Canada's "leverage" or "aid related influence" with that of other donor countries. The concept of leverage—then in vogue in World Bank circles—bore some relation to aid effectiveness and was often a euphemism for degree of success in achieving policy conditionality. Massé was deeply concerned about leverage in both broad and narrow senses but just what the consultants meant was hard to discern.[61] Recognizing that many intangible factors and geo-political realities could not be quantified, they suggested using "leverage index" as a proxy measure. In the case of bilateral aid, the index was defined as the percentage of a donor country's recipients receiving at least 10 per cent of their ODA from that donor.

Whatever the merits of the concept for assessing leverage,[62] it highlighted the degree to which Canada's development assistance program was dispersed and unfocused. For the period 1987-89, Canada's leverage index (12 per cent) was among the lowest in DAC, substantially below that of other middling donors such as Australia, Italy, the Netherlands, Sweden, and the UK. In that comparison group, Canada had the largest number of recipients and made the lowest average contribution.[63] Moreover, of thirteen countries that received 10 per cent or more of their aid from Canada, only Bangladesh and Ghana were outside the Americas (where the so-called "leveraged recipients" were either small or, as in the case of Colombia, received little aid). For multilateral aid, the report concluded that Canada's comparative standing was stronger but eroding.[64]

Organization: Characteristics and dynamics. Secor described CIDA's people, culture, organizational design, and capacities for strategic planning and decision-making. In brief, the people were portrayed as strongly committed to the Agency, plagued by feelings of exasperation and helplessness in the present context, and lacking incentives to change. The culture was characterized as:

- parochial—a reflection of "windows" for different stakeholders (recipient countries, NGOs, universities, business, etc.), and pressure to earmark the budget "so that all groups perceived themselves to be treated fairly";
- bureaucratic—a legacy of controls imposed in the late 1970s, manifested in a shift from content to process and self-protection through extensive paper trails, overplanning, overmonitoring, and belaboured consultant selection and project evaluation;
- idealistic—"respect for the culture and orientation of recipient countries," suspicion of aid linked to Canadian economic interests, and "the 'welfare state mentality' still prevalent in the Canadian public service"; and
- operationally flexible—notwithstanding the other three elements, a pragmatic capacity to cut through red tape in emergencies, and "an ability to

> disburse on time, in spite of complicated bureaucratic procedures, in order to meet Canadian foreign policy and domestic imperatives."[65]

This culture, the report contended, developed "within a closed community of officers . . . rotating among branches," and was reinforced by consensus decision-making as well as periodic assaults and challenges from stakeholders inside and outside of government. "This has encouraged . . . a group think syndrome whereby prevalent, historically established views are not easily challenged, and innovation is tolerated only at the margins."[66]

Turning to structure, the consultants criticized decision-making as too driven by numbers (allocations memos, distribution levels, person years, etc.) and not enough by performance criteria. Branches behaved like separate fiefdoms. Planning was uncoordinated, too mechanical, and too heavily focused on current preoccupations, rather than strategic considerations. Support and operational systems were not linked to one another or the planning system, and the committee-driven decision-making process was informal and unsystematic.[67]

Secor then examined "contingent influences."[68] First, foreign policy imperatives led "Canada to broaden its presence in many countries and areas, potentially further than its financial, technical and managerial capacity [justifies]." Secondly, prudence and probity requirements and central agency directives (reinforced by the Auditor General, parliamentary committees, and the press) exerted pressure on CIDA for "full transparency" and "zero defect," thus breeding overcontrol and risk aversion. Thirdly, disbursement pressures stemming from elimination of non-lapsing authority in 1977 "created an important incentive to 'spend' money, possibly at the expense of well thought-out program decisions."[69] Fourthly, relations with stakeholders involved excessive staff time for recruiting consultants and handling vast numbers of contracts, high monitoring costs, and a loss of control over output.[70]

Having reviewed activities, organizational characteristics, and contingent influences, the report analyzed their dynamic interplay. For example, prudence and probity preoccupations—reinforced by lapsing budgets and breadth of country and sector coverage—meant that managers increased the number of consulting contracts throughout the project cycle to obtain more and more independent opinions on aid content in order to reduce the risk of error. Since conflict-of-interest regulations prohibited consultants and contractors from participating in downstream activities once they had worked on a project, even more consultants were required for any given project, often creating an administrative bottleneck and further delays. The prudence and probity incentive was diverting operational skills from development to process, thus accelerating costs for contracting out and delivery.[71]

"The loss of developmental dexterity and the fact that CIDA's activities are dispersed . . . increase its vulnerability to future developmental challenges; decrease its relevance in third world affairs (leverage); and reduce its reputation as a high-quality development agency." While not absolving management from responsibility for choices, the consultants emphasized that "delivery costs and leverage results would be quite different if the underlying pressure on CIDA was to maximize the impact of the $2 billion aid program, *subject to acceptable prudence and probity practices* instead of *maximizing prudence and probity behavior* subject to delivering a $2 billion aid program."[72] As Clyde Sanger later commented in the North-South Institute's *Review*, "It is a devastating analysis, even if Secor softens it by saying 'CIDA has adapted well to its current context.' "[73]

Diagnosis and recommendations. The report called for a transformation of the ways CIDA defined, planned, and delivered its programs in order to:

- regain control over the development content (as opposed to simple processing of aid delivery) by focusing on core skills, abilities and know-how;
- strengthen its leverage, relevance and dialogue capability in selected third world countries and with all of CIDA's stakeholders by developing more effective planning and communications mechanisms and greater coordination among its units;
- introduce a performance-driven management mode;
- reduce the cost of delivery . . . ; [and]
- [clarify] its accountability.[74]

Recommendations were couched in general terms and clustered around "key strategic orientations." The first concerned "scope and strategic thrust": the consultants called for concentration on fewer countries and sectors, and a more "skills-and-know-how-based" approach positioned at the "cutting edge of development technology."[75] The second was the challenge of building "a governance structure and system" that would enable the Agency to strengthen "its ability to dialogue with and influence its stakeholders"[76] in order to achieve greater coherence based on common knowledge and visions. At the heart of a performance-driven planning process would be a strong "corporate office" responsible for key core and control functions, including research and development of aid policy, establishment of performance objectives and indicators, strategic evaluations of policies and programs, and relations with Canadian government bodies, other donors, and recipient countries.[77]

Relations with executing agencies, delivery costs, and accountability were the main issues in the third cluster, "governance for direct aid delivery." Three alternative models for reform were suggested. The first, a "dual entity" approach, would have CIDA become a strategic planning and policy body, farming out labour-intensive implementation to a new public-sector organization controlled but not managed by the Agency. The consultants suggested that this model, although less costly and complex,[78] might lead to duplication and counter-management; in any case, it would simply transfer current operational problems rather than solving them, and would cut off a vast number of private firms and some NGOs from work in the aid field.[79]

The second model, a "brokerage" or "market" option, would also reduce the Agency to planning and policy functions, but leave considerable scope to business and voluntary sectors for program delivery. While the consultants thought this approach might reduce costs, remove CIDA from micromanagement, and limit the Agency's accountability, it was unlikely to win approval from central agencies and would further erode CIDA's critical skills. Moreover, given the absence of enough Canadian suppliers to create a truly competitive process, the brokerage option would run the risk that CIDA's partners would engage in "opportunistic behavior, [thereby] . . . obtaining unjustified returns and . . . minimizing their downside risk through its transfer to CIDA (e.g. cost overruns, timeliness of completion, higher overhead costs, minimal quality standards, etc.)."[80]

Having essentially disposed of two "straw men," the consultants presented their preferred "comprehensive management model"—"an intermediate solution" that would build "a long term, mutually beneficial relationship" with executing agents that offered them stability and commitment in exchange for a "lower but adequate return." Under this model, "executing agents and consultants would need to be registered, prequalified, and certified by the Agency"; in turn, CIDA would invest in their training, recruiting, and promotion.[81]

CIDA's Strategic Management Review

In releasing the Secor report, Landry emphasized that it represented the views of consultants, and that she would undertake consultations with CIDA staff and partners before making decisions. "And when I *say* consultation, I *mean* it."[82] As we shall see, there were extensive consultations within the Agency, but Canadian partners justly complained about an unsatisfactory external process, as plans to hold several regional meetings were scaled down to just one briefing in Ottawa for selected NGO, NGI, and business representatives. It was held late in January 1992, more than two months after the report's release. Written comments were invited, but few were received, in part because of cynicism about the consultation. In addition, Landry, Lindores, and Groupe Secor appeared in February before a joint meeting of the Standing Committee on Public Accounts and SCEAIT, and SCEAIT's Subcommittee on Development and Human Rights held separate hearings on the report.

The inadequacy of the consultative process was raised in the parliamentary deliberations[83] along with concern about the validity of examining management in a policy vacuum. Landry and Lindores replied that the review was about how best to implement *Sharing Our Future*, but MPs' scepticism was reinforced by Secor's lack of attention to the strategy and perceptions about Massé's policy inclinations.[84] Liberal MP Beryl Gaffney asked if the study proved that contracting out was "a more expensive way of doing business than having it done in-house." Secor's Pierre Richer de Laflèche replied that "I wouldn't go so far as to make a conclusion for the Public Service in general."[85]

CCIC praised the decision to release the report publicly: "it is one of the most open and honest pictures of a complex government agency prepared for and made public by the agency itself."[86] While agreeing with much of the analysis, the Council criticized its portrayal of NGOs simply as stakeholders "rather than as international development agencies with their own legitimacy in the Third World." In this light, fear was expressed that Secor's approach might endanger responsive programming.[87] Eva Egron-Polak of the Association of Universities and Colleges of Canada warned that universities might lose their interest in executing projects if CIDA became even more directive than it was already.[88] Business representatives agreed with much of Secor's analysis, but rejected the comprehensive management model with its notion of a restricted market for suppliers.[89]

Asked about CIDA's response to the report, Vice-President Lindores replied: "The basic conclusions . . . after dropping on the organization with a certain sense of shock and denial . . . have after considerable reflection been generally agreed to." There was doubt about the practicality of some recommendations, however, especially the comprehensive management model, which would "require that we circumvent . . . almost all the existing trends and tendencies in the government about openness, transparency, open bidding, competition, etc."[90]

By that time, February 1992, all Agency branches had brainstormed and developed detailed responses to Secor for Lindores.[91] Employees were invited to submit personal opinions as well. For some, the exercise rekindled the enthusiasm that characterized CIDA 2000 during the Winegard process. As Rawkins reported, however, others held back, not only "from a preference for established ways of doing things" or a resentment of "top-down management," but also from a belief

> that good development projects and programs originate in sound local knowledge, good relations in developing countries, and the designing of initiatives as "unique products" to fit local circumstances. Secor's proposals appeared to reject this view, to threaten the autonomy of project officers, and to question the validity of what was most satisfying in their work.[92]

After a flurry of activity climaxing late in February, the strategic management review disappeared, as one officer put it, into the "vortex of the President's Committee," leaving everyone except senior management and the minister's office in the dark. Landry confidently asserted that decisions would be made by the summer of 1992 but—amid growing uncertainty and anxiety—almost a year elapsed before the process was reopened to the rank and file. Morale sank to new depths.

Towards a "new CIDA." Meanwhile, Lindores took all the submissions to Jamaica, where he wrote his second major report on the state of CIDA. The outcome, "CIDA Strategic Management Review—Discussion Paper," was submitted to the President's Committee in April 1992. It began with a critical assumption: "that the government is no longer prepared to pay the costs of CIDA's broad dispersion." His proposals dealt only with "internally imposed dispersion, but there is no point in proceeding with . . . massive disruption of organization . . . unless concentration is endorsed and supported by the government."[93] Lindores called for a "new CIDA," which "is certainly as much about cultural change as about organizational or operational change." The transformation would require "a full scale effort managed from the top to change the way people think. Many of the consultations have not only urged this, but *insisted upon it*."[94]

Strengthening corporate and service functions. The discussion paper made nineteen main recommendations. The first five sought to strengthen the corporate function by means of an expanded and revitalized Policy Branch,[95] a new Corporate Management Branch, a simplified committee structure, and a strategic planning and coordination network headed by a Corporate Secretary. Two proposals dealt with development education and information: a transfer of the Public Participation Program to Communications Branch (as Public Affairs had become once more), and the development of a new consultation strategy to ensure regular discussions with the Canadian development community. Another recommendation suggested consolidating Finance, along with Personnel and Administration branches, into a new Services Branch.[96]

Strengthening program activities. While the transfer of PPP to Communications to unify development information and education programs (an old chestnut) was bound to be controversial,[97] most recommendations for aid delivery were even more radical, and likely to upset Canadian interests elsewhere in government and in the private and voluntary sectors. The exceptions were proposals aimed at resolving country/sector tensions more productively. Finally following through the intentions of the Corporate Review of the late 1970s, they called for creation of Program Delivery Units (PDUs) in each geographic branch, redistribution of Professional Services personnel to the

PDUs and Policy Branch, and transfer of staff from Operations Services to the PDUs and the new Management Branch. It was suggested that PDUs would also allow planners to learn as project implementation proceeded, and minimize the dangers of being "sucked into counter management . . . every time some difficulty is encountered."[98]

Back in 1984, Lindores had broached the possibility of replacing sectors with programming themes; formal policy in *Sharing Our Future* moved in that direction but operations were still bounded by sectors. Lindores now proposed eliminating both the sector and the project, replacing them with themes and somewhat open-ended thematic programs, perhaps rooted in the "five pillars." In turn, regional and country policy frameworks would "provide for dramatic program concentration with emphasis on limiting the number of thematic programs per country." Agents for thematic programs would then be selected through an open proposal system that would solicit multi-faceted proposals from all elements of the Canadian development community—business, NGOs, and educational institutions. This approach, Lindores suggested, would catalyze the creative capacity of agents, who would design activities to meet defined objectives. It would cut substantially the number of contracts to be managed and allow the development of special relationships with agents without the difficulties inherent in Secor's favoured supplier proposal. Open proposals would also lead "to a new type of demonstrated accountability whereby the agency essentially commits to experiment, but to learn the lessons of its experimentation on a *timely basis*."[99]

Four other recommendations had profound implications for CIDA's responsive programming. First, it would be eliminated in the case of universities. Lindores argued that they were heavily involved in bilateral activities and could expect an even greater role under thematic programs and open bidding. Secondly, for business and NGOs, he expected that the government would still want "to support small-scale activities . . . that contribute to development even if they do not fall within CIDA's strategic thrusts." Beyond a certain threshold, however, INC and NGO programming "should contribute to the general strategic framework for the region in which they are being carried out." It was proposed, therefore, that geographic branches manage "semi-responsive activities" above $50,000. Thirdly, to minimize workload below that level, a "responsive mechanism" would devolve management responsibility to umbrella organizations. Finally, a new Partnership Branch would take over the responsibilities of Multilateral Branch, oversee contracting out small-scale responsive activities, and assume other residual responsibilities of the former Canadian Partnership Branch.[100]

A new approach to accountability. Lindores proposed a statement of CIDA's responsibilities that he hoped would free the Agency of some of the regulatory constraints that hobbled operations and led to risk-averse behaviour. At the most general level, CIDA would be accountable for:

- promoting and defending Canadian government interests in the field of development assistance;
- developing and maintaining an overall program policy base that reflects the three main objectives of Canada's ODA program: developmental, humanitarian, and other national interests;[101] and
- developing appropriate actionable program approaches for those priorities selected for Canadian involvement on global, country or thematic bases.

Rather than being held to account for every detail of aid delivery, the Agency's responsibility would be limited to assessing funded institutions, developing requests for proposals, examining proposals, monitoring implementation according to "key milestones," evaluating program performance, ensuring integrity in the use of public funds, and "demonstrating that systems and qualified personnel are effectively managing the overall accountability framework."[102]

A long hiatus. Lindores' draft was reviewed in detail by the President's Committee and then debated during a two-day retreat at Club Tremblant. Although reservations were expressed, the group agreed that the document was a coherent package and an accurate reflection of dominant views emerging from the in-house consultation. It was presented, essentially unchanged, to Madame Landry in May 1991. The minister was reportedly taken aback by the magnitude of proposed changes, especially for CIDA's mandate and relations with the private and voluntary sectors. Small and medium-size suppliers and consultancy firms, a constituency Landry had courted assiduously, were potentially the biggest losers, and the political implications of taking a major initiative with an election year looming had to be weighed carefully. She and her advisers agonized throughout the late spring and summer. Meanwhile, a transition team worked closely and confidentially with the President's Committee to flesh out Lindores' recommendations and to prepare for action in the event of a positive political decision.

Once she finally decided to support the reform package in September, Landry was an enthusiastic convert. Although some senior officials questioned the necessity of securing cabinet approval, the minister wanted legitimation at that level after obtaining endorsements from McDougall and the Privy Council Office. These might have come quickly in normal circumstances, but action was deferred in the wake, first, of a disruptive three-week strike by federal civil servants in September and, then, of the referendum on the Charlottetown Accord in October. Prime Minister Mulroney asked members of cabinet to set aside all regular business to devote their full attention to the ultimately unsuccessful "yes" campaign. Meanwhile, Marcel Massé had been seconded to the PCO and was spending only a day a week at CIDA. Discussion of an aide mémoire on the proposed changes, by the Cabinet Committee on Foreign and Defence Policy, did not take place until December 3, more than two months after Landry's decision and almost seven months after the President's Committee completed the proposals.

The aide mémoire.[103] The issue put to cabinet committee was whether to proceed with major management and structural changes to streamline CIDA and better focus ODA delivery. The primary objective, the paper advised, was to achieve "better development assistance at a better price." Assurances were given that ODA would continue to serve foreign policy objectives, and that proposals were in accord with the government's efficiency efforts. "Without changes, pressures on CIDA are expected to grow to a point where the Agency will no longer be able to deliver on Canada's international commitments with respect to ODA in a matter consistent with expected levels of program quality, prudence and probity."

Proposals dealt only with "internal reductions" in the number of sectors, projects, delivery channels, and funded institutions; the government was invited to seek advice at a later date on how geographic concentration might be achieved. A section on "a less bureaucratic agency" estimated that a move to thematic programming and open proposals would reduce the number of contracts from 1,050 to 465. Administrative costs would be reduced by about 5 per cent annually during each of the third to fifth years of implementation. "More resources will be dedicated to programs, less to administration. More will be done OUTSIDE government (from project design to implementation), opening the door to Canadian ENTREPRENEURSHIP."

Under the heading "better focus for maximum impact," the authors sought the attention of busy Tory ministers with more short, snappy phrases. CIDA would decide what to do, leaving business, NGOs, and NGIs to determine how to do it. Coherence and impact would be maximized by centralizing management in geographic branches, transferring to them responsibility for "larger scale responsive activities."[104] Proposals for contracting out managerial responsibilities for small-scale responsive programming were labelled "get the government out of managing smaller activities." A "new, more transparent and efficient contracting process" spelled out the mechanics of open proposals,[105] and gave assurance that medium and small firms would have ample scope for subcontracting, monitoring, and evaluation activities. Accountability would be strengthened by specifying clearer lines of responsibility in contracts.

Finally, the aide mémoire proposed a public relations strategy emphasizing government streamlining, improved accountability, and enhanced Canadian private-sector involvement in global markets. It forecast a positive response from large development NGOs, businesses, universities, and cooperatives, but anticipated criticism from "some smaller NGOs who had in the past easy access to some CIDA funds."

A roadblock to implementation.[106] CIDA officials anticipated tough grilling in cabinet committee but were taken aback by a decision to delay consideration. It stemmed from growing unease within EAITC, lobbying from firms and NGOs, and another budget shock. The most important factor was opposition from the Pearson Building, headquarters of External Affairs.

Although McDougall was less inclined than Clark to give relatively free rein to CIDA, her initial response to the reform proposals was reportedly favourable. However, the long delay in getting them onto the agenda of a cabinet committee created scope for detractors in her Department to win support for an alternative scenario. At the most general level, opposition reflected conflicts about bureaucratic turf. The Prime Minister's Office under both Trudeau and Mulroney had usurped much of External's authority, and now CIDA—after several quiescent years under Catley-Carlson—was perceived as encroaching as well.

As far as the Department was concerned, it set foreign policy that the Agency was supposed to implement. In a "Foreign Policy Update," prepared for McDougall and approved by cabinet earlier in 1992, Canada's foreign policy priorities were proclaimed as:

- creating prosperity on a sustainable basis through trade development, environmental awareness and international assistance;
- strengthening cooperative security through non-proliferation, peacekeeping and multilateral membership; and
- securing democracy and respect for human values, through promoting human rights, democratic development and good governance.[107]

Despite these priorities, here was the president of CIDA (not fondly remembered for his tenure as under-secretary of state) talking not only about the desirability of the Agency's becoming more knowledge-based and less process-oriented, but also about playing a stronger horizontal role in shaping Canada's non-aid policies. Indeed, he was being characteristically assertive on many matters in the reconstituted Interdepartmental Committee on Economic Relations with Developing Countries (ICERDC) and other fora.

In the view of one senior official in EAITC, Massé, in proposing that the Agency do policy analysis and contract out the "nitty-gritty," conveyed two worrisome impressions—of wanting to operate too much at arm's length from the Department, and of belittling the importance of the "daily bread" of project implementation. For his part, Massé did not quarrel with External's authority to define the basic parameters of foreign policy to which CIDA would adhere (provided that he had his innings in a consultative process). The policy sphere that he saw as the Agency's preserve was "how to do good development," which of course from his perspective extended well beyond project implementation. How far, and with what implications for overlap and conflict with foreign policy, were questions that senior officials in EAITC wanted to clarify.

McDougall developed her own concerns as well. Unlike Clark, she was dubious about multilateral aid, which she saw as producing too little return for Canada. She also reflected Mulroney's desire to play a more prominent role in assisting states of the former Soviet Union and Central and Eastern Europe. Creation of the International Assistance Envelope had brought the Department and the Agency into direct competition for shrinking resources and there was still considerable jockeying over how the new program would be organized and delivered.

On ODA policy, there was apparent convergence between the two sides on the desirability of concentration and channelling more of the budget to high-growth developing countries. (Within CIDA, opinion was divided over the latter but it was clear that political masters wanted more support from the aid budget for their "prosperity initiative.") Close consultation was the norm between regional and country desks in the two bureaucracies and by and large a meeting of minds on priorities prevailed.

There was, however, a major difference at the senior level over the degree to which there should be flexibility in shifting aid funds to meet short-term priorities and unanticipated contingencies. From the perspective of External Affairs, too much of the ODA budget was tied down to long-term commitments, making it difficult during a time of cutbacks to divert resources to priorities of the day, whether Eastern Europe or peacekeeping in Somalia or a new policy trend such as democratic development. To Massé, Lindores, and other senior officials in the Agency, this viewpoint smacked of political expediency and reflected the antithesis of long-haul commitments they saw as essential for sustainable development and lasting, mutually beneficial relations between Canada and recipient countries.

McDougall's advisers warned that CIDA's suggestions for open proposals and long-term contracting would make it even more difficult to achieve flexibility. In that respect, they argued, the aide mémoire was not simply a "policy neutral" plan for management reform. Why else, the more suspicious asked, was there such a fuss about taking the recommendations before cabinet? Moreover, much had happened since approval of *Sharing Our Future* in 1988, not least the collapse of communism in Eastern Europe, cutbacks in Canada's spending on international assistance, and the approval of EAITC's new foreign policy framework. Before considering Landry's document, they contended, there should be a thorough review of aid policy. Other voices urged caution as well. Consultants, suppliers, and NGOs contacted McDougall's office and officials in EAITC to express their fears about possible outcomes of the strategic management review.

While months of delay allowed opposition to build in and out of government, by happenstance the aide mémoire was presented to the Cabinet Committee on Foreign and Defence Policy the day after Finance Minister Don Mazankowski brought down a mini-budget. Only six months after Prime Minister Mulroney and Environment Minister Jean Charest had reasserted Canada's commitment to the 0.7 per cent ODA/GNP target at the Earth Summit,[108] Mazankowski's December 2, 1992, Economic Statement trimmed $50 million from aid spending in the current fiscal year, and slashed the International Assistance Envelope by 10 per cent in each of 1993-94 and 1994-95. The cumulative reduction in projected spending over the two-and-one-quarter fiscal years was $642 million, the deepest yet.[109] It was again disproportionately severe: 8 per cent of budgetary savings in federal program spending was being carved from an area that accounted for only 2 per cent of expenditures. Defence was also cut, but by less than 4 per cent.[110] Press commentary was critical of this imbalance, but was meagre, less impassioned than in 1989, and now more supportive of fiscal restraint.[111]

The cutback added another argument for delaying CIDA reforms until a review of aid policy took place. When Landry and Agency officials appeared before the committee, External Affairs argued for a full in-house review. However, in view of the imminence of a federal election and CIDA's wish to minimize further delays, the two sides compromised. Under the Department's leadership, but in full consultation with policy analysts from the Agency, an "International Assistance Policy Update" would be prepared quickly and taken to cabinet early in the new year. It would provide a framework for allocating the International Assistance Envelope and create a context for considering management reforms.

A joint meeting was held to discuss broad parameters of the update. Officials in EAITC then hurriedly wrote a draft document to act as a basis for further discussion. The chief author was Barry Carin, assistant undersecretary for economic policy and trade competitiveness. "One of Barbara McDougall's favourite mandarins" (having served under her as an assistant deputy minister in Employment and Immigration), Carin was new to External and had no prior experience in the field of international development.[112] Although much of his first draft reflected ideas CIDA had developed in consultation with EAITC, it went further than Agency officials had contemplated in its approach to country concentration and a redistribution towards middle-income countries. It also made a pitch for substantial diversion of the smaller

International Assistance Envelope to former Soviet bloc countries. These positions might have been viewed within the Agency simply as a bargaining stance open to modification but they were couched in terms that some saw as tantamount to a declaration of war. Though to a lesser extent, there was unease about some recommendations in certain quarters of External Affairs as well.

While CIDA's Policy Branch continued discussions on the document, it was distributed in both the Department and the Agency. As alarm bells went off, MPs, journalists, CCIC and others started receiving brown envelopes and phone calls. By the end of January 1993, an early draft and at least two subsequent modifications were in circulation and the non-governmental development community was mobilizing a campaign to block implementation.

The "International Assistance Policy Update."[113] The leaked document began with a rationale—to enable ministers to adapt to "reduced reference levels" (i.e., funding cuts) and "new foreign policy priorities." These were identified as: (1) demands "for the remainder of the decade" to assist transformation in the former Soviet bloc, (2) emergence of a new development paradigm based on market reform and good governance, (3) desirability of expanded economic cooperation with "growth points" in Asia and Latin America and other efforts to bolster the "prosperity agenda," (4) "strong domestic support" for increased "peacekeeping/enforcement" and humanitarian assistance, and (5) greater prominence of the environment as a major global issue. In view of budget reductions (the 0.7 per cent target was dismissed as no longer relevant), these new priorities necessitated an "overarching policy framework" that moved from "global coverage" to "strategic intervention" at "acupuncture points" that would maximize Canadian influence. The principles that would guide this shift were:

- foreign policy priorities (as above plus "sustainable development abroad as an extension of sustainable development in Canada"[114]);
- concentration/selectivity ("to increase strategic influence and aid effectiveness by transferring resources from lower priority countries, institutions and programme themes to key countries, institutions and programmes of strategic importance to Canada");
- leverage ("multiplier effect") and influence ("persuasion to one's point of view or agenda"); and
- flexibility (to respond quickly to unexpected priorities and emergencies).[115]

"Carin's deck" (as it was derisively labelled by some in CIDA) recommended the following "tough and painful choices":

1. within the overall International Assistance Envelope,
    - an increase in the relative share devoted to former Soviet bloc countries;

2. within the ODA portion,
   - an increase in the relative share of bilateral and geographic programs at the expense of multilateral activities to "restore the balance from past erosion of the geographic programs";
   - a decrease in support for voluntary programs coupled with an assumption that NGOs and NGIs would have more opportunities for funding under revamped geographic programs;
   - an increase in the relative shares for humanitarian assistance, IDRC (because it had been given an expanded mandate in the environmental sphere) and ICHRDD (because of its work in the priority area of democratic development and good governance);
   - a stable level of food aid but with a shift from multilateral to bilateral; and
   - a reduction or even outright elimination of spending on development information;
3. within the geographic programs,
   - abolition of fixed geographic shares to permit greater flexibility;
   - elimination of "core countries" and their replacement by substantially fewer "focus countries," some designated for "development assistance" and others for "economic cooperation";
   - introduction of flexible thematic funds for human rights/democratic development/good governance, the environment, and economic cooperation/private sector development;
   - introduction of a strategic policy reserve "to respond to immediate, one-off needs"; and
   - more funds for CIDA INC and its integration into geographic programs along with "other CIDA instruments to augment economic cooperation activities linking the Canadian and developing country private sectors."

The recommendation to integrate most responsive programming into geographic programs was consistent with plans to implement the strategic management review. So too was the proposal to use new thematic funds to ease the transition for core countries that were dropped. From CIDA's vantage point, however, the unrelenting emphasis on flexibility negated the essence of development assistance as an investment. The virtual dismissal of development information generated anger, as did statements seen as reflecting negatively upon the Agency's performance. Although senior officials in CIDA wanted to maintain the balance between bilateral and multilateral aid (thus implying cuts in both), Massé and Lindores, among others, were also reportedly upset about comments that appeared to devalue the importance of multilateral aid for Canada and the contributions made by international agencies.

As controversial as flexibility and time horizon was the Policy Update's approach to concentration. Reminiscent of the 1973 proposal from trade officials to divide the ODA budget into commercial and pure aid compartments, the document recommended identifying eight to ten countries for a development assistance focus and another six to eight as "economic cooperation countries." In the former, "traditional CIDA multi-dimensional programs would apply" (but would be jointly developed by the Department and the Agency), while the objective in the latter "would be mutually beneficial economic cooperation that assists the Canadian private sector to strategically position itself for long-term market penetration. EAITC/CIDA would formulate strategic frameworks . . . and fully take into account complementary aid and non-aid instruments in programming."

The Agency was still firmly opposed to segregating aid programming in this way, preferring to balance objectives in each recipient country. Moreover, the effort by Carin's group to generate sample lists (including, for example, China and India as "development assistance" and Central America and the Andean region as "economic cooperation") only served to demonstrate the hollowness of the approach. Equally strong were objections to the message that EAITC wanted to intervene much more in areas where CIDA had enjoyed considerable autonomy.

The development community mobilizes. The leaked Policy Update unleashed a furor among NGOs and others who saw in it the most serious threat ever to the integrity of Canadian development assistance. Commentators railed against increasing support for former communist countries at the expense of ODA rather than cuts in defence. Their worst fears were confirmed about the virtual demise of responsive programming, an abandonment of the poorest of the poor, a retreat from multilateralism, and a devaluation of development education.[116] Although EAITC officials complained (with some justice) that the reaction exaggerated the degree of proposed change, there was no denying the directions in which they wanted to move.

The Policy Update presented two funding scenarios for the 1993-94 fiscal year. The more "cautious" one, presumably the bottom line for further negotiations, involved modest reallocations but was characterized as merely postponing pain and disruption. The "aggressive" one more than halved the partnership program for the voluntary sector, cut multilateral by a quarter, and eliminated development information. It doubled funds for the former Soviet bloc (increasing the year-over-year share of a smaller envelope from 3.5 to 7.6 per cent) and for the Industrial Cooperation Program. It suggested putting more than a third of the budget for geographic programs into the new thematic funds and the strategic policy reserve, and 60 per cent of what was left into economic cooperation countries. A later draft predictably produced an intermediate third scenario with a 50/50 split between development assistance and economic cooperation countries—still, of course, a major leap from the existing policy of channelling 75 per cent to low-income and small island countries.[117]

The Policy Update's communication strategy reinforced anxiety and/or cynicism in the development community. If NGOs and the opposition parties "misunderstand" the proposals, "they will attack the government on ethical and emotional grounds, arguing that the government is sacrificing the world poor and betraying Canadian values on the altar of corporate and commercial interests. If this happens, the government must respond aggressively." Citing a recent Decima poll showing support for foreign aid had weakened during the recession, the document asserted that "Canadians appear to be more open than ever to proposals that would reduce the waste of their tax dollars, would tie aid more closely to national interests (including economic interests), and would channel more resources into promoting human rights and democracy." Nevertheless, while the public thus "may not automatically accept what the critics have to say at face value," it would be imperative to assert that the government was not abandoning the poorest by pointing out the proposed increase in emergency aid, naming areas to which "we remain committed" (such as Bangladesh, the Sahel, India, and southern Africa), and emphasizing human rights and the environment.

Even though the Policy Update suggested dropping several core countries in Africa and adding Mexico, Chile, and Argentina as foci for economic cooperation, the communications strategy would nonetheless proclaim: "We're recognizing the importance of hemispheric partners without sacrificing ties to our old friends in the Commonwealth and la Francophonie." Complaints about cuts to voluntary programming would be countered by the claim that "we're opening new avenues for cooperation with NGOs through our geographic programs."

Landry's aide mémoire on restructuring was also leaked in January 1993. It confirmed for critics that, whatever the differences over the former Eastern bloc and other issues, CIDA and EAITC were initiating a drastic modification of aid policy. Moreover, they were doing so in secret just before an election the Tories were almost certain to lose. In speaking out strongly about the direction of proposed changes, CCIC, the North-South Institute, sympathetic journalists, and others agreed that the world had indeed changed dramatically since the publication of *Sharing Our Future*. What was needed, however, was a public review as full and open as the Special Joint Committee and Winegard, but focused on all aspects of foreign policy—trade, defence, peacekeeping, etc.—as well as aid *and* broader international development issues, including debt, economic protectionism in the North, the environment, and human migration. Although the groundwork could be laid now, the review would have legitimacy only if it took place after the election.[118]

The timing of the leaked documents was fortuitous for mobilizing a campaign to discredit them—just a few days before the 1993 International Development Week, an annual educational and informational campaign early each February that was organized jointly by CIDA and the voluntary sector. Already planned media coverage and public events created high-profile opportunities to criticize the Policy Update and publicize alternatives. The highlight in Ottawa was a visit from Mahbub ul Haq, special adviser to the administrator of UNDP and principal author of the *Human Development Report*. He spoke to several organizations and appeared before a joint meeting of several parliamentary committees. In conveying his vision of the current agenda for development, he spoke bluntly about the "very excited debate going on in Canada about a new aid policy." Canada's friends in the international community "will be greatly dismayed by the changes that are being contemplated."[119] His remarks received extensive media coverage, as did concerns aired in community meetings across the country. Active lobbying was stepped up, and both the Liberals and the NDP promised a public review of aid policy after the election.

Massé also appeared before a parliamentary subcommittee during International Development Week. While carefully sidestepping the Policy Update, he spoke forcefully about the value of international financial institutions and maintaining a strong Canadian presence within them.[120] Meanwhile, McDougall promised after the leak to consult the public about any proposed changes in aid policy. Although the Policy Update did influence program reductions (as we shall see in Chapter 10), it was now too late to secure cabinet approval for a new framework that would govern budgetary allocations in 1993-94. The minister was nonetheless determined to move the process forward, and Carin informed an NGO delegation that a document would be made public by the end of February. Six weeks later, McDougall was still assuring the House of Commons that an approved policy paper would soon be available "for normal consultations with the NGO community and others."[121] Not long afterwards, however, she was persuaded to abandon the project. Although the government would not make a commitment to a post-election review, there would be no formal consideration of policy changes before that time.

For CIDA, a changing of the guard. As if the fate of the strategic management review, the implications of budget cuts, and EAITC's intervention were not enough cause for anxiety among CIDA's beleaguered staff in early 1993, the uncertainty was compounded by the departure of the minister and the president. In a New Year's cabinet shuffle, Monique Landry became secretary of state for Canada, while Monique Vézina returned to External Relations and International Development (along with her portfolio as secretary of state for seniors). From the bureaucrats' perspective, while Vézina was easier to work with, she lacked clout to deal with the difficult environment of the moment.

Meanwhile, rumours of Marcel Massé's departure had circulated since his secondment to the Privy Council Office in the fall of 1992. Coinciding with the leaked Policy Update in January 1993, speculation about his unhappiness and an imminent transfer surfaced in the press.[122] Confirmation came on February 11 when, amid several changes at the deputy ministerial level, Massé swapped jobs with Jocelyne Bourgon, secretary to the cabinet for federal-provincial relations.[123] Some CIDA staffers boycotted his farewell reception on February 22, but it was an emotional leave-taking for those in attendance. He had, Massé said, experienced the rare privilege of "dying twice" on leaving the presidency of CIDA. He also expressed regret that the strategic management review had not worked out as he had hoped. That very day, the Agency's sense of headlessness became still more pronounced with the news that Doug Lindores was leaving the senior vice-presidency to take a position as chief executive officer with the Canadian Red Cross. His final days, like Massé's, had not been happy ones.

For Lindores, it was a move from "the frying pan to the fire": he took over the Red Cross just as the tainted blood scandal was breaking. Massé, disillusioned with the Mulroney government's performance, soon resigned from the Privy Council Office. Recruited to run for the Liberals and victorious in the 1993 federal election, he became minister of Intergovernmental Affairs, with special responsibility for civil service reform. Michel Dupuy also won a Liberal seat in 1993, but—with a track record as minister of Canadian Heritage as undistinguished as his CIDA presidency—he was dropped from cabinet in 1996.

Program Profile during Massé's Second Presidency

After the budget cut in 1989, inflation (running at about 5 per cent a year until 1992) negated nominal increases in ODA, which grew from $2,849.9 million in 1989-90 to $3,182.5 million in 1991-92 before falling to $2,972.2 million in 1992-93 (virtually the same current dollar level as in 1988-89).[124] Falling national income during the recession resulted in an ODA/GNP ratio close to 0.5 per cent in 1991-92, before a sharp decline to 0.44 per cent in 1992-93. Other donors also cut back, especially in 1993 when the DAC average was 0.30 per cent, down from 0.33 per cent in 1989. Nevertheless, Canada's share of total OECD development assistance dropped from 5.08 per cent in 1989 to

4.24 per cent in 1993. After having been the fifth largest donor in the mid-1980s, and seventh at the end of the decade, Canada slipped to eighth, behind the Netherlands. In ODA/GNP terms, Canada moved ahead of Belgium into sixth place.

Eligibility and Geographical Distribution

In Asia, with Cold War barriers coming down, modest programming was launched in Vietnam and Cambodia in 1990.[125] While geographic concentration was a major issue for Secor, no further eligibility changes were announced during the second Massé presidency. Bilateral programming became slightly more dispersed.[126]

Shares by income level and region. Between 1989-90 and 1993-94, the proportion of bilateral aid channelled to least-developed and other low-income countries increased slightly at the expense of middle-income recipients.[127] Though the percentage of GNP devoted to LLDCs continued to fall short of the 0.15 commitment, at 0.13 in 1992 it was above the DAC average of 0.08.[128] Official targets for regional shares in *Sharing Our Future* (45 per cent for Africa, 39 per cent for Asia, and 16 per cent for the Americas) were altered after Canada joined the Organization of American States in 1990 and entered negotiations for the North American Free Trade Agreement (NAFTA). Asia was dropped to 37 per cent and the Americas were raised to 18 per cent.[129] Africa received about 48 per cent of actual disbursements in the early 1990s, while the Americas' share grew to 17.6 per cent in 1992-93, and Asia's fell below the policy guideline to 34.6 per cent.[130]

A mixed record on human rights conditionality. The first major test of the commitment in *Sharing Our Future* to sensitizing aid allocations to human rights performance came in June 1989, when the Chinese government violently suppressed the pro-democracy movement in Beijing's Tiananmen Square. Joe Clark and External Affairs took charge of coordinating Canada's response in close liaison with other Western governments.[131] During an emergency Commons debate the day after the crackdown, Clark announced postponement of five aid projects worth $61 million. At the end of the month, following an unprecedented consultation involving Canadians of Chinese descent as well as business and voluntary-sector representatives, he unveiled principles that would guide Canada's relations with China over the months ahead: a preservation of existing links forged by government, industry, and academics over the previous twenty years, a focus emphasizing people-to-people exchanges, and a ban on initiatives that might strengthen the repressive capacity of the Chinese government. Three more projects worth $11 million were cancelled, ostensibly on grounds of falling afoul of this last principle. In addition, Canada suspended indefinitely all involvement in the controversial Three Gorges project (a symbolic act at that stage since the Chinese government had itself announced a postponement.)

Normalization of relations proceeded slowly over the next three years. Nonetheless, China remained Canada's second-largest recipient of government-to-government assistance in 1991-92 and 1992-93, with flows of $66.02 million and $54.9 million respectively. (CIDA grants accounted for 53 per cent of the total, with the rest coming from EDC Section 31 concessional loans.[132]) The prospect of Canadian participation in Three Gorges was revived and then rejected, a decision prompted by intense opposition from environmentalists rather than China's human rights performance. (Subsequently, EDC became involved in the huge dam project, but CIDA did not.) Overall, as Keenleyside suggested, "China is thus illustrative of Ottawa's continuing reticence to take substantive action on aid when the country in question is one with which it has important developmental and other relations."[133]

Another test of this proposition came in November 1991, shortly after Prime Minister Mulroney told Commonwealth and francophone leaders that Canada would strengthen the linkage between aid and human rights performance. After Indonesian troops killed dozens of pro-independence demonstrators in East Timor, Barbara McDougall condemned the action and promised to review the status of Canadian aid to Indonesia.[134] More public attention was drawn to this atrocity than to earlier human rights abuses in East Timor and elsewhere in the republic. Despite reservations within her Department—that action would have negligible impact on Indonesia and damage a valued relationship—McDougall suspended new projects worth $30 million. Most ongoing programming remained unaffected, however, and, at $34.98 million, Indonesia was Canada's fourth largest recipient in 1992-93.[135]

While action on China and Indonesia was largely symbolic, tougher measures were adopted elsewhere. Canada was in the forefront of a successful multi-donor effort (also in November-December 1991) to threaten withdrawal of aid as a lever to force President Daniel arap Moi of Kenya to introduce multi-party elections.[136] The most severe action was in Haiti, historically a large recipient, although one where Canadian interests have been limited to development assistance and human migration. Bilateral programming, suspended during the turmoil of the mid-1980s, was reinstated and expanded after the democratic election of Jean-Bertrand Aristide as president in December 1990. Then, following the military coup of October 1991, Canada withdrew all but humanitarian aid and associated itself with OAS and international efforts to restore Aristide through a process of escalating sanctions.

Allocations to Sri Lanka, long a major recipient, were scaled back considerably as civil strife became more intense and human rights abuses mounted. Other cases associated with deteriorating human rights were Burma (suspension of a marginal program in 1989), Sudan (threat of withdrawal in 1989), Zaïre (suspension of bilateral ODA in October 1991), Malawi (reduction within a small program in 1991), and Peru (temporary curtailment in 1992).[137] There was further questioning of aid to Guatemala and, until the peace settlement in 1992, El Salvador.

Terms of Aid: Debt Relief as a Soft Option in Hard Times

The Department of Finance continued to play the lead role in debt and adjustment policies, though CIDA was represented on a new committee of assistant deputy ministers—the Interdepartmental Coordinating Committee on Structural Adjustment and Debt Issues (ICCSAD). One of ICCSAD's major tasks was to respond officially to *Securing Our Global Future: Canada's Stake in the Unfinished Business of Third World Debt*, a report of the House Standing Committee on External Affairs and International Trade (SCEAIT) prepared in 1990 by a subcommittee chaired by Walter McLean. In the tradition of earlier parliamentary reports, SCEAIT called for Canadian leadership in ending the debt strangulation of the previous decade and reversing the net flow of financial resources from South to North. It accepted the need for adjustment, but criticized the orthodox model for neglecting global imbalances and the impact on the poor. Canada was urged to endorse "less economistic" alternatives that reflected Canadian values—poverty reduction, human rights, democratic traditions, and "recovery from debt to sustainable development that is human-centred, socially equitable, and in harmony with the natural environment."[138]

As Roy Culpeper observed, "the impassioned tone of the report" was in stark contrast with "the cool, complacent response of the government, . . . predictably larded with self-congratulation."[139] Much of that self-congratulation related to forgiveness of official debt in the late 1980s, which, despite positive symbolism, came at slight cost to Canada and yielded little material benefit to debtors. Now, in an era of fiscal restraint, debt relief offered decision-makers an attractive alternative to more substantive and costly measures.

Prime Minister Mulroney used the Commonwealth heads of government meeting in March 1990 to announce that the government would seek parliamentary approval to forgive $181 million of outstanding ODA debt owed Canada by Commonwealth Caribbean countries.[140] With little new aid to offer at the UN Conference on Environment and Development in June 1992, Mulroney again promised debt relief—this time, up to $145 million held by Latin American countries that could be converted, on a case-by-case basis, into local currency funds to help finance environment and other sustainable development projects.[141] During 1993, CIDA signed agreements with El Salvador, Honduras, Nicaragua, and Colombia involving debt swaps of $77.6 million.[142]

Structural adjustment: Softening the rough edges. Within CIDA, Massé's arrival heralded vigorous efforts to strengthen the Agency's capabilities in macro-economic analysis and acquaint key personnel with Bank and Fund policies. The official stance on structural adjustment noticeably toughened. In its 1989 memorandum for DAC, the Agency announced a "significant" realignment of bilateral aid "in many of the poorest countries to provide balance of payments support and structural adjustment assistance." It also stated that sectoral support in countries with IMF/World Bank structural adjustment programs would increasingly depend upon adherence to those programs.[143]

Although the penchant for relabelling was apparent in claims about the extent to which program aid was conditional upon adjustment, considerable new support for anglophone countries in sub-Saharan Africa was earmarked for structural adjustment.[144] So too were increasing shares of Canadian ODA for Jamaica, Guyana, Central America, and the Andean countries (except Colombia).[145] The effort was limited by budgetary stringency, but Canada secured DAC agreement for adding food aid to the more conventional instruments employed by bilateral donors to support adjustment—lines of credit, commodity assistance, and balance-of-payments contributions.[146] Over the five years from 1988-89 to 1992-93, adjustment-related ODA averaged $151.3 million per annum, or 15 per cent of total bilateral disbursements. (The proportions for Africa and the Americas were 21.4 and 29.5 per cent respectively).[147]

As Burdette observed, "People said less and less about the 'human face' " in the early days of Massé's presidency.[148] Subsequently, however, CIDA claimed to have learned from experience (and no doubt from harsh international and domestic criticisms) that "it is essential to integrate issues of social development, political consensus-building, and the environment into decision-making."[149] Disbursements characterized as "poverty mitigation related to structural adjustment" accounted for 14.2 per cent of spending on structural adjustment in 1992-93, above the five-year average of 11.2 per cent; most was in the form of food aid and projects funded from the receipts of counterpart funds.[150] (A CIDA study revealed, however, that some activities financed from counterpart funds, generated by the sale of Canadian food and commodities, conflicted with economic reform objectives.)[151]

The Agency also sought credit for emphasizing such issues as gender, environment, sustainable development, poverty alleviation, and good governance within the development banks and donor consortia.[152] A Development Economics Policy Division was set up in Policy Branch in 1992, with a mandate to develop guidelines for economic reforms and private-sector development, as well as for poverty alleviation.[153]

Procurement untying: Falling short of allowable limits. CIDA reported in 1990 that relaxed restrictions on tying and decentralization had "resulted in a larger untying of funds for the procurement of goods and equipment in the recipient countries or within the regions."[154] However, while the Agency exceeded the old 20 per cent ceiling, the actual use of new untying authorities fell far short of what *Sharing Our Future* permitted. An internal analysis revealed that between 30 and 31 per cent of bilateral disbursements in 1991-92 and 1992-93 were untied in least-developed and sub-Saharan African countries, almost 20 per cent below the allowable threshold. For all other ODA recipients, 24.9 per cent was untied, compared to an authorized limit of 33.3 per cent.[155] DAC data revealed that the proportion of Canadian bilateral ODA tied to domestic procurement in the early 1990s remained above the donor average.[156]

Programming Priorities

Margaret Catley-Carlson's push for an expansion of education and training had already resulted in an increase in bilateral disbursements on human resource development (HRD) from 11.1 per cent in 1986-87 to 15.4 per cent in 1988-89, the year *Sharing Our Future* proclaimed HRD as "the 'lens' through which all of Canada's development efforts are focused."[157] As can be seen in Table 9.1, HRD's share of bilateral ODA rose to 25.4 per cent in 1992-93, making it by far the largest project-based sector during the second Massé presidency. The proportion was even higher for all country-to-country aid (bilateral plus other non-multilateral channels), where HRD surpassed Economic and Financial Support. A good part of the increase was associated with the new programming thrusts on the environment and governance.

Economic and financial support remained larger within the core bilateral program. However, despite Massé's enthusiasm and growing proportions of program and food aid tied to structural adjustment, program aid did not expand much at the expense of project aid in the wake of budget cuts, largely because of a decline in food aid.[158] The official target for food aid growth (5 per cent per annum) was rendered irrelevant along with other volume targets in the strategy. A falling budget and rising needs for emergency relief also thwarted the intention of putting food support on a multi-year commitment basis to facilitate long-term planning.[159]

The shift to HRD was accompanied (as the strategy promised) by a decline in conventional infrastructural projects. Transportation and communications fell from 16.3 per cent of geographic programming in 1986-87 to

11 per cent in 1988-89, and only 5.7 per cent in 1992-93. Though one of six priorities in *Sharing Our Future*, energy also accounted for less—8.2 per cent in 1992-93 compared to 10.9 per cent in 1988-89. A long-serving officer commented: "We were good at transmission lines, bridges, at the engineering level. We've lost that, though I'm not saying that's illegitimate."

Agriculture (including fisheries and forestry) absorbed a higher share of disbursements, as did health and population (which remained low, however, considering the commitment to poverty alleviation).[160]

Human resource development: A dramatic increase but little for basic education. As Karen Mundy and Phillip Rawkins both observed, CIDA embarked on the reorientation to HRD with no clear operational guidelines, other than the objective of increasing scholarships.[161] Efforts to develop a coherent policy began in 1986 when six disparate units (reputedly characterized by Senior Vice-President McWhinney as "all the soft stuff"[162]) were brought together in a new Social and Human Resources Development Division within Resources Branch. The attention paid to HRD by Winegard and *Sharing Our Future* intensified a search for a conceptually rigorous definition of HRD that could be translated into practical programming. After internal and external consultations, the Division proposed in 1991: "the process of developing within an individual, group or organization the capacities for self-sustained learning, generation of technology and implementation of development activities."[163]

As Rawkins argued, HRD can be far more than "a mechanism for improving the life-chances of elites and strengthening the middle class." A sector strategy paper produced by the Social and Human Resources Division devoted considerable attention to higher education, training, and technology transfer, and tried as well to link HRD with the goal of poverty alleviation by stressing institutional capacity-building as a way to strengthen literacy, basic education, primary health care, and the position of women. Basing the case on recent research (by the World Bank among others) and declarations emerging from the World Conference on Education for All in Jomtien, Thailand, in 1990, the paper urged CIDA to devote more resources to strengthening primary education.[164] This recommendation encountered resistance from Canadian universities, as did another one urging that education and training efforts be concentrated more heavily in developing countries rather than in Canada. The President's Committee—preoccupied with the strategic management review as well as policy discussions on sustainable development and good governance—took no action.[165] As Alison Van Rooy observed, "While Jomtien produced a 'blip' in the agency's attention . . . there was not enough sustained senior-level interest to result in a transformation of operations."[166]

Meanwhile, despite budget cuts, the target in *Sharing Our Future* of doubling over five years the number of CIDA-supported students and trainees

Table 9.1

Percentage Distribution of Allocable Bilateral (Geographic Programs) and Country-to-Country ODA by Sector, 1988-89, 1990-91, and 1992-93

	1988-89		1990-91		1992-93	
	Geographic programs	Country-to-country[a]	Geographic programs	Country-to-country[a]	Geographic programs	Country-to-country[a]
Economic and financial support						
Food aid	18.5	14.7	16.1	12.9	13.4	11.3
Other	16.6	12.1	18.6	13.5	17.8	13.2
	35.1				31.2	
Human resource development						
Education	8.1	11.4	8.9	11.0	10.0	12.7
Other	7.3	7.0	12.0	16.5	15.4	17.2
	15.4				25.4	
Agriculture[b]	12.7	13.9	15.5	15.8	14.9	15.0
Energy	10.9	12.0	6.1	7.3	8.2	6.3
Health and population						
Health and nutrition	1.2	4.8	3.0	4.1	2.2	4.2
Population[c]	2.1	3.7	2.6	3.3	2.6	3.9
Water and sanitation	2.2	2.7	2.6	2.3	2.9	2.7
	5.5				7.7	
Transportation and communication	11.0	9.4	5.4	4.9	5.7	6.2
Industry	5.1	4.9	6.3	6.0	5.7	6.1

Other[d]	0.6	1.1	0.8	1.0	0.7	0.9
Multi-sector	3.7	2.7	2.2	1.5	0.5	0.3

a Includes NGO, INGO, and INC channels and the development crown corporations.

b Includes fisheries and forestry.

c Includes human settlements.

d Includes mining and metallurgy, geographical surveys.

Source: Adapted from CIDA, *Annual Report 1988-89*, p. 113; ibid., *1990-91*, pp. S55-56; ibid., *1992-93*, pp. 54-55. Percentages may not total 100.0 because of rounding.

to 12,000 was exceeded by a factor of almost two: there were 21,734 in 1992. However, the enrolment of full-time students on scholarship was 3,986, down from a high of 4,485 in 1991. What had increased more dramatically than envisioned was the number of trainees, mostly in short-term, specialized programs. Whereas 82 per cent of students were enrolled in Canadian institutions, 76 per cent of trainees took courses in their countries of origin and another 9 per cent in third countries. Altogether, the Canadian proportion was 29 per cent—from the perspective of most Agency desk officers, a more developmentally appropriate level than the "about half" promised in the strategy. Providers of education and training, along with recipient countries, were pressed to maximize opportunities for women; in 1992, 34 per cent of students and 38 per cent of trainees were women.[167]

Poverty alleviation: Faltering progress. Poverty alleviation, like HRD, was defined by *Sharing Our Future* as a fundamental commitment of Canadian development assistance. In part because of the intensity of the "human face" debate about structural adjustment, the donor establishment was beginning once more to pay greater heed to the plight of the poor. Poverty reduction was the theme of the 1990 *World Bank Report*, which called for a two-pronged strategy of investing in the productive capacity of the poor, and ensuring broader access to health care, family planning, nutrition, and primary education.[168]

This thinking informed CIDA-commissioned studies that led to a 1990 "Working Paper on Poverty Alleviation" produced by the Area Coordination Group. It emphasized that a successful strategy would have to move beyond welfare-oriented activities "to longer-term programming for endowing the poor with productive capacities and the empowerment of the poor in order to enable them to participate in their own development and ultimately the national development process."[169] Proposals were advanced for making a "first round direct impact on the poor," by improving opportunities for productive employment and access to basic social services, such as education and health. The paper suggested ways of integrating concern for poverty alleviation into various sectoral programs, and strengthening the human and physical assets of the poor; it also highlighted important mechanisms such as credit, new technologies, and participatory approaches to development.[170]

While the working paper suggested useful guidelines for program officers, the effort lost momentum and was not carried forward to the development of an Agency-wide operational strategy—as we have seen, a frequent failing. "Putting poverty first," the first principle of the ODA Charter, was also being sidelined by the new, harder priorities of the 1990s. A CIDA officer lamented in 1993 that

> There is . . . no official policy solely focusing on poverty alleviation, nor any clear guidance for CIDA personnel to address such an immense task. *The need for guidance and policies on targeting ODA towards the poor is becoming an important priority as the development agenda is increasingly focused on governance, trade, private sector development and other issues.*[171]

A 1993 staff discussion paper found that anti-poverty programming had become more prominent since 1988, but "there is little evidence of coherent country strategies and systematic programming."[172] (Work in Asia Branch was seen as the most effective.) The authors of the paper also expressed scepticism about data revealing that projects coded as "poverty alleviation" had increased from 7.2 per cent of all bilateral approvals in the 1983-84/1987-88 period to 30 per cent in the 1988-89/1992-93 period; moreover, food aid accounted for 41 per cent of anti-poverty programming, and basic social reform measures received "relatively little priority."[173] Worries were expressed once more about the debilitating effects of dependency on food aid. CIDA, the authors suggested, needed to define "what it means by poverty alleviation" and take sustainability seriously in determining how best to go about programming for it.[174]

Women in Development: A loss of momentum. CIDA approved in 1992 a new Women in Development Policy Framework for the 1990s. Informed by the gender and development (GAD) critique of early WID programming, it proclaimed a shift from simply promoting equal access of women to the benefits of development to a more comprehensive approach based on gender equity. New emphases included strengthening the role of women as decision-makers, eliminating discriminatory barriers, and protecting and promoting the human rights of women.[175]

Meanwhile, an evaluation of the WID experience from 1984 to 1992 complained about a loss of momentum in the Agency's efforts, though it was positive about accomplishments, especially in the period from 1986 to 1990.

> About half of CIDA's professional staff received WID training, one-third of its country programs developed written WID strategies, and many Posts engaged a WID coordinator. Projects submitted for approval were subject to scrutiny of their gender implications, and the number of WID-specific projects increased substantially. There was a high level of innovation, with new types of WID projects and programs started, and with gender treated in new ways.[176]

Gains in the participation of women in scholarship and trainee programs, an active research profile, and extensive international networking were also praised. The evaluators suggested that success was greatest in institutional support for women's organizations, projects that benefited women only, and activities in the fields of population, health, and nutrition. Programming was judged least effective in eliminating discriminatory barriers, promoting policy dialogue (especially about the gender implications of structural adjustment), and penetrating the spheres of industry, mining, and infrastructure.[177]

The evaluators expressed grave concern about the experience after 1990—a precipitous drop in WID-specific projects (more rapid than cuts overall), stalled progress in increasing the participation rate of women in HRD activities, lack of interest in gender training courses, failure to incorporate WID strategies in a majority of country program analyses, perceptions about declining effectiveness of the WID Steering Committee and Directorate, and (from an internal survey) evidence of growing scepticism about the Agency's commitment. They attributed these difficulties to senior management's preoccupation with other issues, a failure to specify clearly the accountability of vice-presidents and country program directors, a lack of measurable targets (despite the emphasis of the earlier policy), weaknesses in operational mechanisms for planning and monitoring, and ineffectiveness in making WID a consideration in personnel appraisal.

The report made several recommendations to address these deficiencies and reinvigorate organizational momentum. It also called for a refinement of WID policy to reflect more visibly "putting poverty first," "encouraging self-sustainability," and links with other cross-cutting issues such as environment and good governance. Moreover, the expectation that officers should integrate gender perspectives into all of their work required clearer operational conceptions of "WID-integrated" and "gender equity."

Despite internal setbacks, Agency personnel continued to play leadership roles in promoting WID in DAC, the IFIs, UN agencies, and other international fora. In preparation for the UN Conference on Environment and Development, CIDA helped draft Chapter 24 of Agenda 21 on women's issues and gender analysis.

Private-sector development: For whose benefit? Although initiatives for the Third World private sector were promised in *Sharing Our Future*, there was little systematic effort before 1993 to develop a coherent policy for private-sector development in recipient countries. Apart from limited funding for microenterprises, and for the promotion of entrepreneurialism in Africa, the focus was largely on opportunities for Canadian enterprises to develop long-term commercial linkages. Besides expanded lines of credit, four private-sector development funds were set up as pilot projects in 1991 in Pakistan, Morocco, Zimbabwe, and Colombia. While funded bilaterally (initially at a level of $5 million each), they were essentially responsive programs driven by proposals submitted by Canadian firms. As many as twenty were envisaged after the experimental phase was evaluated.[178]

Among special initiatives launched by Asia Branch were Enterprise Thailand-Canada and Enterprise Malaysia-Canada, $12.6 million and $14.9

million projects respectively, designed to promote transfer of Canadian technology and expertise through joint ventures and other "commercial collaborations." CIDA also funded the Canada-ASEAN Centre and the Asia Pacific Foundation to foster closer linkages between Canadian and Southeast Asian private sectors.[179]

Partnership Channels

The division of the ODA budget into equal national initiatives and partnership envelopes was designed to protect bilateral programming in the event of budget cuts. When these occurred, however, the Agency was unable to maintain the balance in favour of national initiatives, in part because it did not wish to hit domestic partners heavily when support for aid was weakening, but largely because of prior commitments to multilateral agencies, especially the World Bank and the regional development banks. The share of national initiatives in the combined envelopes dropped from 51.3 per cent in 1988-89 (when the distinction was introduced) to 46.5 per cent in 1992-93.[180]

Multilateral: Scaling down commitments. While total ODA in current dollars was virtually the same in 1992-93 as in 1988-89, multilateral aid rose from $928.8 million to a high of $1064.23 million in 1991-92 before declining to $1023.15 in 1992-93. The multilateral share of ODA grew to 34.6 per cent in 1992-93, compared to 31.5 per cent five years earlier and 32 per cent in 1989-90.[181] Concerned that cutbacks would squeeze bilateral aid even more, Canadian officials began to negotiate lower levels of international burden-sharing. Whereas Canada agreed in 1989 to maintain a 4.75 per cent share of IDA-9 (covering the years 1991-93), the commitment made to IDA-10 (1994-96) in 1992 was only 4.00 per cent. Reduced shares were taken in regional development bank replenishments, and multilateral technical cooperation agencies were told to expect less.[182] The World Food Program was the only UN agency receiving an appreciable increase in the early 1990s; it came as a diversion of tied food aid from the bilateral channel, mostly in response to rising needs for short-term relief.[183]

Amid the cutting, additional commitments were made to inter-American activities and la Francophonie, among others, and to the new Global Environment Facility.[184] Modest funding was also promised for multilateral initiatives taken at the Children's Summit in New York in 1990, a meeting co-chaired by Prime Minister Mulroney.[185]

Although resources for multilateral ODA were in jeopardy by 1992-93 (and McDougall was more willing than Clark to countenance deeper cuts in the future), the period up to then was marked by continued Canadian activism on governing boards and advisory committees. In the wake of *Sharing Our Future*, and often in conjunction with the Northern European donors, efforts were directed at increasing the sensitivity of the IFIs, the Commonwealth, and la Francophonie to poverty alleviation, HRD, WID, and environmental issues. Later, sustainable development and human rights/democratic development/good governance were added to the agenda.[186]

CIDA initiated a major strategic review of Canadian participation in the IFIs in 1990-91, and Canadian officials were involved in ongoing monitoring and joint donor evaluations of UN agencies.[187] The Auditor General's report for 1992 provided further incentive to improve accountability for multilateral contributions: it called on the Agency to provide better information to Parliament about the management of regional development banks and their effectiveness in promoting development and Canada's objectives.[188]

The voluntary sector: Growing complexity. Even as budget cuts exacted a toll in terms of inflation-adjusted funding, aid channelled through the voluntary sector actually grew in current dollars from $304.6 million in 1988-89 to $355.9 million in 1991-92, before dropping to $337.7 million in 1992-93. (Most of the net addition came from provincial government contributions rather than CIDA.) As a proportion of total ODA, this channel (like the multilateral) experienced an increase—from 10.3 per cent in 1988-89 to 11.4 per cent in 1992-93. (The highest level was 11.5 per cent in 1989-90 when bilateral aid absorbed most of that year's budget cut).[189]

In addition to this funding for strictly responsive programming, NGOs and NGIs continued to serve as executing agents for bilateral projects (including a good many initiated by the voluntary agencies themselves). As noted in Chapter 7, the country focus mechanism was popular among bilateral desk officers, both because they had confidence in the capabilities of NGOs and NGIs, and because the sole-sourcing mechanism for non-profit organizations avoided lengthy contracting and consultant selection procedures. The high point for this practice was 1990-91, when bilateral service contracts for NGOs and NGIs reached $307 million, a further 10 per cent of Canada's ODA. Fears of business backlash, pressure from Monique Landry (part of the Secor agenda), and a declining bilateral budget led to a sharp decrease thereafter—down to $120 million in 1992-93.[190] (Establishment of the Private Sector Development Funds as responsive mechanisms within the bilateral programs, open only to Canadian business, was yet another response to private-sector complaints about heavy use of NGOs and NGIs as executing agencies.)[191]

Within NGO Division, the trend towards program funding was accelerated. By early 1993, fifty agencies (up from twenty-two in 1989) were supported in this way. Continuing a process that began in 1989, twenty-eight of these were on three-year renewable program grants provided after comprehensive institutional evaluations of management systems, financial viability, and accountability. In a move to ease the division's workload and ensure closer scrutiny of smaller NGOs, four regional funds—each administered by an NGI, a consulting firm, or a provincial NGO council—were set up to assess funding applications through a peer review process. These decentralized funds provided grants to 117 organizations in 1993, leaving just 43 on project-only (as opposed to program) funding from CIDA. NGO coalitions continued to assume additional responsibilities for allocating funds on behalf of the Agency.[192]

Despite growing NGO-CIDA tensions—over Massé's policy agenda, cutbacks, and then the leaked Policy Update—these funding arrangements confirmed the observation by Brodhead and Pratt that "there was clearly substantial trust between CIDA's NGO division and the NGO community" in the early 1990s.[193] That trust was shaken, however, when WUSC and Oxfam-Québec experienced major financial and organizational crises.

WUSC (World University Service of Canada), which had become a major contractor under country focus, went into receivership in December 1990 after CIDA turned down a request for a multi-million dollar advance towards future projects. WUSC had become overextended, partly because of mistaken expectations about continued growth in CIDA funding, but largely because of managerial weaknesses and a disastrous real estate miscalculation—it was carrying two mortgages, one for a new office building and another for its old headquarters, which could not be sold in Ottawa's slumping realty market. Following a few days of uncertainty (and panic about implications for overseas workers and WUSC-sponsored refugees studying in Canadian universities), the receivers, Ernst and Young, accepted a contract from CIDA to carry forward existing projects. The Agency also provided a temporary management team. Although there was no commitment initially to save the organization, the government responded to pleas and maintained the arrangement for almost a year until WUSC was once again on its feet.[194]

In December 1991, CIDA froze its quarterly instalment to Oxfam-Québec (a separate entity since its split with Oxfam Canada in 1973), and engaged Ernst and Young to do an independent audit of the organization's finances. Press reports a few months later revealed deep indebtedness and allegations of misuse of substantial sums of money by two former senior executives. Again a successful rescue operation was mounted, this time under a new board of directors who secured a $107,000 grant from the government of Quebec and sold off donated paintings.[195] Chastened by these experiences, CIDA set up a new unit in the summer of 1992 to evaluate the financial viability of NGOs, NGIs, and other partners.[196]

On a more positive note, an evaluation of the NGO Program in 1992 concluded that the rationale for a responsive program based on matching funds was still sound, that NGOs were especially effective in poverty alleviation and grass-roots development, and that delivery costs were low. In recommending continuation, but mindful of the Secor analysis, the evaluators observed that "the NGO Program is at a crossroad." There was a need to address unresolved tensions between CIDA and NGOs over the concept of responsiveness. In addition, "a large percentage of NGOs are involved in too many sectors and countries, which is a major constraint on their limited funds and resources."[197]

Ian Smillie, a former executive director of CUSO and now a prominent aid consultant, did a study of NGO-government relations for CCIC in 1991. He criticized CIDA for having "placed far greater emphasis on expansion of the Canadian constituency than on the quality of overseas programming." Cutbacks were now forcing difficult choices between organizations and activities,

> but in the view of the NGO community, they are not being made on the basis of CIDA's development criteria. They are being made on the basis of the historical funding relationship, on the basis of the public support an NGO can muster in its defence, and on the basis of personal predilections among CIDA officials.

He called for reforms to ensure that decision-making was based "more on program quality than on other considerations."[198] (The evaluation subsequently called for a transparent performance measurement system to guide budget decisions.[199]) Smillie also challenged Canadian NGOs to become more professional, enhance their skills in key sectoral areas, undertake more serious policy research, and work together for a more effective impact on public consciousness. "Divided, fractious and territorial, Canadian NGOs will become increasingly irrelevant, or increasingly co-opted by stronger forces."[200]

The universities: Scaling down expectations. The centres of excellence program promised in *Sharing Our Future* was both badly conceived and short-lived. In its brief to the Winegard committee, the Association of Universities and Colleges of Canada (AUCC) had proposed ways of strengthening interdisciplinary research and teaching in development studies—including a Canadian Institute of Development Studies to "provide bridges between research and practical development and between universities and development agencies," and university chairs in Development Studies "to stimulate teaching and inquiry . . . [and] strengthen ongoing community outreach activities in the sphere of development education."[201]

Guided by Winegard's own experience in higher education, SCEAIT then suggested encouraging centres of excellence or specialization in development studies "not by creating new centres but by developing stronger support for excellence where it already exists or has begun to develop." The report recommended annual funding of approximately $1 million for each of several centres over a five- to ten-year period. Although resources would come from anticipated growth in the budget assigned to CIDA's ICDS division, the centres were an explicit component of Winegard's proposed strategy for strengthening public outreach; "world-class development research centres" and stronger university-based teaching would provide a "solid analytical foundation," without which "development education will remain haphazard and shallow."[202]

Winegard's distinctive conception and approach were lost in *Sharing Our Future*, which promised centres of excellence as a major new initiative for universities, but made no references to development education, interdisciplinary inquiry, stronger links between academics and development practitioners, or potential improvements in the quality of teaching, research, and community outreach on international development.[203] What emerged instead from a subsequent consultative process was a special competition for a higher level of funding for conventional university linkage projects, valuable if done well but hardly ground-breaking as Winegard had hoped. After announcing that eight to ten centres would be supported, CIDA funded two in 1989 and another four in 1990.[204] As budget cuts meant that these ventures were diverting resources from other university-based responsive programming, no further competitions were held.

Meanwhile, paralleling the trend towards program funding and decentralized decision-making in the NGO sector, discussions continued between CIDA and AUCC on ways of devolving greater responsibility to the university community for program management (bilateral as well as responsive). A consultancy report commissioned by AUCC in 1989 explored several options, including creation of a not-for-profit corporation, Canadian Universities International, which would take over from ICDS university-based activities in the Educational Institutions Program (EIP)—university cooperation projects (linkages), centres of excellence, and university initiated scholarships. It would also manage bilateral umbrella programs, such as those for China and Thailand, which AUCC's International Division had already run for some time. What CIDA was seeking, however, was relief in the administrative sphere; as in the late 1970s, it was not prepared to relinquish decision-making authority. AUCC was given a micro-fund to distribute for small projects, but responsibility for major funding decisions stayed in the Agency, though, as the universities requested, with greater reliance on peer review mechanisms.[205]

An evaluation of the Educational Institutions Program in 1992 was generally positive, but pointed out three serious weaknesses—lack of effective participation by developing country partners in the application process (thus perpetuating "the traditional donor-recipient relationship"), insufficient evidence of continuing linkages once funding ended, and failure to plan effectively for outreach and development components of projects.[206]

Seizing the initiative at a time of uncertainty about the future of responsive programming, AUCC commissioned a study later in 1992 to address these concerns and propose another new approach for the EIP. The consultant, Arthur Headlam, criticized universities for failing to make international development an institutional (as opposed to an individual faculty) commitment, and CIDA for overmanaging administrative details at the expense of content. He proposed a new two-tiered program to replace the EIP: Tier 1—integrated university programs that would take two-thirds of the available funding and be managed by CIDA (with peer review input); and Tier 2—projects that would take the other third and be managed by AUCC.[207] As CIDA's still secret strategic management review recommended abolition of responsive programming for universities, the Headlam report proved to be well timed. His recommendations formed the basis of a new program approved in 1993—University Partnerships in Cooperation and Development.[208]

Industrial cooperation: Seeking clearer objectives. Although budget cuts precluded achievement of the 4 per cent share of ODA promised in the strategy for INC, it grew by 20.6 per cent from $60.6 million in 1988-89 to $73.2 million in 1992-93. As a result, the program's share of total ODA rose from 2.1 per cent to 2.5 per cent.[209] The private-sector development funds and other business-oriented initiatives by the geographic branches added yet further resources for INC-type ventures. CIDA's active consultations with Canadian business organizations continued, and three more regional offices were established in Calgary, Winnipeg, and Moncton.[210]

An evaluation of INC in 1992 found that each dollar invested generated three to four dollars in subsequent contracts for Canadian suppliers, although almost a third of the estimated return came from just two of the hundreds of projects funded between 1985 and 1992. About one in seven investment projects and one in five professional service projects yielded returns.[211] Anecdotal evidence suggested positive outcomes in recipient countries in terms of job creation, investment, and strengthened human and physical resources. The report concluded, however, that neither trade nor developmental goals were clearly defined, risking a dissipation of "program impacts." Data on distribution revealed that, while INC made commitments of $341.4 million in 104 countries from 1985 to 1992, over half was earmarked for projects in twelve countries. Not surprisingly, seven were middle-income countries, one (Argentina) was in the high-income category, and four of the five low-income countries were high-growth economies in Asia.[212]

The evaluation called on CIDA to "elaborate a clear and explicit framework of program goals, define the intended results within developing countries and within Canada from each goal, and identify measurable indicators for the intended results." It recommended as well creation of a "proposal evaluation grid" that would focus on developmental implications, responsiveness to CIDA's Country Policy Frameworks, and host country "fit"—as well as track records of firms, viability of projects, and anticipated returns. Noting a significant overlap, the evaluators sought clarification of the relationship between INC and Private Sector Development Funds.[213]

Public Outreach and Support

Sharing Our Future committed the government to increasing expenditures on development education and information from 0.6 per cent to 1.0 per cent of ODA. Once phased in, that meant growth from a 1988-89 budget base of $16 million to almost $28 million per annum. Although this commitment did not survive budget cuts, there was for a time opportunity for innovation. The process of rethinking began in 1988 when, as mentioned in Chapter 8, CIDA hired Manifest Communications to propose a new public outreach strategy.

The Manifest report, produced shortly before Massé's arrival, concluded that there was considerable development-related communication/education taking place across the country, but "the total impact of all this activity is less than it ought to be." Awareness among the general public was low and, though there were charitable impulses, they were rooted in "paternalism, guilt, apathy, frustrated anxiety, a sense of helplessness, and a failure to see the bigger picture." The report called for "a fundamental repositioning of our understanding of development" based on two key ideas:

> The first is global interdependence. . . . [We] share a common destiny. The second is that Canada and Canadians must, can, and do play an active and committed role in international development—not because we have all the answers, but because we cannot, in good conscience and for our own self-interest, stand idly on the sidelines.[214]

The consultants recommended broad-based public outreach and work through such key intermediaries as the development education community, the media, educators and youth, business groups, professional and trade associations, politicians, and CIDA employees. (The Agency was commended for the Global Education Program and other youth-oriented initiatives.)

The most controversial proposal was to transfer outreach activities from Public Affairs (which would then handle only corporate communications) and consolidate them in a new unit along with the Public Participation and Global Education programs. The rationale was to achieve maximum impact through integrated programming, and to allay long-standing fears among NGOs that PPP would be compromised if incorporated into Public Affairs. Landry rejected the recommendation. Instead, a Development Information Program (DIP) was set up to handle outreach activities within Public Affairs (renamed "Communications"), and was urged to work cooperatively with PPP on joint initiatives such as Development Day. With additional resources, the DIP expanded film and video co-production, publications, and media networking. Development of educational and youth-oriented materials remained a priority.

Several of Manifest's recommendations sought to make PPP more accessible and its work more manageable—for example, decentralization of authority for making smaller grants to international cooperation councils operating on a provincial basis. The minister agreed with a proposal to establish a National Advisory Committee on Development Education to advise CIDA on the mandate and funding criteria of PPP and, more generally, "to provide a nurturing ground for fresh, visionary, and constructive approaches and directions."[215]

Douglas Roche, the former MP and long an eloquent champion of international development, was named chairman of the National Advisory Committee; other members were drawn from NGOs, business, and educational institutions. The committee published four reports between April 1990 and December 1991, devoting attention to ways of strengthening outreach to the public and "target audiences" (Manifest's "key intermediaries"). Landry accepted most of its recommendations for revamping PPP, extending funding for the Global Education Program, and establishing ten annual achievement awards to facilitate travel and professional development for staff and volunteers involved in development education.[216] She also agreed with the Committee's suggestion that Development Day be replaced by International Development Week, an annual event scheduled during the first week of February.[217]

Landry rejected a recommendation to increase funding for development information and education to 1.5 per cent of ODA. In fact, the budget was soon cut below the 1 per cent threshold promised in *Sharing Our Future*, and the National Advisory Committee was one of the victims. It was among advisory bodies and commissions abolished in the February 1992 budget—a cruel irony for Roche, who had been the moving force behind the 1 per cent recommendation first made in 1980 by the Breau task force.[218]

International Development Week did survive as a vehicle for achieving greater visibility for local activities undertaken by grass-roots organizations. It also encouraged a closer-than-usual working relationship between NGOs and CIDA's own public outreach personnel. In 1991, however, the event was overshadowed by the Gulf War and somewhat discordant messages at the national level. CCIC chose that week to release a "report card" on the first three years of *Sharing Our Future*; it assigned grades of "F" for volume,

"C" for reaching the poorest, "B–" for protecting the global environment, "C" for human rights conditionality, and "D" for response to Third World debt.[219] The council rehearsed many of its long-standing criticisms of Canadian aid. At a time when polls were showing declining support for foreign aid and growing cynicism about its efficacy, the effort may only have hardened anti-ODA sentiment. The churches' stinging rebuke of CIDA's performance was issued a few months later.

CCIC opted for a different approach in February 1992 when the official theme, highlighting the upcoming Earth Summit, was environmental sustainability. With support from CIDA and considerable cooperation from the media and the NGO community, a four-page insert entitled "Shock of the Possible" was placed in newspapers across the country. It attempted to counter images of poverty and despair with messages of success and hope, quoting UNDP's assertion "that it is too often a lack of political commitment, not of resources that is the ultimate cause of human neglect." The theme the following year was "Together we can change our world," which seemed inane amid the campaign of development activists against the leaked Policy Update paper.

Table 9.2
Percentage Distribution of Polled Opinions About Level of Canadian Aid, 1989-93

	1988 December (Angus Reid)	1990 January (Angus Reid)	1991 January (CRÉATEC)	1992 July (CROP)	1993 March (Focus Canada)
Not enough	31	32	33	15	14
Right amount	45	39	35	34	43
Too much	16	21	25	46	38
No opinion	9	9	7	5	5

Source: Angus Reid Associates, *Report to CIDA: Public Attitudes Toward International Development Assistance* (Hull: CIDA, 1990), p. 9; CRÉATEC, *Report to CIDA: Public Attitudes Towards International Development Assistance* (Hull: CIDA, 1991), p. 12; and data provided by Communications Branch of CIDA.

As the recession deepened and federal debt moved up the political agenda, public support for aid as measured by opinion polls declined precipitously (see Table 9.2). As mentioned above, when given a choice between raising taxes and cutting ODA, almost 70 per cent of respondents to another poll favoured expenditure reductions. For the government, the polls legitimated disproportionate reductions in the ODA budget, and swamped the alternative messages of a public outreach program that was cut back more rapidly than overall aid spending.

Little to Celebrate as CIDA Turns Twenty-Five

Massé's departure in February 1993 coincided with the beginning of CIDA's twenty-fifth year. Unlike the twentieth anniversary in 1988, when *Sharing Our Future* was launched and decentralization was initiated, the quarter century mark was not a time for celebration. The strategy was in tatters, decentralization was dead, poverty alleviation was being shunted aside by other priorities, and there was even backsliding on the commitment to women in development. Canada's ODA was declining, CIDA's relations with External Affairs were strained, and (like all federal public servants) Agency employees were suffering from cutbacks and anti-government sentiment. NGOs, disillusioned with Massé's embrace of the neo-liberal agenda, were angry about the Policy Update and nervous about the fallout from Secor.

Massé once more had put his intellectual mark on CIDA with the framework for sustainable development—but, unlike his time in the early 1980s, his second presidency was marked by unresolved policy and organizational conflicts, and a loss of dynamism. The Agency, already groaning under the weight of multiple mandates when Massé came back in 1989, was by 1993 less certain of its mission and its future. He left before seeing through his major initiative, the strategic management review that he hoped would enable the organization to adapt to changing global and domestic realities. Rank-and-file employees were aware that it had been delayed, but did not know what might be in store for them because proposals had been wrapped in a veil of ministerial secrecy for almost a year. It was a challenging moment for a new president to take office.

Chapter 10

Ebb Tide, 1993-98

Canadian ODA in 1992-93 was $2,972 million. The *Estimates* for 1997-98 projected a comparable figure of $2,146 million,[1] and plans called for a further reduction in 1998-99. The ODA/GNP ratio, which stood at 0.49 per cent in 1991-92, plummeted to 0.34 per cent in 1996-97, and is projected to fall to 0.27 per cent in 1998-99.[2] This dramatic ebbing in Canada's aid effort was the dominant reality during the CIDA presidencies of Jocelyne Bourgon, who served for five eventful months in 1993, and Huguette Labelle, who joined the Agency in July of that year. Amid unresolved questions about the nature of the post-Cold War world, and the role of foreign aid within it, the 1990s continued as a time of uncertainty for CIDA and its partners at home and abroad.

The Agency's twenty-fifth year in 1993 was a particularly anxious one. It began with the Policy Update controversy and the departures of Marcel Massé and Douglas Lindores. Then, in rapid succession, there were three presidents—and, in an election year, four ministers and a change of government. The Auditor General reported again, criticizing CIDA for "losing ground" in its capacity to meet development needs in the 1990s.[3] The Agency's performance was a major concern as Jean Chrétien's new Liberal administration launched a comprehensive review of Canadian foreign policy.

Meanwhile, Bourgon played a crucial role during her short time at CIDA in resolving the impasse over the strategic management review that had sapped morale during the two and one-half years it had dragged on. In doing so, she set in motion some far-reaching organizational changes. Labelle, in turn, committed herself to completing management reforms and attending to the human costs of recent dislocations. Prompted by further criticisms by the Auditor General, she launched a second phase of management renewal focused on "results-based management." She also had CIDA reexamine its programming priorities in readiness for the 1994-95 foreign policy review. As president, Labelle was very much a deputy to André Ouellet, who exercised

---

Notes to Chapter 10 are on pp. 560-80.

tight hands-on control over the Agency as minister of Foreign Affairs from 1993 to 1996.

Non-governmental participants were better prepared than ever for the foreign policy review, hopeful that the Liberals would reverse what they had condemned from the opposition benches: the drift away from the anti-poverty and development-first priorities of *Sharing Our Future*. In the spirit of earlier parliamentary committees, a Special Joint Committee of the Senate and the House of Commons affirmed "the central principle of the development charter, namely to support the poorest people of the world."[4] The process of review, however, was more hurried and less focused than the Hockin-Simard and Winegard studies in the 1980s, and ended up having less impact on foreign policy generally and aid policy in particular.

The Liberal government parted company with *Sharing Our Future* in not declaring poverty reduction as *the* primary objective of Canadian ODA. The official response to the Special Joint Committee proclaimed a more open-ended purpose: "to support sustainable development in developing countries in order to reduce poverty and contribute to a more secure, equitable and prosperous world."[5] An accompanying statement, *Canada in the World*, asserted that the program had to serve "prosperity and employment," "global security," and "Canadian values and culture."[6] The old "trinity" was once again official policy as the ODA Charter was quietly buried as the legacy of a defeated government. Nonetheless, there were promising commitments: to channel 25 per cent of Canadian ODA into meeting basic human needs, to achieve a better fit between policies and programming, to focus less on process and more on results, and to account to Parliament and the public in a more open fashion.

Some encouraging results followed the review on both management and policy fronts. The commitment to manage with a stronger focus on development outcomes rather than process led to new policies for results-based management and performance review as well as simplified contracting procedures. Of potentially great significance was a comprehensive policy on poverty reduction that set out operational strategies for incorporation into all regional/country policy frameworks. CIDA promised that the policy would also guide programming in each of its new programming priorities: basic human needs, women in development, infrastructure services, human rights/democracy/good governance, private-sector development, and environment.

Efforts to make aid more effective had to confront a decline in resources for which there was no end in sight until at least the end of the decade. All programs have been cut back, mostly across-the-board. Two major exceptions stand out: first, a controversial decision early in 1993 to eliminate conventional bilateral programming in some of the poorest African countries, which was reversed after the Liberals came to power; and, second, in 1995, the termination of the Public Participation Program and decentralized funding arrangements for NGOs. The 1995 cuts cast adrift many community-based development education groups, undermined innovative experiments in North-South NGO coalition-building, and—coming on top of other tensions—further strained relations with much of the constituency CIDA had worked so hard to build. Some ground was recovered, however, after changes in ministerial leadership.

All in all, as the 1990s unfolded, it was clear that foreign aid was facing a serious crisis, not simply another round of aid fatigue.

CIDA during the Bourgon Presidency

Jocelyne Bourgon inherited an Agency with "major financial, turf and morale problems."[7] Inexperienced in the field of international development, she came to CIDA from the Privy Council with a reputation as a good "people manager," a skilled administrator, and an excellent communicator. Right at the outset, she proved her diplomatic mettle, spearheading discussions with External Affairs and the Prime Minister's Office that led to formal burial of the International Assistance Policy Update. She had little time to catch her breath, however, before CIDA was embroiled in yet another controversy, this time about how to cope with the budget reduction announced in Finance Minister Don Mazankowski's December 1992 economic statement.

The 1993 Cuts: A Diplomatic Debacle[8]

Outside CIDA, fears of drastic budgetary dislocations—escalated by the leaked Policy Update paper in January—proved well founded on February 25 when the *Estimates* for 1993-94 revealed that several "strategic choices" had been made. These were not as far-reaching as the recommendations in "Carin's deck"—but, as Andrew Clark of the North-South Institute commented, "it seems that CIDA is already well on its way to a *de facto* implementation of the External Affairs 'policy update.' "[9]

The 10 per cent cut in projected spending translated into an absolute reduction in the International Assistance Envelope of 5 per cent. Support for former Soviet bloc countries rose to $147 million, down from the original projection of $163 million, but still up 44 per cent from 1992-93. As a result, ODA cash (the rest of the envelope) declined by 7.4 per cent. A deferral of encashments of some multilateral commitments, mostly to regional development banks, took some immediate pressure off other areas.[10] The only one spared was humanitarian assistance. Some organizational commitments deemed marginal were jettisoned, including—of great symbolic significance historically—the Colombo Plan.[11]

Bilateral programming was relatively protected in this round, but a 4.6 per cent cut still amounted to $45 million year over year. With regional shares pegged at existing levels, each branch was allowed to develop its own strategy for retrenchment. Asia Branch trimmed allocations to all major recipients, in preference to dropping any one of them. Significantly, however, Bangladesh—the poorest major recipient in the region—absorbed a disproportionate reduction, Sri Lanka—racked by civil strife—was downgraded, and programming was dropped or reduced in six minor low-income recipients. No middle-income or high-growth country was appreciably affected.[12] In the Americas, no core country or region was eliminated, but NAFTA and "mutual interest" in South America translated into heavier-than-average cuts in Central America and the Caribbean.

Sub-Saharan Africa experienced the severest repercussions. Soon after the merger of Anglophone Africa and Francophone Africa branches in 1991, the new Africa and Middle East Branch had produced a strategy paper entitled "Africa 21," which projected a vision of a more united, democratic, and entrepreneurial Africa in the twenty-first century. It called on CIDA to play a "catalytic role" in support of greater regional integration and programming.[13] Ostensibly in accord with "Africa 21," the Branch decided to cut along regional lines: full programming would be maintained in the Middle East, the Mahgreb, and West and South Africa, while conventional bilateral assistance to Central and East Africa would be phased out. Of five countries in the downgraded region—Cameroon, Kenya, Rwanda, Tanzania, and Zaïre—three had already experienced a suspension (Zaïre) or curtailment (Kenya and Rwanda) of Canadian aid in response to human rights abuses and political unrest. However, the decision to withdraw from Tanzania, CIDA's largest country program in Africa since the mid-1970s, was shocking. By terminating conventional bilateral aid in Ethiopia as well, the Agency pulled back from the world's second and third poorest countries in terms of per capita income.

While thoughtful work had gone into "Africa 21," including more consultation in Canada and Africa than critics contended,[14] the policy's use for budget-cutting was essentially a rationalization for the difficult decision to drop Tanzania as a core country. Once Africa and Middle East Branch officials decided on greater concentration rather than a "lawnmower approach" (their label for squeezing across-the-board), they determined that the size of the cut required slashing at least one large country program. Alternatives with budgets comparable to Tanzania's were rejected for foreign or domestic policy reasons: Egypt, an External Affairs favourite because of the Middle East conflict and commercial potential; the Southern African Development Community, because of the South African situation, SADC's potential for regional cooperation, and long-term mutual interest; Senegal, because of francophone opposition; and Ghana, because it was the major Commonwealth recipient in largely French-speaking West Africa. Within Central and East Africa, the large program in middle-income Cameroon was also a potential alternative, but it was cut back only modestly in view of its unique bilingual status and commercial promise.[15] Gabon, an even wealthier "non-core" Central African state, was also affected only marginally. In effect, what would have been a compelling case for least-developed Tanzania—if the Development Charter had been taken seriously—lost out to political and commercial considerations. Ironically, it had been scheduled in the first draft of "Carin's deck" as one of few continuing development assistance countries.

The communication of the African cuts caused upset as well. Without prior warning in their home capitals or in Ottawa, ambassadors and high commissioners received letters on February 25, 1993, informing them of decisions and listing projects to be abandoned or completed. No opportunity was given to discuss priorities. Intended to soften the blow in Central and East Africa, but rather patronizing under the circumstances, was an announcement of continuing eligibility for two new thematic funds—one for human rights/democratic development/good governance and the other for private-sector development. The letters were signed by Pierre Racicot, vice-president for Africa and the Middle East, rather than by Barbara McDougall or Monique Vézina, adding insult to injury for protocol-conscious diplomats. Ambassadors and high commissioners were further annoyed when their efforts to see McDougall yielded only a belated meeting with Vézina.[16]

CIDA-watchers in Parliament—including Tories David MacDonald and Walter McLean—expressed dismay about the African decisions and the way they were delivered.[17] McLean's SCEAIT Subcommittee on Development and Human Rights held an unprecedented meeting with ten African ambassadors. Polite praise for Canada's historical contributions to Africa, and an acknowledgement of fiscal pressures, were coupled with deep-seated concerns about lack of consultation and diminished support at a crucial moment in Africa's struggle for economic and political reform. Kongit Sinegioris, ambassador for Ethiopia, asked: "Does it look good for Canada to be cutting assistance to a country that is trying to establish democracy and to have given such big assistance to a country where [before 1991] there was a military dictator?" Expressing appreciation for past emergency relief, she emphasized that what was increasingly needed was support for long-term development.[18]

The subcommittee also heard strong words from the Canadian Council of Churches,[19] and the parent standing committee was hard-hitting when Madame Vézina tried to defend CIDA's actions. Liberal external affairs critic

Lloyd Axworthy told the minister that "you're being set up to take the rap for a very deliberate and insidious change of policy by this government," which, he claimed, was diverting assistance from "those in need to the support of the private sector and developing market opportunities. You're turning CIDA into a business-finance-trade agency."[20] Several sharply critical press editorials saw the African cuts as further evidence that a post-election policy review was needed.[21]

Breaking the Impasse on Management Reform

Meanwhile, Bourgon won respect within the Agency for ending the year-long silence about the strategic management review (SMR), and brokering an approach that enabled several recommendations to move forward. Trying to maintain delicate compromises, Massé and Lindores had insisted that their reform package was a "seamless web" requiring implementation in its entirety. They had also contended that it was "policy neutral," a hard position to defend in view of EAITC's opposition. Bourgon announced a different approach in an upbeat presentation to an Agency forum on April 7.[22] Normally, she said, she had obeyed "one simple rule" in taking charge of an organization—to resist the temptation to make structural or operational changes for at least three months. "This time, I am going to break my rule because it seems essential to me to reduce uncertainty. If there is one message which you have transmitted forcefully to me, it is that the people of this Agency have had enough of studies and work groups. It's time to take decisions. It's time to put our house in order."

Lindores' discussion paper was at last distributed with its recommendations divided into three broad categories: those dealing with internal management reform, those implying mandate or policy changes, and those affecting CIDA's relations with its external partners. Bourgon disclosed that recommendations for internal organizational change would be implemented, while the rest would be set aside for further study and consultation.[23]

As a transition team had laid the groundwork during the long hiatus, action would commence immediately on: strengthening Policy Branch; merging Finance/Corporate Information and Operations Services branches, and several other functions, in a new Corporate Management Branch;[24] creating a Corporate Secretariat in the President's Office; disbanding Professional Services Branch, and transferring its personnel to program, Policy, and Corporate Management branches; and creating in programming branches program delivery units, staffed by people from previously separate units involved with professional, procurement, and financial services. Bourgon assured staff that the "reform is *not* driven by fiscal reasons and there are *no commitments* to cut personnel as a result."[25]

The reorganization left the Agency with nine branches (a reduction of two): four corporate and services branches (Policy, Corporate Management, Communications, and Personnel and Administration), and five program branches (Africa and Middle East, Americas, Asia, Canadian Partnership, and Multilateral). In announcing a streamlined committee structure, Bourgon also signalled a change in leadership style, renaming the President's Committee the Executive Committee.

Early in May, Bourgon held another Agency forum to assess implications of a new federal budget, brought down on April 26, 1993. Although the worst news had come in the December economic statement, the government's new five-year fiscal framework indicated that, at best, the International Assistance Envelope (including support for former Soviet republics) would barely keep pace with inflation. In addition, like all government departments, CIDA would have to shave another 10 per cent from administrative costs during that period. On a more positive note, the president introduced her new management team, which shifted some long-time players and saw others depart.[26]

Then, just six weeks later, Jocelyne Bourgon was gone. After five months of decisiveness and morale-boosting, another shock for CIDA's employees.

More Changes at the Top

Bourgon moved to Transport Canada as deputy minister in July 1993, switching places with Huguette Labelle.[27] A month earlier, when Kim Campbell began her brief tenure as Progressive Conservative prime minister, she dropped the External Relations and International Development portfolio from her slimmed-down cabinet. The president of CIDA reverted to a direct reporting relationship to the secretary of state for External Affairs, now Perrin Beatty (until Campbell and her Tories were defeated in the October general election).

Huguette Labelle Assumes the Presidency

As one senior officer observed, Bourgon—figuratively "sainted" during her short time—was a "hard act" for anyone to follow. Labelle, however, brought to CIDA particular strengths in personnel management and interdepartmental networking. Joining the public service in 1976, she had served until 1980 in the Department of Indian and Northern Affairs. She then held various appointments at the deputy ministerial level, including the chair of the Public Service Commission of Canada from 1985 to 1990. During an earlier career in nursing education and health care planning, she had gained some international experience as president of the Canadian Red Cross and the Canadian Nurses Association and as a CIDA consultant in Haiti and Cuba.[28]

At an Agency forum in September 1993, Labelle expressed concern about the enormous pressures experienced by employees over the past few years. She praised them for their commitment to development, and for holding onto a sense of purpose through all the uncertainties and dislocations of budget cuts, the strategic management review, and the reversal of decentralization. "Your patience has been tested, and there's still a lot of stress in the air." Her priority would be "changing the way we manage our human resources—our people. I'm going to work hard to open up two-way communication, to empower staff, to develop our people, and to strengthen management, particularly of human resources."[29]

Reporting on an executive committee retreat in July, the new president informed staff that there would be another round of management renewal. "The CIDA I see," she proclaimed, "will have cut bureaucracy and process; it will have streamlined costs, and lightened the decision-making process."[30] She promised that Corporate Management Branch would consult widely over the next six weeks as it prepared a two-year plan for the second phase of management renewal. Work was also needed, Labelle advised, on making CIDA's mission to promote sustainable development more meaningful to the Canadian public. When "budgets are shrinking and the world . . . is going through fast and complex change, we need to be thinking hard and carefully about our aid priorities." There might be an aid policy review after the October federal election, and "we need to be the *best* prepared."[31] Ten papers on ODA priorities would soon be circulated as the first step towards creating a short-term strategic plan.[32]

Three developments made CIDA's agenda even more complex later in the fall of 1993. First, following the Liberal victory in October, André Ouellet, a seasoned cabinet veteran from the Trudeau years, was appointed minister of Foreign Affairs.[33] In charge of the renamed Department of Foreign Affairs and International Trade (DFAIT), he assumed direct oversight of CIDA and made his presence and preferences felt throughout the Agency. Secondly, a new round of stinging criticisms from the Auditor General intensified pressure on CIDA to move forward with Phase II of management renewal. Thirdly, in December, Ouellet announced plans for a comprehensive review of foreign policy, including international assistance.

André Ouellet: A "Take-Charge" Minister[34]

Ouellet's assumption of direct responsibility for the aid program, together with the brief experience under Beatty, led many in CIDA to expect a relationship like that with the secretary of state for External Affairs in previous Liberal administrations—arm's length except for political issues, broad policy concerns, and major contracts. The new foreign minister was quick to dispel that notion. Despite his enormous portfolio, he spent several hours a week in CIDA, even more involved in day-to-day decision-making than either Vézina and Landry.

Two junior ministers were assigned to Foreign Affairs. Both Christine Stewart, secretary of state for Africa and Latin America, and Raymond Chan, secretary of state for Asia Pacific, brought relevant experience to their portfolios: Stewart, opposition critic on foreign aid during the 1988-93 Parliament, had long been active in the NGO Horizons of Friendship; and Chan, who emigrated from Hong Kong as a teenager, had been in the forefront of Chinese-Canadian efforts to promote human rights and democracy in China. Speaking frequently on behalf of Ouellet on aid matters, they were given representational rather than line responsibilities, and played virtually no role in managing the Agency.[35]

Ouellet wanted CIDA to be seen as an effective organization that fulfilled its mandate, including developmental objectives. His own priority, however, lay in the Canadian side of the operation, especially in the distribution of work to private-sector suppliers and the use of ODA to promote trade. As Chrétien's senior Quebec minister before the provincial referendum on sovereignty in October 1995, Ouellet was especially diligent in looking after the interests of Quebecers. He was, as journalist Hugh Winsor quoted a senior CIDA official as saying "in an indiscreet moment," "a very *traditional* Quebec minister."[36] Like his Tory predecessors, Ouellet also preferred to see a large number of small cheques being issued to Canadian suppliers. As a result, he disliked proposals for simplifying contracting through the use of fewer executing agencies and more standing offers. His tendency to micromanage with the "Canadian angle" in mind created a situation at the country desk level that prompted considerable second-guessing about his preferences. As one officer put it, "it was almost like having the minister on every project team."

While some CIDA officers regretted Ouellet's narrow vision, he was universally respected as a prodigious worker who moved the paperwork quickly. Tough-minded, he made it clear to both Foreign Affairs and CIDA that he would not tolerate conflict of the sort that erupted over the Policy Update. He also had clout in cabinet, and fought hard for his portfolio. As we shall see, he had strong views on where and how to cut costs.

Ouellet's take-charge approach meant that Labelle was a conventional deputy minister, rather than a somewhat autonomous president. Within the Agency, opinions were mixed about the resulting chemistry. In the eyes of some critics, she was too adaptable and too inclined to anticipate the minister's wishes. At the same time, her skills as a networker and team player, and her tendency "not to rock the boat," were seen as appropriate at a difficult historical moment for Canadian ODA and for CIDA. In addition, while mindful of all the cross-pressures, Labelle—with support from Christine Stewart—took seriously the Agency's briefs for poverty reduction and long-term sustainable development.

Management Renewal: The Auditor General and Phase II

Labelle's appointment coincided with feedback from the Office of the Auditor General on a major audit, this time on bilateral programming and "the lessons that CIDA itself identified in its recent Strategic Management Review."

Of particular concern to the audit team was the "considerable confusion in the minds of many about the sometimes conflicting objectives of the Official Development Assistance program and about how to resolve these conflicts on a daily basis." Examples from an audit of country programs and eighteen projects in Bangladesh, Pakistan, and Sri Lanka were offered as evidence that the issue of conflicting objectives raised by Winegard remained unresolved. "At stake is CIDA's ability to pursue its development mandate effectively."[37]

The report agreed with Groupe Secor and the SMR that "CIDA needs to concentrate its efforts . . . and be more selective." Accepting as well the conclusion about overregulation, the auditors deflected this issue back into the Agency's court:

> On the one hand, CIDA . . . resisted being held accountable for managing results rather than process alone, but on the other, it objected to a proliferation of process-oriented controls. . . . If CIDA could demonstrate that the benefits that accrued from the investments in developing countries were greater that the costs it incurred, one might expect that the pressure for controls on its processes would be lessened, and its ability to innovate would be less constrained.[38]

While controls diverted attention from development to process, other inefficiencies were built into the project cycle, including complex and cumbersome contracting processes. Meanwhile, the "core competence" of CIDA staff had been weakened by the reversal of decentralization, "hands-off" management, and excessive rotation.

The Auditor General called for streamlined management processes and "improvements in staff capability to manage for results, become more adaptive and assume more personal responsibility."[39] More specifically, the "gap between the Agency's broad policy framework for a country and its projects in that country" required "a country-specific strategy linked to an operating plan" that would "focus on specific and measurable results," and allow CIDA "to discuss its operations in a more practical way with its partners and host country officials." Emphasis was needed as well on "more innovative project management skills and practices."[40]

Unimpressed with the sustainability of projects they examined, the auditors kept returning to the imperatives of focusing on development results, rather than process, and of improving results by better management of operating risks and more effective institutionalization of lessons learned. Moreover, "budget constraints . . . make it crucial that CIDA clarify . . . its accountability for achieving results, and "be more forthcoming with full and frank information to the public in Canada and developing countries on what it is trying to achieve and how well it is doing."[41]

The Auditor General's report, released in January 1994, put the Agency back in the public glare when it was still reeling from all the previous year's dislocations. Hugh Winsor of the *Globe and Mail* described the findings as "the portrait of a sick agency."[42]

Managing for results. Rather than reacting defensively (as so often in the past), CIDA drew on the SMR as a springboard for responding to the audit team. Voicing general agreement with the findings, the Agency promised decisive action to make "management of results" a central feature of further reforms.[43]

In the fall of 1993—before the report became public—work on management renewal was reshaped to reflect the Auditor General's concerns. Endorsed by the executive committee in February 1994, the plan for Phase II promised to make "CIDA more results-based, efficient, effective, accountable, and transparent."[44] It included seven main objectives:

- to set clear policy and program directions;
- to establish effective two-way communications and trust between management and staff;
- to improve human resource management policies and practices;
- to implement a results-based management approach;
- to streamline CIDA's decision-making and delivery processes;
- to align operations with the public sector environment and cost reduction; and
- to promote better understanding by the Canadian public of international development cooperation and improvement of CIDA's relationship with stakeholders.[45]

Defined as a three-year exercise, Phase II was worked out in close consultation with the Office of the Auditor General, which agreed to audit progress and report to Parliament in each of 1995, 1996, and 1997. Reflecting an important message from the Secor/SMR process, and from staff dissatisfaction about the way it was handled under Massé, the plan called for all work to be done by internal task forces, without the assistance of outside consultants.[46]

By the time the plan was announced, considerable work had gone into performance review, a new open-bidding system for private-sector service contracting, and consultation.[47] Labelle set the stage for a new standard of openness on information-sharing when she told the Public Accounts Committee in April 1994 that she would "make our evaluations public without being asked."[48] Most of Phase II was only at the conceptual stage, however, and the Auditor General worried that time lines were dauntingly ambitious.[49] As we shall see, efforts on most fronts made little headway until late in 1994.

The 1994-95 Foreign Policy Review

The uproar early in 1993 over the leaked International Assistance Policy Update, and the NGO and media campaign for a full and open review, won sympathetic response from the Liberal opposition. Soon after the leak, Lloyd Axworthy and Christine Stewart—then critics for external affairs and development assistance respectively—"strongly objected to a process which shuts Canadians out of making decisions that can lead to a significant change of policy."[50]

In their election Red Book, *Creating Opportunity: The Liberal Plan for Canada*, the Liberals promised "a comprehensive and public policy review of Canada's foreign aid priorities to ensure that a clear framework is in place for distributing Canadian aid."[51] More broadly, they made commitments to expanding "the rights of Parliament to debate major Canadian foreign policy initiatives . . . and the rights of Canadians to regular and serious consultation on foreign policy issues." The centrepiece of a new consultative process would be a National Forum on Canada's International Relations, drawing parliamentarians together each year with representatives of NGOs and the public "to discuss major issues and directions in Canadian foreign policy."[52]

Although the election campaign ignored foreign affairs (as usual in Canada),[53] the Red Book and a more detailed *Liberal Foreign Policy Handbook*[54] called for a more independent Canadian foreign policy, enhanced multilateralism, and a redefinition of "Canada's security interests to include the emerging issues of environment, population and poverty." Sustainable development was lauded as an overarching principle. On aid, the Liberals castigated the Mulroney administration for budget cuts, a failure to live up to *Sharing Our Future*, and an effort to dismantle CIDA (a reference to the Policy Update proposals). "In contrast to the Conservative government, a Liberal government will not arbitrarily and without prior consultation cut off aid programs to entire regions of the world, such as East Africa, that continue to face desperate poverty and deprivation."[55]

Asserting that "development assistance to the world's poorest fulfils the humanitarian, compassionate side of Canadian society," the *Foreign Policy Handbook* promised a stronger commitment to poverty alleviation through direct human investment—and, reflecting a resolution pushed by Stewart and adopted by the party's policy convention in 1992, an allocation of 25 per cent of ODA to meet basic human needs. It pledged to link aid effectively to promoting human rights and discouraging military expenditures. A Liberal government would also reduce debt for the least-developed, encourage fairer trade agreements, and review international financial institutions and multilateral agencies. All in all, as Cranford Pratt observed, the references to development assistance—"though few and not well integrated"—were "closer to the Winegard Report in spirit and in underlying values than to the main direction of CIDA's policy changes in recent years."[56]

Within days of the Liberal victory, a group of prominent Canadians (including Ed Broadbent, president of ICHRDD, and Flora MacDonald, now chair of IDRC's board) called for a full public review of all aspects of foreign policy.[57] The *Toronto Star* responded favourably: "Entrusted solely to the bureaucracy, foreign policy runs the risk of losing popular support. Enriched by public debate, it would have more enduring foundations. Now is a good time to let Canadians have a say."[58] André Ouellet confirmed immediately that the promised review would take place.[59] Details were revealed in December 1993: it would begin in March with a one-day debate in the House of Commons, followed by the first National Forum on Canada's International Relations, a two-day event; extensive hearings would then be held by a special joint committee of the House of Commons and the Senate, which would complete its work and report within six months.

The foreign minister indicated that subcommittees might be set up on defence and aid, but expressed his conviction that "foreign policy is one whole and this review has to be made globally."[60] To those who hoped that an integrated review would examine the linkages between security and international development, and explore trade-offs between defence and aid spending, it subsequently came as a disappointment to learn that defence-related interests had succeeded in securing a separate joint committee review.[61] In the event, there was little connection between the two reviews, and broader questions about relationships were left dangling.

Extensive Preparations

The foreign policy review was seen in CIDA as an opportunity to gain a more focused mandate at a time of budget cuts. There was also a strong desire to convince MPs that the Agency was serious about improving its effectiveness and accountability. (By early 1994, the Auditor General's recent findings were being examined by two House standing committees.[62])

After the internal review of ODA priorities in the fall of 1993, the minister agreed to publish in June 1994 a list of five "interim programming priorities" to guide allocations, pending the outcome of the foreign policy review.[63]

The first, picking up the Red Book commitment, promised to address basic human needs "by building the human capacity of the poor and responding to emergency situations." The others—full participation of women, democracy/good governance/human rights, private-sector development, and environmental sustainability—reflected the Agency's major policy thrusts during the early 1990s, except for structural adjustment.

Of the priorities set out in *Sharing Our Future* in 1988, only women and environment remained on the interim list. Basic human needs replaced poverty alleviation. Structural adjustment, food security, and energy availability were dropped as explicit priorities, while democracy/good governance/human rights and private-sector development were added.

CIDA's partners get ready for the review. Outside the Agency, preparations were impressive, not least because of activity provoked by the Policy Update controversy. CCIC developed several position papers in close consultation with member NGOs from across the country.[64] Noting that "the traditional notion of military security" had "failed to protect the lives of the vast majority of the world's population," the Council proposed that Canadian foreign policy be based on a new concept of security, defined as "meeting human needs in a just and environmentally sustainable manner."[65] It also called for promotion of human rights in all of Canada's international relations, including trade and investment.

Specifically on aid, CCIC advanced its familiar critique of structural adjustment, and urged that fully 60 per cent of ODA be devoted to sustainable human development and poverty eradication in the poorest countries.[66] Moreover, "*Canada should move away from the norm of a restricted government-to-government framework as a basis for development cooperation*," and involve broader elements of civil society both at home and abroad.[67] CCIC challenged the government to increase to 5 per cent the share of ODA devoted to reaching out and engaging Canadians. It also revived Winegard's recommendations for a national advisory committee and a legislated framework.[68] What it did not address were the implications of fiscal restraint other than in criticisms of cutbacks and broken promises under the Tories.

For its contribution, the North-South Institute published a booklet calling for more effective interdepartmental coordination, and more coherent country strategies to guide all aspects of Canada's North-South relations—including aid, trade, debt, human rights, international migration, environment, and gender equity. Making a plea to concentrate ODA in the poorest countries, the Institute suggested "graduating" the top twelve middle-income countries—except for Thailand and the Philippines, with their substantial numbers of poor. It pushed for further untying, more multilateral assistance, and continued Canadian activism in international agencies. On volume, the

Institute urged—as "more useful than the distant 0.7 percent target"—a restoration of modest, real growth in ODA allocations. It joined CCIC in advocating an advisory council on development.[69]

The Canadian Exporters' Association claimed that business had proven itself since being identified by Winegard as an underutilized resource. Besides seeking more funding for INC, private-sector development funds, and *crédit mixte*, the business lobby regretted that infrastructure programming had been curtailed in recent years. It also argued that Canada lacked the economic and political clout to take effective unilateral action on human rights and environmental standards, thus jeopardizing long-standing economic ties. According to CEA, it was better to work on such issues multilaterally.[70]

The Association of Universities and Colleges of Canada and other educational interests pushed for a continuing priority on human resource development.[71]

The Canada 21 agenda. A major contribution came from the "Canada 21 Council," a group of twenty distinguished business leaders, academics, communicators, and former politicians and public servants. Members with North-South experience included Maurice Strong, Ivan Head, Pierre Trudeau's foreign policy advisor from 1968 to 1978 and president of IDRC from 1978 to 1991, and Tim Brodhead, former president of CCIC. In its report, *Canada and Common Security*, published early in 1994, the group argued that "the distinction between foreign and domestic policy has little meaning" in a post-Cold War world of globalization and growing interdependence. It pushed for a foreign policy rooted in community, civility, and the new common security agenda,[72] and an integration of diplomatic, trade, development, and defence policies.[73]

Canada 21 made several recommendations aimed at making ODA more effective.[74] It suggested that Canada's comparative advantage in development assistance lay not in high technology or heavy infrastructure, but in "the development of social and human capital, and the transfer of knowledge, skills, and technology to address the underlying causes of poverty." "Whenever appropriate," assistance "should be channelled through competent non-governmental organizations (NGOs), universities, colleges, and other associations working in partnership with counterparts in the South and concentrating in areas such as small and micro-business assistance, small-scale agriculture, as well as health care, training and education."[75] The recommendation for more community-to-community and less government-to-government aid was accompanied by an observation that some Canadian NGOs and NGIs spent an "overly large percentage" on organizational, management, and procurement costs; careful monitoring was essential as these organizations "move to the forefront of our assistance programme."[76]

The panel was silent on a positive role for Canadian business—a surprise in view of its "blue ribbon" membership, and the prevailing ideological current in favour of private-sector development and transnational linkages. Instead, it questioned counting as ODA "expenditures that have little to do with what most people regard as assistance to developing nations," and recommended that resources for international assistance be clearly and publicly distinguished from those committed to export development and domestic subsidies.[77]

The report devoted attention to aid management, noting "widespread recognition" that

- CIDA's bureaucracy is cumbersome and slow to respond to new challenges and opportunities;
- CIDA's procedures for the evaluation of the effectiveness of Canadian assistance are unsatisfactory; and
- the Government's budgetary process does not produce understandable records of where Canadian aid is allocated.[78]

Urgent action was needed to rectify these deficiencies.

On the larger question of achieving greater coherence and coordination of North-South policies, Agenda 21 regretted the

> continued segregation of assistance programmes within the policy-making apparatus . . . [and] recommends . . . that an appropriate institutional arrangement be created . . . at the highest levels of policy making, to ensure that the management of Canada's policies toward the South is integrated and coordinated with the broader set of political, financial and military instruments we use to build common security."[79]

Although the group identified Canada's primary domestic task as "getting its own economic house in order," it recommended against any further cuts in the ODA ratio.[80]

The National Forum and the government's "Guidance Paper." The National Forum on Canada's International Relations was held in Ottawa on March 21-22, 1994. Janice Gross Stein of the University of Toronto, project director for Canada 21, was co-chair, and the group's *Canada and Common Security* was among documents circulated. Her co-chair was Pierre Pettigrew—business consultant, Liberal activist, and, for a short time, future minister responsible for CIDA.

The government made available a "Guidance Paper," which asked that views set out in the Red Book and the *Foreign Policy Handbook* be considered, along with "choices the Government will have to make given its overall commitments to job-creating economic growth and responsible fiscal management." It suggested a revised conception of security reflecting sustainable development, and support for democracy and human rights. On development assistance, the paper called for "more balanced, comprehensive policies," aimed at channelling a significant portion of ODA to "direct human investment, basic human needs and environmental sustainability."[81] While trade was emphasized in regional priorities for Latin America and Asia Pacific, the task in Africa was seen as addressing gross economic disparities and social needs.[82]

The two-day forum—which included a plenary session with Chrétien and Ouellet—was too short for disparate voices to articulate concerns, let alone achieve consensus. Although participants talked about the need for hard choices, MPs and observers were unimpressed by the "shapelessness" of much of the discussion.[83] Among generalities in the co-chairs' report, however, was a firm statement that "assistance to the poor is a fundamental priority of Canadian policy." The government was urged to open Canadian markets to developing country exports and "enhanced, reciprocal trading relationships"—but, echoing Canada 21 and long-standing pleas from the development community, the report called for a separation of trade promotion from assistance programs.[84]

The Parliamentary Review

The Special Joint Committee Reviewing Canadian Foreign Policy (SJC-CFP) was chaired by Senator Allan MacEachen, Trudeau's former secretary of state for External Affairs, and Jean-Robert Gauthier, chair of the (renamed) House of Commons Standing Committee on Foreign Affairs and International Trade (SCFAIT). It consisted of nine Liberal MPs, three representatives from each of the Bloc Québécois and the Reform Party (the new populist opposition forces in the Commons), and seven Senators (four Conservatives and three Liberals). Lloyd Axworthy and Christine Stewart were now ministers, and none of the SJC-CFP members had been key participants in the production of the *Liberal Foreign Policy Handbook*. (Michael Pearson—Lester's grandson—who had been heavily involved in its preparation as a member of the Liberal research office, monitored the process closely from his new vantage point as Ouellet's senior policy adviser.)

Amid considerable inexperience, MacEachen emerged as the dominant figure. Apart from urging a more vigorous projection of Canadian culture abroad, however, he was more inclined to defend established positions than to chart bold new directions.[85] Without champions for change, and prompted essentially by the Liberals' commitment to democratize foreign policy-making, the review, as Gerald Schmitz observed, was "more process-driven and uncertain of its destination" than its predecessors in the mid-1980s.[86]

It was also more hurried and disjointed. Operating under instructions to report in October 1994, the SJC-CFP began with round-table discussions on selected themes involving invited witnesses. Like the National Forum, these sessions were broad in scope and did not sharpen issues for the parliamentarians.[87] At the end of May, the SJC-CFP divided into three panels, which heard separate testimony from various parts of the country and later took brief trips to Washington, New York, and Brussels.

The full committee did not reassemble until September, by which time there were hundreds of briefs and presentations to digest and little opportunity to develop a comprehensive and coherent consensus. A 200-page summary by SJC-CFP staff (the "Issues Papers") attempted to provide an overview and raise key questions, additional perspectives emerged from four contracted experts (the "Position Papers"), and still different writers were brought in to draft the final report.[88] Parts of that report, released on November 15, were in turn contested by the Bloc Québécois and the Reform Party.

Briefs and testimony. Like Hockin-Simard in 1985-86, the SJC-CFP was inundated with submissions dealing with North-South issues. Of 561 briefs, 277 came from NGOs, most voicing development concerns and supporting positions adopted during CCIC's consultation process. Surprisingly few environmental NGOs participated. As in earlier reviews, the business sector was less well represented but several of its forty-nine submissions dealt with CIDA's policies and funding practices. Altogether, more than 550 individuals and organizations appeared before the committee or one of its panels.[89]

Extensive NGO involvement emerged as a controversial issue. In its minority report, the Reform Party complained about the absence of participation from "grassroots" (of a rather different character from the community groups that testified):

> Unlike special interest groups, non-governmental organizations and academics which can mobilize presentations for committees on short notice, grassroots Canadians have a very difficult time participating in such a process. Often Canadians are unaware that they even have the opportunity to participate until it is too late. . . . [The] Reform Party Members of the Committee are convinced that an even better report would have resulted from greater participation by the Canadian grassroots.[90]

Although the committee's majority did not challenge the legitimacy of NGO participation, the sheer number of groups testifying raised for some members the question of whether CIDA was supporting too many organizations and diverting funds for development into excessive Canadian overheads. There were also concerns about the breadth of community support for some groups and the dearth of young people among their representatives.[91]

While most MPs and Senators were impressed with the professionalism of NGO presentations (if often bored by their repetitive messages), Liberal members in particular were taken aback by the vehemence with which a few participants attacked not just aid policies and performance, but also CIDA and its officers. At a panel hearing in Halifax, John English, MP for Kitchener,[92] commented: "I'm just wondering how helpful this is to NGOs. . . . [It] seems to me your form of argument is not likely to contribute to your overall goal, which is stronger Canadian support for development assistance. In other words, it seems to me that you're almost killing the messenger."[93] Gauthier expressed similar concerns from the chair[94] and, in Saskatoon, MacEachen reflected his exasperation by commenting that "CIDA can only take so much whiplashing before it disappears."[95]

The Report of the Special Joint Committee

Broadly speaking, as authors of the "Issues Papers" observed, "two alternative visions of Canadian foreign policy" emerged in briefs and testimony—a "Global Market agenda" and a "Global Commons agenda."

> The bottom line is that there are major differences between the two agendas: one is focused on international trade and Canada's economic competitiveness, the other on global security and the problem of world poverty. The tensions between the two become apparent when it comes to policies regarding trade and international assistance. . . . The question arises, is it possible to make a convincing merger of the two agendas?[96]

The SJC-CFP tackled that question, less through creative synthesis than by remaining inconclusive—a reflection of the difficulty of resolving contradictions, the hurried process, and the government's wish to maintain ample freedom to manoeuvre.[97]

The chapter on international assistance was more sharply focused than most of the report, partly because the committee deferred to the "global commons agenda" on most issues. Defining the aid program as an expression of the values and ideals of Canadians ("the bright side of our national character"), and a contribution to common security, the text declared that "Canadian development assistance is a source of national pride and enjoys general public support." Nevertheless, NGOs and other critics had "found CIDA to be excessively bureaucratic and plodding; to be promoting structural adjustment policies that seemed to hurt the poor; to be confusing development objectives with Canada's trade interests; and to be straying far from the stated objectives of the aid program."[98]

Observing that "if reorganization were the solution, CIDA would have been saved many times over," the report urged six practical steps: clarify the mandate, distinguish between aid and trade, reform conditionality, target assistance, improve results, and maintain support.[99]

Clarify the mandate. In the tradition of the Breau, Hockin-Simard, and Winegard committees, the MacEachen-Gauthier report declared that "the primary purpose of Canadian Official Development Assistance is to reduce poverty by providing effective assistance to the poorest people, in those countries that most need and can use our help."[100]

> As repeated public opinion polls have shown, the self-interested justifications for aid (e.g. trade promotion) have never cut much ice with Canadians. Help for those most in need expresses the basic moral vision of aid and corresponds closely to what the vast majority of Canadians think development assistance is all about.

Like its predecessors, the SJC-CFP endorsed a conception of development close to that of the NGO community—a focus on human potential and well-being that is self-sustaining, helps people to help themselves, and involves "a true partnership based on local consensus."[101]

As for areas of special emphasis, the committee was essentially content to back CIDA's interim priorities—basic human needs, human rights/good governance/democratic development, the participation of women,[102] environmental sustainability, and private-sector development. Following Liberal policy, the recommendation on basic human needs called for a minimum allocation of 25 per cent of ODA, "compared to the current total of less than 20%."[103] A sixth priority was added to the Agency's list—public participation, defined as "an essential element in mobilizing a Canadian capacity and commitment to international development."[104]

Agreeing with Winegard and CCIC's submission, the SJC-CFP recommended legislation spelling out the basic principles and program priorities of Canada's development assistance. A legislated mandate would hold CIDA to account, protect "Canadian ODA from random and wayward influences," and provide "stability which comes from knowing that the basic challenges will last beyond the 'fall or spring catalogue.' " Although the report quoted approvingly from the ODA Charter, it did not suggest explicitly that Winegard's principles be enshrined in the proposed legislation. Nor did it favour a national advisory committee, preferring instead to see regular reviews of CIDA and the aid program by SCFAIT and the Senate Foreign Affairs Committee, which would "engage as many Canadians as possible."[105]

Distinguish between aid and trade. In view of testimony claiming that INC "had become little more than a trade promotion program for Canadian exports . . . the Committee is convinced that it is necessary once again to affirm that the purpose of the Canadian aid program is *not* to promote Canadian trade." Accordingly, it recommended (in agreement with Canada 21) "that any functions of CIDA found to be essentially Canadian trade promotion activities" be transferred to DFAIT or EDC "where they belong." The text rather confusingly asserted as well "it is entirely appropriate for the CIDA private sector development program . . . to encourage trading relations with Canada." (Presumably, the intent was to emphasize expanded trade with Canada that promoted development in recipient countries.)[106]

Rehearsing the debate on tied aid, MacEachen-Gauthier observed that unilateral untying would probably lead to Canadian assistance flowing to companies and experts in other rich countries—"a result Canadians would not accept, to put it mildly." Greater untying was best pursued jointly with other donors; the government was urged to work through DAC to lower the tied share of OECD aid to 20 per cent by the year 2000.[107]

Reform conditionality. The report noted contradictory evidence about the effectiveness of structural adjustment programs, as well as the intensity of NGO criticisms of CIDA's role in supporting them. While concluding that "sound economic policies really do matter," the committee recommended "that, in supporting structural adjustment programs, CIDA should pay special attention to their effects on the poor and to the provision of assistance to protect vulnerable groups." It agreed as well with the North-South Institute that Canada should urge the donor community to adopt poverty reduction as a central objective of structural adjustment, not just a compensatory concern. Support was also voiced for making Canadian ODA conditional upon a "reduction in excessive military expenditures" and "increased transparency of government operations."[108]

Devoting less attention to human rights than Hockin-Simard or Winegard, MacEachen-Gauthier urged that human rights/democratic development/good governance be central in Canadian foreign policy and, when bilateral aid was terminated, that poor and vulnerable groups continue to receive assistance channelled through NGOs. The committee echoed business representatives in stressing the desirability of multilateral, rather than unilateral efforts in response to serious violations of rights.[109]

Target assistance. The report pushed several familiar buttons in addressing geographical eligibility and concentration. Observing that Canadian ODA is more dispersed than the OECD average, it called on CIDA "to identify its comparative advantages better and to strive for excellence in a smaller number of areas." In doing so, the Agency "should be guided first and foremost by its mandate of helping the poorest people." The report asked that the current high share for Africa be maintained and, in view of Asia's increasing prosperity, "there may be a case for reducing the share of Canadian assistance going to that part of the world." The "enormous contrasts between rich and poor" throughout the Americas "may offer the greatest potential for refocusing policy reform on poverty reduction."[110]

In discussing geographical priorities, the committee did not address declining resources in the International Assistance Envelope. Nor did it when recommending maintenance of programs of assistance for Central and Eastern Europe and the former Soviet Union—but "not at the expense of ODA priorities." With respect to another new trend—the growth of emergency assistance in response to escalating human conflict—the report suggested a need for eligibility criteria "to ensure that long-term development assistance remains the primary focus of the aid program."[111] A similar concern was apparent in a call for further action to alleviate the debt crisis of the poorest countries, though "not at the expense of funds for long-term development aid."[112]

Improve results. While the SJC-CFP suggested that a poverty-oriented mandate was the most important requirement for promoting effective aid, it cited CIDA's relationship with its partners as another area needing improvement. MPs' scepticism about the number of NGOs and NGIs receiving CIDA support surfaced in a comment that "a point of diminishing returns may have been reached." The report quoted CARE Canada's criticism of CIDA's funding system as preserving "a relationship which has clearly crossed the line separating valuable diversity and distinctiveness from the destructive effects of fragmentation and dispersion." Concerns were expressed about inadequate evaluations of voluntary-sector performance and the apparent lack of popular support for some organizations. Nevertheless, the committee recommended that the share of partnership programs be maintained—"and even increased"—where partners have a strong Canadian support base and "a clearly demonstrated record of effectiveness and efficiency."[113]

In the multilateral domain, the report flagged issues of performance and dispersion. It pushed for closer parliamentary oversight of international financial institutions, as well as efforts to make their operations "more efficient, transparent, accountable and responsive to issues of human rights, social equity, environmental sustainability and public input."[114]

MacEachen-Gauthier lamented that adding "layer upon layer of red tape to ensure that monies are spent properly" had not demonstrably translated into improved results. A stronger role for parliamentary committees in monitoring aid effectiveness was suggested as a better way of strengthening aid performance.[115]

Maintain support. Most of the aid chapter, and indeed the report as a whole, failed to focus sufficiently on the implications of expenditure cutbacks and continued pressure for deficit reduction. It is true that concern about widespread dispersal among countries, Canadian partners, and multilateral agencies reflected a judgement that the "crisis of runaway national debt" required "CIDA to bear down and concentrate its limited resources in the most effective ways possible."[116] However, the SJC-CFP offered only vague and general advice on choices and how to make them.

At the same time, the committee made a positive but, in the prevailing ideological climate, futile gesture on fiscal support for ODA. In contrast to the "Issues Papers," which reviewed a number of options (including a resource transfer from military spending),[117] the report called for stabilizing ODA at the present GNP ratio. While that recommendation implied annual increases of 2 to 3 per cent (in line with GNP growth), the report offered no suggestions about how to exempt ODA—or how to rationalize exempting it—from the substantial expenditure reductions to which the government was committed. A recommendation that progress towards the 0.7 per cent target be made "when Canada's fiscal situation permits" was devoid of operational significance.[118]

Dissenting opinions. Both the Bloc Québécois and the Reform Party issued minority reports, breaking the non-partisan consensus on foreign policy that had prevailed since the contentious Subcommittee on Latin America and the Caribbean in 1981-82. While the Bloc's dissent focused chiefly on jurisdictional issues involving Ottawa-Quebec City relations (actual and potential), it criticized the majority report for a soft line on democracy and human rights, and insufficient emphasis on poverty, basic needs, and sustainable human development. It urged a tougher legislated mandate that "would relieve CIDA of some of the pressure and lobbying efforts which too often divert its attention away from its primary objectives." Decrying cutbacks, the Bloc supported movement towards the 0.7 per cent target as soon as possible.[119]

Besides questioning the representativeness of testimony, the Reform Party attacked the majority for a lack of fiscal responsibility in not urging that bilateral and multilateral both be cut. It also called for a "true legislative mandate" for CIDA, rather than a legislated statement of principles that would merely perpetuate the use of the Agency's $2 billion budget "as a slush fund into which the minister can dip whenever he wants." In an ironic inversion of majority's intent (but in keeping with some business opinion[120]), Reform supported removal of INC from CIDA on grounds "that CIDA is not well placed to do the job."[121]

Media and other commentary. The report was published on November 15, during Prime Minister Chrétien's "Team Canada" trade mission to China and Southeast Asia with provincial premiers and several business leaders. That provided a context for flagging the committee's concerns about human rights. Recommendations for more vigorous promotion of Canadian culture and trade diversification also received attention, as did some specific recommendations on aid.[122] However, MacEachen-Gauthier generated less media attention than either Hockin-Simard or Winegard in the 1980s. The *Globe and*

Mail called the report "tepid and vague. . . . While recognizing the reasons for recasting foreign policy, such as common security and financial constraint, it drowns them in a consommé of clichés and a gruel of déjà vu."[123] Déjà vu was apt for the aid recommendations, which really did little more than recycle the views of Winegard and earlier parliamentary reviews. There were nods to fresh thinking on common security, human development, and civil society, but little sense of connection with new ideas or changing circumstances.

CCIC criticized the absence of a comprehensive framework for Canada's international relations and gave the ODA recommendations a mixed review.[124] Cranford Pratt, who liked the anti-poverty emphasis of the aid chapter, observed that it "lacks the intellectual authority of the Winegard report."[125] Clyde Sanger of the North-South Institute criticized the report's unevenness and its failure to apply convincingly its own recommendation to make sustainable development an overarching foreign policy theme. Observing that the section on international assistance was clearer than the rest of the document, he suggested that the overall incoherence and neglect of fiscal implications meant that André Ouellet had "a big task (and a fairly free hand)" in developing a response, and that Finance Minister Paul Martin "need not feel constrained . . . ahead of his budget in February."[126]

The Government's Response and White Paper[127]

The generality of the committee's report did indeed give the government considerable room for manoeuvre. Meanwhile, Ouellet had conducted his own extensive soundings, and senior officials responsible for drafting a reply to MacEachen-Gauthier already knew where the minister stood on key issues.

The official response and a white paper, *Canada in the World*, were published in February 1995. They presented a more coherent vision of Canadian foreign policy than the SJC-CFP, though one more consistently attuned to the global market agenda. The "key objectives" of Canadian foreign policy were defined as:

- The promotion of prosperity and employment;
- The protection of our security, within a stable global framework; and
- The projection of Canadian values and culture.[128]

Considerable emphasis was put on integrating foreign policy to make these objectives "the focus for the full span of the Government's instruments, including the programs of international trade, diplomacy, and international assistance."[129] It was a clear message that ODA was subordinate to foreign policy and expected to serve objectives that essentially updated the old "trinity" to reflect preoccupations of the 1990s.

The rest of the aid chapter, drafted initially in CIDA's Policy Branch, sought to balance positive responses to the committee with sufficient open-endedness to avoid creating hostages for future criticism of the sort that bedeviled *Sharing Our Future*.[130] "Key commitments" were made to "a clear mandate and set of priorities, strengthened development partnerships, improved effectiveness, and better reporting to Canadians."[131]

Mandate, Priorities, and Scope

The government agreed with MacEachen-Gauthier that an effective aid program must focus on sustainability, human development, and poverty reduction and that it must involve a wide range of partnerships with Canadians, international organizations, and "most importantly, with the people and institutions of the developing world."

However, while the Conservatives had declared help for the poorest countries and people as *the* primary purpose of Canadian ODA—and then often condoned contradictory priorities—the Liberal government adopted a refashioned statement of purpose that promised "to support sustainable development in developing countries, in order to reduce poverty and to contribute to a more secure, equitable and prosperous world."[132] The rationale for aid was thus as broad as the foreign policy objectives (reiterated in a different order). While there was no explicit mention of the needs of the poorest countries, the government did at least flag poverty reduction as an explicit objective, and promise that CIDA's forthcoming policy on poverty reduction would guide programming in all priority areas.[133]

Programming priorities. Five of the preferences expressed by the Special Joint committee were adopted in *Canada in the World*—basic human needs, women in development, human rights/democracy/good governance, private-sector development, and the environment. The government also agreed to channel 25 per cent of ODA to basic human needs but dropped the reference to this as a "minimum" allocation. These five were, of course, CIDA's interim priorities of June 1994. The only one added by the committee—public participation—was rejected, allegedly on grounds that it was integral to the others.[134]

The government substituted "infrastructure services" as a sixth priority, reflecting Ouellet's wishes to deflect business complaints about declining CIDA resources in this area. The initiative was further legitimated by the World Bank, which had recently called for renewed emphasis on infrastructure, especially on providing services that are efficient, environmentally friendly, and responsive to users' needs.[135] *Canada in the World* and subsequent statements made it clear that, largely for financial reasons, this new priority would not restore CIDA support for mega-projects; rather, the stress would be on maintenance, capacity-building, and the interests of "poorer groups."[136] Still, there was the prospect of a significant new role for private-sector expertise, especially, as Martin Rudner observed, in providing "those capabilities in technology and technical expertise that Canadians envisaged as their strategic niches in the emergent knowledge-based economy."[137] Many in the Agency welcomed opportunities to rebuild business support for the aid program and, at a time of budget cuts, to demonstrate new ways in which ODA could support the government's prosperity and employment objectives.[138]

Structural adjustment, already dropped from CIDA's interim priorities, was not reinstated. While policy reform was embedded in official conceptions of sustainable development, private-sector development, and governance, an interdepartmental consensus now favoured reducing financial support for adjustment programming. Prompted by declining budgetary resources and a recognition that Massé's notion of a "high policy" role for Canada was unworkable, the new posture also reflected the Agency's desire to dampen controversy that had damaged relations with NGOs.[139]

An August 1994 CIDA policy paper had already stated that balance of payments support would be made available only in exceptional circumstances. Instead, the Agency's emphasis in supporting economic reforms would "be on the sectors and institutions . . . that are key to poverty reduction and sustainable development. . . . Given CIDA's experience and existing Canadian expertise, the potential that exists to exert influence and add value to the reform process is not in 'gap-filling' exercises but at the sectoral level." The paper urged as well that issues of political sensitivity, poverty, gender, the environment, and human rights be better incorporated in Canada's support for economic reform.[140] In turn, the official response to MacEachen-Gauthier promised to work towards these ends with international agencies, developing countries, and affected groups. It also agreed that excessive military spending and transparency in government operations were relevant factors to consider when making ODA allocations.[141]

A softer line on human rights. In their covering letter introducing *Canada in the World*, Ouellet and International Trade Minister Roy MacLaren declared that respect for human rights was "not only a fundamental value . . . but also a crucial element in the development of democratic societies at peace with each other." They indicated, however, that the Liberal government would be more cautious than the Mulroney adminstration in taking action on human rights violations:

> Our ultimate aim is not to punish countries and innocent populations whose governments abuse human rights but rather to change behaviour and to induce governments to respect their peoples' rights. Responses to specific situations require careful balancing of many considerations, *above all* the effectiveness of the means of influence at our disposal.

Affirming a commitment to ICHRDD and CIDA-funded programming to promote human rights/democracy/good governance, the ministers suggested that "punitive bilateral action in isolation from other countries . . . usually presents the least effective means of achieving results. In the case of trade, it may hurt Canada more than it will change the behaviour of offending governments." They promised that "Canada will continue to lead on human rights issues," but that efforts would be channelled much more through multilateral fora.[142]

Legislated mandate rejected. Like its Conservative predecessor, the government refused to consider a legislated mandate for Canadian ODA, arguing that it would "limit the range of responses that might be required to meet fast-changing conditions in developing countries."[143] In welcoming an enhanced parliamentary role, the official response promised a more consultative foreign policy-making process that would feature an annual National Forum on Canada's International Relations.[144]

No commitments on volume or concentration. The mandate section also touched on aid volume and distribution. A toothless promise to progress towards the 0.7 per cent target, "when Canada's fiscal situation allows it," accompanied a rejection of the committee's call for a stabilization of funding at the current ratio.[145] (The response was published just days before Finance Minister Martin's 1995 budget revealed the biggest cut ever in aid spending.)

On geographical allocations, there was a sharp contrast between the detailed percentage pledges of *Sharing Our Future* and the vagueness of *Canada in the World*, which promised only that most aid would go to low-income countries. Although there was no indication of intent to lower Africa's share, a pledge merely to keep it "highest" hypothetically permitted a drop from 45 per cent—the policy endorsed by MacEachen-Gauthier—to just over a third. The long-standing commitment to 0.15 per cent of GNP for LLDCs was quietly dropped. The possibility of a higher share for the Americas was flagged in a reference to the "growing importance to Canada of our relations with our own hemisphere."[146]

The Liberals' opposition to the East and Central African cuts, together with Ouellet's preference for flying the Canadian flag everywhere, were reflected in this response to the committee's call for greater concentration: "The Government agrees that the effectiveness of ODA can be enhanced by concentrating on a more limited number of priorities and achieving greater targeting and co-ordination of assistance. Canada does, however, have important interests in all areas of the world."[147] The white paper thus essentially rejected geographical concentration.[148] Already in 1994, the Liberal government had declared post-apartheid South Africa eligible for all forms of Canadian aid,[149] and—after a sixteen-year hiatus—had restored aid programming in Cuba.[150] Christine Stewart visited Tanzania in 1995 to mark the "relaunching" of Canadian bilateral ODA in that country.[151] All were praiseworthy decisions, but CIDA did not pull back from other countries to accommodate this renewed expansion.

The government agreed to maintain an active program of assistance to Central and Eastern Europe and the former Soviet Union that would not be funded "at the expense of ODA priorities" (the same wording used by the SJC-CFP, which used a weaker formulation than was perhaps intended). Of particular significance to CIDA was a decision to transfer program delivery from DFAIT to the Agency, with responsibility for policy direction staying with the department. In making this change, the government indicated that the ODA mandate would not apply to the region (except for those former Soviet republics that were ODA-eligible). Instead, the main objectives were security and prosperity.[152] The Countries in Transition program moved to CIDA in a new Central and Eastern Europe Branch in April 1995.

On other concerns, the government gave assurances that emergency assistance and debt relief measures would not come at the expense of long-term development assistance. It also promised to focus more on emergency prevention and preparedness.[153]

The white paper was silent on tied aid, and the official response was unyielding: "current untying authorities, carefully applied, provide CIDA with sufficient flexibility and do not impede programming effectiveness."[154] Subsequently, the Liberal government resisted efforts to ease tying regulations that were spearheaded in DAC by Japan and the Netherlands.[155]

Strengthened Partnerships

Ouellet and MacLaren were adamantly opposed to shifting the Industrial Cooperation Program out of CIDA: INC provided a convenient source of patronage for international business ventures that would be a much easier target for budget-cutting outside the ODA component of the funding envelope.[156] Accordingly, the government declared that the program offered "a unique opportunity for the Canadian private sector to contribute to poverty reduction and sustainable development" and that the participation of Canadian companies generated significant benefits for the private sector in developing countries. Claiming that INC was well regarded by recipient countries and other donors, the official response promised to sharpen the developmental focus of the program, a tacit acceptance of complaints that it was mainly a vehicle for trade promotion.

At the same time—partly in reply to criticisms from business and the Reform Party—greater coordination was pledged among DFAIT, CIDA, EDC, and other departments, including regular project-by-project consultations on INC's activities.[157] Since these other agencies do not have a mandate to promote international development, this recommendation appeared to contradict the commitment to sharpen the developmental focus.[158]

In response to the SJC-CFP's call to maintain or increase funding shares of partnership programs, the government telegraphed its intention to make tough decisions in a "severe budgetary situation," promising to give preference "to those partners who demonstrate the most effectiveness and efficiency." While informing NGOs and NGIs that they would be expected to conform to CIDA's programming priorities,[159] the white paper promised efforts to develop a "renewed relationship between CIDA and Canadian voluntary organizations based on the principle of complementarity of action."[160]

The official position on international partners was in tune with MacEachen-Gauthier, pledging reform that helps to

- better integrate objectives such as respect for human rights, poverty reduction, social and gender equity, and environment into the work of multilateral institutions;
- improve coordination among multilateral institutions;
- increase accountability and transparency; and
- improve developmental and cost effectiveness.[161]

Criticism of excessive preoccupation with domestic interests, to the exclusion of aid recipients, was met with promises to "work with developing countries and their people to help them participate more fully in the international system and global economy; and establish new ways to build longer-term linkages between Canadians and developing country partners to enhance their self-reliance."[162]

Improved Effectiveness

Similar rhetorical sensitivity was apparent in new Guidelines for Effective Programming to ensure that programming is based on:

- *Developing country needs and participation:* by responding to the needs and priorities of developing country partners and placing a strong emphasis on local participation and ownership in all stages of programming.
- *Knowledge of the context:* by basing program design on a thorough knowledge of local conditions and by drawing on the lessons learned, in order to inform policies and ongoing programming.

- *Promoting self-sustaining activities:* by focusing on achieving results that will continue to provide benefits to local citizens and sustain local support after Canadian support ends.
- *Coordination with others:* by working with developing country governments and institutions, international organizations and development agencies to coordinate efforts more effectively.
- *Drawing on Canadian capacity:* by strengthening cooperation with Canadians to ensure that Canadian know-how is put to work for the benefit of developing countries in activities where Canada has a clear comparative advantage.[163]

Policy coherence. The government pledged to integrate more effectively "the foreign policy instruments pertaining to developing countries."[164] The committee's plea for a further opening of Canadian markets to imports from developing countries met cautious endorsement.[165] The white paper also announced creation in DFAIT of a Bureau of Global Issues "to bring greater coherence to the Government's capacity to address internationally such issues as the global environment, population growth, international migration (including refugee issues), international crime, human rights, democratization, preventive diplomacy and post-conflict peacebuilding."[166]

Of greater significance for the aid program was a decision to establish a joint DFAIT-CIDA committee, chaired by the deputy minister of Foreign Affairs, "to oversee systematic policy coordination between the two organizations."[167] Justified as a way of ensuring "the greatest possible coherence and synergy," creation of this committee reflected Ouellet's determination to contain interdepartmental conflict and subordinate the aid program to foreign policy priorities.

Demonstrating Results

Turning to accountability and transparency, the government promised that efforts to make the aid program more effective would be accompanied by better communication of results to Canadians. CIDA's agreement with the Auditor General to move to results-based management, although not mentioned explicitly, was revealed in a commitment to "ensure that results can be demonstrated by establishing clear objectives for programs and projects and by specifying realistic results that are linked to program priorities." Reporting to Parliament and the public would be improved through revisions to Part III of the *Estimates* and more open access to evaluation results and CIDA's summaries of lessons learned.[168]

In contrast to official responses to Breau and Winegard, *Canada in the World* paid scant attention to established forms of public outreach. Less than a sentence confirmed "support for programs which build development awareness and provide Canadians with information on Canada's development activities."[169]

The Immediate Aftermath

Press coverage of the official response and the white paper focused on the government's preoccupation with trade, and speculated that aid would be cut back further in the forthcoming budget; "more trade, less aid" was how the *Toronto Star* sized up the situation.[170] "So long, Dudley Do-right," quipped the *Gazette* (Montreal) in observing that the new foreign policy reflected "self-interests of the '90s."[171] The *Globe and Mail*, in welcoming the priority on the trade promotion, cautioned that "we must strive to preserve that sense of generosity and compassion which has long animated our role in the world." It regretted the absence of a commitment on concentration and the refusal to make aid more distinct from trade.[172]

CCIC criticized what it saw as an agenda mostly geared to promoting prosperity and employment, especially in Canada. While pleased about "the commendable commitment to a values-based foreign policy," it lamented the relegation of values to a third objective that "emphasizes the projection of *Canadian* values internationally, rather than a promotion of the cross cultural dimensions in building cooperative and *global* citizenship for sustainable development."[173] It also condemned backsliding on human rights.[174] Particular concern was voiced about the exclusion of public participation from the list of program priorities, "a move which could affect the future of development education work (as budget priorities are . . . based on [program] priorities)."[175] The fallout from the 1995 budget, brought down three weeks after publication of *Canada in the World*, revealed this to be a well-grounded fear.

An Assessment

In comparison with the Tories' *Sharing Our Future*, the 1995 Liberal policy (1) shied away from declaring the primacy of development, (2) projected less clarity about the priority assigned to poverty alleviation and the human side of development, (3) advanced a weaker position on human rights, (4) offered no further concessions on untying, and (5) downplayed public outreach. Moreover, unlike the Conservatives, who were still committed in 1988 to an increasing ODA/GNP ratio, the Liberals were not even prepared to maintain the existing volume of Canadian development assistance. *Canada in the World* also jettisoned efforts to achieve geographical concentration.

However, many of the central premises and commitments in *Sharing Our Future*, such as decentralization of CIDA and numerous quantitative targets, had soon been breached in practice and formal policy alike. Both politicians and senior officials in the Agency and External Affairs had paid a price in credibility and morale. For those held accountable, the new aid policies in *Canada in the World* were much safer—and a more honest statement of the reality, however lamentable, of multiple and often conflicting ODA objectives. The new mission statement was, as Pratt observed: "of such wide generality that it would cover almost any aid program desired by DFAIT."[176] Indeed, Pratt, concerned as always about "self-serving trade and foreign policy objectives" undermining an aid program that ought to be based on humane internationalism, offered the "severe judgment" that the government's response and *Canada in the World* "seem firmly to deny primacy to CIDA's humanitarian objective. Instead [the Chrétien government] legitimates and indeed requires that CIDA also pursue commercial and foreign policy objectives."[177]

The six program priorities in *Canada in the World* conveyed an impression of specificity and clearly defined focal points for the program. Taken together, however, they also offered such broad scope for programming that, to quote one senior official, "you can drive a truck through them." The virtual absence of quantitative targets made it prospectively much harder to criticize the government for "a gap between rhetoric and reality." Even the one significant exception—the commitment to channel 25 per cent of Canadian ODA to basic human needs—was open to fudging (as we shall see), so that it could be celebrated as an achievement, rather than a goal to be pursued.

While the government's claims about a clear mandate invited cynicism, there were nonetheless other commitments in the white paper that could make Canadian development assistance more effective. The Guidelines for Effective Programming might prove as impotent as the short-lived ODA Charter—but, though open to interpretation, they were operationally focused and they established bench-marks for evaluating and criticizing future performance. As with the commitment to results-based management, action to forge effective links between formal policies and field operations, historically a major weakness for CIDA, could also yield important developmental dividends. Strong statements about working *with* developing countries and their people and emphasizing local participation and ownership were encouraging, though, as Rudner suggested, the domestically driven agenda in *Canada in the World* might lead some in the developing world to see a "presumption of 'cultural supremacy' that neither Canadian aid officials or activists would probably admit even to themselves."[178]

CIDA's accountability to Parliament and the Canadian public could also be strengthened. Despite the Agency's traditional defensiveness and horror-story paranoia, it acted quickly to implement the pledge to open up access to evaluations and summaries of lessons learned. This move, together with improved reporting to Parliament, could lead in time to better evaluation and feedback—and, though there are risks, to a more mature and confident relationship with parliamentarians, the media, and members of the public.

CCIC and other critics saw the government's determination to stress ODA as an instrument of foreign policy, and to create a closer working relationship between CIDA and Foreign Affairs, as evidence of a further weakening of developmental integrity. When Pratt testified before the SJC-CFP in the summer of 1994, he had argued against Canada 21's recommendation for a fuller integration of the Agency within the foreign policy decision-making process:

> past experience strongly suggests that unless CIDA's primary mandate to reach and help the poorest peoples and countries is carefully and especially safeguarded, whatever the public rhetoric, CIDA would be unable to resist the pressures, which experience has shown are irresistible, from within and outside government to promote more immediate commercial and foreign policy objectives, resulting in the situation that your predecessor, the Winegard committee, in the very first line of its report identified CIDA as being beset by a confusion of purpose.[179]

The history of interdepartmental relations suggests, however, that every effort to enhance CIDA's autonomy (under Strong, Gérin-Lajoie, and Massé) provoked a strong reaction, aimed at putting the Agency under the thumb of External/Foreign Affairs and harnessing aid more fully to commercial and foreign policy priorities. Moreover, although PGL's *Strategy for International Development Cooperation 1975-1980* and *Sharing Our Future* reflected interdepartmental compromises, both were seen (incorrectly in view of cabinet approval) as CIDA's policy documents, not the government's. As such, they became targets for whittling away by bureaucratic interests outside CIDA, often with support from disenchanted elements within the Agency.

While CIDA's policy wings were clipped once more, *Canada in the World* at least gave senior Agency officials an opportunity to argue a developmental case based on a policy carrying the imprimatur of senior ministers and DFAIT. And, for all its deficiencies, the Liberal document was more focused on poverty reduction and developmental priorities than the 1992 leaked Policy Update. Many of CIDA's managers were cautiously optimistic after the review about having regained lost ground for development.

CIDA Adjusts to a New Era

Earlier budget cuts, together with concerns about CIDA's effectiveness and accountability, led to the 1990 decision to undertake the strategic management review. By early 1998, it seemed that experience might finally yield positive results for the Agency, its staff, and the people it served. Along the way, there were several more ups and downs after Jocelyne Bourgon rescued the renewal process in 1993, and Huguette Labelle launched Phase II early in 1994.

One objective was partially realized with publication of *CIDA's Policy for Performance Review* in July 1994. It sketched a framework for performance assessment at the branch level, and internal audit and evaluation at the corporate level, emphasizing as well the importance of external reporting. Earlier policies were criticized for using audit and evaluation "as surveillance and control functions, rather than for knowledge building and improved decision-making and overall performance." The new policy promised that CIDA's "defensive culture with respect to performance review" would give way to greater openness.[180] A three-year performance review plan was subsequently put in place.[181]

In August 1994, the Agency unveiled open bidding proposals for private-sector contracting. Aimed at sourcing contracts over $100,000 in a way that was simpler and more transparent (at least up to the level of ministerial discretion over short-listing), the new process replaced the previous in-house list of suppliers with competitive bids for prequalification through a national electronic procurement information system.[182]

While these announcements conveyed a sense of momentum, work on most other tasks moved very slowly. According to a retrospective assessment of the experience,

> The task force leaders and participants were selected and assigned relatively quickly, but found it difficult to move to closure on their assigned tasks. To some observers, it appeared that CIDA was falling into a familiar trap of endless analysis, at the expense of making decisions and taking action. Scepticism started to grow that CIDA would ever proceed beyond the analysis and consultation stage of renewal.[183]

Senior managers, who thought that the worst was behind them, were also taken aback by the results of the employee survey in the spring of 1994. It revealed low morale, high stress levels, serious complaints about uneven workloads and job security, and unhappiness about the high level of contracting out. These particular responses were not surprising in view of the state of siege experienced by federal civil servants since the late 1980s. A majority of respondents also expressed unhappiness about the leadership capacities and "people skills" of senior management and dissatisfaction with the quality of internal information-sharing.[184] The survey confirmed Labelle's message that the Agency still had much to do in the area of personnel management.

Task force activity continued to falter until November 1994 when senior executives were advised of huge expenditure reductions that would accompany the finance minister's budget in February 1995. The news came as a jolt.

> Both the scale of the cuts . . . and the fact that they had been made under the personal direction of the Minister, required the Agency to seize the initiative. If the 1994-95 Renewal Plan had not been in place, the agency would have quickly foundered in its attempts to come to grips with this shock. Instead the plan and its established task forces allowed the Agency to make progress quickly.[185]

Most task forces were on track by July 1995. Especially good progress was reported on efforts to reduce program support costs, and to produce guidelines for linking program priorities and field-based programming in regional/country development policy frameworks.[186] Less headway was made in the crucial area of redesigning geographic programming because "it appears that . . . the distinction between risk management and risky management has been harder to operationalize than anticipated." In contrast, the attempt to implement results-based management had met "unexpected enthusiasm," though there was uncertainty about how to shape an Agency-wide approach.[187] The reform of human resource policies was well advanced and included a five-year renewal plan for recruiting entry-level development officers.[188] The interim assessment claimed as of August 1995:

> CIDA had confounded the sceptics. Not only had something happened, it was agreed both in the Agency and outside that real progress had occurred. At the lowest point in its reputation, many in the government's central agencies doubted that CIDA, with its apparent penchant for endless reflection and self-analysis, would ever take the actions that had . . . been taken.[189]

It was generally acknowledged that much of the credit was due to the outstanding leadership of David Holdsworth, vice-president of Corporate Management (and formerly of Asia Branch), who guided the process until his transfer to the Privy Council Office in June 1995.[190]

The Auditor General's follow-up report in October 1995 was positive about the extent to which the Agency had acknowledged its accountability to Parliament for development results and had taken seriously its search for simpler and more cost-effective program delivery. As the renewal effort had thus far been largely limited to headquarters, the auditors suggested that "it would be timely to extend that effort to the field level." They also urged an acceleration in "the development of indicators that are simple and usable for measuring and reporting on the Agency's results as well as on the success of its programs and, particularly, its projects."[191]

Efforts to operationalize an approach to managing for results led to the introduction of a Results-Based Management (RBM) Policy in March 1996[192] and the parallel development of a new Bilateral Project Performance Review System based on the analysis of results and key factors required for successful development and effective management.[193] The Auditor General's second follow-up report in November 1996 was also supportive, but cautioned that these new measures were largely untested.[194]

Late in 1996, CIDA announced that the Open Bidding System would be further simplified by eliminating the prequalifying stage, with the prospect that contracting time would be halved. Protracted negotiations also yielded an agreement aimed at resolving a long-standing conflict between profit and not-for-profit executing agencies and putting them on a more level playing field. For a fifteen-month experimental period beginning in January 1997, NGOs and NGIs were given access to the open bidding process and private firms the opportunity to participate in sole-sourcing arrangements for non-solicited projects.[195]

There was a positive impact on staff morale arising from a sense that management renewal was working and that, even though resources were declining, the Agency and its people were more in control of their agenda. A second employee survey in 1996 showed an 11 per cent increase in the level of staff satisfaction with CIDA's management style and human resource practices.[196]

While good employee morale is a necessary condition for effective performance, the larger question of whether management renewal will produce better development remains unanswered. In its 1996 report to the Auditor General, CIDA recognized "that it will take time and commitment" to internalize the changes, and "that cultural changes will be needed to facilitate the process."[197] Even if Results-Based Management and related reforms succeed in focusing the Agency more on developmental outcomes and less on process, Rudner speculated that there could be a perverse consequences because of the habitual aversion to risk-taking. Management

> could yield improved "results" by making subtle but nevertheless significant shifts in program composition that favour more easily deliverable and measurable, even if less developmentally challenging pursuits. The "result" would be an aid program that avoids involvement in development initiatives that may be inherently more risky for management, even if these risks are warranted by the prospective developmental benefits for the recipient country.

There is as well a danger, already the focus of complaints by some of CIDA's partners, that implementation of the new RBM policy could become an excessively formalistic exercise more concerned about correct jargon than developmental outcomes.

In addition, it remains to be seen whether the current emphasis on quantitative indicators—also a focus of effort at DAC[198]— will divert energy away from more productive ways of evaluating the qualitative dimensions of human development. One example of the emphasis upon quantification is the new Coding and Counting System for tracking expenditures on each of the six priorities of *Canada in the World*. While the system has been touted as a major advance in accountability, it requires that every activity be assigned to only one priority. How does one classify efforts to improve the access of rural microenterprises to credit? As basic human needs? As private-sector development? Or, under certain circumstances, as women in development or environment? Should basic health, primary education, and birth control be counted as basic human needs or women in development? Ignoring ambiguities of this sort, the system conveys a deceptive aura of precision.

Linking Policy, Program Priorities, and Field Operations

Policy Branch, strengthened by corporate reorganization in 1993, has led the process of creating policy statements designed to provide operational strategies in key areas for all of CIDA's branches and partners. In June 1995, the Agency released an overarching policy on poverty reduction, intended to guide planning (as the white paper promised) in each of the six program priorities.[199]

CIDA's policy on poverty reduction. Produced by the Development Economics Policy Division of Policy Branch, the policy reflected work begun several years earlier by a ginger group of officers who took seriously the commitment of *Sharing Our Future* to "putting poverty first." After impressive research and lengthy internal debate, a draft discussion paper on poverty reduction was circulated in August 1994.[200] It made recommendations for a comprehensive approach, which awaited approval pending confirmation by the government of an anti-poverty thrust in CIDA's mission.

The final version rejected a focus on poverty alleviation or relief—"which addresses the poor's survival needs, their immediate problems, and the effects of . . . inequities"—in favour of poverty reduction—"a process by which the *causes* of deprivation and inequity are addressed."[201] Accordingly, the policy stressed the necessity of challenging the "root causes and structural factors" of poverty, with a focus on enabling the poor to secure "sustainable livelihoods." This could be done by working directly with those living in poverty (targeted poverty programs), strengthening the capacities of organizations which work with the poor (poverty-focused programs), and intervening at the policy/institutional level to remove systemic constraints (policy interventions). Particular emphasis was put on balancing sound economic management with social investments, addressing basic human needs, and ensuring "that food aid is consistent with, and better integrated into, overall poverty-reduction and food-security programming strategies."[202]

Challenging traditional practices of top-down, expert-driven programming, the most radical aspect of the policy called for promotion of participatory approaches to poverty reduction. The text reflected the critique of conventional aid put forward by Robert Chambers[203] and others who advocate empowering the poor and working *with* them. The policy suggested that CIDA had particular advantages to offer, stemming from its experience with local NGO networks, the "gender-poverty nexus," and institutional strengthening.[204]

It remains to be seen whether the Policy on Poverty Reduction will be merely a statement of good intentions or a genuine stimulus to serious and coherent anti-poverty programming. In any case, it will be an important test of the Agency's capacity to harness policy and programming and manage for developmental results. The policy will be carefully monitored within and outside the Agency, and will be formally evaluated after five years.

Basic human needs. While the objectives of sustainable development and poverty reduction supposedly infuse all programming priorities set out in *Canada in the World*, support for basic human needs (BHN) is a crucial component of assistance to the poorest. In estimating that less than 20 per cent of Canadian ODA had been earmarked for this purpose in recent years, the SJC-CFP assumed that a commitment to channel a minimum of 25 per cent to basic needs would have a significant steering effect on aid allocations.

When the government agreed (except for the "minimum" proviso), it referred to expenditures on primary health care, basic education, family planning, nutrition, water and sanitation, and shelter. It also stated that "Canada will continue to respond to emergencies and humanitarian assistance."[205] This definition prompted immediate concerns about the value of the 25 per cent target, if emergency food aid and humanitarian assistance were to count as BHN in the sense of addressing long-term sustainable livelihoods for those living in poverty.[206]

Meanwhile, UNDP had been calling for concerted action by both developing and industrial countries to achieve by 2000 such essential human goals as universal basic education, primary health care, safe water for all, access to family planning, expanded credit, and the elimination of serious malnutrition.[207] The debate over the Canadian government's 25 per cent commitment coincided with a challenge from UNDP before the 1995 World Summit for Social Development: aid recipients and donors were urged to accept a "20:20 compact for human development" that, over ten years, would raise public expenditures in developing countries on these essential human goals from 13 per cent to 20 per cent of national budgets, and increase the proportion of ODA devoted to basic human development from a mere 7 per cent to 20 per cent.[208]

The question of what to include in a definition of basic human needs was central for Alison Van Rooy in *A Partial Promise? Canadian Support to Social Development*, her excellent 1995 study for the North-South Institute:

> The good news is that the government has made basic human needs one of the key priorities in its 1995 white paper . . . and that this promise may serve to lever the whole of Canadian assistance toward a practice of sustainable human development. The bad news is that there is a danger that Canada's contributions may become *counterproductive* to the very goal of sustainable development; Canada may become an ill-equipped international welfare agency, providing inappropriate basic services in lieu of contributing to a country's own capacity to provide services itself.[209]

The good news scenario required exclusion of emergency food aid from the percentage calculation and substantial improvements, quantitative and qualitative, in meeting BHN in the other designated sectors, which accounted for only about 13 per cent of bilateral disbursements and even less in the all-channel total.[210] (Not surprisingly, NGO Division ranked highest, with 29 per cent excluding food aid.[211]) Van Rooy estimated that the inclusion of emergency food aid might raise the share of bilateral aid classified as BHN as high as 21 per cent, thus reducing the pressure to meet the target. Moreover, there "is a real danger that basic human needs spending will be tallied under a multitude of headings simply to have the agency meet the 25 percent number goal alone—in such a case, basic human needs will become an item on a policy shopping list rather than a real commitment to poverty-centred reform."[212] She also pointed out that, while budget cuts may or may not make it difficult to reach the target, they do run counter to the intention of the 20/20 and 25 per cent proposals "to *increase* funding to social sector areas."

As with poverty reduction, it will take time before a verdict can be rendered on CIDA's commitment to basic human needs. On the one hand, emphasis in the anti-poverty policy on tackling the causes of deprivation and inequity, rather than providing relief, suggested a determination to strengthen social-sector programming among the poor. So too did the promise to infuse all program priorities with an anti-poverty focus—not just the obvious ones of BHN and gender.

On the other hand, the Agency ended up adopting a definition of basic human needs that included provision of food aid, for both emergencies and long-term development, and humanitarian assistance. In the *Estimates* for 1996-97, a retrospective application of the new Coding and Counting System revealed that 21.4 per cent of bilateral disbursements went to meeting basic human needs in 1994-95, even without "admissible food aid disbursements."[213] CIDA indicated that food aid and International Humanitarian Assistance would be included when the system was more developed, putting the all-channel target of 25 per cent within easy reach. Indeed, calculations published a year later tracked Agency expenditures of $608 million in 1995-96 on BHN, 37 per cent of its total disbursements.[214] According to

CCIC calculations, however, the percentage dropped to 18.1 when food aid and humanitarian assistance were excluded.[215]

To some extent, adoption of the broader definition of BHN for tracking purposes reflected a desire by bureaucrats to avoid embarrassments like those stemming from the failure to meet the targets of *Sharing Our Future*. Ouellet was also keen to see quick progress in reaching 25 per cent in a way that would maintain flexibility. It remains to be seen whether this easy way out would sap the Agency's will to engage in innovative basic needs programming. In any case, in response to criticism from CCIC and others, CIDA agreed to provide a breakdown of expenditures for both BHN and basic social services—as defined by UNDP and the 20/20 proposal—beginning in 1998-99.[216]

Women in Development.[217] With the dissolution of Professional Services Branch in 1993, WID specialists were assigned to each program branch and a small group was transferred to Policy Branch under a senior policy advisor. The 1992 policy framework, which broadened CIDA's work from women's equality to gender equity, informed an updated Women in Development and Gender Equity Policy in 1995.[218]

After languishing somewhat in the early 1990s, WID programming was given renewed emphasis under Huguette Labelle. A major collaborative project with UNICEF involved efforts in fifteen African countries to improve educational access for girls. In Asia, Canada contributed to a regional network of institutions concerned with promoting business opportunities and labour rights for women and their community-based participation in social and economic decision-making. As many gender-based activities were recorded as contributions to other priorities (especially the 25 per cent target for basic human needs), the 3.2 per cent share of WID-specific disbursements in 1995-96 was understated.[219]

CIDA remained active and visible in international networking on gender issues in DAC, multilateral agencies, and international fora. Canada led an international initiative on Structural Adjustment and Gender in Africa that resulted in agreement among donors on ways of integrating gender analysis into the design of economic policy reforms. Issues of women's human and reproductive rights were advanced by Canadian participants at the Vienna conference on human rights in 1993 and at the International Conference on Population and Development in Cairo in 1994. CIDA was the lead agency in a review and assessment of DAC members' WID policies and strategies. The Agency contributed as well to the development of positions advanced by Canada at the United Nations Fourth World Conference on Women in Beijing in 1995. These included recommendations on poverty reduction, the status and education of the girl child, reproductive health and empowerment, and "women's rights as human rights." In addition, CIDA provided logistical and funding support for the NGO forum held in conjunction with the conference.

Infrastructure services. A working group was set up to develop a policy on infrastructure services after it was designated as a programming priority in the white paper. Preliminary work yielded a definition: "The output or flow of services provided by physical infrastructure which protect health, promote social and economic development and improve the quality of life. These services include, among others, access to clean water and sanitation, good roads and reliable electricity, telephone and information services." Disbursements on additions to physical capital stock, and its maintenance or replacement, would be restricted to "carefully defined circumstances." For the most part, the emphasis would be on strengthening the enabling environment, building institutional and human capacity, and enhancing universal access to basic services "by all levels of society, particularly the poor and women."[220]

Infrastructure services accounted for 13.6 per cent of the Agency's disbursements in 1995-96. Capacity-building and rehabilitation were dominant activities in projects clustered primarily in the transportation, communications, and energy sectors.[221]

Human rights, democracy, and good governance. Many CIDA officials and their DFAIT counterparts were concerned about the inconsistency of the government's application of human rights conditionality (especially in the past under Mulroney and McDougall), and sceptical about the effectiveness of unilateral Canadian action in response to human rights abuses. A September 1993 discussion paper claimed that "experience shows that ODA is best used to support programming in these areas, rather than using it as an on/off switch to try to change behaviour. But, the pressure in favour of 'quick fixes' such as sanctions, when situations erupt, remains strong."[222] As we have seen, *Canada in the World* reflected this disposition, emphasizing that Canada would "continue to lead on human rights issues" through proactive programming and multilateral efforts, rather than unilateral aid or trade sanctions.

A policy balancing positive initiatives in the aid sphere, with caution on the sanctions front, accorded well with the Chrétien-Ouellet trade promotion agenda. Although Ouellet was usually careful in his public statements to project that balance, Canadians with strong convictions about human rights perceived the minister as unsympathetic or even antagonistic.[223] Their suspicions were strengthened in May 1995 when Ouellet, speaking to a meeting of ASEAN foreign ministers, said that Canada would vigorously pursue trade links with developing countries without regard to their human rights records. He later denied allegations from human rights activists and opposition MPs that his statement repudiated official commitments in the white paper. He sparked more anger, however, when he told the House of Commons: "to try to be a Boy Scout on your own, when indeed nobody else is following [trade sanctions], is absolutely counterproductive."[224]

Meanwhile, after extensive preparations, which included participation at the 1993 World Conference on Human Rights in Vienna, CIDA adopted a Policy on Human Rights, Democratization and Good Governance in November 1995. The document committed the Agency to strengthen:

- the role and capacity of civil society in developing countries in order to increase popular participation in decision-making;
- democratic institutions in order to develop and sustain responsible government;
- the competence of the public sector in order to promote the effective, honest and accountable exercise of power;
- the capacity of organizations that protect and promote human rights in order to enhance society's ability to address rights concerns; and
- the will of leaders to respect rights, rule democratically and govern effectively.[225]

The policy also pledged that CIDA would try to ensure that human rights abuses did not result from its policies and programs.[226]

Based on the experience with women in development, proposals were advanced for incorporating rights/democracy/governance objectives into programming guidelines and administrative processes.

Human rights and conflict resolution remained a major focus of CIDA's activities in Sri Lanka, the Middle East, and Central America. New programming in South Africa, and in Haiti after the restoration of President Aristide, was heavily oriented to support for democratic transition.[227]

The Somalia crisis in 1992-93 and the tragedy of Rwanda in 1994 were catalysts in promoting growing interest among international aid donors in the use of aid for conflict prevention and peace-building, as well as post-disaster programming. As declining aid budgets were diverted to humanitarian relief,[228] Canada spent close to $2 billion—an amount equivalent to two-thirds of the annual ODA budget—on the Somalia emergency in support of relief, refugees (including resettlement of many in Canada), and the Canadian Airborne Regiment's disgraceful participation in UN peace-making efforts.[229] It was a harsh lesson in both human and material terms. Peace and security, along with poverty reduction, were defined as major objectives in CIDA's 1995 "Programming Guidelines for Africa and the Middle East." Minister Ouellet also agreed to earmark ODA funds in support of efforts to secure an international treaty banning landmines,[230] an initiative that was successfully carried forward by his successor, Lloyd Axworthy. (Although generally applauded, this use of aid money created some consternation in CIDA at a time when funds for many long-standing projects were being severely reduced.)

Expenditures coded as human rights, democratization, and good governance accounted for 10.5 per cent of CIDA's ODA spending in 1995-96.[231]

Private-sector development. A Policy Branch paper on economic development (written before the foreign policy review) noted the now-prevalent consensus that "a healthy and dynamic private sector is essential to economic growth in particular, and sustainable development in general. This view contrasts starkly with pervasive government interventionist policies of the sixties and seventies." The authors also observed that "pressure is growing . . . for CIDA to be more responsive to Canadian commercial considerations. . . . It is critical that CIDA, within its development assistance mandate, clearly address the needs of the prosperity and trade development elements of the Canadian domestic and foreign policy agendas." Private-sector development was seen as "one of the most efficient ways [of] doing so."[232]

The Development Economics Division of Policy Branch played the lead role (as it had with poverty reduction) in creating an Agency-wide policy on private-sector development. After producing a discussion paper for internal and external consultations,[233] it gained approval from the executive committee and Ouellet for a policy statement. Released in February 1995, the policy sought a balance between developmental objectives—helping to create "an enabling environment for growth of entrepreneurship," and supporting efforts "to enable people living in poverty to participate and contribute to economic development"—and commercial objectives—working "with Canadian partners to develop mutually beneficial relationships in developing countries."[234]

While motivated by the pursuit of long-term benefits for Canadian business, the policy did reflect broader developmental concerns than had been apparent in INC or CIDA's other business-oriented ventures. In this respect, it benefited from ongoing work at the international level. DAC guidelines in 1994 called on donors to help strengthen enabling environments, create efficient financial institutions, develop sustainable grass-roots microenterprises, encourage environmentally sustainable industrial development, and build an informed dialogue between public and private sectors.[235]

CIDA's policy reflected these concerns, in part by distinguishing (along the lines of the long-standing two-track approach to eligibility) between least-developed/low-income countries and those with rapidly growing market economies. In richer countries, the emphasis would be on fostering competitive enterprises and effective financial institutions and promoting private-sector-to-private-sector partnerships. The accent in poorer countries, however, would be on enhancing the enabling environment for private-sector development through support for reform of legal and regulatory regimes, reorganization of the public sector, and capacity-building in public institutions. In addition, "Community-based private enterprises, in the form of microenterprises and co-operatives, are needed to address the goal of social reform and the plight of the poor." Important roles were foreseen for Canadian NGOs, as well as small firms.[236]

The policy also promised to "assist the private sector in developing countries in adjusting to the post-Uruguay Round trade regime and to better integrate into the world economy," and to "sharpen the development focus of the CIDA-INC program."[237] A new statement of INC's objectives subsequently included commitments to strengthen the ability of developing country entrepreneurs to secure "equitable and sustainable livelihoods," and to increase the developmental impact of projects, especially on "job and foreign exchange creation, increased environmental sustainability, and greater participation of women."[238] Again, commitments will bear close monitoring to see if they are translated into effective programming in the field.

CIDA's coding system attributed 10.4 per cent of Agency disbursements in 1995-96 to private-sector development.[239]

Environment.[240] As with WID, the dismantling of Professional Services involved reassignment of specialist expertise to Policy and the geographic branches. The resulting disruption, together with cutbacks, delayed implementation of the 1992 Policy for Environmental Sustainability. Work proceeded, however, on incorporating environmental considerations into guidelines for bilateral programming.[241] Effort went as well into preparations—including training for staff, consultants, and partner organizations—for mandatory environmental assessment of all projects under the new Canadian *Environmental Assessment Act*. After several delays, the *Act* was finally proclaimed in January 1995.

Supporting the assertion of Canadian leadership in international environmental policy-making, CIDA was an active participant in the DAC working party on Development Assistance and Environment. It also funded, and conducted for DAC, a comparative study of environmental assessment procedures of donor countries. As Rudner noted, Canada's own imposition of environmental conditionality "doubtless satisfies domestic concerns," but has complicated relations with recipient countries.[242]

Environmental programming accounted for 7.4 per cent of CIDA's ODA 1995-96. Much of the work in the field focused on strengthening the capacities of local institutions to engage in effective natural resource management.

The Deepest Cuts Yet

While management renewal, policy development, and results-based programming helped revitalize the aid program and CIDA after the dark days of 1992-93, every activity has been coloured by the grim reality of seemingly relentless budget cuts.

In February 1994, the government announced a 2 per cent reduction in the International Assistance Envelope, followed by a frozen budget for two years. Maintenance of a freeze appeared unlikely, however, with increasingly shrill campaigning for deficit reduction by bond-rating agencies, business interests, the media, and the Reform Party—and a well-orchestrated campaign by Finance Minister Paul Martin and his colleagues to prepare the public for unprecedented cuts in federal spending. Meanwhile, a comprehensive cost-cutting review across all departments and programs was supervised by a cabinet committee that was chaired by Marcel Massé in his capacity as minister for public service reform.

Martin's budget of February 27, 1995, announced a three-year reduction of 20.5 per cent in the International Assistance Envelope—not the most severe (the Department of the Environment, for example, lost 30 per cent), but greater than Foreign Affairs (17.3 per cent) or National Defence (14.2 per cent). While the cutback in international assistance was not out of line with reduced program spending in several other areas, it did come on top of several earlier disproportionate cuts by the Mulroney administration.

According to an analysis by the North-South Institute (see Figure 10.1), the result was a decrease in ODA between 1988-89 and 1997-98 of 33 per cent in real terms, compared to 22 per cent for defence and only 5 per cent for all other programs combined.[243] CCIC also lamented the contrast between aid and defence spending: "There has not only been no redistribution of traditional defence expenditures into a common security framework, but there has also been a worsening of the Defence to ODA ratio from 3.94 to one [in 1992-93] to 5.08 to one [projected for 1997-98]," an even higher ratio than in the last few years of the Cold War.[244]

Unlike Foreign Affairs and National Defence—where the brunt of the cutting was scheduled for 1996-97 and 1997-98—the International Assistance Envelope was slashed by 14.4 per cent in 1995-96 (and the ODA component by 14.9 per cent). On the face of the record, there was fear that projections for the following two years—stability in 1996-97 and a further 6 per cent cut in 1997-98—would be overtaken by even steeper reductions.

CIDA was also scheduled for staff reductions of 200 over three years (about 15 per cent)—potentially disruptive, but a modest hit when compared with many other departments and agencies. The Briefing Centre (now known as the Centre for Intercultural Training) was wound down; its responsibilities and some of its staff were transferred to the Canadian Foreign Service Institute.[245] Meanwhile, seventy-seven person years were transferred from DFAIT into the Agency's Central and Eastern Europe Branch.[246]

There was scant media commentary on this deepest cut yet, which was buried in a much broader onslaught on public spending. An editorial in the *Hamilton Spectator* typified the reaction:

> It's unfortunate that Canada's foreign aid was slashed by a hefty 21 per cent, at a time of considerable uncertainty and volatility around the world. Yet with cuts to the civil service; every department of the federal government, except Indian Affairs; Prairie farmers and Quebec dairy farmers, among others, it would have been politically difficult to exempt foreign aid.[247]

Clyde Sanger declared: "It is the end of an era, whether of paternalism or partnership or a bit of both."[248]

Figure 10.1
Index of Real Government Program Spending since 1988
(1988-89 = 100)

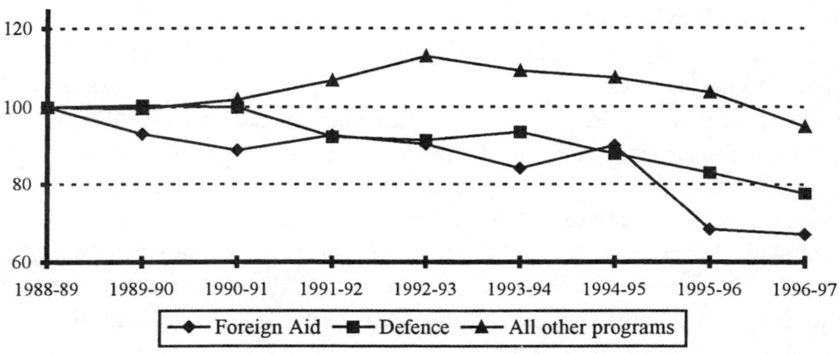

Source: Andrew Clark, "What Next Mr. Martin? Foreign Aid in the Next Budget," *Review* (Ottawa: North-South Institute) (Winter 1996), p. 3.

Columnist John Best, long a sceptical observer of the aid program, wondered what happened to the "compassionate side of Canadian society" touted in the Liberals' *Foreign Policy Handbook*. "Even appeals to donor countries' self-interest no longer have much effect in today's austerity-minded climate. Few seem willing to listen to the time-honoured argument that, with sufficient help, Third World Countries will eventually provide new markets for western industrial goods."[249]

Best observed that the cuts came on the eve of the World Summit on Social Development in Copenhagen. While that gathering involved several heads of state and government, Prime Minister Chrétien and Foreign Minister Ouellet did not attend. Canada's low-key delegation was led by Lloyd Axworthy, then minister of Human Resources—"appropriately, in an ironic way," Best quipped, "since it was Axworthy who, as Liberal opposition foreign affairs critic, led the attack on Tory niggardliness."[250]

Ouellet Uses Cutback to Make Policy

According to CIDA insiders and knowledgeable observers, Ouellet's clout was important in preventing an even more devastating budgetary scenario. Playing a hands-on role in determining where the cuts would fall, the minister also fended off central agency involvement on grounds that priorities were being shaped by the foreign policy review. In fact, however, his approach to expenditure reduction resulted in some dramatic changes in aid policy.

Ouellet decreed that the cuts would respect four principles: first, that existing bilateral commitments and multilateral pledges would be honoured; secondly, that Canada would not withdraw from particular countries or regions; thirdly, that official development assistance would chiefly support projects in developing countries; and, fourthly, that CIDA would manage financial transfers to Canadian institutions directly, supposedly to achieve economies and maximize the resources reaching developing countries.

The principle of maintaining commitments emphasized Ouellet's determination not to lose credibility for Canada in the eyes of recipient country governments or international organizations; though unexceptional, it constrained the range of possible options. While he shared Barbara McDougall's scepticism about the value to Canada of extensive involvement in multilateral assistance, Ouellet deferred to senior advisers in agreeing not to risk Canada's investment in efforts to reform UN agencies by making immediate, drastic cuts in allocations. Estimates for multilateral technical cooperation and food aid were cut by 18.5 and 23.5 per cent respectively.[251] Because of commitments made during Joe Clark's time, the budget for international financial institutions was higher in 1995-96 than in 1994-95, but the government served notice that it would negotiate much lower contribution levels in future, as much as 40 per cent lower for the regional development banks.[252]

The second principle, to stay the course in all regions and countries, was consistent with the white paper—which, as we have seen, reflected Ouellet's judgements that the Conservative government had handled the African cuts badly, and that Canada's national interest lay in maintaining an aid presence virtually everywhere. For 1995-96, each of the geographic programs was cut by 17 per cent on the understanding that the impact would be spread across all recipients (a reversion to the "lawnmower" approach). As regional shares were maintained, Africa and the Middle East suffered the biggest absolute drop in spending ($68 million compared to $56 million for Asia and $27 million for the Americas).[253]

Ouellet's priorities were clear as well in the decision to take only 10 per cent from the Industrial Cooperation Program (out of a base of $72.3 million), compared to 21.2 per cent from the voluntary sector (out of a base of $264.7 million).[254] In contrast to across-the-board reductions in other channels, however, CIDA's non-governmental responsive programming was drastically reshaped by the minister's agenda. His narrow "what's in it for Canada?" attitude and the absence of a Canadian constituency led to a 52 per cent reduction in the allocation for international NGOs (from a base of $20.7 million), compared to a 15 per cent cut for domestic development NGOs, colleges and universities, and other voluntary institutions.[255] Hardest hit was the International Planned Parenthood Federation, which Canada had once helped survive the Reagan/Bush scalpel.[256]

A severe blow for development and global education.[257] Only hinted at in the government's rejection of the MacEachen-Gauthier recommendation that public participation be a programming priority, but rationalized by Ouellet's third principle of giving preference to projects in developing countries, was a decision to abolish the Public Participation Program and cut 100 per cent of the funding received by Canadian development education NGOs. PPP, accounting for only 4.5 per cent of the voluntary-sector budget, absorbed 24.7 per cent of the reduction to that budget.

From now on, there would be no dedicated responsive funding for development education in Canada, a distinctive and vital, if often controversial aspect of CIDA's programming for over twenty years. Upwards of ninety community-based organizations—always funded "on the cheap" compared to other CIDA activities—lost their major, and in many cases sole, source of financial support. Among organizations facing the prospect of extinction was the London Cross Cultural Learner Centre, the prototype for other now-threatened ventures such as the Victoria International Development Education Association, the Arusha Cross-Cultural Centre in Calgary, the One Sky Cross Cultural Centre in Saskatoon, the Kawartha World Issues Centre in Peterborough, Carrefour Tiers-Monde in Quebec City, and the Nova Scotia Global Education Project in Halifax. Ten Days for World Development and other national coalitions involved in development education lost their CIDA funding as well.

Also cancelled by the application of the third principle (perhaps less intentionally than PPP) was the Global Education Program, which funded teachers' associations in their efforts to incorporate global education in the curricula of schools and teacher training institutions. Consistently evaluated highly, it had only just been renewed for a three-year period up to 1997-98. The Youth Initiatives Program was also eliminated, though with a commitment to emphasize international exchanges among young people in regular NGO programming. (Youth internships were introduced in 1997 as part of the government's broader youth employment initiative.)

PPP's demise was announced on March 24, 1995, almost a month after the budget. The action provoked vigorous protests in affected communities, expressions of concern in local media, and some 2,000 critical letters—many more than the minister, his staffers, or CIDA officers had anticipated. A decision had already been taken, however, "to ride it out" in the belief that the development education community was of marginal political significance. While some one-time transitional funding was eventually provided in response to the outcry, the official line expressed regret that the fiscal situation required "tough decisions" not necessarily related to performance criteria.

Ouellet and CIDA officials denied allegations that they were trying to kill development education just when dwindling public support for ODA suggested a greater need than ever. Instead, they claimed that "Development education for Canadians will remain important for CIDA, but will now have to be included in the regular programming of organizations and institutions working in developing countries."[258] What they did not address was how these NGOs and NGIs could shoulder an additional burden when they too were facing cuts, or how—when they were almost all based in Toronto, Montreal, and Ottawa—they could fill gaps in communities across Canada.

Within the Agency, the reaction to the decision was mixed, reflecting long-standing scepticism about the capacity of development education NGOs to engage in effective outreach, tempered by a recognition that many did excellent and often undervalued work at the local level. There were much stronger dissenting opinions about the decision to cancel the Global Education Program because it was seen as having a positive impact on inculcating internationalist values among young people.

Cranford Pratt suggested that the "dev-ed" decision was driven by three factors: first, the general withdrawal of public funding from activist groups (women's, aboriginal, environmental, etc.) that mobilize and articulate popular opinion, and are increasingly seen by the political elite as oppositional elements rather than—as in an earlier era—important contributors to Canadian identity; secondly, the growing impatience and irritation felt within CIDA towards politicized NGOs critical of the Agency's neo-conservative drift since the late 1980s; and, thirdly, CIDA's rejection of pluralism and responsive programming, as evidenced by its preoccupation with policy integration.[259]

Pratt's point about declining public support for activism is especially valid. Perspectives on the NGO community formed during the Joint Committee's deliberations (closely monitored by Ouellet) also appear to have shaped the minister's view that CIDA supported too many marginal organizations. The frustrations of SJC-CFP members in response to attacks on the aid program by some smaller NGOs during the hearings probably influenced the development education cut more than impatience and irritation within the Agency, which was more accustomed to strident criticism.

While it is true that there had always been friction between CIDA and dev-ed organizations, the Agency was at first reluctant to admit publicly that the PPP decision reflected a negative judgement about their value. A year later, however, Janet Zukowsky, vice-president of Canadian Partnership Branch, told SCFAIT that the program

> remained . . . for the most part a creature of CIDA, sustained by ODA dollars, not viable without that flow and in some cases not truly rooted in the community. . . . [The] entire development education community—I speak of all of us, and I'll include government—was essentially stuck in a rut on a dead-end street trying to get across a mix of messages that were fresh and relevant in the 1960s but are increasingly out of sync with realities of the 1990s.

Not all MPs agreed. Philippe Paré of the Bloc Québécois quipped: "when someone wants to get rid of his dog, he claims that he has rabies."[260]

An end to delegated decision-making for NGO funding.[261] Implementation of the fourth principle, which called on CIDA to resume full decision-making responsibility for allocations to NGOs and NGIs, was yet another blow to smaller NGOs, including several that lost PPP funding as well. The Agency cut 100 per cent of the grants to the provincial and Atlantic regional international development councils, which had distributed almost $1.3 million annually in small grants, mostly for Canadian-based community projects. NGOs lost additional funding (distributed through CCIC) for development education, including very short-lived Development Education Awards.

The recentralization decision also affected programming in developing countries. The four regional decentralized funds were disbanded. Only recently established to ease the workload of NGO Division and facilitate peer review of small overseas project applications, they had supported upwards of 100 small overseas programming NGOs. The budgets of most delegated thematic funds were eliminated as well. Among those cut were: the Reconstruction and Rehabilitation Fund, the oldest NGO coalition; the Environment and Development Support Program set up in 1992 to promote partnerships and cooperative programming between Canadian environmental NGOs and their counterparts in the South; and three new funds focused on Children in Difficult Circumstances, Southern Africa, and New Initiatives (involving Canadian Native peoples, among others). The two largest coalitions—Partnership Africa-Canada and South Asia Partnership (with CIDA grants of $15 million and $2.9 million respectively in 1994-95)—retained modest transitional funding while losing their program budgets.

Of approximately $29 million in "repatriated" funds, $15 million disappeared as a budget reduction; the remaining $14 million was put into a new Project Facility Fund to which small NGOs could apply directly to CIDA for project funding. Thus, NGOs previously dependent on decentralized resources for developing country activities lost much more than large NGOs and NGIs that had remained on program funding through CIDA. Moreover, the abandonment of a distinctive experiment, based on delegated decision-making and mutual trust, decimated a substantial investment in interagency networking and cooperation. As with the development education decision, the impact on the morale of many hard-working Canadians and their Southern partners was devastating.

Besides expressing regret for another "tough decision," officials explained recentralization as a measure that economized by reducing Canadian overheads, and strengthened accountability by restoring direct ministerial oversight over public funds. However, Ouellet's desire for hands-on control and his distaste for what he saw as a Tory experiment were probably more important. (While the practice of delegating funding responsibility began under Joe Clark and David MacDonald during the African crisis of 1984-85, it will be recalled that both the Reconstruction and Rehabilitation Fund and the South Asia Partnership had in fact been established during the last Trudeau regime.) The decision also reflected CIDA's lack of knowledge of what many of smaller organizations were doing in the field.[262]

More Cuts and a Plunging ODA/GNP Ratio

Paul Martin's March 1996 budget reiterated plans for an ODA freeze in 1996-97 and a 6 per cent cut in 1997-98, dropping the International Assistance Envelope to $2.1 billion from $2.9 billion in 1994-95. For 1998-99, the finance minister projected a further massive reduction of $150 million.[263]

Lloyd Axworthy, who replaced Ouellet as minister of Foreign Affairs in 1996, pledged in January 1997 that there would be no further cuts after those scheduled in 1998-99.[264] There was, however, no confirmation of this commitment in Martin's February 1997 preelection budget. His speech and accompanying documents, which suggested that improving fiscal balances would permit some expenditure increases in 1999-2000, were silent on the question of whether international assistance would be stabilized or increased. CIDA's own expenditure plans in the *Estimates* merely stated that "for planning purposes, the Agency has assumed that the total budget for 1999-2000 will be maintained at the 1998-99 level."[265]

Martin's next budget in February 1998 projected a zero deficit for the following year and heralded the prospect of fiscal surpluses thereafter. Reflecting an intense lobbying effort by the North-South Institute, CCIC, the NGO community, and several MPs, there was finally a modest respite for international assistance. Although the projected base budget cut of $150 million was not reinstated, the government prepaid $90 million in 1998 dues owed to UN organizations at the end of the 1997-98 fiscal year, thus freeing up an equivalent amount earmarked mainly for health, youth, environment, and governance. It also added $50 million to the IAE to meet a planned cash payment to the Enhanced Structural Adjustment Fund of the IMF, which also reduced pressure for cuts elsewhere.[266] Martin claimed that "this is a signal that, as its fiscal situation allows . . . the Government . . . will make progress towards the ODA target of 0.7% of the GNP."[267]

In the context of Canada's rapid GNP growth in the late 1990s, however, a hugh reinvestment would be needed to reverse an ODA/GNP trajectory that is plummeting downwards. The ratio had already tumbled from 0.49 per cent in 1991-92 to 0.34 per cent in 1996-97.[268] Even with the slight reprieve in the 1998 budget, the ratio is projected to fall to 0.27 per cent in 1998-99,[269] little more than half the level at the beginning of the 1990s and below that of any year since 1965-66. Deduction of various items not counted as ODA before 1980 (including, from 1993-94, imputed costs of resettling refugees during their first year in Canada) yields an even more accurate figure for historical comparison—about 0.20 per cent, which would be the lowest since 1963-64.[270] Ironically, that was the year that Paul Martin's father, then secretary of state for External Affairs, announced the Pearson government's commitment to a rapidly growing aid program.[271]

Paul Martin, Jr. expressed regret that "Canada has slowed down its foreign aid, but not more so than most other major countries."[272] Apart from the dismal performance of the United States and one or two other donors, the finance minister's claim was patently false. In fact, as a result of cutting more rapidly than most other OECD donors, Canada contributed only 3.19 per cent to DAC ODA in 1996, down from approximately 5 per cent in the late 1980s and also the most miserly level since the 1960s.[273] From a respectable fifth in ODA volume within DAC a decade earlier, Canada dropped to ninth in 1996. The collapse in proportional effort was even more pronounced—from sixth among the twenty-one DAC members in ODA/GNP ratio as late as 1994 to eleventh just two years later.[274] When DAC's annual review for 1997 was published, chair James Mitchell was unusually blunt: "reductions in official development assistance raise concerns about Canada's ability to meet expectations both at home and abroad."[275]

The poorest countries have been hit hard by Canada's declining generosity. The shares of Canadian aid channelled to least developed and other low-income countries remained relatively stable in the mid-1990s,[276] but total Canadian aid to the least developed fell from 0.15 per cent of GNP in the mid-1980s to a mere 0.06 per cent in 1996.[277]

Towards a Rekindling of Partnerships and Public Support?

While CIDA's relations with NGOs and NGIs remained more distant than they were in Margaret Catley-Carlson's time, both sides worked hard after the 1995 budget shock to repair damage through extensive consultations on a more transparent approach to NGO funding allocations,[278] a new CIDA policy on the role of the voluntary sector,[279] and other issues.[280]

The prospects of a more trusting relationship with the Liberal government improved when Prime Minister Chrétien shuffled his cabinet early in 1996. In order to open up a Commons seat for Pierre Pettigrew, one of two Quebec federalists brought to Ottawa in the wake of the near loss of the "no" side in Quebec's sovereignty referendum, André Ouellet resigned to become president of Canada Post. His successor as minister of Foreign Affairs, Lloyd Axworthy, had championed a more left-leaning and human-rights-centred foreign policy as opposition critic. The Agency also regained its own junior minister with the naming of Pettigrew as minister for International Cooperation and minister responsible for la Francophonie. (Stewart and Chan retained their regional secretary of state portfolios.)

It was soon clear within CIDA that Pettigrew's interests lay more in policy and the future of Canada than in process and patronage. At a press briefing soon after his appointment, the new minister stated that the government's chief priorities were fighting poverty in developing countries and mobilizing Canadian public opinion in solidarity with these countries. On another occasion, reflecting on his experience as co-chair of the first National Forum on foreign policy, he pledged to promote dialogue between the "two solitudes" of NGOs and business.[281]

Pettigrew's first appearance before SCFAIT came at the beginning of a day-long forum in April 1996 on promoting greater public understanding of international development issues. Called in response to complaints about the PPP decision, it had originally been scheduled in the fall of 1995. Pettigrew pledged efforts to raise the "low level of public knowledge about Canada's contribution to the international community," and harkened back to an earlier era by linking national unity and international solidarity:

> Unfortunately, because of internal squabbles tearing Canada apart . . . we have paid more attention to issues that divide us rather than to those that unite us. At the risk of sounding like an idealist . . . I believe that if we emphasize the contribution that Canada has made to international assistance worldwide, we will help Canadians become aware of the ties that bind them.[282]

During the summer of 1996, Pettigrew undertook extensive consultations with CIDA's domestic partners on how to distribute the funding cuts scheduled for 1997-98 and 1998-99. He promised a report by the end of October that would set out strategic choices reflecting the views of interested Canadians. By then, however, he had been replaced as minister by Don Boudria, the former government whip. When the *Estimates* for 1997-98 were eventually made public in February 1997, it was apparent that Pettigrew's consultative process had little impact on what were essentially across-the-board cuts.[283]

In view of the renewed rhetoric about strengthening public outreach, it was especially disappointing that the Development Information Program was once again an exception to the "lawnmower" approach to cutting. By 1998-99, DIP will have suffered a 61 per cent reduction to $3.2 million from $8.2 million in 1991-92—figures that would be even more dramatic if they included the disbanded Public Participation Program.[284]

Meanwhile, Boudria impressed CIDA's domestic partners, and he too talked of the need to strengthen support for the aid program. He received high marks from Agency personnel for his hard work and helpful demeanour, and for his willingness—reportedly much greater than his predecessor's—to resist pressures from Axworthy to use CIDA funds for immediate political objectives.[285] Boudria's tenure was as short-lived as Pettigrew's, however. Given a more senior portfolio after the June 1997 federal election, he was replaced by Diane Marleau, another bilingual Ontarian. In her case, International Cooperation was clearly a demotion from her earlier responsibilities for Health and then Public Works and Government Services.[286] She maintained a low profile during her first year in office.[287]

Ebb Tide: "Less Aid, but Better Aid"?

Budgetary restraint and sweeping global changes, not least at the ideological level, have marked a new era for all donors and recipients of development assistance during the 1990s. DFAIT's 1996 parliamentary forum focused on whether the apparent aid fatigue associated with declining resources was a transitory phenomenon. One of the participants was Ian Smillie, who had just completed an OECD study on public attitudes towards development assistance. He read a quotation to SCFAIT: "International support for development is now flagging. In some of the rich countries its feasibility, even its very purpose, is in question. The climate surrounding foreign aid programs is heavy with disillusion and distrust." He then pointed out that the words were those of the Pearson Commission in 1969.[288]

In a recent thoughtful paper, Roger Riddell also observed that foreign aid has always been under attack. Addressing the question of whether this latest bout of aid fatigue was temporary, or symptomatic of a "deeper and more far-reaching 'crisis,' " he identified four factors that have made the current situation different:

- the end of the Cold War [and] changing perceptions about security;
- [a] fall in aid volume . . . combined with less aid going to traditional low-income recipients;
- the failure of aid's increasing and now multiple objectives either to maintain or stimulate new interest in aid and development cooperation issues; and
- a series of challenges to traditional notions of aid originating in debate within donor countries about approaches to welfare, the role of the market and the nature of the state.[289]

The Canadian government in *Canada in the World* joined other commentators in pointing out that the threats to common security in the 1990s, though different from those in the Cold War era, are no less challenging. However, while "troubles travel,"[290] they appear more distant and less worrisome to political leaders than the former rivalry between the Americans and the Soviets. What many see as a weaker geo-political case for ODA has certainly contributed to a decline in aid volume and perhaps to public interest. Undoubtedly as well, multiple aid objectives and fashions have made it more difficult to sustain a straightforward humanitarian case for development assistance.

However, an even more important contributor to aid fatigue in the 1990s has been the fourth factor identified by Riddell: the success of neo-liberal ideology in capturing the minds of policy-makers and the public alike. It is unlikely that there will be a rekindling of support for efforts to tackle poverty abroad unless there is a much more fundamental challenge to neo-liberalism aimed at restoring human compassion and solidarity to domestic as well as international policy.

In Canada, the Liberal government's success in deficit reduction and the imminent prospect of fiscal surpluses may open up the possibility of such a challenge. As debates take place about cutting taxes or restoring public services, and about state-market relations in the context of globalization, there may be fresh opportunities to make the case for a renewed commitment to development cooperation. A vital question, therefore, is whether Canadian ODA will become increasingly irrelevant or more effective. The developmental agenda had almost been lost amid commercial and foreign policy pressures and organizational confusion in 1992-93. Subsequently, the Liberal government's commitment to that agenda in *Canada in the World* was weaker than the Tories' in *Sharing Our Future*. And CIDA is still expected to pursue a vast range of mixed and often conflicting objectives.

Bombarded by neo-liberal euphemisms—"leaner and meaner," "more for less," "working smarter," etc.—the observer is inclined to react cynically when the *Globe and Mail* writes an editorial on "Less Aid, but Better Aid" that claims: "Nowadays, though Canada is spending less, at least our officials are trying to spend more intelligently."[291] Nevertheless, there is some evidence of serious efforts in CIDA to improve the quality of ODA: the guidelines for effective programming, the policy on poverty reduction, the emphasis (though feebler than hoped) on basic human needs, the commitment to results-based management, the self-conscious efforts to link policy with operations, and the more open approach to information-sharing and performance evaluation.

Internationally, the Agency contributed to *Shaping the 21st Century: The Contribution of Development Co-operation*, adopted by DAC and endorsed by the OECD council in May 1996. It called for a global effort to achieve selected goals that "seek to give real meaning to the improved quality of life that is the ultimate aim of sustainable development": reduction by at least one-half the proportion of people living in extreme poverty by 2015; universal primary education in all countries by 2015; elimination of gender disparity in primary and secondary education by 2005; reduction of infant and child mortality rates by two-thirds the 1990 level, and of maternal mortality by three-fourths that level by 2015; access through the primary health care system to reproductive health services for all individuals of appropriate ages no later than 2015; and creation of operational national strategies for sustainable development in all countries in 2005. The strategy "places stronger emphasis than ever on the developing country itself as the starting point for development co-operation efforts that reflect local circumstances, encourage local commitment and participation, and foster the strengthening of local capacities."[292]

Since Ouellet's departure, new ministers have also put more emphasis on human rights, NGO relations, and public outreach. In addition, Axworthy has responded positively to the recommendations of a Task Force on Priorities for Canadian Internationalism in the 21st Century, chaired by Maurice Strong, which late in 1996 urged Canada to position itself internationally as a creator and broker of knowledge for sustainable development.[293] The proposals, which foresaw a key role for development assistance within a broader strategy, may offer one avenue for revitalizing interest in ODA beyond the confines of CIDA and the development community. They were also consistent with the reorientation over the past decade from large-scale projects to more people-oriented activities. As with previous initiatives, however, a big question is whether they would contribute to CIDA's relevance and effectiveness, or further complicate its mandate and deflect attention away from staying the course on poverty reduction, basic human needs, and other programming priorities. In addition, though it cannot guarantee good development, reinvestment in a rising ODA budget is essential if Canada is to resurrect its once-proud reputation as a generous international donor.

Chapter 11

Explaining Canadian ODA

A good deal of attention has been paid to the questions of why Canada has had, at least until recently, a substantial Canadian foreign aid program, what it is for, and what it should be for. Perceptions and prescriptions have been advanced to justify and broaden public support for it, and variously to understand, evaluate, reform, and condemn it. The conventional trinity of mixed humanitarian, political, and economic motives has been a focal point in much of the commentary and criticism about what actually drives the aid program. Differing values, interests, and understandings of empirical reality have yielded quite contradictory perspectives.

Amid the diversity of views, developmentalist, dominant-class, and statist approaches deserve fuller elaboration, as each goes beyond an assessment of motives and objectives to offer explanations of Canadian policy-making. Other conceptual approaches have also been helpful in accounting for certain aspects of Canada's foreign aid experience: governmental politics, for the multiple goals and compromises that have emerged from interdepartmental bargaining; regime analysis, for many of the policy thrusts that have been undertaken; and organizational analysis, for some of the constraints that have impinged upon developmental effectiveness.

The main argument advanced in this study's conclusion is that the two most influential schools of thought—statist and dominant class—offer important insights about what determines aspects of the aid program, but fall short of providing a comprehensive framework for explaining the history of Canadian ODA. State actors have enjoyed considerable autonomy in pursuing their political and bureaucratic agendas (as statists argue), although they have been constrained by the imperatives of serving an advanced capitalist state (as the dominant class perspective suggests). Indeed, the evidence supports the case made by both these approaches for rejecting a pluralist model that views state officials as mere mediators among contending societal interests. Neither, however, pays enough attention to the impact of actual processes of political brokerage and interest mediation on objectives, policies, and practices. These

---

Notes to Chapter 11 are on pp. 580-86.

processes—state-societal, state-centred, and transnational—have in turn been mediated by organizational and managerial factors that also have had a significant impact on the way the development assistance program has evolved.

Contrasting Images of Motives and Objectives

The corporate executives on the 1979 Hatch Committee concluded that "the Canadian International Development Agency . . . has, especially since 1970, taken an overly philanthropic giveaway approach to aid."[1] From the left, a sharply contrasting image was projected by Robert Carty and Virginia Smith in their 1981 study, *Perpetuating Poverty: The Political Economy of Canadian Foreign Aid*:

> A review of the content of Agency programs rather than its press releases shows that the humanitarian aim is in fact close to the bottom of Canada's aid agenda. National self-interest rather than philanthropy has always been the basis for Ottawa's development assistance programs. . . . The drive to guarantee western political dominance in the Third World has always been fuelled by the need to secure supplies of raw materials, new markets, and investment opportunities.[2]

According to Carty and Smith, the "real purposes" of Canadian ODA had shown a "basic unity and consistency over the years," and had been "papered over by a rhetoric designed for public scrutiny."[3] They also discounted the desirability of seeking changes in policy and practice: "Lobbying for this and that aid reform in an attempt to create a more nearly perfect assistance program can divert attention from the central issues. It's like fussing over a flat tire on an automobile with a dead battery."[4]

On the extreme right, in opposition to foreign aid altogether, Citizens for Foreign Aid Reform (C-FAR) in its 1981 tract attacked all arguments in the official trinity as "fatally flawed," singling out the case for commercial advantage as "laughable" when compared to alternative means of stimulating the Canadian economy.[5] "Foreign aid should not be, as it is now, resources extracted from an uncomprehending and reluctant donor population to salve . . . consciences and support aid bureaucrats at home and brutal and corrupt elites abroad."

Peyton Lyon dismissed much of the official rhetoric as well, though for quite different reasons. Writing in 1976, the former diplomat who was by then a professor of international relations, saw talk about commercial and political objectives as essentially a tactical ploy to court public support. Most Canadian officials and politicians, he contended, "not only favour a generous response to the needs of the Third World, but would probably do so even if they were not subject to external pressure, or were unable to see clear advantages in terms of Canada's national interest. It is, in their eyes, primarily a matter of self-respect, or conscience."[6] His views coincided with those of a former official, who said of key bureaucratic players involved in the aid program in the early days:

> It wasn't just a job for them. I think all of them were morally committed. . . . I've heard many of them say: "we're in an aid program because we have a moral obligation to be. Whether we're in or out doesn't really matter because we're such a small contributor, but we should be in." I don't think you would find that attitude quite as much today.[7]

Lyon suggested that much more certain means than development assistance were at hand if "the objective is to enhance the wealth, security or influence of Canada." The moral or humanitarian motive was clearly the most important.[8] However, he also expressed regret (in a joint publication with Rod Byers and David Leyton-Brown) that so many in official Ottawa attached a "low priority to meeting the challenges posed by the Third World" because "they perceive Canada's participation in international development to be essentially a matter of altruism . . . and nothing in which Canada has a vital stake."[9]

Journalist Clyde Sanger has been another distinguished commentator on Canadian aid over the years. After visiting several Canadian aid projects for his 1969 book *Half a Loaf*, he offered a poignant "Himalayan" version of the moral argument: "we give aid just because the developing countries are there, with all their mountainous needs so visible even from a distance."[10]

Leonard Dudley and Claude Montmarquette, trying to explain the supply of Canadian foreign aid, discounted altruism as well as commercial factors, seeing instead the political desire to win approval of other donors and recipient countries as the dominant objective.[11] For Michael Tucker, contradictory tendencies in the ODA program reflected a tension between altruism and narrow self-interest.[12] Looking back from the 1990s, Martin Rudner suggested that Canada's self-image as an aid donor was "borne until recently on a tide of developmental romanticism."[13]

Amid these debates about whether humanitarianism *is* a strong motive for Canada's development assistance, disparate views have been advanced about whether it *can* or *should* be the main driving force. Keith Spicer advanced a resolutely "realist" argument in his *A Samaritan State?* in 1966:

> Philanthropy is plainly no more than a fickle and confused policy stimulant, derived exclusively from personal conscience. It is not an objective of government. Love for mankind is a virtue of the human heart, an emotion which can stir only individuals—never bureaucracies or institutions. Governments exist only to promote the public good; and, as a result, they must act purely in the selfish interest of the state they serve.[14]

Years later, Kim Richard Nossal, a leading student of Canada's international relations, agreed with many critics about the low ranking of humanitarianism as a motive, but took issue with those who saw in official pronouncements to the contrary little more than an elaborate exercise in hypocrisy: "Virtually no evidence is offered to demonstrate that officials, particularly those with experience in the Third World, do not have the same personal reactions as private citizens when confronted with evidence of human suffering in other parts of the world."[15] Nor did Nossal assert as categorically as Spicer that a government must act purely in the selfish interest of the state it serves. Rather, he rested his explanation on a "mandated limit to altruism":

> Having never defined its mandate in imperial terms, the Canadian government has no authority over, and thus no real responsibility for, the condition or behaviour of those living outside Canada's borders. A lack of the kind of ethical obligation to other peoples that leads to meaningful and altruistic concrete action follows inexorably.[16]

Cranford Pratt has been cited many times in this study. He has advanced a quite different perspective that laments the Canadian government's failure to respond adequately to ethical concerns, but argues that humanitarian concern ought to be the main rationale for international development efforts. Speaking at a 1970 conference, he put the case in both moral and practical terms:

> Inefficiencies, corruption, authoritarian regimes, these and similar factors in parts of the developing areas would lead to a diminishing Canadian international development effort unless underlying that effort there is a constantly renewed sense of moral obligation. If people are parochial in their acceptance of responsibility for the welfare of fellow human beings, then, I fear, they will quickly be unresponsive to arguments which rest upon enlightened self-interest.[17]

Developmentalist Criticisms

Several authors writing from a policy-oriented outlook have focused on the effectiveness of the Canadian aid program by trying to understand why it has fallen short in achieving developmental objectives. This has been the main concern of Sanger,[18] Douglas Roche,[19] and Peter Wyse,[20] among others. As we have seen, the work on development assistance sponsored by the North-South Institute has been especially significant.

Réal Lavergne was co-author of the Institute's evaluation of Canadian bilateral aid to Senegal. Writing independently in a 1989 essay on determinants of Canadian aid policy, he categorized motives as *international* (ranging from poverty alleviation through desire for peace and security to pursuit of prestige), *national* (as reflected in commercial and foreign policy objectives), and *private* (associated with provision of goods and services and employment opportunities). "The true motives behind foreign aid are difficult to separate, since rhetoric and reality may not match. All three types of motivation—international, national and private—are influential to some degree, and the question is that of identifying the balance existing between them."[21] Noting critics' doubts about official pronouncements that have "given pride of place to the internationalist and humanitarian objective of fostering development in poor countries," he saw value in scepticism about government rhetoric—but it "can also stoke the fires of cynicism."[22]

Lavergne cited several ways in which competing objectives conflict with developmental effectiveness, and criticized the program for becoming more commercially oriented in the late 1970s. He contended nonetheless that the overall balance was such that "Canadian aid objectives are, as the rhetoric suggests, primarily developmental and humanitarian in orientation."[23] Lavergne offered several arguments and observations to support this conclusion, highlighting his sense of how aid objectives have been perceived within CIDA:

> the development objective is definitely primary in their minds. They resent interference in the program by other departments, and they themselves seem as a rule to pay little attention to the long-term commercial implications of the aid program. . . . CIDA documents . . . do, systematically, address commercial and political dimensions as well as development needs. . . . The impression one gains is that someone considers these points important, including perhaps those writing the document, but they do not . . . constitute the primary thrust of the proposal.[24]

Also writing independently, Roger Young—who directed the North-South Institute's bilateral evaluations and did the one on Tanzania—arrived at a different conclusion. He characterized "a confusion of objectives" as the "most enduring crisis" of the Canadian ODA program:

> Foreign aid is variously used to serve Canadian foreign policy interests, domestic economic interests, and policy objectives; to provide humanitarian, short-term relief in emergency situations; and to meet the stated objective of providing external capital for long-term development in the Third World. This is an almost overwhelming set of goals for one single public sector instrument, and it is not surprising that the aid program is so often misunderstood, abused, and misrepresented.[25]

Bernard Wood, Director of the Institute from 1976 to 1989 (who became Director of OECD's Development Directorate in 1994), told the Hockin-Simard Committee in 1986:

> Canadians are not sure what aid programs have been doing and they have been right to wonder. Our studies and others have demonstrated that we and other donors have loaded impossible burdens onto our aid programs. We have made them much less effective than they could be, and sometimes even more harmful than beneficial.[26]

The Dominant-Class Critique

Drawing on Marxist, neo-Marxist, and dependency theories, the dominant-class perspective agrees that foreign aid has served many purposes, but argues that it has been fundamentally an instrument for strengthening and globalizing capitalist relations of production and entrenching the wealth, power, and privilege of dominant classes in both North and South. This tradition informed Carty and Smith in *Perpetuating Poverty*, their well-researched piece of critical journalism for the Latin American Working Group, as well as a companion volume, *Ties That Bind: Canada and the Third World*, edited by Robert Clarke and Jamie Swift, and a follow-up study in 1991, *Conflicts of Interest: Canada and the Third World*, edited by Jamie Swift and Brian Tomlinson.[27]

Writing in the early 1980s, Linda Freeman analyzed Canadian aid from a more theoretically based perspective based on the neo-Marxist concept of the state's relative autonomy, as developed by Poulantzas and O'Connor and extended to the Canadian context by Panitch, Mahon, and others.[28] Public policy in this approach is seen as the outcome of compromises between the dominant capitalist class and subordinate classes, which in turn reflect a dynamic tension between the state's roles in supporting capital accumulation and maintaining long-term legitimacy for the capitalist system. As Freeman explained,

> while the long-term interests of the capitalist system as a whole would be served by the state, it is quite possible . . . that policies will be adopted that will not be in the direct short-term interests of the dominant class or class fraction. . . . A second aspect of the theory . . . is the proposition that there is an unequal representation of class forces inside the state apparatus, an internal structure of dominance which provides a more subtle channel for control than external pressure groups.[29]

In respect of the aid program, contradictory interests

> have set up the two main parameters within which Canada's aid programmes have operated. At one level, the origin and evolution of development assistance has represented a range of political interests—from anti-Communism within the Western alliance to a desire for respectability within the Commonwealth and other donor nations. At another level, the aid programme has been used as a vehicle for the purposes of capital accumulation within Canada.[30]

A humanitarian "commitment to developing human potential" came in only "as a residual trace element" reflected, for example, at an ideological level in attempts to emphasize the needs of the poorest people.[31]

Freeman suggested that the balance was tilted towards political interests until the mid-1970s—first anti-communism, and later the maintenance of international influence and respect and the furtherance of domestic unity. Then—in the wake of growth in aid spending, economic sluggishness, and recession—the much heavier emphasis given to commercial objectives signified a shift to capital accumulation. Although "the relationship between the dominant class and state policy has become closer in this recession [the early 1980s] than in earlier periods, it is important to keep in mind that the effect is not necessarily permanent."[32]

A Statist Perspective

Nossal revisited the debate about the mixed motives of Canadian development assistance in 1988 by undertaking a "heuristic exercise" based on statist and realist theories in international relations. From the statist approach, he argued that "it makes more sense to look at the interests in development assistance from the perspective of the donor government and its officials rather than from the perspective of the beneficiaries of ODA expenditures in either Canada or the Third World." Following realist assumptions, he explored "what the interests of state officials are and why they should give rise to the kind of approach to development assistance so obviously favoured by the Canadian government"—a "policy that is by all accounts so limited, and so wanting in terms of achieving development objectives for the South."[33]

Contrary to assumptions apparent in various versions of the orthodox trinity, Nossal argued, development policy is largely the outcome of preferences of state actors, not those of either recipient countries or Canadian non-state actors such as business and NGOs. There are, to be sure, numerous benefits—concrete and symbolic, macro and micro—for the Canadian and foreign economies, and for individuals, firms, and organizations in Canada and abroad. Also, foreign policy is not impervious to public opinion at the broadest levels of setting political agendas and determining the limits of policy-making ("parameter setting").[34] However, while particular policies may reflect a coincidence of interest between the state and others,

> what statist theory does assert is that when there is a conflict between the state's preferences and the policy preferences of other actors, the state uses its not inconsiderable power to ensure that its preferences prevail. In other words, it is assumed that the primary and most concrete beneficiary of development assist-

ance is the Canadian state itself; other recipients of the benefits of ODA allocations . . . are of distinctly secondary importance.[35]

While conceding that Freeman's version of the dominant-class perspective, unlike some other writings on the left, accepted the relative autonomy of the state and the particular importance of public officials in policy-making, Nossal argued that it suffered like other Marxist analyses from "a rejection of the statist supposition that government officials may have interests of their own in a particular policy area, interests that are autonomous from, and not necessarily linked to, the mode of production or the interests of either the dominant class or society as a whole."[36]

Building on his assumptions, Nossal presented his critique of the trinity. As noted above, he discounted the humanitarian argument on grounds that Canada had a "mandated limit to altruism." Also rejecting claims that aid contributes much to Canada's national security or economic well-being as overstated, Nossal agreed that there was "at least some evidence for the argument that Canadian officials have an interest in aid in order to have a ready tool for the exercise of influence or power." However, given the widespread proliferation of donors and the very few cases where actions appeared to be so directed (such as the expansion into francophone Africa in the late 1960s and the curtailment of aid to India after the 1974 nuclear test), "the assertion that the Canadian government maintains its commitment to development assistance for such periodic attempts at influence stretches credulity."[37]

Nossal offered his own trinity of motives as a substitute. What drives state officials above all else, he suggested, are interests in prestige, organizational maintenance, and limiting real expenditures. His partial characterization of each follows:

Prestige
Development assistance programmes, it might be argued, have evolved . . . from a means to secure limited political or economic ends to being a sine qua non for membership in good standing in the international community for a Western, industrialized, and wealthy state. Demands for adherence to standards of acceptable behaviour on the issue of contributing to development come from both the Third World and other industrialized states, and the costs of ignoring this most elemental of standards are, it might be hypothesized, so great that the alternative to maintaining a development assistance programme of some kind is not even considered.

Organizational maintenance
A statist perspective . . . has little difficulty with the notion that maintaining the very existence of large bureaucracy becomes an interest for the state as a whole, part of its existence, to be nurtured and maintained for its own sake.

> *Limiting real expenditures*
> [During] periods of sluggish economic growth, high government deficits, and domestic pressures to reduce government spending and resist expansion of the public service, it might be suggested that the state has a real and concrete interest in limiting as much as possible its own spending, and in particular real net expenditures. No better means exist to accomplish these conflicting ends than an aid programme which is designed so that development assistance expenditures are largely expended in Canada.[38]

The interaction of the three might be seen in a "minimax calculus," which "in its crudest form, can be put as follows: 'What is the minimum we have to do to maintain our standing in the international community, and how can we do it in a way that both minimizes net external (or real) expenditures and maximizes both bureaucratic maintenance and our international prestige?' "[39]

Cranford Pratt's Synthesis

Pratt has argued in several articles and books over the years that the dominant-class thesis is the most convincing one for understanding Canada's relations with the Third World. In contrast, he contended, pluralist approaches play down the importance of government by treating it as a mere mediator, and fail to account for the vastly superior influence of the corporate sector in comparison with other interests.[40] Pratt also criticized orthodox statist theory for lacking "a developed theory of the determinants of the interests and values which shape decisions taken by the bureaucracy" and for appearing to "attribute to a bureaucratically created foreign policy a superior political and ethical validity."[41] He also criticized Nossal in particular for "inclining heavily towards a narrowly selfish and parochial interpretation" of the motivations of senior officials.[42]

As we have seen, Pratt has been strongly committed to the humanitarian case for ODA, and concerned to explain why Canada's North-South policies have not been rooted in ethical concerns to the extent that public opinion would seem to permit.[43] That reluctance, he argued, has become more pronounced since the mid-1970s with a steadily waning influence of liberal and humane internationalist values on Canadian foreign policy.[44] Tracing this trend historically, he drew on Fred Hirsch's analysis in *The Limits of Growth* to highlight "a distressing conundrum of contemporary capitalism":

> an ethically tolerable capitalism requires the widespread presence of values and attitudes which the practice of capitalism persistently undermines. For a long time . . . religion, education, and various other non-capitalist institutions kept alive those values which are essential to a well-ordered capitalist society though foreign to capitalism itself. However the institutions which have filled that role

> have gradually been weakened by the omnipresence and power in capitalist societies of an acquisitive and materialist individualism. . . . One must therefore anticipate that unless there are features of post-industrial society which will generate a revival of these values, the capacity of political institutions in modern capitalist societies to contain economic individualism in the interests of collective values will continue to decline.

A "Machiavellian amorality in international politics is a far more natural companion" to contemporary capitalism than humane internationalism.[45]

In the 1980s, Pratt was a key participant in "The Western Middle Powers and Global Poverty Project," which compared the North-South policies of Canada, Denmark, the Netherlands, Norway, and Sweden. A team of international scholars collaborated on four volumes exploring why there emerged "in each of these countries a more than average sensitivity to the aspirations and development needs of the LDCs."

Three sets of factors were seen as formative.[46] First, there was strong commitment to a constructive international role among political leaders, senior civil servants, and "active and informed" citizens in the early postwar decades.

> As middle powers in danger of being overshadowed by their much more powerful neighbours, each wanted to demonstrate its capacity to conduct an independent foreign policy. Each was searching for foreign policy initiatives that were congruent with its political culture. The North-South arena offered greater scope for the articulation of distinctive and appropriate contributions to the international scene than they could hope to achieve in regard to national security or to East-West relations.[47]

Secondly, a widely shared sensitivity to cosmopolitan values reflected the influence of Christian churches with their emphasis upon caring for the poor and distressed, the strength of social democracy as a political ideal, and the political force of a social democratic party. These factors were all weaker in Canada than in the Northern European countries, explaining in part why Ottawa has been less willing to champion the cause of international development or accommodate the interests of the developing countries.[48] Thirdly, decision-makers appreciated significant international and domestic advantages that accrued from taking an altruistic stand on certain issues—goodwill among developing countries, considerable influence in multilateral agencies, and reassurance for their electorates that they have the will and capacity to take independent foreign policy initiatives.

Both Pratt and Olav Stokke, who edited a volume on the determinants of aid policies, concluded that public and official support for the values of humane internationalism was weakening in all five countries.[49] As for Canada, while Pratt has been encouraged by signs of continuing vibrancy outside of government in testimony to parliamentary committees (if not in recent opinion polls), he observed that the decline within the bureaucracy is well advanced:

> In a stable capitalist society the senior bureaucracy, for obvious structural reasons, will be likely to accept that one of its primary responsibilities is to ensure the health of the economic system on which depends the prosperity of its society and the revenues of the government. . . . But place the Canadian economy under strain, or introduce economic issues in the equations of foreign policy making, and the advancement of the interests of the Canadian capitalist economy becomes a central preoccupation of the foreign policy makers.

Moreover, in contrast to an earlier era,

> The Canadian foreign service understands its professional duty. . . . Obligations to those beyond Canada's borders, an effective international expression of the ethical values of the Canadian political culture, a long-term interest in greater international equity—these are unconvincing distractions, soft intrusions, into the hard realities of international politics. In contrast, the "natural" objectives of foreign policy, to the policy makers, are a desire to maximize Canadian influence, to gain prestige internationally, to win economic and political advantages for Canada, and to contain those states that are seen as potential enemies.

Pratt argued that these "characteristics of the ideology that is dominant in the foreign policy making elite" provide a good part of the explanation for the limited sensitivity of Canadian foreign policy to ethical considerations.

Also important has been "the special responsiveness of the Canadian political system and the Canadian bureaucracy to the lobbying of quite specific Canadian business interests." As a result, decisions emerge that are more the product of this relationship and less that of the "considered judgment of senior decision-makers on how to advance Canadian interests."[50] In addition, growing preoccupation with international competitiveness associated with weaknesses in the Canadian economy, the challenge of newly industrializing countries, and "extreme dependence on the United States market . . . left little room in policy circles for those who talked the language of Canada's long-term interests in greater international equity or even of Canada's humanitarian obligations as a rich country." Increasingly, except for the fast-growing Asia Pacific area, "the Third World seemed of peripheral interest."[51]

Although Pratt's perspective has been influenced by Marxist and neo-Marxist analysis, his position might better be characterized as a special variant of statism that would accept aspects of Nossal's revised "trinity," but would see it as flawed in ascribing parochial motives to state officials, and deficient in not accounting for specific policy biases and the secular decline of humane internationalism. As well, Pratt firmly rejects the realist conception of the international role of the state.[52] Writing in 1993 on the locus of decision-making, he observed:

> Canadian aid policies have . . . been shaped largely by senior decision makers rather than driven by public opinion or dominated by partisan political calculations. . . . There have been decisions imposed on the bureaucracy by its political masters, and these have increased in number in recent years. However, they have not been so persistent as to undermine the validity of an overall statist view of decision making on aid. Even less has that view been challenged by examples of the importance of public opinion.[53]

In a 1996 essay on competing perspectives on Canadian ODA policy-making, in which Pratt reiterated his judgement about the superior "illumination" provided by the dominant-class approach, he concluded:

> The discussion over the past 12 years of theories about the determinants of Canadian policies towards the Third World has been conducted as if dominant-class and statist perspectives are competing alternatives. Perhaps they are instead complementary, each useful but at different levels of analysis.[54]

An Assessment of Dominant Class and Statist Approaches

Recently, some scholars on the left employing discourse analysis have criticized earlier dominant-class theorizing about Canadian foreign policy. For Mark Neufeld, its strengths are that, like neo-realist writers such as Nossal, it attributes considerable autonomy to the state, but "unlike neo-realism . . . which must be content to affirm the universal pursuit of power, dominant-class theory is able to identify the specific goals pursued by the state apparatus: the reproduction of the capitalist relations of production." The dominant-class approach also acknowledges "the crucial legitimizing function of a dominant ideology." Neufeld suggested, however, that it

> suffers from some lacunae. First, the dominant-class approach as articulated by Pratt is limited to being a theory of "foreign policy," thus leaving largely unanswered the question of how its emphasis on class society at the domestic level relates to the larger global context. Secondly, to the degree that dominant-class theory is derivative of structuralist Marxist theories of the state, it is prone to . . . over-emphasis on determining structures, and the corresponding neglect of human agency.[55]

For Neufeld, Gramscian-inspired theorizing that analyzes public discourse as well as the "material context of Canadian foreign policy" offered a fruitful way of building on the dominant-class model.[56]

Laura Macdonald suggested that "the neo-Marxist perspective provides a valuable analysis of some of the motivations behind Canadian policy, but does not go far enough in its critique." Drawing on the work of Edward Said and other post-colonial writers, she suggested that the ideological patterns established when Canada played the role of junior partner within the British Empire "have continued to affect how Canadians 'see' the Third World and thus affect official policy."[57] So too have the experiences and attitudes of Christian missionaries and growing numbers of Canadians who have worked in developing countries as technical experts, consultants and volunteers: "the sense of mission, and the paternalistic ideology which viewed Canadians as uniquely suited to solve many of the world's problems, particularly the problems of the non-European world, did not diminish. Rather, it took on a more secular tone."[58]

The terminology used to describe those who were to be "uplifted" shifted away from the "weaker races" to the "poverty-stricken," and became more egalitarian in form with an emphasis on partnership and interdependence. However,

> The language of interdependence conceals the real power relations at work in development policy. . . . The hierarchies of power and status created under Empire were recast in the postwar years, but the end of the era of formal imperialism did not eliminate the economic nor the ideological structures of power which were created in that era. . . . [The] history of colonialism and embedded assumptions about the ability of non-whites to govern themselves underlie and facilitate these unequal partnerships.

Thus, Macdonald concluded, "The ideology reflected in the 'discourse of development' was generally supportive of, but not mechanically determined by, the requirements of an increasingly internationalized capitalism."[59]

Discourse analysis in the neo-Marxist tradition, like the earlier concept of relative autonomy of the state, offers scope for transcending the reductionist and deterministic tendencies found in cruder versions of dominant-class theorizing. Nonetheless, while it is able to accommodate an understanding of human agency and non-material motives, the ultimate focus on class, capitalist relations of production, and legitimation of those relations—all without doubt fundamentally significant phenomena—unduly deflects attention from power, prestige, security, and other factors that drive human behaviour.

Understanding Historical Trends: Strengths and Weaknesses of Nossal and Pratt

Nossal's revised trinity—prestige, organizational maintenance, and expenditure limitation—provides helpful insights about Canadian aid policy-making. David Black and Heather Smith observed that "as an explanation for the persistence and relative size of Canadian ODA and for the deep cutbacks of recent years, it is quite compelling."[60] In addition, the search for prestige and international recognition of a distinctive Canadian identity have encouraged the wide geographical dispersion of ODA and the active pursuit of multilateralism. As Nossal himself admitted, however, he offers little to account for most of the specific content of the aid program.[61] Also, although his framework provides a plausible explanation of Canada's middling record among Western donors, as well as budget cuts during periods of fiscal stringency, it does not suggest a way of accounting for performance in the 1960s and 1970s when Canadian ODA grew much more rapidly than the DAC average, and CIDA made especially strong rhetorical commitments to assist the poorest countries and peoples. In this respect, Pratt was correct in criticizing Nossal's narrow and parochial conception of the motives of state officials.

Pratt himself addressed the question of how to explain "the short period, at most from 1968 to 1977" (which arguably should be dated from Maurice Strong's appointment as Director of the External Aid Office in 1966):

> The humane internationalism of these few years was . . . the result of an exceptional conjunction of factors and influences—a conviction that international communism could not be checked by military containment alone; a prosperous economy and rising government revenues; a government wanting an initiative that would demonstrate its capacity to reflect Canadian values in its foreign policy; a prime minister sensitive to global poverty; a shift within the international aid community towards basic needs; a strong team of officials at CIDA committed to poverty-oriented ODA; and an upsurge of community involvement with Third World issues.[62]

There were other factors as well. While the dramatic increase in Canadian aid in the 1960s stemmed initially from American pressure on Canada to take a more equitable share of the burden, Canada's proportional effort soon outstripped that of the US. No longer able to play the formative role in the spheres of security and trade it had enjoyed in the immediate postwar period, Ottawa found that development assistance offered a modest opportunity for international leadership. Moreover, besides providing scope for expressing distinctive domestic values, it extended an opportunity to pursue a more independent foreign policy at a time when the Americans were at war in Vietnam.[63] The Quebec-Ottawa conflict was of course especially important in vigorous efforts to project Canada's bilingualism through the aid program. Also, whether one characterizes the phenomenon as Laura Macdonald does in her post-colonial analysis, or simply as ethical concern, the values of humane internationalism—as Pratt, Lyon, and others have suggested—appear to have been a stronger motivating force at senior levels in Ottawa than in more recent times.

More generally, however, Pratt's portrayal of a relatively progressive period in the late '60s and early '70s, followed by an ever stronger official inclination to harness the aid program to national and commercial interests, tends to oversimplify the complex historical process examined in this book. The period from 1966 to 1977 certainly stands out in terms of Canada's proportional effort and progressive rhetoric, but it was also a time when there were growing doubts about the quality of aid and CIDA's managerial capabilities. Subsequently, attempts to curb the relative autonomy enjoyed by the Agency during the heady days of Strong and Gérin-Lajoie were intensified, and more energy went into promoting longer-term relationships with recipient countries, especially middle-income and high-growth economies. There were as well blatant pressures to divert a larger portion of the aid budget into trade promotion that were most acute during periods of recession. These efforts, however, did not mark the start of a relentless historical process of sacrificing developmental objectives to Canadian self-interest. Since 1977, there have been serious, if not invariably successful, attempts to strengthen programming in basic human needs, poverty reduction, human resource development, women's participation, human rights, and the environment. The recent management renewal efforts may also generate positive developmental outcomes.

The more general point is that every era—before, after, and during 1966-77—has been characterized by contradictory tendencies reflecting competing objectives of officialdom, political and economic interests at home and abroad, organizational dynamics, and the changing global environment.

Questioning the Relative Autonomy of State Actors

Jean-Philippe Thérien and Alain Noël suggested that statist/realist, neo-Marxist, and liberal models of international relations, which see development assistance largely as a foreign policy phenomenon, make assumptions about domestic politics but leave largely unexplored "the articulation of Canadian aid policy to its domestic context."[64] Building on the work of Pratt, Stokke, and others in the Western Middle Powers and Global Poverty Project, Thérien and Noël addressed this issue by exploring further the relationship between Canada's development assistance policies and its welfare state institutions. Their approach involved a comparative analysis of all OECD donors, not just the Northern European countries that were the focus of the earlier studies. After ascertaining that "no simple, unilinear relation" exists between total public expenditures, social transfers, and aid spending, they examined the institutional attributes of various welfare states, employing Esping-Andersen's typology (conservative, liberal, and social democratic). Using this approach, "Canada's welfare state can best be characterized as a liberal institutional arrangement coloured by elements of universalism, inherited from trade union and partisan pressures. The country's aid policy mirrors this characterization, making Canada a generous state among the group of less committed donors." Stressing the need for further research on the linkage, Thérien and Noël found it noteworthy "that recent shifts in aid and social policies follow a strikingly similar and parallel course. In both cases, budget considerations and notions of market efficiency and selectivity have been used to justify a redefinition of the Canadian government's commitments, away from universality."[65]

While the Thérien/Noël study can be seen as consistent with both statist and dominant-class explanations at the level of parameter-setting, it raised the more general question of whether these perspectives overstate the degree of autonomy enjoyed by state actors vis-à-vis societal pressures. It is revealing in this respect that OECD officials interviewed by the author in 1989, when asked to comment on distinctive features of Canadian aid, pointed towards what they saw as an unusual responsiveness among senior officials to movements in public opinion as reflected in polling data.

However, though polls have had some impact on budgetary decisions, Pratt argued correctly that there is little evidence to suggest that they have affected the content of the aid program or the mix of objectives underpinning it.[66] Perhaps the one major exception was the extraordinary level of popular support for relief for the victims of war and drought in Ethiopia in 1984-85. It dampened pressures for aid cuts within the Tory cabinet, and had a profound impact on the review of aid policy by the Winegard committee in 1986-87.

The apparent insensitivity of state officials to polls is an important component of what Pratt saw as "a major paradox in Canadian development assistance policies": "The Canadian public and Parliament have supported aid for over forty years, primarily for humanitarian reasons; nevertheless, most scholarly commentators have concluded that humanitarian considerations have played little role within government in the shaping of those policies."[67] There are many in government, especially in CIDA, who would challenge the extent to which Pratt and others have discounted humanitarianism as a consideration in shaping ODA policy. Apart from that contentious question, there are serious problems with the way he formulated the paradox. First, while polls have consistently shown humanitarian sentiment as the leading reason people give for supporting foreign aid, they have also revealed scant general knowledge about the nature or extent of Canadian development assistance—and, except among a small minority, a low ranking in comparison with other public goods. A committed development community has indeed called for a sharper focus on the needs of the poorest of the poor, but there is no evidence of a widespread public concern to which official Ottawa has been indifferent. As Robert Miller observed, popular support for aid has been at best "a mile wide but an inch thick."[68]

Secondly, Pratt has overstated the gap between parliamentarians and government decision-makers. As he documented with meticulous care,[69] several official policy statements since the late 1970s have in effect rehearsed versions of the conventional trinity of mixed motives and objectives in response to calls from parliamentary committees for reforms to strengthen the developmental coherence and humanitarian mission of the aid program. However, even if diluted (or subsequently neglected like some commitments in *Sharing Our Future*), recommendations from these committees on such issues as human rights and poverty alleviation have had a direct impact on government policies and CIDA's operations. In turn, parliamentarians have made recommendations reflecting humane internationalist values not because of widespread public pressure, but in good measure because articulate, often passionate NGO representatives, academics, and others in a small development community were able to make their case effectively—and often better than state officials or representatives of business. A score of dedicated MPs have also made a difference—most prominently Douglas Roche and William Winegard. So too have some remarkably able parliamentary committee staff.

Private-sector suppliers and consultants, business associations, and representatives of NGOs and NGIs have all exerted pressure on CIDA at various levels, seeking influence upon ODA policies and their implementation, as well as contracts and/or financial support for development work. For its part, the Agency has devoted considerable energy to cultivating these relationships.

The historical evidence confirms Pratt's contention about "the special responsiveness" of state actors to specific Canadian business interests. The success of business lobbyists in thwarting the modest relaxation of aid tying promised by the strategy for 1975-80, in securing access to mixed credit financing, and in curtailing country focus bilateral programming by NGOs and NGIs are examples of private-sector clout when perceived vital interests were at stake. For the most part, however, business lobbying has focused on securing projects rather than influencing policies. Generally speaking, as we have seen, the private sector has had much less interest in CIDA than the Agency has had in courting the private sector—a reflection both of official judgements about what is best for capital and a desire to generate interest and support from the business sector.

Of CIDA's two major domestic constituencies, it has been the voluntary sector that has been the more assiduous in lobbying for changes in aid policy, and often the better organized. Two studies in the early 1980s concluded that NGOs lacked influence on aid policy,[70] and Pratt argued in a 1982 article that consultations with business were more meaningful than those with "counter-consensual" groups within the development community.[71] However, in her excellent comparative examination of NGOs and development policy-making in Canada and Britain, Alison Van Rooy observed a change in the 1980s: "The realization that large-scale projects alone could not engender 'development' has made CIDA dependent on NGOs' activity and expertise in certain areas, and it is this dependence that has opened the doors for NGO influence on policy."[72] More broadly, she argued, "NGOs are *needed* to implement, administer and advise on aid projects, legitimize the official aid program to the public, and support CIDA's policy agenda within government."[73]

At least partly because of these desired forms of cooperation, Agency officials—especially in the 1980s—became more sensitive to meeting demands from Canadian partners than much of the statist and dominant-class literature would have us believe. Representatives of business may have been viewed as more credible and responsible than their NGO counterparts, but the successes of development activists in influencing policy and securing resources have been impressive.

In rebuttal, a statist might argue that the government was the gatekeeper and really determined the limits of sensitivity to NGO and NGI demands. A neo-marxist might see responsiveness to non-business interests as an illustration of how "dominant classes make real concessions (always within limits) to subordinate classes to achieve broad societal consent for their leadership."[74] However, while state actors held the upper hand in relations with their non-governmental constituencies, and tried increasingly to manage those relations, "something for everyone" was a growing phenomenon in the distribution of the aid budget during the Catley-Carlson years. As we have seen, a high point for domestic interests was reached in 1988 with *Sharing Our Future*, a remarkably populist document in its promises, material and symbolic, for all of CIDA's domestic partners.

Relations between CIDA and many in the voluntary sector turned sour early in the 1990s, first as a result of the structural adjustment imperative championed by Marcel Massé, and then when it became apparent that the Mulroney administration was backing off commitments in *Sharing Our Future* and pushing for a greater commercialization of aid. Subsequent soft-peddling of economic reform, a renewed emphasis on improving consultations, and the greater emphasis under the Liberals on poverty reduction and basic human needs can be interpreted in part as evidence of both the continuing effectiveness of NGO lobbying and CIDA's need for support at home and in the field during these lean and mean times. However, drastic budget reductions—especially the decisions to cut off public funding for Canadian-based development education efforts and decentralized NGO coalitions—undermined the rebuilding process.

Contributions from Other Approaches

While the statist perspective suggests that governmental interests will prevail over those emerging from civil society, Nossal pointed out that it

> does not assume that "the state" is a cohesive, monolithic unit. Divergences over policy will occur within the apparatus of the state, with those officials with the weightiest political resources prevailing. Policy is assumed to be the result of "governmental politics"—the struggle for power within government among officials for adoption of policies which fit their particular conception of the national interest.[75]

Bureaucratic politics or governmental politics (to include actors at the political level) has been a significant focus in the bilateral aid evaluations of the North-South Institute and in the work of Lavergne, Rudner, Wyse, Young, Glyn Berry, Phillip Rawkins, Mark Charlton, and Alison Van Rooy.

Governmental Politics

In his pioneering 1974 study of the politics of foreign aid, the British scholar John White observed that the foreign aid agency in an OECD country has "no natural allies" among government departments

> for whom the aid agency's activities are of vital concern. . . . Advocates of aid try to overcome this problem by arguing that in the long term the development of poor countries is in the "enlightened" self-interest of all. . . . But this concept of "enlightened" self-interest is far too vague, when set against the tangible benefits of expenditure on schools, roads, health, etc. . . . Politically, aid is nearly always expendable, and the aid administrator is nearly always on the defensive.[76]

This defensiveness was evident in Berry's account of how CIDA officials acted during interdepartmental consultations leading up to the *Strategy for International Development Cooperation 1975-1980*. As we saw, he also showed how CIDA officials—who sought to advance what they saw as a strong developmental agenda—limited their aspirations in anticipation of resistance elsewhere. As the cabinet wanted any disagreements resolved at the bureaucratic level, the Agency's objectives were still further diluted in arriving at an interdepartmental consensus. The strategy that finally emerged contained modest incremental victories for CIDA, but these were short-lived, not least because other bureaucratic players perceived the Agency's behaviour as excessively aggressive and independent.[77]

Wyse, a former CIDA employee who witnessed this effort in the late 1970s, claimed that

> consensus decision-making within interdepartmental committees was at the heart of many of the problems within the foreign aid program. Each department brought its own objectives to the aid program. Thus, although Cabinet ministers may have claimed the objective of the aid program was to help the Third World poor, the objectives in practice were the objectives of the primary decision-makers.[78]

He reported that the Agency's senior executives felt impelled to load the aid program with objectives appealing to other departments, in the process selling "influence over the aid program in return for verbal support at budget time."[79]

Somewhat more dispassionately, Rawkins agreed that "The logical way to secure support from the centres of bureaucratic power was to accept, at least in part, the agendas of others." Young suggested that, for policy-makers and aid bureaucrats, "trade-offs can become so internalized" that they "can easily conceive of a mutuality of interests between Canadian and Third World governments." The development criterion "in the context of the other priorities and objectives for aid is often the least influential and the easiest to sacrifice."[80] Moreover, when CIDA's leadership was seen as too assertive or as encroaching upon the territorial prerogatives of other departments (in the late 1960s, the early 1970s, and again in the early 1990s), counteractive measures confirmed that the Agency has a "relatively weak bargaining position" within the Ottawa environment[81]— or, to put it more graphically in Van Rooy's words, CIDA is "low man on the totem pole."[82]

Charlton highlighted another significant aspect of CIDA's interdepartmental relations in applying to the Agency the "guardian-spender" framework in public policy analysis. It sees government departments divided between "spenders" who seek increased resources, and "guardians" or central agencies (such as the Department of Finance and Treasury Board) who try to limit spending.[83] He noted that "it is tempting to interpret the . . . argument as implying that most of the pressure to spend comes from CIDA while the pressure to . . . cut costs of the aid program . . . comes from an alliance of 'those who must manage the effects of overall government spending, and from those to whom the benefits of prestige do not accrue directly.' " However, development assistance "is probably unique" in being able to serve several international and domestic interests of a broad range of departments. "Thus the intra-state competition is not just between spenders and guardians, but just as frequently between spender departments. Even in cases where, for developmental and other reasons, CIDA may wish to alter its disbursement patterns, it frequently faces pressures from other departments."[84] Charlton cited as examples the commodity composition of food aid (reflecting conflicting pressures from Agriculture, External Affairs, and Fisheries and Oceans), and repeated failures to reduce the number of recipient countries. The pattern is even more complex, of course, because Finance is one of the guardians, yet also a major spender of Canadian ODA on contributions to the World Bank.

Testifying before the MacEachen-Gauthier Committee in 1994, Van Rooy, then based at the North-South Institute, coined an apt metaphor when observing the difficulty of achieving coherence in Canadian policy towards the South if "CIDA's policy space and its funding are . . . regarded as a parking lot for other departments' aims and ambitions."[85]

As aid policy has largely been a non-partisan affair, political conflict has been less intense than in many policy fields. Political leaders have played an important role in promoting ODA and shielding it somewhat from fiscal pressures—especially Pierre Trudeau up to the mid-1970s, and again during his 1980-84 prime ministerial term; and Joe Clark, when he served as secretary of state for External Affairs from 1984 to 1991. Ministers responsible for CIDA have had an impact on various aspects of aid delivery, not least in expanding the range of recipients of Canadian aid and resisting bureaucratic advice to achieve greater effectiveness through concentration. They have ensured as well that the domestic benefits of the aid program are distributed widely and attuned to electoral advantage. As we have seen, Quebec ministers have been especially attentive to the interests of their constituents.

Regime Analysis

An American sociologist, Robert E. Wood, argued in 1986 that a consistent conception of development has underpinned an "international aid regime" since the Second World War. "From its beginning," he wrote, "aid has been as much about the nature as about the pace of economic growth."[86] Drawing on the work of Krasner and others who developed regime analysis as a tool for the study of international relations, he identified a number of principles, norms, rules, and procedures that had their genesis in the Marshall Plan experience.

Wood's thesis is that the aid regime of the West was structured not only to discredit the Soviet model of development and experiments in radical socialism but also to oppose the growth of national or state capitalism. As well, it has worked "to promote the expansion of the private sector, both domestic and foreign, and the dominance of market principles of exchange; and to encourage 'outward-looking,' export-oriented types of development."[87] Avoiding competition with private capital by refusing loans for productive enterprises, imposing conditions upon the uses of aid, and wielding debt obligations as a lever for ensuring compliance, have been the main features of a regime whose "principal teachers" have been the World Bank and the US AID.[88] In turn, DAC has provided bilateral donors with a locus for international networking, mutual peer review, and collaborative policy-making.

In 1993, David Lumsdaine employed regime analysis to advance a quite different thesis: "Foreign aid is a paradigm case of the influence of crucial moral principles because of its universal scope, as assistance from well-off nations to any in need, its focus on poverty, and its empowerment of the weakest groups and states in the international system."[89] Arguing that any satisfactory explanation of foreign aid must look beyond the economic and political interests of donors to the influence upon them of humanitarian and egalitarian convictions, he cited five historical trends as evidence:

- a rise in ODA as a percentage of GNP (except from the US);
- less exclusiveness in relationships between donors and recipients;
- more assistance channelled through multilateral agencies;
- improved terms (more grants and easier repayment conditions for loans) and fewer conditions tying support to donor procurement; and
- more aid directed "to the poorer nations—particularly the least developed nations of Africa and Asia—and more consciously designed to reach poorer sectors within those (and other) countries."[90]

Wood's dominant-class analysis ignored donors' widespread support for state-led import substitution strategies prior to the triumph of free market ideology in the 1980s. Like many critiques from the left, it also underestimated the significance of humanitarian sentiment as a motive for aid, and failed to acknowledge sufficiently the extent to which alternative perspectives on human development, poverty reduction, women in development, human rights, etc. have influenced donor programming in recent years.

In highlighting important trends often lost in critical commentary, Lumsdaine's liberal, idealist thesis glossed over the tendency for aid agencies to become increasingly directive and heavy-handed in their dealings with recipient countries, especially during the 1980s and 1990s. In addition, his book was published just when most donors began to cut back their ODA in response to pressures for reductions in public expenditures, the end of Cold War tensions, and competing demands for assistance from countries in transition from communism. Nevertheless, while the two authors reflect divergent value orientations, and portray quite different images of an international aid regime, they correctly identified the major impact of a constantly shifting, often contradictory, but dominant transnational discourse on aid policy.

In explaining why CIDA has strongly embraced almost every new programming fashion, one might posit Nossal's prestige motive for bureaucrats wanting to be in good standing with their international peers. That has certainly been a factor, as has enthusiasm for new insights into how to go about a difficult business. However, another rationale was suggested by White in his 1974 study:

> some aid agencies try to insulate themselves from domestic pressures by integrating the aid programme into an international framework. Such aid agencies, of which the Canadian is an example, tend to concentrate on countries for which a coordinating framework exists. . . . In this situation, the bilateral agency can claim that its policy objectives are determined for it by the recommendations of the international agency [such as the World Bank].[91]

In several instances, external legitimation has been useful for CIDA officials trying, amid conflicting pressures, to strengthen the developmental focus of policy. Charlton showed how new principles and norms, centred in the international Committee on Food Aid Policies and Programs and the World Food Program, assisted Agency efforts in the mid-1970s to move to a more developmentally oriented strategy for food aid.[92] In the 1980s, Canadians contributed to a DAC consensus on Women in Development that in turn energized the policy thrust within the Agency. Most recently, international norms helped shape CIDA's new policy on private-sector development, which moved beyond the traditional emphasis on benefits for Canadian business to a focus on strengthening enabling environments, competitive enterprises, and financial institutions in recipient countries.

Without doubt, regime analysis helps make sense of Massé's controversial efforts to redirect CIDA towards a primary focus on macro-economic policy reform in developing countries. In her study of Canada's "conversion to structural adjustment," Marcia Burdette saw the World Bank/DAC consensus as crucial, alongside "the interplay of domestic, bureaucratic, and personal factors" that brought about the Agency's "full endorsement."[93] David Black and Peter McKenna found conventional statist and dominant-class explanations of little help in trying to understand Canada's leadership role in Guyana's structural adjustment process. They looked instead to a Gramscian version of regime analysis highlighting "the transnationalization of social forces and the emergence of 'hegemonic ideas' in the nexus between transnational capital, leading IFIs and international economic organizations, economic thinkers, and senior state officials particularly, though not only, from Northern countries."[94] Black and Thérien, with Andrew Clark, also used regime analysis to explain Canada's acceptance of the recent "standardization" of aid policy in Africa.[95]

Though with different nuances, the official donor consensus has coincided on certain aid priorities with what NGOs in Canada and elsewhere have seen as a progressive agenda for international development. Indeed, the transnational establishment has often been receptive to ideas and pressures from non-governmental activists. As a result, CIDA has been able to draw on both domestic and international support in promoting such priorities as poverty reduction, basic human needs, WID, and civil society. In contrast, when World Bank/DAC and NGO perspectives became intensely polarized over structural adjustment and economic reform in the early 1990s, the Agency lost voluntary-sector support. Not coincidentally, though there were other reasons as well, CIDA became much more vulnerable to the commercial and foreign policy pressures that were embodied in the 1993 International Assistance Policy Update.

Organizational Analysis

Important insights have emerged from the application of organizational and managerial analysis to studies of CIDA's behaviour and institutional arrangements. The findings suggest that constraints on developmental effectiveness imposed by multiple objectives, on top of the already formidable challenges of operating abroad in uncertain environments, have been compounded by organizational characteristics and dynamics.

In his institutional analysis of CIDA, Rawkins observed that the emphasis of much of the academic literature is on "the dominance of outside interests—other government departments or the broad needs of the capitalist state." He argued, however, that it is important "to recognize that government agencies are far more than merely political arenas in which contending social forces struggle for dominance. They are also collections of structures and standard operating procedures, the articulation and character of which serve to define and defend values, norms, interests, identities, and beliefs."[96] Rawkins suggested that some academic criticisms of the gap between rhetoric and reality, or the "considerable time-lag between the formulation of . . . new donor orthodoxy . . . and implementation," fail to appreciate that

> Development *theory* does not—except possibly at the macro-economic level—translate readily into development assistance *policy*, let alone implementation of projects and programs. . . . [Implementation] is never a simple putting-into-practice of policy. It draws on the particular experiences, preferences and expertise, as well as the more immediate professional, bureaucratic and career concerns of those who will be responsible for programming.

Even when there is agreement at all levels to a new policy initiative, "it is likely to take three to five years before changes in programming and expenditure patterns are visible."[97]

Rawkins noted that, for program officers, a key to program survival is "manageability." While this involves taking into account "what will fly" at the political level, "where policies fail to provide clear guidelines on practice (as is often the case), program designers and managers must fill the gap." In doing so, "they will draw on CIDA's conventions and traditions. Thus, 'appropriate behaviour' and 'trade craft' . . . guide organizational practice."[98] Inadequate clarity within the Agency on what constitutes good development—together with an intensely individualistic institutional culture—have both reflected and reinforced a lack of organizational and programming coherence. The challenge of achieving such coherence has had to confront another organizational tendency identified by Rawkins:

> [When] top management attempts to impose new policies or practices . . . such efforts are quickly transformed into discussion of process and implementation procedures. . . . [The] very strength of the organizational culture has often precluded serious, sustained analysis of the presumed development objectives associated with policy initiatives. Instead, process comes first, and process determines objectives.[99]

As the history of CIDA attests, this inclination has been particularly evident in response to disbursement pressures and regulatory controls.

In her 1975 study of organizational behaviour in US AID, Judith Tendler observed that, from the vantage point of the aid agency, there is extraordinary pressure to spend all of the limited funds allocated in order to protect its budget and ensure that unspent funds do not lapse at the end of the fiscal year. However, the "supply of funds as seen from within the donor organization . . . is perceived in relation not to total estimates of need and supply but to the amount of work or time required to commit the funds available." Given the complexities of putting projects together and inevitably long delays, "there may be fewer financeable projects, at any given moment in time, than funds available. From the employee's point of view, the scarce commodity is frequently the project rather than the funds."[100] When the performance of both the agency and the project officer come to be judged by success in moving money, qualitative issues fade away and there is a bias towards mega-projects, lines of credit, and other quick-disbursing options that maximize spending and minimize the amount of staff time required.[101] Moreover, as Roger Ehrhardt noted, "There is no incentive to be innovative since innovative projects, as a rule, require more time to plan and implement than do run-of-the-mill activities."[102]

Ehrhardt and Wyse complained about developmentally perverse outcomes of disbursement pressures when CIDA's budget was growing much more rapidly than staffing resources.[103] Even before 1977—when the Agency lost its authority to carry over unspent funds from one year to the next—criticisms voiced by MPs and other departments about unspent allocations had heightened a sense of vulnerability within the Agency that intensified pressure to disburse. Then, after media horror stories and serious criticisms from the Auditor General—developments not unrelated to disbursement pressures—the response of central agencies was to impose tighter financial and regulatory controls on CIDA's operations. Pressure to disburse continued, but increasingly officers' performance was measured "by the extent to which they adhered to regulations and established plans of operation."[104]

As Rawkins observed, "It is difficult to hold a CIDA manager accountable for rural poverty or the rate of infant mortality in Bangladesh or Malawi but easy to bring her or him to account over improper procedures."[105] The result of putting "squeaky-clean" financial management first is that development comes second;[106] projects get locked into "sub-optimal directions" and project design is biased "toward low-risk, easily verified objectives."[107] In the 1980s, with increasing delegation of more and more of the project cycle to consultants, CIDA's desk officers were transformed into managers of contracts rather than projects, thus becoming even more removed from a concern about developmental outcomes.

Among myriad restructuring efforts over the years, decentralization had the greatest potential for putting hands-on development ahead of bureaucratic process. Its demise coincided with the start of the seemingly endless strategic management review, which finally culminated in the recent commitments to results-based management, stronger links between programming priorities and field activities, and more open performance review.

Conclusion

In assessing the motives and objectives of Canadian development assistance, various commentators have criticized the conventional trinity, but reached disparate conclusions about "real" factors that have shaped the program. It is tempting to agree with Glyn Berry that "attempts to identify a clear hierarchy of objectives in the aid programme seem to arise from misdirected efforts to impose an intellectually satisfying order on policies and events which in reality defy simple structuring."[108] Nonetheless, if one is concerned about the effectiveness of Canada's ODA in promoting sustainable development and reducing poverty, the pursuit by government of multiple and often conflicting objectives is a major problem and therefore an important object of inquiry.

Much of the theoretically inclined literature has discounted the possibility of relieving the aid program of its plethora of motives and objectives. Scholars writing from statist and dominant-class perspectives have concluded that state actors, especially in senior levels of the bureaucracy, have dominated the politics of aid. Kim Richard Nossal and Cranford Pratt in particular have offered different but important insights about the determinants of Canadian aid. While both have argued that state actors enjoy considerable autonomy in pursuing their political and bureaucratic agendas, Pratt has seen these as particularly constrained by the imperatives of serving an advanced capitalist state. What these approaches fail to capture as fully as the evidence in this book warrants is the impact on the aid program of political brokerage and interest mediation at three interacting levels—state-societal, state-centred, and transnational.

Domestic pressures from outside government have had more impact on the aid program than other aspects of foreign policy, or than Nossal has recognized. State actors, as Pratt and others have argued, may in general defer to corporate hegemony but officials within CIDA have invested heavily in building up a strong voluntary sector that can provide political and programming support. In the process, they have become more responsive to lobbying by non-governmental organizations and institutions, and have tried to balance demands from NGOs and NGIs with business interests, which have tended to focus more on obtaining funding and programming opportunities than on influencing policy.

A focus on the black box of governmental politics is essential for understanding the history of Canadian aid policy-making. Nossal's more general analysis of the interests of state actors, though consistent with an intra-state focus, yields little insight about the content of policies that have reflected shifting patterns of conflict and cooperation within the bureaucracy, as well as occasional intervention from the political level. CIDA's junior position within the bureaucracy and a budget that makes it "everybody's billion dollar baby"[109] have been key factors working against coherence in the development assistance program.

Regime analysis focuses attention on the powerful impact of transnational discourse on CIDA's programming priorities, and on how that factor has helped the Agency resist, to some degree, pressures to make ODA serve non-developmental objectives. Fortunately for CIDA, there has often been broad convergence between the NGO agenda, both internationally and domestically, and the consensus among multilateral agencies and other bilateral donors. Macro-economic policy reform was a major exception, and the Agency's open embrace of it in the early 1990s put CIDA in a weakened, cross-pressured situation.

Finally, organizational and managerial analysis serves as an important reminder that aid policy cannot be explained simply by analyzing political dynamics. Throughout CIDA's history, there have been bureaucratic barriers thwarting the translation of formal policy into operational reality in the field. Disbursement pressures, regulatory controls, and the privatization of aid delivery have had a major impact on shaping the aid program and limiting its developmental effectiveness.

Drawing on an interpretation advanced by Agency insiders, Gerald Schmitz likened CIDA "to an overburdened 'Christmas tree.' "[110] To extend this metaphor, if there has been a consistent tendency amid all the twists and turns of aid policy-making, it has been that the Canadian ODA Christmas tree has been weighed down with more and more ornaments of quite different sizes and shapes, often hung with the best of human intentions. The jumble of policies, projects, and priorities that have decorated the tree through the second half of the century reflect the interests and concerns of a mixed variety of actors—Ottawa mandarins and politicians, lobbyists for business and non-governmental Canadian interests, the international aid community, and CIDA officers in particular. The needs and aspirations of the world's poor are reflected much more faintly.

While there is much to criticize about the historical record of development assistance, not least the collapse of budgetary support in the 1990s, the need for ODA is as strong as ever, especially for countries and people who have limited access to other forms of capital. It is true that economic growth has been dramatic in parts of Asia and Latin America, and that many developing countries have experienced remarkable improvements in health, life expectancy, and literacy. However, the gap between the world's richest and poorest has widened alarmingly, much of Africa remains desperately deprived, and poverty and human insecurity—often amid abundance—are on the rise everywhere.

The 1970 Liberal white paper proclaimed: "a society concerned about poverty and development abroad will be concerned about poverty and development at home." That statement was preceded by a corollary that, alas, appears more apt today: "a society able to ignore poverty abroad will find it much easier to ignore it at home."[111] Commitment to collective action ebbed with the end of the Cold War, the success of right-wing efforts to delegitimate the state as an instrument of human betterment, and the onset of a fiscal crisis that weakened the popular will to accept responsibility for the less fortunate at home and abroad. Now, as an obsession with deficit reduction gives way to the prospect of a fiscal surplus, there are strident calls for tax cuts, debt reduction, and reinvestment in domestic health care and education. Weaker voices remind us of the needs of the insecure and the disadvantaged in Canada and around the world, and of the commitment once made to channel a tiny but growing percentage of our national income to support people in developing countries in their efforts to achieve better lives for themselves and their children.

Appendices

Appendix A
Canadian Official Development Assistance: Selected Components, Total, and ODA/GNP Ratio, 1949-50 to 1996-97 ($ million)

Fiscal year	Bilateral	Multi-lateral	Voluntary	Industrial cooperation	Total	ODA/GNP ratio (%)
1949/50	—	12.99	—	—	12.99	0.08
1950/51	0.01	12.49	—	—	12.49	0.07
1951/52	25.27	0.97	0.03	—	27.12	0.12
1952/53	5.52	2.26	0.03	—	7.83	0.03
1953/54	11.72	2.11	0.02	—	14.44	0.05
1954/55	12.55	3.34	0.02	—	16.45	0.06
1955/56	25.32	2.44	0.02	—	29.37	0.10
1956/57	22.44	7.27	0.02	—	29.73	0.09
1957/58	58.13	3.94	0.02	—	62.08	0.18
1958/59	66.93	3.73	0.02	—	70.67	0.20
1959/60	61.17	5.84	0.02	—	68.19	0.19
1960/61	46.74	20.36	0.02	—	73.48	0.20
1961/62	37.04	21.24	0.02	—	59.10	0.15
1962/63	28.15	28.09	0.02	—	57.65	0.13
1963/64	40.19	21.29	0.02	—	64.03	0.14
1964/65	65.44	34.38	0.02	—	100.89	0.20
1965/66	85.78	34.04	0.49	—	122.35	0.22
1966/67	163.18	47.33	0.76	—	212.89	0.34
1967/68	139.02	48.24	1.76	—	190.44	0.29
1968/69	149.15	56.12	3.15	0.02	210.71	0.28
1969/70	198.09	69.82	8.57	—	277.21	0.34
1970/71	264.10	67.46	9.10	—	345.42	0.40
1971/72	267.15	99.89	12.74	0.06	396.66	0.41
1972/73	322.37	156.96	17.29	0.06	513.29	0.47
1973/74	364.84	190.07	22.50	0.14	590.18	0.46
1974/75	495.55	204.35	28.19	0.12	748.21	0.49
1975/76	507.73	331.65	35.29	0.11	903.54	0.53
1976/77	466.41	422.09	42.24	0.09	966.47	0.49
1977/78	541.13	421.24	49.78	0.25	1,046.24	0.49
1978/79	533.45	485.52	73.60	0.46	1,136.45	0.49
1979/80	598.77	493.37	77.50	3.95	1,282.51	0.47

Appendix A (continued)

Fiscal year	Bilateral	Multi-lateral	Voluntary	Industrial cooperation	Total	ODA / GNP ratio (%)
1980/81	581.47	512.93	89.01	7.21	1,308.07	0.43
1981/82	671.35	539.21	117.29	14.16	1,486.68	0.43
1982/83	716.10	588.03	164.32	16.29	1,672.06	0.46
1983/84	678.49	672.24	197.30	28.69	1,797.08	0.45
1984/85	874.63	684.10	190.71	38.50	2,104.56	0.49
1985/86	816.22	864.62	220.33	27.83	2,247.61	0.47
1986/87	967.02	953.11	248.77	32.38	2,551.77	0.50
1987/88	1,101.18	838.36	274.86	38.52	2,624.06	0.48
1988/89	1,177.01	928.78	304.56	60.55	2,946.60	0.49
1989/90	1,026.30	912.47	328.03	58.92	2,849.87	0.45
1990/91	1,106.45	972.22	334.11	62.31	3,035.34	0.45
1991/92	1,125.32	1,064.23	355.85	67.25	3,182.46	0.49
1992/93	979.21	1,023.15	337.66	73.18	2,972.20	0.44
1993/94	891.86	1,046.35	311.48	69.34	3,075.27	0.44
1994/95	1,056.32	976.13	317.80	65.49	3,092.46	0.42
1995/96	898.57	904.16	257.38	63.66	2,683.55	0.36
1996/97	933.42	862.78	257.44	57.42	2,676.44	0.34

Source: CIDA, Canadian Historical ODA System; CIDA, *Statistical Report on Official Development Assistance, Fiscal Year 1995/96* (Hull: Canadian International Development Agency, 1997), pp. 8, 34, 72; and CIDA, *Statistical Report on Official Development Assistance, Fiscal Year 1996/97* (Hull: Canadian International Development Agency, 1998), pp. 1, 2, 28.

Appendix B
Percentage Distribution of Canadian Government-to-Government ODA[a] by Region, Ten-Year Cumulative Totals, 1950-60, and Five-Year Cumulative Totals, 1960-95

Period	Asia	Africa	Americas	Miscellaneous[b]	Totals
1950-51/	99.9	—	0.1	—	100.0
1959-60	(288.66)	(0.11)	(0.29)	—	(289.04)
1960-61/	88.4	6.4	5.2	—	100.0
1964-65	(192.27)	(14.00)	(11.30)	—	(217.57)
1965-66/	76.1	16.9	6.6	0.4	100.0
1969-70	(556.95)	(123.87)	(48.60)	(2.70)	(732.12)
1970-71/	54.7	35.1	8.6	1.6	100.0
1974-75	(937.25)	(601.01)	(146.82)	(28.94)	(1,714.02)
1975-76/	45.1	41.4	11.9	1.6	100.0
1979-80	(1,193.17)	(1,094.86)	(315.21)	(44.39)	(2,647.63)
1980-81/	41.1	47.2	8.2	3.5	100.0
1984-85	(1,408.62)	(1,616.98)	(280.72)	(117.92)	(3,424.24)
1985-86/	38.6	44.8	15.4	1.2	100.0
1989-90	(1,935.77)	(2,250.77)	(775.37)	(59.97)	(5,021.88)
1990-91/	34.5	47.4	17.8	0.3	100.0
1994-95	(1,637.55)	(2,250.92)	(846.15)	(13.06)	(4,747.68)
All years	43.4	42.3	12.9	1.4	100.0
	(8,150.24)	(7,952.52)	(2,424.46)	(266.98)	(18,794.20)

a Government-to-government ODA includes bilateral contributions (less loan repayments) and, since 1986, Export Development Corporation Funds (Section 23, formerly Section 31) that are counted as official development assistance.

b Includes Europe (Turkey is coded as Europe), Oceania, and unattributable bilateral contributions.

Source: Calculated from CIDA, Canadian Historical ODA System; CIDA, *Statistical Report on Official Development Assistance, Fiscal Year 1994/95* (Hull: Canadian International Development Agency, 1996), pp. 14-24. Figures in parentheses are $ million.

Appendix C
Top Twenty Recipients of Canadian Government-to-Government ODA at Five-Year Intervals, 1960-61 to 1995-96 ($ million)

	Government-to-government ODA	Cumulative total	Cumulative percentage[a]	Rank
1960-61				
India	22.37	22.37	47.9	1
Pakistan	14.15	36.53	78.1	2
Thailand	2.09	38.62	82.6	3
Sri Lanka	2.09	40.71	87.1	4
Indonesia	0.86	41.57	88.9	5
Burma	0.64	42.21	90.3	6
Vietnam	0.47	42.68	91.3	7
Malaysia	0.40	43.07	92.2	8
Cambodia	0.13	43.21	92.4	9
Ghana	0.11	43.31	92.7	10
Philippines	0.07	43.38	92.8	11
Nigeria	0.06	43.44	92.9	12
Singapore	0.04	43.47	93.0	13
Laos	0.02	43.50	93.1	14
Sierra Leone	0.01	43.51	93.1	15
Uganda	0.01	43.52	93.1	16
Belize	0.01	43.53	93.1	17
Hong Kong	0.01	43.54	93.1	18
Brunei	0.01	43.54	93.1	19
Nepal	0.01	43.54	93.2	20
Total[b]		46.74	100.0	
1965-66				
India	39.85	39.85	46.5	1
Pakistan	19.35	59.20	69.0	2
Sri Lanka	4.66	63.86	74.4	3
Nigeria	3.79	67.65	78.9	4
Malaysia	3.11	70.77	82.5	5
Ghana	2.04	72.80	84.9	6
Tanzania	1.11	73.91	86.2	7
Rwanda	0.93	74.84	87.3	8
Kenya	0.88	75.72	88.3	9
Uganda	0.83	76.56	89.3	10
Vietnam	0.83	77.39	90.2	11
Trinidad and Tobago	0.64	78.03	91.0	12
Zaïre	0.63	78.66	91.7	13
Burma	0.61	79.27	92.4	14
Cameroon	0.42	79.68	92.9	15
Singapore	0.36	80.04	93.3	16
Guyana	0.36	80.40	93.7	17
Jamaica	0.36	80.76	94.1	18
Malawi	0.29	81.04	94.5	19
Guinea	0.29	81.33	94.8	20
Total[b]		85.78	100.0	

Appendix C (continued)

	Government-to-government ODA	Cumulative total	Cumulative percentage[a]	Rank
1970-71				
India	103.14	103.14	39.1	1
Pakistan	47.50	150.64	57.0	2
Ghana	7.01	157.65	59.7	3
Nigeria	6.63	164.28	62.2	4
Tunisia	5.49	169.77	64.3	5
Sri Lanka	5.18	174.95	66.2	6
Guyana	4.18	179.13	67.8	7
Colombia	4.05	183.19	69.4	8
Algeria	4.01	187.20	70.9	9
Indonesia	3.57	190.74	72.2	10
Cameroon	3.27	194.03	73.5	11
Senegal	3.18	197.21	74.7	12
East African Community	3.14	200.35	75.9	13
Tanzania	3.13	203.48	77.0	14
Burma	2.94	206.42	78.2	15
South Korea	2.60	209.02	79.1	16
Jamaica	2.52	211.54	80.1	17
Niger	2.47	214.01	81.0	18
Malaysia	2.36	216.37	81.9	19
Chile	2.58	218.72	82.8	20
Total[b]		264.10	100.0	
1975-76				
India	98.91	98.91	19.5	1
Pakistan	57.85	156.76	30.9	2
Indonesia	36.70	193.46	38.1	3
Bangladesh	35.29	228.74	45.1	4
Tanzania	24.38	253.12	49.9	5
Ghana	17.63	270.75	53.3	6
Niger	17.38	288.13	56.7	7
Tunisia	16.42	304.55	60.0	8
Malawi	14.92	335.19	66.0	10
Nigeria	13.71	348.90	68.7	11
Cameroon	11.05	359.95	70.9	12
East African Community	15.73	320.28	63.1	9
Algeria	10.70	370.65	73.0	13
Sri Lanka	8.37	379.02	74.6	14
Zambia	6.59	385.61	75.9	15
Kenya	6.48	392.09	77.2	16
Congo	6.46	398.55	78.5	17
Benin	6.35	404.90	79.7	18
Senegal	5.34	410.23	80.8	19
Ivory Coast	4.83	415.06	81.7	20
Total[b]		507.73	100.0	

Appendix C (continued)

	Government-to-government ODA	Cumulative total	Cumulative percentage[a]	Rank
1980-81				
Bangladesh	74.40	74.40	12.8	1
Pakistan	38.13	112.57	19.4	2
Sri Lanka	37.69	150.22	25.8	3
India	29.50	179.71	30.9	4
Tanzania	29.21	208.92	35.9	5
Egypt	22.11	231.03	39.7	6
Cameroon	20.16	251.19	43.2	7
Sahel	19.46	270.65	46.5	8
Turkey	18.98	289.63	49.8	9
Indonesia	17.95	307.59	52.9	10
Kenya	17.10	324.69	55.8	11
Mali	16.91	341.59	58.7	12
Senegal	16.08	357.67	61.5	13
Ghana	14.09	371.76	63.9	14
Tunisia	12.20	383.96	66.0	15
Madagascar	11.58	395.54	68.0	16
Thailand	11.11	406.65	69.9	17
Zaïre	9.70	416.35	71.6	18
Burkina Faso	9.16	425.48	73.2	19
Haiti	7.38	432.85	74.4	20
Total[b]		581.47	100.0	
1985-86				
Bangladesh	100.12	100.12	12.3	1
Indonesia	74.94	175.06	21.4	2
Pakistan	66.68	241.74	29.6	3
India	45.49	287.22	35.2	4
Jamaica	28.78	316.00	38.7	5
Sri Lanka	26.52	342.52	42.0	6
Niger	26.37	368.89	45.2	7
Tanzania	24.29	393.18	48.2	8
Kenya	22.41	415.59	50.9	9
Senegal	20.59	436.18	53.4	10
Sudan	19.00	455.17	55.8	11
Zambia	18.02	473.20	58.0	12
Mali	16.40	489.60	60.0	13
Zimbabwe	15.72	505.31	61.9	14
Zaïre	15.49	520.80	63.8	15
China	15.47	536.26	65.7	16
Burkina Faso	14.48	550.74	67.5	17
Ghana	14.37	565.12	69.2	18
Ethiopia	14.22	579.33	71.0	19
Peru	13.66	592.99	72.7	20
Total[b]		816.22	100.0	

Appendix C (continued)

	Government-to-government ODA	Cumulative total	Cumulative percentage[a]	Rank
1990-91[c]				
Bangladesh	117.24	117.24	10.6	1
China	72.70	189.94	17.2	2
Indonesia	46.16	236.10	21.3	3
Egypt	40.53	276.63	25.0	4
Jamaica	37.45	314.08	28.4	5
Ghana	35.14	349.22	31.6	6
Cameroon	34.98	384.20	34.7	7
Morocco	34.61	418.81	37.9	8
Tanzania	32.40	451.21	40.8	9
Pakistan	27.12	476.41	43.2	10
Philippines	24.42	502.83	45.4	11
Thailand	22.52	525.35	47.5	12
Rwanda	22.25	547.60	49.5	13
Zambia	22.21	569.80	51.5	14
Mali	21.34	591.14	53.4	15
Ethiopia	21.09	612.24	55.3	16
Peru	19.12	631.36	57.1	17
Zaïre	17.41	648.77	58.6	18
Zimbabwe	16.81	665.56	60.2	19
Sahel	16.13	681.70	61.6	20
Total[b]		1,106.45	100.0	
1995-96[d]				
Bangladesh	73.04	73.04	8.1	1
China	62.22	135.26	16.8	2
India	43.89	179.15	22.2	3
Ghana	29.73	208.88	25.9	4
Haiti	25.80	234.68	29.1	5
Peru	22.56	257.24	31.9	6
Bolivia	19.31	276.55	34.2	7
Cameroon	19.27	295.82	36.6	8
Philippines	18.87	314.69	39.0	9
Mali	18.86	333.55	41.3	10
Nicaragua	17.76	351.31	43.5	11
Mozambique	17.26	368.57	45.6	12
Senegal	17.01	385.58	47.7	13
Indonesia	16.76	402.34	49.8	14
Ethiopia	16.21	418.55	51.8	15
Thailand	14.37	432.92	53.6	16
Benin	13.82	446.74	55.3	17
Ivory Coast	12.23	458.97	56.8	18
Egypt	12.17	471.14	58.3	19
Zimbabwe	11.56	482.70	59.8	20
Total[b]		807.53	100.0	

Appendix C (continued)

a Of total government-to-government ODA

b Total government-to-government ODA

c Contributions to the Southern African Development Coordination Conference were $25.08 million.

d Contributions to the Southern African Development Community were $20.76 million.

Source: CIDA, International Development Information Centre. Government-to-government assistance includes bilateral contributions (less loan repayments) and, since 1986, Export Development Corporation Funds (Section 23, formerly Section 31) that are counted as official development assistance. For comparability, 1995-96 figures exclude official debt relief ($91.04 million of $898.57 total).

Appendix D
Core/Category I and Non-Core/Category II Countries, 1978, 1981, 1986

	Asia			
Category	1978		1981	1986
Core (1978); I (1982, (1986)	Bangladesh India Indonesia Nepal Pakistan Sri Lanka		Bangladesh *China* India Indonesia Nepal Pakistan Sri Lanka *Thailand*	Bangladesh China India Indonesia Nepal Pakistan *Philippines* Sri Lanka Thailand
Non-core (1978); IIA and IIB (1982); II (1986)	Malaysia Philippines *Thailand* *Turkey*	IIA IIB	Malaysia *Philippines* *Singapore*	Malaysia Regional

	Americas			
Category	1978		1981	1986
Core (1978); I (1982), (1986)	*Belize* *Bolivia* Colombia *El Salvador* Guyana Haiti Honduras Jamaica Leewards and Windwards Peru		Colombia Guyana Haiti Honduras Jamaica Leewards and Windwards Peru	Colombia Guyana Haiti Honduras[a] Jamaica Leewards and Windwards Peru
Non-core (1978); IIA and IIB (1982); II (1986)	Barbados Brazil Dominican Republic Ecuador Guatemala Trinidad and Tobago	IIA IIB	Barbados Brazil *Costa Rica* Dominican Republic Ecuador *Panama* *Trinidad and Tobago* *Belize* *El Salvador* Guatemala	Barbados Brazil *Caricom* Costa Rica Dominican Republic Ecuador El Salvador Guatemala *Nicaragua* Panama Regional

Appendix D (continued)

	Anglophone Africa			
Category	1978		1981	1986
Core (1978);	Botswana		*Botswana*	Egypt
I (1982), (1986)	Ghana		*Egypt*	Ghana
	Kenya		Ghana	Kenya
	Lesotho		Kenya	*SADCC*
	Malawi		*Lesotho*	Tanzania
	Sudan		*Swaziland*	Zambia
	Swaziland		Tanzania	Zimbabwe
	Tanzania		Zambia	
	Zambia		*Zimbabwe*	
Non-core (1978);	*Egypt*	IIA	Nigeria	*Botswana*
IIA and IIB	*Ethiopia*			*Ethiopia*
(1982); II (1986)	Nigeria	IIB	*Malawi*	*Jordan*
	Sierra Leone		*Sudan*	*Lesotho*
	Uganda			Malawi
				Nigeria
				Sudan
				Swaziland
				Uganda

	Francophone Africa			
Category	1978		1981	1986
Core (1978);	Cameroon		Cameroon	Cameroon
I (1982), (1986)	Guinea		Guinea	Guinea[b]
	Ivory Coast		Ivory Coast	Ivory Coast
	Mali		*Rwanda*	Rwanda
	Morocco		Sahel	Sahel
	Niger		–Mali	–Burkina Faso
	Sahel		–Niger	–Mali
	Senegal		–Upper Volta	–Niger
	Upper Volta		Senegal	–Regional
	Zaïre		Zaïre	Senegal
				Zaïre
Non-core (1978);	Algeria	IIA	Algeria	Algeria
IIA and IIB	Benin		Gabon	Gabon
(1982); II (1986)	*Congo*		Morocco	Morocco
	Madagascar		*Tunisia*	Regional
	Rwanda			Togo
	Togo	IIB	Benin	
	Tunisia		Togo	

a Subsequently expanded to include all Central American republics in a core region.

b Subsequently dropped; see Groupe Secor, "Canadian International Development Agency, Strategic Management Review: Working Document," October 9, 1991, p. 22/1.

Appendix D (continued)

Sources: Adapted from CIDA, "Bilateral Overview 1980/81" (March 1980), pp. 21-22, 26-27; Canadian Council for International Co-operation, "Excerpts from a CIDA Paper on the 'Agency Programming Framework (APF),' December 1981, Annex A" (1982); CIDA, *Memorandum to DAC 1983*, pp. 17-18; and CIDA, "Canadian International Development Assistance Programs: A Briefing Book for Parliamentarians" (Hull: CIDA, 1986), pp. 48-49. First printed in David R. Morrison, "The Choice of Bilateral Aid Recipients," in Cranford Pratt, ed., *Canadian International Development Assistance Policies: An Appraisal* (Montreal and Kingston: McGill-Queen's University Press, 1994), pp. 136-37. Italic type indicates a position different from the preceding or succeeding one.

Appendix E
Publicly Financed Technical Assistance Personnel and Students and Trainees Supported by Canadian ODA, Five-Year Intervals, 1965-95

	1965	1970	1975	1980	1985	1990	1995
Technical assistance personnel[a]	876	3,080	2,159	2,057	4,309	3,626	6,884
Students and trainees	2,274	2,757	2,734	1,723	6,291	15,572	15,693

a These figures include many CIDA-assisted volunteers with CUSO, CECI, etc., as well as Canada World Youth, which is more an educational than a development program.

Sources: OECD-DAC, *Development Assistance: Efforts and Policies of the Members of the Development Assistance Committee 1968* (Paris: Organisation for Economic Co-operation and Development, 1968), p. 273; OECD-DAC, *Development Co-operation: Efforts and Policies of the Members of the Development Assistance Committee 1977*, pp. 216-17; OECD-DAC, *Twenty-Five Years of Development Co-operation: A Review* (Paris: Organisation for Economic Co-operation and Development, 1985), pp. 304-305; and CIDA, *Statistical Report on Official Development Assistance, Fiscal Year 1995-96* (Hull: Canadian International Development Agency, 1997), pp. 64-66.

Appendix F
Canadian ODA: Proportion of DAC Effort and Comparative Standing, Five-Year Intervals, 1960-95

Year	Canadian ODA ($ million US)	Total DAC ODA ($ million US)	Canadian % total DAC	Canadian ODA/GNP percentage	Average DAC ODA/GNP percentage	Number DAC donors[a]	Canadian rank total ODA	Canadian rank ODA/GNP percentage
1960	65	4,676	1.39	0.16	0.51	9	8	9
1965	97	6,489	1.50	0.19	0.48	13	8	9
1970	337	6,949	4.85	0.41	0.34	15	6	5
1975	880	13,846	6.36	0.54	0.35	17	6	8
1980	1,075	27,267	3.95	0.43	0.37	17	7	9
1985	1,631	29,429	5.55	0.49	0.36	17	5	7
1990	2,470	52,961	4.67	0.44	0.33	18	8	8
1995	2,067	58,894	3.51	0.38	0.27	21	7	6

a Besides the commission of the European Economic Community, original DAC members were: Belgium, Canada, France, Germany, Italy, Japan, Netherlands, Portugal, the United Kingdom, and the United States. Accession dates for other members were Norway (1962), Denmark (1963), Austria (1965), Sweden (1965), Australia (1966), Switzerland (1968), New Zealand (1973), Finland (1975), Ireland (1986), Spain (1991), and Luxembourg (1992). Portugal withdrew in 1974 and rejoined in 1991; Portugal is excluded from data prior to 1991.

Sources: OECD-DAC, *Twenty-Five Years of Development Co-operation: A Review* (Paris, 1985), pp. 334-35; OECD-DAC, *Development Co-operation: Efforts and Policies of the Members of the Development Assistance Committee 1987*, p. 201; and ibid., *1996*, pp. A7-A8.

Appendix G
Percentage Distribution of All Attributable Country-to-Country Aid by Region, Canada and All DAC Donors, 1970-71, 1980-81, and 1995-96 (Percentages)

	1970-71		1980-81		1995-96	
Country/Region	Canada	All DAC	Canada	All DAC	Canada	Total DAC
Africa						
• North of Sahara and Middle East	5.7	9.9	6.2	18.3	15.4	15.3
• South of Sahara	19.7	17.1	38.6	28.5	34.2	28.3
Asia	63.6	50.8	40.6	32.4	28.1	34.5
Americas	9.3	12.6	12.7	9.7	18.3	13.2
Other[a]	1.6	9.8	1.9	11.3	3.3	8.7

a Europe and Oceania.

Source: OECD-DAC, *Development Co-operation: Efforts and Policies of the Members of the Development Assistance Committee 1997*, pp. A71, A84. These are averages of two calendar years.

Appendix H
Percentage Distribution of Attributable Country-to-Country Aid by Country Income Level, Canada and All DAC Donors, 1970-71, 1980-81, and 1995-96 (Percentages)

	1970-71		1980-81		1995-96	
Country/Income level[a]	Canada	All DAC	Canada	All DAC	Canada	Total DAC
Least developed	9.3	12.8	37.5	30.2	29.6	23.6
Other low income	71.5	46.1	41.0	30.1	31.3	29.1
Lower middle income	15.6	25.2	19.0	24.0	34.7	33.4
Upper middle income	3.5	12.1	2.4	7.9	4.3	6.3
High income	0.2	3.7	—	7.8	0.1	7.6

a According to the World Bank's classification and using the UN's list of least developed countries.

Source: OECD-DAC, *Development Co-operation: Efforts and Policies of the Members of the Development Assistance Committee 1997*, pp. A71, A84. These are averages of two calendar years.

Appendix I

Canadian Multilateral ODA: Proportion of DAC Effort and Comparative Standing, Selected Years

Year	Multilateral as percentage of Canadian ODA	Multilateral as percentage of DAC ODA	Canadian rank	Multilateral as percentage of Canadian GNP	Multilateral as percentage of DAC GNP	Canadian rank	Canadian Multilateral as percentage of DAC	Canadian rank
1965-66 average	—[a]	13.7	—[a]	.06	.06	5	3.8	5
1974-75 average	30.5	29.1	10	.17	.10	6	7.2	5
1983-84 average	40.6	32.0	4	.18	.12	6	6.5	6
1995-96 average	29.0	30.3	9[b]	.10	.06	5	3.2	8

a Canadian and DAC data for these years are in conflict.

b Excluding Ireland and Luxembourg, both small donors who were not DAC members in earlier years.

Sources: Data and calculations from OECD-DAC, *Twenty-Five Years of Development Co-operation: A Review* (Paris, 1985), pp. 142-43, 147, 296, 322-23; OECD-DAC, *Development Co-operation: Efforts and Policies of the Members of the Development Assistance Committee 1975*, pp. 202-205, 256; ibid., *1976*, p. 165; and ibid., *1997*, pp. A13, A19-A22.

Notes

Chapter 1

1 Up to the end of 1996-97, Canadian ODA totalled $51.96 billion (see Appendix A).

2 Cranford Pratt,"Middle Power Internationalism and Global Poverty," in Cranford Pratt, ed., *Middle Power Internationalism: The North South Dimension* (Kingston and Montreal: McGill-Queen's University Press, 1990), p. 5.

3 Organisation for Economic Co-operation and Development, Development Assistance Committee (hereafter cited as OECD-DAC), *Twenty-five Years of Development Co-operation: A Review* (Paris: Organisation for Economic Co-operation and Development, 1985), p. 11. Much of this special annual report, published to mark the twenty-fifth anniversary of the Development Assistance Committee, was devoted to a history of development assistance efforts. The following account draws on pp. 39-40.

4 Cited in Anne O. Krueger et al., *Aid and Development* (Baltimore: Johns Hopkins University Press, 1989), p. 1.

5 Ivan L. Head, *On a Hinge of History: The Mutual Vulnerability of South and North* (Toronto: University of Toronto Press, 1991), p. 43.

6 Based on a revised text approved by the Development Assistance Committee of the OECD in 1972 (OECD-DAC, *Twenty-five Years of Development Co-operation*, p. 171; emphasis in original).

7 Canada included first-year refugee resettlement costs in reported ODA for the first time in 1993-94, following a 1991 DAC decision to allow them to count (see OECD-DAC, *Development Co-operation: Efforts and Policies of the Members of the Development Assistance Committee 1994* [Paris: Organisation for Economic Co-operation and Development, 1995], p. 118). Henceforth (in this and subsequent chapters), the publication details will not be shown for these annual reports, which, prior to 1972, were entitled *Development Assistance*.

8 As the advanced countries in transition are classified by the Development Assistance Committee of the OECD. Concessional transfers to them are defined as "official aid" rather than ODA. See ibid., pp. 100-101.

9 Responsibility for assistance to these countries at first resided with the Department of External/Foreign Affairs and International Trade.

10 Paul Gérin-Lajoie, *Thoughts on International Development/4—Developmental Administration: CIDA in a Changing Government Organization*, Paper delivered by Paul Gérin-Lajoie, President, Canadian International Development Agency to the Institute of Public Administration Conference in Regina, September 8, 1971 (Ottawa: CIDA, 1972), p. 10.

11 Groupe Secor, "Canadian International Development Agency, Strategic Management Review: Working Document," October 9, 1991, p. 17/2.

12 This summary draws on interviews; Burghard Claus et al., *Coordination of the Development Cooperation Policies of Major OECD Donor Countries* (Berlin: German Development Institute, 1989); and on monographs of several donor countries done for the German Development Institute. Groupe Secor, which undertook a strategic management review for CIDA in 1991, examined the mandates of several other aid agencies (British, Swedish, German, American, EEC, and World Bank). It concluded that "CIDA has a much wider mandate than these agencies, even if some of them may have higher aid budgets to manage" (Groupe Secor, "Canadian International Development Agency, Strategic Management Review: Working Document," p. 167/1. See also pp. 143/1-167/1).

13 See the comparisons in Claus et al., *Coordination of the Development Cooperation Policies*, pp. 95-96.

14 Both cited in Keith Spicer, *A Samaritan State? External Aid in Canada's Foreign Policy* (Toronto: University of Toronto Press, 1966), p. 23.

15 The characterization offered by Bruce Thordarson, *Lester Pearson: Diplomat and Politician* (Toronto: Oxford University Press, 1974), p. 67.

16 From a speech to a Conference on Canadian Aid to Underdeveloped Countries, Ottawa, May 1955, cited in part in R.T. McKinnell and K.H. Tiedmann, "Canada's Development Aid" (unpublished paper, CIDA, 1982), p. 3, and in part in Spicer, *A Samaritan State?*, p. 22.

17 Notes for an Address by the Prime Minister to a Convocation Ceremony Marking the Diamond Jubilee of the University of Alberta, Edmonton, Alberta, May 13, 1968, p. 4. Many of Trudeau's stirring speeches on North-South relations were written by Ivan Head, who served as his foreign policy adviser before becoming President of IDRC.

18 Cited in Peyton V. Lyon and Brian W. Tomlin, *Canada as an International Actor* (Toronto: Macmillan of Canada, 1979), p. 140.

19 Government of Canada, *Canada in the World* (Ottawa: Department of Foreign Affairs and International Trade, 1995), p. 40 (emphasis in original).

20 House of Commons, *Debates*, September 11, 1961, p. 8197, cited in Spicer, *A Samaritan State?*, p. 4.

21 Department of External Affairs, *Foreign Policy for Canadians: International Development* (Ottawa: Queen's Printer, 1970), pp. 9-10, 12-13 (author's emphasis).

22 House of Commons, Standing Committee on External Affairs and National Defence, Subcommittee on International Development, *Minutes of Proceedings and Evidence*, May 29, 1971, session 29, pp. 20, 22.

23 While most government statements ignored the contradictory expectations that have often undermined aid effectiveness, an authoritative official gloss in the early 1970s did recognize that the three categories were "sometimes conflicting." The late Harry Hodder, then vice-president of CIDA's Policy Branch, suggested that the commercial motivation especially "tends to distort CIDA's programs in the direction of satisfying Canadian interests rather than the interests and needs of developing countries whom we are trying to help. This is perhaps to some extent inevitable. It does, however, impose an important and difficult responsibility on CIDA, as Canada's international development agency, to reconcile the differences." Hodder argued that "the purer form of humanitarianism" and shorter-term economic and political arguments fell short of a fully convincing rationale for aid:

"the most satisfactory answer turns on . . . morally enlightened self-interest" (from a speech at the Royal Military College in Kingston in 1972, which was excerpted in CIDA, "Handbook for CIDA Officers Transferred Abroad" [CIDA, 1973], pp. 99-101, 151).

24 *Estimates 1984-85, Part III: Canadian International Development Agency* (Hull: Minister of Supply and Services, 1984), p. 11 (henceforth [in this and subsequent chapters], the publication details will not be shown for these annual reports). This statement appeared as "CIDA's objective" in the Parliamentary *Estimates* every year from 1984-85 to 1996-97 (*Estimates 1996-97*, p. 11). It replaced similar earlier versions. It was superseded by the reformatted "trinity" in *Canada in the World* quoted in this section.

25 Notes for an Address by the Prime Minister to a Convocation Ceremony Marking the Diamond Jubilee of the University of Alberta, Edmonton, Alberta, May 13, 1968, p. 8.

26 See, for example, Spicer, *A Samaritan State?*, p. 30, and the dismissal of security (except as a public relations argument) by participants in the 1969-70 review of Canadian aid policy, discussed in Chapter 3.

27 Government of Canada, *Canada in the World*, p. 40 (emphasis in original).

28 Department of Trade and Commerce, Memorandum to Cabinet on Aid Allocations for 1959-60, cited in Patricia Jean Appavoo, "The Small State as Donor: Canadian and Swedish Development Assistance Policies, 1960-1976" (unpublished Ph.D. dissertation, University of Toronto, 1988), p. 243.

29 See Mark Charlton, *The Making of Canadian Food Aid Policy* (Montreal and Kingston: McGill-Queen's University Press, 1992), pp. 16-25.

30 Department of Industry, Trade and Commerce, International Development and the Canadian Economy, December 1968, p. 27-28.

31 CIDA, President's Office, Directions for the Agency, December 7, 1977.

32 Government of Canada, *Canada in the World*, p. 40 (emphasis in original).

33 Calculated from data expressed in US dollars at 1981 prices and exchange rates, in OECD-DAC, *Development Co-operation: Efforts and Policies of the Members of the Development Assistance Committee 1982*, p. 180.

34 Ibid., *1975*, p. 126.

35 Jean-Philippe Thérien, "Canadian Aid: A Comparative Analysis," in Cranford Pratt, ed., *Canadian International Development Assistance Policies: An Appraisal* (Montreal and Kingston: McGill-Queen's University Press, 1994), p. 327.

36 In Ottawa's federal fiscal year (see Appendix A). In DAC data, which are recorded on a calendar-year basis, Canada's ODA reached 0.55 per cent in 1975 (OECD-DAC, *Development Co-operation: Efforts and Policies of the Members of the Development Assistance Committee 1977*, p. 170).

37 Of all DAC donors, only New Zealand and Australia had worse records in the last half of the 1970s. Calculated from data in ibid., *1982*, p. 180.

38 See ibid., *1997*, pp. A11-A14. As this DAC report pointed out (ibid., p. 94), Canada's performance in the 1996 calendar year—0.32 per cent—may have been understated because the annual contribution to the International Development Association was made later in the 1996-97 fiscal year. Fiscal-year data showed a slightly higher ratio of 0.34 per cent (see Appendix A), which would have moved Canada ahead of Germany into a three-way tie for seventh place. However, with

Canadian aid as a proportion of national income falling more rapidly than that of other donors, data for 1997 and 1998 may well reveal Canada as eleventh or even twelfth or thirteenth.

39 Canada in 1995-96 stood thirteenth behind Denmark ($325), Norway ($289), Netherlands ($213), Sweden ($201), Luxembourg ($185), Switzerland ($152), France ($137), Japan ($101), Belgium ($98), Germany ($94), Austria ($83), and Finland ($79). The figures are averages for these two calendar years. In ranking eleventh in terms of the GNP/ODA ratio in 1996, Canada was behind all of these countries except Austria and Japan. See data in ibid., *1997*, pp. A8, A11-A14.

40 See ibid., pp. A11-A14; Appendix A; Appendix F; and the analysis of budget cuts in Chapter 10.

41 This summary draws from David R. Morrison, "The Choice of Bilateral Aid Recipients," in Pratt, ed., *Canadian International Development Assistance Policies*, pp. 123-55.

42 A term coined in Economic Council of Canada, *For a Common Future* (Hull: Minister of Supply and Services, 1978), p. 98.

43 Canada's bilateral program is the least concentrated in DAC if measured by the proportion of country-to-country aid channelled to a donor's top fifteen recipients. In 1995-96, the Canadian figure was 21.3 per cent, well below typical ranges of 30 to 60 per cent (see OECD-DAC, *Development Co-operation: Efforts and Policies of the Members of the Development Assistance Committee 1997*, pp. A69-A82). Although CIDA restricts bilateral data to government-to-government aid, DAC comparative data use a broader definition of "bilateral": one that is equivalent to CIDA's definition of "country-to-country" aid, which subsumes the voluntary, business, and humanitarian channels as well as contributions from crown agencies like IDRC. While the inclusion of these other elements produces a greater degree of dispersal than for government-to-government ODA alone (which is by far the largest component), the data are nonetheless comparable across all DAC donors.

44 Martin Rudner, "Canada in the World: Development Assistance in Canada's New Foreign Policy Framework," *Canadian Journal of Development Studies* 17, 2 (1996): 211.

45 See data on the regional distribution of Canadian ODA in Appendix B, and Canada's comparative performance in the distribution of aid by region and country income level in Appendices G and H.

46 OECD-DAC, *Development Co-operation: Efforts and Policies of the Members of the Development Assistance Committee 1997*, p. A66.

47 Roger C. Riddell, *Foreign Aid Reconsidered* (Baltimore: Johns Hopkins University Press, 1987), p. 238.

48 According to senior officials at DAC headquarters in Paris interviewed by the author in January 1989.

49 OECD-DAC, *Twenty-five Years of Development Co-operation*, p. 106.

50 See ibid., pp. 106-10, and data in more recent DAC reports.

51 See data for the period 1973-86 compiled from DAC sources in Olav Stokke, "The Determinants of Aid Policies: General Introduction," in Olav Stokke, ed., *Western Middle Powers and Global Poverty: The Determinants of the Aid Policies of Canada, Denmark, the Netherlands, Norway and Sweden* (Uppsala: The Scandinavian Institute of African Studies, 1989), p. 30. CIDA took particular exception

to a table published by DAC in 1985 that estimated that 59.2 per cent of Canada's aid was tied—twice the DAC average, exceeded only by Austria, and 13 per cent above France, which was next highest (see OECD-DAC, *Twenty-five Years of Development Co-operation*, p. 244). The claim that Canada had the second-worst record in the DAC was often flagged in testimony when aid policy was reviewed in 1986-87 by the House of Commons Standing Committee on External Affairs and International Trade. Using a revised statistical approach, DAC pegged the Canadian percentage for 1986 at 35 per cent, roughly the level of Australia, Belgium, Finland, and the United States. The UK and Italy had somewhat higher percentages; France did not report; the Netherlands and the Nordics fell in the 15 to 24 per cent range; and Japan was the lowest at 13 per cent (calculations based on OECD-DAC, *Development Co-operation: Efforts and Policies of the Members of the Development Assistance Committee 1987*, p. 208).

52 See analysis in Chapter 9. The most recent, though incomplete, data on untying suggest that Canada still falls well short of the DAC average (ibid., *1997*, p. A50).

53 See Appendix I.

54 Ibid.

55 House of Commons, Parliamentary Task Force on North-South Relations, *Report to the House of Commons on the Relations between Developed and Developing Countries* (Hull: Minister of Supply and Services, 1980), p. 20.

56 Phillip Rawkins, "An Institutional Analysis of CIDA," in Pratt, ed., *Canadian International Development Assistance Policies*, p. 158.

57 See Kim Richard Nossal, "Mixed Motives Revisited: Canada's Interest in Development Assistance," *Canadian Journal of Political Science* 21, 1 (March 1988): 35-36, and the summary of Nossal's arguments in Chapter 11.

58 Cranford Pratt, "Ethics and Foreign Policy: The Case of Canada's Development Assistance," *International Journal* 43, 2 (Spring 1988): 264.

59 See the discussion of Pratt's writings in Chapter 11.

Chapter 2

1 Keith Spicer, *A Samaritan State? External Aid in Canada's Foreign Policy* (Toronto: University of Toronto Press, 1966), p. 3.

2 Bruce Thordarson, *Lester Pearson: Diplomat and Politician* (Toronto: Oxford University Press, 1974), pp. 65-66.

3 John W. Holmes, *The Shaping of Peace: Canada and the Search for World Order, 1943-1957*, vol. 2 (Toronto: University of Toronto Press, 1982), p. 172. As Douglas LePan noted in his lively memoir on the origins of the Colombo Plan, the meeting was convened primarily to discuss security issues—recognition of China, relations with postwar Japan, and civil strife in Indo-China and Burma—but the authors of the Colombo Plan were able to take advantage of a simultaneous meeting of Commonwealth economic officials to promote their scheme (Douglas LePan, *Bright Glass of Memory* [Toronto: McGraw-Hill Ryerson, 1979], esp. pp. 155-81). The impetus came not simply from desires to promote development in the new Commonwealth countries of Asia and to stem communist advances within them, but also to relieve pressure upon Britain's sterling balances by finding alternative sources of finance for these countries. When still under colonial

rule, the governments of the new states "had accepted large amounts of I.O.U.s from Britain which they now urgently needed to use but which the British were in no position to cash and, after independence, in no position to control" (A.F.W. Plumptre, "Perspective on Our Aid to Others," *International Journal* 22, 3 [Summer 1967]: 487).

4 Lester Pearson, *Mike: The Memoirs of The Right Honourable Lester B. Pearson*, vol. 2 (Toronto: University of Toronto Press, 1973), pp. 109-10.

5 Holmes, *The Shaping of Peace*, p. 176.

6 LePan, *Bright Glass of Memory*, pp. 190, 219.

7 Cited in Pearson, *Mike*, vol. 2, p. 110.

8 LePan, *Bright Glass of Memory*, p. 191.

9 Ibid., p. 218.

10 Thordarson, *Lester Pearson*, p. 66.

11 Interview; see also Holmes, *The Shaping of Peace*, p. 334.

12 LePan, *Bright Glass of Memory*, p. 205.

13 Except where noted, this section is based on CIDA, "CIDA Organizational Manual" (Hull, 1980), pp. 1-13; Spicer, *A Samaritan State?*, pp. 93-100; and interviews and an unpublished private memoir of the period made available to the author.

14 CIDA, "CIDA Organizational Manual," pp. 7, 12.

15 Spicer, *A Samaritan State?*, p. 102.

16 Ibid., pp. 105-106.

17 Ibid., p. 95.

18 Patricia Jean Appavoo, "The Small State as Donor: Canadian and Swedish Development Assistance Policies, 1960-1976" (unpublished Ph.D. dissertation, University of Toronto, 1988), p. 81.

19 Unless otherwise noted, data in this section are drawn from External Aid Office, "Canada's Economic Aid Programmes" (Ottawa, 1961); External Aid Office, *Annual Review 1966-67* (Ottawa: Queen's Printer, 1967), p. 3; CIDA, "CIDA Organizational Manual," pp. 10-13; and A.A. Fatouros and R.N. Kelson, *Canada's Overseas Aid* (Toronto: Canadian Institute of International Affairs, 1964), pp. 15-16, 114-23. Where data conflict, I have deferred to CIDA's Canadian Historical ODA System.

20 Appendix F.

21 Indonesia was the largest at just under 1 per cent ($2.4 million over the decade), followed by Burma ($2.0 million). Quite small amounts were channelled to Cambodia, South Vietnam, and Thailand, and nothing to South Korea. For more details, see data in External Aid Office, *Annual Review 1966-67*, p. 23.

22 Cited in Spicer, *A Samaritan State?*, p. 55.

23 Plumptre, "Perspective on Our Aid to Others," p. 490.

24 This was a Canadian bilateral program, not to be confused with the later establishment within the Commonwealth Secretariat of multilateral programs with similar names, first the Commonwealth Technical Assistance Program and later the Commonwealth Technical Cooperation Program.

25 John G. Diefenbaker, *One Canada—Memoirs of the Right Honourable John G. Diefenbaker: The Years of Achievement 1957-1962*, vol. 2 (Toronto: Macmillan, 1976), pp. 110-11.

26 Cited in Spicer, *A Samaritan State?*, p. 54.

27 Ibid., pp. 54-55. On another occasion, Spicer wrote: "With the imperial rhetoric of Winston Churchill still echoing in their barely post-colonial minds, most English-speaking Canadians could mobilize for almost any cause carrying the Commonwealth label, a zealous, if not unlimitedly generous, idealism" (Keith Spicer, "Clubmanship Upstaged: Canada's Twenty Years in the Colombo Plan," *International Journal* 25 [Autumn 1969]: 15).

28 See Plumptre, "Perspective on Our Aid to Others," p. 495. The Colombo Plan legislation permitted loans, but few were made in the 1950s. The principal ones, totalling some $35 million, were extended to India and Ceylon in 1957 and 1958 for purchases of Canadian wheat and flour (External Aid Office, *Annual Review 1966-67*, p. 3). They were offered at 4.5 per cent with a three-year grace period and repayment over seven years (Spicer, *A Samaritan State?*, p. 206).

29 Walt W. Rostow, *The Process of Economic Growth* (New York: Norton, 1952).

30 Walt W. Rostow, *The Stages of Economic Growth: A Non-Communist Manifesto* (Cambridge: Cambridge University Press, 1960).

31 Fatouros and Kelson, *Canada's Overseas Aid*, pp. 15-16, 121.

32 See Roger C. Riddell, *Foreign Aid Reconsidered* (London: James Currey, 1987), p. 90.

33 See Appavoo, "The Small State as Donor," pp. 239-40.

34 Cited in Theodore H. Cohn, *Canadian Food Aid: Domestic and Foreign Policy Implications* (Denver, CO: Graduate School of International Studies, University of Denver, 1979), p. 22.

35 Ibid., p. 30.

36 Spicer, *A Samaritan State?*, p. 187.

37 See discussion of the "intense confrontation" in the 1950s between supporters of capital and technical assistance, which subsequently gave way to the modernization paradigm and an emphasis on both, in Anne O. Krueger et al., *Aid and Development* (Baltimore: Johns Hopkins University Press, 1989), p. 46.

38 As Spicer noted (*A Samaritan State?*, pp. 193-95), the unexpended balance of funds voted to provide support in the wake of severe flooding in the Low Countries of Europe in 1953 was placed in an International Disaster Relief Fund in 1956. When this fund was exhausted in the early 1960s, however, emergency relief required recourse to unwieldy and time-consuming supplementary estimates. This situation lasted until 1964-65 when an annually lapsing International Emergency Relief fund was established.

39 Spicer, *A Samaritan State?*, p. 16.

40 Ibid., p. 22.

41 David Protheroe, *Canada and Multilateral Aid: Working Paper* (Ottawa: North-South Institute, 1991), p. 17.

42 From a collection of private papers made available to the author.

43 Plumptre, "Perspective on Our Aid to Others," p. 491.

44 OECD-DAC, *Twenty-five Years of Development Co-operation: A Review* (Paris: Organisation for Economic Co-operation and Development, 1985), p. 42.

45 Ibid., p. 43.

46 Spicer, *A Samaritan State?*, p. 102.

47 John Hilliker and Donald Barry, *Canada's Department of External Affairs*, vol. 2: *Coming of Age, 1946-1968* (Montreal and Kingston: McGill-Queen's University Press, 1995), p. 178.

48 Order-in-Council 1960-1476, October 28, 1960, and Memorandum to the Cabinet, August 15, 1960. The cabinet memorandum recommended transferring the functions and the establishment of the Economic and Technical Assistance Branch from the jurisdiction of the minister of Trade and Commerce to that of the secretary of state for External Affairs under whom it would form part of the External Aid Office. The order-in-council, however, effected the transfer to the Department of External Affairs. Possible legal confusion was partially resolved in a subsequent Order-in-Council (1962-490, April 5, 1962), which made the External Aid Office a department under the *Civil Service Act* and confirmed that the director general had deputy ministerial status.

49 Memorandum to the Cabinet, August 15, 1960. The memorandum specified that a member of the External Aid Board would be named chairman by the secretary of state for External Affairs. The director general was appointed as chairman and came to be regarded as *ex officio* in that capacity.

50 Author's interview with H.O. Moran, Ottawa, August 17 and 22, 1989, and Terence Robertson, "The Diplomatic Way to Give Away Millions," *Weekend Magazine* (1965) (undated clipping in a private collection). The following paragraphs are informed by these sources as well as other interviews; Fatouros and Kelson, *Canada's Overseas Aid*, pp. 73-89; Spicer, *A Samaritan State?*, pp. 105-19; and CIDA, "CIDA Organizational Manual," pp. 11-33.

51 External Aid Office, "Nature of Canadian External Aid" (Ottawa, 1963), p. 49.

52 The parliamentary vote for the Colombo Plan program was put on a non-lapsing basis in 1953 in recognition of the difficulty of estimating expenditure patterns within any twelve-month period. A document Moran submitted to the new Liberal cabinet in 1963 noted: "This greatly facilitated the orderly planning and implementation of the program since funds could be earmarked for worthwhile projects over a number of years and fluctuations in the rate of expenditures did not affect the regular progress of individual projects or disrupt the planning of future activities, as frequently happens when one must await the re-vote of funds." While the Diefenbaker cabinet agreed in principle in March 1960 that the newer programs would be treated similarly, and a draft bill was actually prepared by the Department of Justice, no action was taken (External Aid Office, "Nature of Canadian External Aid," p. 32). Non-lapsing authority for all programs was finally conferred in 1964.

53 Fatouros and Kelson, *Canada's Overseas Aid*, pp. 73, 81.

54 Ibid., p. 82.

55 Ibid., pp. 84-85.

56 Clyde Sanger, *Half a Loaf: Canada's Semi-Role Among Developing Countries* (Toronto: Ryerson Press, 1969), p. 227.

57 Spicer, *A Samaritan State?*, pp. 118-19.

58 House of Commons, Standing Committee on External Affairs, *Minutes of Proceedings and Evidence*, March 11, 1960, p. 90.

59 House of Commons, *Debates*, September 11, 1961, p. 8196.

60 See Fatouros and Kelson, *Canada's Overseas Aid*, pp. 13, 113-16.

61 Appendix A.

62 "Canada's Colombo Plan Aid," *Winnipeg Free Press*, November 6, 1962, cited in Peyton V. Lyon, *Canada in World Affairs 1961-1963* (Toronto: Oxford University Press, 1968), p. 352.

63 House of Commons, *Debates*, October 30, 1962, p. 1083.

64 Interviews and OECD, Development Assistance Committee, Minutes of 10th Meeting, July 25, 1962, morning session, pp. 11-14 (in Public Archives of Canada). Earlier, during the annual examination of Canada by DAC, an Italian representative had "noted that Canada, with the second largest per capita income of all the DAC countries, was nevertheless well down on the list of aid givers. He wondered why the Canadian horse, which was a strong one, was not amongst the front runners. Mr. Moran suggested that no owner expected his horse to win every race but nevertheless the record showed that the Canadian horse had been a consistent front runner over the past ten years and one that represented a good bet in the future" (External Aid Office notes on Canadian examination by DAC, June 19, 1962, Public Archives of Canada).

65 See H. Basil Robinson, *Diefenbaker's World: A Populist in Foreign Affairs* (Toronto: University of Toronto Press 1989), pp. 194, 202, and Denis Smith, *Rogue Tory: The Life and Legend of John G. Diefenbaker* (Toronto: Macfarlane Walter & Ross, 1995), pp. 379-88. In his memoirs, Diefenbaker reproduced a "secret memorandum" on "What We Want from Ottawa Trip" that had allegedly been dropped into his wastepaper basket by President Kennedy after the two leaders met in May 1961. Written by none other than Walt Rostow, then policy planning director in the US State department, the text urged the president "to push the Canadians towards an increased commitment to the Alliance for Progress" and towards joining the Organization of American States. Point three called for further pressure on the aid front: "To push them towards a larger contribution for the India consortium and for foreign aid generally. The figures are these: they have offered $36 million for India's Third [Five]-Year Plan, we would like $70 million from them. Over-all their aid now comes to $69 million a year; if they did 1% of GNP the figure would be $360 million. Like the rest of us, they have their political problems with foreign aid; but we might be able to push them in the right direction" (Diefenbaker, *One Canada—Memoirs*, vol. 2, p. 183).

66 "Green Hits Back at U.S. 'Telling Us What to Do,'" *Toronto Daily Star*, March 25, 1963, cited in Lyon, *Canada in World Affairs 1961-1963*, p. 356.

67 Diefenbaker, *One Canada—Memoirs*, vol. 2, p. 144.

68 Fatouros and Kelson, *Canada's Overseas Aid*, p. 56.

69 Lyon, *Canada in World Affairs 1961-1963*, p. 353.

70 Ibid., pp. 356-57.

71 Plumptre, "Perspective on Our Aid to Others," p. 492.

72 A service charge of three-quarters of 1 per cent was imposed but later dropped.

73 House of Commons, *Debates*, November 14, 1963, pp. 4717-21. The quotation from Martin is on p. 4718. Since the late 1950s, the NDP and its CCF predecessor had supported a 2 per cent target, double what was then conventionally seen as a desirable level for donors. Robert Thompson of Social Credit and Real Caouette of the Creditistes also spoke strongly in favour of the proposed increases, although there was an element of "charity begins at home" in Caouette's statement: "We approve and we commend this assistance to the underdeveloped countries but the government should also have some thought for the Canadians who contribute to the development of this country of ours" (ibid., p. 4721).

74 OECD-DAC, *Development Assistance: Efforts and Policies of the Members of the Development Assistance Committee 1965*, p. 115.

75 House of Commons, *Debates*, January 23, 1967, p. 12096.

76 OECD-DAC, *Development Assistance: Efforts and Policies of the Members of the Development Assistance Committee 1967*, p. 178.
77 See ibid., *1969*, pp. 298, 309; OECD-DAC, *Development Co-operation: Efforts and Policies of the Members of the Development Assistance Committee 1974*, pp. 201-202; and Appendix F.
78 Appendix A. Other country-to-country aid, channelled through the Red Cross and other non-governmental agencies, totalled $2.5 million.
79 The problem resulted in part because of the 1965 war between India and Pakistan, which made the implementation of some projects very difficult (OECD-DAC, *Development Assistance: Efforts and Policies of the Members of the Development Assistance Committee 1966*, p. 31, based on a Canadian report). In addition, there was a dramatic increase in workload, largely in the administration of technical aid (see CIDA, "CIDA Organizational Manual," pp. 28-30). The organizational inadequacies discussed above, and the almost total lack of any presence in the field, were contributory factors as well.
80 The data in the first part of this section are derived from Fatouros and Kelson, *Canada's Overseas Aid*, pp. 119-22; External Aid Office, "Nature of Canadian External Aid"; External Aid Office, *Annual Review 1966-67*, pp. 23-25; and CIDA, *Annual Review 1967-68* (Ottawa: Queen's Printer, 1968), p. 22.
81 Appendix C.
82 See Appavoo, "The Small State as Donor," pp. 108-10.
83 John P. Schlegel, *The Deceptive Ash: Bilingualism and Canadian Policy in Africa—1957-1971* (Washington: University Press of America, 1978), p. 88.
84 See ibid., chap. 8, for a detailed account of Canadian-Tanzanian relations. The military assistance programs in Ghana, Nigeria, and Tanzania are discussed on pp. 59-63, 124-26, and 336-39, respectively.
85 Both cited in Spicer, *A Samaritan State?*, p. 56.
86 Hilliker and Barry, *Coming of Age*, p. 223.
87 And the father of Michel Dupuy, a future President of CIDA.
88 Louis Sabourin, "Canada and Francophone Africa," in Peyton V. Lyon and Tareq Y. Ismael, eds., *Canada and the Third World* (Toronto: Macmillan of Canada, 1976), pp. 138-39.
89 Hilliker and Barry, *Coming of Age*, p. 223. Green, anticipating opposition in the cabinet, reduced the proposed allocation from $600,000 to $300,000.
90 Sabourin, "Canada and Francophone Africa," p. 139.
91 Fatouros and Kelson, *Canada's Overseas Aid*, p. 44.
92 Interviews, and Appavoo, "The Small State as Donor," p. 120.
93 Hilliker and Barry, *Coming of Age*, p. 336.
94 Spicer, *A Samaritan State?*, p. 57.
95 Cited in Appavoo, "The Small State as Donor," p. 124.
96 See ibid., pp. 124-25.
97 From a 1965 internal document cited in ibid., p. 125.
98 See, for example, OECD-DAC, *Development Assistance: Efforts and Policies of the Members of the Development Assistance Committee 1965*, pp. 84-85, and ibid., *1966*, p. 105. "Nature of Canadian External Aid," a document submitted to cabinet in 1963, made a strong pitch for maintaining a high level of concessionality, noting DAC concerns (p. 43). See also Plumptre, "Perspective on Our Aid to Others," pp. 494-96.

99 External Aid Office, "A Report on Canada's External Aid Programmes" (Ottawa, 1962), p. 3. The report pointed out that there were occasional exceptions when "certain essential equipment is not ordinarily available in Canada."

100 External Aid Office, Report on the French Program submitted by Henri Gaudefroy to Mr. Maurice Strong, Director General, January 1967, p. 20. Given the structure of the Canadian economy, this regulation presented difficulties for Canadian firms. A draft of EAO's report on the Canadian examination by DAC in 1962 noted: "The French Delegate remarked humorously, with reference to Mr. Moran's explanation of the relatively high U.S. component of Canadian goods, that perhaps the U.S. might claim this component as a part of their aid programme." The final report deleted this reference (External Aid Office notes on Canadian examination by DAC, June 19, 1962, second draft and final report, Public Archives of Canada.)

101 External Aid Office, "Tying of Aid," November 14, 1962 (in Public Archives of Canada).

102 House of Commons, Standing Committee on External Affairs, *Minutes of Proceedings and Evidence*, May 3, 1961, p. 180.

103 Plumptre, "Perspective on Our Aid to Others," p. 497.

104 Ibid.

105 See data in Mark W. Charlton, *The Making of Canadian Food Aid Policy* (Montreal and Kingston: McGill-Queen's University Press, 1992), p. 41.

106 See External Aid Office, *Annual Review 1966-67*, pp. 30-41.

107 Ibid., pp. 6-7.

108 See Spicer, *A Samaritan State?*, pp. 232-33.

109 External Aid Office, Opening Statement by H.O. Moran to the DAC Annual Review of Canadian Aid Programme, May 4, 1965, pp. 8-9.

110 Franc Joubin, *Nor for Gold Alone: Memoirs of a Prospector* (Toronto: Deljay, 1986), p. 369.

111 Overseas Institute of Canada, "Canada's Participation in Social Development Abroad" (Ottawa, 1963).

112 Overseas Institute of Canada, "Canadian Participation in International Development," Report based on Second National Workshop, Ville d'Esteral, November 18-21, 1965, p. 1 (emphasis in original).

113 Except where noted, based on Protheroe, *Canada and Multilateral Aid*, pp. 17-28.

114 In 1966. Percentages calculated from Appendix A and OECD-DAC, *Development Assistance: Efforts and Policies of the Members of the Development Assistance Committee 1971*, p. 34. In 1966, the Canadian government adopted an official policy of channelling 12 to 15 per cent of aid through multilateral channels (Protheroe, *Canada and Multilateral Aid*, p. 19).

115 CIDA, *Annual Review 1967-68*, p. 10, and Protheroe, *Canada and Multilateral Aid*, p. 24.

116 Interviews; Fatouros and Kelson, *Canada's Overseas Aid*, pp. 94-95; and Spicer, *A Samaritan State?*, p. 211. A comprehensive account of the lobbying efforts to secure government funding for CUSO is in Ian Smillie, *The Land of Lost Content: A History of CUSO* (Toronto: Deneau, 1985), pp. 253-58.

Chapter 3

1 In his account of the evolution of the international aid regime, Robert E. Wood reviewed a number of alternatives to development assistance that failed or were rejected by the US and its Western allies: institutional multilateralism, military containment, acceptance of nationalist and socialist revolutions, and trade liberalization (Robert E. Wood, *From Marshall Plan to Debt Crisis: Foreign Aid and Development Choices in the World Economy* [Berkeley: University of California Press, 1986], p. 22). Trade liberalization was "probably the most politically viable alternative to aid. . . . The executive branch has time and again told Congress that failure to liberalize trade necessitates high levels of aid because trade restrictions prevent the underdeveloped countries from earning the dollars they need to finance development and defense" (ibid., p. 25). Wood went on to note that Eugene Black, president of the World Bank when IDA was established, viewed the move as distasteful but necessary in view of the unwillingness of the industrialized countries to lower tariffs.

2 For a history of North-South negotiations, see Nassau A. Adams, *Worlds Apart: The North-South Divide and the International System* (London: Zed Books, 1993).

3 An excellent and carefully balanced survey of critical perspectives is offered in Roger C. Riddell, *Foreign Aid Reconsidered* (Baltimore: Johns Hopkins University Press, 1987). See especially chaps. 4-6, 11-13.

4 Göran Ohlin, "After the End of the Development Era, What?" (paper presented to a Colloquium in Honour of Gerald K. Helleiner, North-South Institute, Ottawa, June 22-24, 1994), p. 5.

5 John Hilliker and Donald Barry, *Canada's Department of External Affairs*, vol. 2: *Coming of Age 1946-1968* (Kingston and Montreal: McGill-Queen's University Press, 1995), p. 337. There was an ironic twist in Strong's appointment to the top job in the EAO. In 1956, wanting "to do something worth the doing," he had applied for a job in the International Economic and Technical Cooperation Division, but was turned down because he lacked the formal educational qualifications ("Strong to Leave CIDA Presidency for UN Environmental Affairs Post," *The Globe and Mail*, September 28, 1970). For a biographical sketch of Strong, including his subsequent career, see Elaine Dewar, "Mr. Universe," *Saturday Night* 107, 5 (June 1992).

6 Much of the information and many of the quotations, except where noted, come from the author's interview with Maurice Strong in London, England on April 14, 1989; additional information is drawn from other interviews.

7 From an interview with Strong, in CIDA, "The 20 Years of CIDA: From Maurice Strong to Margaret Catley-Carlson," *Development* (Summer-Autumn 1988), p. 58. Herb Moran had also supported the emerging wisdom about expanding export markets for the developing countries, and the desirability of integrating aid and trade facilitation policies (for example, in Transcript of a Speech by H.O. Moran, Director General of the External Aid Office to a UNESCO Panel, Ottawa, March 28, 1963). However, the rest of official Ottawa paid little heed at the time.

8 Hudon had been one of the officers seconded from Finance to the EAO for a short time during the early 1960s.

9 The quotations from Strong are from the author's interview with him in London, England on April 14, 1989.

10 Moran had suggested a similar change of name in 1963, in part to distinguish the External Aid Office more clearly from External Affairs. The proposal got as far as cabinet's agenda, but was not implemented. Perhaps more pressing business was the reason. However, the change was strongly opposed by Marcel Cadieux, under-secretary of state for External Affairs, who later objected to much of Strong's agenda on grounds that it would undermine External's supreme authority over foreign policy. Moran had also been rebuffed in efforts to give the aid program and its mandate a legislative basis, despite support from a report commissioned by the Royal Commission on Government Organization (see Hilliker and Barry, *Coming of Age*, p. 207, and Patricia Jean Appavoo, "The Small State as Donor: Canadian and Swedish Development Assistance Policies, 1960-1976" [unpublished Ph.D. dissertation, University of Toronto, 1988], p. 357).

11 Notes for an Address by the Prime Minister to a Convocation Ceremony Marking the Diamond Jubilee of the University of Alberta, Edmonton, Alberta, May 13, 1968, p. 4.

12 "The Canadian International Development Agency," *External Affairs* 20, 11 (November 1968): 42.

13 House of Commons, Standing Committee on External Affairs and National Defence, *Report of the Subcommittee on International Development Assistance*, in *Minutes of Proceedings and Evidence*, session 29, May 29, 1971, pp. 48-52.

14 Memorandum to Cabinet of the Secretary of State for External Affairs, August 29, 1968 (author's emphasis). The change, without any reference to the explanation, was embodied in Order-in-Council 1968-1760, September 12, 1968.

15 William Robb, "New Face on External Aid," *Canadian Business* 41, 5 (May 1968): 12.

16 Clyde Sanger, *Half a Loaf: Canada's Semi-Role Among Developing Countries* (Toronto: Ryerson Press, 1969), p. xii.

17 CIDA, "CIDA Organizational Manual" (Hull, 1980), p. 33.

18 Ibid., pp. 33-46, and Memorandum to All Employees of the External Aid Office from Maurice Strong, September 28, 1967. Noting that programs had expanded rapidly in terms of spending, geographic areas, and complexity, Strong said that it was necessary to improve the effectiveness of aid efforts. He described the broadening scope of the EAO's responsibilities, noting the "policy of the Government" to increase private-sector participation, and another important aspect of his agenda: "There has also been a growing awareness that aid is only one of a number of factors, including trade, tariff, commercial and taxation policies, through which a country like Canada can affect significantly the economic and social progress of developing countries, and the External Aid Office *is being required* to make a contribution to the evaluation of such factors and the development of appropriate policies" (author's emphasis).

19 Based on interviews; CIDA, "CIDA Organizational Manual," pp. 33-46; CIDA, *Annual Review 1967-68* (Ottawa: Queen's Printer, 1968), pp. 29-30. Henceforth (in this and subsequent chapters), the publication details will not be shown for annual reports, which were called *Annual Review* until 1978-79 when the title *Annual Report* was adopted. *CIDA's Year in Review* was used for a time in the early 1980s, but the *Annual Report* citation is used in references for those years.

20 External Aid Office, Report on the French Program Submitted by Henri Gaudefroy to Mr. Maurice Strong, Director General, January 1967, p. 30.

21 CIDA, "CIDA Organizational Manual," p. 36.

22 The documentation—including earlier protocols, an exchange of letters between Strong and Marcel Cadieux, the under-secretary of state for External Affairs, and the texts of agreements—may be found in the CIDA library in Hull. See also the account in Hilliker and Barry, *Coming of Age*, pp. 337-39.
23 CIDA, *Annual Review 1968-69*, p. 53.
24 Dewar, "Mr. Universe," p. 73. Based as well on interviews.
25 CIDA, "CIDA Organizational Manual," p. 48.
26 Tansley recalled in an interview (Ottawa, October 26, 1988) that "what triggered my concern" was an experience in a meeting convened with the high commissioner to Tanzania to review the program in that country. "I was startled to find that, in order to cover all projects going on in Tanzania at the time, there were thirteen officers in the room. And the only one of those officers with an overall view was from the planning side." He put his proposals for reorganization in a memorandum to Strong, who, having just gone through the 1967 exercise, reacted negatively at first but then recognized the logic of what Tansley was advocating.
27 CIDA, "CIDA Organizational Manual," pp. 57-65.
28 George Cunningham, *The Management of Aid Agencies* (London: Croom Helm, 1974), p. 125.
29 CIDA, *Annual Review 1967-68*, p. 29. The activities were coordinated by the Centennial International Development Program.
30 Perinbam did not, however, "retire." He became special adviser to the president of the Commonwealth of Learning, the new distance-learning initiative of the Commonwealth based in Vancouver.
31 Author's interview with Lewis Perinbam, Ottawa, February 27, 1989.
32 CIDA, *Annual Review 1967-68*, p. 29; CIDA, *Annual Review 1968-69*, p. 49; and Appendix A.
33 See North-South Institute, *The Canadian Private Sector and Third World Development* (Ottawa: North-South Institute, 1987), pp. 33-34.
34 Interview with Strong, in CIDA, "The 20 Years of CIDA," pp. 59-60.
35 CIDA, *Annual Review 1968-69*, p. 51.
36 Based on interviews except where noted.
37 Interview with Strong, in CIDA, "The 20 Years of CIDA," p. 59.
38 A.F.W. Plumptre, "The International Development Research Centre and the Role of L.B. Pearson," in Michael G. Fry, ed., *Freedom and Change: Essays in Honour of Lester B. Pearson* (Toronto: McClelland and Stewart, 1975), p. 153.
39 Cited in ibid.
40 Ibid., p. 158.
41 Clyde Sanger, "Canada and Development in the Third World," in Peyton V. Lyon and Tareq Y. Ismael, eds., *Canada and the Third World* (Toronto: Macmillan of Canada, 1976), p. 293.
42 House of Commons, *Debates*, February 20, 1970, p. 3911. See also House of Commons, Standing Committee on External Affairs and National Defence, *Minutes of Proceedings and Evidence*, February 11, 1970, session 13, pp. 3-146.
43 *An Act to Establish the International Development Research Centre*, c. 36, *Statutes of Canada*, vol. 1: *1969-70* (Ottawa: Queen's Printer, 1971).
44 Paul Gérin-Lajoie was president for most of 1970-71, but planning for that year took place while Strong was still in office. The use of a five-year period also permits comparisons with the period 1960-61 to 1965-66 used in Chapter 2 to represent the Moran era. Data in this section are based on CIDA, *Annual Review*

1967-68, p. 3; CIDA, *Annual Review 1970-71*, pp. 10-11; CIDA, *Annual Review 1971-72*, p. 76; CIDA, Canadian Historical ODA System; and Appendix A.

45 Bruce Thordarson, *Trudeau and Foreign Policy: A Study in Decision-Making* (Toronto: Oxford University Press, 1972), p. 71.

46 OECD-DAC, *Development Co-operation: Efforts and Policies of the Members of the Development Assistance Committee 1974*, pp. 201-202.

47 CIDA, *Annual Aid Review 1971: Memorandum of Canada to the Development Assistance Committee of the Organization for Economic Co-operation and Development* (Ottawa: CIDA, 1972), p. 8. Henceforth, in this and succeeding chapters, in order to avoid confusion with Annual Reviews and Annual Reports, CIDA's Annual Aid Reviews for DAC are cited as CIDA, *Memorandum to DAC [date of year reported upon]*.

48 House of Commons, Standing Committee on External Affairs and National Defence, *Minutes of Proceedings and Evidence*, April 29, 1969, pp. 1301-302.

49 Sanger, *Half a Loaf*, p. 229.

50 Cunningham, *The Management of Aid Agencies*, p. 131.

51 The data are drawn from CIDA, *Annual Review 1975-76*, pp. 28-31.

52 See Appendix C.

53 Department of External Affairs, *Foreign Policy for Canadians: Pacific* (Ottawa: Queen's Printer, 1970), p. 20.

54 CIDA, *Memorandum to DAC 1975*, p. 32.

55 John P. Schlegel, *The Deceptive Ash: Bilingualism and Canadian Policy in Africa—1957-1971* (Washington: University Press of America, 1978), p. 141. See pp. 140-77 for his detailed account of the Biafran conflict.

56 J.L. Granatstein and Robert Bothwell, *Pirouette: Pierre Trudeau and Canadian Foreign Policy* (Toronto: University of Toronto Press, 1990), p. 276.

57 Material on the growth of the francophone African program, except where noted, is based on "Canada's Bilateral Grant Aid Programmes," *External Affairs* (February 1964), pp. 82-83; Louis Sabourin, "Canada and Francophone Africa," in Lyon and Ismael, eds., *Canada and the Third World*, pp. 133-61; Schlegel, *The Deceptive Ash*, pp. 208-33, 250-71; Appavoo, "The Small State as Donor," pp. 117-22, 163-65; Granatstein and Bothwell, *Pirouette*, pp. 111-57; and Hilliker and Barry, *Coming of Age*, pp. 339-40.

58 David B. Dewitt and John J. Kirton, *Canada as a Principal Power* (Toronto: John Wiley & Sons, 1983), p. 39.

59 Douglas Anglin, "Canada and Africa: The Trudeau Years," *Africa Contemporary Record* (1983-84), p. A189.

60 Sabourin, "Canada and Francophone Africa," p. 141.

61 The External Aid Office acceded to a number of Gérin-Lajoie's demands that Quebec participate directly in educational components of the aid program. For example, representatives of the provincial Department of Education were included in the process of selecting teachers for overseas service. However, the federal government refused to go along when, in asserting that EAO had no right to employ Quebecois teachers directly, Gérin-Lajoie insisted that monies be transferred to Quebec so that it could issue pay cheques to those in the field.

62 Sabourin, "Canada and Francophone Africa," p. 141.

63 External Aid Office, Report on the French Program Submitted by Henri Gaudefroy to Mr. Maurice Strong, Director General, January 1967, and External Aid Office, Memorandum to Cabinet: Canadian Aid Program for the Independent

French-Speaking African States, 1967. Both documents are in the CIDA library in Hull.

64 Hilliker and Barry, *Coming of Age*, p. 340. See as well Schlegel, *The Deceptive Ash*, p. 251.

65 Schlegel, *The Deceptive Ash*, p. 263.

66 Granatstein and Bothwell, *Pirouette*, p. 131.

67 CIDA, *Annual Review 1967-68*, p. 20.

68 Ibid., *1970-71*, p. 27.

69 Sanger, "Canada and Development in the Third World," pp. 283-84.

70 See J.C.M. Ogelsby, *Gringos from the Far North: Essays in the History of Canadian-Latin American Relations, 1866-1968* (Toronto: Macmillan of Canada, 1976), pp. 200-20.

71 J.C.M.Ogelsby, "Canada and Latin America," in Lyon and Ismael, eds., *Canada and the Third World*, p. 180.

72 Cited in ibid., p. 181.

73 CIDA, *Annual Review 1970-71*, p. 41.

74 Cabinet Document #222-66, April 6, 1966, cited in Department of Industry, Trade and Commerce, "International Development and the Canadian Economy" (December 1968), p. 32.

75 CIDA, *Annual Review 1968-69*, p. 9.

76 OECD-DAC, *Development Assistance: Efforts and Policies of the Members of the Development Assistance Committee 1969*, p. 161.

77 Memorandum to Cabinet: Geographical Allocation of Bilateral Aid Funds for 1969-70, April 1, 1969.

78 See CIDA, *Annual Review 1971-72*, pp. 71-72.

79 CIDA, *Annual Review 1968-69*, p. 19.

80 Letter from S. Cloutier, Assistant Secretary of the Treasury Board, to M.F. Strong, President of CIDA, November 25, 1968.

81 Speech to the International Teach-in by M.F. Strong, President, Canadian International Development Agency, Toronto, September 19, 1970.

82 External Aid Office, *Annual Review 1966-67*, p. 13, and CIDA, *Annual Review 1970-71*, p. 45. See also Appendix E.

83 Theodore H. Cohn, *Canadian Food Aid: Domestic and Foreign Policy Implications* (Denver, CO: Graduate School of International Studies, University of Denver, 1979), pp. 30-31, and Mark W. Charlton, *The Making of Canadian Food Aid Policy* (Montreal and Kingston: McGill-Queen's University Press, 1992), p. 41 and chap. 4.

84 CIDA, *Annual Review 1968-69*, p. 19.

85 Sanger, *Half a Loaf*, pp. 86-87.

86 See Appavoo, "The Small State as Donor," pp. 261-64.

87 Ibid., p. 265.

88 CIDA, *Annual Report 1992-93*, p. 62.

89 See Arnold Smith with Clyde Sanger, *Stitches in Time: The Commonwealth in World Politics* (London: Andre Deutsch, 1981), pp. 110-29.

90 Sanger, *Half a Loaf*, p. 241.

91 Lester B. Pearson, *Partners in Development: Report of the Commission on International Development* (New York: Praeger Publishers, 1969), p. vii.

92 Ibid., p. 152.

93 OECD-DAC, *Development Assistance: Efforts and Policies of the Members of the Development Assistance Committee 1971*, p. 145.

94 Pearson, *Partners in Development*, p. 11.

95 Patricia M. Marchak, *The Integrated Circus: The New Right and the Restructuring of Global Markets* (Montreal and Kingston: McGill-Queen's University Press, 1991), p. 221.

96 Author's interview with Maurice Strong, London, April 14, 1989.

97 CIDA, Review of Policies Governing the Development Assistance Programme, memorandum attached to letters to consultants, December 31, 1968.

98 S.G. Triantis, "Canada's Interest in Foreign Aid," Discussion Paper for Development Assistance Review, April 1969, p. 7. An earlier version served as the basis for discussion in the first meeting of the Development Assistance Policy Review Committee on January 23, 1969.

99 Ibid., p. 13.

100 Ibid., pp. 16, 18. On p. 15, the paternalism was even stronger: "As these people understand us better and develop partly along lines that we comprehend, we should be more ready to yield to somewhat like-minded people and be prepared to share our life and treasures with them."

101 Triantis, "Canada's Interest in Foreign Aid," p. 8.

102 Ibid., p. 4.

103 Ibid., pp. 22-23. However, while it was up to the government to weigh the wisdom "of using questionable or vague and possibly misleading arguments," Triantis counselled against letting a questionable argument influence a bad policy decision (such as shoring up moribund industries). He published a somewhat sanitized version of the paper in S.G. Triantis, "Canada's Interest in Foreign Aid," *World Politics* 24, 1 (October 1972): 1-18. In this article, Triantis suggested that "Aid, more than defence could be a basis of national pride"; in the latter realm, "we see ourselves as a cogwheel in a huge Western machine; aid, on the other hand, is not formally coordinated, and we tend to think of ourselves as being independent and important" (p. 16).

104 CIDA, Aide-Mémoire: Panel Discussion on the Purpose of Development Assistance, January 23, 1969.

105 CIDA, "Background Paper for Development Assistance Policy Review Conference, May 16-18, 1969," pp. 4-6.

106 Ibid., p. 7.

107 Ibid., pp. 8-9 (author's emphasis).

108 Grant L. Reuber, "The Trade-Offs Among the Objectives of Canadian Foreign Aid," *International Journal* 25, 1 (Winter 1969-70): 141.

109 Grant Reuber, "Canada's Foreign Aid Policy: The Strategy and Tactics for Allocating Canadian Funds to Foster Economic Development," Discussion Paper for Development Assistance Review, May 1969, p. 71.

110 Ibid., pp. 36, 41-42. The reference to a "Good Guys Club" in a draft of April 4, 1969 (p. 42) became simply a "group of donor countries" in the final May version.

111 CIDA, "Background Paper for Development Assistance Policy Review Conference, May 16-18, 1969," p. 22.

112 Mitchell Sharp later said that a fixed timetable was seriously debated, but that his earlier experience as minister of Finance had convinced him that a firm plan could be upset by changing circumstances or an emergency situation (House of Commons, Standing Committee on External Affairs and National Defence, *Minutes of Proceedings and Evidence*, May 19, 1971, p. 4).

113 Reuber, "Canada's Foreign Aid Policy," pp. 58-62.

114 CIDA, "Background Paper for Development Assistance Policy Review Conference, May 16-18, 1969," pp. 29-35.
115 Reuber, "Canada's Foreign Aid Policy," pp. 45-52.
116 Benjamin Higgins, "The Terms of Foreign Aid," Discussion Paper for Development Assistance Review, 1969, p. 2.
117 CIDA, "Background Paper for Development Assistance Policy Review Conference, May 16-18, 1969," pp. 40-42.
118 See ibid., pp. 24-28.
119 Louis Sabourin, "Multilateral Aid and the Co-ordination of Aid," Discussion Paper for Development Assistance Review, May 1969.
120 Private Planning Association of Canada, "Ways of Increasing the Involvement of Canadian Private Interests in the Developing Countries," Discussion Paper for Development Assistance Review, May 1969. The paper also dealt in general terms with the voluntary sector.
121 CIDA, "Background Paper for Development Assistance Policy Review Conference, May 16-18, 1969," p. 49.
122 Ibid., p. 50.
123 Department of External Affairs, *Foreign Policy for Canadians: International Development* (Ottawa: Queen's Printer, 1970), pp. 8-9.
124 Ibid., pp. 9-10.
125 Ibid., p. 12 (author's emphasis).
126 Ibid., pp. 12-13.
127 CIDA, "Background Paper for Development Assistance Policy Review Conference, May 16-18, 1969," p. 5.
128 "Canada in the Global Community," Text of a Speech by the Honourable Mitchell Sharp, Secretary of State for External Affairs to the Canadian Manufacturers' Association, Toronto, June 3, 1969, p. 4.
129 Department of External Affairs, *Foreign Policy for Canadians: International Development*, p. 16.
130 Ibid., pp. 18-19.
131 Ibid., p. 19.
132 Ibid., p. 17.
133 Ibid., p. 18.
134 Ibid., pp. 11, 14.
135 Ibid., pp. 18-19. Interestingly, Reuber's list (including a reference to exercising "beneficial leverage"), not that of the white paper, was reproduced in CIDA, *Annual Review 1970-71*, p. 14, as the criteria supposedly informing decisions on geographical eligibility and allocations.
136 Cunningham, *The Management of Aid Agencies*, pp. 127-28.
137 Author's interview with Maurice Strong, London, April 14, 1989.
138 Cunningham, *The Management of Aid Agencies*, p. 128.
139 Ibid.
140 House of Commons, Standing Committee on External Affairs and National Defence, *Report of the Subcommittee on International Development Assistance, Minutes of Proceedings and Evidence*, session 29, May 29, 1971, pp. 1-74.
141 Ibid., pp. 20, 22.
142 Ibid., p. 24. Page references to other issues mentioned are: level, pp. 26-30; untying, pp. 68-70; decentralization, p. 52; economic, social, and human content, pp. 70-72; environmental dimension, p. 72; NGOs, pp. 52-58; and business, pp. 58-66.

143 Ibid., p. 48.
144 Ibid., p. 40.

Chapter 4

1 OECD-DAC, *Development Co-operation: Efforts and Policies of the Members of the Development Assistance Committee 1978*, p. 191.
2 Other proposals included: a more coherent integration of industrial country policies in the spheres of aid, trade, and technology transfer; higher, more stable prices for primary commodities guaranteed by international commodity agreements and financed by a Common Fund; an altered global division of labour in manufacturing and transportation; use of the international monetary system as an instrument of development finance; more effective regulation of multinational corporations; and clearer recognition of national sovereignty over resources.
3 See Robert E. Wood, *From Marshall Plan to Debt Crisis: Foreign Aid and Development Choices in the World Economy* (Berkeley: University of California Press, 1986), p. 197.
4 Cited in ibid., pp. 196-97.
5 Hollis Chenery et al., *Redistribution with Growth* (London: Oxford University Press, 1974).
6 The World Employment Conference of the International Labour Organization in 1976 popularized the concept of basic human needs. Soon thereafter, DAC adopted a statement on "Economic Growth and Meeting Basic Human Needs," which saw BHN "not as a substitute for, but an essential component of more economic growth which involves modernisation, provision of infrastructure and industrialisation." The approach, the statement added, "is not primarily welfare or charity but productivity-oriented, aiming at increasing the productive income of the poor and strengthening the basis for long-term self-generating development" (OECD-DAC, *Development Co-operation: Efforts and Policies of the Members of the Development Assistance Committee 1977*, pp. 149-51).
7 See Raymond F. Mikesell, *The Economics of Foreign Aid and Self-Sustaining Development* (Boulder, CO: Westview Press, 1983), p. 28.
8 Netherlands, Ministry of Foreign Affairs, *A World of Difference: A New Framework for Development Cooperation in the 1990s* (The Hague: Ministry of Foreign Affairs, 1991), pp. 18-19.
9 L. Ian MacDonald, *From Bourassa to Bourassa: A Pivotal Decade in Canadian History* (Montreal: Harvest House, 1984), p. 300. One of Lesage's rivals for the leadership of the provincial Liberals in 1958, Gérin-Lajoie still had strong leadership ambitions after the defeat of the Lesage government. René Lévesque might have been a serious obstacle had he not broken with the Liberals over sovereignty association in 1967. However, by then, as Dale Thomson wrote, Gérin-Lajoie's star "was in eclipse": "Within the rank and file of the party, he was blamed for having contributed to the defeat in 1966 because of the radical changes he had introduced in the educational system; and he had little support in caucus because of his shortcomings as a team player and his frequent absenteeism" (Dale C. Thomson, *Jean Lesage and the Quiet Revolution* [Toronto: Macmillan of Canada, 1984], p. 460).
10 Author's interview with Paul Gérin-Lajoie, Montreal, February 24, 1989.

11 Gérin-Lajoie's emotional commitment was deeply felt. An aide recalled the president's profound culture shock on seeing the urban poverty of Calcutta at first hand. "He wanted to take the whole damn budget of CIDA and remake Calcutta."

12 Gérin-Lajoie's difficulties with the press and opposition MPs started to escalate after anglophones in the Agency, upset about the decision to make French the operating language of the Latin America Division, started leaking embarrassing stories to Ottawa journalists late in 1973. These included confidential documents about Canada's reaction to General Pinochet's coup in Chile earlier that year. Although one of Gérin-Lajoie's fiercest critics in the Tory caucus was Claude Wagner, a former colleague in the Lesage government, several MPs from Western Canada expressed disgruntlement about the Latin American decision and a perceived francophone bias in CIDA. See, for example, Ron Clingen, "MP in Bid to Squeeze 100 CIDA Answers," *Ottawa Journal*, February 14, 1975, and Richard Jackson, "CIDA under Siege: Reynolds Presses French-Only Issue," *Ottawa Journal*, February 18, 1975.

13 The *Thoughts* series was printed in a format copying Robert McNamara's.

14 Paul Gérin-Lajoie, *Thoughts on International Development/1—Canadian International Cooperation: Approaches to the Seventies*, Presentation by Paul Gérin-Lajoie, President, Canadian International Development Agency to the International Development Subcommittee of the Commons Standing Committee on External Affairs and Defence, February 4, 1971 (Ottawa: CIDA, 1971), p. 3.

15 "CIDA: A $424 Million Christmas Stocking?—Not at All," Text of a Speech by Paul Gérin-Lajoie, President, Canadian International Development Agency, to Montreal District Chamber of Commerce, December 7, 1971.

16 Paul Gérin-Lajoie, *Thoughts on International Development/4—Developmental Administration: CIDA in a Changing Government Organization*, Paper delivered by Paul Gérin-Lajoie, President, Canadian International Development Agency, to the Institute of Public Administration Conference in Regina, September 8, 1971 (Ottawa: CIDA, 1972), p. 10.

17 Author's interview with Paul Gérin-Lajoie, Montreal, February 24, 1989.

18 Memorandum from Paul Gérin-Lajoie to All Officers of CIDA re: Strategy for 1975-1980, January 4, 1973, and Memorandum from Paul Gérin-Lajoie to All Officers of CIDA re: the Canadian International Development Strategy 1975-1980, January 30, 1973.

19 Based on interviews; G.R. Berry, "Bureaucratic Politics and Canadian Economic Policies Affecting Developing Countries—The Case of the Strategy for International Development Cooperation 1975-1980" (unpublished Ph.D. dissertation, Dalhousie University, 1981), pp. 109-34; and Thomas C. Bruneau, Jan J. Jørgensen, and J.O. Ramsay, "C.I.D.A.: The Organization of Canadian Overseas Assistance," Working Paper (Montreal: Centre for Developing-Area Studies, McGill University, 1978), p. 18.

20 CIDA, "Report of the Action Committee: Operation 25 Plus on the Least Developed Countries," January 3, 1973.

21 Department of Industry, Trade and Commerce, "International Development and the Canadian Economy," December 1968, p. 1. The priorities were set out on pp. 33-39.

22 The principal author was Bernard Wood, then a young officer in the Aid Operations Division. A CIDA officer in the strategy process recalled to the author years later that the IT&C document was taken very seriously, not least because it was

crafted so cleverly and argued so forcefully. In an ironical twist of history, Wood, as founding director of the North-South Institute from 1976 to 1989, went on to become a consistent and articulate critic of commercialization within the Canadian aid program.

23 Department of Industry, Trade and Commerce, "The Aid-Trade Relationship: A Discussion Draft of a Proposal for a Commercial Aid Programme for Canada," January 22, 1973, p. 7.

24 H.J. Hodder to President's Committee, January 17, 1973, cited in Berry, "Bureaucratic Politics and Canadian Economic Policies," p. 310.

25 Interview, and Berry, "Bureaucratic Politics and Canadian Economic Policies," p. 126.

26 Memorandum from Paul Gérin-Lajoie to All Officers of CIDA re: the Canadian International Development Strategy 1975-1980, January 30, 1973.

27 Memorandum from H.J. Hodder to the President's Committee, January 29, 1973, cited in Berry, "Bureaucratic Politics and Canadian Economic Policies," p. 112. Hodder suggested that it might be desirable "to involve one or two academics on specific issues." However, as the exercise unfolded, the only non-government involvement came in three commissioned papers, one from an academic and two from NGOs. Irving Brecher of McGill, who had been involved in the Strong review, wrote a commentary on Canada's responsibilities in the sphere of development; it had no discernible impact. The other two, by John Dillon of Gatt-Fly and the Development Education Centre, advocated far-reaching and radical changes in Canadian policy, which, as Berry commented, "were not oriented to the slow pace and limited horizons of a bureaucratic review process" (ibid., p. 186).

28 CIDA Strategy Unit, Notes on Strategy 1975-80, February 14, 1973, cited in Berry, "Bureaucratic Politics and Canadian Economic Policies," p. 140. For Harry Hodder, the issue was more one of protecting CIDA's jurisdiction than of rejecting a two-tiered approach as such. In fact, he himself had made such a proposal in November 1972. Thinking through the implications of how CIDA could accommodate an increase in the volume of aid to 0.7 per cent of GNP by 1980, he suggested an untied (and easier to administer) program up to 0.3 per cent, and a program tied to political and commercial interests up to 0.4 per cent. For ease of administration, the latter would rely more on lines of credit and program loans, and involve greater support for middle-income countries (ibid., pp. 131-33).

29 A major consultation with business was organized shortly after the IT&C document was circulated, efforts were made in 1973 to revitalize the low-key Business and Industry Program, and the expansion of the Latin America program was touted for economic benefits that would flow to Canada, as well as recipient countries. Gérin-Lajoie had earlier extolled the contribution of procurement tying for Canadian commerce and industry, but never so forcefully as in a speech to the Montreal Board of Trade in March 1973. See "The Economic Impact of Canada's Foreign Aid Program on the Canadian Economy," Text of speech by Paul Gérin-Lajoie, President, Canadian International Development Agency, to the Montreal Board of Trade, March 12, 1973.

30 Berry, "Bureaucratic Politics and Canadian Economic Policies," p. 159.

31 Ibid., p. 184.

32 CIDA, *Strategy for International Development Cooperation 1975-1980* (Ottawa: Information Canada, 1975), p. 14.

33 Ibid., p. 23.
34 Ibid.
35 Ibid., pp. 20, 14.
36 Ibid., p. 4.
37 Ibid., pp. 5-6.
38 Ibid., p. 8.
39 Ibid., p. 15.
40 Ibid., p. 18.
41 House of Commons, Standing Committee on External Affairs and National Defence, *Report of the Subcommittee on International Development Assistance*, in *Minutes of Proceedings and Evidence*, May 29, 1971, session 29, p. 40.
42 Paul Martin, *A Very Public Life*, vol. 2: *So Many Worlds* (Toronto: Deneau, 1985), pp. 669-70.
43 Based on interviews.
44 CIDA, "Report of the Strategy Task Force on Multidimensional Development," Strategy 1975-1980 Key Policy Papers, vol. 1, September 1974.
45 Berry, "Bureaucratic Politics and Canadian Economic Policies," p. 212.
46 CIDA, *Strategy for International Development Cooperation*, p. 19.
47 CIDA, "CIDA and the Multidimensional Approach to Development," p. 14.
48 Memorandum from J. Gérin, Vice-President for Policy, to President's Committee re: CIDA and the Multidimensional Approach to Development, March 4, 1975.
49 CIDA, *Strategy for International Development Cooperation*, p. 24.
50 Berry, "Bureaucratic Politics and Canadian Economic Policies," pp. 302-303. The only concession to CIDA was an appendix that plotted Canadian ODA expenditures on a trend line that was compared with a hypothetical trend line that would have been achieved with a 0.7 per cent ratio. The hypothetical line was extrapolated to 1980-81, along three alternative paths defined by differing assumptions about future GNP growth rates. However, the trend line of actual expenditures ended in 1975-76 (see CIDA, *Strategy for International Development Cooperation*, p. 48).
51 Parts of this section follow closely David R. Morrison, "The Choice of Bilateral Aid Recipients," in Cranford Pratt, ed., *Canadian International Development Assistance Policies: An Appraisal* (Montreal and Kingston: McGill-Queen's University Press, 1994), pp. 127-30.
52 CIDA, "Report of the Strategy Task Force on Eligibility," Strategy 1975-1980 Key Policy Papers, vol. 1, September 1974, pp. 12-13. The quotation is from p. 12. The countries deleted were: Bolivia, Brunei, Burundi, Central African Republic, Cyprus, Dominican Republic, Fiji, Gambia, Guinea, Hong Kong, Maldives, Paraguay, Philippines, Sierra Leone, Singapore, Somalia, South Korea, and Western Samoa. Of these, only Bolivia, Guinea, and the Philippines subsequently made a "comeback" of any significance.
53 George Cunningham, *The Management of Aid Agencies* (London: Croom Helm, 1974), pp. 129-30.
54 At the same time, External Affairs and IT&C were invited to prepare their own rankings of recipients on political and commercial grounds with the expectation that both would have to resort somewhat to developmental criteria. Neither department followed suit (Berry, "Bureaucratic Politics and Canadian Economic Policies," p. 343).
55 CIDA, "Report of Strategy Task Force on Eligibility," pp. 13-14.

56 Ibid., p. 15.
57 Ibid., pp. 1-3, 15 (emphasis in original).
58 Ibid., p. 32 (emphasis in original).
59 Berry, "Bureaucratic Politics and Economic Policies," pp. 321-22, 348-54.
60 CIDA, *Strategy for International Development Cooperation*, pp. 23, 25-26.
61 According to an interview source.
62 CIDA, *Strategy for International Development Cooperation*, p. 20. Point 3 (p. 21) envisioned possible tripartite arrangements through which oil-exporting countries might provide money, and Canada technology, for aid projects in poorer developing countries.
63 Ibid., p. 27.
64 Interview, and Berry, "Bureaucratic Politics and Canadian Economic Policies," p. 326.
65 See Office of the Prime Minister, Notes for the Prime Minister's Remarks at Duke University, Durham, N.C., May 12, 1974, and Office of the Prime Minister, Notes for Remarks by the Prime Minister at the Mansion House, London, England, March 13, 1975.
66 Interviews, and Berry, "Bureaucratic Politics and Canadian Economic Policies," pp. 334-35.
67 See Berry, "Bureaucratic Politics and Canadian Economic Policies," pp. 188-92, 202, 368-91.
68 CIDA, *Strategy for International Development Cooperation*, pp. 30, 34.
69 According to Berry, "Bureaucratic Politics and Canadian Economic Policies," pp. 433-53.
70 CIDA, *Strategy for International Development Cooperation*, p. 33.
71 The task force on concessionality reported: "A survey of the literature on procurement tying indicates that this cost may be as high as 15-30% of the tied portion of a donor's programme. No empirical study has been undertaken of the Canadian programme but the relatively poor performance of Canadian suppliers against World Bank tenders . . . and numerous specific bilateral examples would suggest that many Canadian goods and services which have been provided under tied procurement financing were not internationally competitive" (CIDA, "Report of the Strategy Task Force on Concessionality," Strategy 1975-1980 Key Policy Papers, vol. 1, September 1974, p. 11).
72 See Berry, "Bureaucratic Politics and Canadian Economic Policies," pp. 414-22.
73 See OECD-DAC, *Development Co-operation: Efforts and Policies of the Members of the Development Assistance Committee 1974*, pp. 124, 191-93.
74 Berry, "Bureaucratic Politics and Canadian Economic Policies," p. 420.
75 "What Worries Exporters about CIDA's New Plan," *Financial Post*, September 13, 1975. See also Linda Freeman, "The Political Economy of Canada's Foreign Aid Programme" (paper presented to the Annual Conference of the Canadian Political Science Association, Montreal, June 1980), p. 44.
76 Interviews. See also correspondence cited in Berry, "Bureaucratic Politics and Canadian Economic Policies," pp. 421-22.
77 CIDA, *Strategy for International Development Cooperation*, p. 32 (author's emphasis).
78 Berry, "Bureaucratic Politics and Canadian Economic Policies," p. 428.
79 CIDA, *Strategy for International Development Cooperation*, p. 23.
80 Ibid., p. 31.

81 Ibid., p. 25.
82 Berry, "Bureaucratic Politics and Canadian Economic Policies," p. 241.
83 CIDA, *Strategy for International Development Cooperation*, p. 36.
84 Ibid., pp. 22, 35.
85 Ibid., pp. 29, 35, 37.
86 Ibid., p. 39.
87 Statement by the Honourable Allan J. MacEachen, Secretary of State for External Affairs, Seventh Special Session, United Nations General Assembly, September 3, 1975, in CIDA, *International Development Cooperation* (Ottawa: CIDA, 1975).
88 See, for example, Peter Thomson, "Canada May Cut Off Aid to 30 Nations," *Montreal Star*, September 3, 1975; "A Sensible Foreign-aid Policy," *London Free Press*, September 30, 1975; Robert Trumbull, "Canada Trims Her List of Foreign-Aid Recipients," *New York Times*, September 7, 1975; Clyde Sanger, "Canada Leads Way in Third World Aid," *The Gazette* (Montreal), November 24, 1975; and "Canada's Red Book," *New Internationalist* (December 1975).
89 Berry, "Bureaucratic Politics and Canadian Economic Policies," p. 454.
90 Author's interview with Paul Gérin-Lajoie, Montreal, February 24, 1989.
91 House of Commons, *First Report of the Subcommittee on International Development*, in *Journals*, April 14, 1976, pp. 1217-39.
92 Ibid., p. 1221.
93 Ibid., p. 1222.
94 Ibid., p. 1223.
95 Data in this section are drawn from Appendix A and Appendix F; CIDA, *Annual Review 1975-76*, pp. 121, 123; CIDA, *Annual Review 1977-78*, p. 32; CIDA, *Memorandum to DAC 1973*, pp. 7-8; OECD-DAC, *Development Co-operation: Efforts and Policies of the Members of the Development Assistance Committee 1978*, p. 191; OECD-DAC, *Twenty-five Years of Development Co-operation: A Review* (Paris: Organisation for Economic Co-operation and Development, 1985), pp. 334-35; and CIDA, *Annual Report 1992-93*, p. 62.
96 Gérin-Lajoie, *Canadian International Cooperation: Approaches to the Seventies*, pp. 8-9.
97 Parts of this section follow closely Morrison, "The Choice of Bilateral Aid Recipients," pp. 130-33.
98 CIDA, *Memorandum to DAC 1972*, p. 18; ibid., *1975*, p. 12; and ibid., *1976*, p. 8.
99 Ibid., *1975*, p. 12.
100 According to a senior associate, PGL insisted that Haiti be included in the Latin American program. It was the only independent French-speaking country in the Western Hemisphere and the least developed. He encountered strong objections from officers in the Planning Division who doubted that it would be possible to do much meaningful development work under the corrupt and dictatorial Duvalier regime. The sceptical position was by and large vindicated.
101 CIDA, *Annual Review 1975-76*, pp. 25, 27.
102 See CIDA, *Memorandum to DAC 1976*, p. 7.
103 See Appendix C.
104 J.L. Granatstein and Robert Bothwell, *Pirouette: Pierre Trudeau and Canadian Foreign Policy* (Toronto: University of Toronto Press, 1990), p. 294.
105 See Patricia Jean Appavoo, "The Small State as Donor: Canadian and Swedish Development Assistance Policies, 1960-1976" (unpublished Ph.D. dissertation, University of Toronto, 1988), pp. 184-89.

106 Gérin-Lajoie, *Canadian International Cooperation: Approaches to the Seventies*, p. 7.

107 CIDA, *Annual Review 1977-78*, pp. 27-40. Each fell to about $90 million in 1976-77.

108 Ibid., *1972-73*, p. 24.

109 Appavoo, "The Small State as Donor," pp. 189-95, and Paul Ladouceur, "Humanitarian Aid for Southern Africa," in Douglas Anglin et al., eds., *Canada, Scandinavia and Southern Africa* (Uppsala: Scandinavian Institute of African Affairs, 1978), pp. 85-102.

110 And future Canadian high commissioner to Tanzania.

111 See "$1 Million to Send Professors to Havana, Ottawa's Plan," *The Globe and Mail*, January 23, 1973; Lionel Martin, "Canada, Cuba Forming Ties through CIDA," *The Globe and Mail*, February 12, 1974; Chris Cobb, "Secret Sugarplum to Cuba Splits Cabinet," *The Globe and Mail*, December 21, 1974; Paul Hellyer, "CIDA's Proposed Agreement with Cuba Shows Need for Review of Aid Programs," *The Ottawa Citizen*, June 6, 1975; "End Aid to Cuba, House Urged," *The Globe and Mail*, January 27, 1976; "Canadian Aid to Cuba Slowly Winding Down," *The Gazette* (Montreal), February 11, 1977; and "Canada Cutting Off All aid to Cuba to Protest Mercenary Role in Africa," *The Gazette* (Montreal), May 24, 1978.

112 CIDA, *Memorandum to DAC 1974*, p. 19.

113 Phillip Rawkins, *Human Resource Development in the Aid Process: A Study in Organizational Learning and Change* (Ottawa: North-South Institute, 1993), p. 5.

114 OECD-DAC, *Development Co-operation: Efforts and Policies of the Members of the Development Assistance Committee 1982*, pp. 240-41. See also data in Appendix E.

115 See CIDA, *Annual Review 1975-76*, p. 123, and ibid., *1977-78*, p. 33.

116 CIDA, *Memorandum to DAC 1974*, pp. 47-48.

117 Ibid., *1975*, p. 23.

118 CIDA, *Sectoral Guidelines 1: Rural Development and Renewable Resources* (Ottawa: CIDA, 1976); CIDA, *Sectoral Guidelines 2: Social Development and Community Services* Ottawa: CIDA, 1976); and CIDA, *Sectoral Guidelines 3: Infrastructure and Environment* (Ottawa: CIDA, 1976).

119 This section is based on Theodore Cohn, "Food Surpluses and Canadian Food Aid," *Canadian Public Policy* 3, 2 (Spring 1977); Theodore Cohn, *Canadian Food Aid: Domestic and Foreign Policy Implications* (Denver, CO: Graduate School of International Studies, 1979), especially chaps. 1 and 2; Mark Charlton, *The Making of Canadian Food Aid Policy* (Kingston and Montreal: McGill-Queen's University Press, 1992), especially chaps. 1 and 2; and press reports: "Canadians Are Best Organized of Non-Governmental Groups Lobbying at Food Conference," *The Globe and Mail*, November 6, 1974; James Rusk, "Canada to Give 10% of World Food Aid for Next Three Years," *The Globe and Mail*, November 7, 1974; Dave Blaikie and John Hay, "Canada Pledges Wheat," *Montreal Star*, November 7, 1974; Ben Tierney, "MPs' Criticism at Home Irks Whelan in Rome," *The Ottawa Citizen*, November 16, 1974; and Ken Whittingham, "Canada's Food Aid Offer Criticized as 'Grandstanding,'" *Montreal Star*, November 16, 1974.

120 Calculated from historical data in Appendix A.

121 David R. Protheroe, *Canada and Multilateral Aid: Working Paper* (Ottawa: North-South Institute, 1991), p. 35.
122 See CIDA, *Annual Review 1972-73*, p. 53.
123 CIDA, *Memorandum to DAC 1973*, p. 13.
124 Protheroe, *Canada and Multilateral Aid*, pp. 43, 30.
125 Appendix A.
126 Based on interviews.
127 Interviews, and CIDA, *Memorandum to DAC 1971*, p. 15.
128 Jean Christie, "A Critical History of Development Education in Canada," *Canadian and International Education* (special issue on Development Education in Canada in the Eighties) 12, 3 (1983): 14.
129 From an unpublished manuscript kindly made available by Blair Dimock.
130 Ibid.
131 See Patrick Best, "Squabbles Plague Overseas University Aid Groups," *The Ottawa Citizen*, December 23, 1974. For a full account of the conflict (from a CUSO perspective), see Ian Smillie, *The Land of Lost Content: A History of CUSO* (Toronto: Deneau, 1985), pp. 103-105, 264-65.
132 Dominick Sarsfield, a former senior financial analyst at Industry, Trade and Commerce, wrote a position paper on the program in 1971 and went on to serve as director from 1972 to 1975. While somewhat beleaguered within a Special Programs Branch where many thought his activities were inappropriate, he managed to achieve a higher profile for the program outside the Agency. (Based on interviews. See "CIDA, Firms to Help Developing Countries," *The Globe and Mail*, March 14, 1973; Jennifer Lewington, "Ottawa Takes Mystique Out of International Financing," *Financial Post*, April 21, 1973; and "CIDA to Boost Private Sector," *Barbados Advocate News*, March 24, 1974, press report of a visit by Sarsfield reproduced in *CIDA Paper Clips*, the Agency's digest of press clippings.)
133 CIDA, *Memorandum to DAC 1975*, p. 29.
134 "CIDA Gets Hand," *The Ottawa Citizen*, July 21, 1976, and CIDA, *Memorandum to DAC 1975*, p. 25.
135 This section is based largely on interviews.
136 According to an interview source. The documents were intended to embarrass the government by showing that Ottawa was more sympathetic towards the coup and American intervention than public pronouncements indicated. An investigation of the leak reportedly traced it back to the Latin America Division.
137 Based on data in an unpublished manuscript by Blair Dimock.
138 Based largely on interviews.
139 CIDA, *Memorandum to DAC 1972*, p. 14.
140 Ibid., *1974*, p. 8, and CIDA, "CIDA Organizational Manual" (Hull, 1980), p. 77.
141 Except where noted, this section is based on CIDA, "CIDA Organizational Manual," pp. 65-75; CIDA's memoranda to DAC for the years under discussion; an unpublished manuscript by Blair Dimock; and interviews.
142 CIDA, *Memorandum to DAC 1971*, p. 2.
143 Ibid., *1974*, p. 9. For a discussion of the genesis and approach of logical framework analysis, see Dennis A. Rondinelli, *Development Administration and U.S. Foreign Aid Policy* (Boulder, CO: Lynne Reiner, 1987), pp. 54-58. The approach has been criticized for placing too much emphasis on process and inputs and not enough on developmental outputs.
144 Clyde Sanger, "Out of Africa," *Canadian Forum* (July/August 1993), p. 22.

145 For example, up to late 1972 when Ed Ritchie was under-secretary of state for External Affairs and Donald Tansley was executive vice-president of CIDA, the relationship between the two organizations was reasonably cordial. CIDA field staff posted to Canadian missions were increased. It was also agreed that senior CIDA personnel could be named as heads of post. Noble Power, later to return to the Agency as a vice-president, was appointed high commissioner to Ghana in 1971. When Tansley left CIDA, the executive vice-presidency was dropped and relations at the senior level deteriorated. (Based on interviews.)

146 "Mixed Reaction Greets Changes in Makeup of Federal Cabinet," *The Globe and Mail*, September 16, 1976; "Dispute Pits Civil Servants against Wish of Minister," *Montreal Star*, October 10, 1976; W.A. Wilson, "The Struggle for CIDA," *The Globe and Mail*, November 1, 1976; and "PM Settles Struggle," *The Gazette* (Montreal), February 8, 1977.

147 House of Commons, Standing Committee on External Affairs and National Defence, *Report of the Subcommittee on International Development Assistance*, in *Minutes of Proceedings and Evidence*, May 29, 1971, session 29, p. 14, and Douglas Roche, "Can Canada Help Achieve a New World Order?" *Saturday Night* (May 1975), p. 15. Professor Irving Brecher, a distinguished political scientist who participated in the 1969-70 review, continued to call for a separate minister (see Irving Brecher, "The Continuing Challenge of International Development: A Canadian Perspective," *Queen's Quarterly* 82 [Autumn 1975]: 341).

148 CIDA, *Memorandum to DAC 1974*, p. 13.

149 Phillip Rawkins, "An Institutional Analysis of CIDA," in Pratt, ed., *Canadian International Development Assistance Policies*, pp. 159-60.

150 See Auditor General, *Supplement to the Annual Report for the Fiscal Year Ended March 31, 1975* (Ottawa: Information Canada, 1975), pp. 138-47, and Auditor General, *Conspectus of the Report of the Auditor General to the House of Commons for the Fiscal Year Ended March 31, 1976* (Ottawa: Minister of Supply and Services, 1976), pp. 26-27, 102-06, 119-20. The list of ninety-two recommendations was appended to House of Commons, Standing Committee on Public Accounts, *Minutes of Proceedings and Evidence*, June 23, 1977, session 38A, pp. 65-79. Five of the ninety-two were directed at IDRC.

151 See discussion of the Lachance committee report in Chapter 3 and, as examples from the press: Alex Campbell, "Self-reliance: Canada's New Direction in Foreign Aid," *The Toronto Star*, June 30, 1972; "CIDA Takes Some Effective Approaches," *The Globe and Mail* (editorial), February 24, 1973; and Eric Downton, "The Kind of Aid that Really Helps," *The Toronto Sun*, July 21, 1973.

152 See, for example, Oxfam of Canada, *Unequal Partners: Development in the Seventies—Where does Canada Stand?* (Report of Unequal Partners Conference, Toronto, May 8-9, 1970).

153 It was constructed in the early 1970s in response to a request from the Tanzanian government for financing of a facility to satisfy growing urban demand for bread. As Roger Young noted in his evaluation of CIDA's bilateral programming in Tanzania: "The SIHA Bakery (Siha is a Swahili word implying goodness) was to become an acute embarrassment to CIDA and a poor investment for the Tanzanian economy. Little or no analysis of the social costs and effects of sophisticated technology imported . . . at high social cost was undertaken prior to the project's approval. The bakery reflected an inappropriate design, experienced poor production records, and initially displaced other more labour-intensive bakeries" (Roger

Young, *Canadian Development Assistance to Tanzania* [Ottawa: North-South Institute, 1983], p. 49).

154 Gordon Pape, "Canada's Goodwill Fund Is Mounting in Africa, but Financial Aid Policy Needs Re-examination," *The Gazette* (Montreal), April 25, 1973.

155 Letter from Paul Gérin-Lajoie, President, Canadian International Development Agency, *The Gazette* (Montreal), May 8, 1973.

156 "Gov't Persisting in Foreign Aid Despite Public Opposition," *Ottawa Journal*, August 10, 1973.

157 Patrick Best, "CIDA Planning Number of Changes," *The Ottawa Citizen*, September 29, 1973.

158 Hugh Winsor, "CIDA to Ask for Restoration of $50 Million Cut in Spending," *The Globe and Mail*, January 31, 1974.

159 See House of Commons, Standing Committee on External Affairs and National Defence, *Minutes of Proceedings and Evidence*, April 30, 1974, session 13, pp. 7-17, and ibid., May 7, 1974, session 16, pp. 24-33. In response to a request from Andrew Brewin of the NDP to treat the matter as one of parliamentary privilege, the Speaker of the House promised to rule later, "perhaps tomorrow" (House of Commons, *Debates*, May 8, 1974, pp. 2133-34).

160 Robert Cameron, "Foreign Aid: Program Needs Revision," *Montreal Star*, July 24, 1974.

161 Interview; see also Berry, "Bureaucratic Politics and Canadian Economic Policies," p. 204.

162 By the mid-1970s, Communications Branch was publishing a bimonthly magazine (*Cooperation Canada*) and a monthly newsletter (*Contact*), which combined information about the Agency's work with news and viewpoints on development issues, as well as a quarterly tabloid (*Action*), which focused on the activities of Canadian and international NGOs. It produced and/or co-produced several audio-visual presentations and developed educational kits and materials for school-age children.

163 Jack Cahill, "Canada Fears Bangladesh Aid Stolen," *The Toronto Star*, November 28, 1974.

164 Cobb, "Secret Sugarplum to Cuba Splits Cabinet."

165 Patrick Best, "MPs Complain of Use of Consultants," *The Ottawa Citizen*, December 21, 1974.

166 Richard Gwyn, "CIDA: Is It a 'Sick Joke'?" *Ottawa Journal*, January 11, 1975.

167 See *Ottawa Journal*, January 18, 23, 24, 25, and 27, 1975.

168 *The Ottawa Citizen*, January 14, 1975, and *Ottawa Journal*, December 28, 1974 and January 14, 1975.

169 "PM Stands Firm on CIDA Issue," *Ottawa Journal*, January 29, 1975; "News Reports Not Enough for CIDA Probe: Sharp," *Ottawa Journal*, January 30, 1975. For additional accounts of critical questioning and commentary by Conservative MPs (especially Steve Paproski, Claude Wagner, Dan McKenzie, and John Reynolds), see *Ottawa Journal*, February 14 and 18, 1975, and *Sun* (Vancouver), February 21, 1975.

170 Cited in Roche, "Can Canada Help Achieve a New World Order?" p. 11. The debate occurred on a day allotted to the Opposition, and was initiated by Conservative Claude Wagner's motion deploring "the government's secrecy in the operation of the Canadian International Development Agency which casts doubt on the quality of management and effectiveness of Canada's international development

assistance program." Wagner had spearheaded the effort a year earlier to obtain the Price Waterhouse report, and continued to make that an issue. While some MPs discussed policy issues, the debate was dominated by partisan attacks on Gérin-Lajoie and the government. See House of Commons, *Debates*, February 25, 1975, pp. 3397-408, 3413-427.

171 Patrick Best, "Door Opened for Watchdog on CIDA," *The Ottawa Citizen*, March 14, 1975.

172 CIDA, "Examples of Problems and Dilemmas in Development Cooperation," April 10, 1975.

173 House of Commons, Standing Committee on External Affairs and National Defence, *Minutes of Proceedings and Evidence*, April 10, 1975, session 11, pp. 15-16. A revised version of the speech was published in CIDA, *International Development Cooperation* (Statement by Honourable Allan J. MacEachen, Secretary of State for External Affairs, Standing Committee of the House of Commons on External Affairs and International Trade, April 10, 1975).

174 Claude Wagner accused MacEachen of contempt (House of Commons, Standing Committee on External Affairs and International Trade, *Minutes of Proceedings and Evidence*, April 10, 1975, session 11, p. 17).

175 House of Commons, Standing Committee on External Affairs and National Defence, *Minutes of Proceedings and Evidence*, 1975, sessions 11, 13, 16, 17, 19, 22, 29. The motions were debated on April 29 and May 16 (sessions 17 and 22). The hearings were extensively covered by the press. See, for example, Patrick Best, "Tories Fail to Force Probe of CIDA Financial Matters," *The Ottawa Citizen*, May 17, 1975; Christopher Cobb, "CIDA 'Misunderstood,' " *Ottawa Journal*, May 1, 1975; Hugh Winsor, "CIDA President Denies Misleading MPs about Size of Canada's Aid Plan for Cuba," *The Globe and Mail*, May 17, 1975; and "The Trouble with Foreign Aid," *Time* (Canadian edition), June 2, 1975. Clyde Sanger penned a humorous essay—with a serious concern—about the hearings: "Peep-hole Politics or 'Now you CIDA, now you don't.' "

176 Roche, "Can Canada Help Achieve a New World Order?" p. 11. Roche wrote several articles during this period, expressing his misgivings about CIDA, but differentiating these from the importance of strengthening Canada's commitment to international development. See, for example, "CIDA: Time for a Parliamentary Review," *The Catholic Register*, February 22, 1975, and "How MPs 'Blew Their Chance' on CIDA," *The Ottawa Citizen*, April 23, 1975.

177 For a report on their tour, arranged by the Canadian Council for International Cooperation, see CIDA, *Action* (Spring 1976).

178 "CIDA to Be More Open—Lajoie," *Ottawa Journal*, June 5, 1975.

179 See MacEachen's preface in CIDA, *Annual Review 1974-75*, p. 3, and Paul Gérin-Lajoie, *Thoughts on International Development/8—25 Years After*, An Address by Paul Gérin-Lajoie, President of the Canadian International Development Agency to the 44th Couchiching Conference, Geneva Park, Ontario, August 8, 1975 (Ottawa: CIDA, 1975), pp. 2-3.

180 CIDA, *Memorandum to DAC 1974*, p. 26.

181 A Gallup poll in 1974 found that 53 per cent of respondents favoured an increase in aid, compared with 35 per cent who did not and 12 per cent who expressed no opinion. A 1976 study found that 35 per cent of respondents did not believe that too much was being spent on aid, but 28 per cent did; 75 per cent revealed that they knew nothing or little about the Canadian aid program. See Peter Wyse,

Canadian Foreign Aid in the 1970s: An Organizational Audit (Montreal: Centre for Developing-Area Studies, McGill University, 1983), pp. 77-78.

182 See Frank Howard's "Bureaucrats" column, *The Ottawa Citizen*, August 27, 1976.

183 "Dupuy's New Job," *The Globe and Mail*, August 30, 1976.

184 See, for example, Ron Clingen, "CIDA Indicted," *Ottawa Journal*, November 24, 1976; "Horrible Stories," *The Globe and Mail*, November 25, 1976; and several stories that coincided with the transition from Gérin-Lajoie to Dupuy early in 1977.

185 Morton Shulman, "CIDA Shenanigans in Haiti," *The Toronto Sun*, January 11, 1977.

186 See "CIDA's Leader Denies Reports," *The Ottawa Citizen*, January 12, 1977, and a series of articles by Dan Proudfoot in *The Toronto Sun*, April 3-7, 1977.

187 See, for example, Ken Pole, "Pressure Mounting for Inquiry into CIDA Spending," *Ottawa Journal*, January 12, 1977; Michael Benedict, "More 'Horror Stories,'" *The Toronto Star*, January 15, 1977; and "Foreign Aid Agency Needs an Open Study," *Montreal Star*, January 14, 1977.

188 Stephen Scott, "CIDA Chief Parts," *Ottawa Journal*, February 24, 1977. At that stage, following rumours that Gérin-Lajoie had turned down offers of ambassadorships, it was thought that he was still being considered for the chairmanship of the CNR. Commentary on his departure was generally more positive and sympathetic, though still mixed, in the French-speaking press. See, for example, Gilbert Brunet, "L'acdi, critiquée mais bien avisée," *Le Droit*, March 1, 1977, and Jean Pellerin, "ACDI: expérience originale et audacieuse," *La Presse* (Montreal), March 3, 1977. Another article quoted Richard Gwyn of the *Toronto Star*, in response to the suggestion that Gérin-Lajoie might receive the CNR appointment, as asking "Pourquoi diable Trudeau tient-il tant à nommer un Gérin-Lajoie? Il va provoquer la ruine des chemins de fer!" It went on to say: "Ce genre de commentaire rend bien l'opinion non seulement de plusiers journalistes et pas seulement des anglophones, mais aussi d'homme d'affaires réputés pour qui M. Paul Gérin-Lajoie constitue l'archétype de l'administrateur irresponsable." However, much of the rest of the article was devoted to an interview in which the former president summarized what he saw as the main achievements during his tenure (Jean Pelletier, "Entrevue avec Gérin-Lajoie," *La Presse* [Montreal], March 5, 1977).

189 See CIDA, *Annual Review 1975-76*.

Chapter 5

1 Cited in Michael Tucker, *Canadian Foreign Policy: Contemporary Issues and Themes* (Toronto: McGraw-Hill Ryerson, 1980), p. 65.

2 It will be recalled that Pierre Dupuy led the fact-finding mission to francophone Africa in 1960 before the extension of Canadian aid to the region.

3 John Best, "Born to Play 'the Game,'" *The Ottawa Citizen*, February 15, 1977; press release from the Office of the Prime Minister, March 11, 1980; and author's interview with Michel Dupuy, Ottawa, March 1, 1989.

4 Cited in Ken Mason, "PM Suggests 'Tighter Ship' to CIDA Head," *The Western Producer* (Saskatoon), March 10, 1997.

5 The first reference came from a press interview: Stephen Handleman, "CIDA's New Broom: Aid Chief Promises No More Scandals," *The Toronto Star*,

October 1, 1977. The second came from the author's interview with Michel Dupuy, Ottawa, March 1, 1989.

6 During that span, Canadian ODA (as measured in 1981 $US) fell by 8 per cent (calculated from data in OECD-DAC, *Development Co-operation: Efforts and Policies of the Members of the Development Assistance Committee 1982*, p. 180).

7 CIDA, *Memorandum to DAC 1978*, pp. 28-29.

8 Considerable detail about changes in financial management, planning and information systems between 1977 and 1979 is contained in *Report of the Auditor General of Canada to the House of Commons, Fiscal Year Ended March 31, 1979* (Hull: Minister of Supply and Services, 1980), pp. 245-92.

9 J.L. Granatstein and Robert Bothwell, *Pirouette: Pierre Trudeau and Canadian Foreign Policy* (Toronto: University of Toronto Press, 1990), p. 290.

10 Except where noted, the account is based on interviews; CIDA, "The Corporate Review" (Ottawa, 1977); CIDA, "CIDA Organizational Manual" (Hull, 1980), pp. 77-104; and an unpublished manuscript by Blair Dimock.

11 CIDA, "The Corporate Review," p. 3.

12 Where, according to interview sources, some saw it as a power play by Pierre Sicard, the vice-president, Corporate Review. Sicard later assumed the position of vice-president of the newly created Resources Branch.

13 CIDA, "The Corporate Review," p. 6.

14 Ibid., pp. 5, 7.

15 See Memorandum from Canadian International Development Agency to Treasury Board, November 29, 1977. Much of the memorandum was reproduced in CIDA, "CIDA Organizational Manual," pp. 76-97.

16 Memorandum to all CIDA officers from Michel Dupuy and Marcel Massé, President's Conference—Cornwall—A-Base and Corporate Reviews, March 31, 1980.

17 See CIDA, Policy Branch, "Evaluation in CIDA: A Proposal for an Integrated Agency-Wide System," September 14, 1978; CIDA, *Memorandum to DAC 1978*, p. 34; ibid., *1979*, pp. 31-32; and CIDA, "Canadian Aid Policy," in Parliamentary Task Force on North-South Relations, *Minutes of Proceedings and Evidence*, June 10, 1980, session 3A, pp. 187-88.

18 Except where noted, based on interviews; Jeffrey S. Steeves, "The Canadian International Development Agency: The Policy Process and the Third World, 1968-1979" (paper presented to Workshop on Development Policy, Centre for Development Projects, Dalhousie University, March 1980), pp. 13-17; Tucker, *Canadian Foreign Policy*, pp. 62ff.; and an unpublished 1991 manuscript by Blair Dimock.

19 Cited in Steeves, "The Canadian International Development Agency: The Policy Process and the Third World, 1968-1979," p. 16.

20 See MacDonald's comments to House of Commons, Standing Committee on External Affairs and National Defence, *Minutes of Proceedings and Evidence*, October 25, 1979, session 1, p. 19. She also made it clear that the aid policy paper prepared for the foreign policy review (discussed below) by CIDA's Policy Branch was for her. The document was referred to as "Flora's strategy" when it was under preparation.

21 See Gilbert Lavoie, "Asselin veut faire le ménage à l'ACDI," *La Presse* (Montreal), July 19, 1979; Robert MacDonald, "Senator Vows Tough CIDA Funds Controls," *Sunday Sun*, August 12, 1979; and House of Commons, Standing Committee on External Affairs and National Defence, *Minutes of Proceedings and Evidence*, November 11, 1979, p. 2.

22 CIDA, *Memorandum to DAC 1976*, pp. 3-5.

23 House of Commons, Standing Committee on External Affairs and National Defence, *Minutes of Proceedings and Evidence*, December 1, 1977, session 4A, p. 11.

24 See the analysis and suggestions for overcoming the bilateral disbursement problem in North-South Institute, *North-South Encounter: The Third World and Canadian Performance* (Ottawa: North-South Institute, 1977), pp. 113-17.

25 House of Commons, Standing Committee on External Affairs and National Defence, Subcommittee on International Development, "First Report," *Minutes of Proceedings and Evidence*, May 5, 9 and 10, 1977, session 9, p. 22.

26 OECD-DAC, *Development Co-operation: Efforts and Policies of the Members of the Development Assistance Committee 1977*, p. 34.

27 CIDA, Policy Branch, "Global Review of Development and of International and Canadian Cooperation in 1977," July 1977, p. iv, n. 13.

28 CIDA, *Memorandum to DAC 1977*, p. 5.

29 Ibid., *1978*, p. 2.

30 CIDA, *Annual Report 1992-93*, p. 62.

31 CIDA, Policy Branch, "A Few Thoughts on the Prospects for Development and Cooperation," October 1978, pp. 24-25. The essay was an internal document, but John Best learned of it and wrote an article, "Gov't May Drop Foreign Aid goal," for *The Globe and Mail*, May 9, 1979.

32 David Humphries, "Foreign Aid Can't Increase Until the Economy Improves, MacDonald Says," *The Globe and Mail*, June 13, 1979.

33 Geoffrey Catton, "Getting Tough: Crosbie Says Canada Can't Afford Aid Demands," *The Globe and Mail*, October 4, 1979.

34 Roger Croft, "We're Tightening Our Belts but Expanding Foreign Aid," *The Toronto Star*, January 21, 1978.

35 CIDA, *Memorandum to DAC 1980*, p. 4; James Rusk, "Restraint Hits Foreign Aid; Inflation Means a Net Drop," *The Globe and Mail*, November 6, 1979.

36 North-South Institute, *In the Canadian Interest? Third World Development in the 1980s* (Ottawa: North-South Institute, 1980), p. 23.

37 Cranford Pratt, "Ethics and Foreign Policy: The Case of Canada's Development Assistance," *International Journal* 43, 2 (Spring 1988): 278.

38 House of Commons, Standing Committee on External Affairs, *Minutes of Proceedings and Evidence*, October 25, 1979, session 1, p. 20.

39 See Appendix A.

40 See Appendix F.

41 Interviews. See Dupuy's testimony in House of Commons, Standing Committee on External Affairs and National Defence, *Minutes of Proceedings and Evidence*, March 20, 1979, session 7, pp. 13-14, and session 7A, pp. 5-7; subsequent discussion in that meeting and *Minutes of Proceedings and Evidence*, November 1, 1979, p. 2; Jan Jelmert Jørgensen, "The Canadian Response to Third World Needs" (paper presented to the Conference on Government, Society and the Public Purpose, Concordia University, Montreal, March 2-4, 1979), pp. 20-22; "Canada Falling Further Behind in Foreign Aid," *The Globe and Mail*, February 24, 1979; Rusk, "Restraint Hits Foreign Aid; Inflation Means a Net Drop"; and "Canada's Cuts Bite," *New African*, February 1980, p. 44.

42 Réal Lavergne claimed, however, "that Dupuy's emphasis on short-term economic benefits was considered by the Cabinet to be too extreme" (Réal Lavergne, "Deter-

minants of Canadian Aid Policy," in Olav Stokke, ed., *Western Middle Powers and Global Poverty: The Determinants of the Aid Policies of Canada, Denmark, the Netherlands, Norway and Sweden* [Uppsala: Scandinavian Institute of African Studies, 1989], p. 46). Subsequent official rhetoric, especially after Marcel Massé assumed the presidency, focused more on long-term mutual benefits.

43 CIDA, Policy Branch, "Global Review of Development and of International and Canadian Cooperation in 1977," p. 17.

44 See ibid., pp. 11-15.

45 CIDA, President's Office, "Directions for the Agency: From Now Until the 1980s," December 7, 1977, pp. ii-iii.

46 Ibid., p. 8. The other recommendations are on pp. 2, 5-7.

47 See, for example, Notes for Remarks by Michel Dupuy, President of CIDA, to the Empire Club of Toronto, November 3, 1977; "The Cooperative Movement and Development Cooperation," Notes for an Address by Michel Dupuy to the meeting of the Conseil de la coopération du Québec, Montreal, November 21, 1977, and "Foreign Assistance: Mature Relationships Leading to Mutual Advantage," Notes for an Address by Michel Dupuy to the Vancouver Club, February 28, 1978.

48 CIDA, Policy Branch, "A Few Thoughts on the Prospects for Development and Co-operation," p. 11.

49 Despite these directives, however, the official list of core (program) and non-core (project) countries that emerged from the exercise reflected little change from the status quo (see Appendix D). A senior CIDA official who participated in the process recalled to the author that bargaining over the formula was long and hard, but that "we ended up getting the numbers right." CIDA participants did fail, however, to secure a commitment on greater concentration, as External Affairs and/or Trade officials invariably had reasons for not dropping any particular country. At the same time, the existence of small Mission Administered Funds in most eligible countries served somewhat as a buffer against even greater dilution of the regular bilateral program.

50 Department of Industry, Trade and Commerce, *Strengthening Canada Abroad: Final Report of the Export Promotion Review Committee* (Ottawa: Department of Industry, Trade and Commerce, 1979), pp. 35-36.

51 House of Commons, *Debates*, December 19, 1977, p. 2022. See also Roche's comments in House of Commons, Standing Committee on External Affairs and National Defence, *Minutes of Proceedings and Evidence*, April 6, 1978, session 10, pp. 7-11.

52 North-South Institute, *North-South Encounter*, especially pp. 5-15 and chaps. 1 and 3.

53 Economic Council of Canada, *For a Common Future: A Study of Canada's Relations with Developing Countries* (Hull: Minister of Supply and Services, 1978).

54 Ibid., pp. 79-81, 104-108.

55 Ibid., pp. 100-10.

56 Ibid., p. 133. The report called for organizational reforms that would either strengthen existing interdepartmental committees with strong coordination by a designated department, probably External Affairs, or establish an independent department based on CIDA with full responsibility for integrating Canada's relations with developing countries.

57 Ibid., pp. 80-81. The Treasury Board was sympathetic, but the suggestion was quickly dismissed in both the President's Committee and ICERDC (interviews).

58 Ibid., p. 97. The report recommended a cap of 35 per cent on non-food multilateral aid—higher than the strategy target but lower than shares in the previous two years.

59 See especially Donald Jamieson's session with the House of Commons, Standing Committee on External Affairs and National Defence, *Minutes of Proceedings and Evidence*, March 29, 1977, session 12, pp. 6-13. David MacDonald of the Conservatives put forward private member's bills in each of 1976-77 and 1977-78 "to prohibit aid to foreign countries violating human rights." The second of these was debated briefly before being talked out on second reading. See House of Commons, *Debates*, March 3, 1977, p. 3610; October 31, 1977, p. 428; and March 21, 1978, pp. 3989-3996. Andrew Brewin of the NDP proposed a similar private member's bill (ibid., October 31, 1977, p. 431).

60 See House of Commons, Standing Committee on External Affairs and National Defence, Subcommittee on International Development, *Minutes of Proceedings and Evidence*, March 30, 1977, session 1A, p. 1.

61 David Blaikie, "Clark Plans Foreign Aid review," *The Toronto Star*, July 31, 1979.

62 Ibid. See Notes for a Speech by the Secretary of State for External Affairs, Flora MacDonald, to the Canadian Club of Montreal, September 17, 1979; and MacDonald's comments to House of Commons, Standing Committee on External Affairs and National Defence, *Minutes of Proceedings and Evidence*, October 25, 1979, session 1, p. 19.

63 Jim Robb, "Tory Caucus Demands Tough Foreign Aid review," *Ottawa Journal*, September 24, 1979.

64 See "Canada Freezes Plans for Aid," *New African* (August 1979), pp. 48-49.

65 Canadian Council for International Cooperation, "A Framework for Canada's Development Assistance," Ottawa, November 1979.

66 See Notes for an Address by the Secretary of State for External Affairs, Flora MacDonald, to the United Nations General Assembly, New York, September 25, 1979; "Protect Human Rights for All or the World Will Scorn You, Flora MacDonald Tells UN," *The Gazette* (Montreal), September 26, 1979; editorial criticisms in "Aid, Trade and Rights," *The Globe and Mail*, October 22, 1979, and "Not by Sincerity Alone," *Ottawa Journal*, September 28, 1979; Peyton Lyon's comments in "Flora Has Chance to Tilt Policy Her Way," *The Ottawa Citizen*, November 27, 1979; and David R. Morrison, "Canada and International Development," *Journal of Canadian Studies* 14, 4 (Winter 1979-80): 142.

67 Wayne Cheveldayoff, "CIDA Policy of Tied Aid Becomes Cumbersome," *The Globe and Mail*, November 12, 1979.

68 See Notes for a Speech by the Secretary of State for External Affairs, Flora MacDonald, to the Canadian Club of Montreal, September 17, 1979, and "Full Review Ordered into Foreign Policy," *Ottawa Journal*, September 18, 1979.

69 "Canada Freezes Plans for Aid," p. 48.

70 Notes for a Speech by the Secretary of State for External Affairs, Flora MacDonald, to the Canadian Club of Montreal, September 17, 1979, p. 5, and Rusk, "Restraint Hits Foreign Aid; Inflation Means a Net Drop."

71 Speech as Delivered by the Secretary of State for External Affairs, Flora MacDonald, to the Empire Club, Toronto, October 4, 1979, pp. 5-6.

72 André McNicoll, "Ottawa's Foreign Aid Policy—Uncertainty Is the Rule," *The Gazette* (Montreal), October 31, 1979.

73 Lyon, "Flora Has Chance to Tilt Policy Her Way." See other critical commentary in Arthur Johnson, "MacDonald Suggests that Politics Should Play Role in Foreign Aid," *The Globe and Mail*, October 5, 1979; "Flora Warns Aid Ingrates," *Ottawa Journal*, October 5, 1979; "Thanks for Nothing," *Sun* (Vancouver), October 6, 1979; John Best, "Clark Regime Must Get Its Act Together on Foreign Policy," *The Leader Post* (Regina), October 10, 1979; and Maurice Western, "New Course for Foreign Aid?" *Winnipeg Free Press*, October 10, 1979.

74 Cited in "MacDonald's Aim Is to Provoke Talks," *The Ottawa Citizen*, October 24, 1979.

75 David Cox, "Leadership Change and Innovation in Canadian Foreign Policy: The 1979 Progressive Conservative Government," *International Journal* 37, 4 (Autumn 1982): 580-81.

76 External Affairs, "The Global Framework," and CIDA, "Canadian Aid Policy," were made available to a Parliamentary Task Force on North-South Relations, appointed in 1980. The Task Force appended them to its *Minutes of Proceedings and Evidence*, June 10, 1980, session 3A, pp. 28-195. "Canadian Aid Policy" is on pp. 136-95.

77 CIDA, "Canadian Aid Policy," pp. 148-49.

78 It was, however, preceded by the semi-official study of Canada's relations with the Third World by the Economic Council of Canada, which had asserted that "moral arguments have obvious force for individual commitment," but "they seldom constitute sufficient reason for action between states." The pursuit of "global peace" and a "stable international economic system" were projected as the most important goals for the aid program and other North-South policies (Economic Council of Canada, *For a Common Future*, pp. 31-32). As far as development assistance itself was concerned, the document eschewed arguments for short-run commercial advantage to the extent that they led to inefficient subsidization of Canadian industries, and made recommendations that would have led to a sharper distinction between investment and trade promotion programs and aid (see ibid., pp. 79-81 and 104-108).

79 CIDA, "Canadian Aid Policy," p. 147.

80 Ibid., p. 159.

81 Ibid., p. 163.

82 Ibid., pp. 166-67.

83 Ibid., p. 167.

84 Ibid., p. 172.

85 In fact, as noted below, the balance had tipped more heavily in favour of Africa.

86 Ibid., pp. 173-75.

87 The claim was largely an ex post facto justification, as Tony Keenleyside observed in "Aiding Rights: Canada and the Advancement of Human Dignity," in Cranford Pratt, ed., *Canadian International Development Assistance Policies: An Appraisal* (Montreal and Kingston: McGill-Queen's University Press, 1994), pp. 246-47.

88 See CIDA, "Canadian Aid Policy," p. 176.

89 Ibid., pp. 177-79.

90 Ibid., p. 155.

91 Ibid., pp. 180-84.

92 Ibid., pp. 184-85.

93 CIDA, *Memorandum to DAC 1980*, p. 19.

94 Calculations based on data in CIDA's annual reports.

95 CIDA, *Memorandum to DAC 1978*, p. 16; ibid., *1979*, p. 21; and ibid., *1980*, p. 18.

96 The upward trend continued, however; using the same standard, middle-income allocations jumped to 16.3 per cent in 1981 (CIDA, *Memorandum to DAC 1981*, p. 26).

97 See Appendix D.

98 CIDA, *Annual Report 1979-80*, p. 14.

99 CIDA, *Memorandum to DAC 1977*, p. 3. Cranford Pratt reported that the cabinet, in part to demonstrate its commitment to the CIEC process, overruled advice from the bureaucracy opposing debt forgiveness for LLDCs. See Cranford Pratt, "Canada: An Eroding and Limited Internationalism," in Cranford Pratt, ed., *Internationalism under Strain: The North-South Policies of Canada, the Netherlands, Norway, and Sweden* (Toronto: University of Toronto Press, 1989), p. 33.

100 CIDA, *Annual Report 1977-78*, p. 15.

101 CIDA, *Memorandum to DAC 1976*, p. 6, and ibid., *1980*, p. 6.

102 Based on interviews; G.R. Berry, "Bureaucratic Politics and Economic Policies Affecting Developing Countries—The Case of the Strategy for International Development Cooperation 1975-1980" (unpublished Ph.D. dissertation, Dalhousie University, 1981), pp. 429-30; and "Ottawa Working Loose Knot Tying Up Foreign Aid loans," *The Globe and Mail*, March 26, 1977.

103 CIDA, "Canadian Aid Policy," p. 177.

104 North-South Institute, *North-South Encounter*, p. 127.

105 Ibid., p. 128.

106 See OECD-DAC, "DAC Aid Review of Canada," Press Release, November 14, 1977.

107 Treasury Board Secretariat, Planning Branch, "The Economic Effects of an Untying of Canadian Bilateral Aid," July 1976, pp. 3-4, 43. The quotation is on p. 4.

108 Ibid., p. 48 (emphasis in original).

109 Ibid., pp. 48-49 (emphasis in original).

110 Roger Ehrhardt, *Canadian Development Assistance to Bangladesh* (Ottawa: North-South Institute, 1983), pp. 110-11.

111 Judith Tendler, *Inside Foreign Aid* (Baltimore: Johns Hopkins University Press, 1975), p. 49.

112 Auditor General, *Conspectus of the Report of the Auditor General to the House of Commons for the Fiscal Year Ended March 31, 1976* (Ottawa: Information Canada, 1975), p. 103.

113 Mark W. Charlton, *The Making of Canadian Food Aid Policy* (Montreal and Kingston: McGill-Queen's University Press, 1992), pp. 29-30. See also Mark W. Charlton, "Reforming Canadian Food Aid Policy, 1975-1980: Bureaucratic Obstacles to Reform" (paper presented to the Annual Conference of the Canadian Political Science Association, Guelph, June 10-12, 1984), pp. 4-5.

114 CIDA, *Memorandum to DAC 1978*, p. 30.

115 See Charlton, *The Making of Canadian Food Aid Policy*, pp. 31, 109-10, 157.

116 CIDA, *Memorandum to DAC 1978*, p. 4.

117 Douglas Williams and Roger Young, *Taking Stock: World Food Security in the Eighties* (Ottawa: North-South Institute, 1981), p. 56.

118 Canadian Council for International Cooperation, "A Framework for Canada's Development Assistance."

119 David R. Protheroe, *Canada and Multilateral Aid: Working Paper* (Ottawa: North-South Institute, 1991), p. 51.
120 Department of Industry, Trade and Commerce, *Strengthening Canada Abroad*, p. 36.
121 Protheroe, *Canada and Multilateral Aid*, p. 61.
122 See Appendix A.
123 Interviews.
124 See Appendix A.
125 Intense political turmoil within CUSO and SUCO led to strained relations with CIDA again in 1979. The Agency used delayed and reduced funding for 1979-80 as leverage to bring about organizational changes. See Ian Smillie, *The Land of Lost Content: A History of CUSO* (Toronto: Deneau, 1985), pp. 117-19; Richard Gwyn, "Political Excesses Hurting Canada's Overseas Projects," *Ottawa Journal*, January 23, 1979; "CUSO Future at Stake in Probe of Its Activities," *The Gazette* (Montreal), March 21, 1979; and David Humphreys, "CIDA Lifts Financial Ban on CUSO after Management Moves Accepted," *The Globe and Mail*, June 8, 1979.
126 This account is based on interviews; CIDA, "Report of a Steering Committee on Cooperation between CIDA and Canadian Institutions of Higher Education," 1972; CIDA, "Higher Education Cooperation Plan: Guidelines for Proposals," 1974; J. King Gordon, "Canadian Universities and Development—A Proposal for Improved Institutional Procedures," 1977; and CIDA, "Social Development in CIDA's Strategy and Programs—Education and Institutional Support" (report by J. King Gordon), 1980.
127 CIDA, *Memorandum to DAC 1980*, p. 9.
128 Ibid., *1978*, p. 37.
129 Ibid., pp. 37-38, and Department of Industry, Trade and Commerce, Ottawa, "Looking to Less Developed Countries: CIDA Launches New Program," *Canada Commerce* (June-July 1979), pp. 19-20.
130 CIDA, *Annual Report 1979-80*, p. 21.
131 CIDA, *Memorandum to DAC 1979*, p. 51.
132 Appendix A.
133 See, for example, Best, "Born to Play 'the Game' "; John R. Walker, "New CIDA Head Cuts Down Waste," *The Ottawa Citizen*, July 12, 1977; and Stephen Handelman, "CIDA's New Broom: Aid Chief Promises No More Scandals," *The Toronto Star*, October 1, 1977.
134 See articles by Dan Proudfoot, *Toronto Sun*, April 3-7, 1977; a letter by Paul Doucet, CIDA's Director General of Communications in *The Toronto Sun*, May 3, 1977; and Dan Proudfoot, "Proudfoot Answers CIDA!" *The Toronto Sun*, May 5, 1977.
135 The article in *The New York Times Magazine* reproduced several of the stories then in circulation, including a claim that "Gérin-Lajoie donated 500 prize Friesian cattle to Idi Amin (which were barbecued by the field marshal's troops)." An exasperated Paul Doucet, CIDA's Director General of Communications, replied: "One clause out of one sentence, and five mistakes! Maurice Strong was president of CIDA, not Paul Gérin-Lajoie, when the cattle went. They were not donated, but provided through a development loan. There were 600 cattle, not 500. Milton Obote was prime minister of Uganda, not Idi Amin. And there is no evidence known to us that the cattle have since been slaughtered" ("CIDA Denies Giving 500 Cattle

for Barbecue to Amin," *The Ottawa Citizen*, June 14, 1977). Doucet might have added that CIDA withdrew from active programming in Uganda after Amin, who deposed Obote in a 1971 coup, expelled Ugandans of Asian descent in 1972.

136 See, for example, Croft, "We're Tightening Our Belts but Expanding Foreign Aid," and "Ten Trudeau Disasters," *The Toronto Sun*, August 25, 1978.

137 *Report of the Auditor General of Canada to the House of Commons, Fiscal Year Ended March 31, 1979*, p. 285. See James Rusk, "Boat, Buildings Head Latest List of Misspending," *The Globe and Mail*, April 17, 1980; "Foreign Aid Spending Is Adrift, Says Auditor-General," *The Gazette* (Montreal), April 17, 1980; Mary Janigan, "Seafaring Saga Has Sad End for CIDA," *Ottawa Journal*, April 17, 1980; Patrick Nagle, "End of the Tale of the Boat that Wouldn't Float," *Sun* (Vancouver), December 11, 1981.

138 *Report of the Auditor General of Canada to the House of Commons, Fiscal Year Ended March 31, 1979*, pp. 252-53 (author's emphasis). See pp. 253-61 and 286-92 for detailed criticisms and recommendations for strengthening financial management.

139 Michel Dupuy to James J. Macdonell, Auditor General, October 22, 1979, *Report of the Auditor General of Canada to the House of Commons, Fiscal Year Ended March 31, 1979*, pp. 294-98.

140 See, for example, Peter Worthington, "Foreign Aid Helps Rich?" *The Toronto Sun*, September 26, 1978; Amanda King, "Mixed Reaction Greets Rexdale's C-FAR Plans on Foreign Aid Cutbacks," *New Toronto Advertiser*, May 9, 1979; letter from Paul Fromm of C-FAR to *The Toronto Star*, August 23, 1979; "Scrambled Aid" (editorial); and Peter Worthington, "An Aid Foul-up for All to See" (based on the *W5* documentary), *Sunday Sun*, October 14, 1979.

141 A summary of the main issues covered is in Peter Wyse, *Canadian Foreign Aid in the 1970s: An Organizational Audit* (Montreal: Centre for Developing-Area Studies, 1983), p. 59. The program received some sympathetic coverage and commentary in the press, especially on the issue of procurement tying. See "CIDA's Monetary Policy Attacked as 'Dishonest,' " *The Toronto Star*, April 5, 1978; "Canada's Aid Policies Come under Fire," *Ottawa Journal*, April 5, 1978; "Strong Raps CIDA Buy-Canadian Policy," *The Ottawa Citizen*, April 6, 1978; and John R. Walker, "CIDA: Challenged by Charges of 'Tied-Aid' Hypocrisy," *The Ottawa Citizen*, July 6, 1978.

142 See CIDA, *Memorandum to DAC 1976*, pp. 33-34; ibid., *1978*, pp. 35-36; and ibid., *1979*, pp. 28-31. A review of the work of the Communications Branch (and the Public Participation Program) is contained in an Appendix to the text of Michel Dupuy's statement to the House of Commons, Standing Committee on External Affairs and National Defence, *Minutes of Proceedings and Evidence*, April 19, 1977, session 13A, pp. 17-26.

143 Several members of the Export Promotion Review Committee, including Hatch himself, had been directly involved in close consultations with CIDA over a number of years.

144 *Financial Post*, February 9, 1980, and David Crane, "Foreign-Aid Opposition 'Shocking,' " *The Toronto Star*, February 12, 1980.

145 "Most Favour Increased Aid," *The Ottawa Citizen*, January 11, 1975; "Foreign Aid—Public Support Cools?" *The Ottawa Citizen*, July 26, 1978; CIDA, *Memorandum to DAC 1978*, p. 36; John O'Manique, "The Response of the Principal Sectors of Canadian Society to the NIEO," in Ervin Laszlo and Joel Kurtzman,

eds., *The United States, Canada and the New International Economic Order* (New York: Pergamon Press, 1980), pp. 124-25.

146 "Most Canadians Would Put Strings on Foreign Aid," *Weekend Magazine*, May 25, 1979.

147 North-South Institute, *In the Canadian Interest? Third World Development in the 1980s*, pp. 6-18.

148 John Best, "Money-Wiser CIDA Now Must Begin Readjusting . . . Back to Status Quo!" *Ottawa Journal*, April 10, 1980.

149 "The Challenge at CIDA," *Ottawa Journal*, April 30, 1977.

Chapter 6

1 Shridath Ramphal, then secretary general of the Commonwealth and a member of the commission, asked in the *Guardian* shortly after the report was published: "where has the moral imperative got us in the post-war period and in particular in the period during which we have been negotiating NIEO?" (cited in Cranford Pratt, "From Pearson to Brandt: Evolving Conceptions Concerning International Development," *International Journal* 35, 4 [Autumn 1980]: 635).

2 Report of the Independent Commission on International Development Issues, *North-South: A Programme for Survival* (Cambridge: MIT Press, 1980), p. 33.

3 See ibid., pp. 267-92.

4 House of Commons, Parliamentary Task Force on North-South Relations, *Report to the House of Commons on the Relations between Developed and Developing Countries* (Hull: Minister of Supply and Services, 1980), p. 5 (hereafter cited as Parliamentary Task Force, *Final Report*).

5 The Dupras Subcommittee on Canada and International Development in the mid-1970s had been confined to a more limited agenda.

6 House of Commons, Parliamentary Task Force on North-South Relations, *Interim Report to Parliament on the Relations between Developed and Developing Countries* (Ottawa: House of Commons, 1980), p. 9. The subsequent references are drawn from pp. 9-11.

7 See "Development: a Global Search for the Future," Notes for a Speech by the Secretary of State for External Affairs, Mark MacGuigan, to the Eleventh Special Session of the United Nations General Assembly, New York, August 26, 1980.

8 "Empty Rhetoric at UN," *The Ottawa Citizen*, August 29, 1980.

9 The decision was taken to the chagrin of officials in the Department of Finance, who worried how the resources would be found. MacEachen is reputed to have replied, "We'll blow up that bridge when we come to it."

10 "The Global Negotiations and the International Development Strategy," Notes for a Speech by the Secretary of State for External Affairs, Mark MacGuigan, to the Eleventh Special Session of the United Nations General Assembly, New York, September 15, 1980.

11 John Best, "Foreign Aid Commitment May Be Hard to Carry Out," *The London Free Press*, September 18, 1980. For editorial comments, see *The Toronto Star*, September 19, 1980; *The Ottawa Citizen*, September 22, 1980.

12 Parliamentary Task Force, *Final Report*, pp. 20-21.

13 North-South Institute, "North-South Relations/1980-85: Priorities for Canadian Policy," Discussion Paper Prepared for the Special Committee of the House of Commons on North-South Relations, Ottawa, November 1980, p. 61.

14 Ibid., p. 20.
15 Parliamentary Task Force on North-South Relations, *Minutes of Proceedings and Evidence*, October 28, 1980, session 19, p. 56.
16 Parliamentary Task Force, *Final Report*, p. 37 (emphasis in original).
17 Ibid., p. 39.
18 Ibid., p. 40.
19 See, for example, the testimony of Geoff Elliot of IT&C, Parliamentary Task Force on North-South Relations, *Minutes of Proceedings and Evidence*, July 10, 1980, session 2, p. 32; and of T.M. Burns of the Canadian Export Association, ibid., November 3, 1980, session 23, p. 6.
20 Parliamentary Task Force, *Final Report*, p. 65.
21 Ibid., p. 38.
22 Ibid., p. 27.
23 Ibid., pp. 40-43.
24 Ibid., pp. 45-53.
25 Ibid., pp. 55-60.
26 Ibid., p. 39.
27 Douglas Roche, "Where's Canada in the Fight to Close the Rich-Poor Gap?" *The Globe and Mail*, June 8, 1981.
28 "PCs Reject Debate on Foreign Policy," *The Gazette* (Montreal), June 9, 1981.
29 Department of External Affairs, "Government Response to the Report of the Parliamentary Task Force on North-South Relations," June 15, 1981.
30 House of Commons, *Debates*, June 15, 1981, pp. 10596-97.
31 Ibid., p. 10613.
32 See statements of Mark MacGuigan, secretary of state for External Affairs, House of Commons, Subcommittee on Canada's Relations with Latin America and the Caribbean, *Minutes of Proceedings and Evidence*, June 8, 1981, session 1, pp. 14-22, and Ed Lumley, minister of state for Trade, June 9, 1981, session 2, pp. 29-35.
33 See Edgar Dosman, Liisa North and Cecelia Rocha, "Canada and Latin America: New Patterns in Development" (October 1981), and Kari Levitt, "Canadian Policy and the Caribbean" (October 1981), Subcommittee on Canada's Relations with Latin America and the Caribbean, *Minutes of Proceedings and Evidence*, session 22A, Appendices LALL-7 (pp. 1-77) and LALL-8 (pp. 78-322) respectively.
34 House of Commons, Standing Committee on External Affairs and National Defence, *Minutes of Proceedings and Evidence*, November 23, 1982, session 78, p. 68. The subcommittee's four reports were bound together in this volume under the title *Canada's Relations with Latin America and the Caribbean*. This title is used in subsequent references.
35 *Canada's Relations with Latin America and the Caribbean*, p. 66.
36 Ibid., pp. 64-65.
37 See John R. Walker, "Worthy Foreign Affairs Group Killed by Tories," *The Ottawa Citizen*, April 20, 1982; John Gray, "PCs Replace MP on Foreign Affairs Committee," *The Globe and Mail*, May 5, 1982; and John Gray, "Concerns for Third World Put MP at Odds with Tories," *The Globe and Mail*, May 31, 1982.
38 See *Canada's Relations with Latin America and the Caribbean*, pp. 126-32 and 27-39.
39 Ibid., pp. 10, 82, 154-55.
40 Ibid., p. 82.

41 Department of External Affairs, "Response to Recommendations of the Final Report of the Sub-Committee on Canada's Relations with Latin America and the Caribbean," 1983.
42 David R. Morrison, "Canada and North-South Conflict," in Maureen Appel Molot and Brian W. Tomlin, eds., *Canada Among Nations 1987: A World of Conflict* (Toronto: James Lorimer, 1988), p. 136.
43 Peter Maser, "Economic Catastrophe Looming, Says Brandt," *The Ottawa Citizen*, December 16, 1982.
44 The Prime Minister's Office announced the appointments in a press release dated March 11, 1980.
45 Author's interview with Marcel Massé, Ottawa, November 3, 1988.
46 CIDA, *Annual Report 1980-81*, p. 2 (President's Preface).
47 "The Intercultural Dialogue: Cornerstone of Development," Notes for an Address by Marcel Massé, President of CIDA, to the Annual Conference of the Society for Intercultural Education, Training and Research, Vancouver, March 12, 1981, p. 14. See also "The Third World: A Canadian Challenge," Notes for an Address by Marcel Massé, President of CIDA, to the Canadian Club, Toronto, April 6, 1981, and "New Trends in Canadian Development Assistance," transcript of a taped address by Marcel Masse, President of CIDA, to the Society for International Development, Ottawa chapter, September 16, 1982.
48 "The Intercultural Dialogue," pp. 15 and 18.
49 Carol Goar, "One Sentimental Journey," *The Toronto Star*, January 18, 1981.
50 Author's interview with Marcel Massé, Ottawa, November 3, 1988.
51 Ibid.
52 Canadian Council for International Co-operation, "Excerpts from a CIDA Paper on the 'Agency Programming Framework (APF),' December 1981" (Ottawa, 1982), pp. 3-4 (author's emphasis).
53 John Tackaberry, "Just What Is Canada's Global Agenda?" *The Global Village Voice* (Fall 1982), reprinted in *CIDA Paper Clips*. In response to a pointed question from Douglas Roche, External Affairs Minister Allan MacEachen denied that potential embarrassment from another North-South Institute report card would dissuade him from authorizing another strategy exercise "if I thought it would make a real contribution" (House of Commons, Standing Committee on External Affairs and National Defence, *Minutes of Proceedings and Evidence*, March 29, 1983, session 86, p. 10).
54 Author's interview with Marcel Massé, Ottawa, November 3, 1988. In a press interview early in 1981, Massé had indicated that the Agency was working on a new strategy for the 1980s that would be ready by that fall; he talked in broad terms both about the priorities that later emerged in the Agency Planning Framework and about the need to better inform Canadians about the challenges of international development (John R. Walker, "How Our 'Aid' Cash Is Spent," *The Nugget* [North Bay], February 6, 1981; see also Jeffrey Simpson, "A New Direction for Canada's Aid Agency," *The Globe and Mail*, January 22, 1981).
55 Canadian Council for International Cooperation, "Consultation on Country Focus: Report on the Proceedings of the NGO-CIDA Meeting in Ottawa, February 17, 1982" (March 1982), Appendix A, p. 5.
56 CIDA, *Memorandum to DAC 1981*, p. 6 (emphasis in original).
57 CCIC, "Consultation on Country Focus," Appendix A, p. 7.

58 The details of Massé's conception of how the approach was to work are spelled out most fully in "Country Focus: Questions and Answers," an internal document based on briefing notes that Massé used for a staff meeting on November 4, 1981. The document was subsequently leaked and circulated by CCIC.
59 Author's interview with Marcel Massé, Ottawa, November 3, 1988.
60 See CIDA, *Memorandum to DAC 1981*, p. 15.
61 Ibid., *1980*, p. 8.
62 Ibid., *1981*, p. 13.
63 CIDA, "Report on More Efficient Project Aid Delivery (MEPAD)," November 1982, p. 1.
64 Ibid., pp. 1-2.
65 Ibid., p. 23.
66 Suteera Thomson, *Food for the Poor: The Role of CIDA in Agricultural, Fisheries and Rural Development* (Ottawa: Science Council of Canada, 1980), pp. 48-69 and 131.
67 CIDA, "Report on More Efficient Project Aid Delivery (MEPAD)," p. 27.
68 The Policy and Expenditure Management System and CIDA's role within it are discussed in considerable detail in CIDA, *Memorandum to DAC 1981*, pp. 2-5.
69 See Kim Richard Nossal, *The Politics of Canadian Foreign Policy* (Toronto: Prentice-Hall, 1985), pp. 139-42; J.L. Granatstein and Robert Bothwell, *Pirouette: Pierre Trudeau and Canadian Foreign Policy* (Toronto: University of Toronto Press, 1990), pp. 228-33; and CIDA, *Memorandum to DAC 1981*, pp. 15-16.
70 Nossal, *The Politics of Canadian Foreign Policy*, p. 141.
71 For the story of early CUSO volunteers abroad, see Bill McWhinney and Dave Godfrey, eds., *Man Deserves Man: CUSO in Developing Countries* (Toronto: Ryerson Press, 1968).
72 CIDA, *Memorandum to DAC 1981*, p. 40.
73 "Trudeau Pledges Millions in New Aid Projects," *The Ottawa Citizen*, October 6, 1981.
74 CIDA, *Memorandum to DAC 1983*, p. 49.
75 As recalculated to include administrative expenses. The total in 1980-81 with these expenses netted out was $1,241.0 million, the figure cited in Chapter 5.
76 Appendix A.
77 OECD-DAC, *Development Co-operation: Efforts and Policies of the Members of the Development Assistance Committee 1990*, p. 268.
78 Douglas Roche criticized the decision to include administrative expenses in ODA in House of Commons, Standing Committee on External Affairs and National Defence, *Minutes of Proceedings and Evidence*, March 29, 1983, session 86, pp. 10-11. DAC made the decision to allow administrative expenses in 1979.
79 The government announced cuts of $75 million and $100 million for 1982-83 and 1983-84 respectively in June 1982 and a further reduction of $55 million for 1983-84 in October 1982. See "Trudeau ampute le budget de l'ACDI de $175 millions," *La Presse* (Montreal), July 17, 1982; Keri Sweetman, "Spending Cuts Upset Foreign Aid Workers," *The Ottawa Citizen*, October 29, 1982; and Michael McDowell, "Canada's Foreign Aid Cuts Spell Third World Hardship," *The Globe and Mail*, January 21, 1983.
80 Data in this section are drawn from Appendix A and Appendix F; CIDA, *Annual Report 1982-83*, pp. 59-60; ibid., *1983-84*, p. 38; and OECD-DAC, *Development*

Co-operation: Efforts and Policies of the Members of the Development Assistance Committee 1985*, pp. 334-35.

81 Parts of this section follow closely David R. Morrison, "The Choice of Bilateral Aid Recipients," in Cranford Pratt, ed., *Canadian International Development Assistance Policies: An Appraisal* (Montreal and Kingston: McGill-Queen's University Press, 1994), pp. 139-46.

82 Canadian Council for International Co-operation, "Excerpts from a CIDA Paper on the 'Agency Programming Framework (APF),' December 1981," pp. 3-5. The category descriptions are the author's summaries.

83 At that time Afghanistan, Cuba, Iran, Kampuchea, Laos, Libya, and Vietnam.

84 These were: in Africa—Mayotte, Reunion, and St. Helena; in Asia—Abu Dhabi, Bahrain, Brunei, Hong Kong, Iraq, Israel, Kuwait, Macao, Oman, Qatar, Saudi Arabia, Syria, Taiwan, and the United Arab Emirates; in the Americas—Bermuda, Falkland Islands, French departments and territories, Netherlands Antilles, and Venezuela; and in Europe—Cyprus, Gibraltar, Greece, Malta, Portugal, Spain, and Yugoslavia.

85 See Appendix D.

86 "Discovering the Third World," interview with Marcel Massé, *Global Report*, reprinted in *CIDA Paper Clips* (September 1981), p. 3.

87 Cited in Phillip Rawkins, *Human Resource Development in the Aid Process: A Study in Organizational Learning and Change* (Ottawa: North-South Institute, 1993), p. 21. See Rawkins' excellent discussion of the new approach (pp. 21-23).

88 CIDA, *Memorandum to DAC 1981*, p. 25, and ibid., *1983*, p. 16. The Canadian delegation played a key brokerage role in securing a compromise resolution enabling the conference to support the 0.15 per cent target, which fell short of the 0.20 per cent goal for 1990 sought by the Group of 77 (Ann Duncan, "Canada Secured Aid Compromise," *The Globe and Mail*, September 18, 1981).

89 See bilateral data for the years 1980-81, 1981-82, and 1982-83 in CIDA, *Annual Report*, for those years. Differences between disbursements and commitments are summarized in CIDA, *Memorandum to DAC 1980*, p. 17; ibid., *1981*, p. 30; and ibid., *1982*, p. 23.

90 See Edgar J. Dosman, "Points of Departure: The Security Equation in Canadian-Commonwealth Caribbean Relations," *International Journal* 42, 4 (Autumn 1987): 826.

91 CIDA, *Annual Report 1981-82*, p. 27.

92 See Appendix C.

93 See CIDA, *Annual Report 1981-82*, p. 26; Lawrence Martin, "Canada Shelves Direct Aid to El Salvador," *The Globe and Mail*, March 10, 1981; and T.A. Keenleyside, "Aiding Rights: Canada and the Advancement of Dignity," in Cranford Pratt, ed., *Canadian International Development Assistance Policies: An Appraisal* (Montreal and Kingston: McGill-Queen's University Press, 1994), p. 248.

94 "Aid Plan $106 Million," *The Sault Daily Star*, March 5, 1982, reprinted in *CIDA Paper Clips*.

95 *Canada's Relations with Latin America and the Caribbean*, pp. 81-82.

96 Ibid., pp. 12-13.

97 Department of External Affairs, "Response to Sub-Committee on Canada's Relations with Latin American and the Caribbean," pp. 1-2.

98 *Canada's Relations with Latin America and the Caribbean*, pp. 14-15.

99 House of Commons, Standing Committee on External Affairs and National Defence, *Minutes of Proceedings and Evidence*, March 29, 1983, session 86, pp. 17-18, and "MacEachen Backs Tougher Aid Policy for Rights Violators," *The Gazette* (Montreal), March 30, 1983.

100 Ingrid Peritz, "Govt. Should Cut Aid to Rights Violators," *The Ottawa Citizen*, April 23, 1983.

101 Department of External Affairs, "Response to Sub-Committee on Canada's Relations with Latin America and the Caribbean," pp. 8-9.

102 T.A. Keenleyside, "Canadian Aid and Human Rights: Forging a Link," in Irving Brecher, ed., *Human Rights, Development and Foreign Policy: Selected Perspectives* (Halifax: Institute for Research on Public Policy, 1989), p. 346.

103 Keenleyside, "Aiding Rights: Canada and the Advancement of Human Dignity," p. 248.

104 CIDA, *Strategy for International Development Cooperation 1975-1980* (Ottawa: Information Canada, 1975), p. 34.

105 CIDA, *Memorandum to DAC 1976*, p. 16.

106 Ibid., *1976*, p. 16, and ibid., *1977*, p. 19.

107 Department of Industry, Trade and Commerce, *Strengthening Canada Abroad: Final Report of the Export Promotion Review Committee* (Ottawa: Department of Industry, Trade and Commerce, 1979), pp. 36, 28.

108 CIDA, "Bilateral Overview 1980/81" (March 1980), p. 32.

109 Department of Industry, Trade and Commerce, "The Economic Benefits of Aid" (June 1980), pp. 8-9, 15-16.

110 CIDA's policy update, *Elements of Canada's Official Development Strategy*, published early in 1984, reported that CIDA and EDC had engaged in parallel financing on twelve occasions since 1978, for a total value of about $740 million (p. 44). Some of the projects in place prior to 1980 were expanded and nine new ones were added, along with lines of credit for Cameroon, Egypt, and Tunisia. The projects were primarily traditional ones in the spheres of transportation (locomotives and rail cars) and energy (power transmission) (see David William Gillies, "Commerce Over Conscience: Canada's Foreign Aid Programme in the 1980s" [unpublished M.A. thesis, McGill University, 1986], p. 178).

111 Linda Freeman, "The Effect of the World Crisis on Canada's Involvement in Africa," *Studies in Political Economy* 17 (1985): 118-20.

112 Martin Rudner, "The Evolving Framework of Canadian Development Assistance Policy," in Brian W. Tomlin and Maureen Molot, eds., *Canada among Nations 1984: A Time of Transition* (Toronto: James Lorimer, 1985), p. 142.

113 Distilled from comments made at the annual External Affairs–Industry, Trade and Commerce–CIDA consultation with the Canadian Association for Latin America (CALA), Ottawa, November 30, 1982. The author was an observer at the meeting. A frequent comment from business participants was that CIDA needed "more realism," i.e., greater sensitivity to Canadian commercial objectives and fewer time-consuming assessments and procedures. A senior official from IT&C (soon to be merged with External Affairs) observed that it was clear that export financing was *the* problem of the day.

114 CIDA, *Memorandum to DAC 1982*, p. 18.

115 Rudner, "The Evolving Framework of Canadian Development Assistance Policy," p. 143.

116 Ibid., p. 217, n. 1.

117 Based largely on Canadian Council for International Co-operation, "Excerpts from a CIDA Paper on the 'Agency Programming Framework (APF),' December 1981," pp. 6-11.

118 See World Bank, *World Development Report 1980* (New York: Oxford University Press, 1980).

119 Canadian Council for International Co-operation, "Excerpts from a CIDA Paper on the 'Agency Programming Framework (APF),' December 1981," p. 9.

120 Based on interviews.

121 CIDA, *Memorandum to DAC 1982*, p. 34.

122 See CIDA, *Annual Report 1983-84*, pp. 38, 74, and other annual reports.

123 Department of External Affairs, *A Review of Canadian Trade Policy* (Ottawa: Minister of Supply and Services, 1983), p. 163.

124 David R. Protheroe, *Canada and Multilateral Aid* (Ottawa: North-South Institute, 1991), p. x.

125 Ibid., p. 61.

126 Calculated from data in Appendix A.

127 In December 1982. CIDA, *Annual Report 1982-83*, p. 9.

128 See CIDA, *Memorandum to DAC 1982*, p. 16, and ibid., *1983*, p. 11. See as well the critique of CIDA's lack of policy and preparedness in this area in Alan J. Taylor, *CIDA in Disasters: A Summary of the Agency's Policies, Procedures and Perceptions* (Toronto: Interchurch Fund for International Development, 1978). It contains considerable detail on the history of the humanitarian channel up to that time.

129 See CIDA, *Annual Report*, various years.

130 See Appendix A. These data included provincial government contributions to NGOs and NGIs, which were $10.8 million in 1980-81 and $10.6 million in 1983-84. CIDA funding for Canadian non-governmental organizations and institutions (derived by deducting provincial contributions and allocations to international NGOs) was $70.2 million in 1980-81 and $167.1 million in 1983-84; these totals include food aid channelled through NGOs ($3.5 million and $10.4 million in 1980-81 and 1983-84 respectively).

131 CIDA, *Annual Report 1983-84*, p. 31.

132 See CIDA, *Memorandum to DAC 1981*, p. 48.

133 CCIC, "Consultation on Country Focus."

134 See Ian Smillie, *The Land of Lost Content: A History of CUSO* (Toronto: Deneau Publishers, 1985), pp. 305-309.

135 See Patricia Williams, "CIDA Has Difficulty Keeping Up with CPPF Aid Requests," *Daily Commercial News and Building Record*, June 13, 1980; Patricia Williams, "CIDA to Double Funds for Project Studies Program," *Daily Commercial News and Building Record*, October 17, 1980; and "CIDA Proves (Again) Small Is Beautiful," *The Financial Post*, April 13, 1981.

136 Author's interview with Marcel Massé, Ottawa, November 3, 1988.

137 See Appendix A.

138 See CIDA, *Memorandum to DAC 1980*, p. 28, and ibid., *1981*, p. 50. CREF was one of the Canadian initiatives announced at the UN Conference on New and Renewable Sources of Energy, held in Nairobi in August 1981.

139 Department of Industry, Trade and Commerce, *Strengthening Canada Abroad*, p. 37.

140 *Canada's Relations with Latin America and the Caribbean*, pp. 118-25.

141 Ibid., p. 152.
142 Letter from Greg Robinson, Director of C-FAR, in *Etobicoke Advertiser*, September 17, 1980.
143 Paul Fromm and James P. Hull, *Down the Drain? A Critical Re-examination of Canadian Foreign Aid* (Toronto: Griffin House, 1981).
144 See, for example, Bruce Ward, "CIDA Goofs Fuel Reform Pleas," *Sunday Star*, July 6, 1980; Sylvia Wright, "Canadian Foreign Aid Money Is Wasted, Lobby Group Charges," *The Whig-Standard* (Kingston), October 9, 1980; Mike Hamilton, "Canadian Foreign Aid 'a Horror,' " *St. Catharines Standard*, from an October 1980 issue reprinted that month in *CIDA Paper Clips*; and Carol Stein, "Canadians First!" *The Calgary Sun*, February 8, 1983.
145 See, for example, Edward Carrigan, "Canada's Foreign Aid Should Be Reviewed," *Kitchener-Waterloo Record*, June 10, 1981; John D. Harbron, "What Is CIDA Doing with Our Foreign Aid Money?" *Examiner* (Peterborough), August 11, 1981; Eric Downton, "Foreign Aid: Global Largesse on a Scale Canadian Taxpayers Simply Cannot Afford," *Sun* (Vancouver), November 8, 1982; and Peter Warren, "Abolish Foreign Aid," *Winnipeg Sun*, October 31, 1983.
146 See "Foreign-Aid Criticism Called a 'Hoary Fairy Tale,' " letter from Yvan Roy of CIDA, in *The Toronto Star*, June 12, 1980, and comments by John de Bondt, another spokesperson, in Ward, "CIDA Goofs Fuel Reform Pleas." Roche's letter to Fromm, dated March 18, 1981, was reprinted in *CIDA Paper Clips* (March 1981).
147 See his comments in *Barrie Banner*, June 30, 1982.
148 Lawrence Martin, "Hard-Liner Gamble Joins PC Race," *The Globe and Mail*, March 7, 1983, and Andrew Cohen, "Slash Foreign Aid: MP," *The Toronto Star*, May 16, 1982. The Conservative Party later refused to renominate Gamble, who ran as an independent and lost.
149 Robert Carty and Virginia Smith, *Perpetuating Poverty: The Political Economy of Canadian Foreign Aid* (Toronto: Between the Lines, 1981).
150 In a poll undertaken for CIDA by Adcom Research in 1980, 65 per cent of the respondents favoured giving aid to developing countries, while 28 per cent were opposed. Asked if aid should be increased, decreased, or ended, 35 per cent opted for an increase, 34 per cent said the amount should be kept at the current level, 15 per cent favoured a decrease, and 5 per cent called for abolition (CIDA, *A Report on Canadians' Attitudes Toward Foreign Aid* [Hull: CIDA, 1981], pp. 19, 37). It is difficult to compare the results with those from the 1974 and 1978 surveys reported in Chapter 5 since the questions differed. CIDA did not publish any more poll results in the Massé years, but confidential surveys apparently demonstrated some slippage in popular support.
151 This account is based on press reports; E. Philip English, *Canadian Development Assistance to Haiti* (Ottawa: North-South Institute, 1984), pp. 80-138, and House of Commons, Subcommittee on Canada's Relations with Latin America and the Caribbean, *Minutes of Proceedings and Evidence*, especially sessions 16 (February 11, 1982) and 17 (February 16, 1982).
152 English, *Canadian Development Assistance to Haiti*, p. 125.
153 Fred Templeman, who had left the public service in 1981, was invited to testify after he appeared on the CTV documentary on the Haiti project. See Subcommittee on Canada's Relations with Latin America and the Caribbean, *Minutes of Proceedings and Evidence*, February 11, 1982, session 16, pp. 5-32, especially p. 10.

Templeman alleged, among other things, that the Canadian consultants had spent $50,000 on a slide show demonstrating achievements of the first five years and making a pitch for continued support (see p. 13).

154 Subcommittee on Canada's Relations with Latin America and the Caribbean, *Minutes of Proceedings and Evidence*, February 16, 1983, session 17, p. 8.

155 Letter to the *Toronto Star*, January 26, 1982.

156 CIDA, "Le Canada suspend sa participation à un projet d'aide en Haiti," Press Release, November 28, 1981.

157 Letter to the *Toronto Star*, January 26, 1982.

158 Subcommittee on Canada's Relations with Latin America and the Caribbean, *Minutes of Proceedings and Evidence*, February 16, 1982, session 17, p. 24. Massé also replied to Cunningham's letter, dismissing CTV's claim and asserting that the decision was taken after repeated warnings to Haitian authorities (*The Toronto Star*, February 1, 1982).

159 English, *Canadian Development Assistance to Haiti*, p. 133.

160 See "Haitians Assail Canada Over Aid Scheme," *The Globe and Mail*, January 20, 1982; John R. Walker, "Canada Aid Plan Just Couldn't Work," *The Ottawa Citizen*, January 21, 1982; Gerald Utting, "This Caribbean Caper Leaves Lot to Be Desired," *The Toronto Star*, January 22, 1982; John R. Walker, "Canada's $21 Million Aid Down the Drain in Haiti," *The Ottawa Citizen*, January 22, 1982; "Probe Entire Haitian Aid Program, Ex-Diplomat Urges House Committee," *The Globe and Mail*, February 12, 1982; John Fraser, "Canada's Foreign Aid Quagmire," *The Globe and Mail*, February 15, 1982; John R. Walker, "DRIPP Mess Costly Lesson," *The Ottawa Citizen*, February 18, 1982; and Douglas Fisher, "W5 and CIDA," *Toronto Sun*, February 19, 1982.

161 Earlier, Massé had exclaimed before the House Standing Committee on External Affairs and National Defence: "We have shown recently, by terminating a major project, that we are prepared to act decisively when, in our opinion, agreements are not being honoured satisfactorily and Canadian dollars are in danger of being wasted" (Standing Committee on External Affairs and National Defence, *Minutes of Proceedings and Evidence*, May 13, 1982, session 72, p. 7).

162 English, *Canadian Development Assistance to Haiti*, pp. 129-30, 134, 156.

163 Roger Young, "Canadian Foreign Aid Policies: Objectives, Influences and Consequences," Working Paper No. A.10, Development Studies Programme, University of Toronto, February 1984, p. 2.

164 Ibid., p. 5.

165 See North-South Institute, *North-South News* (April and October 1981). The other countries were Pakistan, Ghana, Cameroon, and Jamaica. Cameroon was initially selected for intensive study, but Senegal was later substituted.

166 Roger Ehrhardt, *Canadian Development Assistance to Bangladesh* (Ottawa: North-South Institute, 1983); Roger Young, *Canadian Development Assistance to Tanzania* (Ottawa: North-South Institute, 1983); and North-South Institute, *North-South News*, Special Edition on Aid Evaluation (May 1983).

167 Réal Lavergne with E. Philip English, *Canadian Development Assistance to Senegal* (Ottawa: North-South Institute, 1987).

168 See John R. Walker, "New CIDA Chief Well Advised to Study Penetrating Report," *The Ottawa Citizen*, June 21, 1983; Norma Greenway, "Foreign Aid 'Not Meeting Needs,'" *The Ottawa Citizen*, June 24, 1983; James Rusk, "Centralism Hinders Canada's Aid to the Third World, Studies Show," *The Globe and*

Mail, June 24, 1983; Eleanor Boyle, "Foreign Aid Millions: Is Money Well Spent?" *The Gazette* (Montreal), June 25, 1983; and John Best, "Some Troubling Questions about CIDA," *The London Free Press*, June 28, 1982. The *Ottawa Citizen* (July 4, 1983), the *Financial Post* (July 9, 1982), and *The Globe and Mail* (July 18, 1983) also carried editorials calling for reforms. The only uniformly negative coverage of the Institute's findings was predictably in a *Toronto Sun* editorial (July 25, 1983), which complained that "we help the wrong governments because our agencies are staffed by the wrong people . . . left-libbers who like giving money to dreadful African socialist regimes like Tanzania."

169 "Foreign Aid Has Failed, Study Says," *The Toronto Star*, June 24, 1983.

170 Based on interviews and press reports. See Carol Goar, "MacGuigan Announces New Federal Agency in Maiden UN Speech," *Ottawa Journal*, August 27, 1980; "Canada Looks to the Future," *Action for Development* (July 1981), p. 3; André McNicoll, "Great Dream Dissolves into a Big Nightmare," *The Ottawa Citizen*, November 18, 1981; Stephen Hume, "Secretariat Keeps Looking to Its Future," *The Ottawa Citizen*, April 3, 1982; Keri Sweetman, "Futures Secretariat May Be Past History," *The Ottawa Citizen*, April 3, 1982; John Best, "Hard Times Increase Importance of Justifying Foreign Aid," *The Leader-Post* (Regina), May 28, 1982; and John Gray, "How the Road to Global Aid Was Never Paved," *The Globe and Mail*, September 28, 1982.

171 See "Development: A Global Search for the Future," Notes for a Speech by the Secretary of State for External Affairs, Mark MacGuigan, to the Eleventh Special Session of the United Nations General Assembly, New York, August 26, 1980.

172 From transcript of "The World at Six," CBC Radio, August 26, 1980, reproduced in *CIDA Paper Clips*.

173 See Report of the Independent Commission on International Development Issues, *North-South: A Programme for Survival*, pp. 261-62.

174 See comments of Tim Brodhead, then vice-president of CCIC, in transcripts of "The World at Six," CBC Radio, August 26, 1980, and of "The House," CBC Radio, August 30, 1980, reproduced in *CIDA Paper Clips*.

175 "Ex-Minister Heads Group on 3rd World," *The Globe and Mail*, June 10, 1981.

176 CIDA, *Annual Report 1980-81*, p. 49.

177 Gray, "How the Road to Global Aid Was Never Paved."

178 Maureen Hollingworth, "Summary of Major Findings and Recommendations of a National Study," in *Development Education in Canada in the Eighties: Contexts, Constraints, Choices*, special issue of *Canadian and International Education* 12, 3 (1983): 21-31.

179 Included in a survey of Canadians' attitudes toward foreign aid was a question designed to gauge awareness of specific Canadian organizations involved in international development. CIDA was mentioned voluntarily by only 6 per cent of the 1,034 respondents, well below the Red Cross, UNICEF, CARE, Oxfam, and CUSO. In another question, 48 per cent claimed to be aware of CIDA, but, of these, 52 per cent said they were also aware of COA (the Canadian Overseas Assistance Agency), a fictitious organizational name invented by the pollsters (CIDA, *A Report on Canadians' Attitudes Toward Foreign Aid*, pp. 53-54). A subsequent poll not released publicly pegged CIDA's "recognition level" at less than 20 per cent (interview).

180 Cited in David Vienneau, "Foreign-Aid Agency Pushes Propaganda to Protect Budget," *The Toronto Star*, January 25, 1983. This account is based on the Vienneau

article, interviews, and John Best, "Ottawa Needs to Be More Assertive on Foreign-Aid Issue," *The Leader-Post* (Regina), March 7, 1983. See also CIDA, *Memorandum to DAC 1982*, p. 7, for a more "antiseptic" account of the Jamieson review.

181 Vienneau, "Foreign-Aid Agency Pushes Propaganda."

182 From Frank Howard's "Bureaucrats" column, *The Ottawa Citizen*, December 9, 1982. Pitfield was said to be interested, but concerned about whether he would survive a Conservative electoral victory (interview).

183 John R. Walker, "Foreign Aid Agency in Limbo," *The Ottawa Citizen*, March 31, 1983.

184 For the annual discussion of CIDA's estimates, see House of Commons, Standing Committee on External Affairs and National Defence, *Minutes of Proceedings and Evidence*, March 29, 1983, session 86, pp. 8-10. See also John Best, " 'Screw Missing' in Government's Approach to Foreign Aid," *The Leader-Post* (Regina), April 2, 1983.

Chapter 7

1 A number of press and magazine articles carried biographical details about Catley-Carlson. See especially Charlotte Gray, "Our Lady of Perpetual Help," *Saturday Night* (September 1984), and Clyde Sanger, "Canada's Maggie Is Running an Aid Programme for 89 Countries," *Commonwealth Magazine* (December 1984/January 1985); both were reproduced in *CIDA Paper Clips*.

2 See Larry Black, "Poor Nations Hurting Own Cause by Demanding Whole Loaf: Trudeau," *The Ottawa Citizen*, September 30, 1983, and "PM Now Reserved in North-South Relations," *The Toronto Star*, October 1, 1983.

3 OECD-DAC, *Development Co-operation: Efforts and Policies of the Members of the Development Assistance Committee 1984*, p. 193.

4 North-South Institute, *Review '83/Outlook '84* (1984), pp. 10-11.

5 Robert Cassen and Associates, *Does Aid Work?* (Oxford: Clarendon Press, 1986), p. 294. One of the consultants in the project, Paul Mosley, published his own book, which was less sanguine about the historical experience: there was evidence of success at the micro level when one examined individual projects, but "no statistically significant correlation in *any* post-war period, either positive or negative, between inflows of development aid and growth of GNP in developing countries when other causal influences on growth are taken into account." He concluded that fungibility was the culprit (Paul Mosley, *Overseas Aid: Its Defence and Reform* [Brighton: Wheatsheaf Books, 1987], p. 139).

6 Roger C. Riddell, *Foreign Aid Reconsidered* (Baltimore: Johns Hopkins University Press, 1987), p. 271.

7 Graham Hancock, *Lords of Poverty: The Free-Wheeling Lifestyles, Power, Prestige and Corruption of the Multi-billion Dollar Aid Business* (London: Macmillan, 1989), p. xv. An equally strident critique of development practice and discourse was put forward in Wolfgang Sachs, ed., *The Development Dictionary: A Guide to Knowledge as Power* (London: Zed Books, 1992).

8 The *Globe and Mail* was sceptical: "The last thing CIDA's new chief should be contemplating is an education (read public relations) campaign designed to show that one can't make a Third World omelette without breaking a few eggs." The greater need was improving aid effectiveness. "If Mrs. Catley-Carlson insists on an education campaign, it is her Cabinet masters (and her CIDA subordinates) at

whom it should be aimed. The North-South Institute has provided the textbook [in its evaluations of bilateral aid]" ("Foreign Aid Weakness," *The Globe and Mail*, July 18, 1983).

9 As noted in Chapter 6, an approach along these lines had been advocated in the controversial strategy paper prepared by Ann Jamieson, director general of CIDA's Public Affairs Branch, late in 1982. The approach was influenced as well by Catley-Carlson's experience at UNICEF and further refined by Nicole Senécal, who became director general of Public Affairs soon after Catley-Carlson assumed office.

10 Catley-Carlson, in an interview with W.V. Jensen, "CIDA Opens Doors," *Canadian Business Review* (Winter 1987), p. 9.

11 "The Future Role of Canadians in International Development," Notes for an Address by Margaret Catley-Carlson, President of CIDA, at the annual conference of the Canadian Save the Children Fund and the Canadian Hunger Foundation, Orillia, September 30, 1983.

12 "The Business of Development," Notes for Remarks by Margaret Catley-Carlson, President of CIDA, to the 40th annual convention of the Canadian Export Association, Ottawa, October 18, 1983.

13 "World Development and Canadian Aid," Notes for Remarks by Margaret Catley-Carlson, President of CIDA, to the Canadian International Institute of International Affairs, Ottawa, January 9, 1984 (emphasis in original).

14 "Aid, Trade and Manitoba," Notes for an Address by Margaret Catley-Carlson, President of CIDA, at an ITC/REE seminar, Winnipeg, October 12, 1983.

15 "Aid Dimensions and Dilemmas," Notes for an Address by Margaret Catley-Carlson, President of CIDA, to a conference on North-South Dialogue: The Philosophical Issues, sponsored by the Department of Philosophy, Simon Fraser University, October 13, 1983.

16 See, for example, transcript of an interview given to Michael McDowell of *The Globe and Mail* by Margaret Catley-Carlson, September 14, 1983, CIDA Archives, Hull.

17 "Aid, Trade and Manitoba," Notes for an Address by Margaret Catley-Carlson.

18 CIDA, "A Summary Report, 1984," Colloquium on Canada's Official Development Assistance, Ottawa, March 7 and 8, 1984. Policy Branch prepared a compendium of policies and information about all aspects of the aid program for the occasion. Published later that spring as *Elements of Canada's Official Development Strategy* (Hull: CIDA, 1984), it provided a useful summary of policy evolution in the years since the publication of Gérin-Lajoie's *Strategy for 1975-1980*. However, *Elements* was not, and did not purport to be, a new strategy.

19 North-South Institute, *Review '83/Outlook '84*, p. 10.

20 Phillip Rawkins, "An Institutional Analysis of CIDA," in Cranford Pratt, ed., *Canadian International Development Assistance Policies: An Appraisal* (Montreal and Kingston: McGill-Queen's University Press, 1994), p. 162.

21 For details (including a positive evaluation), see National Advisory Committee on Development Education, *Towards a Global Future: Annual Report to the Minister for External Relations and International Development* (Hull: CIDA, 1990), pp. 6-12.

22 CIDA, *Annual Report 1988-89*, p. 49.

23 "The Future Role of Canadians in International Development," Notes for an Address by Margaret Catley-Carlson. See also "Aid, Trade and Manitoba," Notes for an Address by Margaret Catley-Carlson.

24 Department of External Affairs, *A Review of Canadian Trade Policy* (Ottawa: Minister of Supply and Services, 1983), p. 163.

25 Department of External Affairs, "Canadian Trade Policy for the 1980s," Discussion Paper (August 1983), p. 48.

26 Interviews; David Gillies, "Commerce over Conscience: Canada's Foreign Aid Programme in the 1980s" (unpublished M.A. thesis, McGill University, 1986), pp. 175-76; and Dan Turner, "Looking for a Return on Aid," *The Ottawa Citizen*, February 4, 1986.

27 House of Commons, *Debates*, December 7, 1983, p. 2.

28 Ibid., February 15, 1984, p. 1427.

29 "Foreign Aid-Trade Fund formed," *The Chronicle-Herald* (Halifax), February 16, 1984.

30 See, for example, Lynn McDonald (an NDP MP) in House of Commons, *Debates*, February 23, 1984, pp. 1683-84; Gillies, "Commerce over Conscience," pp. 168-70; Martin Rudner, "The Evolving Framework of Canadian Development Assistance Policy," in Brian W. Tomlin and Maureen Molot, eds., *Canada Among Nations 1984: A Time of Transition* (Toronto: James Lorimer, 1985), p. 144; Jack Best, "Canada's Obvious Self-Interest Tilt in Aid Policy Triggers Controversy," *The Ottawa Citizen*, March 31, 1984; Tracey LeMay, "Plan to Link Aid and Trade Worries Critics," *The Globe and Mail*, April 9, 1984; Sheldon E. Gordon, "Ottawa's Aid/Trade Fund a Marriage of Inconvenience," *The Globe and Mail*, April 20, 1984; Maria Elena Hurtado, "The Hard-Nosed Touch," *Charlottetown Guardian*, May 11, 1984; and Jack Best, "Aid-Trade Fund 'a Sell-Out: Critics' " *The Globe and Mail*, September 1, 1984. The last of these was published in the final days of the election campaign, and quoted Bernard Wood of the North-South Institute as saying that the Aid-Trade Fund was a slush fund for Canadian exporters.

31 OECD-DAC, "Aid Review 1984/85: Report by the Secretariat and Questions on the Development Assistance Efforts and Policies of Canada" (Paris, 1984), p. 4. Canadian authorities were asked if they would "agree that CIDA's present appraisal procedures, which ensure the high quality of current Canadian aid, would have to be considerably relaxed if the fund is to become operative at the envisaged scale?" The "DAC Guiding Principles for the Use of Aid in Association with Export Credits and Other Market Funds" were published in OECD-DAC, *Development Co-operation: Efforts and Policies of the Members of the Development Assistance Committee 1983*, pp. 169-70.

32 John R. Walker, "New CIDA Boss Sees Aid as Trade," *The London Free Press*, March 2, 1984.

33 "More Teamwork Needed to Win Overseas," interview with Frank Petrie by Wayne Gooding, *Financial Post*, March 3, 1984.

34 CIDA, "Options for the Future" (Hull, 1984), pp. 1, 8-9.

35 Ibid., p. 1.

36 Ibid., p. 13.

37 Ibid., p. 2.

38 Ibid., pp. 15-16.

39 Notes for an Address to the Canadian Association-Latin America and Caribbean Dinner Club by Sinclair Stevens, external affairs critic for the Progressive Conservative Party, Toronto, August 15, 1984, and Stephen Brunt, "Stevens Doffs Hawk Image to Woo Foreign Trade," *The Globe and Mail*, August 17, 1984. See also an

editorial in *The Globe and Mail*, September 7, 1984, which approved of Stevens' call to concentrate Canadian aid on fewer countries where it could do some good. It took issue with Stevens, however, on the use of aid for promoting Canadian trade and investment, saying that Canadian aid should focus on the alleviation of poverty and oppression.

40 Peter Maser, "Foreign Policy Will Emphasize International Trade, Clark Says," *The Ottawa Citizen*, September 18, 1984.

41 This section draws on interviews; CIDA, *Memorandum to DAC 1985*, p. 13; David Gillies, "Export Promotion and Canadian Development Assistance," in Cranford Pratt, ed., *Canadian International Development Assistance Policies: An Appraisal* (Montreal and Kingston: McGill-Queen's University Press, 1994), pp. 192-204; Wayne Gooding, "Aid-Trade Fund Real Casualty of Cutbacks," *Financial Post*, March 8, 1986; and "Aid/Trade Fund Stillborn," *Canadian Export Association—Export News* (March 1986), p. 3.

42 Government of Canada, "Export Financing Consultation Paper" (January 1985), pp. 16-20.

43 The North-South Institute submitted a dissenting opinion, arguing in terms of the government's own rhetoric that export competition through subsidized financing was inefficient economically, burdensome fiscally, and a classic example of market distortions like those attacked in the cabinet's own "Agenda for Economic Renewal," released in November 1984. A better alternative would be active encouragement for Canadian firms to compete for contracts offered by the multilateral development banks (see North-South Institute, "Third World Markets and Export Financing: Onto a Sounder Footing," Submission to the Minister of Finance and the Minister of International Trade on Export Financing, Ottawa, April 1985).

44 David Stewart-Patterson, "Special Fund Will Offer Help to Canadian Export Trade," *The Globe and Mail*, May 24, 1985.

45 Wayne Gooding, "New Trade-Aid Fund Gathering Steam," *Financial Post*, August 17, 1985, and "Ottawa to Increase Export Subsidies," *The Globe and Mail*, January 20, 1986.

46 Sandra Contenta, "Tories Tie Foreign Aid to Exports," *The Toronto Star*, May 28, 1985. See also a series on the "commercialization of CIDA" by Dan Turner in the *Ottawa Citizen*: "Aid Agency Not Always on Target" and "Profits and Social Services Uneasy Suitors," February 3, 1986; "Looking for a Return on Aid," February 4, 1986; and "Exports, Not Morality, Win Votes," February 5, 1986.

47 "Bad for Aid and Trade," *The Globe and Mail*, May 28, 1985.

48 Bruce Little, "CIDA Busy Consulting on New Aid Approach," *The Globe and Mail*, October 7, 1985.

49 OECD-DAC, "Aid Review 1986/87: Report by the Secretariat and Questions on the Development Assistance Efforts and Policies of Canada" (Paris, 1986), p. 22.

50 Martin Rudner, "Trade cum Aid in Canada's Official Development Assistance Strategy," in Brian W. Tomlin and Maureen Appel Molot, eds., *Canada Among Nations 1986: Talking Trade* (Toronto: James Lorimer, 1987), p. 135.

51 The quotation is from the *Sunday Star*, November 4, 1984. This and some of the following paragraphs draw on David R. Morrison, "The Mulroney Government and the Third World," *Journal of Canadian Studies* 19, 1 (Winter 1984-85): 8.

52 Caitlin Kelly, "Rush of Interest in Ethiopia Won't Last, Officials Fear," *The Globe and Mail*, November 6, 1984.

53 House of Commons, *Debates*, February 13, 1985, pp. 2306-307.

54 See Clark's announcement of additional funding, in House of Commons, *Debates*, February 13, 1985, pp. 2306-307.

55 CIDA, *Memorandum to DAC 1985*, p. 18. The board of Africa Emergency Aid included MacDonald and a CIDA representative but NGO representatives constituted a majority.

56 Canadian Emergency Coordinator/African Famine, *The African Famine and Canada's Response* (Hull: CIDA, 1985).

57 House of Commons, Standing Committee on External Affairs and National Defence, *The Second Report to the House (Response to the Report on the Honourable David MacDonald on the African Famine), Minutes of Proceedings and Evidence*, April 18-19, 1985, session 14, pp. 3-14. The quotation is from p. 10. Sessions 9-12 record the testimony of witnesses before the Committee. MacDonald's own recommendations were presented in session 14, pp. 34-40.

58 See Canadian Emergency Coordinator/African Famine, *No More Famine: A Decade for Africa* (Hull: CIDA, 1986).

59 Such apparently was the judgement within CIDA, which was footing the bill. See Hugh Winsor, "Vézina Shows Some Teeth behind Her Grandmotherly Smile," *The Globe and Mail*, June 2, 1986.

60 Canadian Emergency Coordinator/African Famine, *Forum Africa: Canadians Working Together* (Hull: CIDA, 1986), pp. 37-38.

61 See Canadian Emergency Coordinator/African Famine, *No More Famine*, pp. 36-38.

62 Winsor, "Vézina Shows Some Teeth behind Her Grandmotherly Smile."

63 English translation of Statement by the Hon. Monique Vézina, Minister for External Relations, on the occasion of launching the Africa 2000 initiative, House of Commons, May 6, 1986.

64 Interview with CKO FM, May 6, 1986, reproduced in *CIDA Paper Clips*.

65 "Aid Boss Named Envoy to Ethiopia," *The Gazette* (Montreal), September 13, 1986.

66 "Fixation on Deficit Beggars Africa Aid," *The Ottawa Citizen*, May 8, 1986.

67 Statement by the Hon. Monique Vézina, Minister for External Relations, to the United Nations General Assembly on the Critical Economic Situation in Africa, New York, May 27, 1986.

68 Notes for an address by the Hon. Monique Landry, Minister for External Relations and International Development, to the Governing Council of the United Nations Development Program, New York, June 13, 1989.

69 "CIDA Today and Tomorrow: Views from Margaret Catley-Carlson," in *Development: A Changing World* (Hull: CIDA, 1988), p. 64.

70 See Maureen O'Neil, "The Impact of the Women's Movement on the Canadian Political Agenda," Speech at the School of Policy Studies, Queen's University, November 4, 1989 (printed by the North-South Institute, Ottawa, 1989), and Alena Heitlinger, *Women's Equality, Demography and Public Policies* (New York: St. Martin's Press, 1993), esp. pp. 51-65, 80-94, and 304-11.

71 "Report for CIDA on the United Nations World Conference on the International Women's Year, Mexico City, June 19 to July 2, 1975," p. 9.

72 Except where noted, this historical sketch is based on CIDA, "The Integration of Women in Development: CIDA's Program," July 1983. See also Betty Plewes and Ricky Stuart, "Women and Development Revisited: The Case for a Gender and

Development Approach," in Jamie Swift and Brian Tomlinson, eds., *Conflicts of Interest* (Toronto: Between the Lines, 1991), pp. 107-32. Plewes and Stuart criticized WID and liberal feminism in this article and made a plea for a more radical Gender and Development (GAD) alternative. As we shall see in Chapter 9, elements of the GAD critique were subsequently incorporated into CIDA's WID policy.

73 Suteera Thomson, *Food for the Poor: The Role of CIDA in Agriculture, Fisheries and Rural Development* (Ottawa: Science Council of Canada, 1980), p. 35.

74 See Manon Cornellier, "MATCH," in *Development: Women* (Hull: CIDA, 1987), pp. 13-15.

75 Thomson, *Food for the Poor*, pp. 44-46.

76 Ibid., p. 131.

77 Kathleen Staudt, *Women, Foreign Assistance, and Advocacy Administration* (New York: Praeger, 1985), pp. 24-44.

78 OECD-DAC, *Development Co-operation: Efforts and Policies of the Members of the Development Assistance Committee 1985*, p. 84.

79 Ibid., *1984*, pp. 179-81.

80 CIDA, *Memorandum to DAC 1983*, p. 43 (written at the end of 1984).

81 The account that follows is based largely on interviews, supplemented by Paul Weber, "Bureaucratic Politics: The Case of Women in Development Policy Implementation at the Canadian International Development Agency" (unpublished paper, 1986). See also Rajani E. Alexander, "Evaluating Experiences: CIDA's Women in Development Policy, 1984-94," *Canadian Journal of Development Studies*, Special Issue on Evaluating Experiences: Doing Development with Women (1995), pp. 79-87.

82 CIDA, "Coming of Age: CIDA and Women and Development" (Hull, 1986), p. 2.

83 One of three case examples cited by June Callwood in her account of the Harvard course ("Adding Women to the Aid Equation," *The Globe and Mail*, August 30, 1985).

84 CIDA, "WID Policy Framework," Annex A, in CIDA, *Memorandum to DAC 1984*, pp. 13-14.

85 CIDA, "Canadian International Development Assistance Programs: A Briefing Book for Parliamentarians" (Hull, 1986), p. 122.

86 CIDA, *Memorandum to DAC 1988*, p. 35.

87 CIDA, *Women in Development: CIDA Action Plan* (Hull: CIDA, 1986).

88 "Integrating Women into Development," Notes for a speech by the Honourable Monique Vézina, Minister for External Relations, to mark the publication of CIDA's Plan of Action for Integrating Women into Development, Ottawa, June 11, 1986.

89 Stevie Cameron, "CIDA Blazes Trail for Women's Rights," *The Ottawa Citizen*, June 14, 1986.

90 See CIDA, "Coming of Age"; CIDA, *Memorandum to DAC 1987*, pp. 44-46; and ibid., *1988*, pp. 22, 35-37.

91 OECD-DAC, *Development Co-operation: Efforts and Policies of the Members of the Development Assistance Committee 1987*, p. 164.

92 See Michael Valpy, "Canadian 'Compromise' Puts an End to UN Women's Conference Impasse," *The Globe and Mail*, July 16, 1985. As at earlier conferences, Status of Women Canada played a lead role. Its coordinator (and deputy leader of

the delegation), Maureen O'Neil, was credited with playing a decisive mediating role in a procedural conflict between the American and some of the more radical Third World representatives. O'Neil went on to serve as president of the North-South Institute from 1989 to 1995. She was appointed as president of IDRC in 1997.

93 CIDA, "Coming of Age," p. 4; CIDA, *Memorandum to DAC 1987*, p. 45; and ibid., *1988*, p. 36.

94 Author's interview with Margaret Catley-Carlson, Hull, October 28, 1988.

95 CIDA Press Release, June 20, 1985.

96 Clyde Sanger, "Environment and Development," *International Journal* 28, 1 (Winter 1972-73): 115-16.

97 CIDA, *Sectoral Guidelines 3: Infrastructure and Environment* (Ottawa: CIDA, 1976).

98 See Roger Ehrhardt, Arthur Hanson, Clyde Sanger, and Bernard Wood, *Canadian Aid and the Environment: The Policies and Performance of the Canadian International Development Agency* (Halifax: Institute for Resource and Environmental Studies [co-published by the North-South Institute], 1981), pp. 54, 59-60; Mark Gawn, "Donor Agencies and the Environment: CIDA's Environmental Policy" (unpublished M.A. thesis, Carleton University, 1985), pp. 62-63; and Clyde Sanger, "Environment and Development," in Fen Osler Hampson and Christopher Maule, eds., *Canada Among Nations 1993-94: Global Jeopardy* (Ottawa: Carleton University Press, 1993), pp. 160-61.

99 Ehrhardt et al., *Canadian Aid and the Environment*, pp. 87-93. The study was part of a six-country comparative study sponsored by the International Institute for Environment and Development.

100 CIDA, "Canadian Environment and Natural Resources Assistance" (Hull, 1984). See the critique in Gawn, "Donor Agencies and the Environment," p. 73.

101 See texts in OECD-DAC, *Development Co-operation: Efforts and Policies of the Members of the Development Assistance Committee 1986*, pp. 211-14.

102 CIDA, *Environment and Development: The Policy of the Canadian International Development Agency* (Hull: CIDA, 1987), p. 11. The material that follows is based on interviews.

103 See CIDA, *Environment and Development: A CIDA Perspective*, Submission to the World Commission on Environment and Development (Hull: CIDA, 1986). The quotation is on p. 12. The document claimed on p. 20 that CIDA's environmental performance "is much better than critics contend."

104 CIDA, Memorandum to the President's Committee, Environment and Development Implementation Strategy, June 16, 1986.

105 It is noted in ibid. that this broad typology yielded a level of activity of 27 per cent of the bilateral disbursements in 1985-86. The figure was "surprisingly high and should be used cautiously. The last attempt at categorising projects in 1982/83 indicated that 12% of ODA budget was environment-related. Part of this increase may be due to expansion of the typology, and part may be due to the tendency to include total projects costs for a project which may only have *some* environmental components" (emphasis in original).

106 CIDA, *Memorandum to DAC 1986*, p. 12, and ibid., *1987*, p. 42.

107 CIDA Press Release, April 29, 1987.

108 The occasion this time was World Environment Day. See *The Gazette* (Montreal), June 6, 1987, and CIDA, *Environment and Development: The Policy*.

109 World Commission on Environment and Development, *Our Common Future* (Oxford: Oxford University Press, 1987), p. 43.

110 Letter from Patricia Adams, *The Ottawa Citizen*, July 8, 1987.

111 See CIDA, "Three Gorges Water Control Project Feasibility Study (August 1988) and Background Papers" (February 1989); Patricia Adams, "Canada's Aid Ignores Environmental Concerns," *The Ottawa Citizen*, December 23, 1988; and Ross Howard, "Canadian Study Backs Proposal for Controversial Dam in China," *The Globe and Mail*, February 15, 1989.

112 CIDA, *Memorandum to DAC 1988*, p. 13.

113 Jim MacNeill et al, *CIDA and Sustainable Development: How Canada's Aid Policies Can Support Sustainable Development in the Third World More Effectively* (Halifax: Institute for Research on Public Policy, 1989), p. 15.

114 Ibid., p. 17.

115 Ibid., p. 52.

116 Quoted in "Sustainable Development Holds Key to Future Says CIDA President," *Gleaner* (Fredericton), June 14, 1989.

117 Notes for an address by the Right Honourable Brian Mulroney, Prime Minister of Canada, before the United Nations General Assembly, New York, September 29, 1988, p. 8.

118 She was a key player in organizing Quebec support for Brian Mulroney in his successful campaign to wrest the Conservative leadership from Joe Clark. For more biographical details, see Winsor, "Vézina Shows Some Teeth behind Her Grandmotherly Smile"; Jim Robb, "New Faces Step Forward from Back-Bench Obscurity," *The Ottawa Citizen*, July 2, 1986; and Caitlin Kelly, "Landry: Tough Course Faces Cabinet's Golfer," *The Gazette* (Montreal), October 15, 1986.

119 Writing about another "traditional" Quebec minister (Liberal André Ouellet) some time later, Hugh Winsor recalled: "For former Conservative ministers Monique Vézina and Monique Landry, when they were responsible for CIDA, directing largesse to Quebec firms became such a priority that many non-Quebec-based firms were forced to find Quebec partners or agents in order to win or maintain CIDA contracts" (Hugh Winsor, "Ouellet Illustrates 'Traditional' Style," *The Globe and Mail*, April 8, 1995).

120 Interviews. See also Réal P. Lavergne, "Determinants of Canadian Aid Policy," in Olav Stokke, ed., *Western Middle Powers and Global Poverty* (Uppsala: The Scandinavian Institute of African Studies, 1989), p. 66.

121 Turner Dan, "Think-Tank Slams Foreign Aid Contracting," *The Ottawa Citizen*, January 8, 1987. See also North-South Institute, *Review '86/Outlook '87* (January 1987), p. 3. Under the policy then in place, authority for contracts under $100,000 was delegated within the Agency. For contracts over that amount, CIDA officials presented lists of approximately ten consulting firms to the minister, who short-listed three to five from whom to invite proposals. Civil servants then evaluated the proposals and made a recommendation to the minister, who made the final decision (see CIDA, "Briefing Book for Parliamentarians," pp. 118-19). The process supposedly ensured that contractors were well qualified, but offered scope for political intervention at both the short-listing and final-selection stages. Ministers have had even greater discretion in the responsive programs for business, NGOs, and NGIs.

122 Rudner, "Trade cum Aid in Canada's Official Development Assistance Strategy," p. 132. He cited as a source "Faire du 'bon patronage,' c'est normal," *Le Soleil*,

July 8, 1986. See also Michel Vastel, "Le patronage s'étend à l'ACDI," *Le Devoir*, February 11, 1987; and "Vézina Points Direction in CIDA Contract Awards," *The Ottawa Citizen*, February 3, 1986.

123 See CIDA, "Options for the Future," pp. 30-45. The quoted passage is on p. 35.

124 Rawkins, "An Institutional Analysis of CIDA," p. 169.

125 See "Vézina Points Direction in CIDA Contract Awards"; *Estimates 1989-90, Part III: Canadian International Development Agency*, p. 34; ibid., *1988-89*, Figure 18, p. 54; and ibid., Figure 23, p. 60. CIDA "upgraded" its registry of consultants in 1990 and the number fell to 4,475 (ibid., *1991-92*, p. 33).

126 See the findings of Groupe Secor's strategic management review in Chapter 9.

127 CIDA, "Options for the Future," p. 45.

128 OECD-DAC, "Aid Review 1990-91: Report by the Secretariat and Questions on the Development Assistance Efforts and Policies of Canada" (Paris, 1990), p. 24. The comments were made in the context of contrasting CIDA's "old style"—reactive and project-based—with the 1988 strategy, which sought to be proactive and policy-based.

129 Rawkins, "An Institutional Analysis of CIDA," p. 169.

130 CIDA, "Options for the Future," p. 41.

131 *Report of the Auditor General of Canada to the House of Commons, Fiscal Year Ended March 31, 1984* (Hull: Minister of Supply and Services, 1984), pp. 9-20.

132 Ibid., pp. 2-15, 9-27, 9-31, 9-44, 9-45.

133 Ibid., pp. 2-15, 9-4.

134 CIDA, *Memorandum to DAC 1984*, p. 8; *Estimates 1985-86, Part III: Canadian International Development Agency*, p. 25; ibid., *1986-87*, pp. 33-34; and CIDA, "Briefing Book for Parliamentarians," p. 106.

135 CIDA, *Memorandum to DAC 1985*, p. 11, and ibid., *1987*, p. 34.

136 House of Commons, Standing Committee on Public Accounts, *Minutes of Proceedings and Evidence*, April 25, 1985, session 14, p. 19. See also p. 18.

137 CIDA, "Options for the Future," p. 39. It was a prescient analysis; see the account of the decentralization experience in Chapter 8.

138 Standing Committee on Public Accounts, *Minutes of Proceedings and Evidence*, April 25, 1985, session 14, pp. 14-15.

139 Ibid., April 25, 1985, session 14, pp. 35-36, 41-51; ibid., April 30, 1985, session 15, pp. 37-45; ibid., June 20, 1985, session 20, pp. 7-9, 21-22; Standing Committee on External Affairs and National Defence, *Minutes of Proceedings and Evidence*, March 15, 1985, session 6, pp. 8-12; and *Second Report to the House, Proceedings*, April 18-19, 1985, session 14, pp. 5, 8.

140 Standing Committee on Public Accounts, *Minutes of Proceedings and Evidence*, June 20, 1985, session 20, p. 21.

141 Ibid., October 17, 1985, session 21, p. 7.

142 "Response of the Government of Canada to Certain Recommendations of the Eighth Report of the Standing Committee on Public Accounts Concerning the Canadian International Development Agency Tabled in the House of Commons on October 22, 1985," in ibid., May 8, 1986, session 32A (Appendix "PUBL-32"), pp. 2-3. The response contained as well letters from Catley-Carlson to Aideen Nicholson, MP, chair of the Public Accounts Committee, dated February 21, 1986 and March 26, 1986, session 32A (Appendices "PUBL-33" and "PUBL-34")

pp. 6-20. The first argued that the committee had underestimated the degree of decentralization already achieved by concentrating on public service personnel and neglecting the extensive contracting out of field responsibilities. The second reported that CIDA had obtained approval to delegate the authority to amend contracts in the field to project monitors under contract. "Such delegation will greatly augment the Agency's ability to react in a timely fashion to changing field conditions identified by technical monitors, as specifically recommended by the Auditor General and the Committee."

143 John Best's column, *Star Phoenix* (Saskatoon), June 7, 1984.

144 Canada's GNP in 1990-91 was $673.65 billion (CIDA, *Annual Report 1990-91*, p. 55).

145 Government of Canada, Press Release, August 2, 1984.

146 Notes for a Speech by the Right Honourable Joe Clark, Secretary of State for External Affairs, to the 39th Session of the General Assembly of the United Nations, New York, September 25, 1984, p. 11.

147 David Stewart-Patterson, "CIDA Fights Proposed Cut in Foreign Aid Spending," *The Globe and Mail*, September 24, 1984, and James Rusk, "Studies Point Way for Tories in Quest for Budget Cutbacks," *The Globe and Mail*, October 1, 1984.

148 House of Commons, *Debates*, November 8, 1984, p. 99.

149 Ibid., May 23, 1985, p. 5017.

150 Ibid., and "Foreign Aid Cut by $2.5 Billion: Institute," *The Ottawa Citizen*, June 1, 1985. The difference between the $1.6 billion in budget cuts and the $2.5 billion in the headline was the Institute's estimate of ODA increases that would be diverted into the Trade and Development Facility.

151 North-South Institute, *Review '85/Outlook '86* (1986), p. 11.

152 House of Commons, *Debates*, February 6, 1986, pp. 10982-83.

153 Speech by the Right Honourable Joe Clark, Secretary of State for External Affairs, on Canada's Official Development Assistance, Ottawa, February 28, 1986.

154 See, for example, "Aid Delays Are a Shame," *The Gazette* (Montreal), March 3, 1986; "Broken Promises in Foreign Aid," *The Toronto Star*, March 4, 1986; Terry Glavin, "Tories' Retreat on Foreign Aid Called Betrayal," *Sun* (Vancouver), February 27, 1986; Joe O'Donnell, "Cut in Foreign Aid Funds Worrisome, Official Says," *The Toronto Star*, March 1, 1986; Dan Turner, "Clark Replaces CIDA Loans with Grants," *The Ottawa Citizen*, March 3, 1986; and John Best, "Foreign Aid Hit by Deficit Battle Fallout," *The London Free Press*, March 5, 1986.

155 Data in this section are drawn from CIDA annual reports from 1983-84 to 1989-90 and memoranda to the DAC from 1983 to 1989. See Appendix A.

156 Actual expenditures went up by slightly less because allocations to international financial institutions were counted as ODA on a commitment basis, rather than (as with all other components) on a disbursement basis—and also because of a decision to report as ODA the imputed costs of ODA-sponsored foreign students. (This latitude was allowed by DAC in 1984, but CIDA did not take advantage of it until 1987-88.) Imputed student costs were reported as $12.9 million in 1987-88 and $60.5 million in 1988-89. In addition to formula-driven funds, concessional components of Section 31 mixed credits from the Export Development Corporation were included in the 1987-88 and 1988-89 totals ($2.1 million and $32.1 million respectively).

157 Parts of this section follow closely David R. Morrison, "The Choice of Bilateral Aid Recipients," in Cranford Pratt, ed., *Canadian International Development*

Assistance Policies: An Appraisal (Montreal and Kingston: McGill-Queen's University Press, 1994), pp. 143-46.

158 CIDA, "Options for the Future," p. 9.

159 Minister for External Relations, Press Release, March 3, 1986.

160 "Clark to Request Aid for the Philippines," *Winnipeg Free Press*, July 2, 1986. For an overview of Canadian aid to the Philippines, see Martin Rudner, *Canada and the Philippines: The Dimensions of a Developing Relationship* (North York, Captus Press, 1990).

161 Minister for External Relations, Press Release, October 20, 1986.

162 Interviews; CIDA, *Annual Report 1987-88*, p. 17. See also the report of a 1987 CIDA-NGO mission to Mozambique led by McLean in Dan Turner, "Canada Considers Increasing Aid to Famine-Stricken Mozambique," *The Ottawa Citizen*, March 4, 1987; and David Gillies, "Do Interest Groups Make a Difference? Domestic Influences on Canadian Development Aid Policies," in Irving Brecher, ed., *Human Rights, Development and Foreign Policy: Canadian Perspectives* (Halifax: Institute for Research on Public Policy, 1989), pp. 440-42.

163 CIDA, *Annual Report 1989-90*, pp. 18-19. Mulroney's commitment was reported in "Canada Commits $4.4 Million to Aid Blacks in South Africa," *The Gazette* (Montreal), October 19, 1987.

164 In contrast, the percentages did not change much from 1980-81 to 1985-86 (see Appendix C).

165 See Appendix C. Moreover, sixteen of the top forty recipients over the period from 1988 to 1991 were in the middle-income category. Andrew Clark undertook a statistical analysis of Canadian bilateral aid to these countries, and found that there was no statistically significant relationship between the amount of that aid and a country's per capita income or its ranking in the UNDP's Human Development Index. See Andrew Clark, "ODA Analyzed: Another Canadian Aid Paradox?" *Review* (North-South Institute) (Fall 1992), pp. 7-8.

166 Percentages calculated from data in annual reports.

167 House of Commons, Special Committee on the Peace Process in Central America, *First Report*, *Minutes of Proceedings and Evidence*, July 5, 1988, session 6, p. 42.

168 See the exchange between Lloyd Axworthy and Marcel Massé, in House of Commons, Standing Committee on External Affairs and International Trade, *Minutes of Proceedings and Evidence*, October 31, 1989, session 21, p. 19.

169 See T.A. Keenleyside, "Aiding Rights: Canada and the Advancement of Human Dignity," in Cranford Pratt, ed., *Canadian International Development Assistance Policies: An Appraisal* (Montreal and Kingston: McGill-Queen's University Press, 1994), p. 248; Katharine Pearson and Timothy Draimin, "Public Policy Dialogue and Canadian Aid: The Case of Central America," in ibid., pp. 275-82; and David Close, "Aid and Peace in Central America," in Robert Miller, ed., *Aid as Peacemaker: Canadian Development Assistance and Third World Conflict* (Ottawa: Carleton University Press, 1992), pp. 17-32.

170 Keenleyside, "Aiding Rights," p. 255, and CIDA, *Annual Report 1988-89*, p. 29. See also Catley-Carlson's statement in House of Commons, Standing Committee on External Affairs and International Trade, *Minutes of Proceedings and Evidence*, June 1, 1989, session 5, p. 19.

171 *Estimates, 1987-88, Part III: Canadian International Development Agency*, p. 37.

172 CIDA, *Memorandum to DAC 1985*, p. 2.

173 Statement by the Hon. Monique Vézina, Minister for External Relations, to the United Nations General Assembly on the Critical Economic Situation in Africa, New York, May 27, 1986.

174 "Canada Starts Nice Ripples," *The Gazette* (Montreal), May 30, 1986. See also "Canada Acts in Africa," *The Globe and Mail*, May 29, 1986.

175 "Canada Kills Debts of Seven Countries at Quebec Summit,"*The Globe and Mail*, September 3, 1987; "South Africa on the Agenda Again at Commonwealth Meeting in B.C.," *The Toronto Star*, October 10, 1987; and CIDA, *Memorandum to DAC 1987*, p. 4.

176 See David R. Morrison, "Canada and North-South Conflict," in Maureen Appel Molot and Brian W. Tomlin, eds., *Canada Among Nations 1987: A World of Conflict* (Toronto: James Lorimer, 1988), pp. 147-48.

177 Morrison, "The Mulroney Government and the Third World," p. 10.

178 This section is based on interviews; Marcia Burdette, "Structural Adjustment and Canadian Aid Policy," in Cranford Pratt, ed., *Canadian International Development Assistance Policies: An Appraisal* (Montreal and Kingston: McGill-Queen's University Press, 1994), pp. 216-21; CIDA, *Memorandum to DAC 1984*, p. 8; ibid., *1985*, p. 11; ibid., *1987*, p. 26; and ibid., *1988*, pp. 19-21.

179 According to a senior official interviewed by Marcia Burdette ("Structural Adjustment and Canadian Aid Policy," p. 235, n. 37).

180 Reprinted as Margaret Catley-Carlson, "The Donor's Response—Canadian Aid Policy Towards 2000," *Development: Journal of the Society for International Development* 1 (1988): 41.

181 See Maureen O'Neil and Andrew Clark, "Canada and International Development: New Agendas," in Fen Osler Hampson and Christopher J. Maule, eds., *Canada Among Nations 1992-93: A New World Order?* (Ottawa: Carleton University Press, 1992), p. 224.

182 OECD-DAC, "Aid Review 1984/85: Report by the Secretariat and Questions on the Development Assistance Efforts and Policies of Canada," p. 21. For comparative data for 1983 and 1984, see CIDA, *Memorandum to DAC 1985*, pp. 302-303.

183 CIDA, *Memorandum to DAC 1984*, p. 7, and ibid., *1985*, p. 9.

184 See Karen E. Mundy, "Human Resources Development Assistance in Canada's Overseas Development Assistance Program: A Critical Analysis," *Canadian Journal of Development Studies* 13, 3 (1992): 396-98. The quoted phrase is from the abstract, p. 385.

185 OECD-DAC, *Development Co-operation: Efforts and Policies of the Members of the Development Assistance Committee 1987*, p. 236, and ibid., *1991*, p. 208.

186 See ibid., *1984*, pp. 224-25; ibid., *1985*, pp. 302-303; ibid., *1987*, pp. 206-207; ibid., *1988*, pp. 192-93; ibid., *1989*, pp. 232-33; and ibid., *1990*, pp. 216-17.

187 Mark W. Charlton, "Continuity and Change in Canadian Food Aid," in Cranford Pratt, ed., *Canadian International Development Assistance Policies: An Appraisal* (Montreal and Kingston: McGill-Queen's University Press, 1994), p. 61.

188 See ibid., pp. 59-60.

189 David R. Protheroe, *Canada and Multilateral Aid* (Ottawa: North-South Institute, 1991), p. 160.

190 Ibid., pp. 62-63.

191 Jeffrey Simpson, "The Politics of Aid," *The Globe and Mail*, December 12, 1986.

192 David R. Protheroe, "Canada's Multilateral Aid and Diplomacy," in Cranford Pratt, ed., *Canadian International Development Assistance Policies: An Appraisal* (Montreal and Kingston: McGill-Queen's University Press, 1994), pp. 35-36.

193 Protheroe, *Canada and Multilateral Aid*, pp. 65, 71.

194 See Protheroe, "Canada's Multilateral Aid and Diplomacy," pp. 40-41.

195 Calculated from data in Appendix A.

196 See Protheroe, "Canada's Multilateral Aid and Diplomacy," p. 32. "Moreover, the program habitually gets a boost from unplanned, end-of-fiscal-year transfers; because it is so easily disbursed, this channel functions as a safety-valve to meet targets when disbursement bottlenecks occur in bilateral and other programs." (On balance, the more bilaterally minded executives in CIDA would prefer authority to overprogram other areas so that last-minute transfers to multilateral accounts could be avoided.)

197 Protheroe, *Canada and Multilateral Aid*, pp. 49-50; OECD-DAC, *Development Co-operation: Efforts and Policies of the Members of the Development Assistance Committee 1989*, p. 228; and ibid., *1990*, p. 212.

198 See Appendix A. These data include provincial government contributions to non-governmental organizations and institutions, which were $10.6 million in 1983-94 and $12.9 million in 1988-89. CIDA funding for Canadian NGOs and NGIs (derived by deducting provincial contributions as well as allocations to International Non-Governmental Organizations—in the 18 to 24 million-dollar range per annum) was $167.1 million in 1983-84 and $267.6 million in 1988-89; these totals include food aid channelled through NGOs ($10.4 million in 1983-84 and $25 million in 1988-89).

199 Country focus projects were increasing quickly, and it was feared that data on bilateral aid would have been distorted otherwise. The bilateral branches were also given authority to contract directly for country focus projects, but there was ongoing uncertainty about the respective managerial responsibilities of Special Programs and the bilaterals (interviews).

200 Phillip Rawkins, *Human Resource Development in the Aid Process: A Study in Organizational Learning and Change* (Ottawa: North-South Institute, 1993), p. 20.

201 In some cases, there was serious conflict between CIDA and NGO agendas. Much to the irritation of Agency officials, who had decided to wind the project down, WUSC lobbied successfully at the political level in Canada and Zimbabwe to extend funding for the supply of Canadian secondary teachers to Zimbabwe. See James Travers, "Canadian Aid Plans Worry Zimbabwe," *Calgary Herald*, September 27, 1982; James Travers, "Canada Spikes Zimbabwe Hope for Teachers," *The Ottawa Citizen*, October 13, 1982; Glenn Somerville, "Canada, Zimbabwe Sign Aid Pact," *The Ottawa Citizen*, September 17, 1983; Michael Valpy, "Agency Cools to Aid Project in Zimbabwe," *The Globe and Mail*, June 22, 1984; Michael Valpy, "An Aid Puzzle for Canadians," *The Globe and Mail*, January 23, 1987; and letter from Monique Landry re: "CIDA in Zimbabwe," *The Globe and Mail*, April 1, 1987.

202 For a further discussion of the impact of country focus on NGOs, see Tim Brodhead and Brent Herbert-Copley, *Bridges of Hope? Canadian Voluntary Agencies and the Third World* (Ottawa: North-South Institute, 1988), pp. 59-63, and CCIC, *"Mind if I Cut In?": The Report of the CCIC Task Force on CIDA-NGO Funding Relationships* (Ottawa: CCIC, 1988), pp. 38-39.

203 Rawkins, *Human Resource Development in the Aid Process*, p. 20.
204 See Tim Brodhead and Cranford Pratt, "Paying the Piper," in Cranford Pratt, ed., *Canadian International Development Assistance Policies: An Appraisal* (Montreal and Kingston: McGill-Queen's University Press, 1994), pp. 97, 92.
205 Brodhead and Herbert-Copley, *Bridges of Hope?*, p. 70.
206 CIDA, "Options for the Future," pp. 17-18.
207 Brodhead and Herbert-Copley, *Bridges of Hope?*, p. 70.
208 These arrangements are described in various documents, but are especially well summarized in CCIC, *Mind if I Cut In?*
209 CCIC, *Mind if I Cut In?*, p. 41. See also pp. 39-40 and 62. After efforts to resolve the conflict failed, CIDA wound down its involvement. See as well David Gillies, "The Philippines: Foreign Aid and Human Rights in an Uncertain Democracy," in David Gillies, *Between Principle and Practice: Human Rights in North-South Relations* (Montreal and Kingston, McGill-Queen's University Press, 1996), pp. 76-100, and David Wurfel, "Canadian Aid, Social Change, and Political Conflict in the Philippines: Prospects for Conflict Resolution," in Robert Miller, ed., *Aid as Peacemaker: Canadian Development Assistance and Third World Conflict* (Ottawa: Carleton University Press, 1992), pp. 71-86.
210 CCIC, *Mind if I Cut In?*, p. 46.
211 Brodhead and Pratt, "Paying the Piper," p. 101.
212 Interview. There were some Canadians from church and other groups with local experience but they were not identified as participants initially, thus further exacerbating conflict over the program.
213 A long-standing relationship with the Canadian Association for Latin America and the Caribbean ended after an audit revealed misappropriation of funds and insolvency in 1986. The organization had received $639,000 from CIDA in 1985-86. ("Trade Agency Demise Leaves $300,000 Debt and Many Questions," *The Globe and Mail*, March 17, 1986, and "Ex-Head of Agency Returns Amid Probe," *The Toronto Star*, April 9, 1986.)
214 See a summary of recommendations in David Hatter, "Report Urges Third World Links," *Financial Post*, November 9, 1987.
215 Andrew McIntosh, "Ottawa Set to Improve CIDA Image," *The Globe and Mail*, March 9, 1987. The booklets, published regularly since then under the CIDA imprimatur, include: *CIDA: A Guide for the Business Community*, *Executing Agencies*, *Active Contracts*, and *Lines of Credit*.
216 CIDA, *Annual Report 1988-89*, p. 13.
217 Calculated from data in Appendix A.
218 See data in Gillies, "Export Promotion and Canadian Development Assistance," p. 203.
219 CIDA, "Options for the Future," p. 20.
220 CIDA, *Memorandum to DAC 1988*, p. 28, and ibid., *1989*, p. 33.
221 In 1984, the Auditor General's criticisms of bilateral programming were accompanied by examples that made for dramatic coverage—wheat rotting in the sun in Niger, rails rusting in Tanzania, punctured bags of food aid, etc. Food aid was also a focus of that report; of particular concern was evidence that the federal government's Canadian Dairy Commission was overcharging CIDA for skim milk powder. (See *Report of the Auditor General of Canada to the House of Commons, Fiscal Year Ended March 31, 1984*, chap. 9; "CIDA's Projects are Undermined by Slowness: Dye," *The Globe and Mail*, December 12, 1984, and Iain Hunter, "For-

eign Aid Program Throws Up Its Share of Fiscal Disasters," *The Ottawa Citizen*, December 12, 1984.) The chief focus of the 1988 audit was contracting, which the Auditor General found wanting in about a third of the projects examined. Again there were examples, including CIDA's acceptance of a non-competitive bid from a consortium of potash suppliers that was $1.2 million above an acceptable market price. (See *Report of the Auditor General of Canada to the House of Commons, Fiscal Year Ended March 31, 1988* [Hull: Minister of Supply and Services, 1988], chap. 9, and Sheldon Gordon, "CIDA and Its Pet Contractors Blush on Cue from Mr. Dye," *Financial Times of Canada*, December 26, 1988.)

222 See, for example, a series by Michael Valpy for *The Globe and Mail* on CIDA projects in Tanzania: "African Training Ended by CIDA," October 4, 1985; "CIDA Aid Plan Continues Bleak Record in Tanzania," October 5, 1985; "CIDA Fails to Get Tanzanian Railway on Track," October 8, 1985; and "Tanzanian Railway Abyss Swallowing CIDA Funds," October 9, 1985.

223 For example, in the poll conducted in December 1988, 34 per cent answered "a world leader" and 52 per cent "among the more generous nations." Impressions of Canada's actual role were 7 and 66 per cent respectively (Angus Reid Associates, *Report to CIDA: Public Attitudes towards International Development Assistance* [Hull: CIDA, 1989], p. 21).

224 Ibid., p. 24, and Decima Research, *Report to CIDA: Public Attitudes towards International Development Assistance* (Hull: CIDA, 1988), pp. 30, 32.

225 House of Commons, Standing Committee on External Affairs and International Trade, *For Whose Benefit? Report of the Standing Committee on External Affairs and International Trade on Canada's Official Development Assistance Policies and Programs* (Ottawa: Queen's Printer, 1987), p. 3.

Chapter 8

1 As it became in 1986, replacing what for years had been a Standing Committee on External Affairs and National Defence. The Tories created a separate Standing Committee on National Defence.

2 Its cover was actually grey. See Pierre Tremblay, "Très gris, en effet!" *Le Droit*, May 17, 1985, and Don McGillivray, "Clark's Color: Tattle-tale Grey," *The Gazette* (Montreal), May 15, 1985.

3 External Affairs Canada, *Competitiveness and Security* (Ottawa: Department of External Affairs, 1985), p. 36 (author's emphasis). Earlier the document had asserted: "Canadian understanding of the diversity and complexity of the Third World has deepened and become more sophisticated. So, too, has our appreciation of the interests we have at stake. Trade and investment, immigration, environmental conservation and international peace and security have been added to our original, largely humanitarian objectives" (ibid., p. 9). All these concerns had been present of course since the 1950s, except for the environment.

4 Bob Hepburn, "Tories Propose Closer U.S. Ties, Foreign Aid cuts," *The Toronto Star*, May 15, 1985, and Carol Goar, "Clark's Foreign Policy Lacks Imagination and Excitement," *The Toronto Star*, May 16, 1985.

5 External Affairs Canada, *Competitiveness and Security*, pp. 35-36.

6 Special Joint Committee of the Senate and of the House of Commons on Canada's International Relations, *Independence and Internationalism* (Ottawa: Queen's Printer, 1986), pp. 90-91 (emphasis in original).

7 Ibid., pp. 91-92.

8 Ibid., pp. 92-93. Reflecting ideological differences within the Committee, in particular suspicions on the right about certain NGOs, the report noted that sometimes groups "pop up . . . to ride waves of public concern and generosity for their own benefit. One or two established organizations have been known to support inappropriate political activities in the Third World." As the Committee foresaw an expanded role for NGOs in the future of the aid program, "we urge both CIDA and the voluntary organizations to remain alert to the rare violations of public trust, bring them to public attention, and take effective remedial action" (ibid., p. 93).

9 Ibid., p. 103.

10 On contract from the Parliamentary Centre for Foreign Policy and Foreign Trade, Miller had served in a similar capacity with the parliamentary task force in 1980 and the Subcommittee on Canada's Relations with Latin America and the Caribbean in 1981-82. He went on to work for the Winegard committee in 1986-87 and the Special Joint Committee Reviewing Canadian Foreign Policy in 1994.

11 Ibid., p. 105.

12 Ibid., pp. 89-91.

13 For further discussion of these issues, see North-South Institute, "Foreign Students in Canada: A Neglected Foreign Policy Issue," Briefing Paper (Ottawa, 1985), and David R. Morrison, "Canadian Higher Education and International Development in the 1980s: Policies, Problems and Prospects," in Julia Ballot et al., eds., *Postgraduate Training for Development* (Baden-Baden: Nomas Verlagsgesellschaft, 1989), pp. 277-300.

14 See the convincing evidence presented in Don Page, "Populism in Canadian Foreign Policy: The 1986 Review Revisited," *Canadian Public Administration* 37, 4 (Winter 1994): 573-97. Page, a senior official in External Affairs at the time of the review, cited several examples of recommendations that would have been rejected or brushed off if Clark had not been so insistent on making a mainly positive response.

15 External Affairs Canada, *Canada's International Relations—Response of the Government of Canada to the Report of the Special Joint Committee of the Senate and the House of Commons* (Hull: Minister of Supply and Services, 1986), p. 20.

16 Ibid., pp. 19-21, 65-69. See also Clark's statement and opposition responses in House of Commons, *Debates*, December 4, 1986, pp. 1763-68. Liberal and NDP members criticized the government's unwillingness to speed up the movement towards the 0.7 per cent ODA target.

17 External Affairs Canada, *Canada's International Relations—Response of the Government of Canada to the Report of the Special Joint Committee of the Senate and the House of Commons*, p. 25. See Transcript of an interview given to Michael McDowell of *The Globe and Mail* by Margaret Catley-Carlson, September 14, 1983, CIDA Archives, Hull, and "Aid Dimensions and Dilemmas," Notes for an Address by Margaret Catley-Carlson, President of CIDA, to a conference on "North-South Dialogue: The Philosophical Issues," sponsored by the Department of Philosophy, Simon Fraser University, Vancouver, October 13, 1983.

18 Questioning in particular whether it could do so in international financial institutions "without seriously impairing, through further politicization, the effectiveness of . . . [these] institutions in their critical task of bringing about needed develop-

ment and adjustment in developing countries" (External Affairs Canada, *Canada's International Relations—Response of the Government of Canada to the Report of the Special Joint Committee of the Senate and the House of Commons*, p. 74).

19 Page, "Populism in Canadian Foreign Policy," pp. 587-88.

20 According to Page, it was set up to circumvent conflict between External Affairs and CIDA over how to go about establishing the new institution. See ibid., p. 588.

21 CIDA, *Study of the Policy and Organization of Canada's Official Development Aid: Report to the Minister for External Relations* (Hull: CIDA, 1986), pp. iii-iv.

22 Four other members had experience in business, development consultancy, and NGO work, but none had direct experience within CIDA. The vice-president of Policy was attached to the group as a technical adviser.

23 Detailed terms of reference (not reproduced in the published report) called for studies on a number of issues that received no mention in the task force report. Among these were: trends and challenges in each of the major geographical areas served by the aid program; the sufficiency of CIDA's emergency relief capacity; the Agency's comparative performance within the international donor community; measures for achieving a more equitable distribution of economic benefits flowing from ODA among Canadian regions; ways of increasing returns to Canada from IFI contributions; the role of the provinces in international development; the viability of developing a Canadian Agricultural Services Overseas; and the desirability and feasibility of CIDA programming to complement the American government's Caribbean Basin Initiative (Minister of External Relations, "Study Group on Canada's Development Assistance Programme," October 15, 1985).

24 One of the most bizarre recommendations, ostensibly in support of Canada's commitment to channel 0.15 per cent of Canada's GNP in aid to LLDCs, called for reducing multilateral contributions to 30 per cent of Canada's overall ODA and raising to 40 per cent the share of bilateral aid allocated to the LLDCs (see CIDA, *Study of the Policy and Organization of Canada's Official Development Aid*, pp. 39-40). Earlier arguments for scaling down multilateral in favour of bilateral aid were largely commercially motivated. Here a case was made on behalf of the poorest countries, yet the solutions offered were more aid of a sort the LLDCs were least able to use because of Canadian procurement regulations and less of the multilateral support that had traditionally gone disproportionately to these countries. Moreover, contrary to the impression conveyed by the report, the 0.15 per cent target was in fact achieved during 1985-86 (though not subsequently).

25 Denis Hudon, vice-president of the Planning Branch during the Strong regime, was one of the consultants hired by the task force. He continued to believe in the importance of a powerful planning unit.

26 CIDA, *Study of the Policy and Organization of Canada's Official Development Aid*, p. 79.

27 Ibid., pp. 80-89. The task force also devoted attention to other organizational issues, recommending a weightier role for technical experts within project management, limited restoration of non-lapsing spending authority, and greater field presence.

28 SCEAIT cited the task force only twice: in support of its critique of the existing eligibility framework and its recommendation to allow a limited carryover of unspent funds. See House of Commons, Standing Committee on External Affairs and International Trade (SCEAIT), *For Whose Benefit? Report of the Standing Committee on External Affairs and International Trade on Canada's Official*

Development Assistance Policies and Programs (Ottawa: Queen's Printer, 1987), pp. 64, 125.

29 This account draws in part on David R. Morrison, "Canada and North-South Conflict," in Maureen Appel Molot and Brian W. Tomlin, eds., *Canada Among Nations 1987: A World of Conflict* (Toronto: James Lorimer, 1988), pp. 137-45.

30 SCEAIT, "Discussion Paper on Issues in Canada's Official Development Assistance Policies and Programs," July 1986.

31 SCEAIT, *For Whose Benefit?*, p. xiii.

32 Based on a review of evidence presented to the committee.

33 SCEAIT, *For Whose Benefit?*, p. 7.

34 Ibid., pp. 3, 12.

35 Morrison, "Canada and North-South Conflict," p. 138.

36 SCEAIT, *For Whose Benefit?*, p. 12.

37 In his testimony to the Winegard committee, Strong recalled the conclusion he had reached "that to have CIDA's own legislation was naive and that the mandate had to be vague. If there was legislation it would have been focused on the lowest common denominator." However, in calling for CIDA to be recreated by an Act of Parliament replacing the 1968 order-in-council, SCEAIT commented: "Our own conclusion, looking back over CIDA's first twenty years, is that it was naive not to have had legislation, because the lowest common denominator is more likely to be encouraged than avoided by a vague mandate" (SCEAIT, *For Whose Benefit?*, p. 73). The committee also revisited the old question of whether the aid program would be better served by making CIDA a crown corporation, but on this issue agreed with the position to which Strong had arrived. "Regrettable as it may be, the goals of independence and regular policy input are incompatible" (ibid., p. 72).

38 SCEAIT, *For Whose Benefit?*, p. 74.

39 Ibid., p. 9.

40 Ibid., p. 13.

41 Ibid., pp. 15, 64.

42 Ibid., pp. 16-19.

43 Ibid., p. 15.

44 Ibid., p. 20.

45 Ibid., pp. 57-58, 64.

46 Ibid., p. 64.

47 Ibid., pp. 47-48, 63-64.

48 Ibid., pp. 47, 49.

49 Ibid., pp. 58-60.

50 Ibid., p. 76.

51 Ibid., p. 56.

52 This section follows closely David R. Morrison, "The Choice of Bilateral Aid Recipients," in Cranford Pratt, ed., *Canadian International Development Assistance Policies: An Appraisal* (Montreal and Kingston: McGill-Queen's University Press, 1994), p. 42.

53 SCEAIT, *For Whose Benefit?*, p. 65.

54 Ibid., p. 61.

55 Ibid., p. 61.

56 Ibid., pp. 26-27.

57 Ibid., pp. 27-30. The quotations are on pp. 27 and 29-30. For a good discussion of the work of the Winegard committee on human rights, see Gerald J. Schmitz,

"Between Political Principle and State Practice: Human Rights 'Conditionality' in Canada's Development Assistance," in Irving Brecher, ed., *Human Rights and Foreign Policy: Canadian Perspectives* (Halifax: The Institute for Research on Public Policy, 1989), pp. 467-85, especially pp. 472-78. As noted in the text, Schmitz served as a research adviser to the committee. He also drafted much of the report.

58 According to three respondents who were centrally involved in the process.

59 See, for example, "Submission of the Canadian Chamber of Commerce on Canada's Official Development Assistance to the House of Commons Standing Committee on External Affairs and International Trade," February 9, 1987, pp. 14-17; testimony from the Canadian Manufacturers' Association, in SCEAIT, *Minutes of Proceedings and Evidence*, January 28, 1987, session 13, pp. 7-10; and the comments of Mr. David Page, vice-president, Canada Pacific Consulting Service Ltd., in ibid., February 10, 1987, session 14, p. 7.

60 Both in 1984 and 1986, DAC renewed criticism of the high tied level of Canada's bilateral program, urging CIDA to review possible adverse effects on projects and prices (OECD Press Release on DAC Aid Review of Canada, Paris, December 7, 1984, and OECD Press Release on DAC Aid Review of Canada, Paris, December 4, 1986). Comparative data published by the OECD in 1985 (but based on 1982-83) suggested that a higher percentage of Canada's ODA was tied to domestic procurement than that of any other DAC donor except Austria (see OECD-DAC, *Twenty-five Years of Development Co-operation: A Review* [Paris: Organisation for Economic Co-operation and Development, 1985], p. 299). When CIDA disputed DAC's approach to comparing untying status (CIDA, *Memorandum to DAC 1985*, p. 14), the DAC secretariat concluded that confusion over data on both sides had led to an overstating of Canada's untying ratio. Nevertheless, concern was expressed about the underutilization of CIDA's 20 per cent untying authority. "This situation may point to the need for improved internal programming by CIDA in order to give, in a situation of overall severe procurement restrictions, the maximum benefit of the untying authority to particular participants, and thereby reduce the danger of distortions in aid priorities, and in project selection and design" (OECD-DAC, "Aid Review 1986/87: Report by the Secretariat and Questions on the Development Assistance Efforts and Policies of Canada" [Paris, 1986], p. 18).

61 SCEAIT, *For Whose Benefit?*, pp. 37-38.

62 Ibid., p. 39.

63 Ibid., p. 44.

64 Ibid., p. 35.

65 Ibid., p. 42. David Gillies interpreted the report as being more equivocal on mixed credits and the use of aid for trade promotion. See his "Do Interest Groups Make a Difference? Domestic Influences on Canadian Development Aid Policies," in Irving Brecher, ed., *Human Rights and Foreign Policy: Canadian Perspectives* (Halifax: The Institute for Research on Public Policy, 1989), pp. 449-50.

66 SCEAIT, *For Whose Benefit?*, p. 79.

67 CIDA, "Decentralization: A Question of Balance" (1987), cited in ibid., pp. 86-88.

68 SCEAIT, *For Whose Benefit?*, p. 88 (author's emphasis).

69 Ibid., pp. 82-86. The quotation is on p. 84 (emphasis in original).

70 Ibid., pp. 88-90. The quotation is on p. 90. The report argued that regional offices could also encourage regional cooperation in problem-solving and institution-

building. The inspiration for a regional approach came from the experience of the United Kingdom (with teams of specialists concentrated in regional development missions) and of IDRC (with its regional though, from Winegard's perspective, insufficiently decentralized offices).

71 SCEAIT, *For Whose Benefit?*, p. 115.

72 Ibid., pp. 116-19.

73 Ibid., p. 93.

74 Ibid., pp. 93-97, 104.

75 Ibid., pp. 97-99, 104. The quotation is on p. 99.

76 Ibid., pp. 99-104.

77 Ibid., p. 75.

78 Ibid., pp. 109-11. Winegard was among the sceptics about PPP. Jim Manly, the most active New Democrat on the committee, played an important role as interlocutor for development education groups.

79 SCEAIT, *For Whose Benefit?*, pp. 111-14.

80 Ibid., pp. 123-24.

81 This section draws on interviews as well as relevant documents. See also Martin Rudner, "New Dimensions in Canadian Development Assistance Policy," in Brian W. Tomlin and Maureen Appel Molot, *Canada Among Nations 1988: The Tory Record* (Toronto: James Lorimer, 1989), pp. 149-68; Martin Rudner, "Canada's Official Development Assistance Strategy: Process, Goals and Priorities," *Canadian Journal of Development Studies* 12, 1 (1991): 9-37; and Cranford Pratt, "Ethics and Foreign Policy: The Case of Canada's Development Assistance," *International Journal* 43, 2 (Spring 1988): 263-301.

82 See, for example: Hugh Winsor, "Committee Urges Political Guidelines for Canadian Aid," *The Globe and Mail*, May 29, 1987; Manon Cornellier, "Ottawa devrait couper son aide aux pays répressifs," *Le Devoir* (Montreal), May 29, 1987; "Amnesty Applauds Study Tying Foreign Aid to Human Rights," *The Ottawa Citizen*, May 29, 1987; Canadian Press stories carried in several papers on May 29, 1987; and John Best, "One Way to Measure 'Right' to Foreign Aid," *The London Free Press*, May 30, 1987. There were favourable editorials in the *Sunday Star*, May 31, 1987; *The Globe and Mail*, June 8, 1987; and *The Ottawa Citizen*, June 11, 1987. See also Tim Brodhead, "Editorial: For Those Who Need it Most," *CCIC/Contact* (October 1987), p. 2; John Tackaberry, "Getting Development Right," *International Perspectives* (July/August 1987), pp. 12-14; Ian McAllister, "Aid by Numbers," *Policy Options* 18, 9 (November 1987): 20-22; Morrison, "Canada and North-South Conflict," pp. 137-45; and Pratt, "Ethics and Foreign Policy," especially pp. 283-93.

83 Janine Feretti, Letter to the Right Honourable Joe Clark on behalf of Pollution Probe, September 14, 1987, and Ted Schrecker, "Responding to Brundtland," Report prepared for the Canadian Environmental Advisory Council (1987), p. 34.

84 Beginning with an extensive summary of existing policies and programs in CIDA, "Canadian International Development Assistance Programs: A Briefing Book for Parliamentarians" (Hull, 1986).

85 Government of Canada, *To Benefit a Better World* (Hull: Minister of Supply and Services, 1987). The quotation is on p. 1.

86 CIDA, *Sharing Our Future* (Hull: Minister of Supply and Services, 1987), pp. 22-23. See also Government of Canada, *To Benefit a Better World*, p. 103.

87 For a different reading of the Winegard report and the government's responses, see the thoughtful critique presented by Cranford Pratt in his "Ethics and Foreign Policy," especially pp. 283-93 and 301, and Cranford Pratt, "Humane Internationalism and Canadian Development Assistance Policies," in Cranford Pratt, ed., *Canadian International Development Assistance Policies: An Appraisal* (Montreal and Kingston: McGill-Queen's University Press, 1994), pp. 347-51.
88 *Sharing Our Future* carries a publication date of 1987, but negotiations over decentralization delayed release until March 1988.
89 Best, "One Way to Measure 'Right' to Foreign Aid."
90 Government of Canada, *To Benefit a Better World*, pp. 50-56, and CIDA, *Sharing Our Future*, pp. 31-32.
91 CIDA, *Sharing Our Future*, p. 23.
92 Ibid., p. 25. See also the reference to mixed motives on p. 23.
93 *Estimates 1989-90, Part III: Canadian International Development Agency*, p. 18. As noted in Chapter 1, the text was as follows: "To facilitate the efforts of the peoples of developing countries to achieve self-sustainable economic and social development in accordance with their needs and environment by cooperating with them in development activities, and to provide humanitarian assistance, thereby contributing to Canada's political and economic interest abroad in promoting social justice, international stability and long-term economic relationships for the benefit of the global community."
94 CIDA, *Sharing Our Future*, p. 25. See also Government of Canada, *To Benefit a Better World*, pp. 39-40.
95 CIDA, *Sharing Our Future*, p. 36.
96 Ibid., p. 40.
97 Rudner, "New Dimensions in Canadian Development Assistance Policy," p. 158. See also Karen E. Mundy, "Human Resources Development Assistance in Canada's Overseas Development Assistance Program: A Critical Analysis," *Canadian Journal of Development Studies* 13, 3 (1992): 398-400.
98 CIDA, *Sharing Our Future*, p. 50.
99 See ibid., pp. 59-60.
100 Ibid., pp. 25, 57-58. The quotation is on p. 25.
101 Government of Canada, *To Benefit a Better World*, p. 70.
102 CIDA, *Sharing Our Future*, p. 54.
103 This section follows closely Morrison, "The Choice of Bilateral Aid Recipients," pp. 142-43.
104 With respect to level of economic development, any country that "has been 'graduated' " from World Bank lending would "normally" be excluded. As before, European countries still officially classified as developing—e.g., Greece, Portugal, and Yugoslavia—would be excluded. The "independent" criterion would be qualified, as in the past, to permit the inclusion of some of Britain's Caribbean dependencies (CIDA, *Sharing Our Future*, p. 28).
105 Ibid., p. 30. The Agency continued to publish annually a list of core countries in Part III of the *Estimates* but the practice was dropped in 1995.
106 Ibid., pp. 30, 21.
107 Ibid., p. 30.
108 Ibid., p. 51.

109 Ibid., p. 52. More generally on aid-trade, the government's response to Winegard "accepted" the committee's recommendations on concessional export financing, but reaffirmed commitments both to provide further CIDA-EDC parallel financing (to ensure that Canadian firms were not put at a competitive disadvantage), and to report as ODA any concessional credits granted through EDC that met development criteria. These were defined as: recipient country eligibility for Canadian ODA, a high priority for the project demonstrated by its inclusion in the recipient country's development plan or its approval by the minister of finance or planning, and a justification in writing of its developmental value by the relevant minister who must also certify the country's capacity and commitment to operate and maintain the project once it is completed (Government of Canada, *To Benefit a Better World*, p. 60). As Pratt observed, such a formal certification "in no way constitutes even the beginning of an assurance that the project will be consistent with the proposed Development Assistance Charter" (Pratt, "Ethics and Foreign Policy," p. 289).

110 See CIDA, *Sharing Our Future*, p. 82.

111 Ibid., p. 65.

112 Ibid., p. 68.

113 SCEAIT, *For Whose Benefit?*, p. 125.

114 CIDA, *Sharing Our Future*, p. 77.

115 "Although the Government may participate in shaping policy and programs—for example, through membership on boards of directors of Banks and multilateral organizations, or in funding discussions with NGOs and the business community—decision-making power and questions of eligibility will fundamentally rest with the partners on the basis of their own criteria. The Government will not be directly responsible for choices made by its partners; however, in most cases, the monitoring, evaluation and audit of these programs will be carried out to protect the interests of Canadian taxpayers and to guide the future allocation of funds" (ibid., p. 65).

116 Ibid., pp. 84-85.

117 Ibid., pp. 70-71. For a commentary on provisions dealing with universities, see David R. Morrison, "The Universities and *Sharing Our Future*," *Newsletter: Canadian Universities in International Development* 9, 4 (Spring 1988): 11-13.

118 CIDA, *Sharing Our Future*, pp. 76-79. The quotation in on p. 78.

119 Ibid., p. 63.

120 Ibid., pp. 81-85.

121 See, for example, Daniel Drolet, "Foreign Aid to Be Tied to Human Rights Records" and "Policy Links Foreign Aid, Human Rights," *The Ottawa Citizen*, March 3 and 4, 1988; William Johnson, "Charity Good but Justice Is Better," *The Gazette* (Montreal), March 4, 1988; Don McGillivray, "Poor Will Get Less at End of this Government Rainbow," *Sun* (Vancouver), March 7, 1988; John Best, "Canada's Aid Policies Unsettled," *The London Free Press*, March 7, 1988; Martine Corrivault, "L'aide juste," *Le Soleil* (Quebec City), March 8, 1988; and David Hatter, "Altruism, Self-Interest Still Clash within CIDA," *Financial Post*, May 2, 1988. Editorials were published in *The Gazette* (Montreal), March 9, 1988; *The London Free Press*, March 9, 1988; *Times Colonist* (Victoria), March 10, 1988; and *The Ottawa Citizen*, March 11, 1988. The strategy's statement on aid targets (which merely affirmed existing policy) was mentioned first in the Canadian Press story; as a result, several papers ran headlines like "Foreign Aid Frozen

until 1990-91" (*The Leader Post* [Regina], March 5, 1988) and "Canada Freezing Foreign Aid" (*Guardian* [Charlottetown], March 5, 1988). See as well: "South Survey: Canada," *South* (August 1988), pp. 81-83, and Ross Mallick, "New Thinking on Aid," *Policy Options* (October 1988), pp. 31-32.

122 "Principles of Aid," *The Globe and Mail*, March 5, 1988.

123 *Winnipeg Free Press*, March 13, 1988.

124 North-South Institute, *Review '88/Outlook '89* (1989), pp. 11-12.

125 Ibid., p. 13. Other critical comments dealt with business (capacity and disguised subsidies), universities (the need to monitor developmental content), and multilateral aid (not simply partners) (see pp. 8-17).

126 SCEAIT, *Minutes of Proceedings and Evidence*, March 8, 1988, session 67, pp. 5-25. The quotation is on p. 19. Winegard's statement was in ibid., March 17, session 69, p. 18.

127 Ibid., March 17, 1988, session 69, pp. 4-25. The quotation is on session 69, p. 6. Brodhead also focused on partnership in "Editorial—CIDA Strategy: Artistic Impression 5.7; Technical Merit 4.0," *CCIC Contact* (April 1988), p. 2.

128 SCEAIT, *Minutes of Proceedings and Evidence*, April 12, 1988, session 4, pp. 4-28. The quotations are in session 4, pp. 5 and 17. See also Roland Gaudet, "Untied Aid and Canadian Exports," *Export Is Our Business* (Winnipeg: Canadian Exporters' Association, 1988), pp. 20-25.

129 SCEAIT, *Minutes of Proceedings and Evidence*, April 19, 1988, session 72, p. 5.

130 The quotation is from Pratt, "Humane Internationalism and Canadian Development Assistance Policies," p. 349, but it summarizes his "Ethics and Foreign Policy," published soon after the release of *Sharing Our Future*.

131 SCEAIT, *Minutes of Proceedings and Evidence*, March 8, 1988, session 67, p. 6 (translation of French original).

132 Notes for an Address by the Right Honourable Brian Mulroney, Prime Minister of Canada before the United Nations General Assembly, New York, September 29, 1988.

133 Bill Winegard became minister of Science and David MacDonald reentered the Commons as a backbencher. Either would potentially have been a dynamic replacement for Landry, but Clark's presence in the senior portfolio required a francophone in External Relations and International Development; Landry provided gender balance as well.

134 See Ross Howard, "Don't Trim Aid, Institute Urges," *The Globe and Mail*, January 21, 1989; Hugh Winsor, "Promises Must Be Broken to Keep Promise on Cutting the Budget," *The Globe and Mail*, March 20, 1989; Andrea Gordon and Val Sears, "Expect New Taxes in Wilson's Budget," *The Toronto Star*, March 25, 1989; Andrew Cohen, "Foreign Aid Likely Victim of Deficit-Cutting Drive," *Financial Post*, April 3, 1989. Editorials included "Our Foreign Aid Is Not for Cutting," *The Toronto Star*, March 22, 1989, and "Foreign Aid: Be Gentle in Using the Axe," *The Ottawa Citizen*, April 25, 1989. An open letter from Chris Bryant, executive director of CUSO was published in several papers; see, for example, *The Ottawa Citizen*, April 25, 1989.

135 CCIC and North-South Institute, Press Release: "Severe Impact Seen if Foreign Aid Cut," Ottawa, April 12, 1989.

136 Department of Finance, *The Budget Speech Delivered in the House of Commons by the Honourable Michael H. Wilson, Minister of Finance, April 27, 1989*

(Ottawa: Department of Finance, 1989), Table 1, p. 16, and North-South Institute, Press Release: "The 1989-90 Federal Budget and the ODA Cuts," p. 2.

137 From $595.96 billion to $639.22 billion. See CIDA, *Annual Report 1990-91*, Table A, p. S6.

138 OECD-DAC, "Aid Review 1990-91: Report by the Secretariat and Questions on the Development Assistance Efforts and Policies of Canada" (Paris, 1990), p. 4.

139 CIDA, "Budget Backgrounder: Recent Trends in Canadian Official Development Assistance" (April 1989), p. 3.

140 CIDA, "Budget Backgrounder: Deficit Reduction and the Strategy" (April 1989), p. 1.

141 According to a projection done by the North-South Institute. See Maureen O'Neil, "Foreign Aid Cuts Will Hurt Us, Too," *Sunday Star*, April 30, 1989.

142 See North-South Institute, *Review '89/Outlook '90* (1990), p. 2.

143 As a result, the share of government initiatives in the total for the two envelopes declined from 51.3 per cent in 1988-89 to 48.6 per cent in 1989-90. If unbudgeted EDC Section 31 funds (for *crédit mixte*) are added to government initiatives, the percentages were 51.8 and 49.2 respectively (calculated from data in CIDA, *Annual Report 1990-91*, pp. S6-S7).

144 See CIDA, "Backgrounders: Recent trends in Canadian Official Development Assistance," "Deficit Reduction and the Strategy," "The Private Sector, Voluntary Sector, and Food Aid" (April 1989), and CIDA, "Backgrounder: Deficit Reduction and the Official Development Assistance (ODA) Program" (June 1989). The quotation is from p. 2 of the latter.

145 CIDA, *Annual Report 1990-91*, Table A, p. S5.

146 See, for example, Charlotte Montgomery and Donn Downey, "Harsh Cutbacks Betray Promises to Third World, Groups Charge," *The Globe and Mail*, April 28, 1989; Carol Goar, "Budget Tarnishes PM's Golden Boy," *The Toronto Star*, April 28, 1989; Andrew Cohen, "Critics Charge Betrayal as Ottawa Slashes Foreign Aid," *Financial Post*, April 28, 1989; "Black Day for World's Poor: Ex-envoy," *The Gazette* (Montreal), April 28, 1989; Daniel Drolet, "World's Poor Take Biggest Loss," *The Ottawa Citizen*, April 29, 1989; and Jeffrey Simpson, "Chosen for the Chop," *The Globe and Mail*, May 3, 1989. Several papers carried a separate Canadian Press story on the aid cuts, and many general articles on the budget devoted considerable attention to them. Editorials included: "Fumbling the Budget," *The Gazette* (Montreal), April 28, 1989; "Wilson's Crunch Cause for Pain," *The Toronto Star*, April 28, 1989; and "Odd Timing on Aid," *Winnipeg Free Press*, April 29, 1989. The *Kitchener-Waterloo Record* expressed regret about the aid cuts, but CIDA "could do much to soften the impact on needy aid recipients overseas by taking greater care to eliminate waste and inefficiency." ("Tough, but Reasonably Fair Debt-Battling Budget," April 28, 1989).

147 Hugh Winsor, "Mulroney's Marksmen May Have Had Voters in Sights All Along," *The Globe and Mail*, May 1, 1989.

148 House of Commons, *Debates*, May 2, 1989, p. 1210.

149 Hugh Winsor, "Cutting Food Aid to Third World Hard for Opposition to Swallow," *The Globe and Mail*, May 3, 1989. See SCEAIT, *Minutes of Proceedings and Evidence*, May 2, 1989, session 1, pp. 20-55.

150 SCEAIT, *Minutes of Proceedings and Evidence*, May 2, 1989, session 1, p. 44 (translation from the French original).

151 She gave several speeches similar to Notes for Remarks by the Honourable Monique Landry, Minister of External Relations and International Development,

to a breakfast meeting with representatives of Canadian groups interested in development cooperation, April 28, 1989.

152 OECD-DAC, *Development Co-operation: Efforts and Policies of the Members of the Development Assistance Committee 1991*, p. 214.

153 Aspects of *Sharing Our Future* were praised during DAC's biennial review of Canada's aid policies and performance in December 1988. The official press release welcomed easing of procurement regulations, decentralization, greater priority on human resource development, and other proposed reforms. The emphasis on the poorest of the poor was lauded as well—but tough questions were put during the examination about what poverty alleviation meant, and whether CIDA had thought through concrete implications for programming. Concerns were expressed as well about whether the new strategy was too narrow and insufficiently concerned about large questions of policy reform, infrastructural investment, and broad-based growth (interviews with CIDA personnel in Hull and DAC officials in Paris).

154 Interviews; see also Government of Canada, *To Benefit a Better World*, pp. 82-84.

155 Using External Affairs norms for diplomatic placements (relocation allowances, Canadian housing standards, education benefits, and other perquisites), the cost of maintaining one civil servant in the field was $250,000-$300,000 compared with about $80,000 in Ottawa-Hull.

156 "Memorandum of Understanding on the Decentralization of CIDA Activities to the Field between the Department of External Affairs and the Canadian International Development Agency," December 23, 1987. Other memoranda followed; especially important was "Memorandum of Understanding on the Decentralization of CIDA Activities to the Field between the Department of External Affairs and the Canadian International Development Agency: Human Resource Management," October 11, 1988.

157 CIDA, "Administrative Notices: Special Edition on Decentralization," March 3, 1988.

158 CIDA, *Sharing Our Future*, p. 33. The text, translated and printed in 1987 before some decisions had been finalized, was rather vague on points of detail. It also anticipated a more ambitious plan than that approved by the Treasury Board—370 person years and 23 posts. Some creative accounting was used to reconcile the numbers in a "backgrounder" accompanying the Minister's press release. See CIDA, "Monique Landry Launches New Aid Strategy," Press Release, March 3, 1988, p. 88-16 (N). The summary in the following paragraphs draws on this source and CIDA, "Administrative Notices: Special Edition on Decentralization," March 3, 1988.

159 CIDA, *Sharing Our Future*, p. 35. This commitment was first made in Government of Canada, *To Benefit a Better World*, p. 81.

160 Except where noted, the account of problems associated with decentralization is based on interviews. See also CIDA, "Les 12 Leçons apprises de la décentralisation," December 7, 1993, and Rudner, "Canada's Official Development Assistance Strategy: Process, Goals and Priorities," pp. 18-19.

161 Interviews. See also Catley-Carlson's comments on personnel problems in SCEAIT, *Minutes of Proceedings and Evidence*, April 19, 1988, session 72, p. 15, and Phillip Rawkins, "An Institutional Analysis of CIDA," in Cranford Pratt, ed., *Canadian International Development Assistance Policies: An Appraisal* (Montreal and Kingston: McGill-Queen's University Press, 1994), p. 166.

162 CIDA, *Memorandum to DAC 1990*, pp. 32, 35. Four senior officers interviewed by the author after their return from decentralized posts made similarly positive comments.

163 SCEAIT, *Minutes of Proceedings and Evidence*, April 12, 1988, session 71, p. 6.

164 CIDA and CEA, *Partners in Development: CEA-CIDA Annual Consultations, May 11-12, 1988* (1988).

165 CCIC, "Decentralization of CIDA's Aid Programme," *The Political Scene*, January 7, 1988, and CCIC, *"Mind if I Cut In?": The Report of the CCIC Task Force on CIDA-NGO Relationships* (Ottawa: CCIC, 1988), pp. 13-14; see also pp. 48-49.

166 Interchurch Fund for International Development (ICFID) and Churches' Committee on International Affairs (CCIA), Canadian Council of Churches, *Diminishing Our Future—CIDA: Four Years after Winegard* (Toronto: ICFID and CCIA, 1991), pp. 45-47. The quotation is on p. 47. See Chapter 9 for further discussion of this document and its impact.

167 SCEAIT, *Minutes of Proceedings and Evidence*, June 1, 1989, session 5, p. 11. See Stewart's comments on session 5, p. 8. See also her criticisms and Axworthy's, and Landry's rebuttals, in ibid., May 2, 1989, session 1, pp. 30-34, 50-51.

168 Ibid., October 31, 1989, session 21, p. 15. Joe Clark reaffirmed his support, and the government's, in response to Christine Stewart shortly thereafter. See ibid., November 8, 1989, session 25, pp. 29-30.

169 CIDA, *Memorandum to DAC 1990*, pp. 31-32, and *Estimates 1992-93, Part III: Canadian International Development Agency*, pp. 16, 35-36. Landry continued to praise the experiment. She admitted in March 1991 that administrative expenses were "perhaps a little excessive" but claimed savings of 15 per cent in programming costs (SCEAIT, *Minutes of Proceedings and Evidence*, March 20, 1991, session 104, p. 14).

170 OECD-DAC, "Aid Review 1990-91: Report by the Secretariat and Questions on the Development Assistance Efforts and Policies of Canada," p. 12.

171 Groupe Secor, "Canadian International Development Agency, Strategic Management Review: Working Document," October 9, 1991, pp. 67/1, 41/2-42/2. The quotation is on p. 42/2.

172 See Jonathan Manthorpe, "Canada Kills Key Part of Plan to Improve Foreign Development Aid," *The Ottawa Citizen*, July 17, 1992; John Hay, "CIDA's Better Way to Help the Poor Is Being Eroded by Federal Cuts," *The Ottawa Citizen*, July 24, 1992; and John Best, "Power Struggles May Be Sprouting in CIDA," *The London Free Press*, July 31, 1992.

173 *Estimates 1993-94, Part III: Canadian International Development Agency*, pp. 15-16, 32. See also ibid., *1994-95*, p. 30; CIDA, *Memorandum to DAC 1991*, pp. 32, 35; and ibid., *1992*, pp. 34-35.

Chapter 9

1 CIDA, *Annual Report 1990-91*, p. 5.

2 Pradeep Bandyopadhyay, "Self-Reliance in a New Key: Western Dominance and Socio-Cultural Pluralism" (paper presented to the Conference of the Canadian Association for the Study of International Development, Quebec City, June 1989), pp. 6-13.

3 United Nations Development Program, *Human Development Report 1992* (New York: Oxford University Press, 1992), pp. 34-35.

4 For details, see North-South Institute, "Canada and the Guyana Support Group," *Review '89/Outlook '90* (January 1990), pp. 6-7, and David R. Black and Peter McKenna, "Canada and Structural Adjustment in the South: the Significance of the Guyana Case," *Canadian Journal of Development Studies* 16, 1 (1995): 55-78.

5 Notes for Remarks by Marcel Massé, President of CIDA, to the Standing Committee on External Affairs and International Trade, Ottawa, October 31, 1989, pp. 1-3.

6 House of Commons, Standing Committee on External Affairs and International Trade (SCEAIT), *Minutes of Proceedings and Evidence*, October 31, 1989, session 21, p. 14.

7 Ibid., session 21, pp. 10-12 (the quoted phrase is on p. 10).

8 Ibid., December 7, 1989, session 31, p. 24. See also Massé's intense exchange with NDP MP Bill Blaikie (ibid., pp. 32-34). The occasion was a panel discussion before SCEAIT involving Massé; Michel Chossudovsky, professor of economics, University of Ottawa; Marcia Burdette, director, development cooperation program of the North-South Institute; and Chris Bryant, executive director of CUSO.

9 In view of the neo-conservative agenda of the Mulroney government, it is ironic that Massé's public espousal of structural adjustment became an immediate source of tension between the president's and the minister's offices that set the tone for an uncomfortable relationship between Massé and Landry thereafter. Intrigued by Massé's eloquent defence of a controversial position before SCEAIT, Dave Todd of Southam News sought a follow-up interview. In accordance with protocol, the minister's office was asked for permission. Landry's chief of staff, Gilles Déry, responded that the minister had as yet no policy on structural adjustment, and that there would be no interview until such time as she did. Although she soon began to promote the Massé line in her speeches, three CIDA officials interviewed by the author claimed that the president was thereafter kept somewhat "muzzled" by the minister's office.

10 See, for example, Charlotte Montgomery, "Stand of CIDA Chief Alarms Even Admirers," *The Globe and Mail*, January 30, 1990.

11 Interchurch Fund for International Development (ICFID) and the Churches' Committee on International Affairs (CCIA) of the Canadian Council of Churches, *Diminishing Our Future/CIDA: Four Years after Winegard* (Toronto: ICFID and CCIA, 1991), p. 6. See especially pp. 6-7 and 17-36.

12 John Stackhouse, "Churches Condemn Canada's Aid Policy," *The Globe and Mail*, October 22, 1991.

13 From interviews and Robert Fugere, "Sharing or Diminishing Our Future? A Case Study in Policy Interaction," *Canadian Journal of Development Studies* 15, 3 (1994): 369-81. Fugere, executive director of ICFID, was one of the authors of *Diminishing Our Future*.

14 Transcript of Remarks by Marcel Massé, President of CIDA, to the annual consultation between CIDA and non-governmental organizations, Hull, October 15, 1992.

15 As aptly summarized in Alison Van Rooy, *A Partial Promise? Canadian Support to Social Development in the South* (Ottawa: North-South Institute, 1995), p. 5.

16 CIDA officials later conceded that "pillars" was an unfortunate metaphor for conveying dynamism and interrelatedness, and substituted "elements" or "dimensions."

17 CIDA, Policy Branch, "Sustainable Development Discussion Paper," July 15, 1991, pp. 6, 20.
18 Ibid., p. 2.
19 Gerald J. Schmitz, "Why Words Matter: Some Thoughts on the 'New' Development Agenda" (paper presented to the Conference of the Canadian Association for the Study of International Development, Charlottetown, June 1992), pp. 9, 11.
20 CIDA, "Sustainable Development Discussion Paper," pp. 2-6, 20, 22.
21 CIDA, Asia Branch, "CIDA Programs in Asia: An Overview" (June 1993), p. 2. For details of the distinctive approach taken by Asia Branch in the late 1980s and early 1990s, see Martin Rudner, "Canadian Development Cooperation with Asia: Strategic Objectives and Policy Goals," in Cranford Pratt, ed., *Canadian International Development Assistance Policies: An Appraisal* (Montreal and Kingston: McGill-Queen's University Press, 1994), pp. 292-312.
22 CIDA, *CIDA's Policy for Environmental Sustainability* (Hull: CIDA, 1992), p. 5.
23 See Canadian International Development Agency, "Implementation of CIDA's Policy for Environmental Sustainability: 1992-1993 Progress Report" (October 1993), p. 11, and CIDA, Environment Division, Policy Branch, "CIDA's Environment-Related Activities" (June 1995), p. 10.
24 Ibid., p. 6.
25 Some of this section draws on Nasir Islam and David R. Morrison, "Introduction: Governance, Democracy and Human Rights," *Canadian Journal of Development Studies*, Special Issue on Governance, Democracy and Human Rights (1996), pp. 5-18.
26 Charlotte Montgomery, "Human-Rights Records Ignored in Aid Decisions, Minister Says," *The Globe and Mail*, June 9, 1989.
27 See T.A. Keenleyside, "Aiding Rights: Canada and the Advancement of Human Dignity," in Cranford Pratt, ed., *Canadian International Development Assistance Policies: An Appraisal* (Montreal and Kingston: McGill-Queen's University Press, 1994), pp. 252-53. The quotation is drawn from a statement by Broadbent. See also CIDA, *Memorandum to DAC 1994*, p. 42, and Andres Perez, "The International Centre for Human Rights and Democratic Development," in Robert Miller, ed., *Aid as Peacemaker: Canadian Development Assistance and Third World Conflict* (Ottawa: Carleton University Press, 1992), pp. 145-60.
28 David Israelson, "Canada's Rights Record Flawed, Former MP Says," *The Toronto Star*, June 11, 1991, and Irwin Block, "Focus on Human Rights: Ex-Minister," *The Gazette* (Montreal), September 26, 1991.
29 Bill Schiller, "Foreign Aid May Be Linked to Democracy, Mulroney Says," *The Toronto Star*, October 14, 1991, and Ross Howard, "Mulroney Ties Aid to Human Rights," *The Globe and Mail*, October 17, 1991.
30 Peter Maser, "Canada to Promote Human Rights at Francophone Summit" and "Human Rights Dominate Talks," *The Ottawa Citizen*, November 13 and 21, 1991, and Joel Donnet, "Les droits de l'homme, au coeur du sommet de la francophonie," *La Presse* (Montreal), November 16, 1991. The meeting had earlier been relocated from Zaïre, principally because of Canada's objections to the human rights record of the Mobutu regime.
31 See, for example, "No More Blank Cheques," *The Globe and Mail*, October 16, 1991; "Tying Foreign Aid to Human Rights," *The Toronto Star*, October 22, 1991; "PM's Motives on Rights Suspect," *Star Phoenix* (Saskatoon), October 26, 1991; Carol Goar, "PM's Moral Crusade Has a Hollow Ring," *The Toronto Star*,

October 26, 1991; Gerald J. Schmitz, "Nice Talk, but Will There Be Action?" *The Globe and Mail*, October 24, 1991; and "Hanging in on Rights," *Winnipeg Free Press*, November 19, 1991.

32 See, for example, Holly Nathan, "Canada on Spot for Foreign Aid Cuts," *Times Colonist* (Victoria), September 30, 1989; Dennis Foley, "Agencies Charge Foreign-Aid Cuts Costing Lives," *The Ottawa Citizen*, October 3, 1989; Dave Todd, "Foreign-Aid Cuts Kill Thousands: Coalition," *The Gazette* (Montreal), October 3, 1989; Tim Harper, "Pain of Budget Cuts Felt Around the Globe, Groups Tell Ottawa," *The Toronto Star*, October 3, 1989; "Un appel pour l'aide extérieure," *Le Journal de Montréal*, October 3, 1989; Rosemary Godin, "Halifax Group Protests Cuts to Foreign Aid," *The Chronicle-Herald* (Halifax), October 4, 1989; "Catholic Agency to Cut Aid to Underdeveloped Nations," *The Ottawa Citizen*, November 14, 1989; John Best, "Federal Budget Cuts Hurt Poor, Diseased in the Third World," *Winnipeg Free Press*, November 24, 1989; and Anthony Johnson, "Foreign Aid Agencies Lobby to Save Budget," *Calgary Herald*, November 30. 1989. Other coverage appeared in *Le Devoir* (Montreal), *Le Droit*, *The Globe and Mail*, *Guelph Daily Mercury*, *The London Free Press*, *Kitchener-Waterloo Record*, *Star Phoenix* (Saskatoon), and *The Edmonton Journal.*

33 Margaret Dalton, "USC Needs More Funds, Volunteers," *Evening Telegraph* (St. John's), September 21, 1989; Erica Smishek, "Third World Agencies Struggle with Budget Cuts," *Star Phoenix* (Saskatoon), September 22, 1989; and Jim Durham, "Aid Agency Scrambling for Cash," *Calgary Herald*, September 25, 1989.

34 Carol Goar, "Foreign Aid: Making the Most of a Lot Less," *The Toronto Star*, September 19, 1989.

35 See, for example, Ross Howard, "Clark, Wilson Square Off Over Foreign Aid cuts," *The Globe and Mail*, January 20, 1990; Carol Goar, "Government Cutbacks: Hack First, Plan Later," *The Toronto Star*, January 23, 1990; Ross Howard, "Speculation Rising Clark Could Resign if Foreign Aid Cut," *The Globe and Mail*, January 26, 1990; Tim Harper, "Clark in Battle for Foreign Aid Hike," *The Toronto Star*, January 26, 1990; Andrew Cohen, "If Wilson Cuts Aid, Clark Should Resign," *The Financial Post*, January 29, 1990; Vic Parsons, "Foreign Aid Cuts Take Deadly Aim," *Examiner* (Peterborough), January 31, 1990; Catherine Ford, "Joe Clark Fights a War of the Heart," *Calgary Herald*, February 1, 1990; and Deborah Dowling, "Tory Ministers Learn to Beg," *The Ottawa Citizen*, February 4, 1989. Among editorials opposing cuts and supporting Clark were those in *The Toronto Star*, January 21, 1990; *The Ottawa Citizen*, January 22 and January 28, 1990; *The Gazette* (Montreal), January 29, 1990; *The Hamilton Spectator*, January 30, 1990; *Star Phoenix* (Saskatoon), January 31, 1990; and *The Toronto Star*, February 9, 1990.

36 Transcript of an Address by Marcel Massé, President of CIDA, to a joint meeting of SID, CIIA, UNAC, and CPO, Ottawa, February 13, 1990, p. 12. The quotation is from a response to a question. See also Deborah Dowling, "CIDA Chief Warns Cuts to Aid Budget Will Cost Prestige," *The Ottawa Citizen*, February 14, 1990.

37 Rosemary Speirs, "79% Still Oppose Sales Tax Despite Lower Rate, Poll Says," *The Toronto Star*, February 2, 1990.

38 CIDA, "Backgrounder on Budget and Estimates for 1990-91" (Hull, 1990). See Ross Howard, "Ottawa Gives Foreign Aid Modest Increase in Funds," *The Globe and Mail*, February 21, 1990; Chantal Hébert, "Pas d'augmentation de taxes ni d'impôts," *Le Devoir* (Montreal), February 21, 1990; Daniel Drolet, "Foreign

Aid: Clark Claims Small Victory," *The Ottawa Citizen*, February 21, 1990; John Hay, "Foreign Aid: Was Joe Clark Vindicated?" *The Ottawa Citizen*, February 25, 1990. See also Christopher Neal, "Clark Put Cabinet Job on Line for Foreign Aid and Won," and Chris Bryant, "Clark Defends Third World on Principle and Canadian Interest," *CUSO Advocate* 2, 1 (1990): 1, 3-4.

39 Quoted by Tim Harper, "Overseas Aid Manages to Dodge 'Steamroller,'" *The Toronto Star*, February 21, 1990.

40 CIDA, "Backgrounder on Budget and Estimates for 1991-92" (Hull, 1991); North-South Institute, *North-South News* (Spring 1991). See also Ross Howard, "Defence Spending Rises as Foreign Aid Is Slashed," *The Globe and Mail*, February 27, 1991; William Walker, "Ottawa Slows Aid to Poorer Nations," *The Toronto Star*, February 27, 1991; Dave Todd, "Niggardly Cuts in Foreign Aid Break Promises," *Sun* (Vancouver), March 2, 1991.

41 See Tim Harper, "Agencies Attack Budget Cuts to Foreign Aid," *The Toronto Star*, April 5, 1991; Paul Mooney, "Development Agencies Fume as Funds for Third World Cut," *Winnipeg Free Press*, April 5, 1991; and "Editorial: Aid Cuts," *Central America Update* 12, 5 (March/April 1991): 1.

42 CIDA, President's Office, President's Committee Retreat, March 28, 1991, and North-South Institute, *North-South News* (Spring 1991).

43 Phillip Rawkins, "An Institutional Analysis of CIDA," in Cranford Pratt, ed., *Canadian International Development Assistance Policies: An Appraisal* (Montreal and Kingston: McGill-Queen's University Press, 1994), p. 174.

44 Hugh Winsor, "PCs Reject Aid Cut," *The Globe and Mail*, August 8, 1991.

45 Bill Stadel, "Reformers Urge Cut in Funds for Foreign Aid," *The Edmonton Journal*, October 17, 1991.

46 Tim Harper, "Aid Organizations Fear Budget Cuts," *The Toronto Star*, February 5, 1992.

47 *Estimates 1992-93, Part III: Canadian International Development Agency*, p. 7, and Andrew Clark, "Paradox: ODA Cash Up but ODA Levels Fall," *Review* (Ottawa: North-South Institute) (Summer 1992), pp. 1-2.

48 Department of Finance, *Budget Papers* (Ottawa: Department of Finance, 1992), pp. 127-32. IDRC was also scheduled to lose some of its independence by bringing its administrative regime into conformity with that of the rest of the public service, but enabling legislation was never enacted.

49 Lindores went head-to-head on this issue with the Public Accounts Committee, especially over the Auditor General's criticism of a failed coal-washing project in Pakistan. Since the project had been funded through a line of credit to the Pakistani government rather than through a bilateral agreement, Lindores argued that CIDA should not have been held responsible for the outcome. Having failed to convince the parliamentarians, he was determined to find new ways of defining the Agency's accountability. See House of Commons, Standing Committee on Public Accounts, *Minutes of Proceedings and Evidence*, September 26, 1991, session 4; ibid., October 24, 1991, session 8; and ibid., November 21, 1991, session 11.

50 Interviews. Landry told the Public Accounts Committee that she initiated the review for three reasons: to optimize developmental benefits for the populations of host countries, to keep pace with rapid global change, and "to reconcile our limited means with the increasing need for aid in developing countries" (Committee on Public Accounts, *Minutes of Proceedings and Evidence*, February 12, 1992, session 16, p. 7). See also Landry's comments in House of Commons, Standing

Committee on External Affairs and International Trade, Subcommittee on Development and Human Rights, *Minutes of Proceedings and Evidence*, February 17, 1992, session 12, p. 23.

51 Groupe Secor, "Canadian International Development Agency, Strategic Management Review: Working Document," October 9, 1991, pp. i-ii.

52 Dave Todd, "Employees Fear Canada's Reputation Will Suffer" and "CIDA may Face Radical Changes," *The Ottawa Citizen*, May 22, 1991.

53 Dave Todd, "Minister Tries to Soothe Fears of Agency Staff," *The Ottawa Citizen*, May 24, 1991. Landry also wrote a letter decrying Todd's allegations and an editorial in *The Ottawa Citizen* that criticized her furtive "rewriting of the Canadian book on aid" ("Aid Agency's Job Is More than Writing the Cheques," May 27, 1991); see "Two from Landry," *The Ottawa Citizen*, June 3, 1991. Subsequently, in response to a letter from H.F. Heald complaining about a *Citizen* vendetta against Landry, the paper's ombudsman, noted that Landry was invited by Todd to give her side of the story but had refused an interview (William MacPherson, "Columnist's Strong Views Draw Explosive Reactions from Readers," *The Ottawa Citizen*, June 8, 1991).

54 Dave Todd and Daphne Bramham, "$700,000 Contract Went to Firm Founded by Ex-Adviser to PM," *The Ottawa Citizen*, May 24, 1991; Daphne Bramham, "PM's Aide Admitted Link to Firm in CIDA Deal," *The Gazette* (Montreal), May 25, 1991; "PM's Aide May Not Have Reported Sale of His Shares," *The Toronto Star*, May 25, 1991; and "CIDA Job Was Won with Competitive Bid," letter from Jacques B. Noel of Groupe Secor to *The Gazette* (Montreal), May 27, 1991. Quite incensed about allegations of patronage, CIDA officials claimed that Groupe Secor's submission was by far the strongest on the short list reviewed. However, questions of patronage surfaced again in parliamentary committee hearings later that year. See Committee on Public Accounts, *Minutes of Proceedings and Evidence*, September 24, 1991, session 4, pp. 33-34, 54-57.

55 Groupe Secor, "Canadian International Development Agency, Strategic Management Review: Working Document," and Groupe Secor, "Canadian International Development Agency, Development Agency, Strategic Management Review: Report," October 30, 1991. Although members of the consulting team were francophones, they produced the original documents in English.

56 Cited in CIDA, "CIDA Strategic Management Review—Discussion Paper," April 15, 1992, Foreword (emphasis in original). See also Notes for Remarks by the Honourable Monique Landry, Minister of External Relations and International Development, at a meeting to launch the consultation process on the Strategic Management Review of CIDA, November 7, 1991.

57 Cranford Pratt, "Towards a Neo-Conservative Transformation of Canadian International Development Assistance: The SECOR Report on CIDA," *International Journal* 18 (Summer 1992): 602. Pratt cited one example (from Groupe Secor, "Canadian International Development Agency, Strategic Management Review: Working Document," p. 13/4): "By strategic skills, we refer to systemic analysis skills, pragmatism and realism in utilizing diachronic frameworks, the intimate knowledge of internal factors affecting Third World countries and Canadian executing agencies, innovation and information competencies as well as the capacity to synthesize various analyses and translate them into key operational objectives." In this author's judgement, that passage represented the low point in a text that suffered more from wordiness and imprecision than jargon.

58 Ibid., pp. 8/1-13/1.
59 Ibid., pp. 57/1-63/1, 66/1-67/1, 72/1, 77/1, 84/1.
60 Ibid., pp. 88/1-89/1.
61 When the consultants made a presentation to a joint meeting of the Public Accounts Committee and SCEAIT, they were pushed for clarification. They denied that leverage meant either aid effectiveness or political clout and appeared most comfortable characterizing it as a way of assessing Canada's "market share" or "positioning" (Committee on Public Accounts, *Minutes of Proceedings and Evidence*, February 12, 1992, session 16, pp. 29-30).
62 The report itself noted: "Pushed to the extreme, the concept of maximizing leverage could lead one to the absurd conclusion that the sole objective of aid is to gain influence or leverage with recipient countries. To achieve this objective, on[e] could, for example, simply allocate one's entire aid budget to one recipient country or institution. At the other extreme, one could imagine that in the best of worlds, the ultimate degree of leverage would be attained when a donor has immense influence in a recipient country with very little disbursement" (Groupe Secor, "Canadian International Development Agency, Strategic Management Review: Working Document," p. 95/1).
63 Group Secor's comparison group also included Norway, which had a lower leverage index and a smaller average contribution per recipient (ibid., p. 100/1).
64 Leverage indices were based on representation on governing bodies for IFIs and relative contributions in the case of UN organizations (ibid., pp. 97/1-140/1).
65 Ibid., pp. 9/2, 15/2-17/2. (Except for passages in quotations, this is the author's summary.)
66 Ibid., p. 18/2.
67 Ibid., pp. 25/2-57/2.
68 Ibid., p. 70/2.
69 Ibid., pp. 78/2-80/2.
70 Ibid., pp. 74/2-76/2.
71 Ibid., pp. 83/2-84/2.
72 Groupe Secor, "Canadian International Development Agency, Development Agency, Strategic Management Review: Report," pp. 22-23 (emphasis in original).
73 Clyde Sanger, "CIDA from All Angles," *Review* (Ottawa: North-South Institute) (Winter 1992), p. 4.
74 Groupe Secor, "Canadian International Development Agency, Strategic Management Review: Working Document," p. 18/3.
75 Ibid., pp. 5/4-15/4, and Groupe Secor, "Canadian International Development Agency, Strategic Management Review: Report," p. 30-32. The report recognized, however, that the number of recipients depended largely on political factors outside CIDA's control and that the Agency's sectoral orientation was strongly influenced by Canadian stakeholders.
76 Ibid., p. 32.
77 Groupe Secor, "Canadian International Development Agency, Strategic Management Review: Working Document," pp. 19/4-21/4, 31/4-37/4.
78 The new agency would not be a government department bound by civil service restrictions and regulations.
79 Ibid., pp. 46/4-54/4.
80 Ibid., pp. 66/4-67/4. See also pp. 57/4-65/4.

81 Ibid., pp. 70/4, 80/4-81/4. See also pp. 72/4-79/4, 82/4-83/4.

82 Notes for Remarks by the Honourable Monique Landry, Minister of External Relations and International Development, at a meeting to launch the consultation process on the Strategic Management Review of CIDA, November 7, 1991, p. 4.

83 Committee on Public Accounts, *Minutes of Proceedings and Evidence*, February 12, 1992, session 9, p. 10, and Subcommittee on Human Rights and Development, *Minutes of Proceedings and Evidence*, February 17, 1992, session 12, pp. 19-20. Opposition MPs criticized the consultative process again when Landry appeared for the annual SCEAIT hearing on CIDA's Estimates (SCEAIT, *Minutes of Proceedings and Evidence*, May 6, 1992, session 34, pp. 7-10, 12-13, 17-18).

84 Committee on Public Accounts, *Minutes of Proceedings and Evidence*, February 12, 1992, session 16, pp. 23-26; Subcommittee on Development and Human Rights, *Minutes of Proceedings and Evidence*, February 12, 1992, session 11, pp. 6, 13, 25, 35-36; and ibid., February 17, 1992, session 12, p. 10. Pratt advanced the thesis that "the Secor Report is deeply informed by the neo-conservative development ideology that is now dominant within CIDA and has substantially displaced the humane internationalist orientation of the Winegard Report" ("Towards a Neo-Conservative Transformation," p. 613). However, while Massé had raised the profile of IFI orthodoxy on structural adjustment and moved the policy agenda beyond *Sharing Our Future*, the consultants were if anything insufficiently aware of development discourse. Their support for a knowledge-based reorientation of CIDA reflected the president's vision, but the main foci of the report were on reducing costs and improving management systems (especially for project delivery).

85 Committee on Public Accounts, *Minutes of Proceedings and Evidence*, February 12, 1992, session 16, p. 32. See also Subcommittee on Development and Human Rights, *Minutes of Proceedings and Evidence*, February 12, 1992, session 11, p. 9.

86 See CCIC, "Comments on the Secor Report," December 1991, p. 1. See also Sanger, "CIDA from All Angles," p. 5.

87 The quotation is from CCIC, "Comments on the Secor Report," p. 3. See also CCIC, "CCIC Response to the Secor Report on CIDA's Strategic Management Review," March 2, 1992, and the comments of Tim Brodhead, Executive Director of CCIC, in Subcommittee on Development and Human Rights, *Minutes of Proceedings and Evidence*, February 17, 1992, session 11, pp. 22-25. On the issue of responsive programs, both in the latter (p. 24) and the CCIC Response (pp. 3-4), Brodhead thought it ominous that a Secor consultant at the January 21 briefing said that the question of maintaining responsive programs was essentially a matter for political decision (rather than, by imputation, a developmental issue). Worried about implications of the Secor review for NGOs, the CCIC executive commissioned Ian Smillie in May 1991 to prepare a discussion paper on alternative forms of NGO-government relationships. Smillie's major recommendation was "to convert that part of CIDA which supports the voluntary sector into an independent arm's-length body, operating under its own Act of Parliament." Accountable to Parliament through the minister of External Relations but operating outside the civil service under its own independent board, this body would fund responsive programming through a peer-review process (Ian Smillie, *A Time to Build Up: New Forms of Cooperation between NGOs and CIDA* [Ottawa: Canadian Council for International Cooperation, 1991]; the quotation is on p. 11.) The report

prompted a lively debate, but this recommendation was not endorsed by the Council.

88 Subcommittee on Development and Human Rights, *Minutes of Proceedings and Evidence*, February 17, 1992, session 11, pp. 25-27, 38.

89 See ibid., session 11, pp. 27-33, 44-46.

90 Ibid., pp. 11-15. The quotations are on pp. 12 and 15.

91 Except where noted, the following section is based on interviews.

92 Rawkins, "An Institutional Analysis of CIDA," p. 177.

93 CIDA, "CIDA Strategic Management Review—Discussion Paper" (hereafter cited as CIDA SMR), April 15, 1992, p. 1.

94 Ibid., p. 9 (emphasis in original).

95 "A strong policy base is a prerequisite for a move to a more strategic agency. . . . Although *Sharing our Future* is now four years old, the Agency has not yet developed appropriate policies for its key policy thrusts. Clearly, it will be necessary to improve performance in this area if the Agency is to provide the necessary guidance to its employees, partners and agents, and *to defend itself against external criticism*" (CIDA SMR, p. 19; author's emphasis).

96 Ibid., pp. 14-15, 18-26, 34. Lindores also recommended a new performance assessment branch that would ultimately be folded into Corporate Management, but, by the time changes were implemented (see Chapter 10), audit and evaluation functions had already been assigned to Corporate Management. Some of the terms in his draft were subsequently altered, e.g., Management Branch became Corporate Management Branch and Program Delivery Service Units became Program Delivery Units (PDUs). For simplicity, I have used the names that were eventually adopted.

97 Lindores argued: "even should the government decide to maintain a purely responsive PPP, there is no reason why it could not be managed impartially and with greater communications support from Communications Branch. The difficulties of coordinating Development Week activities between Canadian Partnership and Communications Branch would point out significant efficiency gains" (ibid., p. 25).

98 Ibid., p. 30.

99 Ibid., pp. 16, 29.

100 Ibid., pp. 32-33.

101 Lindores addressed the "considerable confusion in the minds of CIDA staff over the sometimes conflicting objectives of the ODA program—and how to resolve those conflicts on a daily basis." National interests—"peace and security, commercial, environmental, social justice, migration and other interests of Canadians"—could be sought through the aid program and "should be taken in to account in the design of the agency's strategic thrust." However, in accordance with the ODA Charter, national interests should be pursued "only where valid developmental or humanitarian objectives are present" and "where the interests are consistent with the strategic thrust of the ODA program" (ibid., pp. 3-4).

102 Ibid., p. 35.

103 The aide mémoire was leaked during the subsequent furor over another leaked paper—a draft of International Assistance Policy Update produced by External Affairs and International Trade Canada.

104 Examples of programming themes included environment, human resource development, population, women in development, debt and structural adjustment, and "Third World private-sector initiatives." Poverty reduction was not listed.

105 Following public invitation to all potential executing agencies, a two-step process was envisioned for all thematic programs and non-thematic projects: an initial call for proposals, to be assessed on technical and managerial merits, and a second call for proposals from agencies qualified in the first round, to be assessed on the basis of technical merit and price.

106 Except where noted, this section is based on interviews with officials in EAITC and CIDA as well as non-governmental players.

107 Quoted from EAITC, draft of International Assistance Policy Update (January 1993).

108 Albeit without a timetable. "Environmental Pledge Would Cost Extra $2-Billion," *The Globe and Mail*, June 9, 1992, and John Best, "Canada Will Up the Assistance Ante, but Not too Soon," *The London Free Press*, June 12, 1992.

109 *Estimates 1993-94, Part III: Canadian International Development Agency*, p. 6, and Jeff Sallot, "Foreign Aid Takes Heavy Trim," *The Globe and Mail*, December 3, 1992.

110 An analysis by the North-South Institute suggested that the actual reduction for National Defence was 0.8 per cent, not 3.9 per cent, because 80 per cent of the cuts were absorbed by personnel support being transferred out of the defence envelope.

111 See Anne McIlroy, "Critics Slam Huge Cuts to Green Plan, Foreign Aid," *The Ottawa Citizen*, December 3, 1992; Tim Harper, "Foreign Aid Cut but Defence Systems Emerge Unscathed," *The Toronto Star*, December 3, 1992; Jeff Sallot, "A Billion for Guns, Cutbacks for the Hungry," *The Globe and Mail*, December 4, 1992; John Best, "Policy Contradictions Striking," *The London Free Press*, December 9, 1992; and a *Le Droit* editorial ("L'ACDI sur la guillotine"), December 22, 1992.

112 Clyde Sanger, "Out of Africa," *Canadian Forum* (July/August 1993), p. 20.

113 This summary is based on three versions of the leaked document made available to the author.

114 "Sustainable development, in particular, in poorest countries" was added in a later draft, presumably to soften the impression of a total abandonment of the poorest of the poor. The Policy Update summarized existing policy guidelines including the principles and priorities of the Development Charter in *Sharing Our Future* and then stated: "Since 1987 [*sic*], aid programming has evolved and adapted to global changes and foreign policy priorities, with increased emphasis on good governance, the private sector, the environment, and economic cooperation with advanced developing countries. The policy update formalizes many of these changes and furthers the process of adapting to new challenges." Much of the thinking in the Policy Update—including the notion of "sustainable development abroad as an extension of sustainable development in Canada"—came from a 1992 EAITC policy discussion paper, written by Nicolas Dimic.

115 The emphasis on flexibility especially inflamed CIDA. A later version, prepared three weeks after circulation of the first draft in CIDA and two weeks after the leak, contained all these points, but added: "Flexibility must be balanced to ensure continuity and the benefits from long-term strategic cooperation, and to avoid the 'flavour of the month' syndrome."

116 See Dave Todd, "CIDA Overhaul in the Works," *The Gazette* (Montreal), January 23, 1993; Tim Harper, "Revised Policy on Foreign Aid Said to Favor East Europe," *The Toronto Star*, January 23, 1993; Jeff Sallot, "Ottawa to Shift

Foreign-Aid focus," *The Globe and Mail*, January 25, 1993; Dave Todd, " 'Chronic Losers' to Be Written Off Under New Canadian Aid Policy," *The Ottawa Citizen*, January 26, 1993; Tim Harper, "Turning Our Back on Needy," *The Toronto Star*, February 8, 1993; CCIC, "CCIC Review of the Department of External Affairs International Assistance Update," February 8, 1993, and "Defending Canada's Aid Program," February 1993, press release and backgrounder; North-South Institute, "Time for Plain Speaking about Aid," February 15, 1993, a critique widely disseminated to parliamentarians, the media, and the development community; and Andrew Clark, "Secret Paper Steers Aid Policy Changes," *Review* (Ottawa: North-South Institute) (Spring 1993), pp. 1-2. Several columnists (including John Best, Gerry Caplan, John Hay, Jeffrey Simpson, Michael Valpy, and Christopher Young) took issue with the Policy Update and condemned the process. Among critical editorials were those appearing in *The Gazette* (Montreal) and *The Ottawa Citizen* (January 26), *The Edmonton Journal* (January 27), the *Star Phoenix* (Saskatoon) (February 2), *The Toronto Star* (February 8), *Times Colonist* (Victoria) (March 11), and *The Globe and Mail* (March 12). Commentary was generally supportive of concentration in principle, but negative about the other proposals. See also Cranford Pratt's analysis of the "Crisis of December 1992 to March 1993" in his "Humane Internationalism and Development Assistance Policies,' in Cranford Pratt, ed., *Canadian International Development Assistance Policies: An Appraisal* (Montreal and Kingston: McGill-Queen's University Press, 1994), pp. 357-63.

117 The later draft also increased the thematic programs and policy reserve to 60 per cent of geographic programming in all funding models, in effect decreasing the degree of proposed concentration but, after winding down current commitments, setting aside even more for "flexible" programming. The "even focus" model projected equal thematic shares for good governance, the environment, and economic cooperation, while the "more aggressive" one put proportionately more into economic cooperation.

118 The most elaborate proposal was put forward by the CCIC, which had been urging a review of aid policy for over a year. With the furor over the Policy Update, the project suddenly became politically salient. The Council requested and received an invitation to make a submission to the Standing Committee on External Affairs and International Trade. See SCEAIT, *Minutes of Proceedings and Evidence*, February 16, 1993, session 52, pp. 4-23. The formal presentation—"Preparing for the Twenty-first Century: Canadian International Policy from a North/South Perspective"—was printed as session 52A, pp. 1-3.

119 House of Commons, Standing Committee on Finance, Subcommittee on International Financial Institutions, *Minutes of Proceedings and Evidence*, February 2, 1993, session 8, p. 14.

120 Ibid., February 4, 1993, session 9, p. 26.

121 House of Commons, *Debates*, March 26, 1993, p. 17637.

122 See Todd, "CIDA Overhaul in the Works," and Harper, "Revised Policy on Foreign Aid Said to Favor East Europe."

123 Massé's unhappiness with the turn of events at CIDA and internal turmoil were highlighted again in press reports. See Hugh Winsor, "Civil Service Shakeup Signals Inner Troubles," *The Globe and Mail*, February 12, 1993, and Frank Howard, "Public-Service Shuffle Shows PM Plans to Stay," *The Ottawa Citizen*, February 12, 1993. Massé resigned from the public service later in 1993 and stood as a

Liberal candidate in the October general election. He won and became minister of Intergovernmental Relations in the new Chrétien cabinet. He was also given responsibility for civil service reform. The material that follows is based on interviews.

124 See Appendix A.

125 CIDA, *Annual Report 1989-90*, p. 35.

126 Bilateral aid for the top ten and twenty recipients, respectively, fell from 43.2 per cent and 61.6 per cent in 1990-91 to 42.2 per cent and 57.8 per cent in 1993-94 (see Appendix C).

127 Based on an analysis of government-to-government aid flows in 1992-93 using the methodology employed in Table 7.2. The proportions for LLDCs and other LICs increased from 35.7 per cent to 37.6 per cent and from 42.6 per cent to 44.0 per cent respectively. The increased share for the least developed was almost entirely the result of the addition of Zambia to the UN list of LLDCs.

128 OECD, Development Assistance Committee, *Development Co-operation Review Series: Canada 1994 No. 5* (Paris: Organisation for Economic Co-operation and Development, 1994), p. 48.

129 CIDA, *Memorandum to DAC 1990*, p. 22.

130 Calculations based on data in CIDA's annual reports from 1989-90 to 1992-93.

131 The account that follows is based on press reports; Keenleyside, "Aiding Rights," pp. 256-58; and "Canada and China: the Months Ahead," Statement by the Secretary of State for External Affairs, the Right Honourable Joe Clark, Ottawa, June 30, 1989.

132 See CIDA, *Annual Report 1992-93*, p. 16.

133 Keenleyside, "Aiding Rights," p. 257. See also Paul Gecelovsky and T.A. Keenleyside, "Canadian International Human Rights Policy in Practice: Tiananmen Square," *International Journal* 50, 3 (Summer 1995): 564-93; Jeremy T. Paltiel, "Negotiating Human Rights with China,' in Maxwell A. Cameron and Maureen Appel Molot, eds., *Canada Among Nations 1995: Democracy and Foreign Policy* (Ottawa: Carleton University Press, 1995), pp. 165-86; and David Gillies, *Between Principle and Practice: Human Rights in North-South Relations* (Montreal and Kingston: McGill-Queen's University Press, 1996), pp. 140-73.

134 "Canada Will Review Aid Because of Killings, McDougall Says," *The Ottawa Citizen*, November 19, 1991.

135 Interviews; Keenleyside, "Aiding Rights," p. 256; Asia Pacific Foundation of Canada, "Linking Aid to Human Rights in Indonesia: A Canadian Perspective," *Issues* 7, 1 (Winter 1993): 12 pp.; extensive reports and commentary in the press, including Dave Todd, "Canada Cuts Off $30 Million in Aid to Indonesia," *The Ottawa Citizen*, December 10, 1991, and CIDA, *Annual Report 1992-93*, p. 16. For more detailed discussions of Canada's response to human rights abuses in Indonesia, see Gillies, *Between Principle and Practice*, pp. 174-98, and Sharon Scarfe, *Complicity: Human Rights and Canadian Foreign Policy* (Montreal: Black Rose Books, 1996).

136 Steven Greenhouse, "Donor Nations Warn Moi to Introduce Reforms," *The Ottawa Citizen*, November 27, 1991, and "Kenyan Leader Alters Stand, Agrees to Multiparty System," *The Globe and Mail*, December 3, 1991.

137 For more details, see Keenleyside, "Aiding Rights," pp. 254-59.

138 Standing Committee on External Affairs and International Trade, *Securing Our Global Future: Canada's Stake in the Unfinished Business of Third World Debt*

(Ottawa: Queen's Printer, 1990), pp. 21, 25-26. Though to no avail, the committee also urged the government to reverse its rejection of Winegard's recommendations for a legislated framework and funding floor for Canadian ODA (p. 4).

139 Roy Culpeper, "Forgiving Our Debtors Isn't Enough," *The Globe and Mail*, December 14, 1990.

140 CIDA, *Annual Report 1989-90*, p. 29.

141 *Estimates 1993-94, Part III: Canadian International Development Agency*, p. 15. The other aid commitments were $26.6 million for forestry projects, $25 million for the new UN Global Environment Facility, and $50 million for drought relief in southern Africa (see Isabel Vincent and James Rusk, "Jeers Greet Bush at Summit," *The Globe and Mail*, June 13, 1992). The $25 million for the GEF merely recycled an earlier promise, while the $50 million for Africa packaged anticipated commitments that in any case did not address long-term environment/development concerns.

142 *Estimates 1994-95, Part III: Canadian International Development Agency*, p. 30. Others were signed subsequently with Peru and Costa Rica (CIDA, *Memorandum to DAC 1994*, p. 58).

143 Ibid., *1989*, pp. 25-26.

144 Little went to the francophone countries, which did not experience comparable shortages of foreign exchange because of the backing of the CFA franc by the French franc.

145 Some program aid for Bangladesh, Nepal, and the Philippines was linked to economic reform as well, but not formally to IFI-sponsored structural adjustment.

146 OECD-DAC, "Aid Review 1990/91: Report by the Secretariat and Questions on the Development Assistance Efforts and Policies of Canada" (Paris, 1990), p. 19. In its 1994 examination of CIDA, DAC noted: "Clear guidance is not evident in CIDA procedures to assure that such aid does not substitute for current commercial exports or cause distortions, although CIDA officials advise that care is taken in programme designs in this regard" (OECD-DAC, *Development Co-operation Review Series: Canada 1994 No. 5*, p. 41).

147 CIDA Policy Branch, "Economic Reform in Developing Countries: Policy Discussion Paper" (August 1994), Table 1.

148 Marcia Burdette, "Structural Adjustment and Canadian Aid Policy," in Cranford Pratt, ed., *Canadian International Development Assistance Policies: An Appraisal* (Montreal and Kingston: McGill-Queen's University Press, 1994), p. 222.

149 CIDA, *Memorandum to DAC 1993*, p. 27. See also CIDA, "Economic Reform in Developing Countries," pp. 9-19.

150 Calculated from ibid., Table 1. See also p. 22.

151 Ibid., pp. 28-29. See also OECD-DAC, *Development Co-operation Review Series: Canada 1994 No. 5*, p. 41.

152 See ibid.; CIDA, *Annual Report 1990-91*, p. 16; CIDA, *Memorandum to DAC 1992*, p. 27; *Estimates 1993-94, Part III: Canadian International Development Agency*, p. 34; and ibid., *1995-96*, p. 75.

153 Ibid., *1994-95*, p. 66.

154 CIDA, *Memorandum to DAC 1990*, p. 35. Details of the new policy were codified in CIDA, Policy Branch, "Policy Paper and Addendum on Tied Aid, Untied Aid and Partially Untied Aid, and Local-Cost Financing Definitions" (October 1990).

155 CIDA, "Economic Reform in Developing Countries," Table 5. The percentages for the overlapping categories of LLDCs and sub-Saharan African countries were 30.4 and 30.9 respectively.

156 "In 1991/92, 40 per cent of Canadian bilateral commitments were untied, a substantially lower share than the DAC average of 59 per cent reported for 1990/91" (OECD-DAC, *Development Co-operation Review Series: Canada 1994 No. 5*, p. 43). Data for 1992 show Canada closer to the DAC average (see OECD-DAC, *Development Co-operation: Efforts and Policies of the Members of the Development Assistance Committee 1994*, p. F4). As noted earlier, DAC's concept of "bilateral" subsumes all country-to-country programming, hence the difference between 40 per cent and the range of 24.9 to 30.9 per cent reported above for strictly bilateral disbursements.

157 The figure for 1986-87 (the first year that sectoral distribution was reported in this way) is in CIDA, *Annual Report 1986-87*, p. 142. Table 11.2 uses 1988-89 as the base year in order to make comparisons over the first five years of *Sharing Our Future*.

158 Program aid increased from 15.5 per cent to 17.8 of bilateral spending between 1988-89 and 1992-93.

159 See *Estimates 1993-94, Part III: Canadian International Development Agency*, p. 58.

160 Child immunization (supported through bilateral and multilateral channels) and an initiative on AIDS control were the principal new programming thrusts in the health sphere (see CIDA, *Memorandum to DAC 1990*, pp. 37-39, and *Estimates 1992-93, Part III: Canadian International Development Agency*, pp. 30-31).

161 See Karen E. Mundy, "Human Resources Development Assistance in Canada's Overseas Development Assistance Program: A Critical Analysis," *Canadian Journal of Development Studies* 13, 3 (1992): 398-402, and Phillip Rawkins, *Human Resource Development in the Aid Process: A Study in Organizational Learning and Change* (Ottawa: North-South Institute, 1993), pp. 26-28. The following paragraphs draw on these sources as well as interviews and documents.

162 Interview. The six units dealt with social sciences, education, health, population, technical cooperation, and WID.

163 CIDA, "Education, Training and Human Resource Development: A CIDA Sector Strategy Paper" (October 1991), p. 2.

164 Ibid. While commending the paper for emphasizing capacity-building, Mundy was critical of its vagueness: it "does not answer the question of how the balance between general capacity building, institutional development and project related training will be determined. It does not suggest what percentage of HRD sector aid should be spent on increasing the capacity of public sector institutions, what on private sector institutions; . . . or most importantly, what percentage of HRD aid should be tied to Canadian expertise and Canadian training or education" (Mundy, "Human Resources Development Assistance," p. 404).

165 It was redrafted as "Sustainable HRD: A Background Paper" and referred to country programmers for general guidance (Rawkins, *Human Resource Development in the Aid Process*, p. 27). In a public document, the Agency subsequently described HRD activities in a way that gave little quarter to poverty alleviation (apart from a vague reference to community development and participation). It included "encouragement of Canadian firms and institutions to develop viable

partnerships with their counterparts in developing countries" (*Estimates 1992-93, Part III: Canadian International Development Agency*, p. 33).

166 Van Rooy, *A Partial Promise? Canadian Support to Social Development in the South*, p. 37.

167 Data and calculations from CIDA, *Annual Report 1991-92*, p. 56, and ibid., *1992-93*, p. 56.

168 World Bank, *World Development Report 1990* (New York: Oxford University Press, 1990), pp. 1-6, 56-89.

169 CIDA, Area Coordination Group, "Working Paper on Poverty Alleviation for the 4As" (February 1990), p. 2.

170 See ibid., especially chapters 5 to 7.

171 CIDA, Environmental Policy and Assessment Division, "CIDA's Friendly Guide to Agenda 21" (November 1993), p. 8 (cited in CCIC, *Fighting Poverty First: The Development Challenge* [Ottawa: CCIC, 1994], p. 12, with emphasis added by CCIC).

172 CIDA, "Assessment of CIDA's Poverty Alleviation Efforts" (September 1993).

173 In a different way of conceptualizing the post-1988 effort, Van Rooy noted that only about a third of poverty alleviation projects "were actually targeted at the poor (the micro level), and the remainder were projects which worked at the meso level doing 'capacity-building' work" (Van Rooy, *A Partial Promise? Canadian Support to Social Development in the South*, p. 16).

174 CIDA, "Assessment of CIDA's Poverty Alleviation Efforts," pp. 2-5. See also Tables 1 and 2. See as well CIDA, Policy Branch, "Poverty Reduction: Policy Discussion Paper, Part II—Detailed Findings," August 1, 1994, pp. 28-35.

175 CIDA, *Women in Development: A Policy Statement* (Hull: CIDA, 1992). For a discussion of gender and development research and its impact on CIDA, see Jane Parpart, "Who Is the 'Other'?: A Postmodern Feminist Critique of Women and Development Theory and Practice," *Development and Change* 24 (1993): 450-51 and 458, n. 11; Rajani E. Alexander, "Evaluating Experiences: CIDA's Women in Development Policy, 1984-94," *Canadian Journal of Development Studies*, Special Issue on Evaluating Experiences: Doing Development with Women (1995), pp. 79-87; and Joanna Kerr, "Gender Equity: The First Path," in Rowena Beamish and Clyde Sanger, eds., *Canadian Development Report 1996-97: Fairness in a Shifting World* (Ottawa: North-South Institute, 1996), pp. 50-56. See also the critique of WID in Betty Plewes and Ricky Stuart, "Women and Development Revisited: The Case for a Gender and Development Approach," in Jamie Swift and Brian Tomlinson, eds., *Conflicts of Interest* (Toronto: Between the Lines, 1991), pp. 107-32.

176 CIDA, "Gender as a Cross-Cutting Theme in Development Assistance: An Evaluation of CIDA's WID Policy and Activities, 1984-1992, Executive Summary," July 3, 1993, p. 3.

177 Ibid., pp. 8-9.

178 See Minister for External Relations and International Development, "$20 Million Fund to Boost Development," Press Release, March 18, 1991; CIDA, "Invitation Call for Proposals on Private Sector Development Initiatives Fund" (Hull, 1991); and CIDA, *Memorandum to DAC 1991*, p. 51.

179 For details, see CIDA, "CIDA Programs in Asia: Thailand" (June 1993), p. 17; CIDA, "CIDA Programs in Asia: Malaysia" (June 1993), p. 8; and CIDA, "CIDA Programs in Asia: Southeast Asia" (January 1993), p. 6. See also CIDA, Develop-

ment Economics Policy Division, "Private Sector Development in Developing Countries: Policy Discussion Paper" (August 1994).

180 If one adds EDC *crédit mixte* funds to national initiatives and the total of the two envelopes, the percentages rise to 51.8 and 47.0 for 1988-89 and 1992-93, respectively. However, keeping EDC funds in the totals, but deducting from these totals imputed costs (for students in both years and interest in 1992-93), the respective percentages fall from 50.8 to 45.0, which are more appropriate as measures of financial effort (calculations based on data in CIDA, *Annual Report 1990-91*, p. S6-S7, and ibid., *1992-93*, pp. 6-7).

181 Calculated from data in Appendix A.

182 See David R. Protheroe, "Canada's Multilateral Aid and Diplomacy," in Cranford Pratt, ed., *Canadian International Development Assistance Policies: An Appraisal* (Montreal and Kingston: McGill-Queen's University Press, 1994), pp. 35-42. The reduced shares did not necessarily lower the dollar commitment, which for IDA-10 at 4.00 per cent was about the same as for IDA-9 at 4.75 per cent.

183 Contributions to the World Food Program increased from $186.7 million in 1988-89 ($169.5 million in 1989-90) to $214.2 million in 1992-93 (see CIDA, *Annual Report 1990-91*, p. S43, and ibid. *1992-93*, p. 41). As noted above, total food aid declined during this period—i.e., the increase in multilateral food aid was offset by a steeper decline in bilateral food aid.

184 The Global Environment Facility emerged from negotiations leading up to the Earth Summit. Canada made an initial commitment of $38.3 million—$23.3 million from the Green Plan (including $13.3 million for the Montreal Protocol Fund on ozone depletion) and $15 million from CIDA. CIDA manages Canadian participation in the GEF (*Estimates 1992-93, Part III: Canadian International Development Agency*, pp. 31-32).

185 Besides confirming continued support for the Universal Child Immunization Program of the United Nations, the major new commitment—$5 million for projects aimed at eliminating micronutrient (iodine and Vitamin A) deficiencies among children—might have been higher if Madame Landry had not been reminded at the last moment of the $5 million limit on what she could approve without having to go through a lengthy Treasury Board process (interview).

186 See David R. Protheroe, *Canada and Multilateral Aid: Working Paper* (Ottawa, North-South Institute, 1991), pp. 71, 99; Roy Culpeper, *Canada and the Global Governors* (Ottawa: North-South Institute, 1994), pp. 11-12; CIDA, *Annual Report 1989-90*, p. 45; and CIDA, *Memorandum to DAC 1993*, p. 13. Multilateral Branch reviewed its own mission and objectives in 1991, and defined "three strategic entry points" for achieving them—advocacy, monitoring, and funding (see CIDA, *Memorandum to DAC 1991*, pp. 15-16).

187 See CIDA, *Memorandum to DAC 1991*, pp. 19-21; ibid., *1993*, p. 13; OECD-DAC, *Development Co-operation Review Series: Canada 1994 No. 5*, pp. 36-37. CIDA's IFI review was prompted by a proposal initiated by the North-South Institute in 1989 to undertake an in-depth study of the multilateral development banks. CIDA funding was augmented by support from the banks themselves and from Sweden, Norway, and the Netherlands. See Culpeper, *Canada and the Global Governors*, Preface. For an overview of the project's findings, see Roy Culpeper, *Titans or Behemoths* (Ottawa: North-South Institute, 1997). The Institute published as well separate studies of each of the four regional development banks.

188 *Report of the Auditor General of Canada to the House of Commons, Fiscal Year Ended March 31, 1992* (Hull: Minister of Supply and Services, 1992), pp. 273-94.

189 Calculated from data in Appendix A. The totals include provincial government contributions to NGOs and NGIs, which were $12.9 million in 1988-89 and $35.2 million in 1992-93. CIDA's Special Program funding for Canadian NGOs and NGIs (deducting provincial contributions and International NGO Program expenditures of $24.8 million in 1988-89 and $37.1 million in 1992-93) thus amounted to $267.6 million in 1988-89 and $265.4 million in 1992-93 (totals that include $24 million and $28 million in food aid channelled through NGOs). As a percentage of ODA, Special Program funding of the domestic voluntary sector declined slightly from 9.1 to 9.0 per cent.

190 Interviews, and CIDA, "Should CIDA Allow Open Competition Between the Private and Non-Profit Sectors?" (1995), Annex A. Non-profit organizations secured a majority of service contracts once before—$250 million out of $480 million (52 per cent) in 1987-88.

191 See Tim Brodhead and Cranford Pratt, "Paying the Piper," in Cranford Pratt, ed., *Canadian International Development Assistance Policies: An Appraisal* (Montreal and Kingston: McGill-Queen's University Press, 1994), p. 100.

192 See ibid., pp. 97-98; *Estimates 1993-94, Part III: Canadian International Development Agency*, p. 48; and Secoma Ltd./Edpra Consulting Inc., "Evaluation of CIDA's Non-Governmental Organization Program" (February 1992), p. 22. One of the decentralized funds—Camrose International Institute—had been operating since 1984 and provided a model for the other three.

193 Brodhead and Pratt, "Paying the Piper," p. 98.

194 The cost of the bailout operation was about $1 million, plus a $1.8 million loan. See Hugh Winsor, "World University Service Dismisses Staff, Closes Doors," *The Globe and Mail*, December 4, 1990; Daniel Drolet, "Respected Foreign-Aid Agency in Receivership," *The Ottawa Citizen*, December 5, 1990; Minister for External Relations and International Development, "WUSC Receiver and CIDA Agree on Plan for Project Continuation Monique Landry Announces," Press Release, December 7, 1990; James Deacon and E. Kaye Fulton, "Costly Mistakes: A Bankrupt Agency Collapses," *Macleans*, December 17, 1990; Louise Crosby, "Reviving Foreign Aid Group to Cost CIDA Extra $1M," *The Ottawa Citizen*, May 16, 1991; Louise Crosby, "$3M Federal Bailout Rescues WUSC," *The Ottawa Citizen*, June 5, 1991; and Louise Crosby, "After the Fall, WUSC Almost Back Together Again," *The Ottawa Citizen*, September 20, 1991. There were also several editorials and letters urging that WUSC be saved.

195 Michèle Ouimet, "Oxfam n'a plus d'argent," *La Presse* (Montreal), March 23, 1992; Michèle Ouimet, "Un million de dollars disparus en cinq ans chez Oxfam," *La Presse* (Montreal), May 22, 1992; Michelle Lalonde, "Oxfam Quebec tries to rebuild," *The Gazette* (Montreal), May 23, 1992; Michèle Ouimet, "Oxfam-Quebec vend ses Fortin, ses Krieghoff, ses Riopelle," *La Presse* (Montreal), July 10, 1992; and Michelle Lalonde, "Oxfam Québec Rebounds after Spending Scandal," *The Gazette* (Montreal), September 25, 1992. CIDA restored funding to Oxfam-Québec in 1994 (Richard Mackie, "Federal Government Buoys Oxfam-Québec," *The Globe and Mail*, May 6, 1994).

196 *Estimates 1993-94, Part III: Canadian International Development Agency*, p. 34.

197 Secoma Ltd./Edpra Consulting Inc., "Evaluation of CIDA's Non-Governmental Organization Program," esp. pp. 92-100. The quotations are from pp. 99-100.
198 Smillie, *A Time to Build Up*, pp. 16-17. As noted earlier, his major recommendation—a new public arm's-length body—was not endorsed by the CCIC.
199 Secoma Ltd./Edpra Consulting Inc., "Evaluation of CIDA's Non-Governmental Organization Program," p. 100.
200 Smillie, *A Time to Build Up*, p. 47.
201 Association of Universities and Colleges of Canada, "Issues in Canada's Official Development Assistance Policies and Programs: A Submission to the Standing Committee on External Affairs and International Trade" (December 1986), p. 43.
202 House of Commons Standing Committee on External Affairs and International Trade, *For Whose Benefit? Report of the Standing Committee on External Affairs and International Trade on Canada's Official Development Assistance Policies and Programs* (Ottawa: Queen's Printer, 1987), pp. 113-14.
203 See CIDA, *Sharing Our Future* (Hull: Minister of Supply and Services, 1987), pp. 70-71.
204 For details, see CIDA, *Annual Report 1988-89*, p. 49; *Estimates 1990-91, Part III: Canadian International Development Agency*, pp. 30-31; ibid., *1991-92*, p. 29; and "CIDA Funds New Centres," *University Affairs* (January 1991), p. 9.
205 Based on interviews; P. Lacoste and B.C. Matthews, "Administration of International Development Contracts: A Report to the AUCC Board of Directors," September 1, 1989; and AUCC, "Implementation of the Lacoste-Matthews Report," June 1, 1990.
206 Goss Gilroy & Associates Ltd., "Evaluation of the Educational Institutions Program, Vol. 1: The Main Report" (Hull, 1992). The quoted phrase is on p. 39.
207 A. Headlam, "Development of a New Design for University Involvement in CIDA's Educational Institutions Program (EIP), Interim Report to AUCC," September 9, 1992.
208 See CIDA, *University Partnerships in Cooperation and Development* (Hull: CIDA, 1993).
209 Calculated from data in Appendix A.
210 CIDA, *Annual Report 1989-90*, p. 58, and *Estimates 1991-92, Part III: Canadian International Development Agency*, p. 29.
211 Consulting and Audit Canada, "Evaluation Report: Industrial Cooperation Program—CIDA" (December 1992), pp. 68-71.
212 See ibid., Appendix 4.1. The four were China, India, Indonesia, and the Philippines. Senegal was the other low-income country. China and India were the largest recipients. The middle-income countries were (in descending order by level of commitment) Cameroon, Thailand, Morocco, Malaysia, Turkey, and Tunisia.
213 Ibid., pp. xx-xxii.
214 Manifest Communications, "An Outreach Strategy for CIDA," December 22, 1988, p. 6.
215 Ibid., p. 22. See also a summary of the minister's responses in CIDA, "A Public Outreach Strategy for CIDA" (Hull, 1989).
216 CIDA and the Canadian Exporters' Association earlier set up annual awards of excellence for private-sector contributions to international development.
217 See National Advisory Committee on Development Education, *We Journey Together: Preliminary Report to the Minister of External Relations and International Development* (Hull: CIDA, 1990); National Advisory Committee on Devel-

opment Education, *Towards a Global Future: Annual Report to the Minister of External Relations and International Development* (Hull: CIDA, 1990); National Advisory Committee on Development Education, *Special Report on International Development Week* (Hull: CIDA, 1991); and National Advisory Committee on Development Education, *The Impact of Sustainable Development on Development Education: Annual Report to the Minister of External Relations and International Development* (Hull: CIDA, 1991). The minister's responses were circulated with the reports.

218 Shortly after the surprise announcement of the Committee's abolition, Roche gave a correct but frosty report to the Standing Committee on External Affairs and International Trade, *Minutes of Proceedings and Evidence*, March 24, 1992, session 28, pp. 4-7.

219 CCIC, "Report Card on the Government of Canada's Foreign Aid Program" (Ottawa, 1991).

Chapter 10

1 CIDA, *Statistical Report on Official Development Assistance, Fiscal Year 1994/95* (Hull: CIDA, 1996), p. 7, and *Estimates 1997-98, Part III: Canadian International Development Agency*, p. 76. For comparability with 1992-93, the projection forecast for 1997-98 has been adjusted to delete imputed costs for refugees during their first year in Canada ($153 million) and one-time (non-cash) debt relief ($108 million). Canada included refugee resettlement costs in reported ODA for the first time in 1993-94 following a 1991 DAC decision to allow them. See OECD-DAC, *Development Co-operation: Efforts and Policies of the Members of the Development Assistance Committee 1994*, p. 118.

2 See Appendix A and Brian Tomlinson and CCIC Policy Team, "Development Assistance in the 1998 Federal Budget and CIDA's 1998/99 Expenditure Plan Estimates (Part III)" (Ottawa: CCIC, 1998), pp. 3-4.

3 Auditor General, *Report of the Auditor General of Canada to the House of Commons 1993* (Hull: Minister of Supply and Services, 1993), p. 311.

4 Special Joint Committee of the Senate and the House of Commons Reviewing Canadian Foreign Policy, *Canada's Foreign Policy: Principles and Priorities for the Future* (Ottawa: Parliamentary Publications Directorate, 1994), p. 48.

5 Government of Canada, *Government Response to the Recommendations of the Special Parliamentary Committee Reviewing Canadian Foreign Policy* (Ottawa: Department of Foreign Affairs and International Trade, 1995), p. 58.

6 Government of Canada, *Canada in the World* (Ottawa: Department of Foreign Affairs and International Trade, 1995), p. 40.

7 Hugh Winsor, "Civil Service Shakeup Signals Inner Troubles," *The Globe and Mail*, February 12, 1993.

8 For details, see *Estimates 1993-94, Part III: Canadian International Development Agency, passim*, especially pp. 7-19 and 82. The section on cuts in bilateral programming in Africa is based on confidential interviews and documents.

9 Andrew Clark, "Secret Paper Steers Aid Policy Changes," *Review* (Ottawa: North-South Institute) (Spring 1993), p. 2.

10 Multilateral aid to international financial institutions has always been recorded as ODA when commitments are made, rather than when notes are cashed by recipient institutions. In contrast, actual disbursements have been the basis for counting

bilateral and other forms of country-to-country and multilateral aid. Until a change was made in 1998, the official calculation of ODA reflected commitments rather than actual fiscal-year encashments of notes, while the level of encashments rather than commitments determined how much cash was available for the rest of the ODA budget. In the early 1990s, Conservative and Liberal governments kept switching gears, deferring commitments and encashments in some years and accelerating them in others. Although these changes had a major impact on ODA cash, and therefore budget decisions, they were often motivated by deficit "optics." In 1993-94, the Tories wanted to embellish their deficit-fighting record, which reduced multilateral encashments helped achieve. The following year, Liberal Finance Minister Paul Martin was happy to see encashments accelerated as one means of blaming the Tories for fiscal irresponsibility. Erratic patterns of encashment continued to play havoc with ODA cash levels until a decision was taken in the 1998-99 *Estimates* to move to an accrual accounting approach, which considers the full value of the notes to have been expended in the fiscal year in which they are issued rather than when the actual cash is drawn by recipient institutions. See *Estimates 1998-99, Part III: Canadian International Development Agency*, p. 54.

11 That is, the consultative group associated with the Colombo Plan. Others included UNIDO and the Common Fund (OECD-DAC, *Development Cooperation Review Series: Canada 1994 No. 5* [Paris: Organisation for Economic Co-operation and Development, 1994], p. 35).

12 The minor recipients downgraded or cut were Afghanistan, Bhutan, Cambodia, Laos, Maldives, and Burma (Myanmar). However, Cambodia remained on the list of countries of concentration published in the *Estimates* for 1994-95 and 1995-96. Human rights abuses had already led to a suspension of bilateral aid to Burma in 1989.

13 CIDA, Africa and Middle East Branch, "Africa 21: A Vision of Africa in the 21st Century" (October 1991).

14 Widely circulated in 1991, "Africa 21" was reviewed by Monique Landry in a speech to African diplomats in April 1992 (see Notes for an Address by the Honourable Monique Landry, Minister for External Relations and International Development, to Canadian Ambassadors and High Commissioners to Africa, Ottawa, April 29, 1992). There was, however, no suggestion that the policy might have implications for budget decisions other than a steering effect upon future programming.

15 Having decided to justify cuts on the basis of potential for regional cooperation, CIDA was prepared to be as tough with Cameroon as Tanzania, but EAITC insisted on special treatment for Cameroon. There were other inconsistencies in applying the regional rationale: for example, programming in newly independent Namibia in southern Africa was cut back. For details on year-over-year budget shifts in Africa and the Middle East, see Appendix "EXTE-3": Africa and Middle East Branch Reductions, tabled when Vézina appeared before Standing Committee on External Affairs and International Trade, *Minutes of Proceedings and Evidence*, April 21, 1993, session 61A, pp. 1-7. See also CIDA, Africa and Middle East Branch, "East and Central Africa: Regional Profile" (June 1993), and Louise Crosby, "Canada Backs Away from Third World," *The Ottawa Citizen*, April 24, 1993.

16 Based on interviews and Bhupinder Liddar, "Out of Africa Come the Rifts," *Ottawa Sun*, March 24, 1993; Bhupinder Liddar, "Ties that Bind Us to Europe," *Ottawa Sun*, March 31, 1993; and Dave Todd, "Official 'Donor Fatigue' Cuts Off Africa's Poorest," *The Toronto Star*, April 15, 1993.

17 See Todd, "Official 'Donor Fatigue,'" and "Tory MP Condemns More Cutting Aid to Third World," *The Ottawa Citizen*, March 7, 1993. MacDonald was particularly outspoken in statements to the media, which included an extensive interview aired on CBC Radio's *The House*. The issue was raised in the House of Commons by several MPs, including MacDonald (see House of Commons, *Debates*, April 2, 1993, p. 18029; ibid., April 20, 1993, pp. 18180-81; ibid., April 22, 1993, p. 18320; and ibid., June 4, 1993, pp. 20374-75). See as well David MacDonald, "Canada's Trade-Driven Foreign Aid Budget," *Canadian Foreign Policy* 1, 2 (Spring 1993): 99-102.

18 Standing Committee on External Affairs and International Trade, Subcommittee on Development and Human Rights, *Minutes of Proceedings and Evidence*, March 31, 1993, session 37, pp. 20, 25.

19 Ibid., April 1, 1993, session 38, pp. 4-26.

20 See Standing Committee on External Affairs and International Trade, *Minutes of Proceedings and Evidence*, April 21, 1993, session 61, pp. 4-29. Axworthy's comments are on p. 20.

21 "Foreign Aid Cutbacks," *The Ottawa Citizen*, March 3, 1993; "Don't Cut Foreign Aid," *Calgary Herald*, March 4, 1993; "Rethinking Foreign Aid," *The Edmonton Journal*, March 8, 1993; and "Ottawa Spurns Poorest of the Poor," *Kitchener-Waterloo Record*, March 29, 1993. See also Clyde Sanger, "Tanzania Dealt Unkindest CIDA Cut of All," *The Ottawa Citizen*, March 12, 1993.

22 Notes for Remarks to the Agency Forum by Jocelyne Bourgon, President of CIDA, Hull, April 7, 1993.

23 Bourgon announced that the Agency would not proceed with thematic programming or open proposals because both required cabinet-level action. Also set aside were recommendations affecting relations with Canadian partners—integration of most responsive-type programming into geographic branches, merger of Canadian Partnership and Multilateral branches, and transfer of the Public Participation Program to Communications Branch.

24 Finance/Corporate Information was brought into Corporate Management rather than merging it with Personnel and Administration. The new branch also incorporated Audit and Evaluation, the Consultant Selection Secretariat, the Consultant and Industrial Relations Division, and the Cooperant Registry.

25 Notes for Remarks to the Agency Forum by Jocelyne Bourgon, President of CIDA, Hull, April 7, 1993 (emphasis in original).

26 Notes for Remarks to the Agency Forum concerning the 1993-94 Federal Budget by Jocelyne Bourgon, President of CIDA, Hull, May 6, 1993. Bourgon announced one further structural change—rather than appointing a senior vice-president, she named a vice-president Corporate Affairs as the president's alter ego, but at the same level as the other vice-presidents. In the light of experience, budget pressures, and other organizational changes—especially the creation of Corporate Management Branch—this position was dropped in 1995.

27 After the Liberal election victory later that year, Bourgon went on to become the first woman to hold the position of clerk of the Privy Council. For Labelle, the shift from Transport Canada—then about to be embroiled in partisan political conflict during the election campaign over plans to privatize Pearson International Airport in Toronto—was portrayed in the press as a demotion. See Greg Weston, "Shortliffe Could Well Be Reorganization Victim," *The Ottawa Citizen*, July 19, 1993.

28 *Canadian Who's Who* (Toronto: University of Toronto Press, 1994), p. 628.
29 Speaking Notes for Huguette Labelle, President of CIDA, to the Agency Forum, Hull, September 9, 1993.
30 Ibid., p. 9.
31 Ibid., p. 5 (emphasis in original).
32 They focused on economic development, human rights/democracy/good governance, human development, critiques of aid, *Sharing Our Future*, poverty alleviation, aid effectiveness, budgets shares, Canadian prosperity, and definitions of international assistance. The paper on Canadian prosperity argued that CIDA could best serve that objective by promoting long-term sustainable development in recipient countries (see CIDA, "Aid and Canadian Prosperity," September 23, 1993).
33 Instead of secretary of state for External Affairs, a title that reflected an earlier era when Canada was still emerging from a colonial relationship with Britain.
34 Based largely on interviews.
35 Stewart had played a key role in defining Liberal Party policy on international development, and was much more interested in development issues than Ouellet. Insiders reported that she was frustrated about her relatively marginal role in matters related to ODA policy and CIDA's management.
36 Hugh Winsor, "Ouellet Illustrates 'Traditional' Style," *The Globe and Mail*, April 8, 1995. Winsor's report concerned a CIDA contract of $90,000 awarded to Jacques Saada, a former president of the Liberal Party in Quebec and an unsuccessful candidate in the 1993 election. "For this sum, strategically chosen to come just under the threshold for contracts that must be put out for competition," Saada was asked to create a media visibility plan to promote CIDA private-sector funding for the Maghreb. Sceptical about the value of Saada's subsequent work, Winsor commented: "Although Mr. Saada's contract is small change and relatively harmless in relation to CIDA's overall expenditure, it illustrates again how CIDA has been used as a siphon to reward friends of the government of the day by both the Liberals and the Conservatives." See also "Le Bloc accuse Ouellet de patronage," *Le Devoir* (Montreal), April 6, 1995; "A Liberal Education," *The Gazette* (Montreal), April 7, 1995; and "Ouellet's Friend Defends Contract," *The Globe and Mail*, April 7, 1995.
37 Auditor General, *Report of the Auditor General of Canada to the House of Commons 1993*, pp. 311-14.
38 Ibid., p. 316.
39 Ibid., p. 317.
40 Ibid., pp. 317-18, 322.
41 Ibid., pp. 314-21.
42 Hugh Winsor, "External Pressures Take Toll on CIDA," *The Globe and Mail*, January 21, 1994. The Auditor General's report gave rise to extensive press coverage and editorial comment, which tended to focus on the conflict of objectives. See, for example, Allan Thompson, "Aid Agency Told It Must Concentrate on Poverty," *The Toronto Star*, January 20, 1994; Marie-Claude Lortie, "Développement international: les Canadiens n'en ont pas par leur argent," *La Presse* (Montreal), January 20, 1994; Dave Todd, "CIDA Policies Might Be Harming Foreign-Aid Efforts," *The Gazette* (Montreal), January 20, 1994; "For Whose Benefit?," *The Gazette* (Montreal), January 23, 1994; and "In Aid of Foreign Aid," *The Toronto Star*, January 24, 1994.

43 Auditor General, *Report of the Auditor General of Canada to the House of Commons 1993*, p. 330.

44 CIDA, *Memorandum to DAC 1993*, p. 32.

45 *Estimates 1995-96, Part III: Canadian International Development Agency*, p. 21.

46 See CIDA, "Reflections on Organizational Renewal in CIDA," a report by Martyn R. Hulme, HPH Consulting Services, August 29, 1995, pp. 3-4, and Remarks of Huguette Labelle, President of CIDA, to Standing Committee on Foreign Affairs and International Trade, *Minutes of Proceedings and Evidence*, March 10, 1994, session 3, pp. 7, 11-12. On the question of external consultants versus internal task forces, however, the work done by Secor—for all of its flaws—could only have been accomplished by outsiders operating at arm's length.

47 See CIDA, "CIDA's Policy on Consultation with Canadian (Civil Society) Stakeholders," September 22, 1993. Developed through a consultative process after the conflict over the 1992 leaked Policy Update document, it was a model of good intentions.

48 House of Commons, Standing Committee on Public Accounts, *Minutes of Proceedings and Evidence*, April 13, 1994, session 5, p. 24.

49 See the comments of Denis Desautels, the Auditor General, in House of Commons, Standing Committee on Public Accounts, *Minutes of Proceedings and Evidence*, April 4, 1994, session 8, pp. 28, 36.

50 "Axworthy and Stewart Object to CIDA's Major Restructuring without Public Input and Call on McDougall and Vézina to Appear before SCEAIT," Press Release from Axworthy's Office, January 20, 1993.

51 Liberal Party of Canada, *Creating Opportunity: The Liberal Plan for Canada* (Ottawa, 1993), p. 108. See also André Ouellet, "The Commitments of a Liberal Foreign Policy Agenda," *Canadian Foreign Policy* 1, 3 (Fall 1993): 1-6.

52 Liberal Party of Canada, *Creating Opportunity*, p. 109.

53 In an attempt to stimulate awareness and debate about Canada's relations with developing countries, the North-South Institute—in cooperation with NGOs, church groups, academics, labour and business representatives—sponsored public forums in seven Canadian cities during the election campaign. Not surprisingly, participants were atypically sympathetic to continuing Canadian generosity towards the South at a time when general support for foreign aid was declining. When polled, 83 per cent of those in attendance believed that government should exempt the aid program from further cuts and focus on the alleviation of poverty. A mere 7 per cent favoured further cuts, with a priority on deficit reduction, while 10 per cent supported redirecting the majority of ODA to develop export opportunities. See "The North-South Forums," *Review* (Ottawa, North-South Institute) (Winter 1994), pp. 2-3.

54 Office of the Leader of the Opposition, "Liberal Foreign Policy Handbook" (Ottawa, 1993) (no pagination). It was prepared by the Liberal caucus committee on External Affairs and National Defence. The quotation that follows is from a covering letter signed by Lloyd Axworthy as chair and Christine Stewart as vice-chair; other details in this paragraph (except for the Red Book quotation) are drawn from the Handbook. Stewart had already played a lead role in developing positions on development assistance (see her "Discussion Paper/Liberal Party Policy/Official Development Assistance" [1991]). See also Lloyd Axworthy, "Canadian Foreign Policy: A Liberal Party Perspective," *Canadian Foreign Policy* 1, 1 (Winter 1992/93): 7-14.

55 Liberal Party of Canada, *Creating Opportunity*, p. 108.
56 Cranford Pratt, "Canada's Development Assistance: Some Lessons from the Last Review," *International Journal* 49, 1 (Winter 1993-94): 117.
57 Tim Harper, "Liberals Urged to Mount Review of Foreign Policy," *The Toronto Star*, November 4, 1993.
58 "Finding Our Way on Foreign Policy," *The Toronto Star*, November 13, 1993. See also "Foreign Policy Review," *The Ottawa Citizen*, November 8, 1993.
59 "Ouellet Promises Full Foreign Policy Review," *The Toronto Star*, November 5, 1993.
60 Cited in Clyde Sanger, "Twenty Questions for the Foreign Policy Review," *Review* (Ottawa: North-South Institute) (Winter 1994), p. 1.
61 See Clyde Sanger, "Steaming Ahead—or Off Track?—on the Foreign Policy Review," *Review* (Ottawa: North-South Institute) (Summer 1994), p. 1.
62 See House of Commons, Standing Committee on Foreign Affairs and International Trade, *Minutes of Proceedings and Evidence*, February 23 and March 10, 1994, issues 3 and 17, and Standing Committee on Public Accounts, *Minutes of Proceedings and Evidence*, April 13 and May 4, 1994, sessions 5 and 8.
63 CIDA, *Memorandum to DAC 1993*, p. 1.
64 CCIC, *Economic Justice: Toward a Just and Sustainable Canadian Foreign Policy* (Ottawa: CCIC, 1994); CCIC, *Towards a Common Future* (Ottawa: CCIC, 1994); CCIC, *Human Rights and Democratic Development in Canadian Foreign Policy* (Ottawa: CCIC, 1994); and CCIC, *Fighting Poverty First: The Development Challenge* (Ottawa: CCIC, 1994). See also the article by the president of CCIC, Betty Plewes, "Preparing for the 21st Century: Why Canada Needs a Foreign Policy Review," *Canadian Foreign Policy* 1, 2 (Spring 1993): 103-107.
65 CCIC, *Towards a Common Future*, p. 4.
66 CCIC, *Fighting Poverty First*, p. 2.
67 Ibid., p. 21 (emphasis in original).
68 Ibid., pp. 28, 25. Appearing before the Public Accounts Committee just before the foreign policy review, the Auditor General also urged consideration of a legislated mandate as one way of enabling CIDA to resist some of the conflicting pressures (Standing Committee on Public Accounts, *Minutes of Proceedings and Evidence*, April 13, 1994, session 5, p. 20).
69 North-South Institute, *Canada and the Developing World: Key Issues for Canada's Foreign Policy* (Ottawa: North-South Institute, 1994); the quotation is on p. 28. See also Clyde Sanger and Ann Weston, "Caring About the South—With Good Reason," *Canadian Foreign Policy* 2, 2 (Fall 1994): 41-67.
70 Canadian Exporters' Association, "Foreign Policy: The Canadian Challenge in a Competitive World—Brief to the Special Joint Committee Reviewing Canadian Foreign Policy" (1994). See also Business Council on National Issues, "Canadian Foreign Policy: Principles and Priorities—A Statement Before the Special Joint Committee of the Parliament of Canada Reviewing Canada's Foreign Policy" by Thomas d'Aquino, President and Chief Executive, Ottawa, July 25, 1994.
71 See AUCC, "Canadian Universities: Partners in Canada's Foreign Policies—A Submission by the Association of Universities and Colleges of Canada to the Special Joint Parliamentary Committee Reviewing Canadian Foreign Policy," Ottawa, May 25, 1994, and Canadian Bureau for International Education, "Wanted: An International Policy Based on International Education—A Submission to the Special Joint Committee Reviewing Canadian Foreign Policy," Ottawa, May 1994.

72 Canada 21 Council, *Canada 21: Canada and Common Security in the Twenty-First Century* (Toronto: Centre for International Studies, University of Toronto, 1994), pp. 11-12 (emphasis in original).

73 Ibid., p. 12.

74 Gerald Schmitz observed that the Canada 21 report served as a reference point more for the defence than the foreign policy review, especially in the testimony of witnesses (see Gerald J. Schmitz, "The State, the Public, and the Decennial Refashioning of Canadian Foreign Policy: Democratizing Diminished Expectations or Demanding a New Departure" [paper presented to the annual conference of the Canadian Political Science Association, Montreal, June 1995], p. 7). However, the report of the Special Joint Committee Reviewing Canadian Foreign Policy did echo some of the positions taken by Canada 21 on ODA—especially on distinguishing between aid and trade development and coordinating aid more closely with other North-South policies. Its views on NGOs, both positive and negative, were also echoed by the committee.

75 Canada 21 Council, *Canada 21*, p. 36.

76 Ibid., p. 37.

77 Ibid., p. 38. Less surprisingly, this position was strongly argued before the Special Joint Committee Reviewing Canadian Foreign Policy by the International Development Executives Association (IDEA), a body representing several large NGOs (see Special Joint Committee of the Senate and of the House of Commons Reviewing Canadian Foreign Policy [hereafter SJC-CFP], *Minutes of Proceedings and Evidence*, June 8, 1994, session 32, p. 39).

78 Canada 21 Council, *Canada 21*, p. 39.

79 Ibid., p. 40.

80 Ibid., pp. 37-38.

81 "Guidance Paper for the Special Joint Parliamentary Committee Reviewing Canadian Foreign Policy," Appendix "A" of SJC-CFP, *Canada's Foreign Policy: Dissenting Opinions and Appendices* (Ottawa: Parliamentary Publications Directorate, 1994), p. 33.

82 Ibid., p. 34.

83 See Schmitz, "The State, the Public, and the Decennial Refashioning of Canadian Foreign Policy," p. 7. See also Andrew Cohen, "Will Ottawa Take Expert's Advice on Foreign Policy?" *Financial Post*, March 25, 1994.

84 "Report of the National Forum on Canada's International Relations," by Pierre S. Pettigrew and Janice Gross Stein, Co-Chairs of the National Forum, submitted to the Minister of Foreign Affairs, The Honourable André Ouellet, April 15, 1994, p. 4. See also Stein's testimony before the SJC-CFP, *Minutes of Proceedings and Evidence*, April 18, 1994, session 2, pp. 8-11.

85 According to participants and observers interviewed by the author.

86 See Schmitz, "The State, the Public, and the Decennial Refashioning of Canadian Foreign Policy," p. 6. The focus on democratization generated a scholarly debate on what it means to "democratize" foreign policy. See Maxwell A. Cameron and Maureen Appel Molot, eds., *Canada Among Nations 1995: Democracy and Foreign Policy* (Ottawa: Carleton University Press, 1995), especially the editors' introduction and the articles by Nossal and by Draimin and Plewes. See also Kim Richard Nossal, "The Democratization of Canadian Foreign Policy," *Canadian Foreign Policy* 1, 3 (Fall 1993): 95-105.

87 Clyde Sanger reported that "Some members felt the early roundtable discussions were too general, and lacked any hard recommendations" (Sanger, "Steaming Ahead—or Off Track?" p. 1). The round table on development assistance brought together Maureen O'Neil, president of the North-South Institute; Herb Breau, chairman of the 1980 Parliamentary Task Force on North-South relations and now in private business; Raymond Gladu of the Canadian Exporters' Association; and Philip Rawkins of Ryerson Polytechnical Institute. Familiar positions were advanced with eloquence, but scant attention was devoted to the implications of major contextual changes, such as the end of the Cold War, fiscal pressures, and declining public support for aid (see SJC-CFP, *Minutes of Proceedings and Evidence*, April 21, 1994, session 4).

88 The main writer was the late John Halstead, former Canadian ambassador to NATO, who had earlier served as a consultant to Canada 21 and testified before the SJC-CFP. The other major contributor was Albert Breton, professor of economics at the University of Toronto, who did not participate in any of the public sessions of the committee. Halstead was originally scheduled to write the chapter on development assistance, but, under pressure of time, responsibility for the first draft was shifted to Robert Miller. Although subsequently diluted, the text reflected Miller's long-standing commitment to a poverty-oriented ODA program, and his experience serving the Breau task force and the Hockin-Simard and Winegard committees. Gerald Schmitz, who wrote much of the Winegard report, was also a key staff member; he drafted the section on international assistance in the Issues Papers.

89 See the data in SJC-CFP, *Canada's Foreign Policy: Principles and Priorities for the Future*, pp. 85-86, and SJC-CFP, "Charting a Course in Turbulent Times—The Issues Papers" (1994), pp. 15-16. NGO participation was encouraged not only by the CCIC campaign, but also by an invitation from André Ouellet that was sent out to hundreds of organizations and individuals.

90 SJC-CFP, *Canada's Foreign Policy: Dissenting Opinions and Appendices*, p. 32.

91 According to staff members and other observers close to the process. A related concern was voiced by the consultant hired to write the position paper on development assistance—André Martens, professor of economics at the Université de Montréal. He argued that, while some NGOs were well managed and others not, there was no way to ensure adequate performance because they were immune from "the law of the market-place." Martens also criticized many NGOs for their opposition to structural adjustment and their aversion to the market economy. "The market economy will be with us for a long time. NGOs must get used to this idea or flounder in unreality and dreams" (see André Martens, "Foreign Aid & Development Assistance Revisited: Reflections with Special Reference to Canadian Aid," in SJC-CFP, "Canada's Foreign Policy: Principles and Priorities for the Future—The Position Papers" [1994], pp. 64-82; the quotation is from p. 79).

92 And biographer of Lester Pearson. See John English, *The Life of Lester Pearson*, vol. 1: *Shadow of Heaven* (Toronto: Lester and Orpen Dennys, 1989), and vol. 2: *The Worldly Years* (New York: A.A. Knopf Canada, 1992).

93 SJC-CFP, *Minutes of Proceedings and Evidence*, May 31, 1994, session 15, pp. 103-104.

94 Ibid., p. 107.

95 Ibid., May 31, 1994, session 16, p. 78.

96 SJC-CFP, "Charting a Course in Turbulent Times—The Issues Papers," pp. 211-12.

97 Foreign Affairs and CIDA had a direct pipeline to the drafting process, through the presence in each of the co-chairs' offices of seconded officials—Nicolas Dimic from Foreign Affairs (whose thinking had earlier influenced the Policy Update paper) and Stephen Wallace from CIDA. Both Dimic and Wallace later joined Ouellet's staff in preparing the government's response and white paper, *Canada in the World*—a markedly "cosier" arrangement than the Winegard process. For its part, the main concern of CIDA's Policy Branch was to keep to a minimum any recommendations on quantitative targets for ODA allocations that might later prove embarrassing (as those in *Sharing Our Future* had been).

98 SJC-CFP, *Canada's Foreign Policy: Principles and Priorities for the Future*, p. 47. The first draft of the chapter was more scathing in its criticisms of CIDA but the co-chairs and their staffers toned them down.

99 Ibid., pp. 47-48.

100 Ibid., p. 48. The SJC-CFP's formulation was more open-ended than "the poorest of the poor" or "the poorest countries and people." The text went on to state that "need" "should reflect broader measures than simply per capita GNP" and that "can use our help" meant "that countries must have a minimum absorptive capacity for Canadian assistance."

101 SJC-CFP, *Canada's Foreign Policy: Principles and Priorities for the Future*, pp. 48-49. See also the chapter on "Sharing Sustainable Development," pp. 41-46. The committee urged the adoption of sustainable development as an overarching foreign policy theme but its analysis and prescriptions were rather vague.

102 Women in development, missing as a priority in the first draft of the report, was reportedly inserted on the advice of Stephen Wallace, the CIDA official seconded to the co-chairs.

103 SJC-CFP, *Canada's Foreign Policy: Principles and Priorities for the Future*, p. 50.

104 Ibid. In earlier drafts of the chapter, the sixth priority was defined as "culture and education" or "education and communication" and was linked to other recommendations in the report for projecting Canadian culture internationally. As a result, it made references to scholarships and exchange programs (which remained in the final draft). The change from "culture and education" to "public participation" is an example of the hurried way in which the document was put together.

105 SJC-CFP, *Canada's Foreign Policy: Principles and Priorities for the Future*, p. 51. See also pp. 58-59.

106 Ibid., p. 51. The committee went on to say: "Recognizing that expanded trade opportunities are more important than aid to many developing countries, the committee also recommends that the government seek opportunities to open Canadian markets further to developing countries, particularly the least developed" (ibid., p. 58).

107 SJC-CFP, *Canada's Foreign Policy: Principles and Priorities for the Future*, p. 52.

108 Ibid., p. 53. The committee agreed with CCIC and Canada 21 that there ought to be greater reciprocity and shared responsibility for policy changes in the North as well as the South, but did not make a specific recommendation.

109 SJC-CFP, *Canada's Foreign Policy: Principles and Priorities for the Future*, pp. 53-54.

110 Ibid., p. 54.

111 Ibid., pp. 55-56.

112 Ibid., p. 40.

113 Ibid., pp. 56-57.

114 Ibid., p. 39.
115 Ibid., p. 57.
116 Ibid., p. 57.
117 SJC-CFP, "Charting a Course in Turbulent Times—The Issues Papers," p. 134.
118 SJC-CFP, *Canada's Foreign Policy: Principles and Priorities for the Future*, p. 58. Herb Breau, the former MP who chaired the Parliamentary Task Force on North-South Relations in 1980, urged that a clear commitment be made to work towards achieving the target over a ten-year period once the federal deficit had been brought down to 3 per cent of GNP (SJC-CFP, *Minutes of Proceedings and Evidence*, April 21, 1994, session 4, p. 9).
119 SJC-CFP, *Canada's Foreign Policy: Dissenting Opinions and Appendices*, pp. 1-26; the quotation is on p. 19.
120 For example, a business panel commissioned by International Trade Minister Roy MacLaren, which reported a month before the SJC-CFP, included in its recommendations a transfer of INC to Foreign Affairs and International Trade (Barrie McKenna, "Business Panel Wants Trade Tied to Aid," *The Globe and Mail*, October 4, 1994).
121 SJC-CFP, *Canada's Foreign Policy: Dissenting Opinions and Appendices*, pp. 30-31; the full dissent of the Reform Party is on pp. 29-32.
122 See, for example, Jeff Sallot, "Link Trade, Human Rights, Panel Urges," *The Globe and Mail*, November 16, 1994.
123 "Redefining Canada's Place in the World," *The Globe and Mail*, November 17, 1994.
124 CCIC, "Canada's Foreign Policy: Principles and Priorities for the Future / A Review and Analysis of the Report's Recommendations" (Ottawa, 1994), 22 pp.; the quotation is on p. 1.
125 Cranford Pratt, "Development Assistance and Canadian Foreign Policy: Where We Now Are," *Canadian Foreign Policy* 2, 3 (Winter 1994): 81.
126 Clyde Sanger, "The Wise and the Weak in the Foreign Policy Review," *Review* (Ottawa: North-South Institute) (Winter 1995), p. 1.
127 Based on the text of the two documents, supplemented by interviews with key participants. See also Martin Rudner, "Canada in the World: Development Assistance in Canada's New Foreign Policy Framework," *Canadian Journal of Development Studies* 17, 2 (1996): 193-220.
128 Government of Canada, *Canada in the World*, p. i.
129 Ibid., p. iii.
130 My conclusion based on the text and interviews with officials.
131 Government of Canada, *Canada in the World*, p. 42.
132 Ibid., pp. 41-42. Although some CIDA officers wanted a mandate statement with a sharper focus on poverty reduction, the Executive Committee fashioned this compromise formulation, which puts poverty first and then softens the commitment with a safe, catch-all reference to the broad foreign policy objectives.
133 Government of Canada, *Government Response to the Recommendations of the Special Joint Parliamentary Committee Reviewing Canadian Foreign Policy* (hereafter *Government Response to SJC-CFP*), p. 58.
134 Ibid., p. 60.
135 World Bank, *World Development Report 1994* (New York: Oxford University Press, 1994), pp. 1-2.

136 Government of Canada, *Canada in the World*, p. 60. See also CIDA, "Working Group Draft on Infrastructure Services" (1995).
137 Rudner, "Canada in the World," p. 203.
138 According to an interview source, cabinet-level interventions were responsible for white paper commitments to expand ODA "in sectors important to both Canada and developing countries, such as agriculture, forestry and fisheries." See Government of Canada, *Canada in the World*, p. 43.
139 Based on interviews.
140 CIDA, Development Economics Policy Division, "Economic Reform in Developing Countries: Policy Discussion Paper" (August 1994), pp. 30-33; the quotation is on pp. 30-31.
141 Government of Canada, *Government Response to SJC-CFP*, p. 64.
142 Ibid., pp. 4-5; see also pp. 65-66.
143 Ibid., p. 61.
144 Ibid., and Government of Canada, *Canada in the World*, pp. 48-49.
145 Ibid., p. 43.
146 Ibid., p. 43.
147 Government of Canada, *Government Response to SJC-CFP*, p. 67.
148 Some temporizing language about focusing efforts on a limited number of countries was qualified by: "while maintaining programs in other countries through low-cost, administratively-simple delivery mechanisms" (Government of Canada, *Canada in the World*, p. 45).
149 CIDA, "South Africa Eligible for Canadian Aid," Press Release, May 26, 1994. Limited forms of Canadian aid, primarily for the black majority, had of course been provided since 1987.
150 CIDA, "Cuba Becomes Eligible for Canadian Development Assistance," Press Release, June 20, 1994. Subsequent programming emphasized human rights, democratic development, and governance projects and was motivated in part by Canadian opposition to the American *Helms-Burton Act*. When the Tories were still in power, $1 million in emergency food aid was provided to Cuba early in 1993 in response to severe economic crisis, brought on by the loss of Soviet support and magnified by a devastating hurricane. Despite pressure from NGOs and CIDA, however, the Conservative government refused to lift the formal ban on Canadian ODA (Dave Todd, "Federal Government's Dithering Stalls Aid to Cuba, Critics Say," *The Ottawa Citizen*, May 22, 1993, and Dave Todd, "Canada Walks a Fine Line on Aid to Cuba," *The Ottawa Citizen*, August 27, 1993).
151 Department of Foreign Affairs and International Trade, "Secretary of State Stewart Visits Tanzania," Press Release, May 24, 1995.
152 Government of Canada, *Canada in the World*, p. 46. For an account of EAITC/DFAIT support to Central and East Europe and the former Soviet Union, see Jeanne Kirk Laux, "From South to East? Financing the Transition in Central and Eastern Europe," in Maureen Appel Molot and Harald von Reikhoff, eds., *Canada Among Nations 1994: A Part of the Peace* (Ottawa: Carleton University Press, 1994), pp. 172-94, especially 185-94.
153 Government of Canada, *Government Response to SJC-CFP*, pp. 69, 40.
154 Ibid., p. 63.
155 Madelaine Drohan, "Rich Nations Urged to Cut Strings on Aid to Poor Countries," *The Globe and Mail*, September 20, 1996. See also OECD-DAC, *Development Co-operation: Efforts and Policies of the Members of the Development Assistance Committee 1996*, pp. 113-15.

156 Based on interviews.

157 See Government of Canada, *Government Response to SJC-CFP*, p. 62, and Government of Canada, *Canada in the World*, p. 44.

158 The apparent contradiction in fact represented a compromise between trade promotion officials in DFAIT, who wanted to refashion INC into a proactive trade mechanism, and CIDA officers, who insisted that it remain a responsive program. See Rudner, "Canada in the World," p. 210.

159 Government of Canada, *Government Response to SJC-CFP*, p. 70.

160 It proposed as well an expansion of the number and range of personnel exchanges between the Agency and its Canadian partners, especially NGOs (Government of Canada, *Canada in the World*, p. 44).

161 Ibid., p. 44. See also Government of Canada, *Government Response to SJC-CFP*, p. 39.

162 Government of Canada, *Canada in the World*, pp. 44-45.

163 Ibid., pp. 45-46 (emphasis in original).

164 Ibid., p. 45.

165 Apart from general statements in support of open trading regimes and trade liberalization under the Uruguay Round, the government noted that it was conducting a full review of Canada's general preferential tariff scheme "with a view to providing further benefits for the least developed countries and keeping in mind the potential impact on affected industries." It mentioned the eventual phasing out of non-tariff restrictions on textiles and clothing imports under the Multi-Fibre Arrangement. It also promised to seek opportunities for extending technical assistance to help developing countries participate effectively in trade arrangements, such as the World Trade Organization and NAFTA (Government of Canada, *Government Response to SJC-CFP*, p. 72).

166 The creation of the Bureau of Global Issues, subsequently reorganized as the Global and Human Issues Branch, became a renewed source of conflict between CIDA and DFAIT amid bureaucratic jostling over the appropriate jurisdictional boundaries between it and the Agency's Policy Branch. Some senior DFAIT officers advocated merging the two units within Foreign Affairs (see Cranford Pratt, "DFAIT's Takeover Bid of CIDA: The Institutional Future of the Canadian International Development Agency," *Canadian Foreign Policy* 5, 2 [Winter 1998]: 6-10). President Labelle denied categorically that there had been any serious discussion of such a move at the ministerial or deputy ministerial levels (author's interview with Huguette Labelle, Hull, August 18, 1997).

167 Government of Canada, *Canada in the World*, p. 50.

168 As a cost-cutting measure, CIDA replaced the *Annual Report* with a statistical summary. The final two annual reports—1991-92 and 1992-93—contained only statistics and brief messages from the minister and the president.

169 Government of Canada, *Canada in the World*, pp. 46-47. See also Government of Canada, *Government Response to SJC-CFP*, p. 61.

170 When asked in a press briefing if aid would be cut back further, Ouellet answered: "Every department of government, every agency of government has been asked to trim down and participate in this overall effort toward fighting our deficit" (Allan Thompson, "Foreign Policy: More Trade, Less Aid," *The Toronto Star*, February 8, 1995. See also Gordon Barthos, "Radical Foreign Policy Banks on Trade," *The Toronto Star*, February 8, 1995; Chantal Hébert, "La politique étrangère bifurque sur le commerce," *La Presse* [Montreal], February 8, 1995; Manon Cor-

nellier, "Politique étrangère: Ottawa priorise le commerce," *Le Devoir* [Montreal], February 8, 1995; and Dave Todd, "Deal with U.S. 'Trade Irritants': White Paper," *The Gazette* [Montreal], February 8, 1995).

171 "So long, Dudley Do-right," *The Gazette* (Montreal), February 12, 1995.

172 "Foreign Policy and National Interest," *The Globe and Mail*, February 9, 1995.

173 CCIC, *Canada in the World: A Review and Analysis of the Government's Foreign Policy Statements* (Ottawa: CCIC, 1995), pp. 2-3.

174 Ibid., p. 9.

175 Ibid., p. 13. The Standing Committee on Foreign Affairs and International Trade held a post-mortem with CCIC, the North-South Institute, and the Canadian Exporters' Association, whose representatives voiced predictable responses. There was no sense of dissatisfaction with the government's response among Liberal members of the committee. See House of Commons, Standing Committee on Foreign Affairs and International Trade, *Minutes of Proceedings and Evidence*, session 15, February 16, 1995, p. 15.

176 Pratt, "Development Assistance and Canadian Foreign Policy: Where We Now Are," p. 82.

177 Ibid., p. 77.

178 Rudner, "Canada in the World," p. 218.

179 SJC-CFP, *Minutes of Proceedings and Evidence*, August 8, 1994, session 50, p. 115. See also Pratt, "The Institutional Future for the Canadian International Development Agency."

180 CIDA, *CIDA's Policy for Performance Review* (Hull: CIDA, 1994). For a good critical discussion of the debate concerning aid effectiveness and performance review, see Gerald J. Schmitz, "The Verdict on Aid Effectiveness: Why the Jury Stays Out," *International Journal* 11 (Spring 1996): 287-313.

181 Auditor General, *Report of the Auditor General of Canada to the House of Commons October 1995/Canadian International Development Agency: Phased Follow-up of the Auditor General's 1993 Report—Phase I* (Hull: Minister of Supply and Services, 1995), pp. 13-33. See also *Estimates 1996-97, Part III: Canadian International Development Agency*, p. 20.

182 CIDA, "Background to Development: New Contracting Process for CIDA" (Hull, 1994). For more details, see CIDA, "Service Contracting Process" (Hull, 1995). The question of whether to move to open bidding for NGOs and NGIs remained unresolved initially (see CIDA, "Should CIDA Allow Open Competition Between the Private and Non-Profit Sectors?" [Hull, 1995]).

183 CIDA, "Reflections on Organizational Renewal in CIDA," p. 5.

184 See CIDA, "Interim Report: 1994 C.I.D.A. Employee Survey," prepared by Paul de L. Harwood, June 30, 1994. The response rate—87.7 per cent (931/1061) was quite high. There were positive responses as well, but these tended to relate to personal job satisfaction, immediate supervisors, and some aspects of the work environment. While substantial majorities expressed pride in working for CIDA and believed they understood CIDA's mission, 93 per cent strongly agreed/agreed with the statement "I need to know more about CIDA's future direction" and 76 per cent with "I need to know more about why major changes are being made at CIDA."

185 CIDA, "Reflections on Organizational Renewal in CIDA," p. 5.

186 See Auditor General, *Report of the Auditor General of Canada to the House of Commons October 1995/Canadian International Development Agency: Phased Follow-up—Phase I*, pp. 13-26, 13-27.

187 CIDA, "Reflections on Organizational Renewal in CIDA," p. 5. See CIDA, *Results-Based Management in CIDA: Policy Statement* (Hull: CIDA, 1995).

188 *Estimates 1996-97, Part III: Canadian International Development Agency*, pp. 50-51, and ibid., *1997-98*, pp. 9, 60.

189 CIDA, "Reflections on Organizational Renewal in CIDA," p. 6.

190 Years earlier, as a junior officer, Holdsworth had been a key player in CIDA's Strategy Unit during the process leading to the 1975-80 strategy.

191 Auditor General, *Report of the Auditor General of Canada to the House of Commons October 1995/Canadian International Development Agency: Phased Follow-up—Phase I*, pp. 13-13, 13-14. The audit team also offered an analysis of "factors that impact on CIDA's ability to make rapid progress," among them the extent to which the Agency's partners "buy-in" to management of results; the degree to which ministerial and senior management accept the risk of adverse publicity that a more open and objective system for performance review may entail; and the extent to which the Agency deals effectively with perceived conflicts among objectives (ibid., pp. 13-14). Most of the report consisted of CIDA's "Overall Self-Assessment of Progress."

192 *Estimates 1997-98, Part III: Canadian International Development Agency*, p. 39. For further details, see CIDA, *Results-Based Management in CIDA*, and Auditor General, *Report of the Auditor General of Canada to the House of Commons November 1996/Canadian International Development Agency: Phased Follow-up of the Auditor General's 1993 Report—Phase II* (Hull: Minister of Public Works and Government Services, 1996), pp. 26-27.

193 For details, see ibid., pp. 29-29 to 29-38. The system identified "Development Factors" as relevance, appropriateness, cost effectiveness, and sustainability; and "Management Factors" as partnership, innovation and creativity, appropriate human resource utilization, prudence and probity, and informed and timely action.

194 Ibid., p. 29-17.

195 CIDA, "Improvements to the Contracting Regime" (December 1996), and CIDA, "Changes to CIDA's Contracting Regime," *Development* 3, 1 (February 1997).

196 *Estimates 1997-98, Part III: Canadian International Development Agency*, p. 60.

197 Auditor General, *Report of the Auditor General of Canada to the House of Commons November 1996/Canadian International Development Agency: Phased Follow-up—Phase II*, p. 29-37.

198 See OECD-DAC, *Development Co-operation: Efforts and Policies of the Members of the Development Assistance Committee 1995*, pp. 11-13.

199 CIDA, *CIDA's Policy on Poverty Reduction* (Hull: CIDA, 1995), p. 1.

200 CIDA, Development Economics Policy Division, "Poverty Reduction: Policy Discussion Paper," August 1, 1994.

201 CIDA, *CIDA's Policy on Poverty Reduction*, p. 1 (emphasis in original).

202 Ibid., pp. 2-5.

203 See, for example, Robert Chambers, *Rural Development: Putting the Last First* (London: Longman, 1983), and Robert Chambers, "Sustainable Livelihoods, Environment and Development: Putting Poor Rural People First," Paper No. 240 (Brighton: Institute of Development Studies Discussion, 1987).

204 CIDA, *CIDA's Policy on Poverty Reduction*, pp. 5-6.

205 Government of Canada, *Government Response to SJC-CFP*, p. 59.

206 The issue was the subject of considerable debate at a conference in June 1995 at which CIDA's *Policy on Poverty Reduction* was unveiled. The author attended this

meeting which was co-sponsored by CIDA and the Foundation for International Training. See "Poverty Reduction Strategies for Development: Report on the Forum held in Toronto, Canada, June 13 and 14, 1995," especially p. 27 (a summary of a workshop discussion on "Basic Human Needs and Poverty Reduction: What Is CIDA's Role?"). CIDA had tipped its hand to some extent earlier: the Agency's June 1994 list of interim priorities promised to "address basic human needs by building the human capacity of the poor and responding to emergency situations" (CIDA, *Memorandum to DAC 1993*, p. 1).

207 United Nations Development Program, *Human Development Report 1991* (New York: Oxford University Press, 1991), p. 84.

208 United Nations Development Program, *Human Development Report 1994* (New York: Oxford University Press, 1994), pp. 7-8. As part of its campaign to encourage more foreign aid spending on "human development," the UNDP developed three comparative indices for measuring the performance of bilateral donors:

- aid social allocation ratio—the percentage of ODA devoted to social sectors,
- aid social priority ratio—the percentage of social sector ODA spent on the "human priorities" of basic education, primary health care, safe drinking water, adequate sanitation, family planning, and nutrition), and
- aid human expenditure ratio—the percentage of donor GNP earmarked for human priorities.

On the basis of 1989-91 data, Canada's ranking among DAC donors was eighth, seventh, and sixth respectively in these three indices. However, despite the sixth place standing in the last and most significant of these measures, Canada's ODA spending on human priorities was a mere 0.042 of GNP, well behind Denmark (0.255), Norway (0.200), Switzerland, the Netherlands, and Finland. Canada did lead the G7, although it spent a smaller share of its total ODA on human priorities than the United States (ibid., p. 74).

209 Alison Van Rooy, *A Partial Promise? Canadian Support to Social Development* (Ottawa: North-South Institute, 1995), p. 21.

210 See the critique of CIDA's performance in these sectors in ibid., pp. 31-58.

211 Ibid., p. 29.

212 Ibid., p. 70.

213 *Estimates 1996-97, Part III: Canadian International Development Agency*, pp. 14-15. The percentages tracked as spending on basic human needs in 1994-95 varied from a low of 13 per cent in Asia to a high of 32 per cent in the Americas. Africa and Middle East Branch, at 23 per cent, set a target of 30 per cent by 1998-99 (ibid., pp. 36-42).

214 *Estimates 1997-98, Part III: Canadian International Development Agency*, p. 35. The figure for bilateral aid alone in 1995-96, 22 per cent, remained virtually unchanged from the previous year.

215 CCIC, "The February Budget & the 1997/98 Estimates, Part III, Expenditure Plan, CIDA: Analysis and Highlights" (Ottawa, March 1997), p. 14. The 18.1 per cent figure understates the proportion spent on BHN because a significant proportion of long-term food aid could arguably be classified as meeting basic needs. The recalculation nonetheless reveals how slippery data of this sort can be.

216 Ibid. and interviews.

217 See CIDA, *Memorandum to DAC 1993*, pp. 46-47; ibid., *1994*, pp. 45-47; *Estimates 1994-95, Part III: Canadian International Development Agency*, p. 30;

ibid., *1996-97*, pp. 15-16, 36-38; CIDA, *Creating a World of Equality: CIDA, Women and Empowerment in Developing Countries* (Hull: CIDA, 1995); CIDA, Policy Branch, "CIDA and Gender Equity Information Kit" (August 1995); and Rajani E. Alexander, "Evaluating Experiences: CIDA's Women in Development Policy, 1984-94," *Canadian Journal of Development Studies*, Special Issue on Evaluating Experiences: Doing Development with Women (1995), especially pp. 84-87.

218 CIDA, *CIDA's Policy on Women in Development and Gender Equity* (Hull: CIDA, 1995).

219 See *Estimates 1997-98, Part III: Canadian International Development Agency*, p. 35.

220 CIDA, "Working Group Draft on Infrastructure Services" (1995). The definition excluded basic health, primary education, and other aspects of social infrastructure "which, although equally critical for economic and social development, will continue to be supported within CIDA's Basic Human Needs priority."

221 *Estimates 1996-97, Part III: Canadian International Development Agency*, p. 16, and ibid., *1997-98*, p. 35.

222 CIDA, Policy Branch, "Human Rights, Democratization and Good Governance: Draft Discussion Paper," September 23, 1993, p. 4.

223 See, for example, Warren Caragata, "A Change of Heart: Under the Liberals, Foreign Policy Will Stress Economics Over Human Rights," *Macleans*, March 21, 1994, and Allan Thompson, "The Chrétien Doctrine Trades Off Human Rights," *The Toronto Star*, March 26, 1994.

224 "Canada Is No Longer World Boy Scout: Ouellet," *The Gazette* (Montreal), May 16, 1995. See also Ross Howard, "Ouellet Assailed for Remark on Rights," *The Globe and Mail*, May 13, 1995; "Rights Activists Condemn Foreign Policy," *The Edmonton Journal*, May 14, 1995; and Peter O'Neil, "Canada Hasn't Placed Trade Before Human Rights Policy, Ouellet Says," *Sun* (Vancouver), May 16, 1995.

225 CIDA, *Government of Canada Policy for CIDA on Human Rights, Democratization and Good Governance* (Hull: CIDA, 1995), p. 4.

226 Ibid., p. 8.

227 For details, see CIDA, *Memorandum to DAC 1994*, pp. 21, 24.

228 Emergency aid, which accounted for only 1.6 per cent of total DAC ODA in 1989, grew to 5 per cent in 1992 and doubled to 10 per cent in 1994 (OECD-DAC, *Development Co-operation: Efforts and Policies of the Members of the Development Assistance Committee 1990*, p. 217; ibid., *1994*, pp. 2, E4; and Actionaid, *The Reality of Aid 1995* [London: Earthscan Publications, 1995], p. 17).

229 Sanger and Weston, "Caring About the South," p. 44.

230 Interview.

231 *Estimates 1997-98, Part III: Canadian International Development Agency*, p. 36. See also CIDA, Africa and Middle East Branch, "Draft Programming Guidelines for Africa and Middle East" (1995).

232 CIDA, Development Economics Policy Division, "Economic Development," September 23, 1993.

233 CIDA, Policy Branch, Development Economics Policy Division, "Private Sector Development in Developing Countries: Policy Discussion Paper" (August 1994).

234 CIDA, *CIDA's Policy on Private Sector Development in Developing Countries* (Hull: CIDA, 1995), p. 1.

235 *OECD-DAC, Development Co-operation: Efforts and Policies of the Members of the Development Assistance Committee 1994*, pp. 14-15.

236 CIDA, *CIDA's Policy on Private Sector Development in Developing Countries*, pp. 1-2.

237 Ibid., pp. 3-4.

238 CIDA, *Memorandum to DAC 1994*, p. 37.

239 *Estimates 1997-98, Part III: Canadian International Development Agency*, p. 36.

240 See CIDA, *Memorandum to DAC 1993*, pp. 43-45; CIDA, "Implementation of CIDA's Policy for Environmental Sustainability: 1992-1993 Progress Report" (October 1993); CIDA, "Environmental Sustainability: A Priority for CIDA" (March 1994); *Estimates 1995-96, Part III: Canadian International Development Agency*, p. 19; ibid., *1996-97*, pp. 18, 37-42; and ibid., *1997-98*, p. 36.

241 The new Environment Division of Policy Branch also undertook a comprehensive survey of CIDA's environment-related activities during the first half of the 1990s after the Liberal government announced in September 1994 a Canadian Environmental Industry Strategy, "aimed at supporting the development of this spearhead industry in domestic and international markets." CIDA's survey examined how ODA "could continue to support sustainable development in developing countries, while making a greater contribution to strengthening Canada's environmental industry" (CIDA, Environment Division, Policy Branch, "CIDA's Environment-Related Activities—Benefits for Canada's Environmental Industry" [June 1995], p. 1).

242 Rudner, "Canada in the World," p. 206.

243 Andrew Clark, "What Next Mr. Martin? Foreign aid in the Next Budget," *Review* (Ottawa: North-South Institute) (Winter 1996), p. 3.

244 CCIC, "Review of the 1995/96 Spending Estimates for CIDA," March 6, 1995. In the light of a further ODA cut announced for 1998-99—a year when a modest increase was scheduled for National Defence—the ratio is likely to decline to 5.49 to one (CCIC, "1997/98 Federal Budget," p. 1).

245 *Estimates 1996-97, Part III: Canadian International Development Agency*, p. 28.

246 Ibid., pp. 46, 54.

247 *The Hamilton Spectator*, February 28, 1995.

248 Clyde Sanger, "A New Era Breaks for South as Aid Budgets Are Chopped," *Review* (Ottawa: North-South Institute) (Spring 1995), p. 1.

249 John Best, "Aid Cuts Not in Canada's Self-Interest," *Star Phoenix* (Saskatoon), March 9, 1995.

250 Ibid.; see also Paul Knox, "Canadians Face Dilemma Over Aid Cuts," *The Globe and Mail*, March 4, 1995.

251 *Estimates 1995-96, Part III: Canadian International Development Agency*, p. 27. Estimates for multilateral technical cooperation were reduced from \$133.8 million in 1994-95 to \$109 million in 1995-96, and for multilateral food aid from \$141.0 million (and an anticipated actual expenditure of \$166.1 million). Because of prior commitments, estimated contributions to international financial institutions increased from \$148.5 million to \$150.0 million.

252 Sanger, "A New Era Breaks for South as Aid Budgets Are Chopped," p. 2.

253 *Estimates 1995-96, Part III: Canadian International Development Agency*, p. 43.

254 Ibid., p. 27. The base figure for the voluntary sector includes International Non-Governmental Organizations.

255 The average cuts within the NGO and ICDS divisions were: development NGOs, 14.9 per cent; universities and colleges, 15.2 per cent; volunteer-sending organiza-

tions, 14.8 per cent; cooperatives, 12.5 per cent; and professional associations, 8.8 per cent. The small trade union program was increased by 3.8 per cent (see data in CCIC, "Implementing the Cuts: The Implications of Budget Cuts to NGO/NGI Programs in the Partnership Branch of CIDA" [Ottawa, 1995], p. 2).

256 See Knox, Paul, "Canada chops aid-agency grant," *The Globe and Mail*, April 4, 1995.

257 Based on CCIC, "Implementing the Cuts"; interviews; and press reports. See also Zack Gross, "Life after Death: Development Education Confronts the End of Government Funding," *Review* (Ottawa: North-South Institute) 1, 1 (1997): 4-5.

258 Letter from André Ouellet to David Morrison, May 9, 1995.

259 Distilled from Pratt's comments at panel discussions of CIDA's cuts at annual meetings of the Canadian Association of African Studies, Peterborough, May 1995, and the Canadian Association for the Study of International Development, Montreal, June 1995.

260 The exchange occurred during a SCFAIT forum on promoting greater public understanding of international development issues (Standing Committee on Foreign Affairs and International Trade, *Minutes of Proceedings and Evidence*, April 18, 1996, session 8, pp. 29, 30, 45 [of the English version, downloaded electronically]).

261 Based on CCIC, "Implementing the Cuts," pp. 3-5; *Estimates 1994-95, Part III: Canadian International Development Agency*, pp. 42-43; ibid., *1995-96*, pp. 34-36; ibid., *1996-97*, pp. 27-29; and interviews.

262 The Canadian development community was still absorbing the budget blows when a potential scandal involving CARE Canada threatened to weaken already fragile support for the aid program. In May 1995, CBC *Prime Time News* screened a documentary featuring allegations by a disgruntled former CARE official that the NGO had diverted about $400,000 in public donations for relief efforts in Somalia into its general revenues. Although the immediate impact of the story was damaging to CARE and Canadian aid efforts, the tables were quickly turned. CARE held a press conference to announce that it was suing the CBC for libel, just as Christine Stewart was assuring the House of Commons that CIDA audits showed that the NGO had used its public funds properly. Editorial opinion and press commentary generally defended CARE and accused the CBC of shoddy journalism. See "CARE Accused of Not Sending Public Donations to Somalia," *The Ottawa Citizen*, May 31, 1995; Jeff Sallot, "Ottawa to Seek Audit of CARE," *The Globe and Mail*, June 1, 1995; Laura Bobak, "CARE to Sue CBC Over Allegations," *Ottawa Sun*, June 1, 1995; Dave Todd, "Canadian Charities Reeling Over Allegations that CARE Misused Funds," *The Ottawa Citizen*, June 1, 1995; Jeff Sallot, "The CARE Revelations that Weren't," *The Globe and Mail*, June 2, 1995; and John Best, "Integrity—of CARE Canada and CBC—Now at Stake," *The Leader Post* (Regina), June 9, 1995.

263 Budget Speech of the Honourable Paul Martin, PC, MP, Minister of Finance, March 6, 1996, p. 31.

264 John Stackhouse, "Canada to Change Foreign-Aid Focus," *The Globe and Mail*, January 15, 1997.

265 *Estimates 1997-98, Part III: Canadian International Development Agency*, p. 12. See analysis in CCIC, "1997/98 Federal Budget." The distinction between "National Initiatives" and "Partnership" as budget categories—introduced with *Sharing Our Future* in 1988—was dropped in the 1997-98 *Estimates*. It was replaced by seven functional business lines—geographic programs, countries in

transition, multilateral programs, Canadian partnership, policy, communications, and corporate services.

266 *Estimates 1998-99, Part III: Canadian International Development Agency*, pp. 15-18; Tomlinson and CCIC Policy Team, "Development Assistance in the 1998 Federal Budget," pp. 1-3, and Jeff Sallot, "Planned Funding Cuts to Foreign Aid Are Partly Restored," *The Globe and Mail*, February 25, 1998.

267 The quotation from the budget papers was cited by Diane Marleau, minister of International Cooperation, in her introduction to *Estimates 1998-99, Part III: Canadian International Development Agency*, p. iii.

268 See Appendix A.

269 See analysis in Tomlinson and CCIC Policy Team, "Development Assistance in the 1998 Federal Budget," pp. 3-4.

270 See Appendix A. In 1996-97, reported ODA was $2,676.44 million. This included the following items not included in ODA before 1982 (in millions of dollars): EDC and Canadian Wheat Board debt relief, $164.34; administrative costs, $141.45; EDC Section 23, $12.34; imputed service and interest costs, $14.77; imputed student costs, $65.00; and estimated costs of first-year resettlement of refugees from ODA-eligible countries, $163.71. If these items are deducted (a total of $561.61 million), ODA falls to $2,114.83 million and the ratio in 1996-97 drops from 0.34 per cent to 0.27 per cent (calculations based on CIDA, *Statistical Report Report on Official Development Assistance, Fiscal Year 1996/97* [Hull: CIDA, 1998], pp. 2-4). An extrapolation to the estimated level for 1998-99 yields a ratio in the 0.19 to 0.20 per cent range.

271 House of Commons, *Debates*, November 14, 1963, p. 4718. Paul Martin, Jr. alluded to the irony of cutting programs his father had helped to build up, though with a quotation from Paul Sr. about the necessity of governments not living in the past (see Budget Speech of the Honourable Paul Martin, P.C., M.P., Minister of Finance, February 27, 1995).

272 Madelaine Drohan, "Canada's Foreign Aid Inadequate: OECD," *The Globe and Mail*, February 23, 1998.

273 See Appendix F.

274 See OECD-DAC, *Development Co-operation: Efforts and Policies of the Members of the Development Assistance Committee 1997*, pp. A11-A14. As this DAC report pointed out (ibid.: 94), Canada's performance in the 1996 calendar year—0.32 per cent—may have been understated because the annual contribution to the International Development Association was made later in the 1996-97 fiscal year. Fiscal-year data showed a slightly higher ratio of 0.34 per cent (see Appendix A), which would have moved Canada ahead of Germany into a three-way tie for seventh place. However, with Canadian aid as a proportion of national income falling more rapidly than that of other donors, data for 1997 and 1998 may well reveal Canada as eleventh or even twelfth or thirteenth.

275 Quoted in Drohan, "Canada's Foreign Aid Inadequate." See also OECD-DAC, *Development Co-operation: Efforts and Policies of the Members of the Development Assistance Committee 1997*, p. 94.

276 See data for 1994-95 to 1996-97 in CIDA, *Statistical Report on Official Development Assistance, Fiscal Year 1996/97*, pp. 31-34. See also data in annual DAC reports.

277 OECD-DAC, *Development Co-operation: Efforts and Policies of the Members of the Development Assistance Committee 1997*, p. A66.

278 See CIDA, NGO Division, "NGO Division's Allocation Criteria and Process," January 10, 1995, and Universalla, "CIDA NGO Division 1995/96 Assessment and Allocation Process: Trusted Observer Report to the NGO Community" (Hull, 1995).

279 CIDA, *Policy Framework for a Renewed Relationship between CIDA and the Voluntary Organizations* (Hull: CIDA, 1996).

280 Following the elimination of PPP and other budget cuts, NGO Division took over responsibility for International NGOs (previously a separate division) and volunteer-sending programs (from ICDS). ICDS was reorganized as the Institutional Cooperation Division. See *Estimates 1996-97, Part III: Canadian International Development Agency*, pp. 27-28.

281 CCIC, *The Political Scene—February/March 1996*, electronic version.

282 Standing Committee on Foreign Affairs and International Trade, *Minutes of Proceedings and Evidence*, April 18, 1996, session 8, pp. 2-3 (of the English version, downloaded electronically).

283 Interviews; Memo from Betty Plewes, President-CEO, to all CCIC Members Re. CIDA—Voluntary Sector Annual Meeting November 5 and 6, 1996 (November 15, 1996); Andrew Clark, "Problems Ahead? Commitments to the IFIs and UN Agencies Pressure the Aid Budget," *Review* (Ottawa: North-South Institute) 1, 1 (1997); CCIC, "1997/98 Federal Budget"; and *Estimates 1997-98, Part III: Canadian International Development Agency*, p. 12. CIDA claimed that it had little flexibility owing to long-standing international commitments. While the cuts were more or less across the board, the proportional cut in INC's budget continued to decline less than that of the rest of the Agency. In place of a strategic plan, the *Estimates 1997-98* (p. 6) set out a list of broad priorities for coping with reduced resources: greater targeting of efforts to the six official objectives, a shift to more interventions with "multiplier effects," better coordination with other donors, increased leveraging of additional resources from partners, and more effective integration of lessons learned into programming. In addition, the Agency promised to develop "transition mechanisms for the phasing-out of international assistance programming in countries that have made dramatic improvements in their social and economic well-being."

284 See CCIC, "1997/98 Federal Budget," p. 2.

285 Interview. Pratt (in "DFAIT's Takeover Bid of CIDA," pp. 7-9) discussed several instances in which Axworthy looked to ODA resources to support his political initiatives. These included peace-keeping operations in Haiti, funding to prevent the closure of Radio Canada International, a reorientation of the Cuban program towards democratic development and human rights as a means of challenging the American *Helms-Burton Act*, and the active promotion of peace-building initiatives.

286 Axworthy and Chan remained as minister of Foreign Affairs and secretary of state for Asia Pacific respectively. Christine Stewart was promoted to minister of the Environment and replaced as secretary of state for Africa and Latin America by Edmonton MP David Kilgour. None of the parties devoted attention to either foreign policy or development assistance during the campaign. The Liberals were silent about aid volume in their official platform, while both the Reform and the Conservative parties called for more cuts as part of their deficit reduction policies. Only the NDP went on record as favouring phased increases aimed at achieving the 0.7 per cent ODA/GNP target now that the federal deficit had been substan-

tially reduced and there was a looming prospect of fiscal surpluses. See CCIC, "International Affairs and the political party election platforms, 1997" (downloaded electronically).

287 Except shortly before this book went to press, when Marleau was quoted as saying that Canada was considering a resumption of aid to Burma, notwithstanding the Burmese government's notorious record of human rights abuses. Human rights groups were appalled, and Lloyd Axworthy issued an immediate denial. Marleau indicated that she had been misunderstood. See Rod Micklebourgh, "Ottawa May Resume Burma Aid," *The Globe and Mail*, April 22, 1998, and Jeff Sallot, "Burma Gaffe Hooks Junior Minister," *The Globe and Mail*, April 23, 1998.

288 Ibid., p. 7. The quotation was from Lester B. Pearson, *Partners in Development: Report of the Commission on International Development* (New York: Praeger Publishers, 1969), p. 4.

289 Roger C. Riddell, "Trends in International Cooperation" (paper prepared for an Aga Khan Foundation Canada Round Table in June 1996 on Promoting Public Support for Canadian Development Cooperation); see pp. 3-4.

290 A theme advanced forcefully by Mahbub ul Haq, special adviser to UNDP, whose intellectual influence has had a great impact on successive editions of the *Human Development Report*. See, for example, his address to the House of Commons, Standing Committee on Finance, Subcommittee on International Financial Institutions, *Minutes of Proceedings and Evidence*, February 2, 1993, session 8, pp. 7-20.

291 *The Globe and Mail*, June 19, 1996.

292 OECD-DAC, *Development Co-operation: Efforts and Policies of the Members of the Development Assistance Committee 1996*, pp. 5, 12-28.

293 *Connecting with the World: Priorities for Canadian Internationalism in the 21st Century*, a Report by the International Development Research and Policy Task Force, Maurice F. Strong, Chairman, Ottawa, November 1996. The work of the task force and its report were co-sponsored and co-funded by IDRC, the International Institute for Sustainable Development, and the North-South Institute. Minister Axworthy endorsed the thrust of the report and set up a working committee to study ways of implementing some of its recommendations (see Stackhouse, "Canada to Change Foreign-Aid Focus").

Chapter 11

1 Department of Industry, Trade and Commerce, *Strengthening Canada Abroad: Final Report of the Export Promotion Review Committee* (Ottawa: Department of Industry, Trade and Commerce, 1979), p. 35.

2 Robert Carty and Virginia Smith, eds., *Perpetuating Poverty: The Political Economy of Foreign Aid* (Toronto: Between the Lines, 1981), pp. 39, 41.

3 Ibid., p. 38.

4 Ibid., p. 11.

5 Paul Fromm and James P. Hull, *Down the Drain? A Critical Re-examination of Canadian Foreign Aid* (Toronto: Griffin House, 1981), pp. 85-87.

6 Peyton V. Lyon, "Introduction," in Peyton V. Lyon and Tareq Y. Ismael, eds., *Canada and the Third World* (Toronto: Macmillan of Canada, 1976), p. xlv. See also p. xxxii.

7 Interview.

8 Lyon, "Introduction," p. xlii.

9 P.V. Lyon, R.B. Byers, and D. Leyton-Brown, "How 'Official' Ottawa Views the Third World," *International Perspectives* (January/February 1979), p. 12. In this article, they reported responses to a survey of nearly 300 ministers, MPs, and senior officials.

10 Clyde Sanger, *Half a Loaf: Canada's Semi-Role Among Developing Countries* (Toronto: Ryerson Press, 1969), p. xii.

11 L. Dudley and C. Montmarquette, *The Supply of Canadian Foreign Aid: Explanation and Evaluation* (Hull: Economic Council of Canada, 1978), pp. 27, 119.

12 Michael Tucker, *Canadian Foreign Policy: Contemporary Issues and Themes* (Toronto: McGraw Hill Ryerson, 1980), pp. 234-36.

13 Martin Rudner, "Canada in the World: Development Assistance in Canada's New Foreign Policy Framework," *Canadian Journal of Development Studies* 17, 2 (1996): 218.

14 Keith Spicer, *A Samaritan State? External Aid in Canada's Foreign Policy* (Toronto: University of Toronto Press, 1966), p. 11.

15 Kim Richard Nossal, "Mixed Motives Revisited: Canada's Interest in Development Assistance," *Canadian Journal of Political Science* 21, 1 (March 1988): 49.

16 Ibid., p. 50.

17 Oxfam of Canada, *Unequal Partners: Development in the Seventies—Where Does Canada stand?* (Report of the Unequal Partners Conference, Toronto, May 8-9, 1970), p. 20. Much later, Pratt spelled out his views on why social scientists ought to address the ethical aspects of North-South relations and why governments should respond to ethical considerations in their North-South policies (see Cranford Pratt, "Ethics and Foreign Policy: The Case of Canada's Development Assistance," *International Journal* 43, 2 [Spring 1988]: 264-301). For a comprehensive analysis of the ethical foundations for foreign aid, see Roger C. Riddell, *Foreign Aid Reconsidered* (Baltimore: Johns Hopkins University Press, 1987), pp. 1-77. Riddell revisited his analysis from the vantage point of the mid-1990s in "The Moral Case for Post-Cold War Development Aid," *International Journal* 51 (Spring 1996): 191-210. David Lumsdaine challenged the realist paradigm and argued that humanitarianism has been the dominant motivating force for foreign aid (in *Moral Wisdom in International Politics: The Foreign Aid Regime* [Princeton: Princeton University Press, 1993]).

18 See Sanger, *Half a Loaf*, and Clyde Sanger, "Canada and Development in the Third World," in Peyton V. Lyon and Tareq Y. Ismael, eds., *Canada and the Third World* (Toronto: Macmillan of Canada, 1976), pp. 277-307. Over a span of thirty years, Clyde Sanger has written several books, and published widely in newspapers, magazines, and specialized journals. He has also contributed regularly to the publications of the North-South Institute (which have been quoted many times in this book).

19 Douglas Roche, *Justice Not Charity: A New Global Ethic for Canada* (Toronto: McClelland and Stewart, 1976). Both as a journalist and an MP, Roche has written several articles and opinion pieces on Canadian development assistance.

20 Peter Wyse, *Canadian Foreign Aid in the 1970s: An Organizational Audit* (Montreal: Centre for Developing Area Studies, McGill University, 1983).

21 Réal Lavergne, "Determinants of Canadian Aid Policy," in Olav Stokke, ed., *Western Middle Powers and Global Poverty: The Determinants of the Aid Policies of Canada, Denmark, the Netherlands, Norway and Sweden* (Uppsala: Scandinavian Institute of African Studies, 1989), p. 35.

22 Ibid., pp. 35-36.
23 Ibid., p. 71.
24 Ibid., p. 67.
25 Roger Young, "Canadian Foreign Aid: Facing a Crisis of Its Own?" *Journal of Canadian Studies* 19, 4 (1985): 31.
26 Cited in Special Joint Committee of the Senate and of the House of Commons on Canada's International Relations, *Independence and Internationalism* (Ottawa: Queen's Printer, 1986), p. 90.
27 Carty and Smith, eds., *Perpetuating Poverty*; Robert Clarke and Jamie Swift, eds., *Ties that Bind: Canada and the Third World* (Toronto: Between the Lines, 1982); and Jamie Swift and Brian Tomlinson, eds., *Conflicts of Interest: Canada and the Third World* (Toronto: Between the Lines, 1991).
28 See Leo Panitch, ed., *The Canadian State: Political Economy and Political Power* (Toronto: University of Toronto Press, 1977).
29 Linda Freeman, "The Effect of the World Crisis on Canada's Involvement in Africa," *Studies in Political Economy* 17 (1985): 109. See also Linda Freeman, "The Political Economy of Canada's Foreign Aid Programme" (paper presented to the annual conference of the Canadian Political Science Association, Montreal, June 1980), and Linda Freeman, "CIDA, Wheat, and Rural Development in Tanzania," *Canadian Journal of African Studies* 16, 3 (1982).
30 Freeman, "CIDA, Wheat, and Rural Development in Tanzania," p. 482.
31 Freeman, "The Political Economy of Canada's Foreign Aid Programme," pp. 9, 55.
32 Freeman, "The Effect of the World Crisis on Canada's Involvement in Africa," p. 109.
33 Nossal, "Mixed Motives Revisited: Canada's Interest in Development Assistance," pp. 38, 45. For more on Nossal's approach to Canadian foreign policy-making, see his "Analyzing the Domestic Sources of Canadian Foreign Policy," *International Journal* 39, 1 (Spring 1984): 1-22, and *The Politics of Canadian Foreign Policy*, 2nd ed. (Scarborough: Prentice-Hall, 1989).
34 See Nossal's commentary on Denis Stairs' analysis of the impact of public opinion on foreign policy in Nossal, "Analyzing the Domestic Sources of Canadian Foreign Policy," pp. 18-22.
35 Nossal, "Mixed Motives Revisited: Canada's Interest in Development Assistance," p. 45.
36 Ibid., p. 42.
37 Ibid., pp. 47-48.
38 Ibid., pp. 51-54.
39 Ibid., p. 56.
40 Of the authors surveyed in this chapter, Lavergne in "Determinants of Canadian Aid Policy" comes closest to the classic liberal, idealist, and pluralist model, seeing in the contradictory behaviour of states officials conflicting pressures emerging from Canadian society. Some earlier writers like Peyton Lyon who wrote from a liberal, idealist perspective saw foreign policy-makers as a strong, relatively autonomous elite resisting self-interested pressures from societal interests.
41 Cranford Pratt, "Dominant Class Theory and Canadian Foreign Policy: The Case of the Counter-Consensus," *International Journal* 39, 1 (Spring 1984): 107, 111, 114. See also his "Canadian Foreign Policy: Bias to Business," *International Perspectives* (November/December 1982), and "Canadian Policy Towards the Third World: Basis for an Explanation," *Studies in Political Economy* 13 (Spring 1984).

42 Cranford Pratt, "Competing Perspectives on Canadian Development Assistance Policies," *International Journal* 51 (Spring 1996): 252.

43 See Pratt, "Ethics and Foreign Policy," p. 264.

44 Ibid., pp. 293-301, and Pratt, "Canadian Policy Towards the Third World," pp. 47-50.

45 Pratt, "Ethics and Foreign Policy," pp. 296-97.

46 Cranford Pratt, "Middle Power Internationalism and North-South Issues: Comparisons and Prognosis," in Cranford Pratt, ed., *Internationalism under Strain: The North-South Policies of Canada, the Netherlands, Norway, and Sweden* (Toronto: University of Toronto Press, 1989), pp. 194-200; the quotation is on p. 194.

47 Cranford Pratt,"Middle Power Internationalism and Global Poverty," in Cranford Pratt, ed., *Middle Power Internationalism: The North South Dimension* (Kingston and Montreal: McGill-Queen's University Press, 1990), p. 15.

48 Moreover, in Canada, the ideas of "reform internationalism"—which accepts the need for interventions in the marketplace to achieve a more equitable distribution of global power—have "remained outside the consensus supporting the government. They have been prevalent in the NGO community, in the churches, and in the universities in Canada, but have had little, if any influence upon policy." In contrast, in the northern European countries, these ideas have co-existed in the official domain with liberal internationalism, which supports aid and multilateralism but opposes interventionism (Pratt, "Middle Power Internationalism and North-South Issues: Comparisons and Prognosis," pp. 197-98). Patricia Appavoo compared differences between Canada and Sweden in the dominant ideological perspectives on solidarity, justice, equity, and welfare. See Patricia Jean Appavoo, "The Small State as Donor: Canadian and Swedish Development Assistance Policies, 1960-1976" (unpublished Ph.D. dissertation, University of Toronto, 1988), pp. 347-48.

49 Pratt, "Middle Power Internationalism and North-South Issues: Comparisons and Prognosis," pp. 207-19, and Olav Stokke, "The Determinants of Aid Policies: Some Propositions Emerging from a Comparative Analysis," in Olav Stokke, ed., *Western Middle Powers and Global Poverty: The Determinants of the Aid Policies of Canada, Denmark, the Netherlands, Norway and Sweden* (Uppsala: Scandinavian Institute of African Studies, 1989), pp. 312-17. Stokke (ibid., p. 313) reported as a major conclusion of the comparative ODA study (to which Réal Lavergne contributed the chapter on Canada) "that socio-political values in the donors' domestic society have been the main determinants of most dimensions of aid policy."

50 Pratt, "Ethics and Foreign Policy," pp. 297-98.

51 Cranford Pratt, "Canada: An Eroding and Limited Internationalism," in Cranford Pratt, ed., *Internationalism under Strain: The North-South Policies of Canada, the Netherlands, Norway, and Sweden* (Toronto: University of Toronto Press, 1989), p. 58.

52 See Pratt's comparison of realism and humane internationalism in "Middle Power Internationalism and Global Poverty," pp. 10-13.

53 Cranford Pratt, "Humane Internationalism and Canadian Development Assistance Policies," in Cranford Pratt, ed., *Canadian International Development Assistance Policies: An Appraisal* (Montreal and Kingston: McGill-Queen's University Press, 1994), p. 338.

54 Pratt, "Competing Perspectives on Canadian Development Assistance Policies," p. 258.

55 Mark Neufeld, "Hegemony and Foreign Policy Analysis: The Case of Canada as Middle Power," *Studies in Political Economy* 48 (Autumn 1995): 11.

56 Ibid., p. 12.

57 Laura Macdonald, "Unequal Partnerships: The Politics of Canada's Relations with the Third World," *Studies in Political Economy* 47 (Summer 1995): 112-13. See also her "Going Global: The Politics of Canada's Foreign Economic Relations," in Wallace Clement, ed., *Understanding Canada: Building on the New Canadian Political Economy* (Montreal and Kingston: McGill-Queen's University Press, 1997), pp. 172-96.

58 Macdonald, "Unequal Partnerships," p. 123.

59 Ibid., pp. 133, 135-36.

60 David R. Black and Heather A. Smith, "Notable Exceptions? New and Arrested Directions in Canadian Foreign Policy Literature," *Canadian Journal of Political Science* 26, 4 (1993): 755.

61 Nossal, "Mixed Motives Revisited: Canada's Interest in Development Assistance," pp. 51-52. As noted in the text, one could link prestige to adherence to changing fashions within the aid regime, but that is something Nossal only hints at. He does suggest that the bureaucratic interest accounts for the labour-intensive project approach to aid delivery (pp. 52-53), but I would argue that the international regime and inertia have been more significant.

62 Pratt, "Humane Internationalism and Canadian Development Assistance Policies," p. 346.

63 On these points see as well Lyon, "Introduction," p. xlv, and Jean-Philippe Thérien, "Canadian Aid: A Comparative Analysis," in Cranford Pratt, ed., *Canadian International Development Assistance Policies: An Appraisal* (Montreal and Kingston: McGill-Queen's University Press, 1994), p. 328.

64 Jean-Philippe Thérien and Alain Noël, "Welfare Institutions and Foreign Aid: Domestic Foundations of Canadian Foreign Policy," *Canadian Journal of Political Science* 27, 3 (September 1993): 533.

65 Ibid., pp. 555-56.

66 Pratt, "Humane Internationalism and Canadian Development Assistance Policies," pp. 334-38.

67 Ibid., p. 334.

68 Robert Miller, "The People Versus Canadian Aid: A Summary of the Prosecutor's Case," Workshop Paper prepared for IDRC (Ottawa: Parliamentary Centre, 1992), cited in Alison Van Rooy, "The Altruistic Lobbyists: The Influence of Non-Governmental Organisations on Development Policy in Canada and Britain" (unpublished D.Phil thesis, Oxford University, 1994), chap. 2, p. 11.

69 Most recently in Cranford Pratt, "Development Assistance and Canadian Foreign Policy: Where We Now Are," *Canadian Foreign Policy* 2, 3 (Winter 1994): 77-85.

70 Maury Arnold Miloff, "The Role of Canadian Non-Governmental Organizations in Building Support for International Development" (unpublished Master of Arts research essay, Carleton University, 1981), and John S. Clark, "Canadian Non-Governmental Organizations and Their Influence on Canadian Development Policy," University of Toronto Working Paper, no. A.17 (October 1985).

71 Pratt, "Canadian Foreign Policy: Bias to Business," pp. 3-5, and Pratt, "Dominant Class Theory and Canadian Foreign Policy," pp. 129-35.

72 Van Rooy, "The Altruistic Lobbyists," chap. 2, p. 9.

73 Ibid., p. 1.

74 Neufeld, "Hegemony and Foreign Policy Analysis," p. 14. The quotation is drawn from Neufeld's general discussion of the Gramscian notion of hegemony.

75 Nossal, "Analyzing the Domestic Sources of Canadian Foreign Policy," p. 8. See also Kim Richard Nossal, "Allison through the (Ottawa) Looking Glass: Bureaucratic Politics and Foreign Policy in a Parliamentary System," *Canadian Public Administration* 22, 4 (Winter 1979): 610-26, in which he argued that the paradigm has little predictive capability, but is useful in making the linkage between process and policy outcomes, and in suggesting "that accounting for foreign policy behaviour by reference to motives attributed to the government" is a method prone to inaccuracy (p. 626).

76 John White, *The Politics of Foreign Aid* (New York: St. Martin's Press, 1974), p. 51. Based at the Institute of Development Studies at the University of Sussex when he wrote the book, White subsequently joined the DAC secretariat.

77 G.R. Berry, "Bureaucratic Politics and Canadian Economic Policies Affecting Developing Countries—The Case of the Strategy for International Development Cooperation 1975-1980" (unpublished Ph.D. dissertation, Dalhousie University, 1981).

78 Wyse, *Canadian Foreign Aid in the 1970s*, p. 27.

79 Ibid., p. 29.

80 Young, "Canadian Foreign Aid: Facing a Crisis of Its Own?," pp. 32-33.

81 Roger Ehrhardt, *Canadian Development Assistance to Bangladesh* (Ottawa: North-South Institute, 1983), p. 110

82 Van Rooy, "The Altruistic Lobbyists," p. 14.

83 See, in particular, Donald J. Savoie, *The Politics of Public Spending in Canada* (Toronto: University of Toronto Press, 1990).

84 Mark Charlton, "What Motivates Aid Bureaucrats? An Assessment of the Revised Mixed Motives Model" (paper presented to the annual conference of the Canadian Political Science Association, Ottawa, June 1993), p. 15. The quotation is from Nossal, "Mixed Motives Revisited: Canada's Interest in Development Assistance," p. 55.

85 Special Joint Committee of the Senate and of the House of Commons on Reviewing Canadian Foreign Policy, *Minutes of Proceedings and Evidence*, July 26, 1994, session 48, p. 10.

86 Robert E. Wood, *From Marshall Plan to Debt Crisis: Foreign Aid and Development Choices in the World Economy* (Berkeley: University of California Press, 1986), p. 66.

87 Ibid., p. 191.

88 See ibid., pp. 101-106.

89 Lumsdaine, *Moral Wisdom in International Politics: The Foreign Aid Regime*, p. 29.

90 Ibid., p. 268.

91 White, *The Politics of Foreign Aid*, p. 54.

92 Mark Charlton, *The Making of Canadian Food Aid Policy* (Montreal and Kingston: McGill-Queen's University Press, 1992), pp. 194-97. Charlton also argued that the contribution of an "epistemic community" of aid administrators and scholars to "a body of 'consensual knowledge' regarding the uses of food aid as development resource provides a useful basis for understanding how developmental and humanitarian concerns may be incorporated into government aid policy" (ibid., p. 196). In a more theoretical exploration of how regime analysis may

be used to inform the study of Canadian foreign policy, Black and Smith suggested that the literature on epistemic communities may offer a promising avenue for further research ("Notable Exceptions?" pp. 771-73).

93 Marcia M. Burdette, "Structural Adjustment and Canadian Aid Policy," in Cranford Pratt, ed., *Canadian International Development Assistance Policies: An Appraisal* (Montreal and Kingston: McGill-Queen's University Press, 1994), pp. 210-39.

94 David R. Black and Peter McKenna, "Canada and Structural Adjustment in the South: The Significance of the Guyana Case," *Canadian Journal of Development Studies* 16, 1 (1995): 73.

95 David R. Black and Jean-Philippe Thérien with Andrew Clark, "Moving with the Crowd: Canadian Aid to Africa," *International Journal* 51 (Spring 1996): 259-86.

96 Phillip Rawkins, "An Institutional Analysis of CIDA," in Cranford Pratt, ed., *Canadian International Development Assistance Policies: An Appraisal* (Montreal and Kingston: McGill-Queen's University Press, 1994), p. 165.

97 Phillip Rawkins, *Human Resource Development in the Aid Process: A Study in Organizational Learning and Change* (Ottawa: North-South Institute, 1993), p. 13; emphasis in original.

98 Rawkins, "An Institutional Analysis of CIDA," p. 166.

99 Ibid., p. 166. See also a similar analysis of US AID in Dennis A. Rondinelli, *Development Administration and U.S. Foreign Aid Policy* (Boulder: Lynne Reiner, 1987), pp. 150-51.

100 Judith Tendler, *Inside Foreign Aid* (Baltimore: Johns Hopkins University Press, 1975), p. 85.

101 See ibid., especially chaps. 5 and 6.

102 Ehrhardt, *Canadian Development Assistance to Bangladesh*, p. 112.

103 Ibid., pp. 111-15, and Wyse, *Canadian Foreign Aid in the 1970s*, pp. 63-65.

104 Réal Lavergne with E. Philip English, *Canadian Development Assistance to Senegal* (Ottawa: North-South Institute, 1987), p. 144.

105 Rawkins, "An Institutional Analysis of CIDA," p. 163.

106 See ibid., p. 172.

107 E. Philip English, *Canadian Development Assistance to Haiti* (Ottawa: North-South Institute, 1984), p. 142.

108 Berry, "Bureaucratic Politics and Canadian Economic Policies," p. 19.

109 Hugh Winsor (commenting on the Auditor General's 1993 Report), "External Pressures Take Toll on CIDA," *The Globe and Mail*, January 21, 1994.

110 Gerald J. Schmitz, "CIDA as Peacemaker: Integration or Overload," in Robert Miller, ed., *Aid as Peacemaker: Canadian Development Assistance and Third World Conflict* (Ottawa: Carleton University Press, 1992), p. 96.

111 Department of External Affairs, *Foreign Policy for Canadians: International Development* (Ottawa: Queen's Printer, 1970), pp. 8-9. Much later, Monique Landry, Conservative minister for External Relations and International Development, had observed when introducing *Sharing Our Future* in 1988: "Canadians' desire to fight global poverty is an extension of their commitment to combat poverty at home. Fortunately, Canada is a country with the resources to take on both of these challenges" (cited in SJC-CFP, "Charting a Course in Turbulent Times—The Issues Papers" [1994], p. 133).

Index

Adams, Patricia (environment critic) 247
Africa, Canadian ties to 2, 14; Canadian ODA 1, 44, 48, 49, 113; exceeds or equals Asia 163, 201, 258; debts 19; desertification 238; drought crisis 226, 228, 234-38; emergency funds (1984-86) 235, 237; food aid 257; aid in Francophone Africa 14, 17, 28, 49, 51, 58, 75-79, 99, 123, 265, 359; Partnership Africa-Canada launched 237, 266, and cut 419; "Africa 21" strategy paper 372, used to justify East African cuts 372-74, cuts partially reversed 395-96; Winegard committee visit and untying 284 (*see* individual countries)
Algeria 74, 78, 137; aid declines 122; target for aid-trade 229
Aluminum Company of Canada (Alcan) 48
Anglin, Douglas (professor) 76
Angola 199, 234
Argentina, as suggested core country 345
Asia, Canadian ties to 2, 18; Canadian ODA in 1, 18 and equal to Africa 201, 258; communism in 12, 14; cross-board aid cuts 372; decolonization 1; markets 29; poverty 38 (*see* individual countries)
Asselin, Senator Martial (Conservative minister for CIDA) 150, 158
Association of Universities and Colleges of Canada (AUCC) 170, 264, 299, 334, 362-64, 383
Ault, Dr. Orville (aid administrator) 33, 37, 40
Australia 4, 17, 127; and Colombo Plan 28, 29; behind Canada in ODA/GNP 145, 255; but more leverage 330
Axworthy, Lloyd (Liberal foreign affairs minister from 1996) as Liberal critic 310, 374, 380; as human resources minister 385, 414; on landmines 410; pledge on cuts 419; on sustainable development 424

Bangladesh 121, 123, 257, 452; audit in 378; effects of aid cuts 324, 372; human rights 292; Canadian leverage 330; local NGOs 265; NSI study 215
Barbados, as CIDA regional centre 305-308
Bateman, Hylda (CIDA official) 239
Beatty, Perrin (Conservative external affairs minister 1993) 375
Belgium 17
Belize 137, 198
Bene, John (CIDA and IDRC adviser) 65
Bentley, Dean Fred (CIDA adviser) 83
Berry, Glyn (researcher) 107, 108, 116, 119, 443, 450
Best, John (journalist) 175, 254, 414
Best, Patrick (journalist) 138
Black, David (professor) 437, 447
Blakeney, Allan (Saskatchewan premier) 130
Bloc Québecois 386, 391, 418
Bolivia 198, 240
Bothwell, Robert (professor) 75, 146
Botswana 49, 74, 122, 199
Boudria, Don (Liberal minister for international cooperation) 422
Bourgon, Jocelyne (CIDA president 1993) 347, 369, 371, 375, 562 n. 27; SMR 374, 402
Brandt Commission on International Development Issues 177, 178-79, 184
Branham, Daphne (journalist) 328
Brazil 180
Breau, Herb (Liberal MP and chairman, North-South Task Force) 177, 180, 262, 297, 567 n. 87, 569 n. 118
Brecher, Irving (professor and CIDA adviser) 111, 489 n. 27

Brewin, Andrew (NDP MP) 140
Broadbent, Ed (ICHRDD president) 322, 381
Brodhead, Tim (NGO executive and author) 265, 266, 299, 361, 383
Bruce, Geoffrey (CIDA VP Business Cooperation) 232, 244
Brundtland, Gro Harlem, and *Our Common Future* 244-46, 290, 319; defines sustainable development 247
Bryant, Chris (CUSO and CCIC head) 324, 543 n. 8
Bryce, Robert (Finance official) 61
Burdette, Marcia (as NSI researcher) 351, 447, 543 n. 8, 554 n. 148, 586 n. 93
Burma 137, 350, 580 n. 287
Business Council on National Issues (BCNI) 254
Byers, Rod (professor) 427

Cadieux, Marcel (diplomat) 49, 50, 72, 481 n. 10
Cambodia 162, 348
Cameron, Stevie (journalist) 242
Cameroon 49, 78, 80, 257, 258; modest aid cut 372-73
Campbell, Coline (Liberal MP) 239
Campbell, Kim (PM 1993) 375
Canada 2, 14, 15; as honest broker 14, 160; markets in South 2; as middle power 1, 20, 54, 436
Canada: government departments and parastatal organizations
  Agriculture Canada 7, 30
  Auditor General: criticisms of CIDA 23, 451; special 1975-76 audit 135-36, 140, 144, 146, 147, 149, 166, 168; comprehensive 1978-79 audit 173, 176, 193; detailed 1983-84 audit 251, 252, 530 n. 221; 1988 audit 268, 531 n. 221; 1992 report on CIDA 360; and 1993 report 369, 381; positive report (1995) 403; for CIDA decentralization 285
  Bank of Canada 31
  Canadian International Development Agency (CIDA) *see separate entry below*
  External Affairs (and International Trade after 1989; Foreign Affairs and International Trade after 1993): jurisdiction and relations with CIDA 6, 10, 24, 30, 31, 56, 134-35, 149-50, 195-96, 314, 339-46, 377; assumes responsibility for trade promotion 196; declines under Trudeau 133; dominance challenged by Strong 62, 143, but revived under Dupuy 149, 160, 175; drafts International Assistance Policy Update 314, 341-45, 367, 371, 380, 401, 450; unease over Secor-Lindores reports 339; strained relations with CIDA 368; arranges National Forum on Canada's International Relations 381, 384, 421; Bureau of Global Issues created 398, 571 n. 166 (*see various external/foreign affairs ministers, particularly* Axworthy, Clark, Flora MacDonald, MacEachen, McDougall, Ouellet, Pearson, *and* Sharp)
  External Aid Office (1960-68) forerunner of CIDA, established 6, 28, 40-41; growth 16, 21, 42, 56, 60, 65; field offices 44, 72; forerunners: Technical Cooperation Service 30, 31; International Economic and Technical Cooperation Division (IETCD) 30-33, 37; and Economic and Technical Assistance Branch (ETAB) 33, 37, 40, 41
  Export Development Corporation (EDC): cooperation with CIDA 108, 203, 397; *crédit-mixte* program 232, 268; parallel financing 115, 156, 166, 183, 204, 231; EDC loans as ODA 152, 233, 326; Three Gorges 349
  Finance: dominant in policy 30, 31, 32, 56; opposes debt relief 115 and untying 116; leads in debt and adjustment policies 260, 350; protective of IFIs 6, 153, 195,

208, 262; introduction of budget "envelopes" for ODA 195 and for international assistance (IAE) 325-26; slows aid spending 152-53, 255; wary of *crédit-mixte* 228 (*see various finance ministers, particularly* Martin, Mazankowski, *and* Wilson)

Industry, Trade and Commerce: presses commercial interests 31, 51, 56, 112, 143, 175, 183; as Trade and Commerce, runs forerunners of External Aid Office 30, 32, 42; and Hatch committee 156, 169; presses aid to middle-income countries 204; pressure on Gerin-Lajoie 124; opposes untying 116

Interdepartmental Committee on Economic Relations with Developing Countries (ICERDC) 110, 111, 143, 195, 339

National Health and Welfare (now Health Canada): 7, 30, 31, 310

Treasury Board: 7, 42; alarm over CIDA 136, and improved relations 222; assumes more authority 146; caps ODA 133; qualms about NGO funding 70, 128; opposes debt relief 115, and 0.7 per cent target 112; views on decentralization 304, 305; eases terms of tying 81, and reveals costs of tying 165

Canada: international assistance

agricultural assistance 5, 81, 82, 90, 117, 126, 183, 205, 227 (*see* Food shortages and production)

basic human needs 100, 230; as development 4, 102, 117, 120, 155, 370, 382, 393, 406-407; and NGOs 21, 159

commercial returns of aid 15, 79, 106, 145, 153, 155, 160, 161, 204, 284 (*see also* tied aid *below*; Canada: Industry, Trade and Commerce; Canadian International Development Agency, Industrial Cooperation Program; *and* Trade Promotion)

country eligibility and concentration 17-18, 23, 94, 186, 256-57, 272, 294; arguments for greater concentration 89, 112-15, 120, 158, 183, 282, 341, 389-90; program-project categories and two-track approach 122, 145, 198, 200

cutbacks and implications 145, 177, 195, 219, 233, 255, 272, 301, 314, 362, 391, 412-20

debt and debt relief 20, 85, 115, 120, 122, 234, 237, 259, 294, 350

explanations of policy and performance 24-26, *passim* 425-52; developmentalist criticisms 24, 428-30; dominant-class critique 25, 430-31, 433-42, 450-51; statist perspective 431-33, 436-42, 450-51; governmental politics 443-45, 451; regime analysis 445-48, 451; organizational analysis 448-50, 451 (*see in particular* Nossal, Pratt, *and* Rawkins)

food aid 7, 27, 118, 126, 147, 207, 234, 261, 352; for food security and development 19, 83, 130, 168, 183; as surplus disposal 15, 36, 53, 55, 82, 168

human rights and aid 20, 159, 272, 274; action taken 202, 348; human rights in Latin America 186, 258; softer line under Liberals 394; linked with good governance 322, 323, 382, 389, 395, 409-10

international assistance envelope (IAE) 342; 1991 introduction 325-26, 327; reduced 371, 390, 413; and increased 420

lapsing and non-lapsing funds 11, 43, 57, 73; authority removed (1977) 146, 151, 331

aid to least developed 18, 26, 104, 105, 108, 113, 114, 295, 303, 420

mission-administered funds 95, 306

multilateral aid 7, 8; in ascendant 20-21, 23, 27, 47, 54, 83-84, 90, 95, 127-28, 151, 207, 263; com-

mitments reduced 327, 359, 415; debate on and decline of multilateral share 93, 169, 282, 360
ODA volume as percentage of GNP 1, 17, 23, 45, 47, 73, 99, 121, 151, 180, 197, 200, 223, 325, 420; and the 0.7 per cent target 16, 85, 101, 105, 111, 112, 120, 163, 177, 179, 228, 275, 391, 395, 420
opinion polls: 23, 442, 516 n. 179, 531 n. 223; Manifest report 365-66; soft support 140, 219, 514 n. 150; strengthens 268, 269-70, 497 n. 181; declines 313, 325, 345, 367; "aid fatigue" 59, 153, 213, 223, 422-23
poverty reduction 38, 101-102, 154, 271, 275, 292, 356-57, 370, 401; and NGOs 22, 54, 405-406
tied aid 19, 27, 51-52, 71, 95, 116, 135, 162, 164-66, 389, 396; above DAC average 20, 352; critics of policy 22, 90, 96, 120, 157, 237, 284, 383; actions or pledges for untying 72, 81, 85, 94, 100, 116, 271, 295, 352

Canada: parliamentary committees
Special Joint Committee of Senate and House of Commons on Canada's International Relations (1986) 271, 273-75, 386 (*see* Hockin *and* Simard)
Special Joint Committee of Senate and House of Commons Reviewing Canadian Foreign Policy (1994) 385-93 (*see* MacEachen *and* Gauthier)
Standing Committee on External Affairs and International Trade (SCEAIT, previously SCEAND) 150, 159; on African crisis 235, 253; on Human Rights 202; on structural adjustment programs 316, 317; SCEAIT as Winegard committee 279-86, 288, 290
Standing Committee on Public Accounts 252, 333
Subcommittee on Canada's Relations with Latin America and the Caribbean (1982) 178, 185-86, 195, 201-202, 214, 274 (*see* Dupras)
Subcommittee on Development and Human Rights 333, 350 (*see* McLean)
Subcommittee on International Development (1977) 151, 158 (*see* Dupras)
Subcommittee on International Development Assistance (1971) 96, 104, 110, 119, 135 (*see* Lachance)
Task Force on North-South Relations (1980) 177, 179-84, 195, 262, 297 (*see* Breau)

Canada 21 Council 383-84, 385
Canadian Chamber of Commerce 267
Canadian Council for International Cooperation (CCIC) 43, 70; forerunner Overseas Institute of Canada 43, 54, 55, 59; at 1962 COCOA Conference 43, 46, 50, 54; development education (DEAP) 128; Framework paper (1979) 159, 169; critic of tied aid 182, country focus 210, aid-trade 233, direct funding 266, 309, of SAPs 382 and of *Canada in the World* 399; campaigns on budget cuts 301, 324; on Carin and Policy Update 314, 345; Reconstruction and Rehabilitation Fund 209, 418-19; on Secor report 334; on *Sharing Our Future* 299, 366-67; Smillie report on NGOs 362; consultations over SJC-CFP 386
Canadian Executive Service Overseas (CESO) 70, 172
Canadian Exporters' (formerly Export) Association 116, 159, 211, 383; cooperation with CIDA 267; on untying and decentralization 164, 299-300, 307, 309
Canadians for Foreign Aid Reform (C-FAR) 212, 426
Canadian Institute for International Affairs 225, 325
Canadian International Development Agency (CIDA)
Briefing Centre 66, 206, 414
capital assistance 27, 31, 35, 42, 53,

124, 188; failures in Asia 36; large in francophone Africa 49
commodities 5, 19, 27, 36, 166; equals capital aid share 36; important in South Asia 83 (*see* food aid *under* Canada: international assistance)
contracting out 22, 328, 329, 334, 338, 340, 377
country focus 191-93, 263, 360
creation 1, 5, 7, 57; jurisdiction and objectives 6, 7, 10, 14, 18, 23, 63, 182;
decentralization 11, 216; field travel 57, 66; pressure for 97, 135, 194, 195; major moves 252-54, 272, 285-86, 291-92, 303-11, 329
environmental sustainability 14, 19, 92, 97, 221, 321, 412; sustainable development 154, 290, 313, 318-20
evaluation 12, 26, 68, 135, 149, 158, 286-87, 295, 364-65
human resource development (HRD) 205-207, 261, 297, 300, 315, 352, 353, 354, 383
human rights 221, 292, 322 (*see* Canada: international assistance)
Industrial Cooperation Program (INC, formerly Business and Industry) 7, 8, 22, 58, 70, 71, 171, 288, 396, 397, 411, 412 ; increases 210, 230, 267, 297, 343, 344; evaluation (1992) 364-65
under junior minister 24, 135, 222, 227 (*see* Asselin, Boudria, Landry, Marleau, Pettigrew, *and* Vézina)
public education, image and outreach 22-23, 97, 103, 129, 174, 218-19, 227, 297-98, 300, 365-67; development information program (DIP) 422; Futures Secretariat 216-18; parliamentary liaison 137
Public Participation Program (PPP) 21, 218, 227, 289, 297-98, 335, 365-66; termination 371, 416-17, 550 n. 97
reorganizations 65, 68, 131-33, 147, 190, 193, 205, 227, 231, 251, 326, 375
results-based management 370, 378, 379, 398, 404
staffing 131, 137, 250, 307, 328, 402-403, 404
strategic management review (SMR) 314, 327-47, 368, 374, 378
structural adjustment 313, 315, 316-18, 382, 389, 394, 450
technical assistance 5-6, 27, 36, 37, 51, 125; higher priority 53, 82; focus in Latin America 79; education share drops 167, 261 (*see also* HRD)
terms of aid: procurement tying (*see* tied aid *under* Canada: international assistance); soft loans 28, 34, 35; development loans 46; harder terms added 81; all grants 259; debt relief 260, 350 (*see* debt and debt relief)
Women in Development and Gender Equity 14, 19, 162, 221; evolution of program 238-43; Tories affirm 275, 278; momentum lost 357-58; Liberals and new emphasis 382, 408, 409
Canadian Jewish Congress 13
Canadian Labour Congress 179
Canadian Peace Research Institute 46
Canadian University Service Overseas (CUSO) 69, 171; core funding 21, 28, 55; headed by McWhinney 196, Bryant 324 and Smillie 362; hit by cuts 326; learner centre 128; returned volunteers in CIDA 57, 63; SUCO 125, 129; teachers 54, 125
Canadian universities 53, 54, 145, 171, 336, 353; African crisis 237; centres of excellence 289, 297, 300, 362, 363; in country focus 209; promised new Third World scholarships 297, 300; Winegard endorses role 287; University of Alberta 12, 83; Carleton 71, 170; Guelph 277; Laval 50, 141; McGill 111; Ottawa 90; and Western Ontario 43, 88, 141; participation of academics in Strong's aid policy review 86-91 (*see also* Association of Universities and Colleges of Canada)

Canadians abroad: military 2, 64; missionaries 2, 35, 49, 79, 437; recruited into CIDA 64, 123
Carin, Barry (diplomat) drafts Policy Update 341, 344, 346
CARE Canada 59, 210, 264, 390, 577 n. 262
Caribbean 2, 14; Canadian aid to Commonwealth Caribbean 34, 41, 48, 50, 74, 80; banks in 2; ODA debt forgiveness 350; heavy aid cuts 372; special relationship 163, 185, 202; untying for local costs 52
Carty, Robert (broadcaster and author) 212, 426, 430
Cassen, Robert (World Bank consultant) 223, 224
Catley-Carlson, Margaret (CIDA president 1983-89) *passim* 221-68; career 222, 517 n. 1 including CIDA VP 178; gifted in public relations 23, 268; African crisis 236; emphasis on agriculture, HRD and the poorest 227; delivery speed-up 252; and decentralization 253; and environment 245; relations with junior ministers 227; favours multilateral aid 169, 222; strengthens ties with NGOs 224; sceptic on SAP support 260; pushes to implement *Sharing Our Future* 300, 303, 309; promotes WID 240, 243; becomes deputy minister of Health 310
Cavell, Nick (aid administrator) 31, 33, 37
C.D. Howe Institute 254
Central America 372; debt swaps 350; human rights 410; Special Fund for 258; structural adjustment aid 351 (*see* Latin America and Costa Rica, El Salvador, Guatemala, Honduras, *and* Nicaragua)
Centre canadien d'études et de coopération internationale (CECI) 264, 276-77
Chambers, Fergus (CIDA official) 65
Chambers, Robert (professor) 406
Chan, Raymond (Liberal minister for Asia Pacific) 377, 421
Charlton, Mark (professor) 443-44, 447, 585 n. 92
Chile 114, 130; human rights 292; suggested as core country 345
China 27, 344; aid to Africa 48; Canadians in 35, 391; core country for aid 198, 199, 259; shadow of 27, 28; target for aid-trade 229; Three Gorges 349
Chrétien, Jean (PM from 1993) 13, 15, 24, 369; as Liberal external affairs minister (1984) 231; leads Team Canada 391; commercial objectives 400
Christie, Jean (NGO activist) 128-29
Churches 436; Canadian churches' concern for human rights and refugees 185, 273; in African famine 235; about cuts 373; Ten Days for World Development 128
Clark, Andrew (NSI researcher) 371, 414, 449, 527 n. 165
Clark, Joe (PM 1979-80 and Conservative external affairs minister 1984-91) as PM 152, 158 and at Lusaka summit 207; benign influence on aid program 221, 445; African famine 234, 419; protects CIDA from steeper cuts 249, 254, 301, 324-25; pushes decentralization 303, 304; and for ICHRDD 276; 1985 foreign policy paper 272, response to Winegard 290, endorses *Sharing Our Future* 298; in Philippines 257; postpones Chinese projects 348; becomes minister of constitutional affairs 326
Cobb, Christopher (journalist) 138
Colombia 74, 122, 126, 351; fishing vessel debacle 141, 173; private-sector fund 358
Colombo Plan 1, 4, 12, 27, 29, 30, 33, 35; growth 44, 48, 52; decline 45; Canada withdraws 372
Commonwealth 2, 50, 80; Canadian aid through 6, 14, 17, 27, 34; CIDA and 6, 80, 118; Commonwealth Heads of Government Meetings 184, 207, 260, 322, 350; Human Rights Initiative 322; scholarships 34, 41, 261; technical assistance 34, 83-84
Conference Board of Canada 267
Conference on International Economic Cooperation (CIEC) Canada co-chairs

134, 144; Canada's promises 151, 164; issues at 157, 158
Conservatives: Diefenbaker government cuts Colombo Plan contributions 45; MPs criticize spending 138-39, push management review 158; Mulroney government more populist 221, 271; committed to raise ODA 254, 399; poor handling of African cuts 416; reluctant to reduce military spending 324; on trade promotion 257, 444 *(see* Clark, Diefenbaker, Mulroney, Wilson)
Costa Rica 114, 201; and decentralization 306, 308
Cox, David (professor) 160
Crosbie, John (Conservative finance minister) 152
Cuba 124, 375, 396
Culpeper, Roy (NSI president) 350, 554 n. 139
Cunningham, Bill (CTV journalist) 214
Cunningham, George (aid critic) 68, 73, 95, 96, 112

De Bané, Pierre (Liberal MP) 137
de Cotret, Robert (Treasury Board chairman) 310
Denmark 10, 16, 17
Development Assistance Committee (DAC) of the Organisation for Economic Co-operation and Development (OECD) 6, 38; defines ODA 20, 22, 51; Canada above average ODA 256, 263, 347, 420, 440; and above average tied aid 352; Canada low leverage index 330; Canada and environmental guidelines 245; Canadian promises at 151; Canada promotes WID at DAC 243, 358, 408, 449; DAC chides Canada on HRD 261, and on aid cuts 420; criticizes decentralization costs 310; offers mixed review of *Sharing Our Future* 303; questions aid-trade fund 229 and EDC loans as ODA; DAC reports 16, 20, 39, 45
Dewar, Elaine (journalist) 67
Dewitt, David (professor) 75
Diefenbaker, John (PM 1956-63) 47; Commonwealth aid 34, 49, 51; and communism 12; food aid 36, 55
Dimic, Nicolas (foreign policy adviser) 568 n. 97
Dimock, Blair (researcher) 129
Douglas, Tommy (NDP leader) 47
Dudley, Leonard (researcher) 427
Dupras, Maurice (Liberal MP and committee chairman) 119-21, 185
Dupuy, Michel (CIDA president 1977-80) 136, 140, *passim* 143-75; assessment 175; career 143; style 154, 175; concern with foreign policy 153, and CIDA's image 172-73, 174; two-track eligibility 145, 200; WID 239; as ambassador 187; as MP and minister 347
Dupuy, Pierre (diplomat) 49

Economic Council of Canada 157-58, 503 n. 92; abolished 327
Ecuador 122
Egypt 164, 257, 372
Ehrhardt, Roger (as NSI researcher) 166, 215, 449, 523 n. 98
El Salvador 198, 201, 203, 351; human rights 258
English, John (Liberal MP) 387, 567 n. 92
English, Philip (NSI researcher) Haiti evaluation 213-15
Ethiopia 442; drought and civil war 23, 228, 234, 254, 326; aid increased 257, and cut 372, 373; human rights 259, 292; Winegard committee visit 278
Ethnic conflicts 1, 316, 326
Europe, 323; postwar reconstruction aid 28, 36; non-ODA aid to 6, 326, 340, 396; claims half of IAE increase 327, 390, 396
Explanations of Canada's ODA performance (*see* explanations of policy and performance *under* Canada: international assistance)

Food shortages and production 99; as priority 117, 130, 169, 183, 205, 382; in Africa 234, 238; by women 240; CIDA cuts 166; International Fund for Agricultural Development (IFAD) 282
Foreign policy and ODA policy papers
Foreign Policy for Canadians (1970) 13, 74, 79, 86, 91-95, 108, 112, 452

Strategy for International Development Cooperation 1975-1980 (1975) 99-100, 105-19, 154, 191, 443; endorsed 157; evaded 175
"Canadian Aid Policy" (CIDA's 1979 discussion paper) 161-63
Competitiveness and Security (1985), External Affairs' Green Paper paper on foreign policy, section on North-South issues, 272-73
Independence and Internationalism (1986), report of the Special Joint Committee on Canada's International Relations (the Hockin-Simard report) 273-75
For Whose Benefit? (1987, Winegard report) 271-90; visits in Africa 278, 284; report analyzed 277-90; business links 288; ODA Charter and advisory council issues 272, 279; decentralization 285-86; debt 280; fundamental issues 279; heavy emphasis on HRD 280; NGOs 287; ODA/human rights link 283; urbanization 281; use of Trade Facilitation Office 284
To Benefit a Better World (1988, government's initial response to Winegard report) 290
Sharing Our Future (CIDA's 1988 strategy) 222, 238, 271, 272, 291, 300; six priorities 293; on decentralization 297, 311; impact fades 312, 370, but still official policy 314, 319, 328; untying option unmet 352
Canada's Foreign Policy (1994), report of SJC-CFP (the MacEachen-Gauthier report) 387-92, 393, 397,
Canada in the World (1995 foreign policy statement) 13, 15, 16, 370, 392-98, 405, 409, 423
France, as colonial power 70, 77; donor 11, 16, 77; export promotion 156
Francophonie, la 2, 6, 421; Quebec summit 259
Freeman, Linda (professor) 204, 430-31
Gabon 78, 114, 372
Gaffney, Beryl (Liberal MP) 334
Gardiner, Jimmy (Liberal agriculture minister) 29
Gaudefroy, Henri (consultant) 77
Gauthier, Jean Robert (Liberal MP) co-chairs SJC-CFP 385, 387
Gérin, Jacques (CIDA vice-president) 132
Gérin-Lajoie, Paul (CIDA VP 1970-77) *passim* 99-141; appointed 99; career 102-104, 487 n. 9; Quebec education minister 76, 483 n. 61; his booklets 103; links with business 129 and supports tied aid 116, 489 n. 29; sees CIDA as Third World representative 10, and policy-maker for poorest 280; ponders special aid missions 134; growth of disbursements 121; decisions on Haiti project 213, 492 n. 100; interdepartmental conflict 134; Latin America for francophone staffers 80, 99; launches 1975-80 *Strategy* 105; assessment of PGL 100, 448 n. 12, and his heady days 441
Germany 10, 11; donor 45, 48, 263; global reach 17
Ghana 34; aid programs in 47, 48, 74, 80; Canadian leverage 330, 372; SAP support 261
Global markets/globalization 1, 20, 313, 315
Gottlieb, Allan (diplomat) 149, 150, 217
Granatstein, Jack (professor) 75, 146
Green, Howard (Conservative external affairs minister 1959-63) 44-45, 49
G7 (industrialized countries) 16, 184
G77 (developing countries) 58, 109, 223
Groupe Secor 310-11, 314; strategic management report 329-33; focus on four issues 328; leverage concept 330; brokerage concept 333, 425; wins agreement 378, 379
Guatemala 201, 203 (*see* Central America)
Guyana 48, 74; clearing debts 316; human rights 202, 259; SAP support 351, 447
Gwyn, Richard (journalist) 138, 498 n. 188

Haiti 122, 141, 375, 265; rural development 126, 212-15, 223; human rights 259, 410; NSI study 213-14; project cancelled 214, and aid withdrawn 349
Hancock, Graham (aid critic) 224
Harmston, Richard (NGO executive) 218
Hatch, Roger 156, 169; the Hatch report 156-57, 203, 208, 211, 228, 426
Head, Ivan (IDRC president) 4, 62, 110, 383, 470 n. 17
Headlam, Arthur (AUCC consultant) 364
Helleiner, Gerald (professor) as critic 97; NSI founder 111; CIDA-university links 170
Herbert-Copley, Brent (researcher) 265
Higgins, Benjamin (professor and CIDA adviser) 90
Hockin, Tom (Conservative MP) co-chair in 1985-86 of Special Joint Committee 271, 273-75, 431; opposes aid for trade promotion 273; supports multilateral funding 274 and human rights activity 274, 283; government's response 275-76
Hodder, Harry (CIDA VP for Policy) career 105; guides strategy unit 105, 106-107, 115, 470 n. 23, 489 n. 27; leaves CIDA 107
Holdsworth, David (CIDA VP Corporate Management) 403, 573 n. 190
Holmes, John (diplomat) 28-29
Honduras 201 (*see* Central America)
Hong Kong 100, 166, 377
Hopper, David (IDRC president) 72
Howe, C.D. (Liberal trade minister) 32
Hudon, Denis (CIDA VP Planning) 61, 65, 533 n. 25
Hulse, Joseph (as CIDA adviser) 65

India 34, 344; agriculture 83; early aid projects 33, 35, 44, 48, 70, 74; food aid 36; core country 80; freeze after nuclear explosion 122-23; target for aid-trade 229
Indonesia 74, 203, 251, 257; decentralization 306, 308; human rights/East Timor 259, 292
Interdepartmental Committee on Economic Relations with Developing Countries (ICERDC) 111, 340; under Gottlieb 149-50; task force on eligibility 155; demise 195
International Centre for Human Rights and Democratic Development (ICHRDD) 6, 275, 395; under Ed Broadbent 322, 323, 381; Conservative convention demands abolition 326; wider mandate urged 343
International Centre for Ocean Development (ICOD) 6, 178, 197; abolished 327
International Development Research Centre (IDRC) 4; creation 58, 71-73; CIDA and 6, 93, 118, 171, 281; funds International Development Office of AUCC 171; gets high marks 175, 183, 343; in IAE 195; Winegard as governor 277
International Monetary Fund (IMF) 3, 152; Canada at 6, 196; structural adjustment programs 20, 317, 420 (*see* SAPs under CIDA, Massé and World Bank)
Ivory Coast 78, 203; CIDA regional centre 305; effects of cuts 324

Jamaica 48, 70, 114, 122, 257; country focus model 193; concern about turmoil 201; SAP support 351
Jamieson, Ann (CIDA official) 219, 518 n. 9
Jamieson, Donald (Liberal external affairs minister 1976-79) 134
Japan, concentrates aid 80; donor 11, 17, 263; export promotion 156; spearheads untying 396
Johansen, Karl (CIDA official) 124
Jordan 257

Keenleyside, Hugh (diplomat) 30
Keenleyside, T.A. (professor) 202, 349
Kenya 48; threatened withdrawal of aid 349
Kidd, J.Roby (educator) 59
Kirton, John (professor) 75

Labelle, Huguette (CIDA president from 1993) 369, 375, 380, 402, 562 n. 27; relations with Foreign Affairs 571 n. 166; staff pressures 376; focus on WID 408

Lachance, Georges (Liberal MP) chairs 1971 subcommittee 96, 104, 110, 119, 135, 180
Landry, Monique (Conservative minister of external relations 1988-93) 227, 238; career 248, 524 n. 118; criticisms of 249, 524 n. 119; defends cuts 303; pushes decentralization 303, 304, 309; agonizes over Lindores paper 337; pushes management review 327; action on *Sharing Our Future* 272, 297, 298, 311, 334; aide mémoire on restructuring 345; response to Winegard report 290; at Nairobi women's conference 243; transferred 346-47
Langdon, Steven (NDP MP) 299
Latin America, Canadian aid 1, 28, 51, 58, 79-80, 99, 123, 201; commercial interests 123; francophone interests 80, 99, 131, 137; links to Canada 2, 79, 123, and Canadian Association for Latin America (CALA) 211, 231, 512 n. 113
Lalonde, Marc (Liberal finance minister) 229
Laurendeau, André (journalist) 49
Lavergne, Réal (NSI researcher) 215, 428-29, 443
Leger, Jean-Marc (journalist) 49
LePan, Douglas (diplomat) 29, 473 n. 3
Lesotho 49, 74, 122, 126, 199
Lévesque, Father Georges-Henri (educator) in Rwanda 50
Lewis, David (NDP leader) 45
Lewis, Stephen as ambassador to UN 235; accuses government of abandoning Third World 302
Leyton-Brown, David (professor) 427
Liberals: Trudeau government rejects 1 per cent target 23; expands Francophone Africa program 76; refuses to observe Nicaragua elections 186; Liberals recruit Massé 347; election Red Book and Foreign Policy Handbook 380-81 382, 384, 385, 414; Chrétien government cautious on human rights 394-95, focus on poverty 401 (*see various Liberal leaders*)
Lindores, Douglas (CIDA VP Multilateral, later Senior VP) authors study of delivery and aid effectivenesss 229-31, 267; argues for aid-trade, also BHN 230; doubtful on concentration 256; favours decentralizing 252-53; wary on NGO build-up 265; as Senior VP for hands-off management 328, 334, 374, 546 n. 49; authors second major report 335-37; moves to Canadian Red Cross 347
Lumley, Ed (Liberal trade minister) 228
Lumsdaine, David (professor) 446
Lyon, Peyton (professor and former diplomat) 46, 160, 426-27, 438

MacDonald, David (former Conservative MP) 510 n. 59, 539 n. 133; African famine coordinator 234-37, 419; ambassador to Ethiopia 238; dismay at African cuts 373; and Futures Secretariat 217-18
MacDonald, Flora (Conservative external affairs minister 1979-80) 150; friend of aid 152-53, 159; Caribbean a priority 164; and human rights 159, 322; gives mixed messages 159-60, 174; on Sub-Committee on Latin America, 185, 186; as IDRC chair 381
Macdonald, John (civil servant) 31
Macdonald, Laura (professor) 436-38
MacEachen, Allan (Liberal external affairs minister 1974-76 and 1982-84) 114, 119, 226, 134; co-chairs SJC-CFP (1994) 385-86, 387, 388, 389, 390, 392, 393; at World Food Conference 118, 127; on emergency food aid 234; on HRD 206; before parliamentary committees 138-39, 140, 202
MacGuigan, Mark (Liberal external affairs minister 1980-82) 180-81, 201, 210, cancels Haiti project 214, Futures Secretariat 216
Mahbub ul-Haq (UNDP official) 346
MacLaren, Roy (Liberal trade minister) 394, 396
Maione, Romeo (CIDA official) 128
Malawi 49, 74, 122, 199, 452
Malaysia 69; aid programs 33, 48, 80; target for aid-trade 229; technology transfer 358

Marleau, Diane (Liberal minister for international cooperation) 422, 580 n. 287
Marshall Plan 6, 12, 36, 445
Martin, Paul, Sr. (Liberal external affairs minister 1963-68) 45, 46, 50, 53; and CUSO 55; and Maurice Strong 59, 61; as Senator at UNCTAD 110
Martin, Paul, Jr. (Liberal finance minister) 392; budget cuts (1995) 395, 403, 413, 414; and in 1996 Budget 419; respite in 1998 Budget 420
Massé, Marcel (CIDA president 1980-82 and 1989-93) *passim* 177-219, 313-68; 148, 175, 176; career 187; assessment 188; emphasis on human dimension 178, 189; praises NGOs 192; presses program coherence 205, efficient delivery 194, intellectual rejuvenation of CIDA 223 and outreach 218; on Haiti fiasco 213, 515 n. 161; moves to IMF as Canadian director 196, 316; returns to CIDA 310, 313; focus on structural adjustment 313, 316-18, 442, 543 n. 9; disbands foreign service aid stream 311; on governance 314, 323; assertive in ICERDC 330; concern on leverage 330; for strong Canadian presence in IFIs 346; regrets failure of SMR 347, 374; seconded to PCO 337; resigns from PCO and runs for MP 347; as minister 347, 413
MATCH International 170, 239
Mazankowski, Don (Conservative finance minister) 324, 341, 371
McAllister, Elizabeth (CIDA official) 241
McDougall, Barbara (Conservative external affairs minister 1991-93) 314, 327; on Africa cuts 373; promises consultations 346; suspends new aid to Indonesia 349; initiates International Assistance Policy Update 339
McKenna, Peter (researcher) 447
McKenzie, Dan (Conservative MP) 139
McKeown, Robert (journalist) 138
McLean, Walter (Conservative MP) and Africa 257; chairs sub-committee 333, 350; dismay at African cuts 373
McNamara, Robert (World Bank president) 85, 101, 178, 213
McWhinney, Bill (CIDA Senior VP) career and CIDA acting president 196, 219; priority for environmental assessment 245; and HRD 206; commissions MEPAD report 178, 194; rejuvenates CIDA 223; moves to IDB post 310, 327
Media 24, critical of CIDA 100, 103, 136, 137, 212; horror stories 136, 141, 173, 212, 223, 451, 530 n. 221; silence on Nigerian war 74; on World Food Conference 126; CBC 174, 212, 234; CTV 214; *The Globe and Mail* 140, 233, 298, 318, 391-92, 399, 423; *The Hamilton Spectator* 413; *The Gazette* (Montreal) 136, 233, 399; *The Ottawa Citizen* 138, 140, 173, 181, 242; *Ottawa Journal* 138, 143, 175; *Saturday Night* 139; Southam News 328; *The Toronto Star* 219, 381, 399; *The Toronto Sun* 141, 172, 173; *Winnipeg Free Press* 298
Mexico: hosts Cancún summit 187; suggested as core country 345; target for aid-trade 229; women's conference (1975) 239
Miller, Robert (researcher) 274, 278, 440, 567 n. 88
Milne, Glen (civil servant) 111
Montmarquette, Claude (researcher) 427
Monture, Dr. G.C. (as aid critic) 54
Moran, Herbert (director general EAO 1960-66) career 41, 56, 57, 481 n. 10; assessment 42, 44, 56, 477 n. 64; on concentration 80; five-year planning 66, 476 n. 52; and NGOs 55; on tied aid 52; on trade 479 n. 100, 480 n. 7; and universities 47, 53
Morocco 78, 257, 358
Morris, Joe (CLC president) 179
Morrison, David (professor) 279
Mozambique 199, 234, 257, 266
Mulroney, Brian (PM 1984-93) 16, 23, 221; reverses cuts for Africa 235; surprise appointments 235; mild budget curbs 255; co-chairs Children's Summit 359; announces debt relief 350; endorses 0.7 per cent target 254;

launches foreign policy review 271; uses summits for human rights 322; environmental initiatives 298; endorses *Sharing Our Future* 298; touted for UN secretary general 323
Mundy, Karen (researcher) 353

Nepal 122
Netherlands 10, 16, 17; as colonial power 70; exceeds 0.7 per cent 101, and 1 per cent 198; larger donor than Canada 348; untying experience 165, 396
Neufeld, Mark (professor) 436
New International Economic Order (NIEO) 99, 101, 104, 105, 126, 150; Brandt report 179
New Zealand 4, 145
Nicaragua 186, 202; debt swap 350 (*see* Central America)
Niger 78-79, 139
Nigeria 34, 79; aid program 47, 48, 74, 80; aid declines 122; civil war 74-75
Noël, Alain (professor) 439-40
Non-Governmental Organizations (NGOs) 7, 21, 183, 224, 362; CIDA/NGO program 58, 68-70, 102, 145, 169; CIDA responsive to 25, 93, 128, 297, 441-42, 451; NGO critics of CIDA 20, 116, 136, 178, 341; pressures on CIDA to support liberation movements 124; sceptics on food aid 168; Smillie report 362; CIDA and southern NGOs 265-67; Winegard and NGOs 278, 287; (*see* CARE, CUSO, *and* Oxfam; *also* Crossroads Canada 187; International Council for Adult Education [ICAE] 128; International Planned Parenthood Federation [IPPF] 21, 128, 416; *and* Miles for Millions 69)
North-South Institute, The 111; comments on Breau task force 181; on budget cuts 255, 301, 325; CIDA's disarray 226; for decentralization 285; four field studies 215-16, 253, 431, 445; publishes foreign policy booklet 382-83; comments on ODA 152; report card on 1975-80 strategy 157, 175, 191; comments on *Sharing Our Future* 298-99; on Secor report 332; on Policy Update 345; and on tying 164, 203; organizes North-South Forums 564 n. 53
Norway 10, 16, 101, 434
Nossal, Kim Richard (professor and aid critic) 196; statist perspective 25, 431-33, 436, 443, 450-51; trinity of motives 435, 437, 438, 446
Nyerere, Julius (Tanzania president) 124

Official Development Assistance (ODA) defined 3-5 (*see in particular* Canada: international assistance *and* Development Assistance Committee)
Ogelsby, J.C.M. (professor) 79
Ogle, Father Bob (NDP MP) 180, 185
Ohlin, Göran (professor) 59
Oldham, Geoffrey (IDRC consultant) 72
Oliver, Michael (professor) 170-71
O'Neil, Maureen (NSI president, later IDRC president) 521 n. 70, 522-23 n. 92, 567 n. 87
Organization of Petroleum Exporting Countries (OPEC) 100, 109, 204
Ouellet, André (Liberal foreign affairs minister 1993-96) 302, 369, 376-77, 381, 385, 392, 395, 524 n. 119; and *Canada in the World* 396; trade and human rights 409-10; landmines 410, uses cuts to make policy 415-19; resigns 421
Overseas Institute of Canada (*see* Canadian Council for International Cooperation)
Oxfam Canada 126; Oxfam-Quebec 361

Pakistan 34, 41; aid program 33, 35, 48, 74, 80; audit 378; Catley-Carlson visit 222; food aid 36; private-sector fund 358; Warsak dam 35
Pape, Gordon (journalist) 136-37
Parliamentary Centre 111
Partnership Africa-Canada (PAC) 237, 266, 418
Pearson, Lester B. (PM 1963-68) as Liberal external affairs minister (1948-57) 12, 28, 29, 30; as PM 44, 46; aid targets 57, 96; aid to Latin America 51; appoints Strong 59, 61,

announces IDRC 71-72; heads commission for World Bank 84-85, 94, 96, 179, 422
Pearson, Michael (foreign policy adviser) 385
Pelletier, Ireneé (Liberal MP) 140
Perinbam, Lewis (CIDA VP Special Programs) work with NGOs 69, 128, 207; Futures Secretariat 216, 217; leaves CIDA 326, 482 n. 30
Peru 70, 350
Petro-Canada International Assistance Corporation (PCIAC) 6, 178, 196-97; cut 302; abolished 326
Pettigrew, Pierre (Liberal minister for international cooperation) 384, 421-22
Petrie, Frank 229, 299, 307 (*see* Canadian Exporters' Association)
Philippines 256-57, 267, 382; decentralization 306, 308; direct NGO funding 267; human rights 292
Pitfield, Michael (Clerk of Privy Council) 134, 150, 187; and consolidation of foreign service 196; candidate for CIDA president 220
Plewes, Betty (CCIC president) 556 n. 175, 565 n. 64, 566 n. 86, 579 n. 283
Plumptre, Wynne (Finance official) 34, 40, 46, 52; and IDRC 72, 482 n. 38
Population issues 59; become concern 81, 92, 234; Winegard on 281
Pouliot, François (CIDA VP for Policy) 310
Power, Noble (CIDA VP) 495 n. 145
Pratt, Cranford (professor and aid critic) 2, 170, 266, 428; on dominant-class perspective 25, 433-36, 440-41, 450; on CIDA's history 338-39; for autonomy of CIDA 401; on CIDA-NGO links 361, 441; critic of Winegard report 537 n. 87, of *Sharing Our Future* 300, of Secor report 329, of SJC-CFP 392, of *Canada in the World* 400, and of development education cuts 417
Protheroe, David (researcher) 37, 208, 263

Quebec, government of 102; relations with Ottawa 14, 49, 76-79, 438

Racicot, Pierre (CIDA VP Africa and Middle East) 373
Rasminsky, Louis (civil servant) 61
Rawkins, Phillip (professor and author) 24, 443, 567 n. 87; on CIDA as policy-taker 226; on contracting to executing agencies 250, 251; country focus and benefits 264; on HRD 353; CIDA's personnel problems 326; on manageability in CIDA 125, 135, 444, 448-49, 450; on Secor consultations 334-35
Reform Party 326, 386, 391, 397, 413
Refugees 2, 30, 185
Regional development banks 3, 6, 39, 55, 262, 301; reduced Canadian commitments 327, 415; African (ADB) 55, 127, 208, 262; Asian (AsDB) 55, 262; Caribbean (CDB) 84; Inter-American (IDB) 51, 55, 79, 127
Reuber, Grant (as professor and CIDA adviser) 88-90, 94
Riddell, Roger (professor) 18, 224, 422
Ritchie, Ed (diplomat) 59, 495 n. 145
Robinson, Basil (diplomat) 134
Roche, Douglas (former Conservative MP, author and internationalist) 119, 139, 140, 428, 441, 510 n. 78; vice-chair on Breau task force 180, 181, 184; on Dupras subcommittee 185, 186; heads National Advisory Committee on Development Education 366, 560 n. 218; seeks comprehensive aid strategy 220; favours junior minister concept 135, 249; pushes management review 159; on NSI studies 216; opposes aid for trade promotion 157, 174; writings 212, 581 n. 19
Rostow, Walter (professor and US adviser) 35, 477 n. 65
Rudner, Martin (professor) 18, 205, 443; on environment 412-13; on HRD and poverty 293; new role for private sector 394; on procurement 249 and trade subsidies 233; on Canada's self-image 427
Rwanda 198, 372, 410

Sahelian countries 122, 126; Solidarité Canada-Sahel 266
Sabourin, Louis (professor and CIDA adviser) 76, 90

Sanger, Clyde (journalist and author) as CIDA staffer 65; writings 72, 73, 134, 427-28, 523 n. 98, 581 n. 18; on Clark 325; critic of 1995 budget 414, and of SJC 392; on Secor report 332 and 1972 Stockholm conference 244
Sarsfield, Dominick (CIDA official) 494 n. 132
St. Laurent, Louis (PM 1948-56) 29
Schmitz, Gerald (researcher) 278, 319, 385, 566 n. 74; CIDA as Christmas tree 451
Senegal 49, 50, 78, 187, 372; country of concentration 80; drought 234; NSI study 215; Winegard committee visit 278
Sharp, Mitchell (Liberal external affairs minister 1968-74) 61, 62, 114, 131; supports multilateral aid 84; chairs consultations 91-93; aid targets 485 n. 112
Shulman, Morton (as journalist) 141
Sicard, Pierre (CIDA VP Corporate Review) 147, 499 n. 12
Simard, Jean-Maurice (Conservative Senator) co-chairs Special Joint Committee on Canada's International Relations (1985-86) 271, 273-75, 283, 429
Singapore 33, 100; CIDA regional centre 305; tied aid 166
Smillie, Ian (consultant and former CUSO head) 362, 422, 505 n. 125, 549 n. 87, 559 n. 198
Smith, Heather (professor) 437
Smith, Virginia (author and aid critic) 212, 426, 430
Somalia 326, 410
South Africa 396, 410
South Asia Partnership 209, 266, 309, 418
Southern African Development Community (SADC) 198, 199, 257, 372
South Korea 36, 100, 166
Soviet Union (now Russia) aid program to South 38; collapse 313; fear of expansion 27; invades Czechoslovakia 75; non-ODA aid to former USSR 6, 314, 316, 326, 327, 340, 371, 390
Spicer, Keith (as author of *A Samaritan State?*) 13, 27, 32, 44, 50, 427, 428; starts Canadian Overseas Volunteers 55
Sri Lanka (formerly Ceylon) 33, 38, 137; and Colombo Plan 27, 28; aid program 33, 34, 48, 74, 80; audit 378; human rights 259, 292, 410; local NGOs 265; aid scaled back 349, and cut 372
Stein, Janice Gross (professor) 384, 566 n. 84
Stevens, Sinclair (Conservative Treasury Board president) 152, 186, 231
Stewart, Christine (Liberal minister for Africa and Latin America) 377, 378, 385, 421, 579 n. 286; opposition critic 380, 564 n. 54; pushes BHN 380; hedges on decentralization 310; in Tanzania 395
Stokke, Olav (professor) 434
Strong, Maurice (director general EAO 1966-68 and CIDA president 1968-70) *passim* 57-98; career and assessment 59, 103; as EAO director general 57, 60-62, 440; relations with business 22, 129 and with NGOs 21, 118; promotion of CIDA as "third player" 134, 143; takes "President" title 62; 1968 aid review 86-91; seeks statutory foundation for CIDA 279, 280, 534 n. 37; heads UN emergency operations in Africa 235; on Brundtland commission 244, and Canada 21 panel 383; chairs task force on Canadian priorities 424 , 580 n. 293
Students, foreign in Canada 2, 4-5, 53, 82, 237, 261, 275; 50 per cent target for women 242; scholarship growth 293, 353, 356; imputed costs 301-302; third-country training 82
Sudan 228; aid program 257; cuts 324; human rights 259; threat to withdraw aid 349
Swaziland 49, 74, 122, 199
Swift, Jamie (author and aid critic) 430
Sweden 10, 263; SIDA 11, 16, 17, 62; exceeds 0.7 per cent GNP 101, and 1 per cent 198; more leverage than Canada 330; Swedfund 211; at World Food Conference 127

Tackaberry, John (journalist) 191
Taiwan 36, 100

Tansley, Donald (CIDA Executive VP) 65, 67, 132, 470 n. 26, 495 n. 145
Tanzania 48, 70, 122, 199; largest recipient in anglophone Africa 124; decentralization 286, 306, 308; dispute over aid cut 372, 373, 395; horror stories 136, 495 n. 153 (bakery), 173 (forklift), 223; NSI study 215, 431; visits by Stewart 395, and by Winegard committee 278
Tendler, Judith (US aid critic) 449
Thailand 198, 199, 382; small projects 265; technology transfer 358; universities 209
Thérien, Jean-Philippe (professor) 16, 439-40, 447
Thomson, Suteera (researcher) 195, 239
Todd, Dave (journalist) 328
Tomlinson, Brian (researcher) 430
Towe, Peter (EAO official) 60
Trade promotion 1, 20, 106, 157, 196, 313, 315; French *crédit-mixte* 203; aid-trade fund 228-31 and critics 233; reborn as Trade and Development Facility 232-33; Hatch report 156-57, 203, 208, 211, 228; market access for southern countries 91, 109, 110 and CIDA's Trade Facilitation Office 284, 293; reforms in Pearson report 85 (*see also under* Canada: government departments and agencies)
Triantis, Stephen (professor and CIDA adviser) 86-87, 91, 485 n. 103
Trinidad and Tobago 48, 122
Trudeau, Pierre (PM 1968-79 and 1980-84) aid targets 23, 57; on Biafra 61; on External Affairs 133; reviews foreign policy 86, 91-95; suspends nuclear aid to India 123; on North-South issues 12, 13, 14-15, 115, 445; friendship with Nyerere 124; close to Strong 61; surprise visit to CIDA 138; in Togo 77; writes on Latin America 79; government defeated 137 and returns 160, 177; co-chairs Cancún summit 187; tours southern countries 183-84 and criticizes them 223; commits to 0.7 per cent target 228-29, 254
Truman, President Harry 3, 12
Tucker, Michael (professor) 427
Tunisia 49, 50, 74, 78, 122, 137; country of concentration 80; locomotives 204
Turner, John (PM 1984) 231, 302

Uganda 48, 124, 162, 257
United Kingdom 211; aid program 11, 17, 45, 62, 256; aid-trade fund 156; Canadian wartime aid 35; more leverage than Canada 330; opposes Trudeau initiative 177; Thatcher at Cancún 187
United Nations agencies and programs
  Food and Agriculture Organization 30, 234
  United Nations Conference on Trade and Development (UNCTAD) 58, 85, 91, 104, 110, 119, 222;
  United Nations Development Program (UNDP) origins in UN Expanded Program of Technical Assistance (UNEPTA) 30, 37, 55, and in Special UN Fund for Economic Development (SUNFED) 37, 55; UNDP 54, 83, 238, 263, 316, 346, 367, 406
  United Nations Educational, Scientific and Cultural Organization (UNESCO) 30, 69
  United Nations High Commission for Refugees (UNHCR) 30, 54, 209
  United Nations Industrial Development Organization (UNIDO) 129
  United Nations Children's Fund (UNICEF) 30, 223, 408; human face of SAPs 260, 264, 317; hit by Canadian cutbacks 326, 351
  World Food Program 55, 123, 127, 263, 449
  World Health Organization 30
United Nations Development Decades 27, 39, 85, 155; World Food Conference (Rome, 1974) 118, 126, 127, 138, 168; UN Law of the Sea 109; UN Conference on Environment and Development (Rio, 1992) 313, 314, 350, 358, 367; UN Conference on LLDCs (Paris, 1981) 200; UN Confer-

ence on Social Development (Copenhagen, 1995) 406-407, 415; UN Decade for Women 239, 243, 522-23 n. 92; UN Fourth World Conference on Women (Beijing, 1995) 408-409
United States 10, 185; aid program 3, 33, 38, 45, 263; declines 58, 101; food aid 19; Canada's bilateral links 2, 272; pressure on Canada as donor 6, 28, 39, 45, 48, 87; field offices of USAID 11, 253; untying experience 166; under Kennedy 39, and Nixon 100, and Reagan 21, 177, 187, 201

Van Rooy, Alison (NSI researcher) 353, 406-407, 442, 443, 445
Vézina, Monique (Conservative minister of external relations 1984-86 and 1993) 227, 232-33, 233, 235; career 248; criticisms of 249, 524 n. 119; initiates Africa 2000 237-38; appoints task force to review ODA 276-77; transferred 277 and reappointed 347
Vienneau, David (journalist) 219
Vietnam 58, 348, 438

Wagner, Claude (Conservative MP) 139, 488 n. 92, 496-97 n. 170
Walker, John (journalist) 220
Wallace, Stephen (CIDA officer) 568 n. 97
Walmsley, Norma (professor and MATCH International founder) 170
Wenman, Robert (Conservative MP) 186
West Indies aid program 34, 47, 48, 74, 122
Whelan, Eugene (Liberal agriculture minister) on food aid 234
White, John (British aid critic) 443, 446-47
Williams, Douglas (NSI researcher) on food aid 169
Wilson, Michael (Conservative finance minister) cuts aid expenditure 232, 324; budget cuts (1985) 255, (1986) 233, (1988) 272 and (1989) 301; wary on GNP targets 254
Winegard, William (Conservative MP) career and character 271, 291, 441, 539 n. 133; heads aid study 236, 270, 277; identifies human rights violators 292; HRD as focus on people 293, 370
Winsor, Hugh (journalist and columnist) 237, 302, 377, 379, 563 n. 36
Wood, Bernard (NSI executive director) 111, 429-30, 488-89 n. 22, 523 n. 98
Wood, Robert E. (professor) 445-46, 480 n. 1
World Bank (IBRD) 3, 223, 359; Canada at 6, 22, 41, 61, 84; Global Environment Facility (GEF) 359, 557 n. 184; International Development Association (soft loans) 37, 55, 84, 118, 169, 208, 262; McNamara at 101-102, 108, 117; structural adjustment 2, 22, 260, 281-82, 293, 294, 316-17
World Council of Churches 39
World University Service of Canada (WUSC) 171, 210, 264, 361
Wyse, Peter (aid critic) 428, 443-44, 449

YMCA 59
Young, Roger (NSI researcher) 215, 249, 429, 443-44, 495 n. 153

Zaïre (now Democratic Republic of Congo) 137, 372; human rights 259, 260, 349
Zambia 74, 158, 199
Zimbabwe 198-99, CIDA regional centre 305, 306, 307, 308; private-sector fund 358
Zukowsky, Janet (CIDA VP for Canadian Partnerships) 418